R 791.436358 Bolam.S
Bolam, Sarah Miles,
The presidents on film :

The Presidents on Film

*A Comprehensive Filmography of
Portrayals from George Washington
to George W. Bush*

SARAH MILES BOLAM
and THOMAS J. BOLAM

McFarland & Company, Inc., Publishers
Jefferson, North Carolina, and London

LIBRARY OF CONGRESS CATALOGUING-IN-PUBLICATION DATA

Bolam, Sarah Miles, 1934–
The presidents on film : a comprehensive filmography of portrayals from
George Washington to George W. Bush / Sarah Miles Bolam and Thomas J. Bolam.
p.   cm.
Includes bibliographical references and index.

ISBN-13: 978-0-7864-2481-8
ISBN-10: 0-7864-2481-8
(illustrated case binding : 50# alkaline paper) ∞

1. Presidents in motion pictures.
2. Presidents in motion pictures—Catalogs.
I. Bolam, Thomas J., 1933–
II. Title.
PN1995.9.P678B65   2007   791.43'6358—dc22   2006028766

British Library cataloguing data are available

©2007 Sarah Miles Bolam and Thomas J. Bolam. All rights reserved

*No part of this book may be reproduced or transmitted in any form
or by any means, electronic or mechanical, including photocopying
or recording, or by any information storage and retrieval system,
without permission in writing from the publisher.*

On the cover: Charles Edward Bull as Abraham Lincoln in
The Iron Horse, 1924 (Photofest)

Manufactured in the United States of America

*McFarland & Company, Inc., Publishers
Box 611, Jefferson, North Carolina 28640
www.mcfarlandpub.com*

Contents

Preface   1

Introduction   3

1. George Washington (1789–1797)   11
2. John Adams (1797–1801)   38
3. Thomas Jefferson (1801–1809)   45
4. James Madison (1809–1817)   58
5. James Monroe (1817–1825)   61
6. John Quincy Adams (1825–1829)   66
7. Andrew Jackson (1829–1837)   70
8. Martin Van Buren (1837–1841)   84
9. William Henry Harrison (1841)   87
10. John Tyler (1841–1845)   90
11. James K. Polk (1845–1849)   91
12. Zachary Taylor (1849–1850)   94
13. Millard Fillmore (1850–1853)   99
14. Franklin Pierce (1853–1857)   100
15. James Buchanan (1857–1861)   103
16. Abraham Lincoln (1861–1865)   104
17. Andrew Johnson (1865–1869)   168
18. Ulysses Simpson Grant (1869–1877)   172
19. Rutherford B. Hayes (1877–1881)   195
20. James A. Garfield (1881)   198
21. Chester A. Arthur (1881–1885)   202
22. and 24. Grover Cleveland (1885–1889 & 1893–1897)   205

23. Benjamin Harrison (1889–1893)	208
25. William McKinley (1897–1901)	211
26. Theodore Roosevelt (1901–1909)	216
27. William Howard Taft (1909–1913)	238
28. Woodrow Wilson (1913–1921)	240
29. Warren Gamaliel Harding (1921–1923)	251
30. Calvin Coolidge (1923–1929)	253
31. Herbert Hoover (1929–1933)	256
32. Franklin D. Roosevelt (1933–1945)	258
33. Harry S Truman (1945–1953)	275
34. Dwight D. Eisenhower (1953–1961)	286
35. John Fitzgerald Kennedy (1961–1963)	296
36. Lyndon Baines Johnson (1963–1969)	311
37. Richard Milhous Nixon (1969–1974)	315
38. Gerald Ford (1974–1977)	331
39. Jimmy Carter (1977–1981)	334
40. Ronald Reagan (1981–1989)	338
41. George Herbert Walker Bush (1989–1993)	346
42. Bill Clinton (1993–2001)	351
43. George W. Bush (2001–2009)	361
Chapter Notes	365
Bibliography	369
Index	377

Preface

Films—from their flickering beginnings—have provided entertainment for Americans. Moreover, they have provided an interesting record of how filmmakers and the public have viewed the presidents and the presidency. This book addresses that phenomenon and is the first of its kind to treat all presidential films.

The aim of this work is to be inclusive, that is to list all commercial theatrical releases that include an American president as a character. Such films do not necessarily show an actual historical event or necessarily present any framework of fact. But fortunately some do. This book does not include documentary films or television films or series. Nor does it include movies with a fictional president except those obviously referring to a real president such as Richard Nixon in *Dick* (1999), Gerald Ford in *The Pink Panther Strikes Again* (1976), and Bill Clinton in *Primary Colors* (1998).

The Introduction gives a brief overview of the 407 commercial films that include an American president as a character. It also explains the scope of the films, discusses the reactions of historians to these films, describes how films' treatment of presidents have changed over time, and considers how particular films were myth-making in nature. The body of the book is essentially a filmography of these presidential films. It contains individual chapters covering the 42 men who have served as president of the United States with photographs from the films. Each chapter provides a very brief summary of highlights (or lowlights) of the president's administration. In addition, each chapter includes commentary on the overall nature of the films in which the pertinent president appears as a character, and a listing of all the films which include that president. Credits, a plot summary, a description of the appearance of the president, and whenever possible, an assessment of the portrayal are also provided for each film.

Interpretation and a point of view become inevitable because we define historical writing as "critical thinking about the past," as in *The Press and the Presidency from George Washington to Ronald Reagan* (Oxford University Press, 1985), the Pulitzer Prize nominee Sarah Miles Bolam wrote with the late journalist and historian John Tebbel.

We thank our family, friends, colleagues, and especially the librarians who guard these celluloid treasures. During our research, we became dedicated film preservationists. For all their assistance we particularly thank Rosemary Haynes at the Library of Congress, Mark Quigley at the University of California Los Angeles, Jared Case and Antonio Labette at the George Eastman House, Robert Gilliam at the State University of New York College at Brockport, Maxine Fleckner Ducey and Dorinda Hartman at the Wisconsin Center for Film and Theater Research, and Ron Mandelbaum at Photofest.

Sarah Miles Bolam and Thomas J. Bolam
Houston, Texas, and Brockport, New York
Fall 2006

Introduction

As the images of the most esteemed American presidents—Washington, Jefferson, Lincoln, and Theodore Roosevelt—are carved in rock on Mount Rushmore, so are the images of presidents captured on film. But in reality the cinematic images of the presidents are much more mobile and variable than the monumental carvings in the granite of the Black Hills. In fact, over the years, their presentations have changed from respectful to ridiculous.

The public opinion of the U.S. president rests on the messages of the media.[1] Beyond simply influencing public opinion, American cinema portrays American myths and dreams. Throughout American history, different voices assumed this role: the clergy, artists, educators, politicians, and business people. Cultural film historian Robert Sklar emphasizes that there has been a switch from a diverse bunch of spokesmen to a single group—moviemakers—who speak "more truly" about the human experience than anything else.[2] To make his point, Sklar cites a producer's description of F. Scott Fitzgerald's projection room: it is like "Dreams hung in fragments at the far end of the room."

These dreams spin across the silver screens of America matinee after matinee, night after night, week after week for a public eager to escape their own lives to cinematic ones that appear free of care and charged with drama and excitement. Considering how realistic films can be, it is not surprising that from their beginning they have helped to build myths and dreams.

Presidential films particularly reflect this myth-making quality. And over time the nature of the myths has changed. The reasons for the changes in attitudes toward the presidents can be attributed to many influences:

- American cinema's historic role as a popular entertainment, appealing to the broadest public rather than catering to the cultural elite as in Europe;
- the American public's changing attitudes toward its presidents that filmmakers reflect in their constant concern with creating popular entertainment;
- filmmakers' growing independence; that is, the director gaining more control as in the French *auteur* movement of the 1950s. This movement made the director the major creator of a film, allowing him to mold the material into his personal style and endow it with thematic concerns;
- producers' increasing collaboration with foreign investors and foreign production sites and stars to cater to an international audience, although still following the American movie mold;
- historians' varying attitudes toward the presidents and the presidency. This is best illustrated by the "new era of Jefferson historiography" as Merrill D. Peterson names it in his 1960 treatise on Jefferson's image.[3] In the prologue to his 1996 work, Joseph Ellis illustrates that current historiography labels Jefferson as "the American sphinx."[4]

The changing American attitude toward the presidency attracts much attention, from political correspondents and columnists to presidential scholars. The most recently published titles by presidential scholars chronicle the transformation of the office: George C. Edwards II, *The Public Presidency: The Pursuit of Public Support* (1993); Stephen Skowronek, *The Politics Presidents Make: Leadership from John Adams to Bill Clinton* (1993); Louis Fisher, *Presidential War Power* (1995); John P. Burke, *The Institutionalized Presidency, The Presidency and the American Political System* (2000). The extensive literature on the chief executive shows how the presidency evolved from a decision-making office about the formation of a nation by the Founding Fathers into a politically-driven office under Andrew Jackson and Martin Van Buren, and how it navigated the years of angst and compromise over slavery and the nature of America that led to the Civil War under Lincoln. Following Lincoln's leadership came a diminution of power until the imperial and modern presidency evolved under Theodore Roosevelt and was solidified under Franklin D. Roosevelt. Now we have an institutionalized presidency not unlike a giant corporation with the president presiding over numerous councils. Most noteworthy is the number of people in the executive arm of American government and their specializations. Gone are the days when the president met with his cabinet one on one as did Jefferson or with the entire press corps in his office as did Franklin D. Roosevelt. Gone are many other aspects of the presidency.

More concerned about having a "star," Hollywood largely ignores the administrative changes of the monolithic American presidency. With its designated and implied powers held by one executive, the presidency—the first leadership office in the modern Western world to be consciously created as a constitutional position—attracts more attention than the legislative and judicial branches of government. The presidents may not always have "box office appeal" but they still make the cut, however briefly they usually appear in a movie.

Along with the changes in the presidency as mentioned previously are the changes in the depiction of the president. During the early years of cinema, filmmakers made films of romantic solemnity that reflected the public's respectful attitude toward the presidents and the office, then a manageable enterprise with one private secretary and a small cabinet of personal advisers.

The "history written in lightning," as President Woodrow Wilson described D.W. Griffith's *Birth of a Nation* (1915), illustrated the 20th century turn toward films depicting the "normalcy" of the times. Reverential films about the Founding Fathers decreased as did other historical films. What history was filmed became human, really anecdotal and personal, as in *The Beautiful Mrs. Reynolds* (1918) and Griffith's *America* (1924) although respect for the past still received its due. Seemingly tired of turmoil and politics, the filmmakers of the 1920s dealt with the new pattern of private life of fun and adventure as in *In the Days of Buffalo Bill* (1922).

By the next decade and the Great Crash, the longer films of at least five reels strove to capture the contradictions of the morality of the consumptive economy and the uneven distribution of wealth that led some Americans to question their country as in *Turn Back the Clock* (1933). Similarly, Depression era films of the 1930s include plots that told people what kind of situation they were in and how they might or might not handle it. In *The Phantom President* (1932) portraits of past presidents spring to life singing "The Country Needs a Man." With the advent of sound in the 1930s dramatic biographies led the list of important presidential films: Griffith's *Abraham Lincoln* (1930) and John Ford's *Young Mr. Lincoln* (1939) and *Abe Lincoln in Illinois* (1940). That most filmed president proved the perfect subject for inspiring respect for leaders and commitment to patriotic ideals as World War II loomed.

Although the pre–World War I period had its share of propaganda films, the most propagandistic movies appear in the 1940s—before, during, and after World War II. *The Howards of Virginia* (1940) shows conflicts of class and political ideology in 18th century America. Cecil B. DeMille takes liberties with the history of Pontiac's Rebellion in *Unconquered* (1948). *Mission to Moscow* (1943) deals with real-life ambassador Joseph Davies in pre–World War II Russia. *Wilson* (1944) is a wartime propaganda movie about a peace-loving president, while earlier Wilson films take a strong pre–World War I stance against Germany as in *The Prussian Cur* (1918) and *The Kaiser, the Beast of Berlin* (1919).

Later presidential films take several directions: romantic biographies such as *The President's Lady* (1953); *film noir* treatments such as *The Tall Target* (1951); and films of recrimination that search for causes of war and post-war problems such as *The Beginning or the End* (1947). Respect for leaders was dwindling as reverence for the past faded and doubts about the future dawned.

Political and social developments led to a confidence that culminated in the Kennedy era. The 1960s launched a cultural revolution. Whether viewed as reactionary or revolutionary, 60s movies led filmmakers toward candor and realism, accompanied by more complications and ambiguity. Frankness guided the making of *Sunrise at Campobello* (1960) and *PT-109* (1963). Also in the sixties, the studio system collapsed, the Production Code ended, and the struggling industry turned international.

Despite the confidence that marked many films of the 1960s, feelings of doubt about the political process crept into 1970 films such as *The Private Files of J. Edgar Hoover* (1977). This boldness in political themes is a marked difference from the respectful tone of the past and seen clearly in Woody Allen's anti–Black List *The Front* (1976). The ultimate in revisionism and the only bicentennial film, and a musical at that, *1776* (1972) treats the Second Continental Congress as a road show with dancing delegates and wisecracking stars (Howard Da Silva as pundit Benjamin Franklin) yet gives John Adams proper respect as the driving force for action against England. Although MacArthur in the 1977 film of the same name appears as the hero, his presidential adversaries are portrayed as caricatures.

Films of the 1980s revealed optimism and pride in the new political consciousness with an undertone of dubiousness about American fantasies of innocence and power. A sense of ridicule arose when Richard Nixon appeared in a men's room scene in *Where the Buffalo Roam* (1980). And while Dwight D. Eisenhower appeared in a cameo and John F. Kennedy appeared in news footage, Vice President Lyndon B. Johnson played a comic caricature in *The Right Stuff* (1981). Most of the films about the following presidents—Jimmy Carter, Ronald Reagan, George H.W. Bush, Bill Clinton, and George W. Bush—continue this comic characterization. These treatments contradict the conventional wisdom that "People don't expect presidents to be funny."

A new kind of treatment of presidents arrived in the 1990s with Oliver Stone's *JFK* (1991) and *Nixon* (1995). Just call them history as personally interpreted and film as controversy. The 21st century also brings made-for-television movies, rather than films, quickly produced after the event. These TV films sometimes prove to be more historically correct, as was the case with the controversial CBS mini-series "The Reagans," which was yanked off the network in 2003 because of conservatives' complaints and moved to a cable viewing source, Showtime.

The classic genres, best defined by Thomas Schatz, are the western, gangster film, hardboiled-detective film, screwball comedy, musical, and family melodrama.[5] Some, but not all, presidential films fall into one or another of these genres. Nor do the theoretical approaches from a specific point of view (Lancanian, feminist, etc.) apply in our dealing with historically-based film treatments. Furthermore, films about history are often classified as "epics," "period films," or "costume dramas," and thus are not true genres. It would then seem that biography—the biopic genre of the American Film Institute (AFI)—might be the logical classification as many presidential films deal with the life of a president. But few films deal with the complete life of a president. Most presidential films usually depict one aspect of the presidents' lives. The scenarios of many of these films often occur before the men assumed the role of chief executive of the United States. Even films like *JFK* (1991), *Nixon* (1995), and *Wilson* (1944) with titles that suggest a full biographical treatment only cover selected aspects of the presidents' lives. Because of the limitations of the above definitions, we are simply calling our movies "presidential films."

Film style and technique are not covered, because there is little that is revolutionary in these films; the focus is on film as a narrative art. Nevertheless, the revolutionary developments of D.W. Griffith (analytical editing, cross-cutting, and close-ups) and Orson Welles (depth of focus) appear in their films with presidents, *Birth of a Nation* (1915) and *Citizen Kane* (1941), respectively. Most of the films, however, follow the classical Hollywood type of camerawork with the standard angles, range, motion, and *mise-en-scene* (setting)—although there is a preponderance for the long take in battle scenes that gives an impression of inclusiveness. Due to the extensive time period covered in this work, 1903–2005, the very evolution of films is seen: the development of technique from the early un-cinematic theatricality to the dazzling portrayals of the late silent era through wide-angle compositions and greater staging in depth to modernist eclecticism and computer-animated inventions.[6] What continues to endure is an image of the president.

But the production problem in filming American presidents is that their administrative lives involve many complex events not easily translated to film. By its very nature—appealing to a general audience and dealing with a limited time span—film cannot easily deal with complexity. Nor does film tend to follow the daily routine many presidents live—that of desk work, reading, consulting, meeting, and appearing before the public. As Myron A. Levine says in "The Transformed Presidency: The *Real* Presidency and Hollywood's *Reel* Presidency," the daily decisions made by the nation's chief executive did not always make for compelling cinema.[7] What the president thinks about such events as strikes, social unrest, and wars does not provide as much dynamic grist for the Hollywood mill as the events themselves. Action always is easier to depict than thought, as George Bluestone elucidated in his seminal *Novels into Film*.[8] And it's action and conflict that sell tickets, not mental struggles.

Most often, what ends up in presidential films are physical characteristics and personality traits of the presidents. That combination adds up to the icons or images, whether burnished or flawed, respected or ridiculed, that Americans elect and esteem. Yet these icons are not necessarily embodied with obvious tics and mannerisms. They are flesh-and-blood portrayals of leaders of a vast nation closely but not necessarily fully captured on film. Regarding the difficulties of precisely defining a president, Henry Adams said that "Jefferson could be painted only touch by touch, with a fine pencil, and the perfection of the likeness depending upon the shifting and uncertain flicker of its semi-transparent shadows."[9] When a president like Jefferson thinks about his accomplishments differently from historians, another problem arises. Jefferson thought his authorship of the Declaration of Independence and the Virginia Statute for Religious Freedom more deserving of remembrance than his presidency of the United States.

Filmmakers do not necessarily think the same as historians—or as ordinary Americans. They have a vision that they want to capture on film, one that does not always follow history yet conforms to the basic definition of filmmaking—a moving picture. This moving picture of a president reflects the attitudes of the filmmakers as well as the times in which they live.

Historians like Natalie Zemon Davis usually decry feature films attempting to depict history. In *Slaves on Screen: Film and Historical Vision*, she writes of historical film as a "thought experiment."[10] Feature films are often described as creatures of invention, without significant connection to the experienced world or the historical past. Davis establishes two habits of thought, as she terms them, that cause films with much value, both historically and ethically, to "go off track." The first is "too cavalier an attitude toward the evidence about lives and attitudes in the past" that leads to composite characters or changed time frames. The second is "a bad habit of underestimating film audiences."[11] This leads to representation of the past to be exactly like the present, and it also leads to "presentism," the presumption that the past can be judged by standards of the present.

In defense of historical invention in film—compilations of characters, changes of time, switches of statements from one person to another, and condensations of events, for example—history gains dramatic impact and easier understanding. One obvious example is 1776 concluding with the dramatic signing of the Declaration of Independence on July 4, when in reality it was signed over a two-week period. Along with the accent on story and drama are production values that suspend disbelief. Presidential movies tend to look authentic—like the times in which they are set—but not so assertively that the settings dominate.

Coupled with historians' varying attitudes and interpretations is their tendency to assess presidents according to various criteria. With this American love of numbers, of codification, of the top ten of everything, come ever-changing lists of the presidents in order of importance.

The breakdown of the appearances by presidents in the 407 films under study tends to follow the actual popularity of the presidents; Lincoln leads with 123 and is followed by Washington with 52. Somewhat surprisingly, Grant has the third most appearances with 45. This anomaly probably relates both to his being one of America's greatest military leaders and to his close relationship with Lincoln. Following the top three are Theodore Roosevelt with 33, Jefferson with 25, Nixon with 24 (based on notoriety rather than popularity), Franklin Roosevelt with 22, John Kennedy with 21, and Andrew Jackson with 15.

Of the 42 individuals who have held the office there are only three who have not appeared in film; two, Tyler and Buchanan, served in the interregnum between Jackson and Lincoln, and the third is Harding, who served between Woodrow Wilson and Calvin Coolidge. Yet Alexander Hamilton, "the foremost political figure in American history who never attained the presidency,"[12] receives full biographical treatment in two films. Coincidentally, in the most recent ratings of presidents—the Murray-Blessings Ratings—Lincoln, Franklin D. Roosevelt, Washington, and Jefferson stand as "great" presidents. Next as "near great presidents" are Theodore Roosevelt, Wilson, Andrew Jackson, and Truman. An exception is Grant, who appears with Warren Harding at the bottom of the Murray-Blessings Ratings yet appears in 45 films.[13]

Of all the criteria used by the Murray-Blessings Ratings, however, administrations' accomplishments most clearly determined presidential rankings. Administrative accomplishments should create the drama for filmmakers: Lincoln fought to preserve the Union and doing so altered the economic and social standards of the country forever; Washington formed the most impressive cabinet in American history with the best minds available, made formative decisions, and remains beloved as the Father of His Country; Franklin Roosevelt came into office to save the American capitalistic system and remained to not only achieve that goal but led the country in the last of the "good" wars, World War II. But what constitutes greatness in the White House does not always end up on film. In the examples given above, the films about those presidents focused on the young Mr. Lincoln, Washington in staged heroic shots during Revolutionary War battles, and Franklin Roosevelt during his struggle with polio.

This study's treatment expands understanding of presidential films by analyzing individual films in which a real president appears in a major or minor role. In the 407 films examined (the first produced in 1903 and the last in 2005), there are 519 separate appearances by U.S. presidents and 70 films in which two or more presidents appear. These 519 can be categorized as follows:

- Major role—relating to an incident, historical or fictional, in which the president has a significant impact;
- Major role—appearing in a biopic that covers a portion or all of the president's life;
- Minor role—including an incident in which the president acts in his line of duty, either historical or fictional;
- Minor role—including the appearance of a president in a role not related to his responsibilities;
- Minor role—including the appearance of a president in a juvenile or satirical film in which the appearance is either nonsensical or merely satirizing the president.

Playing these roles are 305 actors. The difference between the number of films—407—and the number of actors—305—occurs because many actors played the presidents more than once, particularly in the early films. In addition, there are ten instances where a single actor portrays more than one president. The most notable instances are Anthony Hopkins as John Quincy Adams in *Amistad* (1997) and Richard Nixon in *Nixon* (1995), and James Whitmore in the film of his one-man shows about Teddy Roosevelt in *Bully* (1978) and about Harry Truman in *Give 'Em Hell Harry!* (1975). In the early years of filmmaking (1903–10) more than 70 percent of the presidential films cast the president in a major role. As the industry matured, this presentation of the presidential character changed and fewer of the roles were major: 43 percent in the 1911–20 decade and in the 20 to 30 percent range in the years up to 1980. Since 1980 there has been a further decline in major roles of the presidential character to between 6 and 12 percent by decade.

The movie-going public's interest in the personal lives of the presidents is illustrated by the fact that there has been an average of two presidential biopics in each decade since the 1940s with the exception of the current decade when none have been produced to date. This is a bit misleading because since the 1960s television has produced an increasing number of serious treatments of the presidents and the presidency.

In contrast to television as noted earlier, the movie industry has turned to using the presidents as characters in either nonsensical situations or in biting satires. It appears that Richard Nixon's problems started this movement, and since the 1970s no president has been spared. All of the Carter movies fall in this category and virtually all of the films with Reagan and Clinton are also included. Proving that assassination does not provide armor from this movement, 7 of the 13 movies with a Kennedy character in the 1990s were of this nature. And even the most recent films with a Lincoln character are teenage comedies.

The growth of the use of presidential characters in teenage and satirical films has reversed a long trend of declining presidential appearances; the number of portrayals peaked at 93 in the 1930s and reached a low of 17 in the 1960s. Given the quality of the recent films, this is not necessarily a positive trend. And in almost half of the 407 films examined, the president appears as a minor character acting in the line of duty. Many of these appearances are in westerns when the president sends the hero back to the frontier to save the nation.

Like Maxim Gorky, the Russian writer who wrote after seeing his first motion picture in 1896, "[We have] visited the kingdom of shadows"[14] the industry that started with a magic lantern turned into a dream factory, producing films that tell us what our dreams—and nightmares—are made of. The result is more artistry than history, and for that reason we wrote *The Presidents on Film*.

1

George Washington (1789–1797)

"First in war, first in peace, and first in the hearts of his countrymen" as General Henry "Light-Horse Harry" Lee eulogized him, describes the father of his country. "A deportment so firm, so dignified, but yet so modest and composed, I have never seen in any other person" as young James Monroe characterized him during the Revolutionary War.[1] Washington wished to be a president above politics, above sectionalism, and, above all, above all controversy.[2] He was always above all political contests, writes Gore Vidal: "so far above the battle that he often saw everything more clearly than others."[3] Nature made Washington physically imposing at 6 feet 2 inches and hot-tempered but, as he said "my countenance never betrayed my feelings."[4]

His concern for civility and reputation was founded on his moral nature, developed from his study of Roman notions of nobility and Jesuit manners that gave him great control, particularly over his violent temper. During the Revolutionary War, only at the Kips Bay loss to the British troops caused by the fear and disorder of the Continental Army did Washington vent his rage.[5]

George Washington. (Courtesy of Library of Congress.)

Considered a born leader, Washington crafted his first term as one of precedence, establishing the role of the chief executive in this new nation by executive privilege, a civilian-controlled military, and neutrality. He believed a leader must look and act the part, and that he did with his contentious cabinet.

His second term was tested by the Whiskey Rebellion, the maneuvers of French minister Citizen Genet, and the public uproar over John Jay's Treaty with England.

Despite his status as icon, Washington received as much maltreatment from the press as Jefferson, Lincoln, and FDR. He was, it appeared in print, "treacherous," "inefficient," "despotic," and, according to Tom Paine, "a hypocrite in public life."[6]

THE FILMS

Always among the most respected of presidents by both the public and historians, Washington appears in some of the earliest commercial films and is second only to Lincoln in the total number of films in which he appears as a character (52). Since the 1950s, films including Washington have averaged less than two a decade.

If there is one overriding philosophy in the manner in which Hollywood presents the First President, it could be the "great man" or "heroic leadership" idea of Thomas Carlyle in his book *Heroes and Hero Worship*. All heroes are flawed, believes Carlyle, and their heroism comes from their creative energy in the face of the world's difficulties, not in their moral perfection.

Washington fits this mold. His flaw was his temper that he strove to control in his search for moral perfection. Hollywood almost always portrays him in perfect control of both himself and the situation. However, D.W. Griffith in his last great silent epic, *America* (1924), does show Washington (Arthur Dewey) losing his temper when he learns that the renegade Captain Butler (Lionel Barrymore) used savages in attacking the settlers in New York's Cherry Valley.

But from one of the first films including him, *Washington Under the American Flag* (1909), until the most recent, *The Patriot* (2000), Washington is seen in control, Carlyle's hero—grave, distant, and austere—usually standing upright, frequently in profile shot. In his recent biography, *His Excellency*, Joseph Ellis discusses how Washington's iconic status combined with his aloof personality poses a problem for biographers. The same can be said for filmmakers. How do you film a man of marble and routinized reticence?

The vast majority of Washington films show him as a military leader. He appears as either a participant or in flashback in films about five wars: French and Indian, American Revolution, Civil War, and World Wars I and II. The flashbacks to the "Father of His Country" obviously are the filmmakers' attempt to show Washington's moral support for the correctness of the nation's position in these later wars.

In the 52 films, 32 named actors plus some unidentified individuals have portrayed Washington. Joseph Kilgour leads the list with five impersonations followed by the outstanding Alan Mowbray with three. Kilgour, who was a Canadian born in 1863, began his appearances as Washington in 1909 and concluded with *Janice Meredith* in 1929. Among the many actors portraying Washington were famous stars Noah Beery and Francis X. Bushman. Perhaps Howard St. John's portrayal in the big-budgeted French film, *La Fayette* (1962), was a Washington portrayal at its best. Particularly apt is the typically taciturn statement by Washington to Cornwallis at Yorktown when the dejected Englishman stated he had never surrendered before: "We understand your stubbornness."

Washington at Valley Forge (1908)

Washington: Unnamed actor. *Studio*: Kalem Co. Inc. *Length*: 905 feet.

Moving Picture World (March 21, 1908: 247) states that this "is an interesting picture that appeals to young and old alike." Later (May 9, 1908: 415) the magazine states it "is a good picture, and the scenes are very realistic." This film is not available for viewing.

Benedict Arnold and Major Andre (1909)

Washington: Unnamed actor. *Other Cast*: Charles Kent (Benedict Arnold), William Humphrey (Major Andre). *Director*: J. Stuart Blackton. *Studio*: Vitagraph. *Length*: One reel.

This is a recreation of the Benedict Arnold as traitor plot that illustrates the major events and describes them with well thought out title cards. Included is one short scene showing an uncredited Washington with General Arnold. Also illustrated is Andre being led to the scaffold and Arnold's death in London.

The Life of George Washington (1909)

According to the Internet Movie Database, Vitagraph released this in 1909. The film is not listed in any of the other relevant databases, and IMDb only lists the production company and the interesting fact that it was produced in two reels released separately. This sounds suspiciously like the two *Flag* films discussed below.

Washington Under the British Flag (1909)

Washington: Joseph Kilgour. *Director:* J. Stuart Blackton. *Studio:* Vitagraph. *Length:* 990 feet.

In mid–1909 J. Stuart Blackton directed two silent films for Vitagraph Co. of America about the life of Washington. Both starred Joseph Kilgour as Washington, and they were released almost simultaneously—*British Flag* on June 29, 1909, and *American Flag* on July 3, 1909, in time for Independence Day.

Although it is possible to view *American Flag* there is apparently no copy of *British Flag* available and very little information on the film. From the title it appears to be the story of Washington's adventures as the head of the Virginia militia during the French and Indian War. Since Kilgour's performance is exemplary in *American Flag* as Washington, it is expected that he portrays the young colonel with equal skill.

Washington Under the American Flag (1909)

Washington: Joseph Kilgour. *Other Cast:* William Humphrey, Charles Kent, William Shea, Clara Kimball Young, James Young. *Producer and Director:* J. Stuart Blackton. *Writing Credits:* Charles Kent. *Studio:* Vitagraph. *Length:* 19 minutes.

This silent covers a significant period of Washington's Revolutionary War service to his country. He is played with dignity and pride down to his stately cape by Joseph Kilgour under the direction and production of J. Stuart Blackton.

Washington appears seated on a white horse, sword in place, and compassionately looks at the wounded. His compassion continues through the other battle scenes, especially before his famed crossing of the Delaware River on Christmas night. He defeats the Hessian mercenaries in the surprise battle of Trenton. He sits alone before a campfire, thinking, with a filmed insert of his troops suffering. He rises, paces, clasps his hands to Heaven, and finally falls asleep dreaming of home, Martha and her two children.

The American flag always appears in the foreground during the battle scenes and dominates the screen during the surrender of Great Britain at Yorktown. Washington next appears at home in Mount Vernon, reading the letter requesting him to be president. He clasps it to his breast and kisses a Bible. He enjoys another moment of glory as he joins, on his horse, a parade celebrating independence. The entire film treats Washington with great respect, almost Christ-like.

The Passing Parade (1912)

Washington: Thomas Carnahan Jr. *Other Cast:* Isabel Lamon, Muriel Ostriche, Eileen Hume, Stella Adams, Margaret Prussing (G.A.R. Bazaar Workers), Mathilde Baring (School Mistress), Leslie Stowe (Washington's Father), Julia Stuart (Grandma), Lamar Johnstone (Papa), Evelyn Fowler (Mamma). *Studio:* Éclair American. *Length:* One reel.

Produced by Éclair American and distributed by the Universal Film Manufacturing Company, *The Passing Parade* was released on Aug. 29, 1912. There is little information on the silent film as it is not listed by the American Film Institute or the All Movie Guide. IMDb carries an extensive cast listing, and by deduction it appears that the film is about the happenings at a bazaar given by the ladies of the Grand Army of the Republic. It also appears that the school mistress (Mathilde Baring) tells her students about the truthfulness of the child Washington (Thomas Carnahan Jr.) to his father (Leslie Stowe). Not available for viewing.

The Flag of Freedom (1913)

Washington: Logan Paul. *Other Cast:* Alice Joyce (Betsy Ross), Hazel Neason (Faith). *Studio:* Kalem Co.

This was released on Jan. 4, 1913. Deducing from the character names including Betsy Ross (Alice Joyce) and George Washington (Logan Paul), the assumption is that the scenario includes Washington's request to make the first American flag. Paul was a character actor listed as appearing in 17 films from 1915 to 1922. It seems that this would have to be his first screen appearance. Not available for viewing.

The Spy (1914)

Washington: William Worthington. *Other Cast:* Herbert Rawlinson (Harvey Birch), Edna Maison (Katie), Ella Hall (Frances Wharton), Edward Alexander (Maj. Dunwoodie), Rex De Rosselli (Mr. Wharton), J.W. Pike (Henry Wharton), Frank Lloyd (Jake Parsons). *Director:* Otis Turner. *Writing Credits:* James Fenimore Cooper (novel), James Dayton (scenario). *Length:* Four reels.

Based on the novel *The Spy* by James Fenimore Cooper, this film tells the story of Harvey Birch (Herbert Rawlinson), who although working in Washington's (William Worthington) home, pretends to be a Tory spy. Washington is fully aware of this deception and has given Birch a letter to prove it but only in case of an emergency.

While on a mission, Birch finds he needs to talk with Washington and allows himself to be captured. After receiving the information, the general allows Birch to escape. Complications arise when Maj. Dunwoodie (Edward Alexander) offers a reward for Birch's recapture. Dunwoodie's fiancée Frances Wharton (Ella Hall) is from a Tory family as is her brother Henry (J.W. Pike), a British officer, who is arrested as a spy and sentenced to be executed.

For some reason not revealed on screen, Birch feels that since he is a real spy he is the one who should be punished. After arranging for Henry Wharton to escape, Birch does not show Washington's letter but is saved by a timely arrival of the general. Not available for viewing.

Washington at Valley Forge (1914)

Washington: Peter Leon. *Other Cast:* Francis Ford (The Spy), Grace Cunard (Betty), Ernest Shields (Lafayette), Harry Edmondson (Innkeeper), Harry Schumm (Betty's Brother). *Director:* Francis Ford. *Writing Credits:* Francis Ford and Grace Cunard. *Studio:* Universal Film Mfg. Co. *Length:* Four reels.

Betty (Grace Cunard) is in love with a man who, unknown to her, is a spy (Francis Ford, brother of John and husband of Grace Cunard). She is staying at an inn close to Valley Forge at the same time Washington (Peter Leon) and his forces are camped there. Unwittingly she overhears that the Hessians are planning an attack and tells her fiancé so that he can warn Washington. Again unwittingly, her brother (Harry Schumm) overhears the spy passing her information on to the Hessians and also that the spy is planning to kill Washington while he is staying at the inn.

Betty talks Washington into switching rooms for the night, and the spy stabs Betty. In the morning Washington is found unhurt; Betty, although mortally wounded, denounces the spy, and he is arrested. This film is not available for viewing.

The Battle Cry of Peace (1915)

Washington: Joseph Kilgour. *Other Cast:* Charles Richman (John Harrison), L. Rogers Lytton (Mr. Emanon), James Morrison (Charles Harrison), Mary Maurice (Mrs. Harrison), Louise Beaudet (Mrs. Vandergriff), Harold Hubert (John Vandergriff), Capt. Jack Crawford (Poet Scout), Charles Kent (The Master), Julia Swayne Gordon (Magdalen), Paul Scardon (Gen. Ulysses S. Grant), William J. Ferguson (Abraham Lincoln). *Director and Producer:* J. Stuart Blackton, Wilfrid North. *Writing Credits:* J. Stuart Blackton, Hudson Maxim, based on Maxim's *Defenseless America*. *Cinematography:* Arthur T. Quinn, Leonard Smith. *Music:* S.L. Rothafel. *Studio:* Vitagraph Co. *Length:* 90 minutes.

This pre–World War I silent film specifically aims to preach preparedness. It was given strong support by most of the U.S. military establishment. Although President Wilson upheld a strict policy of neutrality, contemporary reports indicated that those lending support to the film (some to the extent of appearing in it) included Admiral George Dewey, Secretary of State Robert Lansing, Assistant Secretary of the Navy Franklin D. Roosevelt, and General Leonard Wood, Army Chief of Staff. One report states that ex–President Theodore Roosevelt talked General Wood into loaning director Blackton a regiment of marines as extras.

The basic story is of an unprepared United States being invaded and conquered by an unnamed yet obvious German force and the terrible consequences of such an event. The last third of the film is an allegory that includes historical American figures. Joseph Kilgour plays Washington. Since no copies of the film apparently exist, it is difficult to assess this Kilgour portrayal of Washington although he had done it with great skill in earlier appearances. The film generated great controversy over its strong call to arms.

The Dawn of Freedom (1916)

Washington: Joseph Kilgour. *Other Cast:* Charles Richman (Richard Cartwright), Arine Pretty (Elizabeth McLean), Billie Billings (Nancy Cartwright), James Morrison (Dick

Cartwright), Thomas R. Mills (Irving), Templar Saxe (Count), Edward Elkas (Strike Leader). *Directors:* Theodore Marston, Paul Scardon. *Writing Credits:* Marguerite Bertsch, William J. Hurlbut. *Cinematography:* Reginald E. Lyons, Arthur Roth. *Studio:* Vitagraph. *Length:* Five reels.

Fantasy evolves early in the silent film world as Revolutionary War hero Richard Cartwright (Charles Richman) is put in a state of suspended animation after being mortally wounded in an Indian attack. He is roused in 1916 by an explosion on the property where he is buried, set off by laborers striking against a Cartwright relative who has been exploiting his workers.

Cartwright literally arises from the grave, leads the workers, and wins the labor-management battle against his 20th century cousin. Unfortunately both Cartwright and his cousin are killed in the disputes, but the owner's son is obviously more in accord with Cartwright's thinking, so all ends well. Joseph Kilgour appears as Washington in an early scene. The film is not available for viewing.

Betsy Ross (1917)

Washington: George MacQuarrie. *Other Cast:* Alice Brady (Betsy Griscom), John Bowers (Joseph Ashburn), Lillian Cook (Carissa Griscom), Victor Kennard (John Ross), Eugenie Woodward (Mrs. Ashburn), Kate Lester (Mrs. Vernon), Frank Mayo (Clarence Vernon). *Directors:* George Cowl, Travers Vale. *Writing Credits:* Henry A. Du Souchet. *Cinematography:* Max Schneider, Arthur L. Todd. *Studio:* World Film Corp. *Length:* Five reels.

Employing as little history as possible and as much romance as permissible, *Betsy Ross* shows how the American flag could have come to be made. Betsy (Alice Brady, daughter of studio head William A. Brady) and her sister Carissa (Lillian Cook) are Quakers living in Philadelphia. They both have boyfriends who in a complicated affair become enemies. Betsy's friend Joseph Ashburn (John Bowers) thinks that he has killed Carissa's friend Clarence Vernon (Frank Mayo) in a duel and runs away, changes his name, and joins Washington's army.

Washington (George MacQuarrie) chooses Betsy to sew the flag that he has designed and sends his aide Wheatley, who is actually Ashburn, to guard her during the sewing. Ashburn discovers a man living in the Ross house who turns out to be Clarence Vernon, who had only been wounded in the duel. He is captured, tried, and sentenced to be executed.

Betsy finds proof that Vernon is no longer a British officer and, in the nick of time, convinces Washington to commute the sentence. There is every evidence that Carissa and Vernon and Betsy and Ashburn will live happily ever after. George MacQuarrie is one of the silent era regulars and portrays Washington in two films. This film is not available for viewing.

The Spirit of '76 (1917)

Washington: Noah Beery. *Other Cast:* Jack Cosgrove (George III), Howard Gaye (Lionel Esmond), Adda Gleason (Catherine Montour), George Cheeseborough (Walter N. Butler). *Director:* Frank Montgomery. *Length:* Nine or twelve reels.

After being separated from her brother Lionel Esmond (Howard Gaye) during childhood, Catherine Montour (Adda Gleason) grows up and moves to England where she becomes the mistress of George III. She returns to America with the king's blessings and is part of the major events in the Revolution including Revere's ride, the Battle of Lexington, the Declaration of Independence, Valley Forge, the Cherry Valley massacre, and Cornwallis's surrender. During this period she falls in love with Esmond but discovers their relationship prior to marriage.

The historical background of the film is more interesting than the film. Producer Robert Goldstein, who provided costumes for D.W. Griffith's *The Birth of a Nation* (1915), had a great deal of difficulty releasing this film as it was banned by the Chicago censor board. Even with several thousand feet cut, it was confiscated by the police when it opened May 14, 1917, in Chicago.

After further cuts it opened again but was confiscated by the Federal Department of Justice that charged Goldstein with espionage. This seems to have been mainly due to his portrayal of British brutality and the effect it would have on relations with England in the U.S. joint effort during World War I. Goldstein was sentenced to ten years in jail. After this was commuted to three years by Woodrow Wilson in 1919, he served less than two years. This film is not available for viewing.

The Beautiful Mrs. Reynolds (1918) aka The Adventurer

Washington: George MacQuarrie. *Other Cast:* June Elvidge (Mrs. Maria Reynolds), Carlyle Blackwell (Alexander Hamilton), Arthur Ashley (Aaron Burr), Carl Girard (James Reynolds), Hubert Wilke (Jacob Clingman), Evelyn Greeley (Margaret Moncrieffe), Pinna Nesbit (Mrs. Alexander Hamilton), Lionel Belmore (Gen. Israel Putnam), Rose Tapley (Martha Washington), Albert Hart (Thomas Jefferson), Jack Drumier (John Adams), Charles Brandt (James Monroe), Henry West (John Randolph), Betty Peterson (Theodosia Burr), Alec B. Francis (Gen. Philip Schuyler), William A. Brady (Presenter). *Director:* Arthur Ashley. *Writing Credits:* S.M. Weller. *Cinematography:* Lucien Tainguy. *Studio:* World Film Corp.

Since this is essentially the story of the events leading up to the Burr-Hamilton duel, much of the film develops the long-term relationship of the two protagonists. And since historical dramas, no matter how devoted to accuracy, accented romance, this silent starts with Burr's (Arthur Ashley, the director) and Hamilton's (Carlyle Blackwell) attraction to Margaret Moncrieffe (Evelyn Greeley). The two early American figures square off against each other numerous times including compensation for confiscated Tory property, payment of Revolutionary War debt, the Mrs. Reynolds (June Elvidge) scandal, and the New York gubernatorial race. All of these confrontations lead up to the decision by Burr not to accept the apology that would have prevented Hamilton's death.

The January 11, 1918 *Variety* review states, "Director-actor Arthur Ashley has undoubtedly gone to no small pains in working out the many details, any one of which, if incorrect, would bring down upon his head the criticism of the numerous students of American history." Although numerous modern historians would question the accuracy of the film, it is good to note at one time the film industry had some concern for the historical accuracy of its products. It was one of the most pretentious productions World Film Corp. turned out, getting credit for all the care taken for locations, costuming, interior furnishing, and titles in modern colloquial, not stilted English. George MacQuarrie, one of the World Film Corp.'s stock players, again portrays Washington. This film is not available for viewing.

In the Days of Daniel Boone (1923)

Washington: Duke R. Lee. *Other Cast:* Charles Brinley (Daniel Boone), Jack Mower (Jack Gordon), Eileen Sedgwick (Susan Boone), Ruth Royce (Claire de Voe), Herschel Mayall (General Braddock), Albert J. Smith (Capt. Charles Redmond), Frank Farrington (Judge Henderson), Jack Lewis (James Monroe). *Director:* William James Craft. *Writing Credits:* Jefferson Moffit. *Studio:* Universal Pictures.

Universal Pictures produced a very successful series called *In the Days of Buffalo Bill* and attempted to repeat its success with this fictitious story of Daniel Boone's adventures in pioneering. The new 15-episode silent series was first released on June 25, 1923, and starred Charles Brinley as Boone, fighting both Tories and Indians.

Duke R. Lee plays Washington as the leader of the Virginia militia and a character named Simon Girty. The series is not available for viewing. It has to be assumed that Lee does an acceptable job since after directing a film in 1919 he appears as a character actor in 62 films from 1919 until as late as *My Darling Clementine* (1946).

Alexander Hamilton (1924)

Washington: George Nash. *Other Cast:* Allen Connor (Alexander Hamilton), Mabel Taliaferro (Elizabeth Schuyler), Lyndall Olmstead (Martha Washington), J.E. Poole (Sandy McFarlane), Bradley Barker (Tom the Tinker). *Director:* Kenneth S. Webb. *Studio:* Chronicles of America Pictures, Yale University Press. *Length:* 30 minutes.

This depiction of Hamilton's career from 1780 through 1793 was adapted by Allan Johnson from the book *George Washington and His Colleagues*. Although it does not cover his notorious affair with Mrs. Reynolds or the Burr duel, the film provides reasonable coverage of Hamilton's relationship with Washington.

Director Kenneth S. Webb opens the film at Washington's headquarters in Morristown, New Jersey, where Hamilton (Allen Connor) is convincing a farmer that it is his patriotic duty to provide fodder for the army's horses even though the paper money then in circulation is worthless. Washington (George Nash) praises Hamilton, who is his military aide, for his ability to convince people of their duty.

As the years pass, the film shows Hamilton marrying Elizabeth Schuyler (Mabel Taliaferro) and Washington becoming president. After a tableau of the inauguration, Washington offers Hamilton the job of Secretary of the Treasury. At first Hamilton refuses because of personal financial needs but is ultimately convinced by Washington and Mrs. Hamilton to accept it. The film touches very lightly on the serious financial problems that face the new republic and concentrates more on the events leading to the Whiskey Rebellion, obviously the most pictorially exciting event in the early 1790s.

Washington is once more able to play the military leader as he gathers a force in Carlisle, Pennsylvania, to march into Western Pennsylvania. It was not a long campaign and the excitement ends in short order. So does the film that ends immediately after the rebellion is put down. In the final scene Hamilton tenders his resignation to a disappointed President Washington who, understanding Hamilton's need to attend to his own finances, stands and shakes his hand and then places his hand on Hamilton's shoulder. Nash was one of the early Washington impersonators and as usual provides a dignified, serious portrayal in this extended role.

America (1924)

Washington: Arthur Dewey. *Other Cast:* Neil Hamilton (Nathan Holden), Erville Alderson (Justice Montague), Lionel Barrymore (Capt. Walter Butler), Charles Emmett Mack (Charles Montague), Lee Beggs (Samuel Adams), John Dunton (John Hancock), Frank Walsh (Thomas Jefferson), Harry O'Neill (Paul Revere), Carol Dempster (Miss Nancy Montague), Sydney Deane (Sir Ashley Montague), Frank McGlynn Sr. (Patrick Henry). *Director and Producer:* D.W. Griffith. *Writing Credits:* Robert W. Chambers. *Cinematography:* Billy Bitzer, Marcel Le Picard, Hendrik Sartov, Harold Sintzenich. *Editors:* James Smith, Rose Smith. *Production Designer:* Charles Kirk. *Music:* Joseph Carl Breil, Adolph Fink. *Studio:* D.W. Griffith Productions. *Length:* 93 minutes.

America is the last of D.W. Griffith's great silent epics. With an enormous cast, he stages dramatic and authentic scenes of the Battles of Lexington and Concord and Bunker Hill, and the war in Cherry Valley between the settlers and the British with their Indian conscripts. Arthur Dewey as George Washington appears in his War of Independence role in six scenes, always in a deific mode. He is first seen in the second of the film's 28 chapters, *Williamsburg*, where the question is raised: Who will stand against George III? The question is answered two chapters later, in *The House of Burgesses*, when he stands and exhorts the assemblage to aid besieged Boston while Ashley Montague (Sydney Dean) disagrees. The old friends part in the next chapter, *Parting of Old Friends*. With his farewell to Montague's son (Charles Emmett Mack), Washington says, "Charles, you are the son of an honorable man, but do your duty as you see it." Washington then turns to Montague's daughter and says, "Good bye, Miss Nancy."

Later, as general and head of the army during the conflict, Washington prays as his troops face their darkest hours, dressed in rags and almost barefoot (with several telling shots of their ravaged feet) in the Valley Forge chapter. He appears almost Christlike in his pose. Shortly hereafter, when Washington learns of the renegade Butler's (Lionel Barrymore) use of savages to gain his own ends—ruler of a new territory—Washington erupts in a display of temper usually under control through his impeccable manners and morals, but silent as is the film. Finally, Washington accepts Cornwallis's defeat in a stately and sedate manner. The *New York Times* commentary (Feb. 28, 1924) stated that the director "can still be given an 'edge' on any basis of comparison."

Gateway to the West (1924)

Washington: Arthur Vinton. *Other Cast:* Charles Graham (Richard Corbin), Walter P. Lewis (Christopher Gist), John Hickey (Robert Dinwiddie, Governor of Virginia), Louis D'Arclay (Jumonville), Thornton Baston (DeVilliers), Stanley Walpole (William Pitt). *Director:* Webster Campbell. *Writing Credits:* William B. Courtney. *Studio:* Chronicles of America Pictures, Yale University Press. *Length:* Approximately 30 minutes.

One of the Chronicles of America Pictures directed by Webster Campbell, this film highlights the leadership of Washington (Arthur Vinton) as head of the Virginia militia in the fight against the French in Western Pennsylvania in 1753. Washington struggles with his frustrations under British leadership until his commander is killed in battle.

With his command heavily outnumbered, Washington goes against his inclinations that he must retreat. Unable to escape, he decides that his troops must "pick our ground and make a stand." The stand is made at a location now called Fort Necessity and is so much stronger than the French expect that they finally propose very lenient surrender terms. Faced with the ultimate extinction of his men, Washington agrees to the French terms and is allowed to return to Virginia.

Afraid of being sharply reprimanded by Gov. Dinwiddie (John Hickey) for the defeat, Washington is surprised when the governor expresses pleasure, noting that this will mean all-out war with the French. Assuming the triumph of British forces, he sees "thousands of settlers pouring through the gateway to the west."

Vinton portrays a younger Washington than is seen in Revolutionary War films. The role calls for Washington to be indecisive at certain points, and this interpretation does not fit one's preconceived idea of the "father of our country." However, Vinton handles the role well.

Janice Meredith (1924) aka The Beautiful Rebel

Washington: Joseph Kilgour. *Other Cast:* Marion Davies (Janice Meredith), Harrison Ford (Charles Fownes), Macklyn Arbuckle (Squire Meredith), George Nash (Lord Howe), Tyrone Power Sr. (Lord Cornwallis), May Vokes (Susie), W.C. Fields (A British Sergeant), Mrs. Macklyn Arbuckle (Martha Washington), Lionel Adams (Thomas Jefferson), Ken Maynard (Paul Revere). *Director:* E. Mason Hopper. *Producer:* William Randolph Hearst. *Writing Credits:* Paul Leicester Ford (novel), Lillie Hayward. *Music:* Deems Taylor. *Cinematography:* George Barnes, Ira H. Morgan. *Film Editing:* Walter Futter. *Art Direction:* Joseph Urban. *Costume Design:* Gretl Urban Thurlow. *Studio:* Cosmopolitan Pictures. *Length:* 153 minutes.

Although newspaper magnate and film producer William Randolph Hearst produced this as an epic for his mistress Marion Davies, its historical aspects overshadow her screen romance (but she does get her man in the end). Davies as Janice Meredith, "jovial" daughter of New Jersey Royalist Squire Meredith (Macklyn Arbuckle), figures highly in giving information to Paul Revere (Ken Maynard) for his ride and giving George Washington (Joseph Kilgour) the disposition of the Hessian troops in Trenton to spur him to battle.

The lavish—purportedly million-dollar budget—production values of this eleven-reel silent allow for elaborate authentic costumes (more than 20 for Davies alone), original music by Deems Taylor, and realistic war scenes, particularly of Washington crossing the Delaware River. Enveloped in winter gales, Washington leads his men into the small boats that struggle through the ice as they cross the Delaware to surprise the Hessians. Director E. Mason Hopper shows how "impossible" (as even Washington called it) this Christmas attack was by shooting details: the confusion of getting all the men into the small boats, the difficulties with the ice floe, the wind and snow, the fall of one soldier into the frigid water. He does the same with Revere's ride, shooting just the horse's hooves to illustrate Revere's speed, and panning Revere and horse as they gallop across a farmer's porch to accent his intensity.

Kilgour conveys the courage, dignity, dedication, and human understanding of the general in his many scenes. He's especially effective in acting as gracious host at Mount Vernon to Meredith and her husband, Charles Fownes (Harrison Ford) aka Lord John (Jack) Brereton. Washington restores Meredith's Royalist father's home and toasts her, and she in patriotic fervor toasts Washington.

Davies's performance charms: She's alternately coy, mischievous, grave, and daring

Top: Janice Meredith (1924): Joseph Kilgour, the major impersonator of Washington, stands in a boat carrying Colonial troops across the frozen Delaware River to attack the Hessians. Marion Davies (not in this scene) greatly helps the Revolutionary War leader in this Cosmopolitan Productions–Metro-Goldwyn Picture. (Courtesy of George Eastman House.) *Bottom: Janice Meredith* (1924): Joseph Kilgour accepts the surrender of the British forces after the Battle of Yorktown near the conclusion of this Marion Davies vehicle by Cosmopolitan Productions–Metro-Goldwyn Pictures. (Courtesy of George Eastman House.)

between her many romantic swoons. The large cast includes cameo appearances of our Founding Fathers including Thomas Jefferson (Lionel Adams) signing the Declaration of Independence and W.C. Fields imbibing as a British soldier. The *New York Times* review (of Aug. 6, 1924: 13:3) stated that "No more brilliant achievement and ambitious motion picture dealing with historical romances has ever been exhibited."

Yorktown (1924)

Washington: George Nash. *Other Cast:* Lyndall Olmstead (Martha Washington), Sidney Mather (Jean Baptiste Rochambeau), Lionel Chalmers (Count Francis de Grasse), Allen Connor (American Private Soldier), H.P. Woodley (Sir Henry Clinton), Charles Esdale (Lord Cornwallis). *Director:* Webster Campbell. *Writing Credits:* Nathaniel Wright Stephenson. *Studio:* Chronicles of America Pictures, Yale University Press.

The Chronicles of America Pictures produced this silent film based on the Yale University Press Chronicles of America book. It opens in 1781 with Washington reviewing his "desperate" situation with five of his military commanders. Looking solemn and serious, George Nash, who portrays Washington with skill, says the enemy has every advantage while the French fleet, America's last hope, is 3,000 miles away. Nash as Washington dominates the film, appearing in a half dozen scenes and displaying the qualities of boldness and compassion that made him a great leader. Webster Campbell directs for maximum dramatic effect with tight composition and dramatic camera angles.

Washington faces mutiny by his troops unless they are paid, which he has promised to do again and again. Against his judgment, Congress has given the troops permission to disband, which Washington conveys to them, knowing they will. His moral sense surfaces in a subsequent scene with his wife Martha (Lyndall Olmstead) in which she comments how "the men are worried about their families," and he retorts, "What about their duty?"

With the next threat of mutiny, Washington gives stern orders "to march unarmed or be shot." Later, Washington learns that Lord Cornwallis (Charles Esdale) has moved north and sent troops to capture Thomas Jefferson and the Virginia Assembly. Washington despairs, "Now or never; deliverance must come." It does when the French fleet under Count Francis de Grasse (Lionel Chalmers) is spotted by Cornwallis as Washington boldly leads his troops south, his masterful strategy inspiring his troops. The Battle of Yorktown ensues in long shot and smoke, watched over by Washington on his horse. Victory is his, and the stirring British surrender ends the film.

The Flag: A Story Inspired by the Tradition of Betsy Ross (1927) aka The Flag

Washington: Francis X. Bushman. *Other Cast:* Enid Bennett (Betsy Ross), Johnnie Walker (Charles Brandon), Alice Calhoun (Edith Brandon). *Director-Writer:* Arthur Maude. *Music:* Vivek Maddala (2002). *Cinematography:* Ray Rennahan. *Studio:* Loew's Inc. *Length:* 20 minutes.

A restored version of this 1927 film was released in February 2002 and has been shown on TCM. The reason for the restoration and inclusion of a new score by Vivek Maddala is possibly related to the film's being among the few produced using two-strip Technicolor (as contrasted to the three-strip Technicolor of today).

The story is a variation on the theme of Washington's (matinee idol Francis X. Bushman) asking Betsy Ross (Enid Bennett) to produce the first American flag. As directed and written by Arthur Maude, the variation is the fact that Edith (Alice Calhoun), the wife of British officer Charles Brandon (Johnnie Walker) who crosses battle lines to visit her, is staying with Ross. Found hiding by Washington, he is released by the compassionate general.

This early use of Technicolor is particularly effective when the sky changes colors. Ross tells Washington that the twilight sky is the basis for the design of the flag. No doubt because of the technical difficulties in using the new process (high costs of prints, need for high intensity lights, and careful choice of colors), the film lacks dramatic value. Bushman portrays Washington with the skill of an action hero of the day but doesn't have any real action—only tableaux—to make his best showing.

Winners of the Wilderness (1927)

Washington: Edward Hearn. *Other Cast:* Tim McCoy (Col. O'Hara), Joan Crawford (Rene Contrecoeur), Edward Connelly (Gen. Contrecoeur), Roy D'Arcy (Capt. Dumas), Louise Lorriane (Mimi), Tom O'Brien (Timothy), Will Walling (Gen. Braddock), Frank Currier (Gov. de Vaudreuil), Lionel Belmore (Gov. Dinwiddie), Chief John Big Tree (Pontiac). *Director and Producer:* W.S. Van Dyke. *Writing Credits:* Marian Ainslee, Josephine Chippo, John T. Neville. *Cinematography:* Clyde De Vinna. *Editing:* Conrad A. Nervig. *Studio:* Metro-Goldwyn-Mayer. *Length:* 68 minutes.

In the early 1750s, 27 years before the Revolutionary War, French Governor de Vaudreuil (Frank Currier) and the Ottowa chieftain Pontiac (Chief John Big Tree) sign an agreement to fight the British in western Pennsylvania and Ohio. This silent film directed by W.S. Van Dyke introduces a romantic aside to tell in a reasonably historically accurate manner the story of Gen. Edward Braddock and the disastrous defeat in his attempt to take Fort Duquesne (now Pittsburgh) from the French.

An intrepid and unconquerable Col. Dennis O'Hara (Tim McCoy) steals the treaty from the governor and sends it to General Braddock. In making his escape from Quebec, O'Hara also has time to fall in love with Renee Contrecoeur (Joan Crawford), daughter of the commander at Fort Duquesne. By doing this, he makes a fool of the obvious villain (pencil mustache and all), French Captain Dumas (Roy D'Arcy). All this action unfolds using the typical approach of the B-westerns for which McCoy was to become so famous. For example, he stands on a speeding horse while fighting a sword-swinging Frenchman.

O'Hara returns to Virginia where he meets with General Braddock (Will Walling) and George Washington (Edward Hearn) who is the leader of the Virginia militia, the "Virginia Blues." Hearn plays Washington as a serious, intelligent military man who is unsuccessful in convincing Braddock that fighting Indians requires a different approach from the typical British Red Coat military formation. Braddock ridicules Washington through the march to Fort Duquesne (with a film cast of thousands), stating that Indians could not stand up to British military might. Braddock maintains this position until he is mortally wounded in the ambush set up by the French and Indians.

Our hero O'Hara is captured after Braddock's defeat and turned over to the Indians. After almost being burned alive at the stake he finally escapes with his beloved Renee. The lovers arrive in Virginia ready to marry when Governor Dinwiddie (Lionel Belmore) warns against their union as it has international complications: "She is French and he is British. What will their children be?" Washington ends the film, saying, "*American!*"

Its superior production values stem from Clyde De Vinna's cinematography that shows his inventiveness. Van Dyke's direction, especially of the large cast in battle scenes, shows his early training under D.W. Griffith in *Intolerance* (1916). A prolific director, mainly for MGM, Van Dyke made five other films in 1927, all with outdoor settlings like this.

Alexander Hamilton (1931)

Washington: Alan Mowbray. *Other Cast:* George Arliss (Hamilton), Doris Kenyon (Mrs. Hamilton), Dudley Digges (Sen. Timothy Roberts), June Collyer (Mrs. Reynolds), Ralf Harolde (Mr. Reynolds), Montagu Love (Thomas Jefferson), Lionel Belmore (Gen. Philip Schuyler), John T. Murray (Count Talleyrand), Morgan Wallace (James Monroe), John Larkin (Zesial). *Director:* John G. Adolfi. *Writing Credits:* George Arliss, Mary Hamlin, Maude Howell, Julien Josephson. *Cinematography:* James Van Trees. *Film Editing:* Owen Marks. *Art Direction:* Esdras Hartley. *Set Decoration:* Ray Moyer. *Costume Design:* Earl Luick. *Studio:* Warner Bros. *Length:* 73 minutes.

The second most powerful man in the U.S. during the formation of the country was Alexander Hamilton. His efforts at providing for national assumption of the debt to Revolutionary War soldiers became the plot point on which this biographical film turns. The brilliant, complex, relentless patriot receives a fine rendering by George Arliss who wrote this work based on an earlier stage play he wrote with Mary Hamlin. Arliss's biopics were considered the closest Warners came to prestige production. In obtaining approval for the debt assumption that is a first step toward national fiscal responsibility, Hamilton engages in relationships with many other leading political figures of the time, providing both dramatic and character development as well as a view of the mores of the period.

The film opens and closes with Washington very well played by Alan Mowbray who always speaks and acts in Washington's distinguished manner, first as general, then as president. Seated on his horse, Washington delivers his eloquent and "long," as he says, farewell to his troops. He commends their action through eight years of hardship, exhorts their going onto different paths for the country's "future existence," and promises them "ample justice." He ends by raising his hat, his hand, and his horse's legs. Immediately afterward Washington tells his aide, Hamilton, of this farewell, it is "not as hard as it will be to part with you ... and your advice ... you must stand by me."

The question of assumption goes on for some time until it is replaced by the question as to where the permanent capital of the new nation will be located. The seeds for a dual solution are sown by James Monroe (Morgan Wallace), just back from a 700-mile trip through the South to ascertain its feeling for the capital site. Jefferson (Montagu Love) suggests "a little persuasion." The two do just that with Hamilton in the famous compromise, held in Hamilton's home office, not at its actual location in the Philadelphia lodgings of Jefferson. Nothing shakes Hamilton's irrevocable stance until Jefferson says, "Suppose we pass your bill on assumption in return for the capital in the South as we pledged our word."

Secure in this maneuver, Hamilton works late in his office as his beloved wife Betsy is visiting her sick sister in England. He befriends a beautiful young woman, Moira Reynolds, who comes to beg for money from the Secretary of the Treasury so she can flee from her brutal husband. Hamilton gives her $50, "a personal loan." In actual fact, Hamilton had a year-long affair with Mrs. Reynolds, giving her hundreds of dollars to keep her lazy and dishonest husband from blackmailing him about Hamilton's government investments.

When Jefferson, Monroe, and Sen. Roberts (instead of the actual Sen. Venable) visit Hamilton about this "affair," Hamilton displays his temper, saying "you hate me," "this was organized," and "there is no foundation in truth." Jefferson and Monroe apologize, but Roberts continues his plans for Hamilton's vilification through the press. Hamilton finds his wife packing. But the mother of his eight children (never shown) stands by him, as does Washington in the final scene.

The Phantom President (1932)

Washington: Alan Mowbray. *Other Cast*: George M. Cohan (Theodore Blair/Doc Peter Varney), Claudette Colbert (Felicia Hammond), Jimmy Durante (Curly Cooney), Sidney Toler (Prof. Aikenhead), Charles Middleton (Abe Lincoln). *Director*: Norman Taurog. *Writing Credits*: Walter DeLeon, Harlan Thompson, George F. Worts. *Music*: Lorenz Hart, Richard Rodgers, Jimmy Durante, Eddie Leonard, Rudolph G. Kopp, John Leipold. *Cinematography*: David Abel. *Studio*: Paramount Pictures. *Length*: 78 minutes.

In 1932 the country did not need a stand-in for the presidential candidate. With FDR running it was not necessary. However, it got an imaginative film concerning an election in which George M. Cohan plays two roles. The original candidate, Theodore Blair (George M. Cohan) is a complete dud on the campaign trail, and his "handlers" convince his physical double, a carnival pitchman, Doc Peter Varney (also George M. Cohan), to take his place during the electioneering.

Things get out of hand when Varney is fully accepted even by Blair's girl friend, Felicia Hammond (Claudette Colbert), who thinks that Blair has finally "got a life." The handlers decide to shanghai Varney out of the picture, but with the help of sidekick Curley (Jimmy Durante), Blair instead takes a boat ride. This musical comedy, which was Cohan's first talking role, provides all the cast an opportunity to display their talents, presidential or otherwise.

The presidential appearances come in an early satiric scene during which four presidents—George Washington (Alan Mowbray), Thomas Jefferson, Abraham Lincoln (Charles B. Middleton), and Theodore Roosevelt—emerge from large picture frames to do a song-and-dance routine, singing "The Country Needs a Man." Similar in appearance and voice to their respective presidents, the actors do an animated rendition. Mowbray shows his versatility playing this type of light role as well as he did in his serious interpretations of Washington.

The Road Is Open Again (1933)

Washington: Alan Dinehart. *Other Cast*: Dick Powell (The Songwriter), Samuel S. Hinds (Woodrow Wilson), Charles Middleton (Abraham Lincoln). *Director*: Alfred E. Green. *Producer*: Warner Bros. *Music*: Sammy Fain, Irving Kahal. *Length*: Seven minutes.

In a short NRA featurette, the philosophy of this program, instigated by FDR, is supported by three other esteemed presidents. FDR's message is in the words to the title song, "the road to better times is open again."

The song is created in this simple plot that unifies the inspirational, political film—by

Dick Powell (The Songwriter). He's a 1930 musician at his piano, trying to write music, with portraits of Washington, Lincoln, and Wilson on his wall. But he naps, and the three presidents appear reading a newspaper about how the NRA has created one million jobs. When the Songwriter awakes, the presidents address him in historically telling terms. Washington states he's been watching over the country for more than 100 years. As played by Alan Dinehart, he's imposing, sonorous in voice, yet rather portly and pudgy of features, unlike Washington. He serves as the narrator, stating what the NRA will do ("Give more people jobs for a living wage") and saying how Americans can help—by patronizing stores with the blue NRA eagle.

Are We Civilized? (1934)

Washington: Aaron Edwards. *Other Cast:* William Farnum (Paul Franklin Sr.), Anita Louise (Norma Bockner), Frank McGlynn Sr. (Abraham Lincoln, Felix Bockner), LeRoy Mason (Paul Franklin Jr.), Oscar Apfel (Dr. Leonard Gear), Stuart Holmes (Col. Salter), Alin Cavin (Moses), Conrad Siderman (Buddha), Sidney T. Pink (Confucius), Harry Burkhardt (Caesar), Charles Requa (Christ), J.C. Fowler (Mohammed), Bert Lindley (Christopher Columbus), William Humphrey (Napoleon). *Director-Producer:* Edwin Carewe. *Writing Credits:* Harold Sherman. *Cinematography:* Al M. Green, Leon Shamron. *Film Editing:* Dan Milner. *Studio:* Raspin Productions, Inc. *Length:* 70 minutes.

Producer-director Edwin Carewe was a major director during the silent era and was attempting a comeback with this 1934 talkie. By the use of a significant amount of newsreel and stock footage (*Variety* states it was from Cecil B. DeMille historical epics), Carewe appeared not willing to spend a great deal of money on this attempt.

Silent star William Farnum, acting as if he is still in a silent movie, plays the lead as Paul Franklin Sr., a major newspaper publisher from the United States who returns to his home country (obviously Germany). He finds it taken over by boyhood friend Felix Bockner (Frank McGlynn Sr.) and on the road to a brutal dictatorship. For speaking out publicly, Franklin is to be deported but spends most of the film trying to convince Bockner and his sympathizers to change their ways before it is too late.

Franklin's attempt takes the form of a series of episodic flashbacks starting with the "big bang" development of the earth and covering the cave man, Moses, Buddha, Confucius, Caesar, Christ, Mohammed, Christopher Columbus, and Napoleon. He also brings in the major technological advances in the history of man. The stock footage and newsreels are the basis for much of these flashbacks.

Franklin also mentions the advances for freedom made during the American Revolution and a shot of Washington portrayed by Aaron Edwards is flashed on the screen. There are no words or acting involved.

Franklin's warnings were not effective in 1934, and he dies in the film after being hit by a banned book. However, his son Paul Franklin Jr. (LeRoy Mason) promises to continue his work.

The Silk Hat Kid (1935) aka The Lord's Referee

Washington: Sidney Miller. *Other Cast:* Lew Ayres (Eddie Howard), Mae Clarke (Laura Grant), Paul Kelly (Tim Martin), Ralf Harolde (Lefty Phillips), William Harrigan (Brother

Joe Campbell), Billy Lee (Tommy), Raymond Borzage (Lincoln), Frankie Genardi (Theodore Roosevelt). *Director:* H. Bruce Humberstone. *Producer:* Joseph Engel. *Writing Credits:* Lou Bresslow, Edward Eliscu, Dore Schary. *Music:* Samuel Kaylin. *Studio:* Fox Film Corp. *Length:* 68 minutes.

This Depression era film uses gangsters, gamblers, boxers, and a priest to tell a simple story. Tim Martin (Paul Kelly) is a basically good guy who wants nothing to do with bad guy gambler Lefty Phillips (Ralf Harolde). To provide protection he imports old boxing friend Eddie Howard (Lew Ayres). Martin and Howard have their disagreements particularly over Laura Grant (Mae Clarke). Although Phillips and his gang are eliminated, it takes a boxing match arranged by Brother Joe Campbell (William Harrigan) to completely solve their problems.

There are three presidents in the cast listing: Washington played by Sidney Miller, Theodore Roosevelt played by Frankie Genardi, and Lincoln played by Raymond Borzage. Their involvement with this scenario could have been in a short Depression era sermon or a pre–World War II morale building scene.

Give Me Liberty (1936)

Washington: Robert Warwick. *Other Cast:* John Litel (Patrick Henry), Nedda Harrigan (Doxie Henry), Carlyle Moore Jr. (Capt. Milton, Messenger), George Irving (Washington's Guest and Friend), Boyd Irwin (British Commissioner), Gordon Hart (Anti-Rebel Delegate Speaker). *Director:* B. Reeves Eason. *Writing Credits:* Forrest Barnes (also story). *Music:* M.K. Jerome, Jack Scholl. *Cinematography:* W. Howard Greene. *Film Editing:* Louis Hesse. *Art Direction:* Ted Smith. *Studio:* The Vitaphone Corp. *Length:* 21 minutes.

This Vitaphone Technicolor short subject (really a filmed short story) offers moviegoers an opportunity to see and hear Patrick Henry's "Give me liberty" speech although it takes great liberties (no pun intended) with the circumstances. The gifted orator is well played and spoken by John Litel who conveys Henry's political passion. But the film incorrectly focuses on the inspiration his wife Doxie (Nedda Harrrigan) gives him to deliver the speech by coming to Richmond's St. John's Church and the Virginia Provincial Convention.

Equally historically incorrect is Col. Washington's role in suggesting that Henry's wife come to the church to provide Henry with the "lacking" impetus. Robert Warwick as Washington plays the Colonial leader with grace (he dances the minuet in one scene) and command (he urges Henry to arm Virginia so that others will follow upon hearing news of the battles in Massachusetts). Furthermore, in his third appearance in the film during Henry's speech, Washington shows his usual sense of propriety as he rolls his eyes during Henry's melodramatic delivery. The film won Oscars for Best Color Short and Best Live Action Short.

Marry the Girl (1937)

Washington: William Worthington. *Other Cast:* Mary Boland (Ollie Radway), Frank McHugh (David "Party" Partridge), Hugh Herbert (John B. Radway), Carol Hughes (Virginia Radway), Allen Jenkins (Specs), Mischa Auer (Dimitri Kyeff), Alan Mowbray (Dr. Hayden Stryker), Hugh O'Connell (Michael "Mike" Forrester), Teddy Hart (Biff). *Director:* William McGann. *Producers:* Bryan Foy, Jack L. Warner. *Writing Credits:* Pat C. Flick, Sig

Herzig, Edward Hope, Tom Reed. *Music:* David Raksin, Heinz Roemheld. *Cinematography:* Arthur Todd. *Film Editing:* Warren Low. *Art Direction:* Max Parker. *Costume Design:* Howard Shoup. *Studio:* Warner Bros. *Time:* 68 minutes.

Like Theodore Roosevelt in *Arsenic and Old Lace,* Washington appears as a mentally unbalanced person in this madcap comedy. Washington, as enacted with great dignity and bearing by William Worthington, is one of the patients at Dr. Hayden Stryker's Fairview Sanitarium. Dressed impeccably in a lounge suit, Washington strides by without a word as the screwball newspaper owner John B. Radway (Hugh Herbert) and his timid managing editor David Partridge (Allen Jenkins) look behind a Gilbert Stuart portrait of Washington for—of all things—a cartoon, indispensable to the newspaper. Joining Radway for Dr. Stryker's hypnotic cures is Virginia Radway (Mary Boland, the star of the film), sent there to keep her from marrying the egotistic artist Dimitri Kyeff (Mischa Auer).

Logic of course never matters in Miss Radway's romance choices: first the egotistic Kyeff; then Partridge, who turns brave while kidnapping her from the sanitarium. Nor does logic figure in the childlike humor of John Radway who, upon the departure of the couple, shoots a gun at a duck painting, causing the birds to flutter. He shoots again, and they fly out of the frame—1937 special effects.

Sons of Liberty (1939)

Washington: Montagu Love. *Other Cast:* Claude Rains (Haym Salomon), Gale Sondergaard (Rachel Salomon), Donald Crisp (Alexander McDougall), Henry O'Neill (Member of Continental Congress), James Stephenson (Colonel Tillman). *Director:* Michael Curtiz. *Producer:* Gordon Hollingshead. *Writing Credits:* Crane Wilbur. *Cinematography:* Sol Polito, Ray Rennahan. *Film Editing:* Thomas Pratt. *Art Direction:* Hugh Reticker. *Costume Design:* Milo Anderson. *Makeup:* Perc Westmore. *Sound:* E.A. Brown. *Studio:* Warner Bros. *Length:* 20 minutes.

The American Revolution and its ramifications get a probing treatment in this short about patriotic financier Haym Salomon (Claude Rains), a Jewish immigrant who bounced from country to country before he came to the U.S. for freedom. The 20-minute film has superb production values by Warner Brothers and experienced direction by Michael Curtiz.

The plot is one of the many stories that made the Revolution a success. It is of Salomon's joining the Sons of Liberty, a group of rebel stalwarts. Arrested because of his affiliation with them, he works as an interpreter with his multi-lingual gift, but escapes to return to his lucrative import-export business. His generosity receives full distinction from Washington (Montagu Love) who realizes Salomon's patriotism can help his "naked troops leave their quarters" and go into battle rather than desert. Washington asks Salomon to raise $400,000 to support the unpaid troops, which Salomon does. Love achieves Washington's English accent as well as his carriage and demeanor in this scene and a short subsequent shot of him, sitting stalwartly on his horse.

Washington goes on to victory at Yorktown (related in a voice-over), and Salomon achieves immortality for his "sacred trust" in his adopted land of independence, which declaration he quotes on his deathbed.

Holiday Highlights (1940)

Drawn by: Rollin Hamilton, Thomas McKimon. *Music Score and Direction*: Frank Marsales. *Studio*: Warner Brothers.

Part of the Golden Age of Looney Tunes series, this Merrie Melodies cartoon deals with animation of ordinary objects singing songs that reflect the musical style of the period: bouncy rhythm, simple lyrics, humorous bent. George Washington as military commander of the Revolutionary forces appears out of nowhere, unrelated to the plot, crossing the Delaware River. Carrying the American flag (which had yet to be designed), he's en route to New Jersey on Christmas night to battle the Hessians. Drawn in a commanding military manner, the figure looks ahead, saying nothing.

The crux of *Holiday Highlights* deals with a trip to a city dump by a junk wagon which contents come to life. A male doll, for example, plays bed springs as a piano while a female mannequin trio sings the cartoon-stopping number, "A Great Big Bunch of You." There also are dancing shoes, dancing alarm clocks, and three animated toy soldiers who sink Washington's boat, the climax of the great military commander's appearance.

The Howards of Virginia (1940)

Washington: George Houston.

George Washington as played by stately George Houston makes one brief appearance in this Revolutionary War film. Seated on his horse, Washington leads the Virginia troops into battle at the end of the film. He does not speak, and Houston's physical appearance as the general makes a fine impression. For full details see Ch. 3 on Thomas Jefferson.

Meet the Chump (1941)

Washington: Charles Miller. *Other Cast*: Hugh Herbert (Hugh Mansfield), Lewis Howard (John Mansfield), Jean Brooks (Madge Reilly), Anne Nagel (Miss Burke), Kathryn Adams (Gloria Mitchell), Shemp Howard (Stinky Fink), Richard Lane (Slugs Bennett), Andrew Tombes (Revello), Hobart Cavanaugh (Juniper), Charles Halton (Dr. Stephanowsky), Martin Spellman (Champ). *Director*: Edward F. Cline. *Producer*: Ken Goldsmith. *Writing Credits*: Otis Garrett, Alex Gottlieb, Hal Hudson. *Music*: Hans J. Salter. *Cinematography*: Elwood Bredell. *Film Editing*: Milton Carruth. *Art Direction*: Jack Otterson. *Set Decoration*: R.A. Gausman. *Costume Design*: Vera West. *Studio*: Universal Pictures. *Length*: 60 minutes.

This madcap comedy suits the talents of Hugh "Woo Woo" Herbert, a bumbling slapstick comedian. As investment broker Hugh Mansfield he mismanages the ten-million-dollar trust of his nephew John Francis Mansfield III (Lewis Howard), who announces he wants his inheritance and wants to marry Gloria Mitchell (Kathryn Adams). Fearing imprisonment for embezzlement, Mansfield decides to feign insanity. This provokes Mitchell to call off the wedding and young Mansfield to put his uncle in the Stephanowsky Sanitarium. There the uncle meets Revello (Andrew Tombes) who makes ladies' hats from kitchen utensils.

During his sanity hearing, Mansfield masquerades as a psychiatrist, and his nephew is mistaken for him. While trying to escape he asks nurse Madge Reilly (Jean Brooks) to marry him so that he can inherit his estate. More mix-ups occur until government agent Juniper

(Hobart Cavanaugh) informs him the government wants to buy his abandoned mines. He's rich, and his uncle plans to go to Hollywood to design hats with Revello.

Charles Miller is the patient who believes he is Washington—the same situation in an earlier Herbert film, *Marry the Girl* (1937).

The Remarkable Andrew (1942)

Washington: Montagu Love.

Andrew Law (William Holden) is the title character in this patriotic pre–World War II film in which the ghost of Jackson (Brian Donlevy) comes to the assistance of a young bookkeeper accused of embezzlement. Joining Jackson, the seventh president, are the "best legal minds" in the country: Washington, Thomas Jefferson, Benjamin Franklin, and Chief Justice Marshall. Jackson urges these "greatest legal minds" to give advice true to their natures. Washington says, "No violence, General Jackson, please.... We were forced to become heroes." Montagu Love portrays this role with proper Washingtonian morality and dignity. For details, see Ch. 7 on Andrew Jackson.

Don't You Believe It (1943)

Washington: Walter Kingsford. *Other Cast:* John Nesbitt (Narrator), Harry Cording (Rogue), Edward McWade (Wise Man), Ferdinand Munier (Rumor Starter), Ian Wolfe (Aide). *Director:* Edward Cahn. *Writing Credits:* Cran Chamberlin, Gene Piller. *Producer:* John Nesbitt. *Music:* Nathaniel Shilkret, Max Terr. *Cinematography:* Robert Surtees. *Film Editing:* Harry Komer. *Art Direction:* Paul Youngblood. *Studio:* MGM. *Length:* 11 minutes.

In one of his *Passing Parade* shorts, John Nesbitt looks at a number of historical "truths" that aren't true. Among these he included the old saw that George Washington (Walter Kingsford) threw a dollar across the Potomac River. Not true!

Where Do We Go from Here? (1945)

Washington: Alan Mowbray. *Other Cast:* Fred MacMurray (Bill Morgan), Joan Leslie (Sally Smith/Prudence/Katrina), June Haver (Lucilla Powell/Gretchen/Indian), Gene Sheldon (Ali the Genie), Anthony Quinn (Chief Badger), Carlos Ramirez (Benito), Fortunio Bonanova (Christopher Columbus). *Director:* Gregory Ratoff. *Producer:* William Perlberg. *Screenwriter:* Morris Ryskind. *Story:* Sig Herzig. *Cinematographer:* Leon Shamroy. *Songwriters:* Ira Gershwin, Kurt Weill. *Composer:* David Raksin. *Editor:* J. Watson Webb, Jr. *Set Designer:* Thomas Little, Walter Scott. *Studio:* 20th Century–Fox. *Length:* 74 minutes.

This musical of time travel provided by a genie (yes!) takes some unexpected twists, including an interlude with Washington at Valley Forge. It's a World War II propaganda film involving one 4-F man's desire to get into military service. The man is the affable Bill Morgan (Fred MacMurray) who's rejected for military service and also by the woman he desires, Lucilla Powell (June Haver, whom MacMurray later married in real life). She prefers to boost military morale by dancing and dating every available serviceman. Coincidentally, young Sally Smith's (Joan Leslie) adoration of him is unrequited.

While collecting metal for the war, Morgan finds an antique teapot that he rubs clean. Lo! Genie Ali (Gene Sheldon) appears and whisks him to the Valley Forge USO in 1776.

The underlying theme of the film soon surfaces in Morgan's anachronisms and knowledge of the future in this short scene. Morgan warns Washington (Alan Mowbray) that his aide, Benedict Arnold (John Davidson), is a spy. "If only he were," the general replies, mentioning his need of spies. He soon recruits Morgan because he "likes his style." Sent to Trenton to find out how many Hessians are stationed there, Morgan continues his odyssey. This is Mowbray's third and last appearance as Washington and even in this nonsensical role he gives a performance notable for his command in military matters and honesty of character.

Monsieur Beaucaire (1946)

Washington: Douglass Dumbrille. *Other Cast:* Bob Hope (Monsieur Beaucaire), Joan Caulfield (Mimi), Patric Knowles (Duc le Chandre), Cecil Kellaway (Count D'Armand), Marjorie Reynolds (Princess Maria of Spain). *Director:* George Marshall. *Producer:* Paul Jones. *Screenwriters:* Melvin Frank, Norman Panama. *Book Author:* Booth Tarkington. *Cinematographer:* Lionel Lindon. *Music:* Robert Emmett Dolan, Ray Evans, Jay Livingston. *Film Editing:* Arthur P. Schmidt. *Art Direction:* Hans Dreier, Earl Hedrick. *Set Decoration:* Sam Comer, Ross Dowd. *Studio:* Paramount Pictures. *Length:* 93 minutes.

Even in *Monsieur Beaucaire*, a Bob Hope comedy directed by George Marshall, the character of Washington appears as a serious, solemn man. In one brief scene at the end of the film, Douglass Dumbrille as Washington comes to the barbershop of Hope who has fled Europe for his life. He sits in the chair and undergoes "the usual" ministrations of Hope and his wife Mimi (Joan Caufield). His only line is, "Tom and the boys are cooking up a declaration."

Unconquered (1947)

Washington: Richard Gaines. *Other Cast:* Gary Cooper (Capt. Christopher Holden), Paulette Goddard (Abby Hale), Howard Da Silva (Martin Garth), Boris Karloff (Chief Guyasuta), Ward Bond (John Fraser), Katherine de Mille (Hannah). *Director-Producer:* Cecil B. DeMille. *Writing Credits:* Charles Bennett, Fredric M. Frank, Jesse Lasky Jr., Neil H. Swanson. *Music:* Victor Young. *Cinematography:* Ray Rennahan. *Film Editing:* Anne Bauchens. *Art Direction:* Hans Dreier. *Set Direction:* Sam Comer, Stanley Jay Sawley. *Costume Design:* Gwen Wakeling. *Studio:* Paramount Pictures. *Length:* 146 minutes.

This was Cecil B. DeMille's first post-war production, a $5 million, historically inaccurate spectacle about the colonists and the Indians. While the main plot concerns Virginia militiaman Capt. Christopher Holden (Gary Cooper) in maneuvers against the Pontiac Conspiracy, an allegiance of 18 Indian nations dedicated to destroy every colonist on the East Coast, it also includes other events. One is the rescue of Abby Hale (Paulette Goddard), unjustly accused of a crime against the British Crown and forced into servitude. The other is outwitting slave master Martin Garth's (Howard Da Silva), lust for Hale and his firearms trade with the Indians.

Col. Washington (Richard Gaines) makes three appearances, surveying the military import of the territory under dispute. He is especially prescient about the triangle of land around Pittsburgh that he says "may be very important." Gaines displays a commanding military authority that gives credence to his performance.

When the Redskins Rode (1951)

Washington: James Seay. *Other Cast:* Jon Hall (Prince Hannoc), Mary Castle (Elizabeth Leeds), John Ridgely (Christopher Gist), Sherry Moreland (Morna), Pedro de Cordoba (Chief Shingiss), John Dehner (John Delmont), Lewis L. Russell (Gov. Dimwiddie), William Bakewell (Appleby). *Director:* Lew Landers. *Producer:* Sam Katzman. *Writing Credits:* Robert E. Kent. *Music:* Mischa Bakaleinkoff, Paul Sawtell. *Cinematography:* Lester White. *Film Editing:* Richard Fantl. *Art Direction:* Paul Palmentola. *Set Decoration:* Sidney Clifford. *Studio:* Columbia Pictures. *Length:* 78 minutes.

While the French are still trying to control Western Pennsylvania, Col. George Washington (James Seay) is attempting to enlist the Delaware Indians on the side of the British. In this Supercinecolor film set in 1753, Washington's connection to the Delaware is Prince Hannoc (Jon Hall) who has to fight off French spy Elizabeth Leeds (Mary Castle) in order to remain true to the British. In the process his father Chief Shingiss (Pedro de Cordoba) is assassinated, but Hannoc and his true love, Indian maiden Morna (Sherry Moreland), disclose Leeds's duplicity and save the day for Washington at Fort Necessity. James Seay's portrayal of Washington is a bit stodgy for an actor of Seay's experience. However, it is always difficult for one to play the Father of Our Country.

Yankee Doodle Bugs (1954)

Washington. Animation. *Other Cast:* Mel Blanc (Bugs Bunny, voice). *Director:* Friz Freleng. *Writing Credits:* Warren Foster (story). *Studio:* Warner Bros. *Length:* Seven minutes.

Bugs Bunny (Mel Blanc, voice) gets into the act as always in a lecture to his nephew Clyde about American history in order to pass a test. The nephew fails the test, but the ol' rabbit never ceases to amuse as he zips from historical event to historical event, starting with how the Indians got Manhattan for a "song"—and producing the sheet music. As for presidential history, Bugs delivers a missive to Washington at Mt. Vernon, and the esteemed Southern planter says, "Gad zooks, I've been drafted. Martha, you'll have to run the candy store while I'm off to war." Washington appears again at Valley Forge and crossing the Delaware River, standing in a boat that Bugs steers with an outboard motor.

Boyhood Daze (1957)

Washington: Daws Butler. *Other Cast:* Dick Beals (Ralph Phillips). *Director:* Chuck Jones. *Writing Credits:* Michael Maltese (story). *Music:* Milt Franklyn. *Film Editing:* Treg Brown. *Visual Effects:* Harry Love. *Studio:* Warner Bros. *Length:* Seven minutes.

Chuck Jones, the celebrated animator, touches on the fears and fantasies of children who misbehave—like breaking a window with a baseball—in this color cartoon. Jones manages to get the hero, Ralph Phillips (Dick Beals, voice), honored by the president (Daws Butler, voice) although he is not fully visible because of his high position on a throne-like chair. Then Jones lets little Ralph have his revenge for his punishment when his father sends him out to play by morphing into Washington, complete with axe en route to a cherry tree.

In between, young Ralph cries on his bed, lamenting how unappreciated and unwanted he is. Quick as his imagination spurs into action, the wild-haired fellow saves his parents from being boiled alive in Africa, saves the world from evil Martians, and escapes from his prison (really his stunningly colored bedroom) all in minutes. Still his glory isn't complete: The drape from his statue the president unveils falls on him.

Clever as Jones's action is, writer Michael Maltese's lines also amuse with such childish assertions as "My insurance will pay for the window and use whatever is left over to buy yourself a catcher's mitt." The saturated color is especially captivating, notably the blue-green tones of the African scene.

The Story of Mankind (1957)

Washington: Unnamed actor.

Washington appears in one scene without speaking a line. The Spirit of Man (Ronald Colman) describes the great advances made by mankind because of the American Revolution. He specifically mentions Washington with the general shown in profile on horseback (deified, as frequently). For details, see Ch. 16 on Abraham Lincoln.

The Unbearable Salesman (1957)

Washington: Daws Butler. *Other Cast:* Grace Stafford (Woody Woodpecker). June Foray (Knothead and Splinter). *Director:* Paul J. Smith. *Writing Credits:* Dick Kinney. *Producer:* Walter Lantz. *Music:* Clarence Wheeler. *Art Department.* Art Landy. *Studio:* Walter Lantz Productions. *Length:* 7 minutes.

Producer Walter Lantz quite often used a historical event to set the stage for his Woody Woodpecker (Grace Stafford, voice) cartoons. It would appear that this one has to do with a confrontation between young George Washington (Daws Butler) and his father.

John Paul Jones (1959)

Washington: Jack Crawford. *Other Cast:* Robert Stack (John Paul Jones), Bette Davis (Empress Catherine the Great), Marisa Pavan (Aimee de Tellison), Charles Coburn (Benjamin Franklin), Macdonald Carey (Patrick Henry), Jean-Pierre Aumont (King Louis XVI), David Farrar (John Wilkes), Peter Cushing (Captain Pearson), Susana Canales (Marie Antoinette), Georges Riviera (Russian Chamberlain), Tom Brannum (Peter Wooly), Bruce Cabot (Gunner Lowrie), Basil Sydney (Sir William Young). *Director-Writer* John Farrow, with Jesse Lasky Jr. *Producer:* Samuel Bronston. *Music:* Max Steiner. *Cinematography:* Michel Kelber. *Film Editing:* Eda Warren. *Art Direction:* Franz Bachelin. *Set Direction:* Dario Simoni. *Costume Design:* Phyllis Dalton. *Studio:* Samuel Bronston Productions, Suevia Films S.A., Warner Bros. *Length:* 126 minutes.

A biography of John Paul Jones, the rebellious Scot who whipped the U.S. Navy into action during the American Revolution, this swashbuckler gives insight into the heroics of such men as he and George Washington. It follows Jones from his early life on the sea to his service against the king and eventually command of a ship that scores audacious victories, particularly over the British ship *Serapis*. When asked if he will surrender, Jones claims, "I have not yet begun to fight." Robert Stack (later of Eliot Ness fame) displays the toughness of a man who battles the privileged as much as he does his foes. Stack also conveys the devotion Jones shows in urging mentor Benjamin Franklin (a philosophical Charles Coburn) to get French aid and later to establish a strong U.S. Navy. Finally, troublemaker

Jones is sent to aid the fleet of Catherine the Great, played in three languages by a regal Bette Davis.

While director and screenwriter John Farrow shapes Jones's life into dynamic scenes, the battle scenes are so tightly framed that it is difficult to discern the British from the American ships. Max Steiner's original music score, however, signals who wins. Washington (Jack Crawford) appears in but one two-minute scene. Yet he delivers an impassioned speech about the meaning of liberty, telling Jones, "There will be no United States unless all are united ... and [the U.S.] design will be set so the United States will exist as long as we have faith." Washington shows his faith in Jones who, tired of naval politics, comes to serve him as a military officer. The leader of the Colonial forces asks the Navy man if he is "fighting for liberty or promotion." Jones asserts he will "serve on any ship, in any capacity." He is charged to raise a crew and to sail the *Ranger* with papers urging French support for the Revolution through Benjamin Franklin, then envoy in Paris. Tightly framed in a small office and always shot from the rear, his face never seen, Jack Crawford with his imposing physical presence and voice makes for an admirable Washington.

We see the cold and depravation of Washington's men at Valley Forge as Jones makes his way in the snow to Washington's headquarters, a small house. Washington asks Jones's patience as he dictates a "litany of gloom," stating that "in all human probability, the army must dissolve ... the love of freedom is controlled by hunger ... frostbite causes mass amputation."

La Fayette (1962)

Washington: Howard St. John. *Other Cast:* Orson Welles (Benjamin Franklin), Pascale Audret (Adrienne de La Fayette), Jack Hawkins (Gen. Cornwallis), Michel Le Royer (La Fayette). *Director:* Jean Dreville. *Producer:* Maurice Jacquin. *Writing Credits:* Jean Bernard-Luc. *Music:* Pierre Duclos, Steve Laurent. *Cinematography:* Roger Hubert, Claude Renoir. *Film Editing:* Rene Le Henaff. *Production Design:* Maurice Colasson. *Art Direction:* Vlastimir Gavrik, Slobodan Mijacevic. *Studio:* Cosmos, Films Copernic. *Length:* 158 min.

Although Bosley Crowther of the *New York Times* defined this French film as "the American Revolution as a combination of the siege of Ft. Apache and the Crimean War" (April 11, 1963), it appears more like a swashbuckling Errol Flynn pirate adventure as the young La Fayette dashes about defeating the British.

Michel Le Royer appears as the French marquis or "damn brat," as Washington (Howard St. John) affectionately calls him, to lead the ragtag, barefoot, hungry Revolutionaries—with only six cartridges apiece—at Washington's wish. The wise American soldier knows La Fayette's spirit will spur his men to victory. They win, at Saratoga, in a spectacular battle scene, with row upon row of British soldiers marching in orderly ranks to their deaths inspired by the only weapon of La Fayette's—his sword. In one of the scene shifts to the rococo French court, Benjamin Franklin (Orson Welles) receives the news and declares, "We need help from France." He presently receives a proclamation of an alliance with America from the king. Nevertheless, the king is not pleased with the defiant young La Fayette's fighting without his permission. At the queen's suggestion, La Fayette is put under house (his own) arrest. Very soon, however, La Fayette is back in America leading dispirited troops.

Just in time, Washington carefully prepares his tactics for the battle of Yorktown. St. John's deep voice, calm demeanor, and noble head serve him well in the role. His adversary, Cornwallis (played by Jack Hawkins as a fop) fusses over his lack of port and cold punch and claims, "If I don't lay my hands on him [La Fayette] this time, I'll resign my command." Washington is equally worried, feeling, "We will perish if we don't besiege Cornwallis."

Washington's mousetrap strategy "will not squeeze me," says Cornwallis as he observes the battle with his spyglass. He soon spies La Fayette attacking the British fort and raising the American flag. "The damn boy," Cornwallis cries, "I have no desire to die." Under Jean Dreville's suspenseful direction, the French fleet is seen arriving—an impossible feat on the actual terrain of Yorktown.

"Gentleman," declares Washington, "this is the greatest day of the war." Victory soon is his, and the surrender follows in slow and stately pageantry. Guns, bayonets, and flags fall. Then Cornwallis offers his sword, "the first time I've been defeated, but my army never surrenders ... we are stubborn," he says. With his usually dignity and understatement, Washington says, "We have learned your stubbornness." Cornwallis only asks that the British prisoners be treated humanely. La Fayette interjects that "the Americans have been prisoners too long to mistreat others" and reminds the British that "the idea of liberty was born in France." All this pageantry and patriotism ends with the Declaration of Independence scrolling over the final frames.

The Story of George Washington (1965)

Director and Writing Credits: Jack Mendelsohn. *Music:* Winston Sharples. *Art Department:* Robert Little. *Animator:* Al Eugster.

An animated film, not available to us for viewing.

Independence (1976)

Washington: Patrick O'Neal. *Other Cast:* William Atherton (Benjamin Rush), John Favorite (John Lansing), Pat Hingle (John Adams), Ken Howard (Thomas Jefferson), Anne Jackson (Abigail Adams), E.G. Marshall (Narrator), Donald C. Moore (Benjamin Harrison), Scott Mulhern (Alexander Hamilton), John Randolph (Samuel Adams), Paul Sparer (John Hancock), Tom Spratley (George Master), Donald Symington (Richard Henry Lee), James Tolkan (Tom Paine), Eli Wallach (Benjamin Franklin). *Director:* John Huston. *Producers:* Joyce Ritter, Lloyd Ritter. *Writing Credits:* Tom McGrath, Joyce Ritter, Lloyd Ritter. *Cinematography:* Owen Roizman. *Film Editing:* Eric Albertson. *Costume Design:* Ann Roth. *Studio:* U.S. National Park Service, 20th Century–Fox. *Length:* 30 minutes.

To celebrate the Bicentennial at Independence Hall, Philadelphia, director John Huston and a host of actors (the Founding Fathers) made this short film about the drafting of the Declaration of Independence. Washington (Patrick O'Neal) figures less than Adams (Pat Hingle), the driving force, and Jefferson (Ken Howard), the author of the Declaration.

The film covers the First and Second Continental Congresses, the Revolutionary War, the Constitutional Convention, and the election of Washington. As Washington, O'Neal displays noble qualities.

Revolution (1985)

Washington: Frank Windsor. *Other Cast:* Al Pacino (Tom Dobb), Donald Sutherland (Sgt. Maj. Peasy), Natassja Kinski (Daisy McConnahay), Joan Plowright (Mrs. McConnahay), Steven Berkoff (Sgt. Jones), Dexter Fletcher (Ned Dobb). *Director:* Hugh Hudson. *Pro-*

ducers: Chris Burt, Irwin Winkler. *Writing Credits:* Robert Dillon. *Music:* John Corigliano. *Cinematography:* Bernard Lutic. *Editor:* Stuart Baird. *Production Designer:* Assheton Gorton. *Length:* 126 minutes.

This is an interesting look at the American Revolution with enough serious problems to make it a disaster for the distributors, namely Warner Brothers. A trapper, Tom Dobb (Al Pacino), and his son Ned (Sid Owen) are reluctantly dragged into the Revolution when they arrive in New York City to sell their skins. One of their first acquaintances is Daisy McConnahay (Natassja Kinski), a zealous patriot from a rich Tory merchant family, framed in shots that would serve on a coin. These three characters meet occasionally—and incredibly coincidentally—from the Battle of Brooklyn Heights (1776) until after the Battle of Yorktown (1781), usually at very dramatic moments.

Unfortunately for the well produced movie, one of the half dozen that deals in serious detail with the Revolutionary War, numerous long periods unwind when virtually nothing is happening—except for beautifully filmed shots of historically impossible landscapes by Bernard Lutic. Among his locations are the Adirondacks that look like the Grand Tetons and the coast at Yorktown that looks like California's. Pacino's voice switches from a reasonable facsimile of colonial American to straight modern New Yorkese, but his looks never change from those in *Serpico* (1973). Kinski, as a daughter of upper class Tories, has an Eastern European accent. The moviegoing public saw these problems immediately, according to reviews, and the film was a financial disaster.

Although credited as Washington, Frank Windsor's appearance is so fleeting that in the Valley Forge and Philadelphia scenes, it is almost impossible to find him.

A More Perfect Union: America Becomes a Nation (1989)

Washington: Michael McGuire. *Other Cast:* Craig Wasson (James Madison), Fredd Wayne (Benjamin Franklin), Morgan White (George Mason), Douglas Seale (Lord Carmarthen), Bruce Newbold (Edmund Randolph), James Walch (James Wilson), Ivan Crosland (John Adams), H.E.D. Redford (Roger Sherman), Jesse Bennett (John Dickinson), Roderick Cook (Nathaniel Gorham), Derryl Yeager (Alexander Hamilton), James Arrington (Gouverneur Morris), Scott Wilkinson (Thomas Jefferson). *Director:* Peter N. Johnson. *Producers:* Nicholas J. Gasdik, Peter N. Johnson. *Writing Credits:* Tim Slover. *Cinematography:* Gordon Lonsdale. *Film Editing:* Peter G. Czerny. *Music:* Kurt Bestor. *Production Design:* Richard Jamison. *Costume Design:* Yvonne Robertson. *Art Department:* John R. Uibel.

Of the films about the birth of this nation, this deals more with the philosophical and political positions of the Founding Fathers. Madison (Craig Wasson) expresses his opinions on states rights vs. a strong federal government and a workable separation of powers. Michael McGuire as Washington weathers the debate on a title ("American King or President") and accepts the latter with composure and equanimity as Franklin (Fredd Wayne) tells him, "God governs the affairs of men."

Sometimes Santa's Gotta Get Whacked (1998)

Washington: Vince Palmieri. *Other Cast:* Anthony Russell (Santa), Maureen Kedes (Mrs. C.), Cutter Mitchell (Lil' Petey), Bob Bouchard (Rudy), Wayne Thomas (Leon), Frankie Pace (Frosty), Tom Katsis (Lincoln), Len Matgnus (Tommy T.), Jason Ensler (Chanukah Harry),

Stephen Gatta (Cupid). *Director:* Robert Markopoulos. *Producer:* Milan Petrovich. *Music:* Charles Swanson. *Film Editing:* Andre Tan. *Length:* 25 minutes.

A comedy short with little or no distribution, this film somehow combines Mafia and Santa Claus. A plot outline states that Santa's "family" of organized holidays suffers attacks from a power-hungry outsider. Because this film is not available for viewing, it is difficult to assess the appearance of Washington.

The Patriot (2000)

Washington: Terry Layman. *Other Cast:* Mel Gibson (Benjamin Martin), Heath Ledger (Gabriel Martin), Joely Richardson (Charlotte Selton), Jason Isaacs (Col. William Tavington), Chris Cooper (Col. Harry Burwell), Tom Wilkinson (Gen. Cornwallis). *Director-Producer:* Roland Emmerich. *Screenwriter:* Robert Rodat. *Cinematographer:* Caleb Deschanel. *Composer:* John Williams. *Editor:* David Brenner. *Studio:* Columbia Pictures. *Length:* 164 minutes.

Despite the drama inherent in the American Revolution, it has not been a favorite subject for Hollywood, especially in recent years. Finally, two centuries after the war, Roland Emmerich directs and Mel Gibson of *Braveheart* (1985) stars as Benjamin Martin in *The Patriot*, a Revolutionary War epic about a South Carolina planter drawn into the conflict after one of his sons is killed by the British. Based very broadly on the exploits of Francis Marion, "The Swamp Fox," the film follows Martin's adventures as the leader of Carolina guerrilla patriots until the end of the war at Yorktown.

Although Martin was associated with Washington in the French and Indian War during the brutal fighting of the Wilderness Campaign at Fort William where he was named the hero, this haunting relationship of the humbled Martin is never shown. However, Washington (Terry Layman) appears in a single scene, leading troops (stunningly created through digital photography). Layman displays the resolute leadership of the general. This action is narrated by another of Martin's patriotic sons soon after the boy has enlisted in the Revolutionary army.

The Master of Disguise (2002)

Washington: Unnamed actor. *Other Cast:* Dana Carvey (Pistachio Disguisey), Brent Spiner (Devlin Bowman), Jennifer Esposito (Jennifer Baker), Harold Gould (Grandfather Disguisey), James Brolin (Fabbrizio Disguisey), Austin Wolff (Barney Baker), Edie McClurg (Mother Disguisey), Buddy Bolton (Abe Lincoln). *Director:* Perry Andelin Blake. *Producers:* Jack Giarraputo, Adam Sandler. *Writing Credits:* Dana Carvey, Harris Goldberg. *Music:* Marc Ellis. *Cinematography:* Peter Lyons Collister. *Film Editing:* Peck Prior, Sandy S. Solowitz. *Production:* Alan Au. *Art Direction:* Susan Detrie, John B. Josselyn, Dominic Silvestri. *Set Decoration:* Robert Greenfield. *Costume Design:* Mona May. *Makeup:* Ann Pala. *Studio:* Happy Madison Productions, Out of the Blue ... Entertainment, Revolution Studios. *Length:* 80 minutes.

Dana Carvey co-wrote and stars in more than three dozen disguises in this family-oriented film. His parents are kidnapped by the evil thief Devlin (Brent Spiner) from their restaurant where Carvey as Pistachio Disguisey waits (on table). Disguisey learns from his grandfather of the family's mystical means of changing identity from Washington to George W. Bush.

Washington appears in a one-shot scene as a little boy who can't chop down the cherry tree because it's running away. The tree's running because it is one of the family's disguises.

2

John Adams (1797–1801)

John Adams. (Courtesy of Library of Congress.)

Long before he assumed the presidency, John Adams served his state of Massachusetts, starting in 1770 as a representative to the state legislature, and the fledgling states of the union as envoy to France and to England. Along with John Hancock, president of the Continental Congress and three others, he represented Massachusetts at the Continental Congress, beginning in 1774, and established a reputation as the voice of independence. A scholar and a proud Harvard graduate, Adams considered teaching and the ministry before studying and practicing law in his native Massachusetts. His passion for legal justice led him to take the unpopular case of defending the English soldiers and their captain involved in the Boston Massacre. He not only defended them but his "virtuoso performance"[1] (although not recorded) resulted in a not-guilty verdict.

Adams's presidency was plagued by problems not necessarily of his making. His often overweening ego would not permit him to think that he might be wrong, a failing he shared with other men; but, toward the end, vanity and frustration produced in him a bitterness that led him to blame his own misfortunes as well as those of his party on both the Federalist press and relentless Republican papers.[2] Of particular importance was the XYZ Affair which, in effect, defined the confrontation between those who supported France, led by Jefferson, and those who suspected France's ambitions. Like many Americans, Adams vacillated on his feelings toward France. He, the Roman stoic of simplicity, deplored French duplicity and avarice.[3]

Further exposure of the political enmity between the Republicans and Adams's Federalists surfaced in his signing the Alien and Sedition Acts. This legislation was politically inspired to silence political opposition, particularly in the press. Such abridgment of personal liberty inflamed Jefferson and his followers and contributed to the split between the two old friends until their old age. Many other differences contributed to that split, starting with Jefferson's letter to Robert Livingston in July 1783 about Adams's performance in their negotiating the Treaty of Paris: "He means well for his country, is always an honest man, often a wise one, but sometimes and in some things, absolutely out of his senses."[4] Shortly thereafter in 1791, the two old friends became embroiled over Adams's comments on Thomas Paine's *The Rights of Man* claiming they were "political heresies." As often happened, Jefferson recanted, blaming the indiscretion of a printer and saying he has cordial esteem despite "his apostasy to hereditary monarch" to friend Adams.[5]

Although equally supportive of personal liberty but less politically agile than Jefferson (Adams was really quite innocent of the reverberations of the Alien and Sedition Acts), Adams and his old protégé corresponded in their old age and coincidentally both died on the same day, July 4, 1826, the 50th anniversary of the adoption of the Declaration of Independence. So much happened in John Adams's life as his most recent biographer David McCullough states: "[H]e had done so much, taken such risks, given so much of himself heart and soul in the cause of his country that he seems not to have viewed the presidency as an ultimate career objective or crowning life achievement."[6]

THE FILMS

Despite the importance of John Adams as one of the greatest of the Founding Fathers he was not exciting enough to warrant a great deal of film attention in Hollywood's eyes. With the exception of *1776*, which is an adaptation of a Broadway musical and in which Adams is the main character, there are only five additional films in which he appears as a character.

The Beautiful Mrs. Reynolds (1918) aka *The Adventurer*

Adams: Jack Drumier.
Jack Drumier, one of the World Film Corp.'s stock players, plays Adams in a cameo appearance in this silent drama of the rivalry between Alexander Hamilton and Aaron Burr. For details, see Chapter 1 on George Washington.

The Declaration of Independence (1938)

Adams: Ferris Taylor. *Other Cast:* John Litel (Thomas Jefferson), Ted Osborne (Caesar Rodney), Rosella Towne (Betsy Kramer), Richard Bond (Thomas Lynch Jr.), Owen King (Edward Rutledge). *Director:* Crane Wilbur. *Writing Credits:* Charles L. Tedford. *Music:* Howard Jackson. *Cinematography:* W. Howard Greene. *Film Editing:* Everett Dodd. *Art Direction:* Hugh Reticker. *Costume Design:* Milo Anderson. *Length:* 17 minutes.

This featurette on the drafting and signing of the Declaration of Independence takes as much liberty with history as the delegates took stands on it during the famous First Continental Congress at (now) Independence Hall, Philadelphia.

For dramatic effect the film focuses on the difficulties of assuring Caesar Rodney's (Ted Osborne) of Delaware deciding vote for the Declaration. He's left Philadelphia for Dover, Delaware, to see his fiancée Betsy Kramer (Rosella Towne). But her father (William Ormond) is holding a secret Tory meeting at his mansion and tries to hold Rodney and forbid the marriage. In swashbuckling gunplay, a mark of Osborne's physical acting style, Rodney flees, recovers from a shot that throws him from his horse, and rides to Philadelphia to cast the crucial vote for independence. While the depiction of the vote is historically correct, the romantic circumstances of Rodney are as stretched as they were about his health in 1776 (1972).

Thomas Jefferson (John Litel) reads from the document he penned. Jefferson figures almost as much as Rodney in this film. John Adams (Ferris Taylor) appears in only one scene compared to his central role in 1776. In offering his advice to Ben Franklin (Walter Walker) on Jefferson's draft of the Declaration, Adams stresses that "New England can't afford a slavery clause," and Jefferson drops the inflammatory slavery issues from the document. Taylor gives a passable performance, never revealing all the qualities of Adams, in this dramatized view of history.

John Paul Jones (1959)

Adams: Robert Ayres.

The cameo appearance of Robert Ayres as John Adams is too short for a meaningful assessment. For details, see Chapter 1 on George Washington.

1776 (1972)

Adams: William Daniels. *Other Cast:* Howard Da Silva (Dr. Benjamin Franklin), Ken Howard (Thomas Jefferson), Donald Madden (John Dickinson), John Cullum (Edward Rutledge), Roy Poole (Stephen Hopkins), David Ford (Congressional President John Hancock), Ron Holgate (Richard Henry Lee), Ray Middleton (Col. Thomas McKean), William Hansen (Caesar Rodney), Blythe Danner (Martha Wayles Skelton Jefferson), Virginia Vestoff (Abigail Smith Adams), Emory Bass (Judge James Wilson), Ralston Hill (Congressional Secretary Charles Thomson), Howard Caine (Lewis Morris). *Director:* Peter H. Hunt. *Producer:* Jack Warner for Columbia Pictures. *Writing Credits:* Peter Stone, Sherman Edwards (also play). *Music-Lyrics:* Sherman Edwards (also play). *Cinematographer:* Harry Stradling, Jr. *Length:* 166 min. Panovision.

At the Continental Congress in Philadelphia during the drafting of the Declaration of Independence, Adams was respected by the 53 other delegates for his solidity and virtuous character, qualities extolled by McCullough and other historians. Yet, in the film that captures this event and the best cinematic treatment of Adams he was told—in the opening song of the musical based on the hit play 1776—to shut up and "Sit Down John." Like the Broadway 1776, the film is about the days leading up to July 4, 1776, of the Continental Congress meeting in Independence Hall, Philadelphia.

Peter Stone (book) and Sherman Edwards (music-lyrics), authors of *1776: A Musical Play*, used Adams as the protagonist of their 1969 production. This was done in spite of Adams being obnoxious and unpopular during the Congress—charges that also surfaced during his presidency. In a brief "Historical Note" that follows the published version of the libretto, Stone and Edwards admit, "John Adams is, at times, a composite of himself and his cousin[7] Sam Adams." Those times when John becomes Sam are so hard to discern that they are not treated in this analysis.

What is significant is that the film is the best of all feature films about our second president. It deals with him at length, it reveals his humanity and qualities of character, and it shows him in relations with his fellow patriots and especially with his wife. Adams's character is solid as the Liberty Bell; candor, probity, and decision being his self-proclaimed strongest attributes[8] that shaped his life and those of his children, particularly those of his son John Quincy Adams who also became a president of the United States. As Adams, William Daniels compensates for his lack of his character's girth (connoting solidity) with such force of movement and with such assured and resounding speech that he commands attention.

Persevering as he was, Adams never shut up or stopped urging his colleagues to vote for "independency" from England. It was he who coerced Jefferson to write that bold and comprehensive document, the Declaration of Independence. Similar in many ways, in particular their love of words and scholarship, they became protégé (Jefferson) and mentor (Adams). It was Adams also who worked with the aged and withdrawn Benjamin Franklin to persuade the recalcitrant colonies to join their side for independency. It was he who sustained the debate for nine hours and made the greatest speech in his life for the expediency of the measure,[9] unfortunately not recorded.

All these actions appear in the film, former studio mogul Jack Warner's first independent production. Furthermore, under Peter H. Hunt's direction the film faithfully follows the plot and score of the stage version—although the Nixon White House pressured Warner into deleting a song critical of conservatives, "Cool, Cool Considerate Men." In short, the plot follows the long hot Philadelphia days from May 8 to July 4, 1776 (marked by a calendar on the Chamber wall) of debate on whether or not to become independent of England. Another prop, a tally of the votes, adds to the tension of this historical event.

Playing to his colleagues' indifference to his resolve to vote for independency, the decisive Adams bemoans in song his colleagues' "Piddle, Twiddle and Resolve" as they debate about everything but independency. Adams uses one argument after another to sway the vote. He is supported by the vain and wisecracking Franklin (Howard Da Silva) and the silent and studious Jefferson (Ken Howard) whose idea of simply writing a document of independence Adams upholds. To inspire the newlywed Jefferson, Adams sends for his bride Martha.

More difficult to move than Jefferson's pen is the desire of the Conservatives (led by Donald Madden as John Dickinson) to remain faithful to England and the South Carolina delegation whose slave-based way of life does not fit with a document promising liberty for all. John Collum as Edward Rutledge of South Carolina sings a show-stopper, "Molasses to Rum," to decry the hypocrisy of the Northerners who gain as much from the slave trade as the Southerners.

While the debate ensues, a courier comes to the Chamber with message after message (numbering to one thousand) from Washington who is valiantly and, to a large extent, unsuccessfully leading patriot troops in the battles in the New York–New Jersey area. The losses of this revolution surface in Stephen Nathan as the courier's plaintive vocal reminiscence of the Battle of Bunker Hill, "Momma Look Sharp" (to see your dying son).

Besides the historical depiction, character portrayal, and humanization of these momentous days, the play and film provide diverting moments such as the song "The Egg" in which Franklin, Adams, and Jefferson debate about a national bird. Franklin is for the turkey, a native bird; Adams, the eagle; and Jefferson, the dove.

1776 (1972): William Daniels (left) as John Adams and Howard Da Silva as Benjamin Franklin enjoy the dancing of Thomas Jefferson's new wife Martha (Blythe Danner) in the Columbia Pictures version of the successful stage musical. She's also singing a romantic ballad extolling her husband, "He Plays the Violin." (Courtesy of George Eastman House.)

Invariably in the Hollywood tradition, the film opens up the stage version's settings of the Chamber of the Continental Congress to its Anteroom, High Street, and Jefferson's room in Philadelphia. While the expanded setting detracts from the hot, stifling atmosphere of the Chamber, it offers comic opportunity for the wit and enthusiasm of Ron Holgate as Richard Henry Lee to make puns about his family name as he sings "The Lees of Old

Virginia" while he mounts his horse for an errand of patriotic support. The expanded setting also provides a garden on High Street outside Jefferson's room for Blythe Danner as Martha Jefferson to extol the virtues of her husband in song, "He Plays the Violin." This clever song with its sexual innuendo stops Adams and Franklin from prying into the young bride's life with the author of the Declaration of Independence.

In addition the film is much more effective than the stage version in its treatment of "certain reaches" of John Adams's mind as he reveals his frustrations to his beloved and supportive wife. In soft focus, he appears on one side of the screen and Abigail (Virginia Vestoff) appears on the other. It is more convincing a device of handing thought than the stage characters stepping forward and voicing their inner thoughts.

Most writers for film and stage find it necessary to take some theatrical license in their efforts for dramatic impact. Stone and Edwards, the writers of *1776*, assert that the events of the musical are factual. However, what the filmmakers do with their theatrical license is:

- downplay the respect Adams engendered from his esteemed colleagues, second to none, as mentioned above, according to his most recent biographer, David McCullough in *John Adams*. Only Adams used the word "obnoxious" to describe himself and only he wrote disparagingly of himself at the Continental Congress, says McCullough.[10] In the film, Adams quotes his colleagues as calling him "obnoxious" and "unpopular."
- diminish the mutual interest in words, books, and scholarship and mutual admiration of the (six-years) younger Jefferson who wrote the Declaration of Independence at Adams's urging and who called Adams "the colossus on the floor."[11]
- expand the outspoken commentary by Franklin who never liked floor debate and at age 70 spent much time sleeping in his chair during the deliberations.
- change the emphasis on disagreement led by Edward Rutledge of South Carolina over Jefferson's passage on slavery and the slave trade when the debate was at heart more centered on the rupture of the colonies from England. Of the more than 80 changes, this hurt Jefferson the most. He finally acquiesced to its deletion but clung to the term "tyrant" to describe George III.
- obscure the voluntary absence of the disputatious John Dickinson and Robert Morris of Pennsylvania from the proceedings because they understood the need for Congress to speak unanimously. The film most dramatically focuses on the change of heart in voting for independence of modest, politically unambitious James Wilson.
- ignore that the signing of the document, one of the most dramatic scenes in the film, was on August 2 not on July 4. But it makes for a heart-rending scene as each delegate affixes his name after the first of John Hancock.

Regardless of the factual shortcomings of *1776*, the film treats with great esteem future presidents at the Congress, Adams and Jefferson, and the first future president, Washington, an unseen but often-heard-from character. This film shows great respect for historical figures. The early song "Sit Down John" merely sets the stage, showing the extent to which Adams was the leading exponent and driving force for independence in the Congress. It was Adams who urged his colleagues to action, who urged Jefferson to write the declaration, and who worked with Jefferson on the more than 80 changes that were made to the draft of the Declaration. Adams is continually presented as a persistent, intelligent leader, a devoted husband, and one who would honorably hold the office of the presidency.

Independence (1976)

Adams: Pat Hingle.

Pat Hingle as John Adams joins the Founding Fathers in this 30-minute film for the Bicentennial celebration of the Declaration of Independence in 1976. John Huston directs this authentic-looking enactment of the making of this important American document. He creates a *mise-en-scene* that resembles Trumbull's famous painting of the signing.

The action occurs at the First and Second Continental Congress in Independence Hall, Philadelphia, during the deliberations of the colonies' protests against Great Britain and their desires for independence. Hingle airs Adams's fears of violence during a revolution. He also is shown reading a letter from his wife Abigail that states her philosophy about independence: "The King is no longer if people are discontent." Adams also states that he thinks Colonel Washington will take the job of leading the Revolutionary army. Although not as stout as Adams, Hingle looks and acts much like the forceful leader of independence, outspoken and dynamic. For details, see Chapter 1 on Washington.

A More Perfect Union: America Becomes a Nation (1989)

Adams: Ivan Crosland.

Contrary to 1776, John Adams (Ivan Crosland) plays a minor role in this film covering the early years of the United States. For details, see Chapter 1 on Washington.

3
Thomas Jefferson (1801–1809)

Washington is the major symbol of the independent Republic itself, Lincoln of the preserved Union, but Jefferson surpassed both of them in the rich diversity of his achievements. For his writing of the Declaration of Independence alone he is a major apostle of individual freedom and human dignity. He has long belonged, not merely to his own compatriots, but to the human race. His fame dimmed toward the middle of the 19th century, when slaveholders tended to deride his sayings about human equality and Unionists to deplore his emphasis on States' rights. It is ironic that the most extensive account of him appeared at that time: The three-volume *Life* by Henry S. Randall was issued shortly before the Civil War. Now he is considered the Slave President not for his purported children with slave Sally Hemings but for his protection and extension of slavery through the three-fifths clause in the Constitution.[1]

Thomas Jefferson. (Courtesy of Library of Congress.)

A man of such expansive accomplishments and elusive character "could be painted only touch by touch, with a fine pencil" wrote Henry Adams.[2] The ever-elusive Virginian with the glacial exterior and almost eerie serenity served in the Continental Congress, as American minister to France, governor of Virginia, first Secretary of State, and second vice president. As president, the accomplishments that gave Jefferson most satisfaction were the Louisiana Purchase and the retirement of a substantial portion of the national debt.[3] His first term ranks as one of the most successful in presidential history in achieving its objectives, but his second was not[4] mainly because of his solution to British harassment on American seas, the Embargo Act.

The American embodiment of the Enlightenment man, he expressed interest in everything, some of which he developed during his presidency such as the commissioning of the Lewis and Clark expedition to increase knowledge of the uncharted West. He also developed the country's first viable opposition party, the Democratic-Republican, and supported a party press even though he suffered the worst newspaper attacks on any president (with the possible exceptions of Washington and Lincoln). Still he championed a free press but at the same time a press free of libel.[5]

THE FILMS

With 25 films in which he appears, Jefferson is one of Hollywood's favorite presidents. The interest has grown of late and resulted in a major biopic in 1995, *Jefferson in Paris*, stressing his relationship with Sally Hemings. Despite his attitude toward slavery and his own slaves, Jefferson's fame is probably greater in our generation than it has been at any other time since his death. It seems ironic that this major film about him, *Jefferson in Paris*, is so narrow in scope. Many of the other films deal with his writing the Declaration of Independence, which he considered his major accomplishment.

The Heart of a Hero (1916)

Jefferson: Charles Jackson. *Other Cast*: Robert Warwick (Nathan Hale), Gail Kane (Alice Adams), Alec B. Francis (Colonel Knowlton). *Director*: Emile Chautard. *Writing Credits*: Clyde Fitch (play), Frances Marion. *Length*: Six reels.

In this fictionalized story of the death of Nathan Hale (Robert Warwick), Hale is a teacher in a small town who falls in love with Alice Adams (Gail Kane). When the Revolutionary War begins, Hale joins the Revolutionaries and through acts of heroism advances in rank. Despite Adams's objection he volunteers for a spy mission.

One of Adams's relatives spots Hale while he is on the mission and tricks her into revealing his identity. As is well known from grammar school history, he is captured by the British, tried for spying, and hung. However, before this is done he passes the information he has obtained to his sweetheart, and she is able to pass it on to the rebels.

Charles Jackson appears as Jefferson in a brief scene in this silent.

The Beautiful Mrs. Reynolds (1918) aka *The Adventurer*

Jefferson: Albert Hart.

Albert Hart portrays Jefferson in a brief appearance in this drama of the Alexander Hamilton-Aaron Burr rivalry. For details, see Chapter 1 on George Washington.

My Own United States (1918)

Jefferson: P.R. Scammon. *Other Cast*: Arnold Daly (Lt. Philip Nolan I, II, III, IV). Charles Graham (Aaron Burr), Mrs. Allen Walker (Mrs. Philip Nolan I), F.C. Earle (Andrew Jackson), Frank Murray (Gen. Ulysses S. Grant), Gerald Day (Abraham Lincoln). *Director*: John W. Noble. *Producer*: William L. Sherill. *Writer*: Anthony Paul Kelly. *Photography*: Herbert O. Carlton. *Art Direction*: W. Bruce Bradley. *Studio*: Frohman Amusement Corp.

Based on Edward Everett Hale's 1863 story, "The Man Without a Country," this film goes a step further and becomes propaganda for World War I. Philip Nolan (Arnold Daly) is convicted of being involved with Aaron Burr (Charles Graham) in an attempt to set up a separate country in the Southwest. Nolan does not realize that his new bride (Mrs. Allen

Walker) is pregnant when he begins his sentence that includes receiving no information about the United States. Thus he does not know that he has a son. His son, grandson, and great grandson (all played by Arnold Daly) are all called Philip Nolan. The thrust of the story is to convince the great grandson, Philip IV, to become a patriot and join the army in World War I. That he does after hearing the story of his progenitor.

No copies of this black-and-white silent film exist. However, because it is based on all of the other "Man Without a Country" films, it can be surmised that all of the presidents listed in the cast performed the same role. Jefferson (P.R. Scammon) was president when Nolan was first convicted. *Variety* reported in its review, "All of the impersonators were good."

America (1924)

Jefferson: Frank Walsh.

Frank Walsh appears briefly in this film. For details, see Chapter 1 on George Washington.

Janice Meredith (1924)

Jefferson: Lionel Adams.

Among the many historical figures in this Revolutionary war epic, Jefferson (Lionel Adams) appears signing the Declaration of Independence. Adams barely looks the part. For details, see Chapter 1 on George Washington.

Ace of Spades (1925)

Jefferson: John Herdman. *Other Cast:* William Desmond (Dan Harvey), Mary McAllister (Olive Heath), Albert J. Smith (Joe Deneen), William A. Steele (Jim Heath), Cathleen Calhoun (Parker Dice Ann), Jack Pratt (Gideon Trask), Clarke Comstock (Martin Heath), Frank Lanning (Francois), William P. De Vaull (Napoleon Bonaparte), John Shanks (Talleyrand), Aaron Edwards (Lucien Bonaparte), Bert Sprotte (James Monroe). *Director:* Henry MacRae. Writing Credits: Isadore Bernstein, William Lord Wright. *Studio:* Universal Pictures. *Length:* 15 episodes.

The basic story of this 15-episode Western serial concerns cattle rustling during the time of the Oklahoma land rush, requiring detective work by Dan Harvey (William Desmond). Although the films are not available, it is obvious from the cast of characters that the history of the Louisiana Purchase also is included. In addition to Thomas Jefferson (John Herdman) and James Monroe (Bert Sprotte) there are appearances by Napoleon (William De Vaull) and Tallyrand (John Shanks).

Alexander Hamilton (1931)

Jefferson: Montagu Love.

This biopic treats Secretary of the Treasury Hamilton's efforts to ensure national assumption of the debt to Revolutionary War soldiers. A secondary problem also addressed in this film concerned the location of the permanent capital for the United States. The seeds for a solution to both problems are sown by James Monroe, just back from a 700-mile trip through the South to ascertain its feeling for the capital site. Jefferson (Montagu Love) suggests "a little persuasion." The two do just that with Hamilton in the famous compromise, held in Hamilton's home office, not at the actual dinner in the Philadelphia lodgings of Jefferson. Hamilton is at his diplomatic best, first suggesting Albany because it "commands commerce," then New York or Philadelphia because of their "great traditions." Monroe wonders if this is "a bait."

Love, who also has played Washington, does his usual splendid job of showing emotions, in this case Jefferson's antagonistic relations with Hamilton and their compromise on debt assumption and the location of the capital. For details, see Chapter 1 on George Washington.

The Phantom President (1932)

Jefferson: Unidentified actor.

The actor portraying Jefferson is not identified and an assessment of his abilities is difficult given the length of his appearance. Nevertheless, he is involved in a spirited rendition of "The Country Needs a Man" campaign song in this musical comedy about an unusual presidential candidate. For details, see Chapter 1 on George Washington.

Hearts Divided (1936)

Jefferson: George Irving. *Other Cast:* Dick Powell (Capt. Jerome Bonaparte), Marion Davies (Betsy Patterson), Henry Stephenson (Charles Patterson), Clara Blandick (Ellen Patterson), Charles Ruggles (Sen. Henry Ruggles), Arthur Treacher (Sir Harry), Claude Rains (Napoleon), Edward Everett Horton (Sen. John Hathaway). *Director:* Frank Borzage. *Producers:* Harry Joe Brown, Marion Davies. *Screenwriters:* Laird Doyle, Casey Robinson. *Cinematographer:* George Folsey. *Composers:* Alexis Dubin, Harry Warren. *Editor:* William Holmes. *Studio:* Cosmopolitan. *Length:* 87 minutes.

George Irving as Jefferson presents the historical aspect of this musical love story in the opening scene about the acquisition of the Louisiana Territory. In the White House with proponents of the purchase, he says, "As Thomas Jefferson I agree heartily, but as President I don't like the [$20 million] cost." After discussion about France's probability of yielding the territory and the French need for funds to combat the British as well as reducing the cost of the territory, the president says, "That's what Monroe and Livingston are doing" (negotiating a reduction in Paris).

Jefferson appears in two more speaking scenes: the first when he visits his friend Charles Patterson (Henry Stephenson) who interrupts their conversation to search for his daughter Betsy (Marion Davies). He finds her in a tree surrounded by three suitors: Sen. Ruggles (Charles Ruggles), Sen. Hathaway (Edward Everett Horton), and Sir Harry (Arthur Treacher). Jefferson says, sarcastically, that they are "all business." Jefferson's second appearance is at Patterson's ball to introduce Jerome Napoleon (Dick Powell), on a good-will tour of America for his brother Napoleon Bonaparte. The last Jefferson appearance, non-speaking, is also at this gala (that includes Burr, Hamilton, and Gallatin) when stately Jefferson stands next to Patterson and his sister, Ellen (Clara Blandick), as Betsy reveals her marriage plans to Jerome, who all think is her French tutor.

Hearts Divided (1936): George Irving as Thomas Jefferson (on stairs) gives Henry Stephenson (foot of stairs) as Charles Patterson and his ball guests a greeting watched intently by Marion Davies as Betsy Patterson and Dick Powell (in uniform) as Napoleon Bonaparte's brother Jerome. This romantic musical with a score by Richard Rodgers and Lorenz Hart, based on a true story, was a Cosmopolitan Production–First National Picture. (Courtesy of George Eastman House.)

This romance as directed by Frank Borzage comprises most of the film and ends with Jerome's renouncing a kingdom in Europe. His brother, *the* Napoleon (Claude Rains), again finds his expansion plans thwarted. In real life, Jerome divorces Betsy in order to be politically paired and become King of Westphalia. Irving portrays Jefferson in a very formal and direct manner throughout. However, Rains as Napoleon gets "A-1 for characterization" by *Variety* (June 17, 1936) because he "believes in the role."

Old Louisiana (1937) aka Louisiana Gal

Jefferson: Allan Cavan. *Other Cast:* Tom Keene (John Colfax), Rita Hayworth as Rita Cansino (Angela Gonzales), Will Morgan (Steve, Colfax's Pal), Robert Fiske (Luke E. Gilmore), Ray Bennett (Flint), Budd Buster (Kentuck), Carlos de Valdez (Gov. Juan Buenaventura), Ramsay Hill (Secretary of State James Madison), Wally Albright (Davey). *Director:* Irvin Willat. *Producer:* E.R. Derr. *Writing Credits:* Mary Ireland, John T. Neville. *Music:* Abe Meyer. *Cinematography:* Arthur Martinelli. *Film Editing:* Donald Barratt. *Art Direction:* Edward C. Jewell. *Studio:* Crescent Pictures Corp. *Length:* 60 minutes.

The Spanish governor of Louisiana plans to tax all American goods moving through

New Orleans in this adventure drama. This starts a battle between John Colfax (Tom Keene) and Luke Gilmore (Robert Fiske) of the Louisiana Fur Co. Colfax presents the problem of the Americans to President Jefferson (Allan Cavan). Since he is in the process of buying the territory from France, Jefferson gives Colfax a letter to the Americans asking them to follow his leadership.

On the return trip to Louisiana, Colfax meets Donna Angela Gonzales (Rita Cansino, later to be known more famously as Rita Hayworth). After escaping with him from the villains, she returns to her father in St. Louis. Colfax continues to fight Gilmore until Gilmore is arrested and jailed, and Colfax and Cansino marry.

The Declaration of Independence (1938)

Jefferson: John Litel.

Jefferson (John Litel) figures almost as much as Caesar Rodney (Ted Osborne) whose deciding vote for the Declaration provides the plot of this featurette. Jefferson is first seen en route to Philadelphia with Richard Henry Lee (Tom Chatterton) airing their political views about a declaration of independence from England. Then Jefferson appears with his draft for advice from his colleagues John Adams (Ferris Taylor) and Ben Franklin (Walter Walker). They urge him to drop his slavery clause "to stop debate" over the inflammatory issue and proceed with debate on the Declaration. In the final signing scene Jefferson reads the Declaration as the Liberty Bell tolls. Litel's imposing posture and mellifluent voice gives him Founding Father presence.

Beautifully filmed and produced, the film looks authentic, although its history is not. For details, see Chapter 2 on John Adams.

The Romance of Louisiana (1938)

Jefferson: Erville Alderson. *Other Cast:* Addison Richards (James Monroe), Gordon Hart (Robert Livingston), Suzanne Kaaren (Empress Josephine), Ian Wolfe (Talleyrand), Alphonse Ethier (Marbaugh), Theodore Osborne (Ross of Pennsylvania). *Director:* Crane Wilbur. *Producer:* Gordon Hollingshead. *Writing Credits:* Charles L. Tedford. *Music:* Howard Jackson. *Cinematography:* W. Howard Greene. *Film Editing:* Everett Dodd. *Studio:* The Vitaphone Corp., Warner Bros. *Length:* 18 minutes.

In this short, the purchase of the Louisiana Territory is reenacted for a radio dramatization commemorating the 150th anniversary of the event. The main participants include President Jefferson (Erville Alderson) and his ministers to France who negotiated the purchase, Robert Livingston (Gordon Hart) and James Monroe (Addison Richards). Although Empress Josephine (Suzanne Kaaren) is represented, the main French participant, Napoleon, does not appear (or speak since this is a radio dramatization).

The Howards of Virginia (1940)

Jefferson: Richard Carlson. *Jefferson at 11:* Buster Phelps. *Other Cast:* Cary Grant (Matt Howard), Martha Scott (Jane Peyton Howard), Cedric Hardwicke (Fleetwood Peyton), George Houston (George Washington). *Director-Producer:* Frank Lloyd. *Writing Credits:* Sidney Buchman, Elizabeth Page. *Music:* Richard Hageman. *Cinematography:* Bert Glennon. *Film Editing:*

3—Thomas Jefferson (1801–1809) 51

Paul Weatherwax. *Art Direction:* John B. Goodman. *Set Decoration:* Howard Bristol. *Studio:* Columbia Pictures. *Length:* 117 minutes.

This period costume drama serves to stir patriotism for the United States during the period of its release. Its central character, Matt Howard, as played by Cary Grant, is properly called an "imposter" by his future wife, Jane Peyton Howard (Martha Scott), when he tries to survey her family's plantation, Fleetwood. He's struggling to find himself (and a way to handle his role). Offering advice is Richard Carlson who plays his friend Jefferson. Grant made this film during one of the busiest years of his career, between his delightful screwball comedy roles in *His Girl Friday* and *My Favorite Wife* and before his signature witty, super-sophisticated role opposite Katharine Hepburn in *The Philadelphia Story*. Unfortunately, Grant retains much of his native Cockney accent and many of his screwball comedy techniques in *The Howards of Virginia* that detract from the serious intentions of his American colonialist character.

Yet his underlying patriotic seriousness is understood by Jefferson who inveigles Howard to be a surveyor, then to run for a seat in the House of Burgesses. Howard goes home to western Virginia on the day of the Boston Tea Party, and finally gives his support to Jefferson who's writing the Declaration of Independence. Not only is Jefferson an inspiring friend, he utters inspiring words to Howard such as, "You fight for the very thing you love

The Howards of Virginia (1940): Richard Carlson (center) as the young Thomas Jefferson tries to convince Cary Grant as Matt Howard to join the Revolutionaries while Martha Scott (playing Jane) looks on in this Columbia Pictures film. (Courtesy of George Eastman House.)

[legality]" and "Home ... where men can be free." Carlson handles his short appearances in a weighty yet youthful role with the dignity that characterized Jefferson.

The film lost money at the box office as did most Hollywood films about the Revolutionary War. To Grant's credit, he donated his $40,000 salary towards the war effort.

The Tanks Are Coming (1941)

Jefferson: John Litel. *Other Cast:* George Tobias (Malowski), William Travis (Pete), Gig Young as Byron Barr (Jim Allen), Frank Wilcox (Colonel), Walter Walker (Benjamin Franklin), Franklin D. Roosevelt (Himself from archive sound), Knox Manning (Narrator). *Director:* B. Reeves Eason. *Producer:* Gordon Hollingshead. *Writing Credits:* Owen Crump. *Music:* William Lava. *Cinematography:* Bert Glennon. *Film Editing:* Everett Dodd. *Studio:* Warner Brothers.

Just before the United States' entry into World War II, Warner Brothers in cooperation with the U.S. Army made this semi-documentary short regarding the production and use of tanks by the military. As background for the necessity of preparedness, the speech given by Jefferson (John Litel) in *The Declaration of Independence* (1938) is shown. For details on *The Declaration of Independence*, see Chapter 2 on John Adams.

The Loves of Edgar Allan Poe (1942)

Jefferson: Gilbert Emery. *Other Cast:* Linda Darnell (Virginia Clemm), Virginia Gilmore (Elmira Royster), Jane Darwell (Mrs. Mariah Clemm), Frank Conroy (John Allan), Mary Howard (Frances Allan), Shepperd Strudwick as John Shepperd (Edgar Allan Poe), Hardie Albright (Mr. Shelton). *Director:* Harry Lachman. *Producer:* Bryan Foy. *Screenwriters:* Art Caesar, Samuel Hoffenstein, Tom Reed. *Cinematographer:* Lucien Andriot. *Editor:* Fred Allen. *Studio:* 20th Century–Fox. *Length:* 67 minutes.

Virginia figures in this film on the life of Edgar Allan Poe (John Shepperd, later known as Shepperd Strudwick). He was born and raised in Richmond; he attended the University of Virginia at Charlottesville, then headed by its architect and founder, Jefferson (Gilbert Emery). Elsewhere, as this biographical film depicts, Poe pursued his writing in Philadelphia, New York City, and Baltimore where he died.

The loves of Poe receive less attention than his problems with his stepfather John Allan (Frank Conroy), his "tempestuous spirit," his drinking, and his zealous belief in his talent and work. Jefferson recognized Poe's talent when he was a troublesome student at the University of Virginia. The former president said, "You young men cause me more trouble... than running a country." Then Jefferson says Poe "did him the service by writing 'The Gold Bug' that kept him awake" and, he believed, Poe "was on to something new." But Jefferson says that Poe has gone deeper into debt than the most gentlemanly fashion (gentlemanly being a trait University of Virginia encourages) and he shall "greatly regret your leaving here."

Looking very much like Jefferson with his curly hair, distinguishing upturned nose, and cultured manner, Emery creates a convincing characterization, particularly with some parting advice: "Never raise your voice, and count to ten if you think you are going to lose your temper."

As for Poe's loves, Elmira Royster (Virginia Gilmore) weds a Mr. Shelton (Hardie Albright) when her father learns Poe would never inherit his stepfather's fortune (because Poe's parents were actors). Virginia Clemm (Linda Darnell), Poe's childlike cousin, becomes his muse, his inspiration, and "his life's care." Poe also is influenced by his loving stepmother Frances Allan (Mary Howard) and Aunt Mariah Clemm (Jane Darwell). Under Harry Lachman's direction, this follows a Hollywood pattern of films about geniuses by stressing how they are misunderstood, go from bad to worse, and yet attain immortality.

The Remarkable Andrew (1942)

Jefferson: Gilbert Emery.

Andrew Law (William Holden) is the title character in this patriotic pre–World War II film in which the ghost of Jackson (Brian Donlevy) comes to the assistance of the young bookkeeper accused of embezzlement. Joining Jackson are the "best legal minds" in the country: George Washington, Thomas Jefferson, Benjamin Franklin, and Chief Justice Marshall. The "greatest legal minds" Jackson knows, give advice true to their natures. Jefferson (Gilbert Emery), in his familiar philosophic way, states, "I fail to see your reasoning." Emery portrays this role with proper Jeffersonian Enlightenment spirit. For details, see Chapter 7 on Andrew Jackson.

The Magnificent Doll (1946)

Jefferson: Grandon Rhodes.

In a subplot, Jefferson (Grandon Rhodes) appears briefly, having tied the election for the presidency with Aaron Burr. Jefferson wins by buying some votes that cheapens him, Dolley says. Yet, he invites her to be hostess in the White House to make it "warm and friendly." For details, see Chapter 4 on James Madison.

Barbary Pirate (1949)

Jefferson: Holmes Herbert. *Other Cast:* Donald Woods (Maj. Tom Blake), Trudy Marshall (Anne Ridgeway), Lenore Aubert (Zoitah), Stefan Schnabel (Yusof, the Bey of Tripoli), Ross Ford (Sam Ridgeway), John Dehner (Murad Reis), Matthew Boulton (Tobias Sharpe). *Director:* Lew Landers. *Producer:* Sam Katzman. *Writing Credits:* Frank Burt, Robert Libott. *Cinematographer:* Ira Morgan. *Editor:* James Sweeney. *Studio:* Columbia Pictures. *Length:* 65 minutes.

"Quickie king" Sam Katzman was responsible for this "small-budget supporter for secondary slotting," according to *Variety* (Aug. 3, 1949). "Yet the theme is ambitious and stock shots and similar production tricks cloak the corner-cutting."

The story is set in the post–Revolution era when Barbary pirates preyed on American shipping vessels off the shores of Tripoli. Taking the offensive, President Jefferson (Holmes Herbert) unofficially dispatches undercover Army officer Maj. Tom Blake, aka Brighton, an Englishman (Donald Woods). Blake soon is captured, befriends Yusof, the Bey of Tripoli (Stefan Schnabel), who is receiving shipping tips from American traitor Tobias Sharpe (Matthew Boulton), and engages in swordplay. Anne Ridgeway (Trudy Marshall) uncovers Woods's English Tory pose and succumbs to his romantic persona.

Mr. Whitney Has a Notion (1949)

Jefferson: Erville Alderson. *Other Cast:* Lloyd Bridges (Eli Whitney), Howard Negley (Military Committee Man), Harry Hayden (Senatorial Committee Man), Mitchell Lewis (Whitney's Workman), John Nesbitt (Narrator). *Director:* Gerald Mayer. *Writing Credits:* John Nesbitt. *Length:* 11 minutes.

Eli Whitney has been presented to American schoolchildren as the inventor of the cotton gin. In fact, in this short film he is shown to have inventiveness much beyond agricultural equipment: He pioneers the principle of mass production with each worker manufacturing and assembling individual parts for the finished goods. Directed by Gerald Mayer, this short is part of the *Passing Parade* series, with narration by John Nesbitt.

In 1798 Whitney (Lloyd Bridges) with the support of Jefferson (Erville Alderson) convinces a government committee that he could produce ten thousand usable muskets in two years. Pressed for proof that he could meet the contract, Whitney is successful in illustrating to the government committee his ability in a scene made dramatic by close-ups of Whitney and his workers assembling a musket in just 16 minutes.

Alderson is obviously much older than Jefferson would have been at this period in his life. In addition, he does not seem to project the erudition for which the third president is noted. Yet he ruminates on a name for Whitney's invention, suggesting "production by the mass" and comments that "the results will yield millions of low priced articles for all problems."

Ben and Me (1953)

Jefferson: Hans Conried, voice. *Other Cast:* Sterling Holloway (Amos Mouse, voice), Charles Ruggles (Ben Franklin, voice). *Director:* Hamilton Luske. *Producer:* Walt Disney. *Writing Credits:* Robert Lawson, Bill Peet. *Music:* Oliver Wallace. *Animator:* Ollie Johnson. *Studio:* Walt Disney Pictures. *Length:* 20 minutes.

Once more a Disney mouse, Amos, takes center frame, and influences Ben Franklin (voice of Charles Ruggles) and the founding of the American Republic. This short, part of a Disney package that includes *The Living Desert* and *Storm*, is based on Robert Lawson's classic 1939 story of the same name. Scriptwriter Bill Peet retains the original's whimsy, featuring a slightly bumbling Franklin. According to Amos Mouse, he inspired Franklin's inventions and work on the Declaration of Independence.

The Far Horizons (1955) aka Blue Horizons and aka Untamed West

Jefferson: Herbert Heyes. *Other Cast:* Fred MacMurray (Meriwether Lewis), Charlton Heston (William Clark), Donna Reed (Sacajawea), Barbara Hale (Julia Hancock), William Demarest (Sgt. Cass), Alan Reed (Charboneau). *Director:* Rudolph Mate. *Producer:* William H. Pine, William C. Thomas. *Writing Credits:* Della Gould Emmons, Winston Miller, Edmund H. North. *Music:* Hans J. Salter. *Cinematography:* Daniel L. Fapp. *Film Editing:* Frank Bracht. *Art Direction:* A. Earl Hedrick, Hal Pereira. *Set Decoration:* Sam Comer, Otto Siegel. *Costume Design:* Edith Head. *Makeup:* Wally Westmore. *Studio:* Paramount Pictures. *Length:* 108 minutes.

Untamed West is the reissue and better title of this western telling of the Lewis and Clark expedition of 1803–06 to explore the Louisiana Purchase. That purchase, the greatest real estate deal in the U.S., was made by President Jefferson for $20 million because the French under Napoleon needed money to fight the English. It doubled the size of the U.S.

Lewis and Clark's charge from Jefferson was to explore the territory to the western coast because, as he says, "We'll never be secure until our land stretches to the Pacific." Herbert Heyes as Jefferson makes three appearances in this film, his first in Jefferson's private quarters while shaving when Meriwether Lewis (Fred MacMurray) answers his request to report for an assignment. The president's administrative struggles surface in his explanation to Lewis of his monetary request: "Dealing with Congress is like shaving. No matter how well you do it, you have to get up in the morning and do it all over again." Jefferson's second appearance is greeting Lewis and Clark (Charlton Heston) upon their return. Again he's dealing with Congress—dictating a request for the budget. Jefferson's Virginia manners also surface when Clark insists he meet their Indian guide Sacajawea (Donna Reed) and Jefferson says, "It's an honor to receive you, my dear." Two scenes later, after Jefferson reads Lewis and Clark's report (another historically impossible feat as it was voluminous unlike the movie version), he congratulates them both and says he thinks it "so meticulous ... yet found five pages missing."

Much is missing concerning Jefferson's reaction to this journey of discovery: A man of manifold interests, he was truly enthralled by Lewis and Clark's work. Still, Heyes conveys Jefferson's serene presidential behavior and manner of speaking, although he is much shorter than the third president; and his features, much fuller.

Even more is missing of historical accuracy in depicting the expedition. The film is really a western, a standard story of two men feuding over two women (Reed and Barbara Hale as Julia Hancock) and fighting with Indians, played generally as savage as was the style of 50s westerns. And it's anachronistic with clichéd dialogue delivered in 20th century colloquial English.

There are several fine scenes showing the explorers' accomplishments: bestowing the famous Jefferson medals on the Indians, taking readings for their maps, noting the wildlife, struggling with the wilderness, and battling the Indians on the Columbia River as they push to the Pacific Ocean. The Technicolor-and-Vistavision cinematography of Daniel L. Fapp truly dramatizes the splendor of the American west—purple mountains' majesty and all. Perhaps the film's inaccuracy could be traced to its being based on Della Gould Emmons's novel, *Sacajawea of the Shoshones*.

1776 (1972)

Jefferson: Ken Howard.

One of the major subplots of the musical concerns Jefferson's writing the Declaration of Independence. Tall, slim, and red-headed, Ken Howard portrays Jefferson with musical skill and physical dexterity. He especially exudes Jefferson's youthful ardor for his bride who comes to break his writer's block. For details, see Chapter 2 on John Adams.

Independence (1976)

Jefferson: Ken Howard.

Ken Howard as Jefferson joins the Founding Fathers in this 30-minute film for the Bicentennial celebration of the Declaration of Independence in 1976. John Huston directed this authentic-looking enactment of the making of this important American document. He creates a *mise-en-scene* that resembles Trumbull's famous painting of the signing.

Howard expresses the guiding philosophy of Jefferson: "All our devotion is to the public good." He also is seen in a close-up drafting the Declaration. He looks and acts much like the Virginian, especially his taciturn nature. For details, see Chapter 1 on George Washington.

A More Perfect Union: America Becomes a Nation (1989)

Jefferson: Scott Wilkinson.

Scott Wilkinson appears briefly as Jefferson in drafting the Declaration of Independence. His most notable line is "Rebellion is liberty's natural manure." For details, see Chapter 1 on George Washington.

Jefferson in Paris (1995)

Jefferson: Nick Nolte. *Other Cast:* Greta Scacchi (Maria Cosway), Jean-Pierre Aumont (D'Hancarville), Simon Callow (Richard Cosway), Seth Gilliam (James Hemings), Thandie Newton (Sally Hemings), Gwyneth Paltrow (Patsy Jefferson). *Director:* James Ivory. *Producer:* Ismail Merchant. *Writing Credits:* Ruth Prawer Jhabvala. *Cinematographers:* Pierre Lhomme, Larry Pizer. *Editors:* Isabelle Lorente, Andrew Marcus. *Production Designer:* Guy-Claude Francois. *Studio:* Ivory-Merchant. *Length:* 139 minutes.

Reputed for their historical films based on novels that observe British class and social issues—*A Room with a View* (1986) and *Howard's End* (1992)—through a lens of lavish and accurate productions, director James Ivory, producer Ismail Merchant, and scriptwriter Ruth Prawer Jhabvala turn to an American subject, Thomas Jefferson, in one period of his life before his presidency. Accurate as the production values appear, the script draws on imagined interpretations of Jefferson's behavior while ambassador to Paris. All the key events are true: that he loves France and things French, that he negotiates a loan at the Hague, that his daughters Patsy and then Polly join him in Paris, that he "romances" Maria Cosway.[6] His paternity of his slave Sally Hemings's child was in debate at the time of this film's release, although since then genetic evidence supports it as a possibility.

What's missing in Nick Nolte's enigmatic rendering of Jefferson is his rich inner life, his thoughts and emotions. Well documented as Jefferson's enigmatic character is, most recently by Joseph Ellis in *American Sphinx*, he did show some passion toward Maria Cosway (Greta Scacchi), the wife of a homosexual English painter (Simon Callow), particularly in his letters to her. But Jefferson was more in love with love itself. This subtle difference in Jefferson's emotions never surfaces on film. He just forgets her soon after she leaves for England, and he's suffering with a broken wrist, his excuse for not writing her. Nor are Jefferson's feelings toward Sally Hemings made clear. As portrayed by Thandie Newton, the 15-year-old slave seems simple-minded, as much taken by ghost stories as she is by her master. The most overt manifestation of Jefferson's emotion toward her is his grabbing her wrist when she attends to him in his bedroom and reacting to her flirtatious movements with him in front of Cosway.

In the film's longest scene, Jefferson promises Sally and her brother James (Seth Gilliam) their freedom, then calls in Patsy (Gwyneth Paltrow) to witness the bargain and promise to fulfill it if he is unable. Patsy reacts with religious indignation upon learning that Hemings is pregnant by her father. She is angry with him for breaking her mother's deathbed vow not to marry again and for not letting her become the nun she wishes. Earlier, when he enrolled her in a French convent, Jefferson expounded about freedom of religion. (Scriptwriter Jhabvala manages to weave many of Jefferson's pronouncements, however contrary, into the script.) Now Jefferson wants Patsy to go home to Virginia and be a lady.

The film ends as it begins with Madison Hemings (James Earl Jones) recounting the family history, or semblance thereof. What remains are the images of the Paris Jefferson so loved, even on the cusp of revolution: the sumptuous drawing rooms, the elegant opera, the colorful balloon ascensions.

4
James Madison (1809–1817)

Both before and during his presidency, James Madison left his intellectual imprint on the formation of this country: He created the plan for three branches of government in the Constitution, he helped write the *Federalist* papers in support of the Constitution, and he wrote the Virginia Resolutions that advocated the free-speech-and-press amendment of the Bill of Rights.[1] Undecided about a career, he turned to scholarship, concentrating on the Enlightenment philosophers who shaped his constitutional thought (exactly which one is debated by modern historians).

His career, nevertheless, saw him as the youngest delegate to the Continental Congress, delegate to the Constitutional Convention, four terms in Congress as floor leader for important legislation, member of the Virginia legislature, and Secretary of State under Jefferson. As president, Madison balanced his friend Jefferson's philosophy of state sovereignty and strict construction against the principle of strong central government needed for debt reduction, internal improvements, and the War of 1812.

James Madison. (Courtesy of Library of Congress.)

One of the most unpopular wars this country ever waged, the War of 1812 divided the country: New England Federalists were anti–French and eager to revive shipping, Republicans in the South and West under Henry Clay were anti–English and for expansion into Canada. Madison tried diplomacy, and then declared war despite lack of government funds and competent generals. The perceptive Alfred Gallatin noted after working daily (as Secretary of State) with Madison for eight years that "Mr. Madison is, as I always knew him, slow in taking his ground, but firm when the storm rises."[2] Still, "under [his wife] Dolley's presiding genius, and with her husband's entire approval, both in Washington and at Montpelier, the years of Madison's presidency were a social triumph. The honor and dignity of the republic, never separate in Madison's mind from the success of the experiment in republican government, seemed to require some elegance and style in its social life."[3]

THE FILMS

Not one of the more popular presidents, this most literate and political man never received full treatment in a film; Madison appears in only three films and has a major role in only one, *Magnificent Doll*. While Dolley is the star, his high-minded character and soft-spoken personality appear most strongly. His other roles are so minimal, filmgoers do not see the full measure of the man.

Old Louisiana (1937) aka Louisiana Gal

Madison: Ramsay Hill.

Although there is some confusion in contemporary versus modern casting lists, it now appears that Ramsay Hill portrays then Secretary of State James Madison in this western. For details, see Chapter 3 on Thomas Jefferson.

Magnificent Doll (1946)

Madison: Burgess Meredith. *Other Cast:* Ginger Rogers (Dolley Payne Madison), David Niven (Aaron Burr), Peggy Wood (Mrs. Payne), Stephen McNally as Horace McNally (John Todd), Robert H. Barrat (Mr. Payne), Grandon Rhodes (Thomas Jefferson). *Director:* Frank Borzage. *Producers:* Bruce Manning, Jack H. Skirball. *Screenwriter:* Irving Stone. *Cinematographer:* Joseph A. Valentine. *Composer:* Hans Salter. *Editor:* Ted Kent. *Production Designer:* Alexander Golitzen. *Musical Direction:* David Tamkin. *Set Designers:* Russell A. Gausman, Ted Offenbecker. *Costume Designers:* Travis Banton, Vera West. *Studio:* Universal. *Length:* 95 minutes.

While it remains difficult to picture Ginger Rogers of *Kitty Foyle* (1940) and *The Barkeleys of Broadway* (1949) as Dolley Madison, "a political pinup girl" and the subject of this film, it proves even more difficult to see her torn in her love between Aaron Burr and James Madison. Perhaps she ignored Burr's self-centered scheming and political conniving as well conveyed by David Niven because, as she says, he has "an odd way of making danger attractive." In choosing idealistic, solemn, soft-spoken Madison, convincingly and modestly portrayed by Burgess Meredith, she put herself in the social spotlight she enjoyed. The charm and sociability of Dolley do suit these characteristics of Rogers, however, and carry the film when historical accuracy fails.

Quaker-bred Dolley's story begins with her unhappy marriage to John Todd (Stephen McNally) who dies with their son in a yellow fever epidemic in Philadelphia, the then capital. Dolley helps her mother (Peggy Wood) run a boarding house where the likes of Burr and later Madison take rooms. While Burr escorts Dolley to the theater, Madison quietly plays chess, symbolically showing their differences. Upon Dolley's return, the brilliant Madison, architect of the United States Constitution, tells her of his bill in the Senate to prohibit slavery on ships. Unlike Burr, he subtly romances Dolley by asking her "if she's thinking of marrying again." Later, in Congress, when he defines freedom, Dolley knows that she loves him and "no man has ever made a more beautiful proposal." Meredith, indeed, gives credibility to Madison's political statements. His physicality also resembles Madison's.

Meanwhile, Burr plots to overthrow the U.S. and writes Dolley to come with him. She shows the letter to Madison who nobly says he "can't tell her what to do." Because Burr

Magnificent Doll (1946): Ginger Rogers (right) as Dolley Payne Madison appears torn between the affections of Aaron Burr, played by David Niven (far left), and James Madison, played by Burgess Meredith (center), in this Universal film on the wife of the fourth president. (Courtesy of George Eastman House.)

once did her a great favor, she goes to his cell to give him sympathy and prevent his being hanged as Madison arrives. He delivers ringing words to the mob around Burr, "This is your trial and you who want to hang him would abolish law ... let him pass to the oblivion he has chosen for himself."

The film does not go on to show Dolley's bravery in saving important state documents and the famous Gilbert Stuart portrait of George Washington when British troops invaded Washington in 1814, thus ignoring one of the most dramatic and significant incidents in the Madison era.

A More Perfect Union: America Becomes a Nation (1989)

Madison: Craig Wasson.

Craig Wasson plays Madison with reflection as well as assertiveness in expressing his philosophical and political positions in this film about states rights vs. a strong federal government and workable separation of powers. He notes how "loyalty to sovereign states threatens to ruin us as small states insist on equal representation." For details, see Chapter 1 on George Washington.

5

James Monroe (1817–1825)

Soon after election, James Monroe toured the country, as had Washington, ostensibly to view federal fortifications but really to restore national unity after the War of 1812. His visit was described by the Boston *Columbian Centinel* as a demonstration of an "ERA OF GOOD FEELINGS" that characterized his two terms, covering change with the air of consistency. Like Washington, Monroe was a military hero of the Revolution, calm in disposition, opposed to partisan politics, a believer that everyone should work together for the greater glory of the nation as he did in a lifetime of public service.[1] Monroe's most memorable legacy, the Monroe Doctrine, also was Washingtonian.

When minister to France for Washington, however, Monroe's defense of the Jay Treaty brought him rebuke from the Father of the Country. Yet, Monroe was seen as a man "whose soul might be turned wrong side outwards without discovering a blemish to the world," said Jefferson.[2] Monroe, the last of the Virginian Dynasty, was more interested in foreign policy than domestic politics, and his wife was not interested in politics at all. The prevailing issues of his first term were internal improvements. This included national expansion which involved a hard-fought compromise to add the states Missouri and Maine (the first a slave state, the second not), as well as treaties about the borders of Oregon and Florida.

James Monroe. (Courtesy of Library of Congress.)

These issues heightened during Monroe's second term when antislavery factions wanted to nullify Missouri's admission. Monroe reluctantly signed Henry Clay's Missouri Compromise that postponed a decision on the expansion of slavery, for which as his Secretary of State Madison knew, the Constitution provided no solution. With Russia extending territory down the Pacific coast, and Spain with French aid threatening to re-enter its former colonies, Monroe refused English support and "avowed his principles." The result was the Monroe Doctrine, written by Secretary of State John Quincy Adams, and delivered by Monroe to Congress, proclaiming "that the American continents ... are henceforth not to be considered a subject for future colonization by any European powers."[3]

THE FILMS

As the presidential author of one of the United States' longest lasting foreign policy positions, Monroe could be expected to provide grist for Hollywood's mill. However, he appears in only eight films and has a major role in only two short films. Even in *The Monroe Doctrine* about Monroe's philosophy of American integrity, Monroe does not receive full treatment. He appears in almost cameo roles in the other patriotic films.

The Beautiful Mrs. Reynolds (1918) aka The Adventurer

Monroe: Charles Brandt.

Charles Brandt makes a cameo appearance as Monroe in this silent historical drama of the rivalry between Alexander Hamilton and Aaron Burr. For details, see Chapter 1 on George Washington.

In the Days of Daniel Boone (1923)

Monroe: Jack Lewis.

Jack Lewis plays Monroe in this serial concerning Daniel Boone's adventures in the wilderness. For details, see Chapter 1 on George Washington.

Ace of Spades (1925)

Monroe: Bert Sprotte.

It would seem from the cast of characters that the Louisiana Purchase is involved in the plot. For details, see Chapter 3 on Thomas Jefferson.

Alexander Hamilton (1931)

Monroe: Morgan Wallace.

Morgan Wallace portrays Monroe who is working with Jefferson to situate the new U.S. capital in the South. He returns from a tour of the South and together with Jefferson reaches a compromise with Hamilton on both the capital location and the assumption of Revolutionary War debts. He also visits Hamilton later in the film because of the scandal of Hamilton's "affair" with Mrs. Reynolds. Although his facial features do not resemble Monroe's, Wallace's stature does, and he imbues his characterization with Monroe's dignity and sincerity. For details, see Chapter 1 on George Washington.

The Man without a Country (1937)

Monroe: Unnamed actor.

In an uncredited appearance, Monroe is visited in 1817 by Philip Nolan's wife. He informs her that there is nothing he can do since there are "no records" relating to her husband, the man without a country. For details, see Chapter 7 on Andrew Jackson.

Alexander Hamilton (1931): Morgan Wallace as James Monroe (left) assists Montagu Love as Thomas Jefferson (center) in confronting George Arliss as Alexander Hamilton (right) on his marital infidelity in this Warner Brothers biopic. (Courtesy of George Eastman House.)

The Romance of Louisiana (1938)

Monroe: Addison Richards.

Addison Richards portrays James Monroe in this short concerning the Louisiana Purchase. For details, see Chapter 3 on Thomas Jefferson.

The Monroe Doctrine (1939)

Monroe: Charles Waldron. *Other Cast:* Grant Mitchell (John Quincy Adams), James Stephenson (Dellatorre), Sidney Blackmer (Theodore Roosevelt), Nanette Fabray as Nanette Fabares (Rosita Dellatorre), George Reeves (John Sturgis), Frank Wilcox (Henry Clay), Edwin Stanley (James K. Polk), Millard Vincent (Millard Fillmore), Stuart Holmes (Grover Cleveland). *Director:* Crane Wilbur. *Writing Credits:* Charles L. Tedford. *Cinematography:* Wilfrid M. Cline. *Film Editing:* Everett Dodd. *Art Direction:* Hugh Reticker. *Costume Design:* Leah Rhodes. *Makeup:* Perc Westmore. *Sound:* Dolph Thomas. *Studio:* Warner Brothers. *Length:* 16 minutes.

To boost the patriotism of the American public just before and just after World War II began, a number of shorts were made, particularly by Warner Brothers. Quite often Amer-

The Monroe Doctrine (1939): The Monroe Doctrine with its importance in American political history features six presidents who implemented this doctrine. President James Monroe, the author, as portrayed by Charles Waldron (seated), confers with his Secretary of State John Quincy Adams (Grant Mitchell) on America's response to attempts by Spain to interfere in South America, the action that prompted the doctrine. The other presidents in the Warner Brothers film are James K. Polk, Millard Fillmore, Grover Cleveland and Theodore Roosevelt. Crane Wilbur directed this short patriotic film. (Photofest.)

ican presidents were used as characters in these films, and they weren't necessarily the more famous presidents.

In this film, writer Charles L. Tedford tells the story of President Monroe's (Charles Waldron) actions to eliminate Spanish interference in Latin America by instituting the doctrine using his name. Other presidents included are John Quincy Adams (Grant Mitchell), James K. Polk (Edwin Stanley), Theodore Roosevelt (Sidney Blackmer), Millard Fillmore (Millard Vincent), and Grover Cleveland (Stuart Holmes). Obviously the use of Adams, Polk, Roosevelt, Fillmore, and Cleveland is to illustrate how future presidents implemented the Monroe Doctrine.

March On, America! (1942)

Monroe: Charles Waldron. *Other Cast:* Richard Whorf (Narrator), Grant Mitchell (John Quincy Adams), Sidney Blackmer (Theodore Roosevelt), Douglas Kennedy (Paratrooper), John Litel (Patrick Henry), Frank McGlynn Sr. (Abraham Lincoln), Addison Richards (Man at Map), Franklin D. Roosevelt (Himself, voice), Hugh Sothern (Andrew Jackson), Douglas Wood (President McKinley), Donald Woods (Francis Scott Key). *Director:* Crane Wilbur.

Producer: Gordon Hollingshead. *Writing Credits:* Owen Crump. *Music:* Howard Jackson, Henry Carey, Francis Scott Key, Samuel A. Ward. *Cinematography:* Charles P. Boyle. *Film Editing:* Everett Dodd. *Art Direction:* Charles Novi. *Studio:* Warner Bros. *Length:* 21 minutes.

In this 1942 film, writer Owen Crump uses the same presidents (and the same actors) who appeared in *The Monroe Doctrine*, with the exception of Polk, to illustrate the history of the United States. In addition, Crump wrote in appearances by Lincoln (played by the top impersonator Frank McGlynn Sr.), Jackson (Hugh Sothern), and McKinley (Douglas Wood). Furthermore, there is a vocal-only appearance by Franklin Roosevelt himself.

The presidential appearances are very short, and an assessment is difficult. However with Blackmer, McGlynn, and Sothern in their patented roles, reasonable impersonations are assured. Charles Waldron plays Monroe in this patriotic story of America.

6

John Quincy Adams (1825–1829)

Besides following his father John Adams, the second president of the United States, in that office, John Quincy Adams served as Secretary of State, senator, and U.S. minister to the Netherlands, Prussia, Russia, and Great Britain. These achievements can be divided into three "careers." The first, the longest, and the most successful, was in diplomacy, culminating with his tenure as Secretary of State to James Monroe from 1817 to 1825. The second, the shortest, and the least successful, was his presidency from 1825 to 1829 that he achieved mainly on his reputation as a diplomat and spokesman on foreign policy.[1] The third, and easily the most spectacular, was as a congressman from Massachusetts from 1831 to his death in 1848.[2]

John Quincy Adams (Courtesy of Library of Congress.)

He confronted private crises as well: a less-than-happy marriage, irresponsible siblings, frustrating children, and financial stress. His diary chronicles all of these achievements and crises, reflecting both his great strengths as a dogged and often courageous defender of principle and his weaknesses as a censorious and uncharitable critic of those who crossed him.[3] He was seldom content, neither abroad where his stubbornness made him regarded as a "bulldog among spaniels," nor in Washington where his reticent nature kept him outside the social and political circles.[4] Besides being stubborn, he describes himself in his diary as "dogmatical," "peremptory," "cold," "overbearing," and "harsh."[5]

In that diary that he started as a teenager and kept faithfully until a few weeks before his death, he chronicles that his term in presidential office was a failure. One of the main reasons, say most historians and biographers, was the means by which he was elected. It was the so-called "corrupt bargain" with Henry Clay who as Speaker of the House swung the necessary votes for Adams over Andrew Jackson and William H. Crawford. Clay then served as his Secretary of State.

The second reason attributed to Adams's failure was the theme of his first Annual Message, calling in foreign affairs for the United States to take a leading role in inter–American affairs and in domestic affairs for the federal government to undertake an ambitious program of economic, education, technological, and social improvement. In pursuit of these goals, he proposed a package of measures that came to pass—but not in his day. They included a national bankruptcy law, a national astronomical observatory, a national academy, national research and exploration, and a new Department of Interior to help administer increasing federal business.

The third reason for his failure was his signing the partisan Tariff of Abominations and his siding against Native Americans, particularly in the controversy in which all Creek lands were ceded to Georgia. This action veered from his usual support of Native Americans as well as Blacks, later expressed in his undertaking of the *Amistad* case while in Congress where he depicted himself as an upholder of the public good against the forces of evil.

Finally, Adams refused to push his ideas, protect himself from political enemies, especially in the press, and reward his friends through patronage. While his vision of federal government supporting the economic and intellectual development of the country proved ahead of his time by almost a century, his abhorrence of organized politics recalled an earlier time and ultimately led to his downfall as a leader.

THE FILMS

The worldly Adams followed a father to the presidency after a career that involved more diplomatic posts than practically any other man in government—and a cabinet position. He seemed trained for the job. Yet, it was his work as a congressman and legal counsel on the *Amistad* case that gained him screen coverage with the star role performed by one of the leading actors of the day, Anthony Hopkins. Adams earlier had been portrayed in two minor roles in two shorts.

The Monroe Doctrine (1939)

Adams: Grant Mitchell.
The story of President Monroe's response to attempts by Spain to interfere in South America. For details, see Chapter 5 on James Monroe.

March On, America! (1942)

Adams: Grant Mitchell.
Grant Mitchell also plays Adams in this patriotic story of America. For details, see Chapter 5 on James Monroe.

Amistad (1997)

Adams: Anthony Hopkins. *Other Cast:* Nigel Hawthorne (Martin Van Buren), Djimon Hounsou (Cinque), Morgan Freeman (Joadson), Matthew McConaughey (Baldwin), David Paymer (Secretary Forsyth), Keith Postlethwaite (Holabird), Arliss Howard (John C. Calhoun). *Director:* Steven Spielberg. *Producer:* Debbie Allen. *Writing Credits:* David Franzoni. *Cinematography:* Janusz Kaminski. *Film Editing:* Michael Kahn. *Music:* Debbie Allen, John Williams. *Production Design:* Rick Carter. *Art Direction:* Chris Burian-Mohr, Tony Fanning,

Amistad (1997): Steven Spielberg (left) is the focus of attention as he directs Anthony Hopkins as the former president now congressman and Morgan Freeman as former slave Theodore Joadson in this courtroom drama concerning an actual slave rebellion that John Quincy Adams defended before the Supreme Court. The film was produced by Dream Works/SSKG. (Courtesy of George Eastman House.)

Jim Teegarden. *Set Decoration*: Rosemary Brandenburg. *Costume Design*: Ruth E. Carter. *Studio*: Dream Works. *Length*: 152 minutes.

Steven Spielberg spins this little-known 19th-century tale of the *Amistad*, a Spanish ship whose slave cargo breaks their chains in search of freedom. They find it through the efforts of former president, now Massachusetts Representative John Quincy Adams, who successfully argues their case before the U.S. Supreme Court.

A.O. Scott, the *New York Times* film critic, calls this film "well-intentioned"[6] in an otherwise paean of praise for what he calls "the greatest living American director." Natalie Zemon Davis, Professor of History, Emerita, Princeton University, and author of *The Return of Martin Guerre*, is critical. While she believes viewers would come away from *Amistad* with a general sense of the events, interests, arguments and the popular excitement and missionary zeal stimulated by the Africans, she asserts that the film is not the "mirror [of] actual events as they unfolded." Regarding Adams, she concludes from Adams's diaries that he was advising the Africans from the beginning of their case, rather than needing to be persuaded.[7]

Anthony Hopkins as Adams appears after the main action of the slaves' revolt, an exciting sequence reminiscent of some of the torture scenes in Spielberg's *Schindler's List* (1993). Adams is sleeping as he is wont to do during a Congressional session. Afterward he limps down the Capitol steps and goes home to shuffle among the botanical specimens in his greenhouse where Abolitionist Joadson (Morgan Freeman) finds him and urges him to take on the *Amistad* case. With his usual New England pragmatism, Adams agrees and says he learned whoever tells the best story wins. His renewed interest in botany led to his filling his nursery with seedlings from all over the world, including an African violet that attracts his principal *Amistad* client, Cinque.

Depicting himself as an upholder of the public good against the forces of evil, Adams in the 11-minute long film version of his eight-hour, two-day argument before the Supreme Court makes his key point the Declaration of Independence (that hangs on the wall of the chamber). He also argues that the term "merchandise" is not to be applied to human beings, and that the Africans were not robbers. Missing in the film are his more complex arguments about the wrongful complicity of the president (Van Buren) with the demands of the Spanish government and his interference with the courts. Adams's "story" was based on his mastery of a multitude of documents, as Davis notes in her book. And win he does in an eloquent appeal that he says "concerns the very nature of man." In his summation he cites the principle of that Declaration (pointing to the Declaration of Independence on the wall) and states like Adams did in his published *Argument* "that says that every man is endowed by his Creator with certain inalienable rights.... I ask nothing more in behalf of these unfortunate men, than this Declaration."[8]

Hopkins, a British actor known for his outstanding technique, gives this role great importance through the use of his voice and mannerisms. But history is the loser in this film by such truncating of court testimony, combination of persons into other characters, and omission of significant events.

7

Andrew Jackson (1829–1837)

Whatever the view on Andrew Jackson, man of the people or ruthless political entrepreneur, he ranks as one of the great American presidents. He was the first modern president in that he used his office for purposes of national leadership to bring the people and their government closer together, a use of presidential authority that influenced Lincoln, both Roosevelts, and Woodrow Wilson.[1] Jackson's presidency affirmed the power of the president against two foes: Nicholas Biddle's National Bank and John C. Calhoun's nullifactionist South Carolina.[2]

Different as the historians' overall views of Jackson, views of his character unite on his temper, ardent patriotism, and strong opinions. Unlike the six men that preceded him as president, outsider Jackson was born poor and was self-made, particularly as a military commander at New Orleans in the War of 1812. Tall, craggy,

Andrew Jackson (Courtesy of Library of Congress.)

and rough, this man of the frontier assumed office mourning the death of his wife Rachel against whose "adulterous" reputation he dueled, carrying that shot and another bullet to add to his constant physical pain. But his presidency was more than personal character and impulses, standing for states' rights and an agrarian-based nation, nominating presidential candidates by inventing political conventions, and forming a new party—the Democrats of Jeffersonian principles. Like Jefferson, Jackson championed the people and rewarded loyalists with patronage, the spoils system.

He substituted the ideas of democracy for republicanism as "the last of the great ideologues of the early national period."[3] He wrote, "There is nothing that I shudder at more than the idea of a seperation [his usual misspelling] of the Union." On this principle he fought Calhoun over nullification. Another of Jackson's principles, "The majority is to govern," determined his stance against a National Bank he saw serving the interests of the privileged. Yet his idea of serving the Indians was removal and his idea of slavery was supported by the Constitution.

7—Andrew Jackson (1829–1837)

THE FILMS

Jackson appeared as thin and sharp as his sword, standing at 6' 1" and weighing 140 pounds. His belief in male dominance influenced his behavior as did his military background of daring and courage. Those characteristics resonate throughout the film treatments of him, usually as a warrior. Charlton Heston, who plays him in two films, *The President's Lady* and *The Buccaneer*, stands out as the best impersonator. Heston's physical bearing and commanding voice surface in his interpretations.

My Own United States (1918)

Jackson: F.C. Earle.

See the discussion of the film under Chapter 3 on Thomas Jefferson. Andrew Jackson (F.C. Earle) obviously turns down a request to pardon Nolan. Earle received special comment from the *Variety* reviewer: "F.C. Earle as Andrew Jackson suggested in the most artistic of the brief bits the reserve power of the statesman." What more needs to be said?

The Eagle of the Sea (1926)

Jackson: George Irving. *Other Cast:* Florence Vidor (Louise Lestron), Ricardo Cortez (Captain Sazarac), Sam De Grasse (Colonel Lestron), Andre de Beranger (John Jarvis), Mitchell Lewis (Crackley), Guy Oliver (Beluche), James Marcus (Dominique), Ervin Renard (Don Robledo), Charles Anderson (Bohon), Boris Karloff (Pirate). *Director:* Frank Lloyd. *Producer:* B.P. Schulberg. *Writing Credits:* Charles Tenney Jackson, Julien Josephson. *Cinematography:* Norbert Brodine. *Studio:* Famous Players-Lasky Corp. *Length:* Eight reels.

This black-and-white silent is the first of a number of films relating the relationship between Jackson and pirate Jean Lafitte. Based on Charles Tenney Jackson's novel *Captain Sazarac*, this centers on Lafitte (Ricardo Cortez). He saves Louise Lestron (Florence Vidor) while attending a ball in New Orleans in honor of Jackson (George Irving). Unfortunately, in the process Lafitte is unmasked by John Jarvis (Andre de Beranger) and told by Jackson to leave by dawn.

From this point the film moves onto the oceans with numerous abductions from ships and swashbuckling sea battles. When Lafitte returns to New Orleans, he is imprisoned but freed with the aide of Lestron. Irving plays Jackson in a manner that would make the "People's President" proud.

The Frontiersman (1927)

Jackson: Russell Simpson. *Other Cast:* Tim McCoy (Captain John Dale), Claire Windsor (Lucy), Tom O'Brien (Abner Hawkins), Lillian Leighton (Mrs. Andrew Jackson), Louise Lorraine (Athalie Burgoyne), May Foster (Mandy), Chief John Big Tree (Grey Eagle), Frank Hagney (White Snake), John Peters (Colonel Coffee). *Director:* Reginald Barker. *Writing Credits:* Tom Miranda, L.G. Rigby, Madeleine Ruthven, Ross B. Wills. *Cinematography:* Clyde De Vinna. *Film Editing:* Frank Sullivan. *Art Direction:* Edward Withers. *Costume Design:* Andreani. *Studio:* MGM. *Length:* 53 minutes.

After the War of 1812, the Tennessee Militia under Jackson was concerned with Creek

Indians. Capt. John Dale (Tim McCoy) makes an attempt to forge peace, but tribal leader White Snake (Frank Hagney) will not agree.

Dale is reprimanded by General Jackson (Russell Simpson) when he engages in a duel with an army compatriot over their mutual love of Athalie Burgoyne (Louise Lorraine). Dale changes his mind and then falls in love with the general's ward Lucy (Claire Windsor) who is captured by marauding Creek Indians. Dale rescues Lucy, and the militia stops the Indians.

The Gorgeous Hussy (1936)

Jackson: Lionel Barrymore. *Other Cast:* Joan Crawford (Margaret "Peggy" O'Neal Eaton), Robert Taylor (Lt. "Bow" Timberlake), Franchot Tone (John Eaton), Melvyn Douglas (John Randolph), James Stewart (Roderick "Rowdy" Dow), Charles Trowbridge (Van Buren), Beulah Bondi (Rachel Jackson). *Director:* Clarence Brown. *Writing Credits:* Samuel Hopkins Adams, Stephen Morehouse Avery. *Studio:* MGM. *Length:* 102 minutes.

Hollywood's star icon Joan Crawford takes the title role of Margaret "Peggy" O'Neal Eaton who brings down the cabinet of Jackson (Lionel Barrymore) in this "fiction founded on fact," as the introduction states. Clarence Brown, one of MGM's top directors, suppresses history for pictorial splendor and sentimental romanticism.

Historically, O'Neal, an innkeeper's daughter, attracted many suitors including John Eaton. Conveniently her Navy purser husband, Lt. "Bow" Timberlake, committed suicide so O'Neal and Eaton married at Jackson's insistence. Then Jackson named Eaton Secretary of War. Nevertheless, wives of other cabinet members, led by Floride Calhoun, the vice president's wife, shunned O'Neal. Jackson staunchly defended O'Neal, mindful of the scorn his recently deceased wife, Rachel, endured. Ultimately, at the "oddest cabinet meeting in U.S. history," Jackson defended O'Neal ... and dismissed his cabinet. O'Neal left Washington and married a wealthy Italian dance-master who took her considerable assets and her granddaughter.

Although Barrymore remains true to Jackson's fighting spirit, the film does not remain true to O'Neal's history. Timberlake (Robert Taylor) dies, rather than commits suicide. Eaton (Franchot Tone, Crawford's husband from 1935–39) does not enjoy the love of O'Neal that she bestows on Virginia Senator John Randolph (Melvyn Douglas) who never figured in her actual life. And Roderick "Rowdy" Dow (James Stewart), another fictitious character, aids O'Neal in puppy-like devotion.

Barrymore as Jackson first appears in 1823 with his beloved Rachel (Beulah Bondi) whom he teases and teaches how to smoke a pipe. Next, in 1828, as he awaits the results of the presidential election, he debates Randolph in Congress about the need to preserve the Union: "Union and liberty, now and forever," says Jackson. Later, Jackson's views on a national bank surface as he dictates a letter. He continues to defend O'Neal, notably at that famous cabinet meeting when he accuses them of not having "proof" of their "malicious slander" that is "a treasonable persecution." Last, he bids farewell to O'Neal and Eaton as they sail to Spain where Eaton will serve as ambassador. Barrymore plays an older Jackson in *Lone Star* (1952) but with the same commanding presence.

The Man Without a Country (1937)

Jackson: Erville Alderson. *Other Cast:* Gloria Holden (Marian Morgan), John Litel (Lt. Philip Nolan), Ted Osborne (Jack Morgan), Donald Brian (Col. Morgan), Holmes Herbert

7—Andrew Jackson (1829–1837)

The Gorgeous Hussy (1936): "Bewitching hussy," says Lionel Barrymore as Andrew Jackson to Joan Crawford as Peggy O'Neal as she slips a stalk of celery into his buttonhole in this scene. Crawford stars as the daughter of an innkeeper who rose to become the wife of cabinet member John Eaton during Jackson's tenure in the early 19th century. Playing Jackson's wife Rachel is Beulah Bondi (right), whom Jackson taught to smoke a pipe. Because of the scorn Rachel received, Jackson defends O'Neal against similar malicious slander. Clarence Brown directed and Joseph Mankiewicz produced this MGM romantization of Samuel Hopkins Adams's novel. (Photofest.)

(Aaron Burr), Charles Middleton (Lincoln). *Director:* Crane Wilbur. *Writing Credits:* Edward Everett Hale, Forrest Barnes. *Music:* Howard Jackson. *Cinematography:* Allen Davey. *Film Editing:* Ben G. Liss. *Art Direction:* Ted Smith. *Sound:* Oliver S. Garretson. *Studio:* The Vitaphone Corp., Warner Bros. *Length:* 21 minutes.

In this classic story based on clergyman and author Edward Everett Hale's novel of the same name (the screenplay was written by Forrest Barnes), Lt. Philip Nolan (John Litel), a supporter of Aaron Burr's desire to establish a new country, is exiled from the United States he damns—forever. Burr was arrested, tried for treason, and acquitted in 1807 for attempting to form a republic in the Southwest that he was to head.

Marian Morgan (Gloria Holden) spends 56 years seeking a pardon for "the only man I could ever love." She first visits President Jackson and later President Lincoln in the White House. Nolan has been transferred to *The Hawk* and is told he will never see his country again. Jackson tells Morgan "I'm sorry, I can't interfere." Alderson's performance as Jackson is matter of fact, no temper tantrums, no exhortations.

The Buccaneer (1938)

Jackson: Hugh Sothern. *Other Cast:* Fredric March (Jean Lafitte), Franciska Gaal (Gretchen), Akim Tamiroff (Dominique You), Margot Grahame (Annete de Remy), Walter Brennan (Ezra Peavey), Ian Keith (Sen. Crawford), Anthony Quinn (Beluche), Beulah Bondi (Aunt Charlotte), Montagu Love (Admiral Cockburn), Spring Byington (Dolley Madison). *Director-Producer:* Cecil B. DeMille. *Writing Credits:* Harold Lamb, Jeanie Macpherson. *Music:* George Antheil. *Cinematography:* Victor Milner. *Film Editing:* Anne Bauchens. *Art Direction:* Roland Anderson, Hans Dreier. *Studio:* Paramount Pictures. *Length:* 124 minutes.

Cecil B. DeMille made two films 20 years apart with the same name and almost the same story. He directed the 1938 version while his son-in-law, Anthony Quinn, directed the 1958 version. More than 15,000 people saw the opening of the original film in New Orleans as a result of the publicity concerning the authenticity of the story. Almost as many people play in this epic film of the War of 1812 as participated in the British attack. During the attack, Dolley Madison (Spring Byington) saves the Declaration of Independence when the White House is burned by the British.

The story is how pirate Jean Lafitte (played with a suspicious French accent by Fredric March) helps to save New Orleans from the British. Lafitte and his men live in the swamps that are part of the Mississippi delta south of the city. They are protected from U.S. law enforcement by the impassable nature of this bayou country. The British try to bribe Lafitte into leading them through the swamps to ease their capture of New Orleans. Lafitte convinces his men to side with the Americans, but confusion, distrust, and a traitorous Sen. Crawford (Ian Keith) cause the Americans to attack Lafitte, capture, and imprison a number of his men.

General Andrew Jackson (Hugh Sothern) arrives to save the city but is extremely short on flints and powder. Lafitte negotiates to supply these upon certain conditions. Jackson agrees to pardon Lafitte and his men if they agree to fight on the American side. The Battle of New Orleans takes place (actually after the treaty ending the War of 1812 was signed) with the joint forces of Americans and pirates giving the British a terrible beating, as wave upon wave of trained British regulars fall before Jackson's rag-tag forces, singing as they slaughter.

The Buccaneer (1938): Hugh Sothern (center) as Andrew Jackson bemusedly eyes Fredric March as Jean Lafitte paying respect to his lady-love, Louisiana belle Annete de Remy, played by Margot Grahame. The first of Cecil B. DeMille's two *Buccaneer* films on the Battle of New Orleans was a Paramount Pictures production. (Courtesy of George Eastman House.)

Although appearing somewhat older than Jackson would have been at the time, Sothern gives a credible portrayal of "Old Hickory." He conveys toughness in dealing with both Lafitte and Sen. Crawford who leads the citizens of New Orleans and who wants to surrender the city. In addition, Jackson is shown to be a respected and experienced military officer.

Akim Tamiroff gives a highly esteemed and comic portrayal of Lafitte's second-in-command, Dominique, who shepherds the camp follower, Gretchen (Franciska Gaal). Margot Grahame supplies the romantic interest for Lafitte as Annette de Remy and Anthony Quinn plays a bristling young pirate, Beluche.

Man of Conquest (1939)

Jackson: Edward Ellis. *Other Cast:* Richard Dix (Sam Houston), Gail Patrick (Margaret Lea), Joan Fontaine (Eliza Allen), Ralph Morgan (Stephen F. Austin), Robert Barrat (David Crockett), Victor Jory (William B. Travis), Robert Armstrong (Jim Bowie), George "Gabby" Hayes (Lannie Upchurch), C. Henry Gordon (Santa Ana). *Director:* George Nichols Jr. *Writing Credits:* Harold Shumate, Wells Root. *Stunts:* Yakima Canutt. *Studio:* Republic Pictures. *Length:* 105 minutes.

As a dramatization of the life of Sam Houston (Richard Dix), this film does not try to cover up the problems and blemishes that were inherent in this lauded Texan-American. After briefly covering his early public life serving under Jackson (Edward Ellis) and being wounded at the battle of Horseshoe Bend, the film treats his rise in politics including two terms as governor of Tennessee. This sequence also includes the scandal and divorce from Eliza Allen (Joan Fontaine) that resulted in his resignation from the governorship and return to a sodden life with the Cherokee Indians.

From Tennessee the film quickly shifts to the Texas revolution including the massacre at the Alamo and an extended scene of the highly outnumbered Texans routing Santa Ana's sleeping troops at San Jacinto. The film then quickly moves through the era of Texas independence until the annexation to the United States seven years later.

The historical treatment is not bad for a film of its time, and the sentiment expressed seems almost modern in a quote from Jackson in the film as reported by the *New York Times*: "Up in Washington you said we'd buried freedom under a pile of dirty politics, well just remember that America is still the land of the free—and there's many a brow beaten people who'd trade their dictatorships in a minute for a good dose of our dirty politics. Not that our brand of freedom ain't got its faults—couldn't help it being run by ornery humans like congressmen and you and me. But I recon [sic] that the United States is still the only place in the world where a man can cuss the president out loud and all the president can do is cuss back or go fishin.'"

Edward Ellis is an excellent impersonator of Jackson in an extended role. Although many of the lines make Jackson a saint and/or a prophet, Ellis "with a lift of an eyebrow or a twitch of the mouth has managed to suggest that the halo is gilded, that Andy was the wily old rascal history proves him to be, a statesman of highly practical idealism," according to the *New York Times* review of the film upon its release.

Old Hickory (1939)

Jackson: Hugh Sothern. *Other Cast:* Nana Bryant (Rachel Jackson), George Renavent (Jean Lafitte), John Hamilton (Governor of Louisiana), Ray Bennett (Vice President John C. Calhoun), Emmett Vogan (Daniel Webster), Edwin Stanley (Sen. Kane), Frank Wilcox (Abraham Lincoln). *Director:* Lewis Seiler. *Writing Credits:* Owen Crump, Don Ryan. *Cinematography:* Charles P. Boyle. *Film Editing:* Benjamin Liss. *Art Direction:* Charles Novi. *Studio:* Warner Bros. *Length:* 17 minutes.

This very brief biopic of Jackson (Hugh Sothern) starts with his military success at New Orleans, ending the War of 1812, and finishes with the somewhat surprising position he took in defending the republic regarding the tariff question during his presidential years.

The Battle of New Orleans and Jackson's agreement with the pirate Jean Lafitte (George Renavent) are skipped over very quickly. More time is spent on the political aspects of the legitimacy of Jackson's marriage to Rachel (Nana Bryant) and her death prior to his inauguration on March 4, 1829. Although the National Bank question was one of the most serious faced by Jackson, it is not covered at all. His other major issue, the tariff question, is fully reported including the debate in the Senate between Daniel Webster (Emmett Vogan) of Massachusetts and Sen. Kane (Edwin Stanley) of South Carolina. Destined for history, Webster carries the day with his "liberty and union, now and forever, one and inseparable" speech.

Jackson had been expected to side with his southern colleagues but turns to them and says, "Our federal union must and shall be preserved." He then tells John C. Calhoun, his vice president, that it is "not a question of tariff but disunion."

Hugh Sothern has a similar appearance to Jackson but possibly a bit less haggard. However, he handles the role with seriousness and realism, displaying Jackson's noted irascibility and strength of character through a forceful delivery.

March On, America! (1942)

Jackson: Hugh Sothern.

Hugh Sothern again plays Jackson in this patriotic story of America. For details, see Chapter 5 on James Monroe.

The Remarkable Andrew (1942)

Jackson: Brian Donlevy. *Other Cast:* William Holden (Andrew Long), Ellen Drew (Peggy Tobin), Montagu Love (George Washington), Gilbert Emery (Thomas Jefferson), Brandon Hurst (John Marshall), George Watts (Benjamin Franklin), Rod Cameron (Jesse James), Richard Webb (Randall Stevens). *Director:* Stuart Heisler. *Producer:* Richard Blumenthal. *Writing Credits:* Dalton Trumbo. *Music:* Victor Young. *Cinematography:* Theodor Sparkuhl. *Film Editing:* Archie Marshek. *Art Direction:* Hans Dreier, A. Earl Hedrick. *Costume Design:* Edith Head. *Studio:* Paramount Pictures. *Length:* 81 minutes.

Andrew Long (William Holden) is the title character in this patriotic pre–World War II film in which the ghost of Jackson (Brian Donlevy) comes to the assistance of the young bookkeeper accused of embezzlement. Joining Jackson are the "best legal minds" in the country: Washington, Jefferson, Benjamin Franklin, and Chief Justice Marshall.

The citizens of Shale City, Colorado, set their watches by the appearance of the disciplined Long on his way to work at City Hall. He finds a discrepancy of $1,240, reports it, refuses to charge it to another (wrong) department, and is suspended. Compounding his situation is his fiancée Peggy's (Ellen Drew) distress when he's late for the country club dance.

While dressing in his rented room, Long sees the real Jackson, heretofore only a portrait on his wall with the inscription: "One man with courage makes a majority." Jackson's life was saved at New Orleans by Long's great-great-grandfather, "a fighting fool," says Old Hickory. The general's quick temper and readiness for action, especially dueling, surface in the interpretation of Donlevy. Although Donlevy in no way looks like Jackson, he behaves like him in: politically scheming, storming, and strutting. He's come to do as Long's ancestor did and suggests "the only good politician has his heels 15 feet above the ground."

Peggy arrives to find out who Long's "friend" is, can't see or find him (even with a wildly swinging umbrella), and calls Long crazy. Long's boss tries to bribe him with a raise (to $25 weekly) that Long righteously refuses. Then Long faces his fiancée's ultimatum: her or a ghost. Long gets another blow with a warrant for embezzlement. But Jackson's ghost comes to the jail, proclaiming his animosity against politicians. The "greatest legal minds" he knows, true to their natures, will give advice. Washington: "no violence, General Jackson, please.... We were forced to become heroes"; Franklin, "What sort of men are you dealing with?"; Jefferson, "I fail to see your reasoning"; Marshall, "Democracy isn't a gift, it's a responsibility."

When Long becomes his own counsel, his historical heroes take advantage of their invisibility and do a little spying. They find a recording in the mayor's office that incriminates all parties involved with the embezzlement, even the judge. It's used as Long's only evidence, following his testimony on democracy quoting the famous men, being quite contrary to the prosecution's hollow patriotic accusations. Long's exonerated, the judge marries him and Peggy, and Jackson finally leaves, urging Long "not to betray the future."

Ironically, Dalton Trumbo was the screenwriter of this poetic definition of democracy before he was convicted of contempt of Congress by the House Un-American Activities Committee for refusing to answer questions about membership in the Communist Party.

Lone Star (1952)

Jackson: Lionel Barrymore. *Other Cast:* Clark Gable (Devereaux Burke), Ava Gardner (Martha Ronda), Broderick Crawford (Thomas Craden), Beulah Bondi (Minniver Bryan), Moroni Olson (Sam Houston). *Director:* Vincent Sherman. *Producer:* Z. Wayne Griffin. *Writing Credits:* Borden Chase, Howard Estabrook. *Music:* David Buttolph. *Cinematography:* Harold Rosson. *Film Editing:* Ferris Webster. *Art Direction:* Cedric Gibbons, Hans Peters. *Studio:* MGM. *Length:* 94 minutes.

It is dark as lone horseman Devereaux Burke (Clark Gable) arrives at "The Hermitage," Andrew Jackson's Tennessee home. The rider carries information that Sam Houston, leader in Texas independence and a friend of Jackson's, has reversed his position and now opposes annexation of Texas into the United States. Andrew Jackson is played with his usual commanding presence by Lionel Barrymore in his next-to-last screen appearance, similar to his enactment in *The Gorgeous Hussy* (1936), but a far different role from Barrymore's avaricious role in *America* (1924). The ex-president is certain that Houston has not changed his mind and asks profiteer Burke to take a message to Houston (Moroni Olson) who is negotiating with the Mescaleros Apaches somewhere in West Texas.

In this opening scene Jackson is shown continuing the efforts that started during his administration to bring Texas, newly independent from Mexico, into the U.S. Because Texas would be a slave state, opposition to the annexation continued throughout the administration of Jackson's hand-picked successor, Martin Van Buren, and was still in existence as James Polk took office. Jackson felt that northern opposition to annexation could be reduced if somehow Texas could claim California in its territory. Much of this historical information is used by director Vincent Sherman and writers Borden Chase and Howard Estabrook in the extended opening scene to prepare the audience for what turns out to be a routine western, touched with Sherman's taste for melodrama.

Burke, assuming the name of Bill Jones to shield his pro-annexation position, rides from Tennessee to Texas, and tries without success to find Sam Houston. However, he just happens to run into, and save from the Indians, the main opponent of annexation, Thomas Craden (Broderick Crawford). After their skirmish with the Indians, they ride to Austin together and immediately meet the lovely editor of *The Austin Blade*, Martha Ronda (Ava Gardner, who outdoes her seductive self by singing a song in a love scene with Burke). Gable as Burke and Crawford as Craden develop a strong antagonism for both political and romantic reasons as the love interest between Burke and Ronda becomes evident. Burke finally finds Houston and the Apaches. As was expected, Houston informs Burke that he has not

7—Andrew Jackson (1829–1837)

Lone Star (1952): An elderly Andrew Jackson portrayed by Lionel Barrymore (left) sends Clark Gable as Devereaux Burke to find Sam Houston in the story of Texas Independence by Metro-Goldwyn-Mayer Pictures. (Courtesy of George Eastman House.)

changed his position on annexation, and Burke returns to Austin on an obviously very fast horse since he is able to cover hundreds of miles in a few days. He ultimately convinces the Texas Congress of Houston's real position. This sets the stage for a wild fight in Austin between the pro and anti-annexation forces.

Just as things look bad for the pro forces, Houston arrives on horseback. Usually the cavalry is expected to save the day, but Houston is accompanied by mounted Apache Indians—hardly a sight to bring relief to a small Texas town in the mid–19th century. Burke and Craden continue to fight it out personally and to the surprise of all, Burke wins. After all, as Ronda says, "He's quite some guy." The annexation of Texas by the U.S. is ensured, and all the boys, led by Burke and Craden virtually arm in arm, head for the border to join "Zach" Taylor in fighting the Mexican horde.

Of note: Barrymore, who played on the stage with the young Gable, once got him an unsuccessful screen test at MGM.

The President's Lady (1953)

Jackson: Charlton Heston. *Other Cast:* Susan Hayward (Rachel Donelson Robards), John McIntire (Jack Overton), Fay Bainter (Mrs. Donelson), Ralph Dumke (Col. Stark). *Director:* Henry Levin. *Producers:* Sol Siegel, Henry Levin. *Writing Credits:* John Patrick,

Irving Stone. *Music:* Alfred Newman. *Cinematography:* Leo Tover. *Film Editing:* William B. Murphy. *Art Direction:* Leland Fuller, Lyle R. Wheeler. *Studio:* 20th Century–Fox. *Length:* 96 minutes.

Of the 15 films about Jackson, this is the most complete biography. Based on Irving Stone's novel, it covers 40 years of his life, as narrated in voice-overs that explain the events by both his wife, Rachel (Susan Hayward, one of the few female stars in biopics), and Jackson himself (Charlton Heston). While their marriage and Rachel's influence (the lady and the great man plot) provide considerable drama, Jackson's rise to military and political power is of more historical interest.

In top billing, Hayward made her reputation in fallen women roles as Rachel Donelson Robards, a woman without a legal divorce; she nobly endures throughout her marriage to Jackson. Heston rises to the Jacksonian stature, rugged facial features, and commanding presence of the seventh president. Under Henry Levin's sure-handed direction of adventure, these two performances dominate. Fay Bainter gives one of her fine sympathetic interpretations as Mrs. Donelson, Rachel's mother.

The story follows Jackson's arrival to start a law practice in Tennessee where he meets Rachel. They flee to Mississippi, marry, and return to Tennessee where Jackson soon trains a militia to fight the Creek Indians. Rachel endures humiliation, death of an orphan Indian baby Jackson brings her, his habitual gambling and bad temper. On the eve of a duel over her good name, pious and selfless Rachel says she must leave him if he continues to suffer for her. Jackson cries he will "lift you up so high, no one will dare touch you." He goes off again, gains fame in the battle of New Orleans, returns to politics with a term in the Senate, and ultimately wins the presidency as she dies, leaving him "enough memories to sustain me all of my life," he says.

This is the first of two appearances of Heston as Jackson as he reprises his role in *The Buccaneer* (1958). In both instances he epitomizes the president in physique and manner. *Variety* (March 11, 1953) says his "forthright, steely-eyed portrayal [in *The President's Lady*] surely will establish him in topflight ranks of stardom."

The President's Lady (1953): Charlton Heston as General Andrew Jackson in a publicity photo for the production in which he co-starred with Susan Hayward in the title role as Rachel Jackson. Heston became known as the best Jackson impersonator when he repeated his role in Cecil B. DeMille's *The Buccaneer* in 1958. (Courtesy of George Eastman House.)

Davy Crockett, King of the Wild Frontier (1955)

Jackson: Basil Ruysdael. *Other Cast:* Fess Parker (Davy Crockett), Buddy Ebsen (George Russel), Kenneth Tobey (Col. Jim Bowie), Hans Conried (Thimblerig). *Director:* Norman Foster. *Producer:* Bill Walsh. *Cinematographer:* Charles P. Boyle. *Songwriter-Screenwriter:* Tom Blackburn. *Songwriter-Composer:* George Bruns. *Editor:* Chester Schaeffer. *Studio:* Walt Disney Pictures. *Length:* 93 minutes.

Walt Disney saw the success of a 1954 TV Davy Crockett miniseries as an opportunity and combined three episodes to produce this 1955 feature film under the direction of Norman Foster. Continuity is not the greatest but the frontiersman Davy Crockett (Fess Parker) and his sidekick George Russel (Buddy Ebsen) are shown to advantage in the three distinct sequences. Parker, in coonskin cap, looks the "half horse, half alligator" Crockett says he is. In the first sequence, they effectively eliminate the warlike challenge of the Indians in Southeastern U.S.; in the second sequence, Crockett overcomes the duplicity of Congressional politicians to protect the now peaceful Indians; and, in the third episode, the fall of the Alamo and the deaths of Crockett and Russel show how far one must be willing to go for one's beliefs.

Jackson is played by Basil Ruysdael who looks nothing like the president. He appears in three brief scenes. As General Jackson in the Indian fighting segment, Ruysdael, in a neat blue uniform, is completely overdressed and appears uncomfortable. There is obviously no attempt at historical accuracy in the portrayal as Jackson was known for his earthy characteristics. It seems unlikely that Crockett and Russel would have left the military camps as they did against orders as Jackson, a strict disciplinarian, looked on.

In the second sequence, Jackson is at his Tennessee estate, The Hermitage, where he greets Crockett. He wants Crockett to run for Congress. "I want men I can trust," Jackson explains and shows Crockett a laudatory book about him to make his point. Ever the humble woodsman, Crockett replies in the affirmative but asserts he would only answer to his constituents. Jackson happily says, "That's the answer I hoped."

In the third sequence, Jackson is in Washington, D.C., where he again greets Crockett and asks his favor. He says the presidency is a "tougher job than fighting Indians" and sends Crockett to the Alamo to assist Col. Jim Bowie (Kenneth Tobey).

The First Texan (1956)

Jackson: Carl Benton Reid. *Other Cast:* Joel McCrea (Sam Houston), Felicia Farr (Katherine Delaney), Jeff Morrow (Jim Bowie), Wallace Ford (Henry Delaney), Abraham Sofaer (Don Carlos), David Silva (Santa Ana), James Griffith (Davy Crockett). *Director:* Byron Haskin. *Producer:* Walter Mirisch. *Writing Credits:* Daniel Ullman. *Music:* Roy Webb. *Film Editing:* George White. *Art Direction:* Dave Milton. *Studio:* Allied Artists Pictures Corp. *Length:* 82 minutes.

This film describes the history of the Texas Revolution, using events in the life of Sam Houston (Joel McCrea). Many of the historical events are questionable, particularly with regard to Houston's life. A completely fictitious romance was developed to add spice to the story, and Houston is portrayed as being reluctant to become involved in the cabal leading up to the split from Mexico when this is known not to be the case.

The most amusing scene in the film, and certainly unintentional, occurs at the Battle of San Jacinto. The actual battle took place near the current city of Houston (named after our hero) that is as flat as can be with no elevations much higher than 20 feet over sea level. The mountains in the film's battle scene would indicate a great deal of geologic activity since the 1830s.

Although the scene in which President Jackson appears is historically reasonable, it is completely fictional. Houston had known Jackson (Carl Benton Reid) most of his life, having served under him in the War of 1812 and having been a political associate of Jackson's in Tennessee and Washington. In addition, it is well known that Jackson was very interested in Texas and the possibility that Texas would eventually become a state. However, for Jackson to have summoned Houston, using a message carried by Davy Crockett (James Griffith) from Texas to Washington for a quick talk about the state of the revolution and to tell Houston that he could provide no help to the revolutionaries is improbable. Yet Reid shows Jackson's common sense in his arguments about bringing the country into another war. Reid also provides a good physical impersonation of Jackson with similar craggy looks and down-to-earth disposition. Reid even delivers such Jackson homilies as "a horseshoe in hell." Besides Jackson's triumph over Santa Ana (David Silva), the battle of San Jacinto is a triumph of movie-making.

The Buccaneer (1958)

Jackson: Charlton Heston. *Other Cast:* Yul Brynner (Jean Lafitte), Claire Bloom (Bonnie Brown). Charles Boyer (Dominique You), Inger Stevens (Annette Claiborne), Henry Hull (Ezra Peavey), E.G. Marshall (Gov. William Claiborne). *Director:* Anthony Quinn. *Writing Credits:* C. Gardner Sullivan, Harold Lamb, Jesse Lasky, Jeanie Macpherson, Edwin Justus Mayer, Bernice Mosk, Lyle Saxon. *Executive Producer:* Cecil B. DeMille. *Music:* Elmer Bernstein. *Cinematography:* Loyal Griggs. *Film Editing:* Archie Marshek. *Art Direction:* Albert Nozaki, Hal Pereira, Walter Tyler. *Set Decoration:* Sam Comer, Roy Moyer. *Costume Design:* Edith Head, John Jensen, Ralph Jester. *Studio:* Paramount Pictures. *Length:* 119 minutes.

A remake of the 1938 film of the same name, this *Buccaneer* follows the same story of pirate Jean Lafitte's (Yul Brynner) escapades off the Louisiana coast. To save Dominique You (Charles Boyer) and other pirates he offers help and provides munitions to Gen. Andrew Jackson.

As Jackson, Charlton Heston brings his commanding presence to this swashbuckling VistaVision treatment of the War of 1812. More shaded and subtle than in his performance as Moses in DeMille's epic *The Ten Commandments* (1956) with Yul Brynner, Heston shows many sides of the complex Jackson character. Wrapped in a flowing black cape and with a head of flowing white hair, he first appears on a desolate field where he finds a young soldier complaining of his hunger. To this Heston as the tough Old Hickory admonishes, "You're not hungry until you can wipe your eyes with the slack of your stomach." Such toughness earns Jackson the nickname of "Old Hag Face" by a passing soldier. He then heads for New Orleans to block the six major water routes through the Mississippi Delta.

The action shifts to the plight of Jean Lafitte, played with his usual bravado by Yul Brynner. He's wanted by Gov. William Claiborne of Louisiana (E.G. Marshall) whose daughter Annette (Inger Stevens) he loves. Despite these obstacles, Lafitte continues to plunder the seas, seizing the booty of the sunken American ship *The Corinthian* on which Claiborne's other daughter sailed.

With his usual cunning, Lafitte stalls the British and their bribes for assistance as he confers with the American governor about aiding Jackson. He returns to find his Bariteria port hideaway burned by the Americans. Overriding hatred of the British—and love for the American southern belle—prompts Lafitte to negotiate with Jackson. Incensed by the cowardly New Orleans politicians who want to surrender, the angry Jackson declares "before the British take it, I will burn this city [New Orleans]." He drives a hard bargain with Lafitte, demanding to have the 8,000 flints and powder before he turns over the imprisoned pirates.

Jackson readies for the attack, ordering his unit of Kentucky and Tennessee frontiersmen to build a barricade against the British. His rough men are joined by Creole dandies, free Negroes, Choctaw braves, and Lafitte and his pirates. Jackson then demonstrates his military bravery in the long battle scene. He walks up and down the line, urging his "boys" to "stand fast." He compliments Dominique You (Charles Boyer) on his cannon fire tactics "learned under Napoleon." Jackson shows his understanding of British military tactics as he holds his fire during the "loudest quiet" while the British ranks slowly march toward his ragtag army. He wins the Battle of New Orleans, a victory that furthers his reputation and career. At the victory dance, Heston shows his manners by thanking the Louisiana governor "for these honors" and again displays his love for his wife by saying, "If my Rachel were here, she'd teach you dances."

The battle scene benefits from the lavish production by DeMille in his last screen effort, and direction by his then son-in-law Anthony Quinn (his only such effort). The marching lines of 12,000 Redcoats seem endless; the scrambling efforts by the American forces seem inspired. The flat overgrown cane field of a battleground provides no cover for the British men and artillery batteries. Instead they shoot warning rockets. Jackson's forces retaliate with relentless crossfire. While there is original music by the esteemed Elmer Bernstein, the pirates do not sing as they did in the previous version of this story.

8

Martin Van Buren (1837–1841)

Martin Van Buren. (Courtesy of Library of Congress.)

The "Little Magician's" rise from obscurity to eminence was a lesson in statecraft, and his lasting contribution was a patronage system that became at once the strength and curse of both parties.[1] Another epithet, the "American Talleyrand," also described his skill at political manipulation. Besides being wily, this meditative, cool, distant, and equivocal man had a character of great paradox: Although Van Buren committed himself to Andrew Jackson, the Hero of the People, he himself had no love for people and a great love for patrician luxury. His basic philosophy was that the federal government had no right to interfere with business and that the president had no duty to restore prosperity, leaving that to the private sector.

This belief led to troubles in the Panic of 1837 which prompted Van Buren to fight for an Independent Treasury to solve the national depression as it would take control from the moneyed class. With that exception, his administration was the apotheosis of *laissez-faire* government.[2] Guided by the philosophy of another of his heroes, Jefferson and his views of limited federal government, he viewed the Constitution as a sacred instrument; yet, paradoxically he supported an elected judiciary.

In the judicial matter of the *Amistad* case, Van Buren took, not unexpectedly, a very legalistic and pro–Southern approach, pointing to the treaty that dictated that the Africans be returned to Spanish authorities.[3] As he wrote in his autobiography, he "acted the part of listener rather than contestant" ultimately becoming known as less of a chief executive and more of a transforming political figure in American history. He was the chief architect of the Democratic Party, the first mass body of its type in the world.[4] His contributions came from his belief in the inevitability of political conflict and an expanding and demanding electorate.[5]

8—Martin Van Buren (1837–1841)

THE FILMS

Van Buren, the strong follower of Jackson, had none of the charismatic attraction of Jackson and suffered Hollywood film attention with two minor roles.

The Gorgeous Hussy (1936)

Van Buren: Charles Trowbridge.

Van Buren (Charles Trowbridge) makes a forgettable appearance in this film about President Jackson's problems with the notorious Margaret "Peggy" O'Neal Eaton (Joan Crawford). For details, see Chapter 7 on Andrew Jackson.

Amistad (1997)

Van Buren: Nigel Hawthorne.

Van Buren was president during this 1839 revolt by Africans on the slave ship *Amistad*

The Gorgeous Hussy (1936): Andrew Jackson's wife Rachel (Beulah Bondi, left) learns that her reputation has been attacked unwarrantedly in this scene. Onlooking is star Joan Crawford (Peggy O'Neal) who receives similar attacks that Andrew Jackson (Lionel Barrymore, not pictured) denounces. Also observing are Melvyn Douglas (right), seen as John Randolph, and (behind Bondi and Crawford) Sidney Toler as Daniel Webster and Charles Trowbridge as Martin Van Buren. Douglas is one of Crawford's four leading men in this MGM picture; Robert Taylor, Franchot Tone, and James Stewart share the honors. (Photofest.)

and their subsequent trial in the United States Supreme Court with then Rep. John Quincy Adams in their defense. Unlike Adams, played by Anthony Hopkins, whose appearance dominates the action, Van Buren only appears briefly. He is played by Nigel Hawthorne, known for his lordly presence, most recently before this film in the title role of *The Madness of King George* (1994). For that stunning display of "madness" he received an Academy Award nomination for Best Actor. The English actor stands much taller than Van Buren, known as "The Little Magician" because of his short stature and highly skillful political ability, although Hawthorne exudes the command and dignity of the then president.

Van Buren seems to ignore the historical import of this incident that might have helped avoid the Civil War. He haughtily reviews the slaves in captivity in New England and drives away in splendor in his carriage, more intent on his re-election than the slaves' freedom. He dismisses the *Amistad* case, saying, "Why concern myself with forty-four, when there are two million in the United States?" He overturns the lower court's decision in favor of the Africans. Former President John Quincy Adams is reluctant to become involved, but when the case moves to the Supreme Court, Adams mounts a successful defense. (For details, see Chapter 6 on John Quincy Adams.)

At a dinner Van Buren hosts in the White House for the Spanish ambassador (under whose flag the *Amistad* sailed) he spends most of his time in political talk with John C. Calhoun (Arliss Howard), his defeated adversary for the presidency. His political self surfaces as he questions Calhoun's calling anti-slavery immoral when the real question is "Must we raise swords?" This prescient inquiry underlies the constant threat of civil war that haunted Van Buren's administration.

Steven Spielberg's meticulous attention to historical detail (rather than facts) suffuses this film. From the darkness of the New England prison to the brightly lit White House state dining room, Van Buren and the other cast appear as if in the 19th century. But, as Spielberg says, "No matter how earnest the artist's effort, he or she can never really capture, 'pin down,' or fully re-create the lives of great men and women."[6]

9
William Henry Harrison (1841)

William Harrison died at 68 of pneumonia just three weeks after his inauguration. The first president to die in office, he said on his deathbed, "Sir [meaning Tyler]—I wish you to understand the true principles of Government. I wish them carried out. I ask nothing more."[1] He was dubbed "General Mum" by the Democratic press when his managers tried to silence their candidate because they doubted his intellect. So his stand was never known on the issues of slavery in the western territories, statehood for Texas, and an Independent Treasury.

Yet Harrison proved very outspoken about the press. He was asked about the subsidized press and said, "What governs its operations, and it will open its iron jaws and answer you in a voice loud enough to shake the pyramids—*Money! Money!* I speak not at random—facts bear me testimony."[2] In his inaugural address

William Henry Harrison. (Courtesy of Library of Congress).

(written by Daniel Webster who served as his Secretary of State), Harrison stated:

"There is no part of the means placed in the hands of the Executive which might be used with greater effect for unhallowed purposes than the control of the public press.... A decent and manly examination of the acts of the Government should be not only tolerated, but encouraged."

Having spoken, Harrison made one of his first, and few, acts in office the dismissal of the *Globe* as printer to Congress. That was understandable, however, since its editor, Francis Blair, accused him of fraud and of profiting from English capitalists to win the presidency, as well as charging his party with maneuvering a puppet who would be controlled by Webster and Henry Clay.[3]

But Harrison was more than the "log cabin and hard cider" Whig candidate. He was a military hero—at Tippecanoe and the Thames during the War of 1812—and had long experience in government. Under Jefferson as governor of the Indiana Territory he negotiated the Treaty of Fort Wayne, transferring 2.5 million acres of Indian land to the United

States over the great Tecumseh's objection. Harrison also served without distinction as congressman, senator, and minister to Colombia. He was admired for his character rather than his political record, which was mediocre at best.[4]

THE FILMS

Like several other presidents (namely John Quincy Adams), Harrison's non-presidential endeavors received film treatment instead of his presidency. Granted, Harrison only served three weeks in office, but the hullabaloo of his Whig candidacy, based on the "log cabin and hard cider" slogan, was one of the first colorful political campaigns and screams for film treatment.

Ten Gentlemen from West Point (1942)

Harrison: Douglass Dumbrille. *Other Cast:* George Montgomery (Joe Dawson), Maureen O'Hara (Carolyn Bainbridge), Laird Cregar (Maj. Sam Carter), John Sutton (Howard Shelton), Shepperd Strudwick as John Shepperd (Henry Clay), Victor Francen (Florimond Massey), Harry Davenport (Bane), Ward Bond (Sgt. Scully). *Director:* Henry Hathaway. *Producer:* William Perlberg. *Writing Credits:* Ben Hecht, Richard Maibaum, George Seaton, Malvin Wald, Darryl F. Zanuck. *Music:* Alfred Newman. *Cinematography:* Leon Shamroy. *Film Editing:* James B. Clark. *Art Direction:* Richard Day, Nathan Juran. *Set Decoration:* Thomas Little. *Costume Design:* Dolly Tree. *Makeup:* Guy Pearce. *Studio:* 20th Century–Fox. *Length:* 102 minutes.

The "ten gentlemen" are early West Point cadets who refuse to reveal the identity of the correspondent to Congress over the incompetence of their commander Maj. Sam Carter (Laird Cregar) and are severely punished. Carolyn Bainbridge (Maureen O'Hara) wrote the letter and finally wins the affection of poor and principled Kentuckian Joe Dawson (George Montgomery).

The ten gentlemen and other West Pointers report to Gen. William Henry Harrison (Douglass Dumbrille) in the Indiana Territory where he's seeking Tecumseh. Employing the strategy they learned (and Carter despised) in West Point classes, the cadets, led by Dawson, free Carter from the Indians. Carter praises the cadets, they graduate, and Dawson marries Brainbridge.

Brave Warrior (1952)

Harrison: James Seay. *Other Cast:* Jon Hall (Steve Ruddell), Christine Larson (Laura Macgregor), Jay Silverheels (Tecumseh), Michael Ansara (The Prophet), Harry Cording (Shayne Macgregor), George Eldredge (Barney Demming), Leslie Denison (Gen. Proctor), Rory Mallinson (Barker), Rusty Wescoatt (Standish). *Director:* Spencer G. Bennet. *Producer:* Sam Katzman. *Writing Credits:* Robert E. Kent. *Music:* Mischa Bakaleinikoff. *Cinematography:* William V. Skall. *Film Editing:* Aaron Stell. *Art Direction:* Paul Palmentola. *Set Decoration:* Sidney Clifford. *Studio:* Columbia Pictures Corp. *Length:* 73 minutes.

What begins as a cloak-and-dagger tale of counter-plotting of Americans and British sympathizers just before the War of 1812 turns into an Indian fight film, according to *Vari-*

9—William Henry Harrison (1841)

Brave Warrior (1952): James Seay (right) as William Henry Harrison, governor of the Indiana Territory, listens to Jon Hall as Steve Ruddell explain his plans for a model village to gain support of the Shawnee Indian Tribes. The highlight of the film is the Battle of Tippecanoe that made Harrison's reputation as a soldier. This Sam Katzman Technicolor production was released by Columbia Pictures. (Photofest.)

ety (May 14, 1952). The story centers on Steve Ruddell's (Jon Hall) efforts as Indiana Governor William Henry Harrison's emissary to find traitors to the U.S. who are stirring up Indians for the British cause. He's helped by the title character, legendary Shawnee chief Tecumseh (Jay Silverheels). Although it includes the Battle of Tippecanoe, the screenplay is "too reminiscent of other Indian stories," says *Variety*. The low-budget Sam Katzman production is not helped by obviously painted backdrops.

10

John Tyler (1841–1845)

John Tyler. (Courtesy of Library of Congress).

John Tyler's campaign slogan with William Henry Harrison—"Tippecanoe and Tyler too"—implied that he shared the views of his running mate whom he succeeded upon death after Harrison's three weeks in office. On the contrary, Tyler did not support Harrison's Whig positions. A Southerner and a strict constructionist, he consistently opposed protective tariffs, the national bank, and federally sponsored internal improvements.

Tall, slender, sharp-featured with a strong code of proper political behavior, he took the side of principle almost at once when he vetoed a new bank bill as unconstitutional. His Harrison-appointed cabinet resigned in protest except for Secretary of State Daniel Webster who alone upheld the president's executive power. Tyler continued to veto presidential aspirant Henry Clay's bills reviving the Bank of the United States and repealing the Independent Treasury. What Charles Dickens wrote about Tyler "being at war with everybody"[1] no doubt explained his being expelled from the Whig Party and almost being impeached.

At 51, the youngest president yet, Tyler had more experience in government than any president before. He had spent his life in politics: the Virginia House, Senate, and governorship, then the Federal House and Senate. In foreign affairs he settled boundary disputes with the Webster-Ashburton Treaty and gained Senate support for annexation of Texas. His second wife, Julia Gardiner, aided him in charming senators and congressmen.

THE FILMS

There are no films with John Tyler as a character.

11

James K. Polk (1845–1849)

James K. Polk. (Courtesy Library of Congress.)

"Who is James K. Polk?" the Whig press inquired sarcastically when the Democrats nominated him as the "dark horse" in 1844.[1] Polk turned out to be a great president,[2] achieving the four goals he set for his single term: a reduction of the tariff, an Independent Treasury, settlement of the Oregon boundary question, and the question of California.[3] In acquisition of land, which involved war with Mexico, he added more than a million square miles of land to the United States.

Following the peaceful settlement with England of the Oregon boundary at the 49th parallel, the Mexican War started when Polk's preferred diplomacy failed. Mexico refused to cede its land for up to $20 million for Upper California, New Mexico, and the Rio Grande as a boundary for Texas. This provoked Polk to a war as controversial as the War of 1812 and the Vietnam conflict, stirring cries of Manifest Destiny on one side and antislavery and antiwar on the other. With his usual administrative skill and mastery of political detail, Polk managed the war with the aid of his two top military commanders, Winfield Scott and Zachary Taylor.

Polk's command of his administration supported his self description: "the hardest-working man in this country."[4] His extremely helpful wife, Sarah Childress, was considered more popular than the intense, humorless Polk. Nevertheless, this moderate man presided over a country in expansion and transition with increasing sectional antagonisms and kept his promises.

THE FILMS

Although one of the great U.S. presidents, Polk is unheralded by Hollywood with only four minor role appearances. The importance of Polk particularly in settling the boundaries of the U.S. raises the question of why Hollywood overlooked this president.

The Monroe Doctrine (1939)

Polk: Edwin Stanley.
This is a story of President Monroe's response to attempts by Spain to interfere in South America. For details, see Chapter 4 on James Monroe.

Can't Help Singing (1944)

Polk: Edward Earle. *Other Cast:* Deanna Durbin (Caroline Frost), Robert Paige (Johnny Lawlor), Akim Tamiroff (Prince Gregory Stroganovsky), David Bruce (Lt. Robert Latham), Leonid Kinskey (Koppa), June Vincent (Jeannie McLean), Ray Collins (Sen. Martin Frost), Andrew Tombes (Sad Sam), Thomas Gomez (Jake Carstairs), Clara Blandick (Aunt Cissy Frost), Olin Howlin (Bigelow), George Cleveland (U.S. Marshal), William Sundholm (Lincoln). *Director:* Frank Ryan. *Producer:* Felix Jackson, Frank Shaw. *Writing Credits:* Lewis R. Foster, John D. Klorer, Frank Ryan, Leo Townsend, Curtis B. and Samuel J. Warshawsky. *Music:* H.J. Salter, Jerome Kern. *Cinematography:* Woody Bredell, W. Howard Greene. *Film Editing:* Ted J. Kent. *Art Direction:* Robert Clatworthy, John B. Goodman. *Set Decoration* Russell A. Gausman, Edward R. Robinson. *Costume Design:* Walter Plunkett. *Makeup:* Jack P. Pierce. *Length:* 89 minutes.

This is a major vehicle for Deanna Durbin who at the time was slightly past her peak (at age 23) of a career in which she became the most famous female star in Hollywood. In her first Technicolor film, a western musical (by Jerome Kern, among others), she plays Caroline Frost who follows a young cavalry officer, Johnny Lawlor (Robert Paige), to California in the early gold rush days. Her father, Sen. Martin Frost (Ray Collins), sent the young man there because he believes him unsuitable for her. Ironically, his singing daughter encounters prospectors, bandits, and Indians in pursuit of her love. The presidential cameo with Edward Earle playing James Polk sets the historical time period.

California (1947)

Polk: Ian Wolfe. *Other Cast:* Ray Milland (Jonathan Trumbo), Barbara Stanwyck (Lily Bishop), Barry Fitzgerald (Michael Fabian), George Coulouris (Pharaoh Coffin), Anthony Quinn (Don Luis Rivera y Hernandez), Roman Bohnen (Col. Stuart). *Director:* John Farrow. *Producer:* Seton I. Miller. *Writing Credits:* Frank Butler, Boris Ingster, Seton I. Miller, Theodore Strauss. *Music:* Earl Robinson, Victor Young. *Cinematography:* Ray Rennahan. *Film Editing:* Eda Warren. *Art Direction:* Roland Anderson, Hans Dreier. *Set Decoration:* Sam Comer, Ray Moyer. *Costume Design:* Edith Head, Gile Steele. *Makeup:* Wally Westmore. *Studio:* Paramount Pictures. *Length:* 97 minutes.

A typical western with pretensions including a well-known cast, *California* tells the story of the redemption of Jonathan Trumbo (Ray Milland), an army deserter, by the love of a tough woman, Lily Bishop (Barbara Stanwyck), and a tough old Irishman, Michael Fabian (Barry Fitzgerald). The three join to stop the scheming of the appropriately named Pharaoh Coffin (George Coulouris) in his efforts to gain control of California.

The hard action of the film contrasts with cinematographer Ray Rennahan's picture-postcard shots of California over the sound of a chorus. John Farrow's direction is as misguided as the villain's imperious plans. The scene that includes Ian Wolfe as President Polk obviously is cut from the print reviewed of this sprawling film. It spends too much finely shot footage on the wagon trek west. No doubt expansionist Polk was discussing the fate of California.

The Oregon Trail (1959)

Polk: Addison Richards. *Other Cast:* Fred MacMurray (Neal Harris), William Bishop (Capt. George Wayne), Nina Shipman (Prudence Cooper), Gloria Talbott (Shona Hastings), Henry Hull (George Seton), John Carradine (Zachariah Garrison), Lumsden Hare (Ambassador Sir Richard), Ollie O'Toole (James Gordon Bennett). *Director:* Gene Fowler Jr. *Producer:* Richard Einfeld. *Writing Credits:* Gene Fowler Jr., Louis Vittes. *Music:* Charles Devlan, Paul Dunlap, Will Miller. *Cinematography:* Kay Norton. *Film Editing:* Betty Steinberg. *Makeup:* Del Acevedo. *Studio:* 20th Century–Fox. *Length:* 86 minutes.

"The single most important element in the film," according to *Variety* (Aug. 19, 1959), "is Fred MacMurray's portrayal of a New York newspaperman (Neal Harris)." He is sent to Oregon to dig up a story by the *New York Herald* editor James Gordon Bennett (Ollie O'Toole) who believes President Polk (Addison Richards) is sending military troops to the Oregon territory disguised as pioneers.

With his usual wit, MacMurray gets his story, but getting it to New York City proves difficult. He's taken prisoner by Indians, and he's helped to escape by one of their beautiful maidens. In a reversal, he joins the troops to fight the Indians, leaves journalism, and rides off with the maiden.

This Deluxe Color–CinemaScope vehicle uses segments from other films much better than bits of the new backdrop footage. MacMurray also appeared in a similar film, *The Far Horizons* (1955), about the Lewis and Clark expedition.

12

Zachary Taylor (1849–1850)

After 16 months in office, Zachary Taylor died of acute gastroenteritis, leaving a compromise to be made on the crucial issues of expansion and slavery. Like Harrison, who died in office, he was a military man, showing leadership for 40 years, something that he unfortunately did not do as president. Known as "Old Rough and Ready" from his military service, Taylor campaigned for the gold standard and against party domination but lacked political connections and experience to rally the public.

Despite his promise not to be a party president, he established an administration newspaper and put fellow Whigs in hundreds of offices, including the Customs position in Salem, Massachusetts, given to Nathaniel Hawthorne. This provoked as much outrage as did his unpopular cabinet appointments of which three members engaged in a legal but suspect activity that garnered Secretary of War George Crawford nearly $100,000.[1]

Zachary Taylor. (Courtesy of Library of Congress.)

The most memorable action during Taylor's administration was Sen. Henry Clay's Compromise of 1850 that Taylor opposed. Enacted as five separate measures, it made New Mexico a free territory, California a free state, Utah a territory, the Fugitive Slave Act more stringent, and the District of Columbia free from slave trade. But it merely postponed the crisis over slavery.[2]

THE FILMS

With such a short lived administration Taylor is more often shown in minor roles in films as a military leader. The four films in which he is the military leader are split between the Seminole Wars and the Mexican War. Taylor's longest appearance as president, and one of the two films with him in this role, is *The Yankee Clipper,* an early Cecil B. DeMille epic about the British-American rivalry in the tea trade.

The Yankee Clipper (1927)

Taylor: Harry Holden. *Other Cast:* William Boyd (Hal Winslow), Burr McIntosh (Hal Winslow Sr.), Elinor Fair (Jocelyn Huntington), John Miljan (Paul de Vigny), Walter Long (Portuguese Joe), Louis Payne (Huntington), Frank Coghlan Jr. (Mickey). *Director:* Rupert Julian. *Producer:* Cecil B. DeMille. *Writing Credits:* Denison Clift, Garrett Fort, John W. Krafft, Garnett Weston. *Cinematography:* John Mescall. *Film Editing:* Claude Berkeley. *Art Direction:* John Hughes. *Studio:* DeMille Pictures Corp. *Length:* 68 minutes.

Cecil B. DeMille had the ability to turn a boat race into an epic. The tea trade with China is the reward for winning this race between British merchantman *The Lord of the Isles* and the newly designed *Yankee Clipper,* and DeMille made the most of it in this silent film.

Young Hal Winslow (William Boyd in his pre–Hopalong Cassidy days) takes the new vessel on its maiden voyage to China to obtain a cargo of tea. In Foochow he meets Lord Huntington (Louis Payne) and his beautiful daughter, Lady Jocelyn (Elinor Fair, at the time Boyd's wife). He learns the lady's fiancé Paul de Vigny (John Miljan) is a cad who has taken up with a Chinese woman. Winslow kidnaps Jocelyn and de Vigny to ensure that she doesn't marry the cad. He forces both of them onto the *Yankee Clipper* on its racing voyage back to Boston. Although delayed by a wild typhoon while rounding the Horn, the Clipper wins by the narrowest of margins, and Winslow and Jocelyn live happily ever after.

Early in the film Taylor (Harry Holden) meets with Hal Winslow Sr. (Burr McIntosh) and tells him that he pictures the *Yankee Clipper* as the forerunner of hundreds more like her, which will enable the U.S. to control the seas. Holden bears no resemblance to Taylor, but he gives a performance that would make Old Rough and Ready particularly proud by his sense of command and presence.

Rebellion (1936) aka Lady from Frisco

Taylor: Allan Cavan. *Other Cast:* Tom Keene (Capt. John Carroll), Rita Hayworth as Rita Cansino (Paula Castillo), Duncan Renaldo (Ricardo Castillo), William Royle (Harris), Gino Corrado (Pablo), Roger Gray (Honeycutt), Robert McKenzie (Judge Moore), Jack Ingram (Hank), Lita Cortez (Marquita), Theodore Lorch (Gen. Vallejo), W.M. McCormick (Dr. Semple). *Director:* Lynn Shores. *Producers:* E.B. Derr, Bernard A. Moriarty. *Writing Credits:* J.T. Neville. *Music:* Abe Meyer. *Cinematography:* Arthur Martinelli. *Film Editing:* Donald Barratt. *Art Direction:* Edward C. Jewell. *Makeup:* Steve Corso. *Studio:* Crescent Pictures Corp. *Length:* 62 minutes.

The Treaty of Guadalupe-Hidalgo has just been signed and already the American settlers are taking Mexican land in California. President Taylor (Allan Cavan) will not stand for this action and sends his aide Capt. John Carroll (Tom Keene) to solve the problems. He works with Paula Castillo (Rita Cansino) and her brother Ricardo (Duncan Renaldo). Under the direction of Lynn Shores, Carroll keeps up the pace in this standard western, disguised as an historical work by producer E.B. Derr (who made *The Glory Trail* with Keene). With the usual fights with "brigands," kidnapping and saving of the heroine, and a hand-to-hand fight between Carroll and villain Harris (William Royle), the film ends with a big fiesta.

There seems to be some confusion as to who portrays Taylor in the film. Screen credits and AFI list Allan Cavan while a 1938 review in *Variety* lists Robert McKenzie. In either case Taylor, in a short appearance, is well represented.

Distant Drums (1951)

Taylor: Robert Barrat. *Other Cast:* Gary Cooper (Capt. Quincy Wyatt), Mari Aldon (Judy Beckett), Richard Webb (Lt. Richard Tufts), Ray Teal (Pvt. Mohair), Arthur Hunnicutt (Monk). *Director:* Raoul Walsh. *Producer:* Milton Sperling. *Writing Credits:* Niven Busch, Martin Rackin. *Music:* Max Steiner. *Cinematography:* Sidney Hickox. *Film Editing:* Folmar Blangsted. *Art Direction:* Douglas Bacon. *Set Decoration:* William Wallace. *Wardrobe:* Marjorie Best. *Makeup:* Gordon Bau. *Studio:* United States Pictures, Warner Brothers. *Length:* 101 minutes.

Filming in the Florida Everglades, director Raoul Walsh uses a typical western genre approach to tell the romantic story of this event in the Second Seminole War in 1840. Capt. Quincy Wyatt (Gary Cooper) leads a small band of soldiers across Lake Okeechobee to destroy a fort manned by gunrunners and Seminoles. After missing the rescue boat, he and his trusty sidekick Monk (Arthur Hunnicutt) lead the soldiers and the civilians rescued from the fort, including Judy Beckett (Mari Aldon), in a perilous journey across the Everglades while continually fighting the Seminoles. In true western fashion, Wyatt saves the day by fighting the Indian Chief Oscala (Larry Carper) underwater hand-to-hand (in special underwater processes created for the film), proving the superiority of Hollywood stars like Cooper with his deliberate, soft-spoken, and heroic demeanor.

The initial title states that the film depicts "how our greatest general, Taylor, was thwarted." Throughout the film the military leader Taylor (Robert Barrat) attempts to locate and support Wyatt in his escape. It was during the Battle of Lake Okeechobee that Taylor earned his nickname "Old Rough and Ready" for his informal, homespun approach to military command and uniform. It appears that Marjorie Best, the wardrober for this film, got her generals confused by dressing Taylor to look like "Old Fuss and Feathers" Winfield Scott. Taylor is seen throughout the film in full regalia with a feathered hat.

Barrat has a good physical resemblance to Taylor and maintains a serious military demeanor, which would be expected of the general and future president.

Seminole (1953)

Taylor: Fay Roope. *Other Cast:* Rock Hudson (Lt. Lance Caldwell), Barbara Hale (Revere Muldoon), Anthony Quinn (Osceola/John Powell), Richard Carlson (Maj. Harlan Degan), Hugh O'Brian (Kajeck). *Director:* Budd Boetticher. *Producer:* Howard Christie. *Writing Credits:* Charles K. Peck Jr. *Music:* Joseph Gershenson, Henry Mancini, Milton Rosen. *Cinematography:* Russell Metty. *Film Editing:* Virgil W. Vogel. *Studio:* Universal International Pictures. *Length:* 87 minutes.

The film opens with a court scene headed by Col. Zachary Taylor (Fay Roope) in which Lt. Lance Caldwell (Rock Hudson) is being tried for killing a guard in an attempt to free the Seminole chieftain Osceola (Anthony Quinn) from a military prison. All of the action takes place in flashback as Lt. Caldwell tries to explain what happened.

Caldwell had returned to Florida to participate in a military campaign against the Seminoles. The fact that he was born and grew up in the area made him a potentially valuable officer. Instead he is greeted by a bigoted, rule-driven commanding officer, Major Harlan Degan (Richard Carlson), who is determined to either move the Seminoles west of the Mississippi River or exterminate them. As it happens, Caldwell's boyhood friend John Powell/Osceola (Quinn) is leading the Seminoles against the American troops. When the

12—*Zachary Taylor (1849–1850)* 97

Seminole (1953): Rock Hudson (right) as Lt. Lance Caldwell is being court-martialed for insubordination in a trial chaired by Col. Zachary Taylor played by Fay Roope (seated in the center of the table left of the American flag). *Seminole* was released by Universal-International Pictures. (Courtesy of George Eastman House.)

lovely Revere Muldoon (Barbara Hale) appears, the military problems multiply and numerous good men are killed in a disastrous raid by Degan on Osceola's camp.

Director Budd Boetticher and writer Charles K. Peck Jr. attempt to use some historical facts in the film, but the actual history apparently did not satisfy them. Osceola was a half-breed with a British trader father and a Creek Indian mother. He was taken prisoner while under a flag of truce, not by Maj. Degan but by General Thomas Jesup. He did die while imprisoned, not in Fort King, Florida, but in Fort Moultee, Charleston, South Carolina.

Roope looks a bit older than the 51 years Taylor would have been in 1836. However, he portrays the future president as a tough and reasonable officer but without giving him the characteristics that would have justified calling him "Old Rough and Ready."

Old Shatterhand (1964)

Taylor: Charles Fawcett. *Other Cast:* Lex Barker (Old Shatterhand), Guy Madison (Capt. Bradley), Pierre Brice (Winnetou), Daliah Lavi (Paloma), Rik Battaglia (Dixon), Gustavo Rojo (Capt. Bush), Ralf Wolter (Sam Hawkens), Kitty Mattern (Rosemary), Alain Tissier (Tujunga). *Director:* Hugo Fregonese. *Producer:* Artur Brauner. *Writing Credits:* Ladislas Fodor, Karl May, Robert A. Stemmle. *Music:* Riz Ortolani. *Cinematography:* Siegfried Hold. *Production Design:*

Otto Pischinger. *Art Direction:* Veljko Despotovic. *Costume Design:* Mira Glisic, Trude Ulrich. *Studio:* CCC Filmkunst. *Length:* 122 minutes.

This is the second of a series of German movies based on the novels of Karl May (the first being *Winnetou* and the third *Winnetou II*). Old Shatterhand, played by Lex Barker (long-term expatriate to Germany), is the blood brother of the Apache chief Winnetou (Frenchman Pierre Brice). Although filmed in Yugoslavia, May's story is true wild west.

General Zachary Taylor (Charles Fawcett) is in charge of a cavalry unit in Apache territory. He leaves for Washington D.C. on business; problems start immediately. Comanches in cahoots with white bad guys start attacking ranches and place the blame on the Apaches. Behind all of the problems is cavalry Capt. Bradley (another expatriate, Guy Madison) who takes Old Shatterhand prisoner along with Chief Winnetou's son Tujunga (Alain Tissier). Winnetou attacks the fort and saves Shatterhand, but Tujunga dies while destroying the fort's ammunition.

All ends well when General Taylor returns to interrupt the fighting, arrest Capt. Bradley, and sign a peace treaty with the Apaches. From numerous user comments on IMDb it is clear that these films were well received in Germany and throughout Europe. The running time for the film in Germany is 122 minutes while AFI reports that the U.S. release in 1967 runs 89 minutes.

One Man's Hero (1999)

Taylor: James Gammon. *Other Cast:* Tom Berenger (John Riley), Joaquim de Almeida (Cortina), Daniela Romo (Marta), Mark Moses (Col. Benton Lacey), Stuart Graham (Corp. Kenneally). *Director:* Lance Hool. *Producer:* Lance Hool, Conrad Hool, Tom Berenger. *Screenwriter:* Milton Gelman. *Cinematography:* Joao Fernandes. *Composer:* Ernest Troost. *Editor:* Mark Conte. *Studio:* Orion/Silver Lion Films. *Length:* 121 minutes.

Based on a little known historical event, *One Man's Hero* is the story of Irish deserters from the American army who fought on the Mexican side during the war with Mexico. Many young men fled their home country to the United States when the potato famine hit Ireland during the 19th century. A great number of them joined the U.S. Army with the promise of a regular salary and U.S. citizenship. Instead of citizenship, many of the Irish soldiers were mistreated because of their foreignness and their Roman Catholic religion.

In the film a few Irish soldiers led by Sgt. John Riley (Tom Berenger) desert into Mexico. They are chased by American troops but are finally captured and imprisoned by Mexican guerillas. Upon the beginning of the war with the U.S. they decide to side with the Mexicans and formed the Saint Patrick Brigade (San Patricio) in honor of the patron saint of Ireland. After fighting bravely for the Mexicans they are captured by the American army near Mexico City. Fifty members of San Patricio are executed. This is reported to be the largest single execution by the U.S. Army in its history. Although the historical event is virtually unknown in the United States, it is still well remembered in Ireland.

Taylor (James Gammon) plays a minor role in the film as the commanding officer of the army in the Texas border region. He is characterized as a rustic, tough but respected officer, which is in agreement with the historical assessment of the man who served 40 years in the U.S. military but only 16 months in office as the twelfth president.

13

Millard Fillmore (1850–1853)

In his three-year term, Millard Fillmore accomplished much for America abroad. But, like Zachary Taylor whom he succeeded, he lacked the capacity to settle the nation's most serious internal problem—slavery. Although Fillmore suffered abuse from the public and political leader Thurlow Weed, he "possessed extraordinary strength of character and an enviable tenacity of purpose as well as an admirable personality."[1]

Born in a log cabin (helpful in campaigning) he devoted his life to politics, serving in the New York State and U.S. legislatures before becoming vice president. Rather than follow Taylor's policies, Fillmore signed the Fugitive Slave Law of the Compromise of 1850. Then he sent troops to prevent Southern insurrection and threatened to send troops to the North to force Abolitionists also to comply with the Constitution. From party man he changed to defender of the national welfare, anticipating Lincoln's position.

Millard Fillmore. (Courtesy of Library of Congress.)

To that end Fillmore encouraged economic growth through subsidized railroad construction. Abroad he strove to open new markets, particularly in Japan; create diplomatic harmony with Mexico and Peru; favored plans for a canal through Nicaragua; and thwarted French imperialism in Hawaii. From his first day in office he said he would not seek a second term, but he ran and lost on the Know-Nothing ticket in 1856.

THE FILMS

The Monroe Doctrine (1939)

Fillmore: Millard Vincent.

Fillmore (Millard Vincent) appears with five other presidents in this 22-minute film about the importance of the Monroe Doctrine. For details, see Chapter 5 on James Monroe.

14

Franklin Pierce (1853–1857)

Even his friend Nathaniel Hawthorne in a campaign biography admitted that "he did not at the outset, give promise of distinguished success."[1] Franklin Pierce, well mannered and well intentioned as he was, could not cope with the events of his era: Eastern industrialization and urbanization, Western expansion, and above all, the questions of slavery and states rights. He lacked inspiration and initiative.

He had served as a brigadier general during the Mexican War and defeated his former commander, Whig Winfield Scott, as the Democratic candidate in the presidential election of 1852. Although only 48, Pierce had been a member and speaker of the New Hampshire legislature and a U.S. congressman and senator. His wife, Jane, a religious woman, saw the deaths of all their three children as a divine signal for her husband to be a better president.[2]

Franklin Pierce. (Courtesy of Library of Congress.)

The Kansas-Nebraska Act became the downfall of his administration. It overturned the Missouri Compromise by providing for "popular sovereignty" in the new territories. Pierce hoped it would provide a way out of the slavery dilemma; instead it turned the territories into a battleground. Elsewhere, Southerners urged acquisition of Cuba, which Pierce unsuccessfully tried to purchase; he also tried to annex Hawaii. Abroad, however, Pierce oversaw a trade treaty with Japan and another with Canada defining fishing rights and eliminating import duties.

THE FILMS

The single film including Pierce has him in a minor role, acting very un-presidential in a historically inaccurate film.

The Great Moment (1944)

Pierce: Porter Hall. *Other Cast:* Joel McCrea (W.T.G. Morton), Betty Field (Elizabeth Morton), Harry Carey (Prof. Warren), William Demarest (Eben Frost). *Director:* Preston Sturges. *Producer:* Buddy G. DeSylva, Preston Sturges. *Writing Credits:* Rene Fulop-Miller, Preston Sturges. *Music:* Victor Young. *Cinematography:* Victor Milner. *Film Editing:* Stuart Gilmore. *Art Direction:* Hans Dreier, Ernst Fegte. *Studio:* Paramount Pictures. *Length:* 83 minutes.

Preston Sturges, leading writer and director of satire from 1940 to 1944 (*The Great McGinty* [1940] and *The Lady Eve* [1941]), turns his talents with writer Rene Fulop-Miller to biographical drama in 1942 to film the story of an obscure and unrewarded Boston dentist. This film follows the popularity of the bio dramas about Alexander Graham Bell, Thomas Edison, and Louis Pasteur. While these films deal with stories of medical and scientific success, William Thomas Green Morton's story shows failure. Sturges struggled with Paramount Pictures, his producer, to make the film his way, but Paramount wanted something upbeat for World War II audiences. The result was shelving Sturges's film and then releasing it in

The Great Moment (1944): Porter Hall as President Pierce (right) in the only film in which he appears. It's director Preston Sturges's story of W.T.G. Morton, an unrewarded Boston dentist who invents anesthesia. Joel McCrea (center) plays this role, shown seeking support from Pierce for his pain-saving invention, in the president's White House office (far different from today's Oval Office). Paramount Pictures forced Sturges to make this picture upbeat for World War II audiences. (Photofest.)

altered form two years later. What is left is a disjointed biography told through flashbacks and confused sequences under a changed title from the original *Triumph Over Pain*.

Joel McCrea, Sturges's star in his 1942 *Sullivan's Travels* and *The Palm Beach Story*, convincingly portrays the handsome, dedicated, and energetic dental surgeon who invents anesthesia. He sees ether as a way to help patients and himself. Unfortunately, his Harvard professor and a fellow student make claims on discovery of the anesthesia, while Morton continuously struggles with the Patent Office and Congress.

As a final resort Morton seeks support from President Pierce who, in his usual evasive way, suggests that before he signs an act of Congress authorizing payment to Morton, that Morton bring suit against a Navy doctor who has infringed upon Morton's patent. Porter Hall appears as Pierce, in a Victorian solarium setting that looks very un-presidential. So does Hall's manner; he tells Morton he'd "rather be you than president." Other performances also fail to ring true: Betty Field is the doting but dull wife Elizabeth, and Sturges regular William Demarest as Morton's friend and guinea pig. The better story of Morton rests on Paramount's cutting room floor and in the *Cambridge Sketches* of Francis Preston Stearns.

15

James Buchanan (1857–1861)

James Buchanan (Courtesy of Library of Congress.)

Physical characteristics define James Buchanan's presidency: Because he was near-sighted in one eye and far-sighted in the other he cocked his head down and to one side while speaking and listening, ever the compromiser in a weak position. The mounting turmoil over slavery and the various compromises to settle the issue finally took its toll when this cautious Democrat took no action against Southern secession. Unlike the decisive Washington in the Whiskey Rebellion and Jackson in the Nullification Crisis, he believed the solution was a Constitutional amendment guaranteeing slavery to states that desired it.

No one had seemed better prepared for the presidency since John Quincy Adams.[1] Buchanan served in the Pennsylvania legislature, U.S. Congress as congressman and senator, and Pierce's cabinet as minister to Great Britain and Russia. "The great object of my administration," he wrote, "will be to arrest, if possible, the agitation of the slavery question at the North, and to destroy sectional parties."[2] But he did not; neither did the Senate ratify any of his treaties for South American solidarity nor did the House pass any of his ambitious legislation.

Abroad, Buchanan achieved diplomatic success. Through his contacts in Great Britain he strove to guarantee nonintervention in Central America by both countries in an interpretation of the 1850 Clayton-Bulwer Treaty. Beset with Congressional threats for investigation and press accusations involving his niece, ward, and White House hostess Harriet Lane, he spent his retirement defending his presidential record.

THE FILMS

There are no films with James Buchanan as a character.

16

Abraham Lincoln (1861–1865)

Abraham Lincoln. (Courtesy of Library of Congress.)

"If elected, I shall be thankful; if not, it will be all the same,"[1] said Abraham Lincoln humbly before his first run for elective office (which he lost). Of course, it would not be all the same; he continued in politics, and the United States is not the same. From his legendary log cabin birth, he became a store clerk and owner, ferry pilot, surveyor, postmaster, and lawyer. He also served in a volunteer company during the Black Hawk War before he became a member of the Illinois General Assembly and U.S. congressman. Self-educated, he drew attention by his literary art of precision, vernacular ease, rhythmical virtuosity, and elegance, such as his biblical "A house divided against itself cannot stand" regarding the nation and slavery.[2]

His words and actions fill libraries as poets, like Walt Whitman, and scholars like Arthur Schlesinger, Jr., attempt to define and redefine him: "He asserted the right to proclaim martial law behind the lines, to arrest people without warrant, to seize property, to suppress newspapers, to prevent the use of the post office for treasonable correspondence, to emancipate slaves, to lay out a plan of reconstruction. His proclamations, executive orders and military regulations invaded fields previously the domain of legislative action. All this took place without a declaration of war by Congress."[3] Lincoln took these extra–Constitutional steps to ensure the maintenance of the Union using a detachment in concert with saint-like forbearance.[4]

Lincoln devoted himself wholly to the preservation of the Union, a principle he placed above the abolition of slavery. In so doing he faced a divided and personally ambitious cabinet; abolitionists calling for total war on slavery and the unconditional surrender of an occupied South; defeatists demanding peace over Union; uncooperative states; insubordinate generals; Army deserters; and an abusive press. Even his family life with Mary brought sorrow and depression, "the hypo," he called it. Always revealing "the better nature of our angels,"[5] he and his pervasive humanity prevailed.

Barely into his second term as the newly formed Republican Party candidate, Lincoln approved the Thirteenth Amendment to abolish slavery. His developing plans for Reconstruction stressed reconciliation, never retribution or revenge. But he never could carry them out as another bloody bullet ended his life on Good Friday, April 14, 1865. The Great Emancipator was mourned beyond measure. The worldly-wise John Hay, his secretary, who knew him about as well as he permitted himself to be known, called him "the greatest character since Christ."[6] His Secretary of State William Seward, most devoted member of his contentious cabinet, praised him "without limitation" as "the best and wisest man he [had] ever known."[7]

THE FILMS

Without question Abraham Lincoln has appeared as a character in motion pictures more than any other individual. His films represent almost one-third of the total number presented in this book. This fact can be attributed to his continually being listed by historians as the greatest of the presidents, to the public perception of his legendary personification of the American spirit, to his being the first widely photographed president, and to his role in the Civil War.

Invariably Lincoln is treated with respect bordering on reverence. He receives iconic status, primarily as Father Abraham "to bind up the nation's wounds" to use his words from his second inaugural address.

As Mark S. Reinhart states in his *Abraham Lincoln on Screen* filmography, "Lincoln's life has been examined from every conceivable angle: a godlike leader, a folksy man of the people, or a terribly depressed man driven by the dark sides of his personality."[8] Unfortunately overlooked by filmmakers is the historical drama of the political revolution from 1856 to 1860 that led to his election. On a personal basis, the reverential treatment plays down his complex personality, his political shrewdness, his military leadership, and the manner in which he was able to control his many adversaries during his presidential terms.

Because of the number of Lincoln films and the similarity of plot in many, it is worthwhile to categorize them according to their scenarios:

• Clemency Acts. Numerous are the films in which Lincoln acts as the president (or God) to pardon an individual sentenced to death. Lincoln pardons Union soldiers (mainly sentries) in seven films; he pardons Union officers in two films; he pardons Southern soldiers in three films; he pardons Southern officers (including Shirley Temple's film father, John Boles) in four films; he pardons the man without a country, Philip Nolan, in three films; and, somewhat differently, in *Of Human Hearts* (1938) he tells Jimmy Stewart he will not pardon him unless he writes to his mother. Obviously the myth of Father Abraham is nurtured and burnished in these films that conform to an actual pardoning as detailed in one chapter of Carl Sandburg's biography. Father Abraham was not merely a nickname to Lincoln. As Sandburg said—he cared. His followers trusted him as he trusted them. There was this kinship between him and a certain legion of loyalists. He seemed to reason that if they wanted him to go on as president they would have their way—and if they didn't want him, he could stand that if they could;

- Lincoln as commander-in-chief. Of the 39 films in this category, 20 concern the president acting as the Union leader in the Civil War. Eight of these films are westerns, quite often with the president sending some stalwart like Joel McCrea to save gold for the union as in *Wells Fargo* (1937);
- Lincoln as a soldier. Lincoln acted as the head of an Illinois company in the Black Hawk War. There are two films with brief scenes recreating this historical event.
- Lincoln biographies. There are 11 biopics covering various periods in Lincoln's life including *Lincoln the Lover* about his relationship with Ann Rutledge; the more extensive *Abraham Lincoln, Young Mr. Lincoln* and *Abe Lincoln in Illinois*; and later *Lincoln in the White House*, a 21-minute film chronicling the presidency. Only *The Dramatic Life of Abraham Lincoln* (1924) and *Abraham Lincoln* (1930) attempt to cover most of his life;
- Lincoln's assassination. Of the eight assassination films, seven relate to the actual event in Ford's Theatre. The last of these films, *The Tall Target*, concerns a fictional attempted assassination, stopped by Dick Powell as a New York detective, prior to the inauguration;
- Unknown roles. There are 13 early silent era films that list an appearance by a Lincoln character but little is actually known about either the film or the role.
- Lincoln as a walk-on. Starting with *The Fortune Cookie* there have been eight films with cameo-type appearances by a Lincoln character, apparently to garner some respect for the film. For example, in the teen-age comedy *Bill & Ted's Excellent Adventure*, the Lincoln character gets to say "Party on, dudes."

For all of the Lincoln films, 64 actors undertook the part with 44 actors playing him once and 13 several times. Probably the most skillful and close in resemblance to the president was Frank McGlynn Sr. with 12 impersonations. McGlynn Sr. was born in San Francisco in 1866 and made his stage debut on Broadway in *The Gold Bug* in 1896. His first reported appearance as Lincoln in a film was in 1915 in *The Life of Abraham Lincoln* and his last was in the World War II 1942 film *March On, America!* In 1919 he starred on Broadway in the play *Abraham Lincoln*. Starting in 1934 with *Are We Civilized?* he appeared as Lincoln in 12 films during the next eight years. Although primarily known as a Lincoln impersonator, McGlynn appeared in more than 100 films during his extended career and during the period 1910–1915 directed six films.

Lincoln was 51 when he was elected to the presidency. McGlynn was 68 in 1934 when he started his eight-year run as the primary film Lincoln. Because of the adulation of Lincoln this age difference probably benefited McGlynn in his role as Father Abraham. McGlynn's strength as a Lincoln impersonator came from his striking physical resemblance to Lincoln and his overall acting ability. His movements and gestures were suitably Lincolnesque although he, along with the other Lincoln impersonators, failed to reproduce what is know to be Lincoln's Midwestern nasal speaking voice.

Ralph Ince was second to McGlynn as a Lincoln impersonator on film. He was born in Boston in 1887, the youngest of three brothers, all of whom made their mark in films. Ince started as a cartoonist with Vitagraph in 1906 and first appeared as Lincoln in *Under One Flag* (1911). He continued in ten films until 1921 with *The Highest Law*. As was the case with McGlynn, Ince was extremely well known as a Lincoln impersonator but had a much broader career in film. He acted in 105 films starting in 1907 and ending just prior to his death in a road accident in 1937. In addition he was a major director with 169 films to his credit starting in 1910 and ending in England in 1937 with *It's Not Cricket*.

Today Raymond Massey is the most remembered Lincoln actor because *Abe Lincoln in*

Illinois is still widely shown on TV. The apocryphal anecdote is that Massey would never be satisfied until he was assassinated.

In these impersonations, the most difficult characteristic of Lincoln to realize was his voice—a tenor intonation that ultimately settled down in a clear, shrill, monotone style yet highly audible.[9] Equally difficult are his facial expressions. His secretary John G. Nicolay said, "Graphic art was powerless before a face that moved through a thousand delicate gradations of line and contour, light and shade, sparkle of the eye and curve of the lip, in the long gamut of expression from grave to gay, and back again from the rollicking jollity of laughter to that far-away look."[10]

The vast majority of Lincoln films were produced prior to World War II. Since *Abe Lincoln in Illinois* in 1940 there has been only one film in which Lincoln is a major character, *Abe Lincoln: The Freedom Fighter* (1978), and that it probably was made for TV. In fact, the last nine portrayals of Lincoln in film until 2005 have been nonsensical in juvenile films. In 2005 there were two short films of a serious nature but with limited commercial exposure. Much of the Lincoln material produced since World War II has been made for TV and, to an extent, has presented a more truthful look at Lincoln. Nevertheless, the view of Lincoln as Father Abraham, Honest Abe, the rail-splitter, and the man on the penny has remained intact because the audiences wanted him that way.

Uncle Tom's Cabin (1903) or Slavery Days

Lincoln: No actor listed. *Director:* Edwin S. Porter. *Based on the novel by* Harriet Beecher Stowe. *Studio:* Edison. *Length:* Approximately five minutes.

This earliest appearance of a president in a film is that of Lincoln in a silent Edison Film Company presentation of *Uncle Tom's Cabin.* Since Harriet Beecher Stowe's novel was published in 1851, a full decade before Lincoln took office, the film is also one of the first instances in which the filmmaker and history are not in agreement. Yet, the film's end is a tableau shot of Uncle Tom's death, including a prescient showing of Lincoln freeing a slave.

There is no information on the actor who portrays Lincoln in the single scene of his appearance.

The Blue and the Grey (1908) aka The Days of '61

Lincoln: Unknown actor. *Director:* Edwin S. Porter. *Studio:* Edison Mfg. Co. *Length:* 1000 or 1085 feet.

In film after film during the silent era, President Lincoln acts as the court of last resort. In this film, two friends from childhood attend West Point but at the onset of the Civil War go to opposite sides in the conflict. The Union officer refuses to capture his friend, a Confederate officer, and is sentenced to death in a court martial. Lincoln acts to pardon the condemned man.

The film no longer exists, and the actor portraying Lincoln is not identified.

The Life of Abraham Lincoln (1908)

Lincoln: Unknown actor. *Studio:* Essanay Film Mfg. Co. *Length:* Approximately 15 minutes, 958 or 975 feet.

In the fall of 1908, Essanay Films released the initial attempt to cover the entire life of Lincoln as the first of a series, "Flashlights of American History." *Variety*, in its issue of October 17, 1908, describes the film as "an American historical lecture in motion" and was generally favorable in its critical review. The trade newspaper notes that the film "shows the great American statesman as a boy, his father and mother, and other personages." While the actor who portrays Lincoln is not identified, the reviewer felt that the actor had "evidently studied the personality of the martyred President." Most of the familiar episodes are based on the memoirs of Lincoln's former law partner, Herndon, an advocate of the president.

The Reprieve: An Episode in the Life of Abraham Lincoln (1908)

Lincoln: Unknown actor. *Director*: Van Dyke Brooke. *Studio*: Vitagraph Company of America. *Length*: 400 or 440 feet.

This story is based on an actual incident concerning a Union soldier, William Scott, who in 1861 fell asleep on guard duty and was sentenced to death. In his definitive filmography *Abraham Lincoln on Screen* Mark Reinhart provides details on the actual events concerning Scott's pardon.

Lincoln (actor unknown) pardons the young man and this act becomes the basis for not only this film directed by Van Dyke Brooke but other later films, *Abraham Lincoln's Clemency* (1910) and *The Sleeping Sentinel* (1910), for example, and a general part of the Lincoln mythology. The film has not survived and the actor who plays Lincoln is not identified.

Abraham Lincoln's Clemency (1910)

Lincoln: Unknown actor. *Other Cast*: Leopold Wharton. *Director*: Theodore Wharton. *Studio*: Pathe Freres. *Length*: One reel.

Based on the poem "The Sleeping Sentinel" by Francis De Haas Janiver, which in turn was based on the William Scott event, this film serves as the basis for the numerous silent era films depicting Lincoln the pardoner. This film concerns a young soldier who falls asleep while on duty. He is convicted and sentenced to be shot. After an appeal from the boy's mother President Lincoln provides a pardon at the last minute. Unfortunately, the boy is killed in the next battle but knows his death is with honor rather than in front of a firing squad.

Lincoln (played by an unidentified actor) appears throughout the film and is not a very believable representation of the president either in his personal appearance or his acting ability.

The Sleeping Sentinel (1910)

Lincoln: George Stille. *Studio*: Lubin. *Length*: Approximately 10 minutes.

Released less than a year after *Abraham Lincoln's Clemency*, this film also tells the story of Lincoln's pardoning young William Scott. Although no prints of the film seem to be in existence, it is assumed that it was based on the poem of the same name by a government clerk named Francis De Haas Janiver. It has been reported that the character of Lincoln is played by George Stille.

Battle Hymn of the Republic (1911)

Lincoln: Ralph Ince. *Other Cast:* Julia Swayne Gordon (Julia Ward Howe), Maurice Costello (Jesus Christ), Edith Storey (The Virgin Mary), Edward Thomas (Tolstoy), Anita Stewart (Angel). *Directors:* J. Stuart Blackton, Laurence Trimble. *Producer:* J. Stuart Blackton. *Writing Credits:* Betta Breuil, Julia Ward Howe. *Studio:* Vitagraph Co. of America. *Length:* Approximately 10 minutes.

Without any question the song "The Battle Hymn of the Republic" became the anthem for the North during the Civil War. This film purports to tell the story of how Julia Ward Howe (Julia Swayne Gordon) came to write the song after a fictionalized trip with President Lincoln (Ralph Ince) to a dispirited Union recruiting center. This lost film had to have more to it because the cast of characters includes Jesus Christ (Maurice Costello), the Virgin Mary (Edith Storey), Tolstoy (Edward Thomas), and an Angel (Anita Stewart). Ralph Ince also appears as Lincoln as he did in *Under One Flag* later that year.

The Fortunes of War (1911)

Lincoln: Unknown actor. *Director and Writer:* Thomas Ince. *Studio:* Independent Motion Picture Co. of America (IMP). *Length:* Approximately 10 minutes.

There are no copies of this black-and-white silent film in existence, and the actor who portrays Lincoln is unknown although IMDb reports, unconfirmed, a William Clifford as doing the role. The film is the first listed to have been written and directed by Thomas Ince, the most famous early director of Lincoln films.

Reportedly, the film covers the adventures of two brothers during the Civil War, and Lincoln appears reviewing the troops and talking with officers and members of his cabinet.

Grant and Lincoln (1911)

Lincoln: Unknown actor. *Studio:* Champion. *Length:* Approximately 10 minutes.

Another film for which no copy exists, *Grant and Lincoln* tells the story of a Southerner who is fighting for the Union and is mistakenly arrested for spying. His highly capable sister, using a gun, demands that General Grant pardon him. Grant refuses but somehow she gets to see President Lincoln who, everybody knows, will pardon anyone—in Hollywood films. In real life Lincoln also showed such compassion, as he did to Grant when a number of Republicans and "the tide of popular sentiment" were against Grant. A.K. McClure, Lincoln's friend and a Republican spokesman, urged Grant's dismissal from the service so that the president could retain the confidence of the country. Lincoln said "in a tone of earnestness that I shall never forget," said McClure, 'I can't spare this man—he fights!'"[11]

His First Commission (1911)

Lincoln: Charles Brabin. *Studio:* Edison Film Manufacturing Co.

Very limited information is available on this film other than the fact that President Lincoln is played by Charles Brabin for the only time.

Lieutenant Gray of the Confederacy (1911)

Lincoln: James Dayton. *Other Cast:* Alvin Wyckoff (Ulysses S. Grant). *Director-Writer:* Francis Boggs. *Studio:* Selig Polyscope Co. *Length:* Approximately 10 minutes.

This is another Lincoln clemency film concerning a Confederate soldier sentenced to be shot for spying and pardoned by Lincoln. The film no longer exists, although it is known that James Dayton portrays Lincoln.

A Romance of the 60's (1911)

Lincoln: Unknown actor. *Other Cast:* Jack Standing, Frances Gibson. *Studio:* Lubin Manufacturing Co. *Length:* Approximately 10 minutes.

In this lost film, Lincoln is again asked to grant a pardon, which he does.

Under One Flag (1911) aka One Flag at Last

Lincoln: Ralph Ince. *Other Cast:* Earle Williams (Capt. Jack Meyers), Rose Tapley (Southern Boy's Sister), Harry Benham (Southern Boy). *Studio:* Vitagraph. *Length:* 10 minutes.

In another variation on the Lincoln clemency theme, a Southern girl (Rose Tapley) reluctantly falls in love with a wounded Northern officer, Captain Jack Meyers (Earle Williams). Her reluctance comes from the fact that her brother has been captured and is in a Yankee prison. When Union forces rescue Meyers he promises the girl that he will try to save her brother.

Captain Jack is able to get a hearing from President Lincoln (Ralph Ince), and the brother (Harry Benham) is freed. As the Civil War ends, Meyers and the Southern girl reunite and become engaged.

The most memorable aspect of the film is the first appearance of Ralph Ince as Lincoln. Ince subsequently appeared in nine more silent films as the president and was always considered the greatest of Lincoln silent impersonators.

The Fall of Black Hawk (1912)

Lincoln: H. G. Launsdale. *Director:* William Lee. *Studio:* American Film Manufacturing Co. *Length:* Approximately 10 minutes.

In his filmography *Abraham Lincoln on Screen*, Mark Reinhart reports that elements of this film exist at the Library of Congress, but that there are no appearances by Lincoln. He further reports that in a 1961 article in *Films in Review* Robert C. Roman noted that the film was based on Lincoln's experiences in the Black Hawk War, and that Lincoln was portrayed by H.G. Launsdale. Lincoln did serve 80 days in the war for which he received $95. Assessing those days, Carl Sandburg wrote that Lincoln had seen deep into the heart of the American volunteer soldier, why men go to war, march in mud, sleep in rain on cold ground, eat pork raw when it can't be boiled, and kill when the killing is good. On a later day an observer was to say he saw Lincoln's eyes misty in his mention of the American volunteer soldier.

The Higher Mercy (1912)

Lincoln: Ralph Ince. *Other Cast:* Julia Swayne Gordon (Mrs. Brinton), James Morrison (Jasper Brinton), Rose Tapley (Mrs. Lincoln), Kenneth Casey (Tad Lincoln), Norma Talmadge (Alice), Florence Ashbrook (The Nurse), Hal Wilson (Servant). *Director:* William V. Ranous. *Writing Credits:* Charles L. Gaskill. *Studio:* Vitagraph Co. of America.

This film is no longer in existence, and little has been written about it. It was another of the Lincoln films starring Ralph Ince who did such a good job in these early films. It also stars Julia Swayne Gordon who had starred with Ince in *The Battle Hymn of the Republic* (1911).

Lincoln's Gettysburg Address (1912)

Lincoln: Ralph Ince. *Directors:* J. Stuart Blackton, James Young. *Writing Credits:* Betta Breuil, Abraham Lincoln. *Studio:* Vitagraph Company of America. *Length:* Approximately 10 minutes.

As the title suggests, this film is a re-enactment of Lincoln's most famous address at the dedication of the National Soldier's Cemetery on November 19, 1863. Rather than just showing the speech (not a very interesting choice in a silent film) there are scenes illustrating the speech from the Revolutionary War, slavery, Lincoln's cabinet, and the battle at Gettysburg.

The Seventh Son (1912)

Lincoln: Ralph Ince. *Other Cast:* Mary Maurice (Janet Grant, a widow), James Morrison (Harry Grant, Janet's seventh son), Tefft Johnson (Stanton), Robert Gaillard (Tom). *Director-Writer:* Hal Reid. *Studio:* Vitagraph Company of America. *Length:* Approximately 10 minutes.

A variation on the Lincoln clemency theme, *The Seventh Son* also uses a historical event to satisfy the horde of Lincoln admirers. Toward the end of the Civil War, Lincoln sent a letter of condolence to a Mrs. Lydia Bixby of Boston who was reported to have lost five sons in the war. As it turns out, she had lost only two sons, but this did not deter the writer from enhancing the story for the screen.

In the film a widow, Mrs. Grant (Mary Maurice) has already lost six sons in battle when her youngest, seventh son Harry (James Morrison) joins the Union Army. Out of fear and inexperience he deserts during his first battle, is court-martialed, and sentenced to death. Mrs. Grant is, of course, able to convince President Lincoln (Ralph Ince) over the objections of Secretary of War Edwin Stanton (Tefft Johnson) to pardon the boy. In another screen appearance as Lincoln, Ralph Ince gives a credible performance.

The Battle of Bull Run (1913)

Lincoln: Unknown actor. *Director:* Francis Ford. *Other Cast:* Grace Cunard (Grace), Ray Myers (Her Brother), William Clifford (Confederate Colonel), Victoria Forde (May). *Studio:* 101-Bison. *Length:* Approximately 30 minutes.

This film and the name of the actor who portrays Lincoln have been lost. The basic story concerns a female Union spy during the first battle of Bull Run. Lincoln appears in a scene with Secretary of State Seward.

Battle of Gettysburg (1913)

Lincoln: Willard Mack. *Other Cast:* Charles K. French, Herchel Mayall, Walter Edwards, J. Barney Sherry, Ann Little, George Fisher, J. Frank Burke, Enid Markey. *Directors:* Thomas

Ince, Charles Giblyn. *Producer*: Thomas Ince. *Writing Credits*: Charles Brown, Thomas Ince. *Studio*: New York Motion Picture Corp. *Length*: Approximately 50 minutes.

Although there are no known copies of this film in existence, it is considered one of the most important Civil War films of the silent era. Directed by Charles Giblyn and Thomas Ince, probably the most serious rival of D.W. Griffith for being the best of the day, it concentrates on the narrative flow. Differing from Griffith on characterization and the implied symbolism, Ince's direction develops rhythm, emotion, and ideas to keep the story moving.[12] This film mixes a typical North-South love story and the action of the battle of July 1–3, 1863. *Variety* reports that the love story "got lost" and further states, "It isn't history, but it's smashing, thrilling warfare...."

Willard Mack portrays Lincoln giving his Gettysburg address. The use of Mack is somewhat surprising since Ralph Ince, brother of the director, was one of the top Lincoln impersonators of the time and had been used as Lincoln in numerous short silent films earlier than 1913. In addition, from stills Mack does not appear to bear much resemblance to Lincoln.

From Rail Splitter to President (1913)

Lincoln: Francis Ford. *Other Cast*: Grace Cunard, Edgar Keller, Fred Montague. *Director*: Francis Ford. *Writing Credits*: Grace Cunard. *Studio*: Gold Seal, Universal Film Mfgr. Co.

From the title it would appear to be a biopic of the 16th president, but this is another of the missing Lincoln films with little known about the actual film or the actors. It is known, however, that Francis Ford both directs and stars as Lincoln. Furthermore, Grace Cunard wrote the scenario and appears in the film.

Lincoln for the Defense (1913)

Lincoln: Unknown actor. *Studio*: Pilot. *Length*: 10 minutes.

Based on Lincoln's years in legal practice in Springfield just prior to his national political fame, the story involves a young boy accused of murdering his employer. Supposedly the case is to come to trial on the same day, November 2, 1858, that Lincoln is scheduled to debate Stephen Douglas in their run for Congressional office. Lincoln's political advisors try to convince him that to miss the debate will cost him the election.

Lincoln ignores them to defend the boy whose parents are his friends. Quite naturally he is successful in convincing the jury that the death was accidental as the boy defended himself against a brutal employer.

The story is completely fictional. So is the scheduled date of the debates that actually occurred between August and October. Despite his success in the seven debates, Lincoln lost the election even though he received significantly more votes than Douglas. Douglas won the seat by receiving the majority of votes in the Illinois Legislature.

Although the actor who portrays Lincoln is unnamed, he is reported to have done an exceptional job in this fictional but enjoyable film.

Song Bird of the North (1913)

Lincoln: Ralph Ince. *Other Cast*: Anita Stewart (Elida Rumsey). *Director-Writer*: Ralph Ince. *Studio*: Vitagraph Company of America.

By 1913 Ralph Ince had expanded the scope of his involvement in Lincoln films to include both writing and directing as he did for *Song Bird of the North*. Mrs. John Fowle (Anita Stewart) had actually sung for wounded Union soldiers during the Civil War, and this is supposedly her story, under the name of Elida Rumsey. In one unlikely scene Lincoln gives Mrs. Fowle away at her wedding. Ince continues his run as a credible Lincoln.

The Toll of War (1913)

Lincoln: William Clifford. *Other Cast:* Francis Ford, Ethel Grandin (Southern girl). *Director:* Francis Ford. *Writing Credits:* Grace Cunard. *Studio:* 101-Bison. *Length:* Approximately 10 minutes.

By combining two of the favorite silent era Lincoln themes, i.e., the pardoning of a military prisoner and the assassination, director Francis Ford was assured of a real winner. The fact that the story had nothing to do with history is incidental.

Lincoln (William Clifford) pardons a young Southern girl (Ethel Grandin) for spying. After Lincoln is shot in Ford's Theatre he is carried across the street and placed in a bed in a room being rented by the girl.

When Lincoln Paid (1913)

Lincoln: Francis Ford. *Director:* Francis Ford. *Writing Credits:* William Clifford. *Studio:* Kay-Bee. *Length:* Approximately 20 minutes.

In a variation on a regular Lincoln theme, President Lincoln (Francis Ford) is called upon to pardon another soldier. It is payment for an I.O.U. to a mother and her son who sheltered Lincoln during a violent storm that occurred while he was a traveling lawyer in Illinois.

During the Civil War the son is captured and executed as a Union spy by a Confederate general. In a strange coincidence the general's son ends up hiding in the mother's home and, seeking revenge, she sees that he is captured and is sentenced to be executed as a spy.

Having second thoughts about her duplicity, the mother hurries to Washington to try to obtain a presidential pardon for the boy. At first unable to see the president, she produces the I.O.U. and is admitted to make her plea. As would be expected, Lincoln grants the pardon.

Francis Ford, the older brother of John Ford, bears almost no resemblance to Lincoln and generally appears as bad-tempered rather than solemn and sympathetic. He later took lesser roles in his brother's *The Prisoner of Shark Island* (1936) and *Young Mr. Lincoln* (1939).

When Lincoln Was President (1913)

Lincoln: Unknown actor. *Studio:* Pilot. *Length:* 10 minutes.

Another of the numerous Lincoln-as-pardoner films, this one uses the same name, William Scott, for the soldier in the historical case in which Lincoln actually did pardon a soldier sentenced to death for sleeping on guard duty. The difference in this film is that he is standing in for a sick cousin when he falls asleep. After his conviction Scott's aunt, the cousin's mother, convinces Lincoln that Scott was doing a good deed and did not deserve to die. Lincoln agrees and pardons the soldier.

No copies exist of this fictional representation of an actual event in Lincoln's presidency.

With Lee in Virginia (1913)

Lincoln: Hugh Ford. *Other Cast:* Henry King (William Girard). *Director:* Thomas Ince.

Famed Civil War film director Thomas Ince adds a romantic line to this story detailing Robert E. Lee's turning down a position in the Union Army to support his state and join the Confederate Army. After a brief introduction of the romance between Miss Blair and William Girard, President Lincoln's agent is shown offering a major military position to Lee and being rejected. Lee then writes a letter to General Winfield Scott resigning his commission in the Union Army. In the next scene Lincoln (Hugh Ford) appears completely despondent over the news of Lee's refusal as he meets with his advisors to decide about the call-up of more troops.

William Girard (Henry King) becomes a spy for the South and is caught but escapes during the fighting at the First Battle of Bull Run. Miss Blair has also been imprisoned for spying but escapes when she kills a Union officer who assaults her. Her black slave is captured and executed when he takes the blame for the killing.

Hugh Ford is an excellent Lincoln look-alike and his intensity as Lincoln is quite good. Critics of the day raised the question as to why Thomas Ince did not use his brother Ralph in the role.

Lincoln the Lover (1914)

Lincoln: Ralph Ince. *Other Cast:* Anita Stewart (Ann Rutledge), E.K. Lincoln, Logan Paul, Johnny Hines. *Director:* Ralph Ince. *Writing Credits:* Ralph Ince. Catherine Van Dyke. *Studio:* Vitagraph Company of America. *Length:* Approximately 10 minutes.

Directed by and starring Ralph Ince, this film brings to the screen for the first time the early love life of the man who would be the 16th President of the United States. It is not clear that the flyers for *Lincoln the Lover* included these words but they should have.

Based on the known relationship between Lincoln and Rutledge (Anita Stewart), the film has the newly inaugurated Lincoln pondering this in front of a roaring fire in the White House. Although a stilted dramatization, it covers the basic elements of a relationship recalled by those who knew both Lincoln and Rutledge. The two were friends, but she became engaged to a man named John McNeil (or John McNamar) in 1833. McNeil went back East for financial reasons and never returned to New Salem. While waiting for McNeil's return, Rutledge and Lincoln became closer, but their relationship tragically ended when she died, probably from typhoid, in 1835. Ince does his usual excellent job of portraying Lincoln both as a young man and as president.

The Man Who Knew Lincoln (1914)

Lincoln: Ralph Ince. *Writer:* Unknown. Based on "He Knew Lincoln" by Ida M. Tarbell. *Studio:* Vitagraph. *Length:* 10 minutes.

Billy Brown claims to have known Lincoln in Illinois and reminisces about those days in a series of flashbacks. Ralph Ince portrays Lincoln in these fictional events with his usual skill.

Battle Cry of Peace (1915)

Lincoln: William J. Ferguson.
For details, see Chapter 1 on George Washington.

The Birth of a Nation (1915)

Lincoln: Joseph Henabery. *Other Cast:* Henry Walthall (Ben Cameron, the Little Colonel), Miriam Cooper (Margaret Cameron), Mae Marsh (Flora Cameron, the Little Sister), Lillian Gish (Elsie Stoneman), Robert Harron (Tod Stoneman), Ralph Lewis (The Honorable Austin Stoneman, Leader of the House), Raoul Walsh (John Wilkes Booth), Donald Crisp (Gen. U.S. Grant). *Director-Producer-Film Editor:* D.W. Griffith. *Writing Credits:* Thomas F. Dixon, D.W. Griffith. *Music:* Joseph Carl Breil, D.W. Griffith. *Cinematography:* G.W. Bitzer. *Studio:* D.W. Griffith Corp. *Length:* 175 minutes.

Griffith's first masterpiece is a textbook of filmmaking techniques, the best and worst silent of all time, and one of the greatest box-office attractions in the history of motion pictures. From 1915 to 1947, two hundred million people viewed the film in the U.S. and abroad. It is the story of the American Civil War told through two fictitious families. Griffith corresponded with President Woodrow Wilson, sympathizing with his Progressivism that would restore the past as symbolized by the family and the virtue in its sanctity. As Griffith wrote, "*The Birth of a Nation* is not an historical document any more than are Walt Whitman's poems about the [Civil] war or Shakespeare's historical plays."

In Griffith's film on the Civil War, families are represented by the Stonemans who reside in Washington, D.C., and represent Northern Union attitudes, and the Camerons who reside in Piedmont, South Carolina, and represent Southern Confederate attitudes. Of particular interest is Ben (The Little Colonel) Cameron's creation of the Ku Klux Klan after the war to continue Southern supremacy over Blacks that raised much criticism of the film at the time and thereafter. The film's message is literally written in blood: Before riding off to redeem the white South, Klansmen dip their emblems into the blood of a blonde white virgin who has been terrorized to death by a Black brute.

Woodrow Wilson supplied scholarly footnotes for the film, although he is not credited. Wilson called *The Birth of a Nation* "history written in lightning." And his only regret is that is that it is all so terribly true. But the Lincoln scenes, like the others, are not historical: Two of the four scenes concerning Lincoln are based on typical, not specific actions.

In the first scene, barely one minute long, Lincoln signs the first proclamation, calling for 75,000 soldiers. He is sitting, then stands and gets the document, sits again, and signs it. Ten congressmen surround him in what purports to be his office; they leave after his signing. Lincoln then takes off his glasses, wipes his eyes, and assumes a position signifying prayer.

In the second scene, two minutes long but not based on any recorded event, Lincoln again appears sitting in his office receiving visitors. Mrs. Margaret Cameron (Miriam Cooper) comes with Elsie Stoneman (Lillian Gish), seeking "The Great One" to appeal for her wounded and hospitalized son, Ben. He stands to greet the two women, signals "No," then reverses his action and touches Mrs. Cameron's arm. He quickly writes a document and gives it to Mrs. Cameron, who passes it to Elsie Stoneman. They happily depart as more plea-seekers arrive.

In the third scene, also not based on any recorded event, Lincoln meets after the war with Austin Stoneman (Ralph Lewis), the staunch Unionist, who asserts, "[The Confederates'] leaders should be hanged." Ever the conciliator, Lincoln replies, "I shall deal with them as if they have never been away" as the background music "America" swells. Stoneman storms out of Lincoln's office.

In the fourth and final scene, the longest at four minutes and the most important and historically accurate, including the recreated theater, Lincoln arrives at Ford's Theater on April 14, 1865, to see "Our American Cousin" with his wife and another couple. He is greeted with applause, including that of Elsie Stoneman and Ben Cameron who are seated in the front section. During the performance, Lincoln holds his wife Mary's hand and appears rapt in the stagecraft. As the intertitle states, the bodyguard leaves his post to get a view of the play. Griffith then uses one of his innovative techniques, the iris shot, showing John Wilkes Booth (Raoul Walsh), the assassin. To build suspense, Griffith shows Lincoln wrapping his shawl about himself in a typical gesture. Then Booth enters the president's box, shoots him in the head, and leaps to the stage. Turmoil ensues, graphically depicted. The scene concludes with Lincoln's removal from the box.

All these Lincoln scenes reflect Griffith's innovations in filmmaking: underacting, a lexicon of gesture and movement, and key artistic principles of the stage—melodrama, suspense, pathos, and purity. Assisting Griffith was Henabery who played Lincoln and 13 other parts in this film. Born in Nebraska in 1888, Henabery was best known as a director, making 108 films until his death in 1976.

Much of the press in 1915 loved *Birth*. A March 4 *New York Times* account was typical: "A great deal might be said concerning the spirit revealed in ... the unhappy chapter of Reconstruction and concerning the sorry service rendered by its plucking of old wounds. But of the film as a film, it may be reported simply that it is an impressive new illustration of the scope of the motion picture camera.... It made movie-going a middle-class activity."

The Heart of Lincoln (1915)

Lincoln: Francis Ford. *Other Cast:* Grace Cunard (Betty Jason), Ella Hall, William Quinn, Elmer Morrow, Lew Short. *Director-Producer:* Francis Ford. *Writing Credits:* Grace Cunard. *Studio:* Universal Gold Seal. *Length:* Approximately 30 minutes.

Grace Cunard and Francis Ford again unite to present another Lincoln clemency film—with a twist. Cunard wrote the scenario for this black-and-white silent film and stars as Betty Jason, a Southern belle who intercedes with Lincoln on behalf of her father, a Southern colonel sentenced to death for spying. Ford directs the film and stars in the title role. Naturally, Lincoln grants the pardon but complicates it by issuing secret orders to allow the colonel to escape. For allowing this escape, a Northern lieutenant is arrested, but Betty Jason also convinces Lincoln to pardon him.

Ford plays Lincoln well but his performance is overshadowed by his lack of resemblance to the president.

The Heart of Maryland (1915)

Lincoln: Unknown actor. *Other Cast:* Leslie Carter (Maryland Calvert), William E. Shay (Alan Kendrick), J. Farrell MacDonald (Col. Thorpe). *Director:* Herbert Brenon. *Writing*

16—Abraham Lincoln (1861–1865)

Credits: Based on a play by David Belasco. *Studio:* Tiffany Feature Film Co. *Length:* Approximately 50 minutes.

David Belasco, the impresario, wrote a play called "The Heart of Maryland" that was produced and became a hit in New York in 1895. Because of its success it went on the road, starring Mrs. Leslie Carter as Maryland Calvert and was seen throughout the country nearly 3500 times. In 1915 the work became the first film produced by the Tiffany Film Co. and again starred Mrs. Carter. Obviously the story was enticing as it was produced twice again, in 1921 and 1927 under the same title.

It's the story of lovely Southern belle Maryland Calvert (Leslie Carter) whose fiancé Alan Kendrick (William E. Shay) joins the Union army at the outbreak of the Civil War and a Col. Thorpe (J. Farrell MacDonald) who also is in love with Calvert and joins the Rebels. Through normal cinematic (unlikely) circumstances Kendrick is captured by the rebels, and Thorpe sentences him to be hanged as a spy. Calvert helps Kendrick escape and prevents his recapture by acting as a damper on the clapper of a large bell used to call the rebels during an escape. This act of daring seems to be the reason for the success of the play and the film. Needless to say, Calvert and Kendrick live happily ever after.

In the original play there was no Lincoln role and the cast listings in AFI and IMDb do not include a Lincoln character. However, in his book *Abraham Lincoln on Screen*, Mark Reinhart notes an unknown Lincoln actor.

There is also no Lincoln character listed for the 1921 version of the film. See the 1927 version for a discussion of the appearances of both Grant and Lincoln in that release of this film.

The Life of Abraham Lincoln (1915)

Lincoln: Frank McGlynn Sr. *Other Cast:* Nellie Grant (Mary Todd Lincoln), Guido Colucci (Stephen Douglas), Charles Sutton (Mudge Davis), Charles McGee (Edwin McMasters Stanton), James Harris (Gen. Ulysses S. Grant), Robert Kegerreis (Gen. Robert E. Lee), Richard Peer ("Tad" Lincoln), Richard Tucker (John Wilkes Booth). *Director:* Langdon West. *Studio:* Edison. *Length:* Approximately 20 minutes.

All of the important events in the life of Lincoln flash across the screen in this short film made for the State of Illinois in commemoration of the 50th anniversary of the death of Lincoln. There is very little time spent on any single event, therefore resulting in a less than satisfactory episodic film.

For the first time Lincoln is played by a young Frank McGlynn Sr. who for the only time in his long career as a Lincoln impersonator is actually close to Lincoln's age.

The Lincoln Cycle (1915–17) aka The Cycle of Photodramas Based on the Adventures of Abraham Lincoln and aka Son of Democracy

Lincoln: Benjamin Chapin. *Director-Writer:* Benjamin Chapin. *Cinematography:* Walter Blakely, Harry A. Fishbeck, J. Roy Hunt. *Studio:* Benjamin Chapin–Charter Features Corp. *Length:* Each two reels, approximately 30 minutes.

Benjamin Chapin established himself as the premier Lincoln impersonator during the 1910s by appearing as the president in a one-man stage play he wrote, "Abraham Lincoln in the White House." This success, lauded by Mark Twain and John Hay who knew Lincoln, induced him to undertake the production of a series of films highlighting important real or imagined events in the life of Lincoln. In an attempt to at least give the impression of historical accuracy, the films include locations that are central in Lincoln's life such as the White House (reportedly, Woodrow Wilson granted approval to film it there).

As could be expected Chapin was the guiding light for the films as he wrote the scenarios, produced and directed, and starred not only as Lincoln but also as his father Thomas and his grandfather Abraham. Although there is a great deal of confusion in contemporary reporting about the *Cycle*, it appears that Chapin made seven two-reel films; the first, *Old Abe*, was released in 1915. This first release reportedly did quite well at the box office, but Chapin was still unable to get a distributor for the remainder of the series. For this reason on May 27, 1917, he released four additional films at the same time under the following names: *My Mother: The Spirit Man*, *My Father: The Physical Man*, *Myself: The Lincoln Man*, and *The Call to Arms: Humanity's Man*.

Because of the success of the 1917 releases Chapin was able to arrange a distribution contract with Famous Players–Lasky for the remainder of his footage under the title of *Son of Democracy*. Although *Variety* reported that ten films were included in the contract, it appears that only eight were released under the individual titles *My Mother*, *My Father*, *The Call to Arms*, *My First Jury*, *The President's Answer*, *Tender Memories*, *My Native State*, and *Under the Stars*. These eight covered Lincoln's early life up to the years of the presidency.

Chapin died of tuberculosis in 1918, and he was never able to complete his planned total coverage of Lincoln's life. In the copyright of the final two films of the ten in the contract with Famous Players–Lasky it states that Chapin wrote, produced, and directed. However, both contemporary and modern sources indicate that John M. Stahl actually directed.

As noted previously, Chapin stars in each of these films not only as the president but also as his father and grandfather. Even with little makeup Chapin bears a striking resemblance to Lincoln, and his portrayals are consistently excellent, particularly in showing the broad range of seriousness and homespun humor of this western president. In addition, in his portrayals of Thomas Lincoln and grandfather Abraham Lincoln, it appears that Chapin is careful to ensure that they are not just variations of the presidential impersonation. *The New York Times* (May 28, 1917) noted that "Abe's first adventure as advocate for the persecuted is rarely approached in effectiveness."

The films available for viewing are six of the eight released under the *Son of Democracy* agreement:

My Mother: The Spirit Man

Lincoln: Benjamin Chapin (also Tom Lincoln), Charlie Jackson (Lincoln as a boy), Madelyn Clare (Nancy Hanks Lincoln), John Stafford (Carter). *Director:* John M. Stahl.

Abraham Lincoln (Benjamin Chapin), after having been elected president in 1860, leaves Springfield, Illinois, for his boyhood home in Gentryville, Indiana, to visit his old friends before going to Washington, D.C. While in Gentryville, he reminisces about his early years, particularly those with his natural mother Nancy Hanks in Hogenville, Kentucky.

After a scene showing his birth and his mother Nancy (Madelyn Clare) writing his name in the family Bible, a few years are skipped and Abe is fighting with his boyhood enemy, Huck Carter, over who caught a fish. Abe's mother elicits a promise of "no more fighting" by using Biblical examples. To illustrate the importance of reading and writing to Lincoln, the film uses a flashback to show that Abe's father Tom Lincoln (also Chapin) promises Nancy that he will become literate. Over the years Tom has not fulfilled this promise, and Nancy feels that Abe will be the one to use literacy for advancement.

Nancy becomes mortally ill and, before dying, gets Abe to promise that he will win his battles by "love and service" and will no longer rely on fighting. The tenderness between mother and child appears in scene after scene, particularly in her death scene when Abe appears completely distraught.

My Father: The Physical Man

Lincoln: Benjamin Chapin (also Tom Lincoln).

Still talking with his friends in Gentryville, Indiana, Abe tells the story of how Huck Carter, the villain in this series, was dunked in the rain barrel by Tom Lincoln, Abe's father. Tom feels that Abe is wasting his time and coincidentally shirking work around the house by reading all the time. To cure Abe's bad habit, Tom, opposed to "book-larnin,'" takes the books from Abe that had been given to him by his mother. Abe is greatly disturbed by this action both because of his love of reading and because the books were from his mother.

Later, Tom Lincoln is on the verge of being cheated out of his farm by his neighbor Endell Carter, mainly because he cannot read the paper that he is signing. Abe is able to protect his father from being cheated by reading the document to him. After Tom wins a fight with Endell Carter over the paper, he dunks Huck Carter in a rain barrel.

Showing appreciation of Abe's literacy skills, Tom recovers the books that he had taken away and hid in the woods and returns them to Abe. Both actors convey the tension between father and son based on their different approaches to life by their expressions and movements.

My First Jury

Lincoln: Benjamin Chapin.

By the time of this event Abe Lincoln has been inaugurated and settled in Washington. He has become inured to the Civil Service scams and sees the humor in the request from Bill Jenks in Gentryville that he, Lincoln, replace Huck Carter as postmaster. As a result of the postmaster change in Gentryville, Carter tells Lincoln's cousin Dennis Hanks that Abe had stolen a cutting sickle from him.

Hanks writes to Abe regarding this charge, and Abe invites him to Washington to hear the true story of the sickle. Abe informs Hanks that the sickle was lost when Black Jim (a small Negro boy) stole a chicken from the Carters, and Abe decides to help Black Jim avoid punishment. Abe convinces Huck Carter that Black Jim deserves a "trial by jury," and that Abe will defend him. After selecting a jury of farm animals, Huck Carter prosecutes the trial while Abe defends Jim. As expected, Abe Lincoln wins the case.

Back in Washington in 1861, Lincoln tells Hanks where the sickle has been located for all these years. Hanks returns to Gentryville and makes a fool of Huck by telling him where to find the sickle.

Native State (*originally released in 1915 as* Old Abe)

Lincoln: Benjamin Chapin.

In this fictional story, Lincoln runs into the intransigence of his Secretary of War Edwin Stanton who is set on confiscating the property of any Southern sympathizers living in Washington. High on Stanton's list is one Edward Daniel Boone, a veteran of the War of 1812 and a grandson of *the* Daniel Boone.

Shortly after the soldiers begin taking the property from the blind Edward Boone's home, Lincoln arrives and begins to tell Edward that their grandfathers were close friends. His story goes back to pre–Revolutionary War days in frontier Kentucky where there was a major Indian problem.

President Lincoln's grandfather, also named Abe, was working in the woods and his youngest son Tom (President Lincoln's father) was sent to take lunch to him. Unexpectedly, Tom's baby sister followed him, and they both got lost in the forest. Fortunately, they were found by a friendly Indian maiden, Fawn, who protected them.

Fawn was discovered by Crow Eye, a mean Indian, who wanted to scalp the children. In the meantime, all of the white settlers, including Daniel Boone, searched for the children. After numerous adventures, Daniel Boone and Abe's grandfather rescued the children.

After telling of the safety of the children, President Lincoln reverses the confiscation order and Edward Daniel Boone is saved. Although the blind Edward is not sure who his benefactor is, he will undoubtedly find out.

Tender Mercies

Lincoln: Benjamin Chapin.

Again, Benjamin Chapin begins the film with a scene illustrating one of Lincoln's problems as president, the continual crowd of office seekers at the White House. To compound his problem, these pests not only disagree with everything Lincoln is attempting to do but cannot even agree among themselves. Treating them like children, Abe leaves them with a single word to consider: "Union."

As was his habit, the president quite often visits the troops in the field, and after a small skirmish he remarks to a soldier burying his comrade that this action reminds him of the death of his mother when he was a child. He relates to the soldier the story of his mother's death and ties it in with a "My First Jury" scene. The scene is that of Pastor David Elkins arriving to say prayers at Lincoln's mother grave only to find Abe fighting with Huck Carter. Thinking that Abe is at fault, the preacher scolds him and supports Huck.

Huck's father goes off to Abe's house to tell Tom Lincoln of Abe's fighting and gets a face full of corn mush from Tom for his trouble. In the meantime, the preacher overhears Abe praying at the grave and telling his mother what actually happened. From this point on, everything works out well, and Elkins performs a service at the grave the following morning.

Chapin ends this episode with a documentary view of Nancy Hanks Lincoln's grave as it was in 1918. Among his other directorial touches is his use of footage from one episode to another, both refreshing the viewers' memories and saving himself footage.

A President's Answer

Lincoln: Benjamin Chapin.

What appears to be one of the later films in the cycle opens with Lincoln sitting on a park bench with the White House in the background. A title card is used to explain that the White House in Lincoln's time is essentially the same as in Woodrow Wilson's tenure, the time of the filming.

Lincoln is reading a newspaper story about treason spreading in his childhood home area in Southern Indiana. The scene immediately shifts to Gentryville and notes that Abe's old nemesis, Huck Carter, is a Southern spy recruiting troops for the Confederacy. One of his recruits happens to be the son of Pastor Daniel Elkins who had read the prayers at Nancy Lincoln's grave.

As unlikely as it may seem, young Elkins has been captured but is seen walking on the White House grounds by Lincoln who asks, "Who induced you to join the Confederate army?" Before the young man can answer, he is struck by his brutal Union guard and kills the guard in defense.

Elkins Jr. is convicted of the murder and is to be executed. Pastor Elkins and his wife rush to Washington to plead for their son's life and not unexpectedly Lincoln suspends the sentence and paroles the son to his parents.

Two of the Famous Players–Lasky films were not available for viewing. In *The Call to Arms* Lincoln is portrayed during the first few days of his administration. When Fort Sumter is attacked he is forced to call for 75,000 volunteers. *Under the Stars* would appear to be the same film as that released in 1917 under the title *Myself*. In this film, Lincoln is an attorney becoming interested in a political life.

The Magistrate's Story (1915)

Lincoln: Unknown actor. *Other Cast:* Gertrude McCoy (Bess Howard), Richard Tucker (Tom Weldon), Pat O'Malley (John Sterrett), William West (John Sterrett as an Old Man). *Studio:* Edison. *Length:* Approximately 10 minutes.

There are no known copies of this film. It is the basic Lincoln-as-pardoner story with the sweetheart, Bess Howard (Gertrude McCoy), asking Lincoln to show clemency to her fiancé Tom Weldon (Richard Tucker), who fell asleep on guard duty. As usual, Lincoln does.

The Crisis (1916)

Lincoln: Sam D. Drane. *Other Cast:* Eugenie Besserer (Mrs. Brice), Marshall Neilan (Clarence Colfax), Matt B. Snyder (Col. Comyn Carvel), Tom Santschi (Stephen Brice), Bessie Eaton (Virginia Carvel), George Fawcett (Judge Silas Whipple). *Director:* Colin Campbell. *Writing Credits:* Colin Campbell (scenario), Winston Churchill (novel). *Cinematography:* G. McKenzie. *Art Direction:* Gabriel Pollock. *Studio:* Selig Polyscope Co. *Length:* Approximately 40 minutes.

Opening with a stark scene of Lincoln (Sam D. Drane) unchaining a slave, this black-and-white silent film obviously deals with the Civil War, a popular topic since *The Birth of a Nation*. To set the tone, the Lincoln scene is immediately followed by short views of a slave market, an abolitionist meeting, and Lincoln campaigning in Illinois. Based on a popular novel by an American named Winston Churchill, it is the story of two families on opposing sides of the slavery issue in pre–Civil War St. Louis.

Col. Carvel (Matt B. Snyder) and his daughter Virginia (Bessie Eaton) are Southern sympathizers. Judge Silas Whipple (George Fawcett) and his young apprentice attorney Stephen Brice (Tom Santschi) represent the North. Virginia has a suitor, Clarence Colfax (Marshall Neilan), who is also a believer in slavery. Although Col. Carvel and Judge Whipple argue constantly they are obviously the best of friends.

During the period prior to the Civil War the story concentrates on the complications arising from the love triangle of Virginia Carvel, Colfax, and Brice. Virginia basically won't admit that she loves Brice because he is a Black (conservative) Republican. Brice even goes to Illinois to meet Lincoln while he is debating Stephen Douglas, hears the "nation cannot exist half-slave and half-free" speech, and vows he will not forget him.

There is little resolution to the love triangle until Lincoln's election and the beginning of the war. At that point, all of the men except the judge leave for the front; Colfax and Col. Carvel head south; and Brice becomes a Northern officer.

With an exceptionally large cast well directed by Campbell, the film shows serious fighting but gives scant indication as to what is going on or who is winning. At last the audience is told that Colfax has been injured. Brice helps to get him home to St. Louis. Brice, also slightly injured, ends up in St. Louis too. This is opportune because Judge Whipple is dying, and even Col. Carvel gets back to the city to say goodbye to his friend.

After the judge dies, the colonel goes back to the front and is killed by a sniper. Colfax is captured, tried as a spy, and sentenced to die. This presents everybody with an opportunity to test Lincoln's empathy. Separately, and unknown to each other, Brice and Virginia go to Washington to ask Lincoln to free Colfax. Lincoln asks Virginia if she is going to marry Colfax, and she answers, "I don't love him." This gives the president the opening to bring Brice into the room for reconciliation with Virginia. It also allows Lincoln to spare Colfax and to give Virginia a lecture on his love of the South.

Drane does an exceptional job as Lincoln. In the scenes of Lincoln's early years he shows both the fun-loving and the serious nature of the future president. In the Washington scenes the role requires a deeper, more reserved character that Drane handles well.

The Slacker's Heart (1917)

Lincoln: Tony West. *Other Cast:* Edward Arnold (Frank Allen), Byrdine Zuber (Phyllis Montgomery), Phea Catto Laughlin (Bessie Myers), Lillian De Turck (Madame Garcia), T.H. Westfall (President Wilson), Marion Skinner (Mrs. Allen), Gustave Kleeman (Gustave Myers), Chester Woods (Fred Allen), Oscar Briggs (Von Litz), Hilda Holberg (Col. Montgomery). *Director-Writer:* Frederick J. Ireland. *Cinematography:* John J. Pasztor. *Studio:* Emerald Motion Picture Co.

IMDb indicates that this is a World War I propaganda film.

The Birth of a Race (1918)

Lincoln: Unknown actor. *Other Cast:* Louis Dean (The Kaiser), Harry Dumont (Crown Prince), Carter B. Harkness (Adam), Doris Doscher (Eve), Charles Graham (Noah), Ben Hendricks (Fritz Schmidt), Alice Gale (Frau Schmidt), John Reinhardt (Pat O'Brien), Mary Carr (Mrs. O'Brien), Jane Grey (Jane O'Brien), Edward Elkas (Herr Von H.). *Director-Producer:* John W. Noble. *Writing Credits:* George F. Wheeler, Rudolph De Cordova, John W. Noble, Anthony P. Kelly, Tom Bret. *Music:* Joseph Carl Breil. *Cinematography:* Herbert O. Carleton. *Art Direction:* W. Bruce Bradley. *Studio:* Birth of a Race Photoplay Corp. *Length:* 87 minutes.

Although the release of D.W. Griffith's *The Birth of a Nation* in 1915 created a great stir both for its cinematic advances and its racist storyline, the development of this film in response to *Nation*'s racist nature stirs interest of a different type. It has been variously reported that the idea for the film originated with either Booker T. Washington or the National Association for the Advancement of Colored People (NAACP) to present a more positive picture of the black race than that shown in Griffith's highly popular epic.

The original intent of *The Birth of a Race* was to show the progress that blacks had made over time. Unfortunately, by the time the film was released in December 1918, it had turned into a reprise of issues of World War I and had little to do with race. The reviews of the day were scathing. Made with the best of intentions, this film died a quick death. *Variety* reported that the production of the film was highly troubled from the beginning, having an association with numerous production companies including the Birth of a Race Photoplay Corp., Selig Polyscope Co., and the Frohman Amusement Corp. By the time the film was released in December, 1918, there was little evidence that American blacks were to be defended from Griffith's excesses, and it almost seemed that the writers-producers were selling the theme that Americans are a race unto themselves.

In addition to the confusion in the production of the film, there appears to be two different films currently in existence with the same title. The film as reviewed by IMDb and All Movie Guide is in two parts with the first part covering the highlights of the history of the world including Bible stories and ultimately great moments from American history. The second part of the film is a story concerning a German-American family that is torn between their loyalty to Germany and to the United States.

In the print viewed at the Library of Congress, which was 87 minutes long, the second part of the film was missing. Of the 87 minutes, around 77 were episodic coverage of Adam and Eve (with a bit of full frontal nudity), Moses (without any attempt at parting the Red Sea), the passion of Christ, Christopher Columbus, Paul Revere, and the signing of the Declaration of Independence. These episodes are followed by two scenes with Lincoln played by an unidentified actor: the signing of the Emancipation Proclamation, and Lincoln's death. Unfortunately the deathbed scene includes Lincoln awake and speaking, which did not and could not happen. Regardless, the actor does a credible job in imitating the president.

The final scenes seem to have been added to make the film timelier with the ending of World War I. In them, battle scenes are interspersed with a mother and child praying for peace. As an obvious reference to the original intent of the film, there is also a scene of two men plowing a field. One is a black man and the other white, and their farming clothes fade to military uniforms as they march off together to save Europe from the Kaiser.

Madam Who (1918)

Lincoln: Clarence Barr. *Other Cast:* Bessie Barriscale (Jeanne Beaufort), Edward Coxen (John Armitage), Howard C. Hickman (Henry Morgan), Joseph J. Dowling ("Parson" John Kennedy), David Hartford (Alan Crandall), Fanny Midgley (Mrs. Howard), Nick Cogley (Mose), Eugene Pallette (Lt. Conroy), Bert Hadley (General Grant). *Director:* Reginald Barker. *Writing Credits:* Clyde De Vinna, Monte M. Katterjohn, Harold McGrath (story). *Cinematography:* Clyde De Vinna. *Production Design:* Roger Brunton. *Studio:* Peralta Plays, Inc. *Length:* Seven reels.

In one of the stranger Civil War spy tales Jeanne Beaufort (Bessie Barriscale) is a secret agent for the South because both her father and brother were killed by Unionists early in the war. She is captured while spying and forced to marry a masked man with a tattoo on his wrist.

After escaping she begins spying in Washington, D.C., working for Henry Morgan (Howard C. Hickman) who is actually a double agent. Caught again for spying, Beaufort must leave for Richmond. Morgan, who is finally identified as the masked husband, follows her to Richmond, but in a drunken brawl is killed by "Parson" John Kennedy (Joseph J. Dowling) who rescues Beaufort and marries her after the war.

Clarence Barr portrays Lincoln in a brief cameo appearance. As *Variety* (Jan. 18, 1918) reports, the film "has no blood and thunder of the battlefield until near the close. Then there is enough to make the lover of thrills sit up."

My Own United States (1918)

Lincoln: Gerald Day.

In most of these "Man Without a Country" films the mythological Lincoln is always the one to provide clemency. The final scene in this film is no different. Of course, it's too late for Nolan. For details, see Chapter 3 on Thomas Jefferson.

Victory and Peace (1918)

Lincoln: Rolf Leslie. *Other Cast:* Matheson Lang (Edward Arkwright), Marie Lohr (Barbara Towntree), James Carew (Karl Hoffman), Ellen Terry (Widow Weaver), Renee Mayer (Jenny Banks), Hayford Hobbs (Charlie Caine). *Director:* Herbert Brenon. *Writing Credits:* Hall Caine. *Studio:* National War Aims Committee. *Length:* Eight reels.

During World War I, Great Britain established the National War Aims Committee to produce propaganda film to boost public morale. *Victory and Peace* is one of these films. The film was not available for our viewing, but it is assumed that the inclusion of Lincoln (Rolf Leslie) as a character is simply another means of reminding the public of the sacrifices necessary to defeat a vile enemy.

The Copperhead (1920)

Lincoln: Nicholas Schroell. *Other Cast:* Lionel Barrymore (Milt Shanks), William P. Carleton (Lt. Tom Hardy), Francis Joyner (Newt Gillespie), Richard Carlyle (Lem Tollard), Harry Bartlett (Dr. James), Jack Ridgeway (Theodore Roosevelt), Anne Cornwall (Madeline), Francis Haldorn (Elsie). *Director-Producer:* Charles Maigne. *Writing Credits:* Frederick Landis, Charles Maigne, Augustus Thomas. *Cinematography:* Faxon M. Dean. *Studio:* Paramount/Artcraft. *Length:* Approximately 70 minutes.

Lionel Barrymore's most successful stage role was the lead in *The Copperhead* by Augustus Thomas based on a novel by Frederick Landis. Charles Maigne directs this black-and-white silent film. Copperheads, members of "a circle of gold" but treated like their namesakes, drew Northerners dedicated to the Southern cause in the Civil War. Short as is his appearance, Nicholas Schroell lends presidential dignity to the role of President Lincoln who recruits his old Springfield friend Milt Shanks (Barrymore) to serve as spy. Shanks acts as a double agent out of loyalty but never defends himself when captured by the Union and is imprisoned. Through his son's heroism he is pardoned, yet never reveals himself.

With son killed, wife dead, and all but his granddaughter Madeline (Anne Cornwall) despising him, Shanks passes the years in silence. In 1904, his loyal granddaughter refuses marriage to Tom Hardy (William David), grandson of her grandfather's Union accuser Lt. Tom Hardy (William P. Carleton). It is "Reunion Day" and Theodore Roosevelt appears (in archival footage) and in oratory by Jack Ridgeway. In a long confessional scene, Shanks shows his letter from Lincoln about his "great service" as his meeting with Lincoln flashes before his eyes. All is forgiven, all ends happily.

The Land of Opportunity (1920)

Lincoln: Ralph Ince. *Studio:* Selznick Co.

In *The Land of Opportunity* Lincoln is defending a young man accused of a murder he did not commit. Lincoln proves that the witness was lying because the moon was not full and bright as the witness claimed when the murder occurred. The same storyline is used in other Lincoln films and is based on an actual 1858 trial defended by Lincoln. Ralph Ince again portrays the 16th president.

The Highest Law (1921)

Lincoln: Ralph Ince. *Other Cast:* Robert Agnew (Bobby Goodwin), Margaret Seddon (Mrs. Goodwin), Aleen Burr (The Girl), Cecil Crawford (Tad). *Director:* Ralph Ince. *Writing Credits:* Lewis Allen Browne (story). *Studio:* Selznick Co. *Length:* Six reels.

Two men begin chatting with an elderly veteran of the Civil War after a 1920 Memorial Day parade. He tells them a story about Lincoln's belief that intelligent use of humanity was more important than strictly following the law.

President Lincoln (Ralph Ince) and Secretary of War Stanton argue at a Cabinet meeting about Lincoln's continual use of clemency for deserters. After strongly reiterating his position, Lincoln closes the meeting and begins telling his son Tad (Cecil Crawford) a story about a clemency case.

In the case, the mother of three boys, two of whom had been killed in the war, was dying and asking for her third son Bobby Goodwin (Robert Agnew). When his requests for leave are refused, he goes home anyway to comfort his mother. Lincoln sees the correctness of the situation and, in spite of Stanton, pardons Bobby. The elderly man telling the story rises at the end and says that he is Bobby Goodwin.

This is the last film in which Ralph Ince employs his special talents in impersonating Lincoln.

In the Days of Buffalo Bill (1922)

Lincoln: Joel Day, J. Herbert Frank. *Other Cast:* Art Acord (Art Taylor), Duke R. Lee (Buffalo Bill Cody), George A. Williams (Calvert Carter), Jay Morley (Lambert Ashley), Otto Nelson (Alden Carter), Pat Harmon (Gaspard), Jim Corey (Quantrell), Burton C. Law (Allen Pinkerton), William P. Devaull (Edwin M. Stanton), Clark Comstock (Thomas C. Durant), Charles Colby (William H. Seward), Joe Hazelton (Gideon Welles), John W. Morris, Tex Driscoll (Gen. U.S. Grant), Lafayette McKee (Gen. Robert E. Lee), Harry Myers (Andrew Johnson), Ruth Royce (Aimee Lenard), Chief Lightheart (Sitting Bull), William Knight (Jack Casement), Buck Connors (Hank Tabor), M.K. Wilson (Tim O'Mara), William Moran (John Wilkes Booth), Silvertip Baker (Gen. Grenville M. Dodge), Charles Newton (Maj. North),

Alfred Hollingsworth (Chief Justice Chase). *Director-Producer*: Edward Laemmle. *Writing Credits*: Robert Dillon. *Cinematography*: Herbert J. Kirkpatrick, Howard Oswald. *Studio*: Universal Pictures. *Length*: 18 episodes.

In the silent era the serial became a favorite of audiences, and *In the Days of Buffalo Bill* was one of the earliest under pioneer director Carl Laemmle. Unfortunately there do not appear to be any prints in existence. Buffalo Bill's show captured Americans' desire to turn brutal history into make-believe and to feel good about themselves in a western industrial society as the apogee of human development. Thus Buffalo Bill was destined to become one of the most successful mass entertainers in history and receive much screen treatment.[13]

Released on Sept. 11, 1922, and starring new cowboy hero Art Acord as Art Taylor, the episodes reveal the adventures of Taylor as he saves rancher Calvert Carter (George A .Williams) and his daughter Alice (Dorothy Woods) from the clutches of Eastern financier Lambert Ashley (Jay Morley) and foreign agent Gaspard (Pat Harmon). In an 18-episode serial, it is obvious that Ashley and Gaspard cannot be Taylor's only problem so, in addition, there is a Sioux uprising and a gang of vigilantes.

Many historical figures are involved in this typical western. There is another interesting feature in that Abraham Lincoln and Ulysses S. Grant are both played by two different actors; Lincoln by Joel Day and J. Herbert Frank and Grant by John W. Morris and Tex Driscoll. It is assumed that in an 18-episode serial it is possible to switch actors without confusing the audience. In addition to these two presidents a third one, Andrew Johnson, is also included, played by Harry Myers.

Wild Bill Hickok (1923)

Lincoln: Unnamed actor. *Other Cast*: William S. Hart (Wild Bill Hickok), Ethel Grey Terry (Calamity Jane), Kathleen O'Connor (Elaine Hamilton), James Farley (Jack McQueen), Jack Gardner (Bat Masterson), Carl Gerard (Clayton Hamilton), William Dyer (Col. Horatio Higginbotham), Bert Sprotte (Bob Wright), Leo Willis (Joe McCord), Naida Carle (Fanny Kate), Herschel Mayall (Gambler). *Director*: Clifford S. Smith. *Producer*: William S. Hart. *Writing Credits*: William S. Hart, J.G. Hawks. *Cinematography*: Arthur Reeves, Dwight Warren. *Studio*: Famous Players-Lasky Corp. *Length*: 6,893 feet.

Returning from the East at the end of the Civil War, Wild Bill Hickok (William S. Hart) sets aside his weapons and retires in Dodge City. Unfortunately, his retirement cannot last as he is asked to help rid the city of lawlessness. Although gang head Jack McQueen (James Farley) escapes, Hickok tracks him down for a fight to the finish.

In the opening scenes, Washington, D.C., is depicted at the end of the war. These scenes include a brief uncredited appearance of Lincoln.

Barbara Frietchie (1924)

Lincoln: George A. Billings. *Other Cast*: Florence Vidor (Barbara Frietchie), Edmund Lowe (William Trumbull), Emmett C. King (Col. Frietchie), Joe Bennett (Jack Negly), Charles Delaney (Arthur Frietchie). *Director-Adaptation*: Lambert Hillyer. *Producer*: Thomas H. Ince. *Writing Credits*: Agnes Christine Johnston. *Cinematographer*: Henry Sharp. *Studio*: Regal Pictures. *Length*: Approximately 85 minutes.

While the John Greenleaf Whittier poem of the same name appears in the title, this film is inspired by the Clyde Fitch play. Although the Whittier poem had been filmed previously in 1908 and 1915 this is the first time that a Lincoln character is included. This is another story of star-crossed lovers from the North and South. Barbara Frietchie (Florence Vidor) falls in love with Captain Trumbull (Edmund Lowe), a West Point friend of her brother Arthur (Charles Delaney). But she denounces Trumbull when he heads North at the start of the war. When he returns to take over Frederickstown, where the Frietchies live, Barbara realizes her love for him triumphs over her Southern patriotism. A Confederate advance in which Arthur wounds Trumbull prevents their wedding. Because she believes her lover is dying, Barbara hangs the Union flag at half mast out her window as the Confederates march by. She impresses Stonewall Jackson who orders her protection. However, one of Barbara's rejected suitors and Trumbull's rival, Jack Negly (Joe Bennett), wounds her.

Variety's critic asserts that for dramatic brevity director Lambert Hillyer should have ended the film there (Oct. 8, 1924). But he doesn't. Another scene and a closing montage with Lincoln giving the Gettysburg Address unfold. An earlier montage, also not in the play, includes Lincoln contemplating the coming Civil War. George Billings, star of another 1924 film, *The Dramatic Life of Abraham Lincoln*, impersonates the president helping the young lovers get back together.

The Dramatic Life of Abraham Lincoln (1924)

Lincoln: George A. Billings, Danny Hoy (Lincoln at 7). *Other Cast:* Alfred Allen (Gen. George Meade), W.B. Clarke (Thomas Lincoln), Ruth Clifford (Ann Rutledge), Nick Cogley (Simon Cameron), Nell Craig (Mrs. Abraham Lincoln), T.G. Dixon (Gideon Welles), Newton Hall (Tad Lincoln), Jules Hanft (Mr. James Rutledge), Pat Hartigan (Jack Armstrong), William Humphrey (Stephen A. Douglas), Irene Hunt (Nancy Hanks Lincoln), Willis Marks (William H. Seward), Fay McKenzie (Sarah Lincoln), Ida Mae McKenzie (Sarah Lincoln at 10), William F. Moran (John Wilkes Booth), Walter Rodgers (Gen. U.S. Grant), James Welch (Gen. Robert E. Lee). *Director:* Phil Rosen. *Producers:* Al and Ray Rockett. *Writing Credits:* Frances Marion. *Cinematography:* H. Lyman Broening, Robert Kurrie. *Music:* Joseph Carl Breil. *Studio:* Rockett-Lincoln Film Co. *Length:* 120 minutes.

Of the 11 biographical films on Lincoln only two attempt to portray his life in full, D.W. Griffith's *Abraham Lincoln* (1930) and this black-and-white silent film. It treats Lincoln's life in four sections: "The Kentucky and Indiana Period," "The New Salem Period," "The Springfield Period," and "The Washington Period." The *New York Times* (Jan. 31, 1924) considered it one of the ten outstanding films of 1924. Before production, it took months of research for copies of old paintings, etchings, and drawings from which many of the scenes were reproduced. The research contains some errors: Lincoln's Gettysburg Address is treated as improvised. More importantly, the lack of sound omits Lincoln's speeches, crucial in his political life, and his other memorable utterances. The scenes run from Lincoln as a boy, his mother's death, Lincoln as rail-splitter, his meeting Ann Rutledge, and his wrestling Jack Armstrong.

George Billings's strong resemblance to Lincoln overcomes his lack of acting experience. He is considered "splendid" in the touches of kindliness by Lincoln as postmaster of New Salem, and he also is cited by the *New York Times* for his look of "grim, unswervable determination." Nell Craig as Mrs. Lincoln is termed "extremely efficient in her grumbling and also in portraying her ambition for her husband."

The presidency scenes include fighting the war, the pardon of Pvt. William Scott for falling asleep at his post, and the ball to mask Lincoln's desperation over his dying son Tad. Finally, Lincoln signs the Emancipation Proclamation, Sherman marches to the sea, and Lincoln is assassinated.

The Iron Horse (1924)

Lincoln: Charles Edward Bull. *Other Cast:* Winston Miller (Younger Davy), George O'Brien (Davy Brandon), Peggy Cartwright (Younger Miriam), Madge Bellamy (Miriam Marsh), James Gordon (David Brandon Sr.), Cyril Chadwick (Peter Jesson), Fred Kohler (Deroux). *Director-Producer:* John Ford. *Screenwriters:* Charles Kenyon, John Russell. *Cinematography:* George Schneiderman. *Composers:* Erno Rapee, John Lanchbery. *Studio:* Fox Film Corp. *Length:* 133 minutes.

Director John Ford invents what will become the western's clichés with this film of human-interest subplots in the story of the building of the transcontinental railroad following the reconciliation and assimilation theme of Civil War films. In the building of a railroad, metaphor for civilized society, this great American populist director shows the arguments of the working class, especially the Irish; the torn affections of the young woman between her true love and the seemingly successful man; the inevitable traitor; and the hero devoted to family and purpose. Ford also paints a celluloid canvas of beautifully executed shots of natural beauty juxtaposed with masses of people or solitary figures in a wilderness. The black-and-white tinted silent film is considered to be the finest western of the silent era.

The Iron Horse claims to be "accurate and faithful" to the history it conveys. And it does, through the use of a regiment of U.S. troops and cavalry (3,000 railway workmen; 1,000 Chinese laborers; 800 Pawnee, Sioux, and Cheyenne Indians; 2,800 horses; 1,300 buffalo; and 10,000 Texas steers). Amidst these epic proportions stands the personal story of a young man, David Brandon (George O'Brien) from Springfield, Illinois, whom Lincoln (Edward Bull, the very picture of the president) knew as a lad. The lad heads west with his visionary surveyor father (James Gordon) to find a path for a cross-country railroad. Later, in 1862, Lincoln answers all of his cabinet's questions about the folly of signing a bill supporting the railroad during the Civil War. He states he just wants it.

That is the last of the well-portrayed Lincoln in the film, but the lad goes on to serve as a Pony Express rider and surveyor. He suggests a route to the head of the Union Pacific, outlasts the skullduggery of the traitor (the archetype Fred Kohler), survives an Indian attack, and wins the childhood sweetheart. The film ends with an image of Lincoln's head over the title card: "His Truth is marching on."

Wide Open Spaces (1924)

Lincoln: Charles Dudley. *Other Cast:* Stan Laurel (Gabriel Goober), Billy Engle (Phil Sheridan), Al Forbes (General Custer), Mae Laurel (Calamity Jane). *Director:* George Jeske. *Writing Credits:* H.M. Walker. *Producer:* Hal Roach. *Cinematography:* Frank Young. *Film Editing:* Thomas J. Crizer. *Studio:* Hal Roach Studios Inc. *Length:* 20 minutes.

Prior to teaming up with Oliver Hardy, Stan Laurel made *Wide Open Spaces* and other two-reel comedies with Hal Roach. *Wide Open Spaces* was a disaster of a film mainly because of considerable editing. It was filmed as a parody of Wild Bill Hickok and originally named

Wild Bill Hiccough; Pathe would not release it, and Laurel was not available for additional shooting. Thus the cuts and new name. The historical characters including A. Lincoln (Charles Dudley) did not add to the quality of this film.

Man Without a Country (1925)

Lincoln: George A. Billings. *Other Cast:* Edward Hearn (Lt. Nolan), Pauline Starke (Anne Bissell), Lucy Beaumont (Mrs. Nolan), Richard Tucker (Aaron Burr), Albert Hart (Thomas Jefferson), Emmett King (James Monroe), Edward Martindel (Adm. Decatur), Wilfred Lucas (Maj. Bissell), Harvey Clark (Peter). *Director:* Rowland V. Lee. *Writing Credits:* Robert E. Lee (adaptation). *Studio:* William Fox. *Length:* Approximately 100 minutes.

The Edward Everett Hale 1863 story takes another fictitious twist in this dramatic version. American Army Lt. Nolan (Edward Hearn) is exiled from his country when he refuses to arrest Aaron Burr (Richard Tucker). Anne Bissell (Pauline Starke), his sweetheart, tries for a half century to have him pardoned. She approaches Jefferson, Monroe, and finally Lincoln who does pardon him.

Hands Up! (1926)

Lincoln: George A. Billings. *Other Cast:* Virginia Lee Corbin (Alice Woodstock), Charles K. French (Brigham Young), Raymond Griffith (Jack, Confederate Spy), Noble Johnson (Sitting Bull), Montagu Love (Capt. Edward Logan), Marian Nixon (Mae), Mack Swain (Silas Woodstock). *Director:* Clarence G. Badger. *Writing Credits:* Monte Brice, Lloyd Corrigan, Reggie Morris. *Cinematography:* H. Kinley Martin. *Studio* Famous Players-Lasky Corp. *Length:* 50 minutes.

Hands Up! is a silent comedy relying on the skills of Raymond Griffith who plays Jack, a confederate spy vying with a Yankee in search of gold to win the war. The search is instigated by Lincoln (George A. Billings), low on funds as the Civil War continues to rage during 1864.

The opening title states that this is "An historical incident of variation." Varied it is, with serious scenes followed by comic routines in the silent tradition of Chaplin, Turpin, and the Keystone Cops. Of historical import, however, is the opening scene with Lincoln meeting with an agent, Pinkerton, who has found in Nevada "all the gold" Lincoln needs. Lincoln, in rather uncharacteristic bold gestures of fellowship and certainly not leadership, urges Capt. Logan to get the gold. Smiling, Lincoln returns to a cabinet meeting and sits, relaxed, with one foot dangling over the other.

The film segues with this shot to General Lee who sits in his headquarters, a cabin, with one foot dangling over the other. The cabin is shot out from under him. The next scene is in Fort Laramie, billed as the last Union outpost. There, the comic Confederate spy faces a "strictly private execution." He cleverly escapes by encouraging the Union soldiers to shoot at plates, rather than at him.

Soon, "the man from Lincoln," Capt. Logan, arrives for the first of the other three horses he requires for his trip. He runs into the mine owner, Woodstock, and all seems assured until the spy, in the wagon with the needed gold, woos Woodstock's two daughters simultaneously. His repertoire dazzles: card tricks, story reading, and insect killing while Capt. Logan and Woodstock shoot rabbits and Indians.

As might or might not be expected, the spy ends up teaching the Indians the Charleston dance step and eventually takes over the Woodstock Lode mine, blowing it up in what he thinks is destruction but turns out to be a new vein. That event's result is a shot colored gold. All this mayhem ends when the citizens of the mining town post a sign that Lee has surrendered. Their exuberance saves the spy from hanging and terminates in his Chaplinesque solitary walk down the dusty street. This is the last of Billings's appearances as Lincoln and the first available to be reviewed. His looks are reminiscent of the president and his acting, even in this comedy, is a credible representation.

The Heart of Maryland (1927)

Lincoln: Charles Edward Bull. *Other Cast:* Dolores Costello (Maryland Calvert), Jason Robards Sr. (Alan Kendrick), Walter Rodgers (Ulysses S. Grant), James Welch (Robert E. Lee), Francis Ford (Jefferson Davis), Harry Northrup (Joseph Hooker), Lew Short (Allan Pinkerton), S.D. Wilcox (Winfield Scott), Madge Hunt (Mary Todd Lincoln). *Director:* Lloyd Bacon. *Screenplay:* C. Graham Baker (based on a play by David Belasco). *Cinematography:* Hal Mohr. *Studio:* Warner Bros. *Length:* Approximately 60 minutes.

Using the David Belasco play on which the 1915 film of the same name was based, Warner Brothers starred Dolores Costello as Maryland Calvert and Jason Robards Sr. as Alan Kendrick. Belasco and co-writer C. Graham Baker obviously expanded the scope of the story since the cast listing includes President Lincoln (Charles Edward Bull) and Mrs. Lincoln (Madge Hunt), Confederate States of American President Jeff Davis (Francis Ford), and Gen. U.S. Grant (Walter Rodgers), R.E. Lee (Jim Welch), and Winfield Scott (S.D. Wilcox).

The story seems to be much the same as that described in the 1915 film review. Bull plays the role of Lincoln as he had done admirably in John Ford's 1924 film, *The Iron Horse.*

Lincoln's Gettysburg Address (1927)

Lincoln: Lincoln Casewell.

Another of the favorite subjects of films about Lincoln is his address at the Gettysburg cemetery, starting with the 1912 silent film starring Ralph Ince (although a silent film is an odd choice to have a speech as the subject). The Gettysburg Address is also highlighted in the 1922 production by Joseph Tykocinski-Tycociner, a research professor of electrical engineering at the University of Illinois. His colleague Ellery Paine read the address. This is the first film to include sound-on-film technology but never was released to theaters.

This 1927 version, for which very little information is available, is reported by Mark S. Reinhart in his book *Abraham Lincoln on Screen* to have been an early talkie, released the same year as *The Jazz Singer,* and stars a famous Lincoln stage impersonator, Lincoln Casewell. According to Reinhart, his appearance and delivery of the speech is excellent.

Court-Martial (1928)

Lincoln: Frank Austin. *Other Cast:* Jack Holt (Capt. James Camden), Betty Compson (Belle Stone), Pat Harmon (Bull), Doris Hill (General's Daughter), Frank Lackteen ("Devil" Dawson), Zack Williams (Negro). *Director:* George B. Seitz. *Producer:* Harry Cohn. *Writing*

Credits: Mort Blumenstock, Anthony Coldeway, Elmer Harris. *Cinematography:* Joseph Walker. *Film Editing:* Arthur Roberts. *Art Direction:* Robert E. Lee. *Studio:* Columbia Pictures Corp. *Length:* 40 minutes.

While *Court-Martial* follows a familiar formula of Lincoln films—the search for a spy—it takes an unusual twist. President Lincoln (Frank Austin) orders Capt. James Camden of the U.S. Army (Jack Holt) to capture a bandit who is ruthlessly destroying property and personnel of Union forces. As film plots turn, the bandit is beautiful Belle Stone (Betty Compson). This "terror of the wild frontier" is out to avenge the shooting of her father by Union troops on his plantation steps. Upon giving Camden this order, Austin (looking much like Lincoln) slumps, head bowed over his desk, weighed down by his responsibilities over the Civil War.

With more twists and turns than is necessary even for a disjointed western, Camden is finally able to stop the terrorizing and win Belle over. However, she is shot in the final scene uttering melodramatically before she dies, "It wasn't to be." Although disjointed, this is considered an above average Columbia production with fine performances by Austin, Holt, and Compson, and directing by Seitz. The Library of Congress print reviewed runs only 40 minutes, although listed at 75 by IMDb, perhaps explaining its disjointedness.

Two Americans (1929)

Lincoln: Walter Huston. *Director-Writer:* John Meehan. *Studio:* Paramount. *Length:* Approximately 20 minutes.

As reported by Mark S. Reinhart in his book *Abraham Lincoln on Screen*, this film was among the first sound films to feature Lincoln and stars Walter Huston in that role, a year before his appearance in the same role in D.W. Griffith's *Abraham Lincoln*. Supposedly the film concerns the problems that Lincoln encounters when naming U.S. Grant to be commander of the Northern forces. There are apparently no copies of the film in existence and no information available from AFI, IMDb, or AMG.

Abraham Lincoln (1930)

Lincoln: Walter Huston. *Other Cast:* Una Merkel (Ann Rutledge), William L. Thorne (Tom Lincoln), Lucille La Verne (Midwife), Helen Freeman (Nancy Hanks Lincoln), Otto Hoffman (Offut), Edgar Dearing (Armstrong), Russell Simpson (Lincoln's employer), Charles Crockett (Sheriff), Kay Hammond (Mary Todd Lincoln), Helen Ware (Mrs. Edwards), E. Allyn Warren (Stephen A. Douglas), Jason Robards Sr. (Herndon), Gordon Thorpe (Tad Lincoln), Ian Keith (John Wilkes Booth), Cameron Prud'Homme (John Hay), James Bradbury Sr. (Gen. Winfield Scott), James Eagles (Young soldier), Oscar Apfel (Secretary of War Edwin Stanton), Frank Campeau (Gen. Philip Sheridan), Hobart Bosworth (Gen. Robert E. Lee), Henry B. Walthall (Col. Marshall), Fred Warren (Gen. U.S. Grant). *Director-Producer:* D.W. Griffith. *Writing Credits:* Stephen Vincent Benet, John W. Considine Jr., Gerrit Lloyd, D.W. Griffith. *Cinematography:* Karl Struss. *Music:* Hugo Reisenfeld. *Editors:* John Considine Jr., James Smith, Hal C. Kern. *Set-Art Decorator:* William Cameron Menzies. *Costume Designer:* Walter J. Israel. *Studio:* Feature Productions. *Length:* 97 minutes.

This is also known as *D.W. Griffith's Abraham Lincoln*, as well it should be since it was the first talkie of the single most important figure in the history of American film. It embod-

Abraham Lincoln (1930): Walter Huston (left) in the title role of the biopic considers clemency for the unnamed young soldier played by James Eagles (center) in D.W. Griffith's epic next-to-last picture, produced by Feature Productions, Inc. At its time of release it was the only talking picture to encapsulate the entire life of Lincoln, from cradle to grave. (Courtesy of George Eastman House.)

ies Griffith's signature use of cinematic techniques to create art, such as changing camera angles, intercutting, crosscutting, parallel action, camera movement, dramatic lighting, the close-up, the full shot, and rhythmic editing. After *America* (1924) and *Birth of a Nation* (1915), in *Abraham Lincoln* Griffith expands his film subjects to the presidency in what was his next-to-last film.

Larger in scope than many Lincoln films, but not a great Griffith epic, it is criticized as slow, too episodic, and historically incorrect, especially by Mark S. Reinhart in his *Abraham Lincoln on Screen*. Nevertheless, *Abraham Lincoln* features Griffith's beloved spectacle and accurate period detail. Carl Sandburg, fresh from his successful Lincoln biography, *Abraham Lincoln—The Prairie Years*, was replaced by Stephen Vincent Benét in the last drafting of the scenario. However, the final screenplay, written by Griffith and Gerrit Lloyd, follows the life of the 16th president from his birth, his overblown romance with Ann Rutledge, his early prowess in Illinois, his debates with Stephen Douglas, and his efforts to win the war and preserve the Union during the Civil War. Following the assassination, the final scene features cuts from the log cabin to the Lincoln Memorial and ends with a backlit aureole of Lincoln's statue at the Memorial with a chorus singing *The Battle Hymn of the Republic*.

Walter Huston's sober yet slyly witty portrayal of The Great Emancipator, a moving and natural performance, earned enthusiastic reviews. His subtle acting skills show early here as they did in his Academy Award–winning supporting role in *The Treasure of the Sierra Madre* (1948), directed by his son John. Close-up after close-up reveals his fatigue over the war. Moreover, Huston evolved his characterization from eager young lawyer to aged statesman. There is one battle scene late in the war, of Sheridan turning his men around and defeating Lee, but the earlier scene of the retreat at Bull Run with Karl Struss's shots of men marching and horses galloping conveys even better the great Union loss.

Una Merkel, a Lillian Gish lookalike, is perhaps correct for the period and the romantic role of Ann Rutledge but off-putting with her high voice. Kay Hammond as Mary Todd Lincoln, Fred Warren as Gen. Ulysses S. Grant, Hobart Bosworth as Gen. Robert E. Lee, Ian Keith as John Wilkes Booth, and Jason Robards Sr. as Herndon, Lincoln's partner, are most effective.

Two-Fisted Justice (1931)

Lincoln: Joe Mills. *Other Cast:* Tom Tyler ("Kentucky" Carson), Barbara Weeks (Nancy Cameron), Bobby Nelson (Danny), William Walling (Nick Slavin), John Elliott (Mr. Cameron), Gordon De Main (Marshal Houston), Yakima Canutt (Perkins), Pedro Regas ("Cheyenne" Charlie). *Director-Writer:* George Arthur Durham. *Producer:* Trem Carr. *Cinematography:* Archie Stout. *Film Editing:* J. Logan Pearson, Len Wheeler. *Studio:* Monogram Pictures Corp. *Length:* 63 minutes.

This typical western has little to recommend it except a boy named Danny (Bobby Nelson) and his dog Sagebrush. Fortunately, "Kentucky" Carson (Tom Tyler), who has been delegated by President Lincoln (Joe Mills) to keep the West safe during the Civil War, is in town to ensure that justice triumphs over the villain Nick Slavin (William Walling). Director George Arthur Durham, production supervisor of the Tom Tyler unit at Monogram, attempts to direct former silent stars, particularly Walling, with little experience in sound film.

Apparently there is more than one copy of the film in existence with somewhat different scenes. *Variety* reports an opening scene that includes a "crude picturization of Lincoln [Joe Mills] with some of his Cabinet" while AFI did not note such a scene.

The Phantom President (1932)

Lincoln: Charles Middleton.

In this satirical musical comedy, Lincoln (Charles Middleton) appears in a portrait as do three other presidents—Washington, Jefferson, and Theodore Roosevelt—singing a Rodgers and Hart song, "The Country Needs a Man." Similar in appearance and voice to their respective presidents, the actors do an animated rendition, and Middleton appears Lincolnesque. Middleton plays Lincoln in *They Died with Their Boots On* (1941) and Lincoln's father Thomas in *Abe Lincoln in Illinois* (1940). For details see Chapter 1 on George Washington.

The Road Is Open Again (1933)

Lincoln: Charles Middleton.

Lincoln appears in this short about the National Recovery Act with fellow Presidents Washington and Wilson, reading a newspaper about how the NRA has created one million jobs. All the presidents address star Dick Powell, a songwriter, in historically telling terms.

Lincoln (Charles Middleton) says, "I've lived to see the freeing of the slaves, but this is the freeing of the sweat shops." Middleton looks much like Lincoln and speaks in a similar way. For details see Chapter 1 on Washington.

Are We Civilized? (1934)

Lincoln: Frank McGlynn Sr.

Among the many famous leaders of history cited by newspaper publisher Paul Franklin Sr. (William Farnum) is Lincoln, played by the most famous Lincoln portrayer Frank McGlynn Sr. This is the first Lincoln portrayal by McGlynn after a 19-year hiatus. As was the case with Washington, there are no words or acting in these impersonations since a shot of the president is merely flashed on the screen. One of the more interesting aspects of this appearance by McGlynn is that he also plays Felix Bochner, the dictatorial Director of the Censorship Bureau who was the Hitler representation in the film. McGlynn is not known for portraying anyone other than Lincoln, and this good/evil characterization is somewhat surprising. For details, see Chapter 1 on George Washington.

Operator 13 (1934)

Lincoln: Unnamed actor.

The sad state of the Union after its fall at the Second Battle of Bull Run appears on President Lincoln's face as he gazes out a White House window. It's only a one-shot by cameraman George Folsey, but it punctuates his opening montage of the battle. For details, see Chapter 18 on Ulysses S. Grant.

The Littlest Rebel (1935)

Lincoln: Frank McGlynn Sr. *Other Cast:* Shirley Temple (Virginia Cary), John Boles (Capt. Herbert Cary), Jack Holt (Col. Morrison), Karen Morley (Mrs. Cary), Bill Robinson (Uncle Billy), Guinn "Big Boy" Williams (Sgt. Dudley), Willie Best (James Henry), Bessie Lyle (Mammy), Hannah Washington (Sally Ann). *Director:* David Butler. *Producer:* Buddy G. DeSylva. *Writing Credits:* Edwin J. Burke, Edward Peple, Harry Tugend. *Music:* Sidney Clare, Cyril J. Mockridge. *Cinematography:* John F. Seitz. *Film Editing:* Irene Morra. *Art Direction:* William S. Darling. *Set Decoration:* Thomas Little. *Costume Design:* Gwen Wakeling. *Studio:* 20th Century–Fox. *Length:* 70 minutes.

Continuing the "old magnolia" whitewashed portrayal of the Old South (with much female ultra-femininity) and the Shirley Temple-adorable-child tradition of films, this musical comedy is a "Shirley Temple Civil War Family Film." It twists the Lincoln-as-pardoner clemency theme to a heart-rending Civil War North-South reconciliation story making it a "decidedly chummy little war," according to the *New York Times* review (Dec. 20, 1935). This lavish black-and-white production was based on Edward Peple's play.

Set on a Southern Virginia plantation, the action concerns the littlest rebel, Virginia "Virgie" Cary (Shirley Temple) with her stalwart and cheery forbearance (or just her usual sunny film personality) during the devastation of Southern life by the Yankee invasion. Most

16—Abraham Lincoln (1861–1865) 135

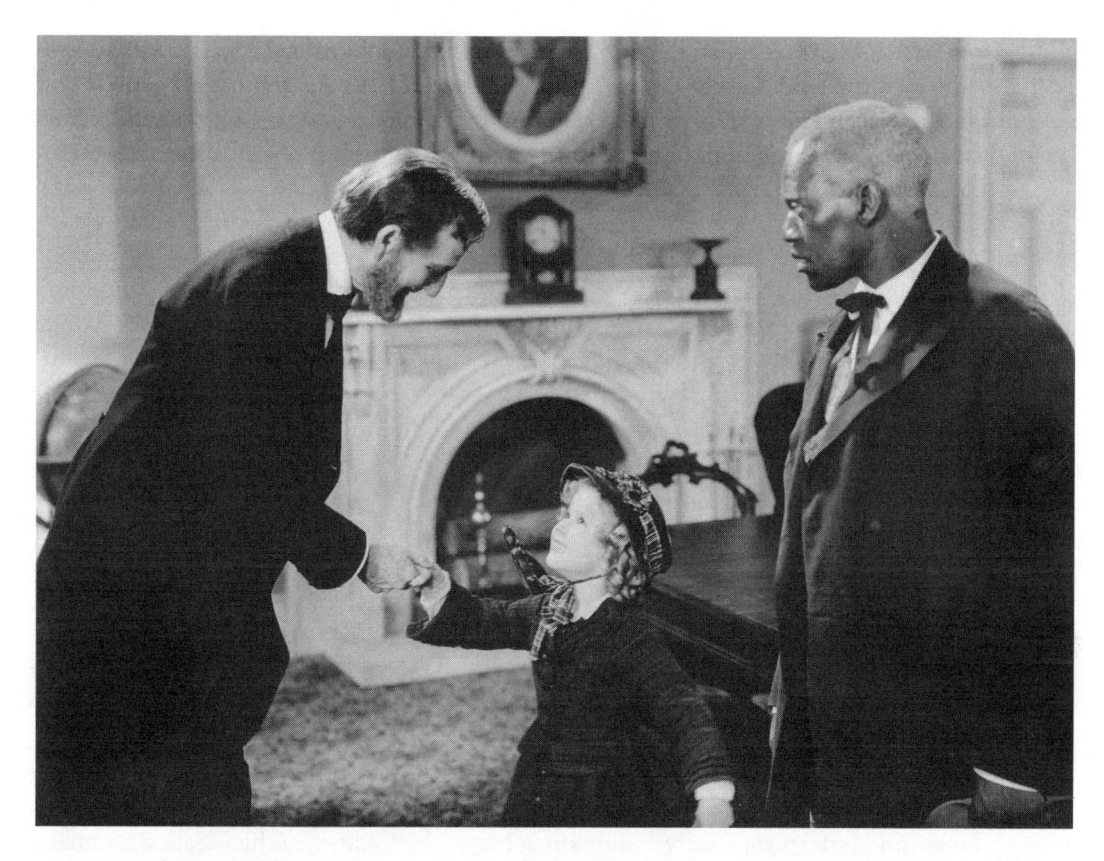

The Littlest Rebel (1935): The most prolific Lincoln impersonator, Frank McGlynn Sr. (left), greets one of the greatest child stars, Shirley Temple, while the top song-and-dance man of the time, Bill Robinson, watches his young mistress persuade the president to grant her Rebel father clemency. John Boles played the father, Capt. Herbert Cary, in this 20th Century–Fox film. (Courtesy of George Eastman House.)

revealing of Virgie's character—and that of the president's—is her scene with Lincoln (Frank McGlynn, Sr.), the only scene of the president in the film, another clemency treatment. She exhibits her honest devotion and Lincoln reveals his lighter side. Virgie suffers the looting and burning of the family plantation, the death of her mother (Karen Morley) as a result of living under debilitating conditions, and the capture of her beloved father (John Boles), Capt. Herbert Cary, a Confederate spy, by the sympathetic Northern Colonel Morrison (Jack Holt). So spunky Virgie (slingshot at the ready as a true-rebel-David vs. a Goliath-of-a-Yankee) decides to take her father's case to the president. She's escorted by the faithful family retainer, Uncle Billy (Bill "Bojangles" Robinson) to the White House. Robinson was one of the great black entertainers of his day and shows it in his dancing with Temple.

The Great Emancipator graciously greets the six-year-old and her devoted slave with whom she has charmingly danced to raise the train fare to D.C. With "The Battle Hymn of the Republic" playing in the background, Lincoln places Virgie on his desk and asks her to "Tell me all about it." She recounts her family's travails as Lincoln in his usual understanding way poses questions to her that the mighty tyke can readily answer. Without lying, an important precept to the littlest rebel, she responds to "What color was his uniform?" and "Did your father write anything down when he was captured?" The great

Lincoln lookalike listens attentively and sympathetically as Virgie carefully answers. Ever adorable, she says she doesn't know if her father is a spy, but "he wouldn't do anything bad." Avuncular Lincoln comments, "How could he with a little one like you." When she describes her mother's death she cries and Lincoln lifts her onto his lap.

Throughout this poignant encounter, Lincoln peels an apple and offers slices to Virgie, some of which she sweetly refuses because "she had the last piece." And Lincoln listens to the stalwart Uncle Billy clarify what happened to this Confederate family.

Lincoln signs Col. Carey's pardon. This is McGlynn's most faceted Lincoln interpretation. The story climaxes with Virgie again singing "Polly Wolly Doodle" to the assembled Union troops, her freed father, and Col. Morrison who's befriended him. Director David Butler ends the film in a typical three-shot embrace of Little Curlytop and her two "fathers." As the *Times* notes, "She continues to be the most improbable child in the world."

The Perfect Tribute (1935)

Lincoln: Charles "Chic" Sale. *Other Cast:* George Ernest (Benjamin Blair), Oscar Apfel (Stratton), Walter Brennan (Stone Cutter), William Henry (Soldier), Claude King (Everett), William V. Mong (Old Story Teller), Edward Norris (Orderly). *Director:* Edward Sloman. *Writing Credits:* Mary Raymond, Shipman Andrews, Ruth Cummings. *Cinematography:* Jackson Rose. *Studio:* MGM. Length: 20 minutes.

This really is a "perfect" little short with the script by Ruth Cummings from a 1906 story of the same name by Mary Raymond Shipman Andrews. It's about the audience reaction to Lincoln's Gettysburg Address. Lincoln's played by Charles "Chic" Sale who give a credible performance although he is known for his comic roles. He appears very serious, very melancholy, and very much like the Lincoln of our current myth.

The story is told in flashback by an Old Story Teller (William V. Mong) to a Stone Cutter (Walter Brennan). It concerns Lincoln, at home with Mary, broken-hearted about the poor reception of his Gettysburg Address. She asks if he's seen the morning newspaper and if he thought a little walk would be good. He takes a walk and bumps into a Southern boy named Benjamin Blair (George Ernest) who is seeking a lawyer to write a will for his dying older brother.

Next Lincoln appears visiting the Washington prison hospital in the room of the brother, Capt. Blair, a blind Confederate soldier (William Henry), resting in his bed, blindfolded. He dictates his will to the unknown lawyer, then turns to his guest and comments on the news of the day, declaring Lincoln's Gettysburg Address "one of the great speeches in history.... You can't applaud a speech like that," he continues, "It would have been sacrilege ... the most perfect tribute was the crowd's lack of applause."

Blair then recites the speech. Lincoln, reading, drops his paper, and finishes the speech, agreeing, "I believe it's a good speech." He concludes, stating, "We're not Northerners, we're not Southerners, we're Americans ... and I am Abraham Lincoln, your friend" as the background music, "America," swells and the soldier dies, seeming to have given the president the will to go on.

Different from the original story that ends without either brother knowing Lincoln's identity, this version is sentimental fiction and questionable history. The audience did applaud his Gettysburg Address but not to the extent Lincoln wished.

The Silk Hat Kid (1935) aka The Lord's Referee

Lincoln: Sidney Miller.

Sidney Miller portrays Lincoln in a short scene in this urban drama. For details, see Chapter 1 on Washington.

Cavalry (1936)

Lincoln: Budd Buster (also Wagon Boss Jake). *Other Cast:* Bob Steele (Capt. Ted Thorpe), Frances Grant (Betty Lee Harvey), Karl Hackett (Gavin Rance), Hal Price (Horace Leeds), Earle Ross (Col. Lafe Harvey), Edward Cassidy (Bart Haines), William Welsh (Gen. John Harvey). *Director:* Robert N. Bradbury. *Producer:* A.W. Hackel. *Writing Credits:* Robert N. Bradbury, George H. Plympton. *Cinematography:* Bert Longnecker. *Film Editing:* Roy Cline. *Studio:* Republic Pictures Corp. *Length:* 63 minutes.

The Civil War is over but President Lincoln (Budd Buster who also plays Wagon Boss Jake) is still alive and sends Capt. Ted Thorpe (Bob Steele) to protect a telegraph line that a group of Confederates, hoping to form an independent nation, attempt to take over. Thorpe finds himself involved in protecting a wagon train from Indians, helping a blind ex–Confederate general, and generally sustaining the action until the cavalry arrives to stop any damage to the new telegraph line.

This typical 30s western has an appearance of Lincoln (in shadow) by Budd Buster mainly to set the stage for the development of the storyline.

Hearts in Bondage (1936)

Lincoln: Frank McGlynn Sr. *Other Cast:* James Dunn (Kenneth), Mae Clarke (Constance), David Manners (Raymond), Charlotte Henry (Julie), Henry B. Walthall (Buchanan), Fritz Leiber (Ericsson), George Irving (Commodore Jordan), Irving Pichel (Secretary of War Sumner Welles), J.M. Kerrigan (Paddy), Ben Alexander (Eggleston), Oscar Apfel (Capt. Gillman), Clay Clement (Worden), Douglas Wood (Farragut), Bodil Rosing (Mrs. Adams), Erville Alderson (Jefferson Davis), John Hyams (Bushnel), Etta McDaniel (Mammy), Warner Richmond (Bucko), Lloyd Ingraham (Timekeeper), George "Gabby" Hayes (Ezra). *Director:* Lew Ayres. *Producers:* Nat Levine, Herman Schlom. *Writing Credits:* Karl Brown, Olive Cooper, Wallace MacDonald, Bernard Schubert. *Music:* Hugo Riesenfeld, Marlin Skiles. *Cinematography:* Jack A. Marta, Ernest Miller. *Film Editing:* Ralph Dixon. *Studio:* Republic Pictures Corp. *Length:* 72 minutes.

The epic sea battle between the USS Monitor and the Merrimac serves as the basis for this Civil War love story that was the only Hollywood feature directed by Lew Ayres. Using a typical Civil War plot, Kenneth Reynolds (James Dunn) is a Northern naval officer engaged to Constance Jordan (Mae Clarke) whose brother Raymond (David Manners) joins the Confederate navy to be with his fiancée Julie Buchanan (Charlotte Henry).

Raymond is an officer working on the iron cladding of the Confederate's Merrimac, and Kenneth is involved with John Ericsson (Fritz Leiber) in the design and construction of the Northern ironclad, the Monitor. Both ships are completed around the same time and meet in the battle of Norfolk. After a grand cinematic ocean batttle, the Monitor wins, but Raymond is killed. Constance cannot forgive Kenneth for his role in Raymond's death until they meet President Lincoln (Frank McGlynn Sr.) whose strong arguments for peace change her mind.

Variety says that McGlynn's Lincoln impersonation shows "rare perception." The stars of the film, however, are Republic's special-effects masters Howard and Theodore Lydecker whose scale models of the ships confront each other in realistic, exciting, and convincing force.

The Prisoner of Shark Island (1936)

Lincoln: Frank McGlynn Sr. *Other Cast:* Warner Baxter (Dr. Samuel Mudd), Gloria Stuart (Peggy Mudd), Claude Gillingswater (Col. Dyer), Arthur Byron (Mr. Erickson), Harry Carey (Commandant of Fort Jefferson ["Shark Island"]), Francis McDonald (John Wilkes Booth), O.P. Heggie (Dr. MacIntyre), John Carradine (Sgt. Rankin), Leila McIntyre (Mary Todd Lincoln). *Director:* John Ford. *Producers:* Darryl F. Zanuck, Nunnally Johnson. *Writing Credits:* Nunnally Johnson. *Music:* R.H. Bassett, Hugo Friedhofer. *Cinematography:* Bert Glennon. *Film Editing:* Jack Murray. *Art Direction:* William Darling. *Costume Design:* Gwen Wakeling. *Studio:* 20th Century–Fox. *Length:* 96 minutes.

One of the most historically inaccurate of films about Lincoln, *The Prisoner of Shark Island* was remade as *Hellgate* (1952) and a TV movie, *The Ordeal of Dr. Mudd* (1980), in efforts to clear the name of the doctor involved in the Lincoln assassination. So deceitful was Dr. Samuel "Sam" Alexander Mudd about his actual relationship with John Wilkes Booth that he inspired the phrase, "Your name is mud." The current perception of Mudd's innocence is due to 70 years of efforts by Dr. Richard Dyer Mudd, his grandson.

As written by Nunnally Johnson and co-produced with Darryl F. Zanuck, the film presents Mudd (Warner Baxter) as innocent of any relationship with Booth except for setting his broken leg. Yet, Mudd is tried by a military tribunal told not to be influenced by "law or reasonable doubt," escapes hanging, and suffers the cruelty of Confederate hater Sgt. Rankin (John Carradine) in Fort Jefferson on Shark Island in the Dry Tortugas. Although the film is early in the distinguished career of John Ford, it benefits from expressionist passages, especially in the prison: the shots of the entrance with "Leave hope who enter here," the sharks feeding around the prison's moat, the "hell hole" where Mudd is punished. Despite the efforts of his wife, Peggy (Gloria Stuart), Mudd is released only after he takes over the medical duties of the prison's deceased doctor during a yellow fever epidemic. How Mudd succeeds is not depicted and historically suspect considering the medicine available at the time.

Frequent Lincoln impersonator Frank McGlynn Sr. conveys the relief of the war-weary president when he appears on the White House balcony during victory celebrations. "You want a speech," the sensitive leader says. "I must have opportunity to think ... as undue importance might be given." As president and commander, he asks for the playing of "Dixie," the South's song and the Union's "contraband of war," he says. Later, in the Ford Theatre scene, McGlynn, seated in a larger-than-reality box with Mary (Leila McIntyre), laughs at *Our American Cousin*, then slumps and drops his hand (filmed in close-up) upon the shot of Booth. A gauze curtain draws around Lincoln, revealing only an impression of the man now made myth.

Trailin' West (1936) aka On Secret Service

Lincoln: Robert Barrat. *Other Cast:* Dick Foran (Lt. Rod Colton), Paula Stone (Lucy Blake), Bill Elliott (Jefferson Duane), Addison Richards (Curley Thorne), Joseph Crehan

(Col. Douglas), Fred Lawrence (Lt. Dale), Eddie Shubert (Happy Simpson), Henry Otho (Hawk), Stuart Holmes (Edwin M. Stanton), Milton Kibbee (Henchman Steve), Carlyle Moore (Hotel Clerk), Edwin Stanley (Maj. Pinkerton), Jim Thorpe (Black Eagle). *Director:* Noel Smith. *Producer:* Bryan Foy. *Writing Credits:* Anthony Coldeway. *Music:* M.K. Jerome, Jack Scholl, Howard Jackson. *Cinematography:* Sidney Hickox, Ted D. McCord. *Film Editing:* Frank McGee. *Art Direction:* Hugh Reticker. *Costume Design:* Milo Anderson. *Studio:* First National Pictures Inc., Warner Bros. *Length:* 56 minutes.

Variety describes this film as a throwback to the silent era with Indians, spies, renegades, and fistfights rather than gun fights. During the Civil War, President Lincoln (Robert Barrat) sends Secret Service Agent Lt. Rod Colton (Dick Foran) to Kent City to investigate Southern sympathizers. With normal western unbelievability, Colton loses his credentials, and they are used by Jefferson Duane (Bill Elliott) to learn about the big gold shipment.

Colton goes undercover in a saloon job to not only investigate the Confederate spies but to sing two nondescript songs and fall in love with Lucy Blake (Paula Stone). With a good deal of "overhearing" on both sides, the Union is saved in Kent City, and Lucy (who turns out to be a Union spy) and Foran return to Washington. Robert Barrat is reported by *Variety* as being "an almost believable Lincoln" in his short scene.

Courage of the West (1937)

Lincoln: Albert Russell. *Other Cast:* Bob Baker (Jack Saunders), Lois January (Beth Andrews), J. Farrell MacDonald (Buck Saunders), Harry Woods (Al Wilkins), Fuzzy Knight (Hank Givens), Carl Stockdale (Rufe Lambert). *Director:* Joseph H. Lewis. *Producer:* Trem Carr. *Writing Credits:* Norton S. Parker. *Cinematography:* Virgil Miller. *Film Editing:* Charles Craft. *Studio:* Universal Pictures. *Length:* 56 minutes.

This western served as the debut for Bob Baker as Jack Saunders, head of the Free Rangers. In the opening scene President Lincoln (Albert Russell) appoints Buck Saunders (J. Farrell MacDonald) to be head of the newly established Free Rangers whose main task is to protect gold shipments coming from the West to finance the Civil War. Physically, Russell is a passable Lincoln, but his acting is not. One of the first shipments is robbed by Al Wilkins (Harry Woods) and his gang. Everyone involved is killed except Buck Saunders. Buck swears revenge and ultimately captures Wilkins. But before that, assuming Wilkins has been hung, Buck adopts Wilkins's son Jack and raises him in the spirit of the Free Rangers. Eighteen years go by and Jack is the head of this white-hatted pinto-riding group, still protecting trains and Wells Fargo from gangs of thieves.

As is the case in this genre of western, Wilkins turns out to have escaped hanging and is still a bad guy. However, in the end, he discovers Jack's true identity and his fatherly conscience makes him change his life-long stealing ways before he is shot in a battle while working with Jack.

John Ericsson—Victor at Hampton Roads (1937)

Lincoln: John Ericsson. *Other Cast:* Victor Sjostrom (John Ericsson), Marta Ekstrom (Amelia Ericsson), Anders Henrikson (Taylor), Hilda Borgstrom (Ann Cassidy), Carl Barcklind (Stephen Mallory), Marianne Aminoff (Mary Mallory), Kotti Chave (Lieut. James Kerrigan), Edvin Adolphson (Commander Sanders), Ivar Kage (Harry Delamater), Olof

Winnerstrand (Commander Smith), Richard Lund (Commander Paulding), Eric Rosen (Capt. Davis), Sigud Wallen (Karl Petterson), Helga Gorlin (Jenny Lind). *Director:* Gustaf Edgren. *Writing Credits:* Gustaf Edgren, Oscar Rydqvist. *Music:* Eric Bengtson. *Cinematography:* Ake Dahlqvist. *Film Editing:* Edvin Hammarberg. *Art Direction:* Arne Akermark. *Studio:* Svensk Filmindustri AG. *Length:* 94 minutes.

Produced entirely in Sweden, this film tells the story of Swedish inventor John Ericsson (Victor Sjostrom, one of the most famous Swedish directors) and his involvement in the construction of the *Monitor* during the Civil War. Ericsson had a long list of inventions in the locomotive field in both Sweden and England before moving to America in 1839. His leadership in the development of the *Monitor* has been noted in a number of films and TV productions.

To boost audience interest the writers include a romance between Confederate Lt. James Kerrigan (Kotti Chave) and Amelia Ericsson (Southern belle Marta Ekstrom). To illustrate the importance of the *Monitor* project to the Northern cause, Lincoln (portrayed by an actor named John Ericsson) makes a cameo appearance.

The Man Without a Country (1937)

Lincoln: Charles Middleton.

In this classic based on clergyman and author Edward Everett Hale's story of the same name, Lt. Philip Nolan (John Litel), a supporter of Aaron Burr's desire to establish a new country, is exiled from the United States. His wife, Marian Morgan (Gloria Holden), spends years seeking a pardon for "The only man I could ever love." She first visits President James Monroe, then President Andrew Jackson, and later President Abraham Lincoln (Charles Middleton) in the White House. Standing, hands characteristically on his lapels, Lincoln tells Morgan he has "good news. I've arranged for the return of Philip Nolan to this country." Morgan falls asleep in her chair as "Beautiful Dreamer" plays in the background. Her husband soon dies with the American flag he made hidden under his pillow. For complete details, see Chapter 5 on James Monroe.

The Plainsman (1937)

Lincoln: Frank McGlynn, Sr. *Other Cast:* Gary Cooper (Wild Bill Hickok), Jean Arthur (Calamity Jane), James Ellison (Buffalo Bill Cody), Charles Bickford (John Latimer), Helen Burgess (Louisa Cody), Porter Hall (Jack McCall), Paul Harvey (Yellow Hand), Victor Varconi (Painted Horse), John Miljan (Gen. George A. Custer), Anthony Quinn (Cheyenne Indian). *Director-Producer:* Cecil B. DeMille. *Screenplay:* Waldemar Young, Harold Lamb, Lynn Riggs, Jeanie MacPherson (based on the stories *Wild Bill Hickok* by Frank J. Wilstach and *Prince of the Pistoleers* by Courtney Riley Cooper, Grover Jones). *Cinematography:* Victor Milner, George Robinson. *Musical Score:* George Antheil. *Editor:* Anne Bauchens. *Music Director:* Boris Morros. *Art Directors:* Hans Dreier, Roland Anderson. *Set Director:* A.E. Freudeman. *Costumes:* Natalie Visart, Dwight Franklin, Joe De Yong. *Special Effects:* Gordon Jennings, Farciot Edouart, Dewey Wrigley. *Studio:* Paramount. *Length:* 113 minutes.

Put Lincoln, Wild Bill Hickok, Calamity Jane, Buffalo Bill Cody, and hordes of Cheyenne Indians in a Cecil B. DeMille film and what do you get? "An entertaining compression of many years and many lives," as the title card states. You do not get history.

Lincoln (Frank McGlynn Sr.) opens the film with a close-up of his meeting with his Cabinet and Speaker of the House Schuyler Colfax (all uncredited) on the eve of his assassination. Colfax cites a newspaper about the possibilities of the West for the post-war labor problems. Lincoln agrees, saying that *some* men are coming home. Several Cabinet members raise the dangers of Indian attacks. Lincoln stresses, in a most thoughtful way, "The frontier must be made safe for the plough." He then waxes like Carl Sandburg on the places where soldiers can settle. The discussion ends when Mary Lincoln interrupts to tell Lincoln they must leave for Ford's Theater.

In reality, Lincoln did meet with Colfax earlier that day to discuss Western mining profits as possibilities for reducing the national debt. They also met that evening. The Cabinet and Gen. Grant met with Lincoln that morning, but Western expansion was not discussed, Moreover, the setting for the final scenes of the film, the Badlands of South Dakota, is far from what appears on screen.

There is no better DeMille spectacle than thousands of Indians attacking Hickok, Cody, and a band of soldiers awaiting help from Custer, and the action provides suspense. Hickok (Gary Cooper) single-handedly stops John Lattimer (Charles Bickford) from continuing gun sales to Indians. Calamity Jane (Jean Arthur) offers a hard-boiled love interest to his equally hard-boiled gunman. In her memoirs, Calamity Jane says she was a scout with Hickok and captured his killer, Jack McCall. But she was en route with her family from Missouri to Montana in 1865, the time of this film As for the historical accuracy of Hickok, he also says Calamity Jane was a scout with him. But his death by McCall avenged the death of McCall's brother, not gun smuggling.

One of the film's other historical lowlights is Anthony Quinn (DeMille's son-in-law) as a Cheyenne Indian telling in the Cheyenne language the story of Custer's death at Little Big Horn.

Stand-In (1937)

Lincoln: Charles Middleton. *Other Cast:* Leslie Howard (Atterbury Dodd), Joan Blondell (Lester Plum), Humphrey Bogart (Douglas Quintain), C. Henry Gordon (Ivor Nassau), Alan Mowbray (Koslofski), Marla Shelton (Thelma Cheri), Jack Carson (Potts). *Director:* Tay Garnett. *Producer:* Walter Wanger. *Screenwriter:* C. Graham Baker, Glen Towne. *Cinematographer:* Charles Clarke. *Composers:* Heinz Roemheld, Alfred Newman, David Klatzin. *Editors:* Otho Lovering, Dorothy Spencer. *Art Director:*Alexander Toluboff. *Studio:* Walter Wanger Productions, Inc. *Length:* 91 minutes.

You know you are in Hollywood when a stand-in for Abraham Lincoln (Charles Middleton) answers the door at a rooming house. He's waiting for a remake of *The Gettysburg Address* in which he starred but which he does not remember. It's "C-i-v-i-l" War says Atterbury Dodd (Leslie Howard), comporting himself as the noble Britisher, ever brains over brawn. He makes the correction because he's a brilliant mathematician, out to save Colossal Studios for his wealthy banker client. But he's in a London fog about Shirley Temple and Clark Gable

The course of this Hollywood comedy is less adulating than *A Star Is Born* (1937) of the same year yet subdued in sexual and anti-business overtones according to PCA (Production Code Authority) suggestions. To list the cast is to understand the film. It stars the honest stand-in, Lester Plum (Joan Blondell); the ruthless producer, Ivor Nassau (C. Henry

Gordon); the brilliant but alcoholic producer, Doug Quintain (Humphrey Bogart); the snake of an untalented star, Thelma Cheri (Marla Shelton); and the temperamental foreign director, Koslofski (Alan Mowbray).

Tay Garnett directs, nine years before his masterpiece, *The Postman Always Rings Twice*. He got this mood right, too, as Dodd says, "The only thing that matters is to be true to yourself."

Victoria the Great (1937)

Lincoln: Percy Parsons. *Other Cast:* Anna Neagle (Queen Victoria), Anton Walbrook (Prince Albert), Walter Rilla (Prince Ernest), Mary Morris (Duchess of Kent), H.B. Warner (Lord Melbourne), Felix Aylmer (Lord Palmerston). *Director-Producer:* Herbert Wilcox. *Writing Credits:* Miles Malleson, Charles de Grandcourt. *Music:* Anthony Collins. *Cinematography:* William V. Skall, Freddie Young. *Film Editing:* Jill Irving. *Production Design:* Tom Hesslewood, Doris Zinkeisen. *Art Direction:* Lawrence P. Williams. *Studio:* Imperator. *Length:* 112 minutes.

A British star vehicle and a spectacle, *Victoria the Great* traces Victoria's life from her 1837 coronation to her Jubilee celebration 60 years later. As the beloved Queen Victoria, Anna Neagle demonstrates why she was voted one of "the most durable leading actors" and the United Kingdom's best-loved star for seven straight years in the 40s. She was discovered and developed into this leading screen star position by producer, director, and husband Herbert Wilcox. Wilcox directs her, as he had in all but two of her films. He achieves a majestic performance from Neagle and an epic portrayal of royal life in all its splendid castles. He varies the grand depiction of royal splendor, in Technicolor for the Jubilee, to revealing personal scenes between Victoria and Albert at their meeting and in Albert's trying to establish his position with a monarch who happens to be his young wife.

The close collaboration that the couple develops appears when they work together to send a "temperate and conciliatory, courteous and friendly" message to American President Lincoln regarding the boarding of a British vessel by an American naval party. The British vessel had American Confederates aboard and was boarded by Unionists. Lord Palmerston tells the Queen that the "honor of the country is at stake." She confronts him with both his disobedience to the crown and his pushing the country toward war with the U.S. and vows to abdicate if it happens again. Albert spends the night crafting the conciliatory letter. As Lincoln receiving the message, Percy Parsons distinguishes himself especially with his voice, similar to the president's. The setting for this scene equals others in the film for its elegant depiction of the Oval Office.

After this and Wilcox and Neagle's subsequent film, *Sixty Glorious Years* (1938), the couple came to the United States for RKO in 1939 with less success.

Wells Fargo (1937)

Lincoln: Frank McGlynn Sr. *Other Cast:* Joel McCrea (Ramsay MacKay), Frances Dee (Justine), Lloyd Nolan (Del Slade), Porter Hall (James Oliver), Bob Burns (Hank York). *Director-Producer:* Frank Lloyd. *Writing Credits:* Gerald Geraghty, Frederick J. Jackson. *Music:* Ralph Freed, Burton Lane, Victor Young. *Cinematography:* Theodor Sparkuhl. *Film Editing:* Hugh Bennett. *Art Direction:* Hans Dreier, John Goodman. *Costume Design:* Edith Head. *Studio:* Paramount Pictures. *Length:* 97 minutes.

Using an episodic approach that the director, Frank Lloyd, had a tendency to employ, this film shows the growth of Wells Fargo as a transportation-banking company paralleling the growth of the United States into a continental country. The film and the company starts in Buffalo, New York, in 1840 (although Wells Fargo's current history notes the company was founded in California in 1852). In the persona of Ramsay MacKay (Joel McCrea) the company extends its service to St. Louis. By 1852 it extends all the way to San Francisco.

Two years later Wells Fargo has grown to be a major banker and saves the city of San Francisco by barely meeting depositors' demands during a panic caused by a gold mine failure. In 1860 the company is awarded the overland mail contract by the U.S. government. MacKay and his sidekick (one must have a sidekick in a western) Hank York (Bob Burns) establish more than 100 way stations across the southern route for use by Wells Fargo stages and its Pony Express. The problems with delivery, particularly with Indians, are most graphically filmed.

A presidential appearance occurs when MacKay is called to Washington, and President Lincoln (Frank McGlynn Sr.) stresses the importance of Wells Fargo's gold shipments to the Federal cause. McGlynn does his usual impeccable job as the president, but the incident never could have happened. MacKay returns to California and, in spite of Civil War–related family problems with his Southern bride, Justine Pryor MacKay (Frances Dee, McCrea's real-life wife), overcomes the Confederate seizure of gold shipments.

There is a second Lincoln appearance at war's end, showing him at his desk writing a letter concerning Reconstruction.

Western Gold (1937) aka *The Mysterious Stranger*

Lincoln: Frank McGlynn Sr. *Other Cast:* Smith Ballew (Bill Gibson), Heather Angel (Jeannie Thatcher), LeRoy Mason (Fred Foster), Howard C. Hickman (Thatcher), Ben Alexander (Bart), Otis Harlan (Jake), Victor Potel (Jasper), Lew Kelly (Ezra), Al Bridge (Holman), Tom London (Clem). *Director:* Howard Bretherton. *Producer:* Sol Lesser. *Writing Credits:* Forrest Barnes, Earle Snell, Harold Bell Wright. *Music:* Arthur Lange. *Cinematography:* Harry Neumann. *Art Direction:* F. Paul Sylos. *Studio:* 20th Century–Fox, Principal Productions Inc. *Length:* 57 minutes.

Smith Ballew plays Bill Gibson, a nightclub crooner turned singing cowboy in this western story about stopping the gold shipment. He must prevent Northern gold from being stolen by Southern spies. Besides confronting the familiar problems, he must face having to arrest his lifelong pal Foster (LeRoy Mason).

Mark S. Reinhart in his *Abraham Lincoln on Screen* notes two historically inaccurate appearances of Frank McGlynn Sr. as Lincoln: the first conferring with his Cabinet about the gold, the second meeting with the Army sergeant at his camp.

Of Human Hearts (1938)

Lincoln: John Carradine. *Other Cast:* Walter Huston (Ethan Wilkins), James Stewart (Jason Wilkins), Beulah Bondi (Mary Wilkins), Guy Kibbee (George Ames), Charles Coburn (Dr. Charles Shingle), Ann Rutherford (Annie Hawks), Gene Lockhart (Quid, the Janitor). *Director-Producer:* Clarence Brown. *Writing Credits:* Bradbury Foote (based on the story *Benefits Forgot* by Honore Morrow). *Music:* Herbert Stothart. *Cinematography:* Clyde De Vinna. *Film Editing:* Frank E. Hull. *Art Direction:* Cedric Gibbons. *Studio:* MGM. *Length:* 103 minutes.

A prodigal son story, *Of Human Hearts* was produced and directed by Clarence Brown, a renowned MGM director from the 1920s into the 1950s. This 1938 film with a very strong cast is representative of Brown's pictorial skills—the bucolic scenes fairly sparkle in Clyde De Vinna's cinematography—and a tendency toward sentimentalism.

The story would be considered a close relation to soap operas by modern audiences. Jason Wilkins (James Stewart) grows up in a small Ohio River farming community with his strong-willed preacher father the Rev. Ethan Wilkins (Walter Huston who played Lincoln eight years earlier) and his loving mother Mary Wilkins (Beulah Bondi). Both father and son are self-centered and selfish; thus resentful Jason is in continual conflict with his stern and righteous father who forces his family into poverty to set an example for his parishioners. These conflicts usually end with his mother supporting the father but ultimately letting Jason get his way. After a physical confrontation with his father, Jason leaves home and studies medicine in Baltimore, inspired by the local physician, "rascal" Dr. Charles Shingle (Charles Coburn). During his studies and throughout his early career as a doctor, Jason continually asks for financial support from his mother who sells her meager personal possessions to provide him with money.

When the Civil War begins, Jason becomes a medical officer in the Northern Army and makes the excuse of work pressure to neglect to write to his now widowed mother for more than two years. Thinking her son dead, Mary Wilkins writes to President Lincoln (John Carradine) asking his assistance in finding the grave of her son. President Lincoln finds the missing son and orders him to Washington where he strongly upbraids Jason for the neglect of his mother. Duty triumphs, and all ends well as mother and son reunite in the final scene of the film, set as all others by Cedric Gibbons accurate to period.

Although the film is mawkishly sentimental and continually tugs at the heartstrings of the audience, a major scene with Lincoln and Jason, seven minutes long, is well-handled by Lincoln look-alike and act-alike Carradine. He obviously is represented as a stern father figure, congratulating Jason on doing "Great things in the field ... more than your share," admiring his policy of not amputating, and asking him about his medical education. Slowly and skillfully probing the young doctor, Lincoln learns that Jason doesn't know how his mother is and admits he neglects to write her.

"She must have done something terrible for you to drop her," Lincoln says. He then catalogs a mother's work and states that his mother wants to see his grave. Calling Jason "an ungrateful fool," Lincoln commands him to sit in "that chair and write a letter." He threatens Jason with a court marital if he ever again fails to write his mother at least once a week. The similarity between Lincoln the president and the Rev. Ethan Wilkins, the father, is reinforced when Lincoln stares out the window of his office and recites lines from a poem, *Winter Skies*: "Freeze, free thou bitter sky/ Thou does not bite so hard as benefits forgot."

Strange Faces (1938)

Lincoln: Charles Middleton. *Other Cast:* Frank Jenks (Nick Denby), Dorothea Kent (Maggie Moore), Andy Devine (Hector Hobbes), Leon Ames (Joe Gurney, gangster posing as William Evans), Mary Treen (Lorry May), Frank M. Thomas (Ward), Spencer Charters (Mason City Sheriff), Robert Emmett Keane (Newspaper Editor Hammon), Joe King (Police Lieutenant Hennigan), Renie Riano (Mrs. Keller), Frank Jaquet (Henry Evans), Eddie "Rochester" Anderson (William). *Director:* Earl Taggert. *Producer:* Burt Kelly. *Writing Credits:*

Charles Grayson, Arndt Guisti, Cornelius Reese. *Original Music*: Frank Skinner. *Cinematography*: Elwood Bredell. *Film Editing*: Charles Maynard. *Art Direction*: Jack Otterson. *Set Decoration*: R.A. Gausman. *Studio*: Universal Pictures. *Length*: 65 minutes.

This gangster film has it all: doubles, impersonators, impostors, and an appearance by Lincoln. Inspired by Nick Denby's (Frank Jenks) column on "Look-Alikes," gangster Joe Gurney (Leon Ames) murders his "twin" William Evans (also Ames), arranges the killing as if he were the victim, then steals the corpse from his home town to avoid a post-mortem and to continue his criminality. Columnist Denby (Frank Jenks) investigates with his girlfriend Maggie Moore (Dorothea Kent), both Universal actors moving from supporting to leading roles.

Gurney as Evans commits another murder to hide his identity, and Denby and Moore quarrel about its newspaper treatment. While after the story, Moore interviews Gurney and then witnesses his marriage to Lorry May (Mary Treen), an heiress. But Moore's threatened by Gurney, and she hits him on the head. He gets his justice; she gets her story; the audience gets laughs from them and newspaper editor Hector Hobbes (Andy Devine).

Strange Glory (1938)

Lincoln: Frank McGlynn Sr. *Other Cast*: Carey Wilson (Narrator), Fay Helm (Anna Ellis Carroll). *Director*: Jacques Tourneur. *Writing Credits*: Morgan Cox. *Music*: David Snell. *Cinematography*: Harold Lipstein. *Studio*: MGM. *Length*: 11 minutes.

This short concerns an interesting yet little known involvement of Anna Ellis Carroll of Maryland in Civil War developments. According to the Maryland Women's Hall of Fame biography, early in the war President Lincoln sent Ms. Carroll to the Western front. She returned with her strategic suggestions for the invasion along the Tennessee River. This was apparently one of numerous contacts between the president and Ms. Carroll with the biography indicating Lincoln's strong appreciation for her efforts.

The film tells the basic story regarding the Tennessee River plan but has Ms. Carroll (Fay Helm) presenting her strategic suggestions in a personal meeting with Lincoln (Frank McGlynn Sr.) There is no historical information that the two ever actually met.

Lincoln in the White House (1939)

Lincoln: Frank McGlynn Sr. *Other Cast*: Dickie Moore (Tad Lincoln), John Harron (John Hay), Raymond Brown (Secretary of War Edwin M. Stanton), Erville Alderson (Secretary of State William H. Seward), Sibyl Harris (Mrs. Scott), Nana Bryant (Mary Todd Lincoln). *Director*: William C. McGann. *Writing Credits*: Charles L. Tedford. *Cinematography*: Wilfrid M. Cline. *Film Editing*: Everett Dodd. *Art Direction*: Charles Novi. *Costume Design*: Milo Anderson. *Studio*: The Vitaphone Corp. *Length*: 21 minutes.

In one of the last appearances by Frank McGlynn Sr., he portrays the highlights of Lincoln's presidential years in this patriotic short. It covers Lincoln's presidential career from his first inauguration to the Gettysburg Address. It also includes insights into Lincoln. While talking to his son Tad (Dickie Moore), Lincoln covers such topics as his clemency for the Union soldier who was court martialed and his request that "Dixie" be played by the Union band. The highlight of the short is McGlynn's superb reading of the

Gettysburg Address. A contemporary review in *Variety* states, "If visual education ever assumes the wide proportions its advocates have been urging, this excerpt alone is surefire for every classroom." The short Technicolor film also is notable for its general historical accuracy and fine portrayal of Lincoln during the same year as the highly touted *Young Mr. Lincoln*.

The Mad Empress (1939)

Lincoln: Frank McGlynn Sr. *Other Cast:* Medea de Novara (Empress Carlotta of Mexico), Lionel Atwill (Bazaine), Conrad Nagel (Maximilian), Guy Bates Post (Napoleon), Evelyn Brent (Empress Eugenie), Jason Robards Sr. (President Benito Juarez). *Director-Producer:* Miguel Contreras Torres. *Writing Credits:* Jean Bart, Jerome Chodorov, Miguel Contreras Torres. *Music:* Heinz Roemheld. *Cinematography:* Arthur Martinelli, Alex Phillips. *Film Editing:* Carl Pierson. *Art Direction:* F. Paul Sylos. *Length:* 72 minutes.

The saga of Austrian Archduke Maximilian's (Conrad Nagel) noble efforts in Mexico and romantic devotion to his consort Carlotta (Medea de Novara) get full Hollywood treatment in this historical melodrama. It's filmed with authenticity for the Mexican locales and monuments involved in the French effort to unseat the Republic under President Benito Juarez (Jason Robards Sr.)

With a cast of thousands, the action moves from the splendor of Maximilian's Austrian palace to the Mexican battlefields where he is defeated. His execution is a small masterpiece of stark cinematic structure by director Miguel Contreras Torres. He films Maximilian walking to his death, the shooting, and then cuts to Carlotta playing the piano. None of his devoted wife Carlotta's efforts with Napoleon III or the Pope save what she naively calls "our empire." Dejected and alone in Europe, she learns that her beleaguered husband must die and goes mad; therefore, the "mad empress" title.

Amidst all this melodrama, Lincoln learns of France's military action and immediately states that Secretary of State Seward should inform the French ambassador that the United States still sees Juarez as president. While "not exactly a threat to America," he terms the French action a violation of the Monroe Doctrine. He also expresses the sympathy of the American people and will "always be for democracy." Frank McGlynn Sr. delivers these lines with simple dignity and dutifulness. These attributes also are attributed to Maximilian in his French figurehead capacity as ably portrayed by Conrad Nagel.

Old Hickory (1939)

Lincoln: Frank Wilcox.

In the final scene of this Jackson biopic there is a shot of Lincoln (Frank Wilcox) as the leader of a small militia group in the Black Hawk War. He is reading Jackson's position on the tariff question stating that the "federal union must and shall be preserved." Lincoln states that if he is ever in a position of power in the federal government, "I will shape my course by the words of Andrew Jackson."

This may have been one of Lincoln's few agreements with Jackson's policies since he returned from his stint in the military to run for a seat in the Illinois general assembly as an anti–Jackson Whig. Wilcox appears young, tall, and thin and could have been a 23-year-old Lincoln. For details, see Chapter 7 on Andrew Jackson.

16—Abraham Lincoln (1861–1865)

Young Mr. Lincoln (1939)

Lincoln: Henry Fonda. *Other Cast:* Alice Brady (Abigail Clay), Marjorie Weaver (Mary Todd), Arleen Whelan (Hannah Clay), Pauline Moore (Ann Rutledge), Richard Cromwell (Matt Clay), Eddie Quillan (Adam Clay), Donald Meek (John Felder), Ward Bond (John Palmer Cass). *Director:* John Ford. *Producer:* Darryl F. Zanuck. *Screenwriter:* Lamar Trotti. *Cinematographers:* Bert Glennon, Arthur C. Miller. *Composer:* Alfred Newman. *Film Editor:* Walter Thompson. *Art Directors:* Richard Day, Mark-Lee Kirk. *Set Designer:* Thomas K. Little. *Studio:* 20th Century–Fox, Cosmopolitan Productions. *Length:* 100 minutes.

John Ford's vision of Lincoln dominates *Young Mr. Lincoln* as Sherwood Anderson's dominates *Abe Lincoln in Illinois* (1940). Ford's panegyric to Lincoln is myth. Underlying this directorial choice is Lincoln's statement in the important trial scene when Lincoln says, "I may not know much about the law, but I know what's right." The prosecutor attempts to force the mother of the two sons involved in a killing to identify one as the murderer. Lincoln makes sure that this does not happen. Screenwriter Lamar Trotti admits that the trial is not based on Lincoln's life but a trial Trotti covered as a young reporter. It is another example of Darryl Zanuck's themes in biopics: motivation and a bending of facts to fit ticket

Young Mr. Lincoln (1939): Director John Ford had to persuade Henry Fonda to take the title role in this highly imaginative early life story of Lincoln. Both Ford and Fonda considered this 20th Century–Fox release to be among their best work. Note that a Gilbert Stuart portrait of George Washington looks over Lincoln's shoulder in this law office scene. (Courtesy of George Eastman House.)

sales. Throughout *Young Mr. Lincoln,* Lincoln in the person of Henry Fonda narrates his own story of his early life and his first important court case, removed from the rest of the film that is unnarrated action about events in his early life. From the first shot Fonda moves slowly, deliberately, thoughtfully, even passively or statically on the edge of the frame as he takes on a different persona, his mythical one, from the rest of the characters. Fonda, the compassionate, taciturn American film hero, was reluctant to play "the Great Emancipator," but patriotic Ford convinced himself to direct and one of his favorite actors to play "a jack-legged lawyer who rides a mule because he can't afford a horse." Still, Fonda as Lincoln looks and talks like Fonda with "youthful exuberance," according to one critique. He's a homespun star persona with a flat Midwestern accent as he delivers homely similes and backwoods colloquialisms. Fonda delivers the same persona that year in *Jesse James, Let Us Live, The Story of Alexander Graham Bell,* and *Drums Along the Mohawk.*

In creating *Young Mr. Lincoln,* Ford worked at a slow pace, irritating producer Zanuck. To avoid post-production changes, Ford destroyed his least favorite footage and edited on camera with many montages and dissolves to create the popular images of Lincoln. Ford also employed natural surroundings, as he did in his westerns in Monument Valley that make symbolic statements: the river that ripples when Fonda throws a stone into it while courting Ann Rutledge (Pauline Moore) and the lightning-lit stormy sky that ends the film as Fonda leaves the courthouse, Alfred Newman's version of "The Battle Hymn of the Republic" echoing in the backgound.

Ford directed two more pictures that legend-creating year of his career, *Stagecoach* and *Drums Along the Mohawk.* While *Young Mr. Lincoln* won no Oscars, Lamar Trotti was nominated for best original screenplay although he had fictionalized the trial, a key sequence in the film.

Abe Lincoln in Illinois (1940)

Lincoln: Raymond Massey. *Other Cast:* Gene Lockhart (Stephen Douglas), Ruth Gordon (Mary Todd Lincoln), Mary Howard (Ann Rutledge), Minor Watson (Joshua Speed), Alan Baxter (Billy Herndon), Harvey Stephens (Ninian Edwards), Howard Da Silva (Jack Armstrong), Dorothy Tree (Elizabeth Edwards), Aldrich Bowker (Judge Bowling Green), Maurice Murphy (John McNeil), Louis Jean Heydt (Mentor Graham), Clem Bevans (Ben Mattingly), Harlan Briggs (Denton Offut), Herbert Rudley (Seth Gale), Andy Clyde (Stage Driver), Elisabeth Risdon (Sarah Lincoln), Charles Middleton (Tom Lincoln), Erville Alderson (Andrew Jackson). *Director:* John Cromwell. *Producer:* Max Gordon. *Writing Credits:* Robert E. Sherwood, Grover Jones. *Music:* Roy Webb. *Cinematography:* James Wong Howe. *Film Editing:* George Hively. *Art Direction:* Van Nest Polglase. *Set Decoration:* Casey Roberts. *Studio:* RKO Radio Pictures. *Length:* 110 minutes.

Raymond Massey's close physical resemblance and realistic (albeit wooden) impersonation of Lincoln makes him the best-known interpreter of America's favorite president. He played the role in the Pulitzer Prize–winning stage version of this film (the film rights were sold to RKO for $225,000) and in many other productions for his remaining career. Massey's was the only Lincoln portrayal to receive an Oscar nomination (in 1940 when James Stewart won for *The Philadelphia Story*).

The film covers Lincoln's life from the early 1830s when he arrived in New Salem until 1861 when he left Springfield for Washington, D.C. Perhaps the single most famous scene in all the Lincoln movies is the religious farewell to his neighbors when he is presented as a tired, somber old man. It was filmed in darkness to stimulate the laconic Massey. Although the script rings true to Lincoln's complex behavior, especially his gloominess, the history does not.

Because Sherwood relied heavily on Lincoln's law partner William Herndon's biography for his relationships with the two women in his life, Ann Rutledge (Mary Howard) and Mary Todd Lincoln (Ruth Gordon), and because Sherwood, with Grover Jones, expanded the earlier part of Lincoln's life in the play to appeal to film audiences, there are many historical inaccuracies. Ann Rutledge's death of brain fever on the night of Lincoln's first legislative victory—New Salem's representative to the State Legislature—with Lincoln holding her hand but being mistaken for her true love John McNeil (Maurice Murphy) is but a popular myth.

Even more serious, attributed to Herndon's and Sherwood's negative feelings about Mary Todd Lincoln, is

Abe Lincoln in Illinois (1940): Raymond Massey has become the most known portrayer of Lincoln in modern times in spite of his stilted and unrealistic performance under John Cromwell's direction. Of note in the RKO Radio Pictures production is James Wong Howe's cinematography. (Courtesy of George Eastman House.)

her depiction as an ambitious schemer and outright termagant. Although the troubled Lincoln marriage was a "house divided" in their differing characters, it was still a happy one. More importantly, Lincoln was an ambitious and driven self-made man who says he "hated Mary's infernal ambition." The film further shows Mary's undocumented unleashing of her fury at Lincoln on the eve of his election in front of many of his friends and his rebuttal to her: "You're never to do that again, make a fool of me."

Most seriously, Lincoln's complicated personality does not emerge. He seems dutiful and doomed rather than ambitious. Still, Massey, in his stiff performance, conveys the unattractive man's attractive qualities of wit and likability. He also debates against Stephen Douglas with great conviction, although his words come from other of the debates and Lincoln's private correspondence, speeches, and writings, not from the "house divided" debate itself.

Other liberties taken by Sherwood with Lincoln's speeches appear in the final scene when Lincoln bids farewell to his fellow citizens of Springfield with his Farewell Address, political philosophy far from the personal comments made on February 11, 1861. Nevertheless, Sherwood filed a suit (that he lost) about the plagiarizing of his work by 20th Century-Fox in *Young Mr. Lincoln* (1939) and its prior release to *Abe Lincoln in Illinois* that hurt its profits.

Under John Cromwell's direction the film adds many scenes from Lincoln's early life: the arrival of Tom Lincoln and his family in the Illinois wilderness, young Lincoln's job hauling a flatboat of hogs from Springfield to New Orleans, Lincoln's meeting with Ann Rutledge in New Salem, his return there to clerk in Denton Offut's store and its later failure, his triumphant fight with the local bully, and his appointment as a milita captain during the Black Hawk Indian War. Then the film returns to the play's script with Lincoln's conversation with the inspirational local schoolteacher, his job as postmaster, his political career in the state capital, and his rise to national prominence through the Lincoln-Douglas debates.

Critically well received at its release and one of the mostly widely shown and well-known screen dramatizations of Lincoln's life, the film lost $750,000 for producer Max Gordon and RKO. These low box office receipts are attributed to the public's loss of interest in dramatically embellished film biographies of earnest heroes (Alexander Graham Bell, Thomas Edison, Louis Pasteur, etc). Of note is the Oscar nomination of James Wong Howe for black-and-white cinematography (he lost to George Barnes for *Rebecca*). Howe's work for the interior sets is convincing; some of the backwoods exteriors appear all too much like studio sets.

A Failure at Fifty (1940)

Lincoln: Edmund Glover. *Other Cast:* Bebe Anderson (Ann Rutledge), Truman Bradley (Lincoln's Friend). *Director:* Will Jason. *Writing Credits:* Howard Dimsdale, Arno B. Reincke. *Producer:* Carey Wilson. *Cinematography:* Paul Vogel. *Film Editing:* Adrienne Fazan. *Studio:* MGM. *Length:* 10 minutes.

A man (Emmett Vogan) contemplating his lack of success at age 50 is told a story of an anonymous man who also felt he was a failure at 50. As it turns out, the man in the story was Abraham Lincoln (Edmund Glover) who in two years became the 16th president.

Hi-Yo Silver (1940)

Lincoln: Frank McGlynn Sr. *Other Cast:* Lee Powell (Allen King/The Lone Ranger), Bruce Bennett (Bert Rogers), Chief Thundercloud (Tonto), Lynne Roberts (Joan Blanchard), Stanley Andrews (Jeffries), George Cleveland (George Blanchard), Lane Chandler (Dick Forrest), Wally Wales (Bob Stuart), George Montgomery (Jim Clark), Billy Bletcher (Lone Ranger voice), Raymond Hatton (Smokey), Dickie Jones (The Boy). *Director:* John English, William Witney. *Producer:* Sol C. Siegel. *Writing Credits:* Franklin Adreon, Ronald Davidson. *Music:* Alberto Colombo. *Cinematography:* William Nobles. *Film Editing:* Edward Todd, Helene Turner. *Studio:* Republic Pictures Corp. *Length:* 69 minutes.

That this is an abridgement of the 1938 Republic serial *The Lone Ranger* is very evident in that the story about the beginning of the Lone Ranger myth continually jumps back and forth. To flesh out this mystery of the masked man's adventures, the film departs from the continuity of the radio program and uses a basic old western plot with an evil man, Jeffries (Stanley Andrews), brought to justice by a series of five men, any one of whom could be the Lone Ranger. They come forth as the "masked rider of the plains" to fight the power-hungry Jeffries in his quest to control Texas and its silver. Interestingly, Bruce Bennett is credited as Herman Brix and George Montgomery as George Letz in masked rider roles before their stardom under their more famous names.

President Lincoln (played by the great Lincoln actor Frank McGlynn Sr.) appears because Jeffries is pretending to be a Federal tax collector. First, Lincoln calls on the Lone Ranger for help. In a second scene, Lincoln, wearing a shawl and clasping his hands behind his back in typical fashion, "gives full authority" to the Lone Ranger because "the initial reports of harshness by Jeffries in collecting taxes trouble me." This Lincoln scene is short yet effectively realistic. The scene ends with Lincoln saying "Godspeed" and casting a big shadow on the wall of his office.

Virginia City (1940)

Lincoln: Victor Kilian. *Other Cast:* Errol Flynn (Kerry Bradford), Miriam Hopkins (Julia Hayne), Randolph Scott (Vance Irby), Humphrey Bogart (John Murrell), Frank McHugh (Mr. Upjohn), Alan Hale (Olaf "Moose" Swenson), Guinn "Big Boy" Williams (Marblehead). *Director:* Michael Curtiz. *Producer:* Hal B. Wallis. *Writing Credits:* Robert Buckner. *Music:* Max Steiner. *Cinematography:* Sol Polito. *Film Editing:* George Amy. *Art Direction:* Ted Smith. *Studio:* Warner Bros. *Length:* 118 minutes.

With a film that had been promoted as a sequel to the successful *Dodge City* (1939), the decision had obviously been made to make it as complicated as possible while generally using the same cast of characters. As such, director Michael Curtiz turned out a Civil War spy western, including a wagon train of gold, an attack by Mexican bandits (instead of Indians), the main character undergoing a court martial and a sentence to death—but receiving a presidential pardon.

Kerry Bradford (Errol Flynn) escapes from a Confederate prison with his companions "Moose" Swenson (Alan Hale) and Marblehead (Guinn "Big Boy" Williams) after maltreatment by Capt. Vance Irby (Randolph Scott). Confederate spy Julia Hayne, aka Julie Adams (Miriam Hopkins), convinces Irby to move gold from Virginia City, Nevada, to Richmond to save the Confederate cause. Coincidentally, the newly escaped Bradford is assigned to stop the gold shipment. Complications mount when Bradford falls in love with Julia Hayne, discovers Irby in Virginia City, and fails to stop the wagon train from getting on the road to Richmond.

Irby leads his people toward Texas aided by the Mexican bandit chief with the unbelievable name of John Murrell (Humphrey Bogart in the funniest role of his career with a Spanish accent that comes and goes like a migrant worker). However, Murrell comes back to steal the gold but is ultimately thwarted by a U.S. Cavalry charge after Irby is killed, leaving the road open for Bradford to woo Julia.

Complications continue as Bradford refuses to tell the cavalry where the Confederate gold is hidden. He is subsequently court martialed and sentenced to death on the very day the Civil War ends. Meanwhile, Julia Hayne rushes to Washington and convinces President Lincoln (Victor Kilian) to offer clemency for Bradford. Lincoln commutes the sentence but not before his normal practice of giving a speech concerning the need for unity in the nation: "I'm not a military man," he says. "He won't be killed.... You came over 2,000 miles to save a man who was once your enemy. That's a symbol of what we can do for our country." He then reads from his Gettysburg Address about "malice toward none."

Kilian's face is not shown in the film as he appears in a shadow profile, and his voice is much more polished than Lincoln's is reported to have been. However, his act of clemency certainly fits the Father Abraham stereotype developed by Hollywood.

March On, America! (1942)

Lincoln: Frank McGlynn Sr.

Frank McGlynn Sr. is credited with doing his usual excellent job as Lincoln in this World War II morale builder. For details, see Chapter 5 on James Monroe.

Tennessee Johnson (1942)

Lincoln: Ed O'Neill.

Lincoln appears twice but barely visibly in this chronicle of the life of Andrew Johnson, Lincoln's vice president who followed him in office. Lincoln is seen on his deathbed, his face hidden from view, after the attack in Ford's Theater. His distinctive hat is all that is shown during the other scene, of Johnson's swearing in as vice president. For details, see Chapter 17 on Andrew Johnson.

Scrap Happy Daffy (1943)

Lincoln Duck: Mel Blanc, voice. *Director*: Frank Tashlin. *Writing Credits*: Don Christensen. *Length*: 8 minutes.

This is a World War II Daffy Duck cartoon with a message to save all the scrap metal possible to win the war. Daffy defeats a goat sent by Hitler to eat his scrap pile by using many of his ancestors, including a Lincoln Duck from the Civil War. Besides Lincoln Duck, the gifted Blanc voices the characters of Hitler, Nazi Soldiers, Submarine Captain, Billy Goat, Great-Great-Great-Great-Great-Uncle Dillingham Duck, Minuteman Duck, Pioneer Duck, Admiral Duck, and Daffy's Ancestors.

The Battle of China (1944)

Lincoln: Walter Huston (voice). Archival footage of Claire Chenault, Chiang Kai-Shek, Madame Chiang, Winston Churchill, Anthony Eden, Admiral W.F. Halsey, Hirohito, General D. MacArthur. *Directors*: Frank Capra, Anatole Litvak, *Producer*: Anatole Litvak, *Writing*: Julius J. Epstein, Phillip G. Epstein. *Music*: Dimitri Tiomkin. *Film Editing*: William Hornbeck. *Studio*: U.S. Army Signal Corps. *Length*: 65 minutes.

Frank Capra uses his directing skills during the World War II effort to turn out seven films in the "Why We Fight" series. In *The Battle of China*, the sixth of the seven films, Walter Huston supplies the voice of Lincoln to this propaganda effort. Huston had portrayed Lincoln in two previous films and does not disappoint with his homespun vocal delivery in this effort.

Can't Help Singing (1944)

Lincoln: William Sundholm.
For details, see Chapter 11 on James Polk.

Rock Island Trail (1950)

Lincoln: Jeff Corey. *Other Cast*: Forrest Tucker (Reed Loomis), Adele Mara (Constance Strong), Adrian Booth (Aleeta), Bruce Cabot (Kirby Morrow), Chill Wills (Hogger McCoy),

Grant Withers (David Strong). *Director:* Joseph Kane. *Producer:* Paul Malvern. *Screenplay:* James Edward Grant (based on a novel by Frank J. Nevins). *Music:* R. Dale Butts, Billy Roy. *Cinematography:* Jack Marta. *Film Editing:* Arthur Roberts. *Art Direction:* Frank Arrigo. *Set Decoration:* John McCarthy Jr., George Milo. *Costume Design:* Adele Palmer. *Studio:* Republic Pictures Corp. *Length:* 90 minutes.

Taking considerable historic license, *Rock Island Trail* tells the story of the building of the Rock Island Line from Chicago to the Mississippi River and beyond. The completely fictional railroad man Reed Loomis (Forrest Tucker) pushes the railroad with the assistance of banker David Strong (Grant Withers) and the banker's daughter, Constance Strong (Adele Mara). Loomis's sidekick is Hogger McCoy (Chill Wills), the bad guy is shipping mogul Kirby Morrow (Bruce Cabot), and the other romantic interest is Indian princess Aleeta (Adrian Booth).

Director Joseph Kane's use of a villainous shipper allows for the introduction of Lincoln (Jeff Corey) who in actual fact did act as a lawyer for the railroad and its right to build bridges across navigable rivers. Although the film shows Lincoln winning the case, in actual fact the case went to the Illinois Supreme Court before the railroad won. Corey does a reasonable job with the role of Lincoln as the corporate lawyer. He delivers Lincoln's homespun humor in questioning a hostile witness, saying, "I'm as serious as an unfed mule." The highlight of the film is the Sioux Indians fighting the Sac and Fox Indians led by Chief Keokuk. Unfortunately it is impossible to tell the Indian tribes apart.

Stage to Tucson (1950)

Lincoln: James Griffith. *Other Cast:* Rod Cameron (Grif Holbrook), Wayne Morris (Barney Broderick), Kay Buckley (Kate Crocker), Sally Eilers (Annie Benson), Carl Benton Reid (Dr. Noah Banteen), Roy Roberts (Jim Maroon), Harry Bellaver (Gus Heyden), Douglas Fowley (Ira Prentiss). *Director:* Ralph Murphy. *Producer:* Harry Joe Brown. *Writing Credits:* Frank Bonham, Bob Williams, Frank Burt, Robert Libott. *Music:* Paul Sawtell. *Cinematography:* Charles Lawton Jr. *Film Editing:* Charles Nelson. *Art Direction:* George Brooks. *Set Decoration:* Frank Tuttle. *Studio:* Columbia Pictures Corp. *Length:* 81 minutes.

This war-between-the-states-affair goes beyond the routine with "some good action," according to *Variety*, particularly of skullduggery over money-grabbing schemes by Atlanta confederates to steal from Arizona stagecoaches on an important line from St. Louis to Georgia. *Variety* raises the question of "just how much coin could be realized by stealing a stage in Arizona and then freighting it via wagon train to Georgia" (Dec. 20, 1950).

Regardless of the implausibility, Lincoln (James Griffith) recognizes the importance of the Butterfield Stage and enlists the aide of Grif Holbrook (Rod Cameron) and Barney Broderick (Wayne Morris) to ensure that the North is not damaged. Although continually quarreling, particularly over Kate Crocker (Kay Buckley), Holbrook and Broderick end up going off to fight for the Union as part of Lincoln's request for 75,000 volunteers. But the camerawork by Charles Lawton Jr. of rugged western landscapes never falters.

New Mexico (1951)

Lincoln: Hans Conried. *Other Cast:* Lew Ayres (Capt. Hunt), Marilyn Maxwell (Cherry), Robert Hutton (Lt. Vermont), Andy Devine (Sgt. Garrity), Raymond Burr (Pvt. Anderson),

Jeff Corey (Coyote), Lloyd Corrigan (Judge Wilcox), Verna Felton (Mrs. Fenway), Ted de Corsia (Acoma, Indian Chief), John Hoyt (Sgt. Harrison). *Director:* Irving Reis. *Producers:* Irving Allen, Joseph Justman. *Writing Credits:* Max Trell. *Music:* Rene Garriguenc, Lucien Moraweck. *Cinematography:* Jack Greenhalgh, William Snyder. *Film Editing:* Louis Sackin. *Art Direction:* George Van Marter. *Set Decoration:* Edward Ray Robinson. *Studio:* United Artists. *Length:* 76 minutes.

A (fictional) treaty between President Lincoln (Hans Conried) and Acoma (Ted de Corsia) leads to an Indian uprising on a high mesa in New Mexico that a friend of the chief's, Capt. Hunter (Lew Ayres), must put down. According to *Variety* (May 2, 1951) Irving Reis's direction points up the bloody warfare between the Indians and the soldiers trapped on the mesa with long-range en masse shots. It's a cavalry vs. Indians picture with a script that "could have presented some characters with more clarity," says *Variety*.

There's plenty of action with Hunter rescuing saloon girl Cherry (Marilyn Maxwell) from an Indian attack and defending an Army fortress from the enraged Chief Acoma whose son was accidentally killed by a soldier.

The Tall Target (1951)

Lincoln: Leslie Kimmell. *Other Cast:* Dick Powell (Jack Kennedy), Paula Raymond (Ginny Beaufort), Adolphe Menjou (Col. Caleb Jeffers), Marshall Thompson (Lance Beaufort), Ruby Dee (Rachel). *Director:* Anthony Mann. *Producer:* Richard Goldstone. *Writing Credits:* Art Cohn (based on a story by George Worthington Yates and Geoffrey Homes). *Cinematography:* Paul Vogel. *Film Editing:* Newell P. Kimlin. *Art Direction:* Cedric Gibbons, Eddie Imazu. *Set Direction:* Ralph S. Hurst, Edwin B. Willis. *Studio:* MGM. *Length:* 78 minutes.

Based on a true story, this film becomes more than interesting because of its dark nature, the attempted assassination of Lincoln as he was heading toward his inauguration on a train. Director Anthony Mann takes the story developed by Art Cohn and George Worthington Yates into the noir genre with dark shadows, unclear motives, and beautiful women not to be trusted.

Dick Powell stars as John Kennedy, a New York City detective who pursues the Lincoln assassination plot despite his superiors' doubt. He resigns, boards the "Night Flyer" to Baltimore and tries to stop the plot. He encounters a double-crossing Caleb Jeffers (Adolphe Menjou), intent on leading his Zouaves to Baltimore; earnest Lance Beaufort (Marshall Thompson), eager to return to the South; Ginny Beaufort (Paula Raymond), his trustworthy sister; and her devoted slave Rachel (Ruby Dee). Kennedy proves a smart cop.

Leslie Kimmell is Lincoln, of proper resemblance and speech, who is seen only in a three-quarter shot, looking out the window after he boards the train at Baltimore. He says, "Did ever any president come to his inauguration like a thief in the night?" That line sums up the continual suspense. The climax is the view of the capital with the "Battle Hymn of the Republic" playing in the background.

San Antone (1953)

Lincoln: Richard Hale. *Other Cast:* Rod Cameron (Carl Miller), Arleen Whelan (Julia Allerby), Forrest Tucker (Brian Culver), Katy Jurado (Mistania Figueroa), Rodolfo Acosta (Chino Figueroa), Harry Carey Jr. (Dobe), George Cleveland (Allerby). *Director-Producer:*

Joseph Kane. *Writing Credits:* Curt Carroll, Steve Fisher. *Music:* R. Dale Butts. *Cinematography:* Bud Thackery. *Film Editing:* Tony Martinelli. *Costume Design:* Adele Palmer. *Studio:* Republic Pictures Corp. *Length:* 90 minutes.

Republic Pictures occasionally tried to make a different western. However, mixing the U.S. Civil War, cattle drives, racial problems, and ousting Emperor Maximilian and the French from Mexico leads to difficult continuity. Carl Miller (Rod Cameron) is a Texas cattleman supplying beef to the Confederate Army. He becomes the lifelong enemy of Confederate officer Lt. Brian Culver (Forrest Tucker) when he insults Culver's fiancée Julia Allerby (Arleen Whelan) who is the duplicitous daughter of a Texan (George Cleveland), owner of a San Antonio "plantation" (a Tara-like mansion with square brick pillars instead of round white ones). The insult takes place when Julia accuses Miller's friend, Chino Figueroa (Rodolfo Acosta) of attempted rape because Chino is leaving her to fight for Benito Juarez in Mexico. More complexity follows.

The action, under Joseph Kane's direction, is continual. However, the Civil War action scenes do not last too long since Miller spent most of it in a Yankee prison. Returning to San Antone, Miller finds that Culver, who killed Miller's father during the war, had been captured by Figueroa and is in a Mexican prison. Miller rounds up 700 head of cattle to use as ransom for Culver so he can settle their score. All this activity is complicated by the presence of Julia and Miller's true love who is also Chino's sister, Mistania Figueroa (Katy Jurado).

Lincoln (Richard Hale) appears briefly in two scenes. In the first he gives a solemn statement about the need for union as the war is about to begin. The second is his voice-over reading, pronounced with a decided drawl, of the Gettysburg Address with battle scenes in the background. As is the case in films of this nature and period, Lincoln is the typical Father Abraham figure.

Apache Ambush (1955)

Lincoln: James Griffith. *Other Cast:* Bill Williams (James Kingston), Richard Jaeckel (Lee Parker), Alex Montoya (Joaquin Jironza), Movita (Rosita), Adele August (Ann), Tex Ritter (Traeger), Ray Corrigan (Mark Calvin), Ray Teal (Sgt. O'Roarke), Don C. Harvey (Maj. McGuire), James Flavin (Col. Marshall), George Chandler (Chandler), Forrest Lewis (Silas Parker), George Keymas (Tweedy), Victor Milan (Manuel), Harry Lauter (Bailey), Bill Hale (Bob Jennings), Robert Foulk (Red Jennings). *Director:* Fred F. Sears. *Producer:* Wallace MacDonald. *Writing Credits:* David Lang. *Music:* Mischa Bakaleinikoff. *Cinematography:* Fred Jackman Jr. *Film Editing:* Jerome Thoms. *Studio:* Columbia Pictures Corp. *Length:* 68 minutes.

In this B western, Lincoln, in one of his last official but historically inaccurate acts before his assassination, sends Union scout James Kingston (Bill Williams) and Sgt. Tim O'Roarke (Ray Teal) to Texas to protect a cattle drive over a thousand miles to Abilene, Kansas. Lincoln leaves for Ford's Theater, and Kingston and O'Roarke leave for Texas and all of the convolutions that a western can take.

The enemies of these Union and Confederate soldiers are Apaches, Mexican revolutionaries, and distressed Confederate veterans. In addition to the thousands of cattle, this strange mix of enemies are also interested in a cache of Henry repeating rifles hidden somewhere in the wagon train. Kingston and O'Roarke finally sort this all out after considerable bloodshed and the loss of at least half of the credited cast. In a politically correct note, the

All Movie Guide warns "more sensitive viewers" that "neither the Apaches nor the Mexicans are shown in a particularly sympathetic light."

Prince of Players (1955)

Lincoln: Stanley Hall. *Other Cast:* Richard Burton (Edwin Booth), Maggie McNamara (Mary Devlin Booth), John Derek (John Wilkes Booth), Raymond Massey (Junius Brutus Booth), Charles Bickford (Dave Prescott), Elizabeth Sellars (Asia Booth), Eva LeGallienne (Gertrude in *Hamlet*), Christopher Cook (Edwin Booth at 10), Sarah Padden (Mary Todd Lincoln), Dayton Lummis (English Doctor), Ian Keith (Ghost of Hamlet's Father in *Hamlet*). *Director-Producer:* Philip Dunne. *Writing Credits:* Moss Hart, Eleanor Ruggles. *Music:* Bernard Herrmann. *Cinematography:* Charles G. Clarke. *Film Editing:* Dorothy Spencer. *Art Direction:* Mark-Lee Kirk, Lyle R. Wheeler. *Set Direction:* Paul S. Fox, Walter M. Scott. *Costume Design:* Mary Wills. *Studio:* 20th Century–Fox. *Length:* 102 minutes.

This is a play-within-a-play with more drama offstage than on by John Wilkes Booth (John Derek) in his role as President Lincoln's assassin. The play's excerpts from Shakespeare, with esteemed actress Eva LeGallienne as special consultant, are more accurate than the history. She appears as Gertrude in *Hamlet* and as Juliet with Richard Burton in *Romeo and Juliet*.

Historically flawed is the Ford's Theater scene in which John Wilkes Booth escapes through the audience, not backstage, and a Union soldier guard for Lincoln is seen laughing although actually a Washington police officer, John Parker, deserted his guard post. Burton is Edwin Booth, the older of the Booth brothers who launches his own career as Richard III when his drunk, carousing father, Junius Brutus Booth (Raymond Massey), can no longer act. Edwin also struggles with the family "madness" with the help of actress Mary Devlin (Maggie McNamara) who becomes his devoted wife. But John Wilkes Booth, not as well disciplined and trained for the stage as Edwin, takes up with hotheads in the South. Trying to save him as he did his father, Edwin suggests that John Wilkes alternate roles with him in London. John Wilkes responds that there is "more glory to life than bowing" and "to destroy greatness is to be great."

Lincoln's appearance in the assassination scene is very short, just one shot; he sits with Mary (Sarah Padden, lornette in hand), watching the play on stage. Stanley Hall as Lincoln comports himself with little emotion as does Padden. Writer Moss Hart continues the drama, although the date may be historically inaccurate, following Edwin Booth's resolute reaction to the angry audience as he later performs *Hamlet*, beginning with the line, "Murderer." Bernard Herrmann's original music enhances the drama and Director-Producer Philip Dunne allows the innate drama of the plays and events to create emotion.

The Story of Mankind (1957)

Lincoln: Austin Green. *Other Cast:* Ronald Colman (The Spirit of Man), Hedy Lamarr (Joan of Arc), Groucho Marx (Peter Minuet), Harpo Marx (Sir Isaac Newton), Chico Marx (Monk), Virginia Mayo (Cleopatra), Agnes Moorehead (Queen Elizabeth), Vincent Price (The Devil), Peter Lorre (Nero), Charles Coburn (Hippocrates), Cedric Hardwicke (High Judge), Cesar Romero (Spanish Envoy), John Carradine (Khufu), Dennis Hopper (Napoleon Bonaparte), Marie Wilson (Marie Antoinette), Helmut Dantine (Anthony), Edward Everett

Horton (Sir Walter Raleigh), Reginald Gardiner (William Shakespeare), Marie Windsor (Josephine). *Director-Producer:* Irwin Allen. *Writing Credits:* Irwin Allen, Charles Bennett, Henrik Van Loon. *Music:* Paul Sawtell. *Cinematography:* Nicholas Musuraca. *Art Direction:* Art Loel. *Studio:* Cambridge Productions, Inc., Warner Brothers. *Length:* 100 minutes.

Using a novel by Henrik Van Loon as the basis, Irwin Allen wrote the screenplay and directs this longwinded and, ultimately, boring film regarding the future of Earth as a planet. Before an outer space court of elders headed by a High Judge (Cedric Hardwicke), the Devil (Vincent Price), and the Spirit of Man (Ronald Colman) argue the case as to whether the human race should be allowed to continue to exist or should be destroyed by a newly invented "high hydrogen bomb."

Their arguments take the form of a series of historical flashbacks, a sort of history of mankind, used to illustrate either the evilness or the goodness of humans. It appears that the real reason for the flashbacks is to use all of Warner Brothers' old footage of ancient Egypt and Greece as well as the U.S. West. The cast of characters includes Hedy Lamarr as a hard-to-believe Joan of Arc; Agnes Moorehead badly overacting as Elizabeth I; Virginia Mayo as a blonde Cleopatra; and Groucho, Harpo, and Chico Marx in three separate (and unfunny) sequences as Peter Minuet, Isaac Newton, and a Monk, respectively. The list goes on and on but the acting does not get any better. Needless to say, the decision to destroy humanity is deferred. The High Judge gives us another chance to mend our ways.

There are two American presidents shown in separate sagas, an uncredited Washington and Austin Green as Lincoln reading a portion of the Emancipation Proclamation about which the Devil says, "at least something good came out of the Civil War." Green makes a highly acceptable Lincoln with both the sincerity and humanity with which he delivers his lines. Although his speaking voice is undoubtedly unlike Lincoln's, his appearance is quite close to the 16th president's.

How the West Was Won (1962)

Lincoln: Raymond Massey. *Other Cast:* Spencer Tracy (Narrator), James Stewart (Linus Rawlings), Henry Fonda (Jethro Stuart), Gregory Peck (Cleve Van Valen), Debbie Reynolds (Lilith Prescott), Richard Widmark (Mike King), George Peppard (Zeb Rawlings), Karl Malden (Zebulon Prescott), John Wayne (Gen. William Tecumseh Sherman), Harry Morgan (Ulysses S. Grant). *Directors:* John Ford, Henry Hathaway, George Marshall, Richard Thorpe. *Producer:* Bernard Smith. *Writing Credits:* John Gay, James R. Webb. *Cinematography:* Joseph LaShelle, Charles Lang Jr., William Daniels, Milton Krasner, Harold Wellman. *Music:* Alfred Newman, Ken Darby. *Film Editor:* Harold F. Kress. *Art Direction:* George W. Davis, William Ferrari, Addison Hehr. *Set Direction:* Henry Grace, Don Greenwood Jr., Jack Mills. *Studio:* MGM, Cinerama Productions Corp. *Length:* 162 minutes.

John Ford directs the "Civil War" third section of this extended, award-wining Cinerama western. Henry Hathaway directs the first two chapters ("The Rivers" and "The Plains"), George Marshall directs the fourth ("The Railroad"), and Hathaway directs the fifth and last ("The Outlaws").

As a saga of the settling of the West, the film tells the story of three generations of a family and their adventures and misadventures in the period between 1839 and 1889. Spencer Tracy provides the continuity between five separate yet related stories, all of which fit into the classic western mode. With its all-star cast including James Stewart, Henry Fonda, Gregory Peck, Karl Malden, John Wayne, Debbie Reynolds, etc., the film won three Oscars and was the top-grosser of 1962.

In "The Civil War" chapter, Ford takes the opportunity to show two of his favorite historical characters, Abraham Lincoln and U.S. Grant. Grant's appearance is covered in Chapter 18. Lincoln is portrayed by Raymond Massey in a non-speaking short scene. It appears to be pre-presidential in his Illinois office as a non-bearded Lincoln ponders the fate of the nation and slavery. Even without lines or action, Massey does his usual capable job.

Treasure of the Aztecs (1965) aka Der Schatz der Azteken

Lincoln: Jeff Corey. *Other Cast:* Lex Barker (Dr. Karl Sternau), Gerard Barray (Count Alfonso di Rodriganda y Sevilla), Rik Battaglia (Capt. Lazoro Verdoja), Michele Girardon (Josefa), Alessandra Panaro (Rossita Arbellez), Theresa Lorca (Karja), Fausto Tozzi (Benito Juarez), Hans Nielsen (Don Pedro Arbellez), Gustavo Rojo (Lt. Potoca), Kelo Henderson (Frank Wilson), Jean-Roger Caussimon (Marshal Bazaine), Ralf Wolter (Andreas Hasenpfeffer). *Director:* Robert Siodmak. *Producer:* Artur Brauner, Gotz Dieter Wulf. *Writing Credits:* Karl May, Ladislas Fodor, Robert A. Stemmle, Georg Marischka. *Music:* Erwin Halletz. *Cinematography:* Siegfried Hold. *Film Editing:* Walter Wischniewsky. *Production Design:* Hertha Hareiter, Kosta Krivokapic, Otto Pischinger. *Art Direction:* Veljko Despotovic, Miodrag Miric, Milan Todorovic. *Costume Design:* Edith Almoslino. *Studio:* Avala Film. *Length:* 101 minutes.

After the film opens with a mysterious trek across an active volcano by a blond-haired Aztec priest, one can only note that Italians aren't the only filmmakers who made spaghetti westerns. Using a novel written by the noted German western author Karl May, director Robert Siodmak brings the Germans into competition with a sauerbraten western.

Dr. Karl Sternau (Lex Barker well beyond his 1949–53 Tarzan days) attempts to obtain financial support for deposed Mexican President Juarez (Fausto Tozzi) who is in turn attempting to depose the French installed emperor Maximilian. Sternau's first appointment is in Washington, D.C., where President Lincoln (Jeff Corey) is perfectly willing to stop worrying about the Civil War while he listens to Mexico's problems. Lincoln shows the effectiveness of Dr. Sternau's request by immediately writing an official note to Juarez offering U.S. support. Corey is much too short to portray Lincoln and, in fact, looks much more like President Grant. He also depicts Lincoln as a more exuberant person than usually portrayed, wagging his finger to emphasize his supportive position.

After the visit to the White House the plot turns into a stagecoach ride attacked by Mexican bandits, a firing squad execution ordered by Juarez, unknown young ladies abducted by strangely dressed Indians who then tie them to a post and dance around it, the saving of the ladies by a few cowboys who then race across the plains followed by Indians on horseback (who have different costumes from the original Indians), etc.

These events are not tied together, perhaps because the film was originally planned to be a three-hour epic, but was released in Germany in two parts with the second called *Pyramid of the Sun God*.

The Fortune Cookie (1966)

Lincoln: John Anderson. *Other Cast:* Jack Lemmon (Harry Hinkle), Walter Matthau (Willie Gingrich), Ron Rich (Luther "Boom Boom" Jackson), Judi West (Sandy Hinkle),

Cliff Osmond (Purkey), Lurene Tuttle (Mother Hinkle), Harry Holcombe (O'Brien), Les Tremayne (Thompson), Lauren Gilbert (Kincaid), Marge Redmond (Charlotte Gingrich). *Director:* Billy Wilder. *Producers:* Billy Wilder, I.A.L. Diamond., Doane Harrison. *Writing Credits:* Billy Wilder, I.A. L. Diamond. *Music:* Andre Previn. *Cinematography:* Joseph LaShelle. *Film Editing:* Daniel Mandell. *Art Direction:* Robert Luthardt. *Set Decoration:* Edward G. Boyle. *Studio:* Mirisch Company, Phalanx-Jaelam. *Length:* 125 minutes.

The initial joint effort of Walter Matthau and Jack Lemmon, in a Billy Wilder comedy, cannot be all bad, and it isn't. Matthau gives an Academy Award–winning Best Supporting Actor portrayal of Willie Gingrich, a shyster lawyer who always has an angle to turn a buck. His brother-in-law is Harry Hinkle (Lemmon), a CBS-TV cameraman who is slightly injured by return specialist "Boom Boom" Jackson (Ron Rich) while covering a Cleveland Browns football game. Gingrich is able to expand the injury into something medically significant and develops a major suit against the Browns, the NFL, and anybody else he can think of.

The comedic aspects of the film arise mainly from Matthau's ability with verbal dexterity and facial malleability and his satiric rendition of a sleazy tort lawyer coupled with the spineless behavior of nice-guy Hinkle that finally turns to righteous indignation. Written with I.A.L. Diamond by the celebrated Wilder, a cynical moralist, the script often sags in its singular action, dragging on for more than two hours. But Wilder's sharp direction never falters. He elicits further comedy from secondary roles of Hinkle's greedy ex-wife Sandy (Judi West), bumbling private detective Purkey (Cliff Osmond), and a sympathetic performance from footballer Rich.

Lincoln (John Anderson) joins the plot when Hinkle is in the hospital recovering from his accident and just beginning to become involved in Gingrich's scheme. There is an old movie on TV in which Lincoln gives his famous statement, "You can fool some of the people...." This gives Hinkle pause, but he goes on with the scam anyway. The choice of this wise aphorism proves especially apt and surprising.

The Faking of the President (1976)

Lincoln: William J. Daprato.

This satire uses Nixon's voice from 250 hours of tapes, speeches and press conferences, re-edited word by word, resulting in the 37th president making the most outrageous accusations, confessions, *faux pas* and *non sequiturs*. Visuals come from newsreel stock footage and comic vignettes created by actor Richard M. Dixon. Lincoln's (William J. Daprato) appearance is just a cameo. The comedy is similar in style to the Abels' earlier film, *Is There Sex After Death?* (1971). For details, see Chapter 37 on Richard Nixon.

Guardian of the Wilderness (1977) aka Mountain Man

Lincoln: Ford Rainey. *Other Cast:* Denver Pyle (Galen Clark), John Dehner (John Muir), Ken Berry (Zachary Moore), Cheryl Miller (Kathleen Clark), Don Shanks (Indian Friend, Teneiya). *Director:* David O'Malley. *Producer:* Charles E. Seller, Jr. *Screenwriters:* Casey Conlon, Charles E. Sellier Jr. *Cinematography:* Henning Schellerup. *Music:* Bob Summers. *Film Editing:* Sharon Miller. *Art Direction:* Paul Staheli. *Makeup:* Mike Bacarella. *Studio:* Sunn Classic Pictures Inc. *Length:* 112 minutes.

This is a family film supposedly based on the life of Galen Clark (Denver Pyle) who was responsible for saving California's Yosemite Valley from commercial development. As a family film there are numerous friendly animals doing wondrous deeds aided by friendly Indians. The only despicable characters are loggers who intend to destroy the valley and the mountain lions that abound in the area.

Aided by his friend Zachary Moore (played by longtime Disney family film specialist Ken Berry) and his association with famous naturalist John Muir (John Dehner), Clark maps the Yosemite Valley in preparation for the passing of a preservation law in the California Legislature. Unfortunately, his arrival is too late in Sacramento, the state capital, to make his case, but he learns that the federal government is interested in such a law.

By a feat of transportation wizardry for the 1860s, Clark says that all he needs is ten days to get to Washington, D.C., to plead his case. In a final desperate scene he gets to see President Lincoln (Ford Rainey) by sheer accident—and stirs the president's curiosity about his documents that have fallen on the executive's floor. Convinced of the plan, Lincoln issues an executive order saving the Yosemite area from the loggers. Rainey plays the Lincoln role well but suffers from his physicality: He is much heavier in the face than the 16th president and has a scraggly beard.

The Lincoln Conspiracy (1977)

Lincoln: John Anderson. *Other Cast:* Bradford Dillman (John Wilkes Booth), John Dehner (Col. Lafayette C. Baker), Robert Middleton (Edwin M. Stanton), James Green (Capt. James William Boyd), Whit Bissell (Sen. John Conness). *Director:* James L. Conway. *Producers:* Raymond D. Jensen, Charles E. Sellier Jr. *Writing Credits:* Jonathan Cobbler (based on the book by David Balsiger and Charles E. Sellier Jr.). *Music:* Bob Summers. *Cinematography:* Henning Schellerup. *Film Editing:* Martin Dreffke. *Art Direction:* William Cornford. *Set Decoration:* Charles C. Bennett. *Costume Design:* Cheryl Beasley. *Studio:* Sunn Classic Pictures Inc. *Length:* 90 minutes.

In addition to its wildly inaccurate history, *The Lincoln Conspiracy* is a poorly made, directed, and acted film. Supposedly based on "newly discovered evidence" (that has never been seen by any recognized historian), the story implicates Secretary of War Edwin Stanton (Robert Middleton) in a plot to kidnap Lincoln (John Anderson) on the same day and in the same place that the president is actually killed by John Wilkes Booth (Bradford Dillman). Stanton's motive is to negate Lincoln's reconstruction policy for the South. As has been seen in the case of John F. Kennedy's assassination, conspiracy theorists come out of some archive regardless of the assuredness of the evidence otherwise. In this film Stanton's purported kidnaper is killed while searching for Booth, and then is passed off as Booth by Stanton. The actual Booth is never caught.

John Anderson, who played Lincoln in an earlier TV film, gives a stiff although reasonable portrayal in this instance given the absurdity of the story and the poorness of the production.

Czarodziej z Harlemu (1988)

Lincoln: Okon Jones. *Other Cast:* Bodgdan Baer (Sylwester Baczek), Leszek Teleszynski (Romuald Straczek), Piotr Skarga (Jagodka), Jan Monczka (Szwed), Jerzy Lustyk (Black-Market

16—Abraham Lincoln (1861–1865)

Money Changer), Wojciech Nizynski (Grynszpan), Malgorzata Boratynska (Jola, Baczek's Secretary), Anna Gornostaj (Hot Dog Seller/Massage Therapist). *Director:* Pawel Karpinski. *Writing Credits:* Pawel Karpinski, Leszek Konarski, Wojciech Nizynski. *Music:* Krzysztof Marzec. *Cinematography:* Zdzislaw Kaczmarek. *Film Editing:* Anna Wilska. *Sound:* Stanislaw Bokowy. *Studio:* Studio Filmowe Perspektywa, Zespol Filmowy "Perspektywa." *Length:* 76 minutes.

This Polish film was not available for our viewing and the only information we could find was a list of credits. Lincoln appears in six scenes, initially stressing "trust ... to handle peace ... and to keep the country together" before his assassination scene and a voice-over of his Gettysburg Address.

Two Idiots in Hollywood (1988)

Lincoln: Richard Craycroft. *Other Cast:* J.B. McGrath (Murphy Wegg), Jeff Doucette (Taylor Dupp), Cheryl Anderson (Marianne Plambo), Lisa Lack Robins (NBA Casting Secretary), Joe Clark (Himself), Jenny Bourgeois (Lynn Jett). *Director-Writer:* Stephen Tobolowsky. *Studio:* New World Pictures. *Length:* 85 minutes.

Anyone over 12 years of age would deserve the name of the title of this film if they were to spend money to see it because this is another teenage film with the intelligence and humor at a level to entertain the least thoughtful teenager. It is an expansion of director Tobolowsky's cult theatrical production of the same name.

Talyor Dupp (Jeff Doucette) and Murphy Wagg (J.B. McGrath) of Dayton, Ohio, decide to go to Hollywood to seek their fortunes. (They should have stayed in Dayton.) There is a cameo appearance in the last sequence of scenes with the ghost of Lincoln played unconvincingly by Richard Craycroft. Virtually the same scene appears in a much better picture, *Happy Gilmore* (1996), when Lincoln shows up in the sky with one of the dead characters from the film.

The Big Picture (1989)

Lincoln: Richard Blake. *Other Cast:* Kevin Bacon (Nick Chapman), Emily Longstreth (Susan Rawlings), J.T. Walsh (Allen Habel), Jennifer Jason Leigh (Lydia Johnson), Martin Short (Nick's Agent), Walter Olkewicz (Babe Ruth). *Director:* Christopher Guest. *Producer:* Richard Gilbert Abramson. *Writing Credits:* Michael Varhol, Christopher Guest, Michael McKean. *Music:* David Nichtern. *Cinematography:* Jeff Jur. *Film Editing:* Martin Nicholson. *Studio:* Aspen Film Society. *Length:* 100 minutes.

In his first film directorial effort, *Saturday Night Live* comedian Christopher Guest tackles a very uneven comedy. Since the release of this film, Guest has developed an almost cult-like following with three writing, directing, and performing efforts, *Waiting for Guffman* (1997), *Best in Show* (2000), and *The Mighty Wind* (2003). Unfortunately the quiet, subtle humor of these later films is not evident in his first effort.

The story of *The Big Picture* concerns aspiring filmmaker Nick Hampman (Kevin Bacon) who turns out an interesting film as his final exam before graduating from film school. It attracts the attention of a major studio executive, Allen Habel (J.T. Walsh). Through working with Habel, who changes Chapman's idea of a serious film into another of his teenage beach party movies, Chapman experiences, in a satiric manner, all of the strangeness and insincerity of Hollywood. Included is a wild agent, Neil Sussman, an uncredited appearance by Martin Short. The development of this role for Short shows director Guest's genius for comic characterization.

Fighting to maintain his artistic integrity during his Hollywood education into corruption, Chapman lapses at times throughout the film into replacing current events with similar traditional film genre scenes. For example, when he breaks up with his girlfriend, Susan Rawlings (Emily Longstreth), he pictures her in a film noir gangster and moll scene. Another of these imaginary scenes entitled "Abe and the Babe" shows President Lincoln (Richard Blake) using an axe to fashion a baseball bat for Babe Ruth (Walter Olkewicz). Lincoln, working in what appears to be a California farm setting, wears (inappropriately for his time) a beard, a clean white shirt, and a stovepipe hat. In Chapman's take on history, this strange combination is supposed to be a buddy movie. The film is best considered as an inside Hollywood joke complete with unbilled celebrity cameos.

Bill & Ted's Excellent Adventure (1989)

Lincoln: Robert V. Barron. *Other Cast:* Keanu Reeves (Ted Logan), Alex Winter (Bill S. Preston, Esq.), George Carlin (Rufus), Bernie Casey (Mr. Ryan), Hal Landon Jr. (Captain Logan), Terry Camilleri (Napoleon), Dan Shor (Billy the Kid), Tony Steedman (Socrates), Rod Loomis (Dr. Sigmund Freud), Al Leong (Genghis Khan), Jane Wieedlin (Joan of Arc). *Director:* Stephen Herek. *Producers:* Scott Kroopf, Michael S. Murphey, Joel Soisson. *Writing Credits:* Chris Matttheson, Ed Solomon. *Music:* Gary Cherone, David Newman. *Cinematography:* Tim Suhrstedt. *Film Editing:* Larry Bock, Patrick Rand. *Costume Design:* Jill Ohanneson. *Studio:* Interscope Communications/Nelson Entertainment/Orion Soisson-Murphy Productions. *Length:* 90 minutes.

This goofy comedy includes Lincoln as an unlikely character after a dozen years' absence from the big screen. President Lincoln (Robert V. Barron) turns up during two inseparable numbskull teenagers' trip through time to assemble historical figures for their history report. Devoted to becoming rock stars, although admitting they can't even play the guitar, they will flunk history unless their report is what their supportive and long-suffering teacher Mr. Ryan (Bernie Casey) terms "something very special." They are to "ace" an oral exam about how a famous historical person would react today. If not, Ted's father (Hal Landon, Jr.) vows to send his garage band son to military school in Alaska and their "Wild Stallions" band would break up. George Carlin as Rufus turns up in a time machine from a world where Bill & Ted's rock music is the bedrock of society. He dials them up.

The film led to an animated and a live-action TV series as well as a sequel, *Bill & Ted's Bogus Journey* (1991). In the sequel, the same actors, Keanu Reeves and Alex Winter, under the same director, Stephen Herek, go to Heaven.

In *Excellent Adventure* the young adventurers' controlling line is "Party on, dudes." They do, seeing life as such and mispronounce history or reduce every encounter to an anachronistic joke of misunderstanding. That is, every historical figure's dialogue and actions are historically based so that they do not work or seem funny in the 20th century. For example, the only thing Bill learns is that Caesar is a salad dressing. The longest scene for the Lincoln character is at the final high school assembly where students present their history projects. Arriving on stage at the last minute with Bill, Ted, and his historical colleagues (Genghis Kahn, Joan of Arc, Sigmund Freud et al.), Lincoln enters with dignity and para-

Bill & Ted's Excellent Adventure (1989): Lincoln, along with many other presidents, appears in modern teenage movies such as this Keanu Reeves (left) and Adam Winter (center) comedy. Robert V. Barron is an obviously young Lincoln, joined at the table by Rod Loomis as Freud and Clifford David as Beethoven, in this time-travel story of how historical figures help two teenagers pass their history course. Photo by Phil Caruso for Orion Pictures Corp. (Courtesy of George Eastman House.)

phrases his Gettysburg Address: "Four score and seven minutes ago we your forefathers were brought forward on a most excellent adventure ... dedicated to the proposition to be excellent to each other ... and to party on, dudes."

Such tortured twisting of history annoys serious educators yet delights others in making history fun, fun, fun. There's just too much of that, particularly a too-long scene in an amusement park with Terry Camilleri as Napoleon taking over—as Napoleon did—a water slide.

Bebe's Kids (1992)

Lincoln: Voice of Pete Renaday. *Other Voice Cast:* Rich Little (President Nixon), Faizon Love (Robin Harris), Vanessa Bell Calloway (Jamika), Wayne Collins Jr. (Leon), Jonell Green (LaShawn), Marques Houston (Kahill), Tone Loc (Pee Wee), Myra J. (Dorothea), Nell Carter (Vivian), Bebe Drake (Bebe Drake-Massey). *Director:* Bruce W. Smith. *Producers:* Reginald and Warrington Hudlin. *Writing Credits:* Robin Harris, Reginald Hudlin. *Music:* John Barnes. *Film Editing:* Lynne Southerland. *Production Design:* Fred Cline. *Studio:* Hyperion Pictures. *Length:* 70 minutes.

This is the first mainstream animated feature film developed for African American audiences. Based on a comedy routine by the late Robin Harris (Faizon Love), it is a romantic comedy gone crazy. To romance Jamika (Vanessa Bell Calloway), Harris takes her son as well as her friend Bebe's three kids on their date. They careen from one childhood amusement to another, satirizing hip-hop music, urban riots, and whitebread theme parks. Understandably, they are charged with aggression. President Lincoln (Pete Renaday) defends them as the kids present their rap defense with a chorus about freedom. President Nixon (Rich Little) waves his arms in familiar gestures in his prosecution of these little monsters. They are exonerated and go on merrily to more mayhem in Las Vegas.

Happy Gilmore (1996)

Lincoln: Charles Brame. *Other Cast:* Adam Sandler (Happy Gilmore), Chris McDonald (Shooter McGavin), Julie Bowen (Virginia), Frances Bay (Grandma), Carl Weathers (Chubbs). *Director:* Dennis Dugan. *Producers:* Brad Grey, Sandy Wernick. *Writing Credits:* Tim Herlihy, Adam Sandler. *Music:* Mark Mothersbaugh. *Cinematography:* Arthur Albert. *Film Editing:* Jeff Gourson, Steve R. Moore. *Studio:* Universal Pictures. *Length:* 92 minutes.

In an attempt to cross the violence and speed of hockey with the gentility of golf, Adam Sandler, who writes and plays the part of Happy Gilmore, does little to appeal to the fans of either sport. Nor does he satirize class warfare and sports, as Stephen Holden noted in the *New York Times*. As an excessively violent hockey player he obviously knows nothing about the game's skills, and when he turns his violence to golf it may be funny to his teenage audience, but it does nothing for serious golfers.

Making a guest appearance at a tournament, game show host Bob Barker brawls with Gilmore, whose hyperkinetic shtick finally triumphs over his golfing nemesis, Shooter McGavin (Chris McDonald). Gilmore uses his hockey-stick putter to sink the winning stroke in a fallen tower that resembles a miniature golf obstacle. Gilmore's aided in his golfing quest to get money for his grandma's (Frances Bay) confiscated house by a PR woman (Julie Bowen) and Chubbs, a disfigured golf pro turned teacher (Carl Weathers).

After an untimely death, Chubb appears in the sky with Lincoln (Charles Brame) in the final scene, both unexplained and unnecessary.

Sometimes Santa's Gotta Get Whacked (1998)

Lincoln: Tom Katsis.
For details, see Chapter 1 on George Washington.

Wrongfully Accused (1998)

Lincoln: Mark Francis. *Other Cast:* Leslie Nielsen (Ryan Harrison), Richard Crenna (Lt. Fergus Falls), Kelly LeBrock (Lauren Goodhue), Melinda McGraw (Cass Lake), Michael York (Hibbing Goodhue), Sandra Bernhard (Dr. Fridley), Aaron Pearl (Sean Laughrea), Leslie Jones (Sgt. Tina Bagley), Ben Ratner (Sgt. Orono), Bev Martin (Mary Lincoln). *Director-Producer-Screenwriter:* Pat Proft. *Cinematographer:* Glen MacPherson. *Editor:* James Symons. *Production Designer:* Michael S. Bolton. *Art Director:* Sandy Cochrane. *Set Designer:* Lin MacDonald. *Sound:* Rob Young. *Stunts:* Guy Bews. *Studio:* Constantin Film Produktion Gamble-I/Morgan Creek Productions. *Length:* 87 minutes.

Leslie Nielsen plays Ryan Harrison, but he appears as he has in his many films, mostly the *Naked Gun* series—bumbling. He's wrongfully accused of a murder that a one-armed, one-legged, one-eyed man has done. Mark Francis appears as Abe Lincoln and Bev Martin as Mary Lincoln but they are not discernible in this fast-paced satire of *The Fugitive* (1993), the Harrison Ford action film.

Many other films receive lampooning include *Titanic* (1997), *Clear and Present Danger* (1994), *Chinatown* (1974), *Mission: Impossible* (1996), *North by Northwest* (1959), *Field of Dreams* (1989), *Braveheart* (1995), and *Superman* (1978). Pat Proft made his directing debut as well as being the producer and screenwriter. He's obviously adept, knows films, and his opening characterization of Nielsen as a virtuoso violinist is clever.

Some Kinda Joke (2001)

Lincoln: Howard Chester. *Other Cast:* Steve Seagren (Guy), Jimmy Pardo (Johnny "Who's There"), Lenny Schmidt (Joe the Bartender), Tom Tully (Shot Drinking Man), Sarah Rachelle (Arm Pit Lady), Ted Lyde (Drunk "Ballerina" Admirer), Karen Rontowski (Lady with Duck), Jeff Tully (Priest), Brenda Hill (Nun), Tony Dimond (Rabbi), Christina Grandy (Genie), Mike Lukas (Bad Guy with Frog on Head), Franko (Arab Sheik), Hannes Phinney (Farmer), Cathryn J. Brockett (Farmer's Daughter). *Director-Producer-Writer:* Alan Altur. *Other Writing Credits:* Steve Seagren. *Music:* Steve Davis. *Film Editing:* Ryan Reilly. *Cinematography:* Brett Smith. *Production Design:* Deborah Davis. *Costume Design:* Charlene McCabe. *Makeup:* Madlen Sarkisyan. *Art Department:* Connie Condos, Dave Cox. *Sound:* Kenny Klimak. *Studio:* Hammerscotch.

This film was not available for our viewing.

Zoolander (2001)

Lincoln: Charles Brame. *Other Credits:* Ben Stiller (Derek Zoolander), Owen Wilson (Hansell), Will Ferrell (Mugatu), Christine Taylor (Matilda), Milla Jovovich (Katinka), Jerry Stiller (Maury Ballstein), Jon Voight (Larry Zoolander), David Bowie (Himself). *Director-Producer-Screenwriter:* Ben Stiller. *Producer:* Scott Rudin. *Cinematography:* Barry Peterson. *Composer:* David Arnold. *Editor:* Greg Hayden. *Studio:* NPV Entertainment. *Length:* 89 minutes.

Comic actor Ben Stiller co-wrote, directed, and stars in this spoof of the fashion industry that originated as a short skit for the 1996 VH1 Fashion Awards. Stiller does what he calls "the most extreme manifestation of vacuous self-love" as a male model in this overdrawn lampoon. For years the top model, Stiller loses that position when Hansen (Owen Wilson) defeats him in a "walk-off" that mocks the posturing of male models. In Zoolander's attempt to recover his status he's invited to a day spa by fashion designer Jacobim Mugatu (Will Ferrell). Katinka (Milla Jovovich) brainwashes Zoolander, programming him into assassinating the prime minister of Malaysia to help the U.S. balance of trade.

Lincoln (Charles Brame), previously *Happy Gilmore*'s Lincoln, appears in one scene showing that all of the major assassinations in history have been accomplished by male models. Neither the scene nor the movie deserve serious comment.

Stiller's real-life wife Christine Taylor appears as his love interest Matilda, as does his father Jerry Stiller along with a host of personalities, led by Donald Trump, who play themselves.

The Master of Disguises (2002)

Lincoln: Buddy Bolton.

Buddy Bolton appears as Abe Lincoln in a one-shot scene during which the grandfather of star Dana Carvey as Pistachio Disguisey explains the family's mystical means of changing one's identity that Disguisey does dozens of times in this family-oriented film. One of these disguised characters, a hip-hop dancer, replaces Lincoln in the scene. Lincoln surreptitiously leaves the stage, saying he has to go get a glass of water. For details, see Chapter 1 on George Washington.

From Surveyor to President (2003)

Bearded Lincoln: Charles Ott. *Young Lincoln:* Jode Woodard. *Other Cast:* Gillette Ransom (Mary Todd Lincoln). *Director:* Dean Williams. *Producers:* Paul Beaver, Cindy Mclaughlin, Dean Williams. *Film Editing:* Mike Unland. *Studio:* Dean Williams Productions.

The title might suggest a film about George Washington but the cast list does not. IMDb notes that it was estimated to cost $100,000.

The Man Who Invented the Moon (2003)

Lincoln: Charles Brame. *Other Cast:* Sean Gunn (Sammy Hughes), Nicolette DiMaggio (Haley/Megan), Julie Dolan (Haley 2), Brent Saxton (Tommy), Matt Gunn (Dan McMahon), "Santa Dave" Barnes (Santa Claus), Eddie Ebell (Jesus the Christ), Michael Cornacchia (Babe Ruth), Robert Gantzos (Davey Crockett). *Director:* John Cabrera. *Producers:* Sean Gunn, Lee Kirk, Larry Fitzgibbon. *Writing Credits:* Lee Kirk. *Music:* Willie Wisely. *Cinematography:* Ken Seng. *Film Editing:* John Cabrera. *Art Direction:* James Clark. *Studio:* Normandie County. *Length:* 33 minutes.

This film was shown at the St. Louis Film-maker's Showcase. From the cast listing it would appear to be a wild fantasy since it includes Jesus Christ, Davy Crockett, and Babe Ruth, to name a few. Lincoln is portrayed by Charles L. Brame, who also had the role in *Happy Gilmore* and *Zoolander*.

Lincoln vs Bush (2004)

Lincoln: Tom Katsis. *Other Cast:* DeMorge Brown (Andre Johnson), Nicholas M. Muccini (VP Cheney), Danny Murphy (Moderator), Cathy Shambley (Dr. Solomon). *Director-Writer-Film Editing:* Pat Battistini.

This seeming duel is one among many comedy shorts released recently to cover the supposed shortcomings of President Bush. This one obviously compares the greatness of Lincoln with the problems of Bush by having a secret society try to thaw the cryogenically frozen Lincoln to save the country. What these perpetrators do not realize is that Lincoln was attacked by political opponents and the press during his presidency in much stronger terms than has Bush. However, with a $3,000 budget and one person, Pat Battistini, serving as director, writer, and film editor, it is difficult to include complexities in a film. The cast list does not even include Bush.

The Legend of Zorro (2005)

Lincoln: Pedro Mira. *Other Cast:* Adrian Alonso (Joaquin), Nick Chinlund (Jacob McGivens), Antonio Banderas (Zorro/Alejandro), Catherine Zeta-Jones (Elena), Rufus Sewell

(Armand). *Director:* Martin Campbell. *Writing Credits:* Roberto Orci, Alex Kurtzman, Ted Elliott, Terry Rossio, Johnston McCulley. *Producers:* Laurie MacDonald, Walter F. Parkes, Lloyd Phillips. *Music:* Eduardo Gamboa, James Horner. *Cinematography:* Phil Meheux. *Film Editing:* Stuart Baird. *Production Design:* Thomas Owen. *Art Direction:* Tomas Owen. *Set Decoration:* Jon Danniells. *Costume Design:* Graciela Mazon. *Studio:* Amblin Entertainment/Spyglass Entertainment. *Length:* 129 minutes.

A sequel to the 1998 *The Mask of Zorro, Legend* garnered mixed reviews. The plot is pretty straight Zorro: Zorro *nee* Don Alejandro de la Vega (Antonio Banderas) still upholds the fight for justice in pre-statehood California. His wife Elena (Catherine Zeta-Jones) has become somewhat of a nag, wanting Zorro to spend more time at home with their child. Nevertheless, they work together long enough to foil a plot designed to block statehood. This leads to the interesting presidential appearance of Lincoln (Pedro Mira) who in 1850 was a politically ambitious, small town lawyer in Springfield, Illinois, at the signing ceremony welcoming California into the Union. Hollywood still has the right to use its historical license.

Lincoln's Eyes (2005)

Lincoln: William Schallert, voice. *Other Cast:* Stephen Wozniak (The Yankee Merchant). *Director:* Charles Otte. *Producers:* Tisa Poe, Bob Rogers. *Music:* David Kneupper. *Cinematography:* Reed Smoot. *Production Design:* Chuck Roberts. *Costume Design:* Christina Wright. *Special Effects:* Stan Winston Studio: *Studio:* BRC Imagination Arts. *Length:* 17 minutes.

The concept for this 17-minute film is interesting in that an artist is trying to understand everything he sees in Lincoln's eyes as he paints a portrait, a challenge described by many of Lincoln's associates and chroniclers. The film's brief write-up in IMDb indicates that there are dazzling special effects. Although the director, Charles Otte, and cast have limited experience, Reed Smoot, the cinematographer, has broad experience in the field since 1971 including an award from Kodak for IMAX work. In addition, the special effects were done by the Stan Winston Studio that has considerable experience in such films as the *Terminator* series, *Big Fish* (2003), and *Pearl Harbor* (2001).

The Persistence of Dreams (2005)

Lincoln: Jeffrey DeMunn. *Other Cast:* Rosemary Knower (Mary Todd Lincoln), Sean Hagan (John Wilkes Booth), Jane Beard (Mrs. Mountchessington). *Director-Writer-Film Editing:* Erik Courtney. *Producers:* Chip Bartlett, Ben Brunkhardt, Erik Courtney. *Music:* Marcus Trumpp. *Cinematography:* Ben Brunkhardt. *Production Design:* Paul Falcon. *Costume Design:* Thomas F. Timlin Jr., Martha R. Timlin. *Makeup:* Frank Rogers. *Sound:* Chris M. Jacobson. *Studio:* Arrowhead Productions. *Length:* 4 minutes.

In a four-minute film, first-time director, writer, producer, and film editor Eric Courtney attempts to portray the last conscious moments of Lincoln's life in real time.

Untitled Steven Spielberg/Abraham Lincoln Project (2007)

Lincoln: Liam Neeson. *Director:* Steven Spielberg. *Writing Credits:* Doris Kearns Goodwin (biography).

This project upcoming.

17

Andrew Johnson (1865–1869)

Andrew Johnson. (Courtesy of Library of Congress.)

Alone among senators from seceding states, Andrew Johnson, a Jacksonian Democrat and staunch Constitutionalist, stood by the Union during the Civil War. In 1862 Lincoln named him war governor of his native Tennessee where he had served in the Legislature, as governor, U.S. congressman, and senator. For his remarkable service, the Republicans nominated him in 1864 for the vice presidency, giving presidential candidate Lincoln a ticket that was both nonpartisan and non-sectional. Charles Dickens wrote one of the best descriptions extant: "He is a man with a remarkable face, indicating courage, watchfulness, and certainly strength of purpose.... Figure, rather stout for an American; a trifle under the middle size; hands clasped in front of him; manner, suppressed, guarded, anxious. Each of us looked at the other very hard."[1] Johnson sought to continue Lincoln's magnanimous Reconstruction plan but without regard for freed peoples' rights because unlike Lincoln, Johnson was a bitter racist.[2] The result was conflict with the Radical Republicans who dominated Congress and Johnson's unwillingness to compromise with them. Johnson either vetoed or opposed many measures including the Freeman's Bureau Bill and the Fourteenth Amendment providing citizenship to all persons born or naturalized in the country. The conflict ended with impeachment for attempting to remove his disloyal Secretary of War Edwin M. Stanton. Johnson was acquitted, most importantly because several senators believed to convict a chief executive for mere political reasons undermined the tripartite system of American government. Besides, Johnson had only nine more months left in office—during which his loyal Secretary of State William Henry Seward purchased Alaska, the most famous achievement of the administration. Vindicated after leaving office by election to the Senate three times, Johnson served there until his death in 1875.

THE FILMS

With but two films available to assess his film treatment, Johnson can only be remembered by the dynamic portrayal of him by Van Heflin in *Tennessee Johnson*. It is a biopic of his adult career, starting as an illiterate tailor and ending with his triumphant return to the Senate after his besmirched presidency by impeachment of which he was acquitted.

In the Days of Buffalo Bill (1922)

Harry Myers appears as Johnson in this 18-episode series. For details, see Chapter 16 on Lincoln.

Tennessee Johnson (1943)

Johnson: Van Heflin. *Other Cast:* Ruth Hussey (Eliza McCardle), Lionel Barrymore (Thad Stevens), Marjorie Main (Mrs. Fisher), Regis Toomey (McDaniel), Morris Ankrum (Jefferson Davis), Ed O'Neill (Lincoln). *Director:* William Dieterle. *Producer:* J. Walter Ruben. *Writing Credits:* John L. Balderston, Milton Gunzburg. *Music:* Herbert Stothart. *Cinematography:* Harold Rosson. *Film Editing:* Robert Kern. *Art Direction:* Cedric Gibbons. *Studio:* MGM. *Length:* 100 minutes.

Johnson has not been one of Hollywood's favorite presidents, although his administration included some of the most dramatic and controversial events in American history. However, the one movie about his life is an excellent biopic that with reasonable accuracy covers the political highlights in this politician's life. Thaddeus Stevens's supporters felt he was treated unsympathetically in the film. Given Hollywood's tendency to write its own history, *Tennessee Johnson*, with MGM's opening caveat of "certain dramatic liberties," is not a bad film.

Van Heflin gives a strong performance as Johnson who is first seen in Greenville, Tennessee, in the spring of 1830, having escaped from an apprenticeship as a tailor "back East." As in Johnson's actual life, the film shows how he quickly opens his own business, learns to read and write from schoolteacher Eliza McCardle (Ruth Hussey), marries her, and has a child—and naturally gets into politics. The film then breezes through Johnson's rather turbulent political life in which he held all of the major offices in Tennessee including congressman, governor, and senator. In 1860 Senator Johnson is back in his hometown shown giving a speech against Lincoln but stating that the nation would have to support Lincoln if he is elected. Even in non-slave holding eastern Tennessee, this message is not well-received.

The speech segues into the Senate chambers in Washington where Johnson is giving essentially the same speech and being attacked by Southern senators. As the scene ends, Jefferson Davis (Morris Ankrum) tells the Senate that Mississippi has seceded. All of the Southern senators walk out with the exception of Johnson.

The war years pass quickly with no mention of Johnson's being Lincoln's choice as

Opposite: Tennessee Johnson (1942): Van Heflin as President Andrew Johnson defends himself from impeachment charges in the Metro-Goldwyn-Mayer biopic. It is one of the few presidential films that covers the full political life of a president. Directed by William Dieterle, it was a Metro-Goldwyn-Mayer production. (Courtesy of George Eastman House.)

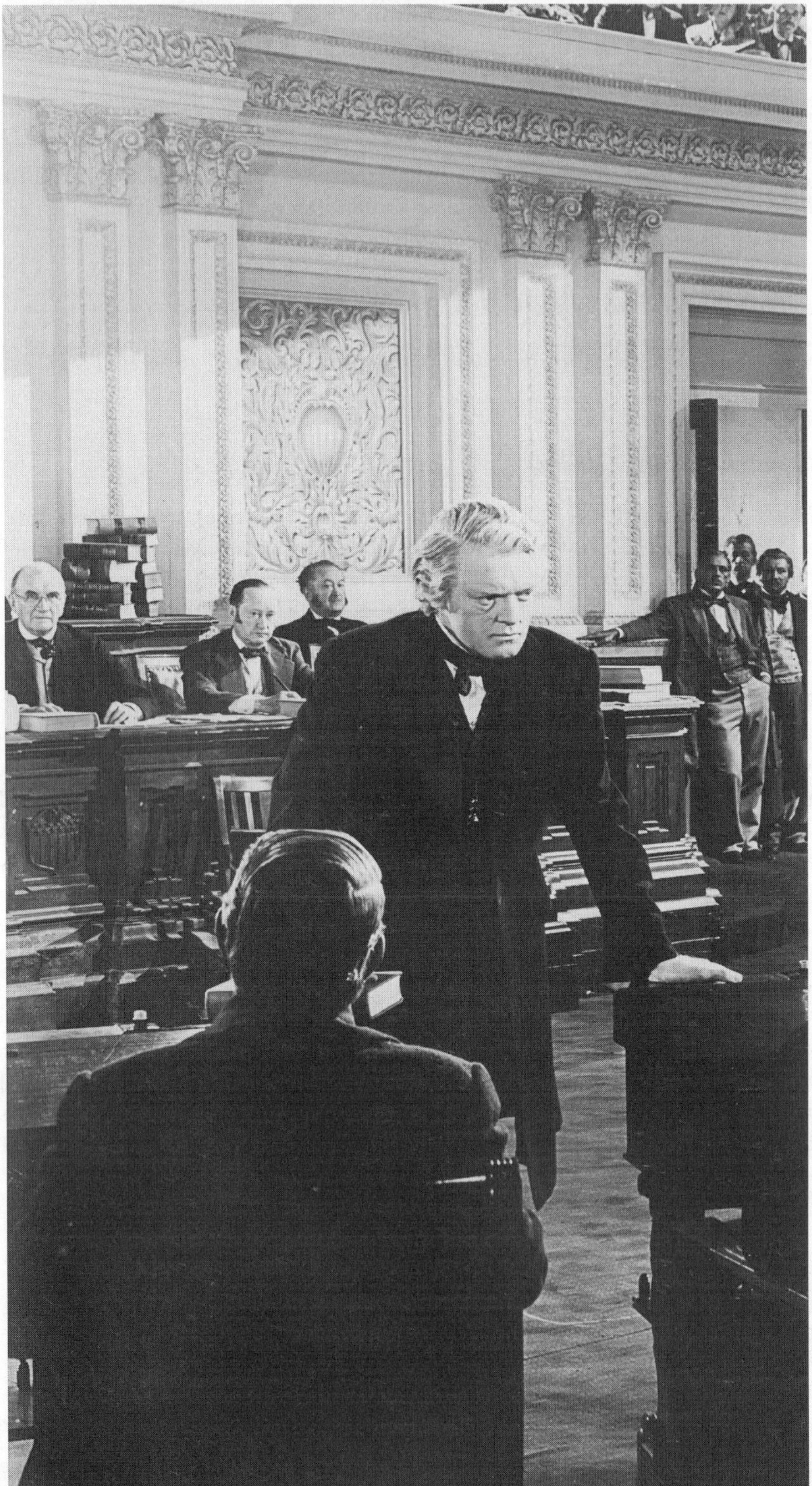

wartime governor of Tennessee. In 1864 the villain of Johnson's presidency and of this picture, Thaddeus Stevens (Lionel Barrymore), is introduced when Lincoln passes him over to insist that Johnson be his vice presidential running mate. Lincoln and Johnson win. Lincoln (Ed O'Neill) attends Johnson's swearing-in ceremony. Only his distinctive hat shows on camera. Lincoln appears again, face invisible, in his deathbed scene. The accuracy of his appearances in this film is questioned by Mark S. Reinhart in his *Abraham Lincoln on Screen* because of the depiction of a historically inaccurate speech given by Johnson several hours before the assassination.

Upon Lincoln's assassination, Johnson takes the office and makes clear that he does not feel fit for the job, but that he will try to do what Lincoln had planned, particularly with regard to Reconstruction. To this end he meets the opposition of the Radical Republicans led by Stevens who are for strict, vengeful reconstruction. Stevens rightly says Johnson is "a great stickler for the Constitution." Yet Stevens gets his reasons to impeach Johnson when Johnson fires one of his Cabinet officers in violation of the "Tenure of Office Act."

The drama of the Senate impeachment trial is overstated in this film by director William Dieterle's having Johnson appear to defend himself (which he did not do). But it is impossible to make the actual vote any more dramatic that it was—acquittal by one vote. In the final scene Johnson returns to the Senate chamber as the newly elected senator from Tennessee, the only former president to be elected senator, and makes a speech about the unity of the nation. Heflin was an excellent actor who presents Johnson's strengths—his moral uprightness—and shortcomings—his touchy pride of the self-made man—with equal skill. Many of Johnson's problems came from his inability to control his anger and his unwillingness to compromise once he had made up his mind. Fortunately, Heflin had the skills to illustrate these complex characteristics without denigrating the president's positive points. Although less stocky than Johnson, Heflin uses his haunted eyes, terse speaking voice, and noted temper to great credit.

18

Ulysses Simpson Grant (1869–1877)

Again, Americans voted a war hero into office, Ulysses Simpson Grant. But the man who could effectively and efficiently command troops failed to handle the complexity of commanding a country. His list of failures in office—bad selection of cabinet and other appointees, failure to formulate policy, inability to learn from mistakes, and blindness to widespread corruption in his administration—cannot be denied. Yet, throughout his eight years in office the public adored him.

His notable achievement in foreign affairs was the settlement of Civil War controversies with England by the Treaty of London negotiated by Secretary of State Hamilton Fish, "the jewel in his toad" of a cabinet. In national affairs during his first term, he advocated prompt payment of the war debt of $500 million and the Fifteenth Amendment giving Black Americans the right to vote. Following Grant's lead in his second term, Congress endorsed equal pay for equal work for women in federal agencies and passed his Resumption Act providing for specie payment.

Ulysses Grant. (Courtesy of Library of Congress.)

After years of political party newspapers of note was the rising independence of the press and investigative reporting that exposed Grant's problems. It began with the source of much greed—gold that he sold as did his son-in-law Abel Rathbone Corbin in collusion with Wall Street speculators Jay Gould and Jim Fisk. The precious metal fell in price but Grant's reputation did not. Next were Caribbean problems as many Americans wanted to acquire Cuba and the Dominican Republic, but Congress did not. In the Credit Mobilier affair in which there was a fraudulent diversion of profits from the Union Pacific Railway to his vice president and other highly placed Republicans, Grant was able to wrap himself in the flag and blame others.[1] Intrigue was completely foreign to Grant's nature ... though humility of character may have put him at an initial disadvantage.[2]

Grant never declined in popularity with the electorate, but a congressional resolution stated a third term "unwise,"[3] and he himself declined physically because of throat cancer.

In almost the final effort of his life he wrote his memoirs that kept his beloved wife Julia and family from poverty.

THE FILMS

Although continually placed near the bottom of any list ranking the quality of American presidents, Grant was always popular with both the American people and Hollywood. The popularity among filmmakers arose from both his outstanding military leadership during the cataclysmic Civil War and his presidency during one of the major pushes to settle the American West.

As such Grant is a character in 45 films, more than many other more successful presidents. In these films 19 actors portray him. Joseph Crehan plays him the most, in seven films, followed by Walter Rodgers with six appearances. The focus is on Grant as a general during the Civil War in 15 films with the remainder mainly westerns taking place while he was president. The western's ideology fitted Grant.[4] The frontier provides the basis of a national public myth. Its ethos and codes are bound up with America's sense of itself as the nation for which no frontier was uncrossable, no enemy unbeatable, no mountain too high, no forest too dense for conquest. In other words, the western gives the assembly instruction for an empire, regeneration through violence.[5]

Despite his legendary military career, the 18th president is never the subject of a film, is never treated fully, and with the exception of ten of the films winds up as a bit character in films about Lincoln, Custer, and even Mark Twain, his friend. Grant is seen pardoning a spy, reuniting two lovers separated by the war, commuting a death sentence, or nodding his head in conversations with Lincoln. Grant is given few lines but usually seems to have a *good* cigar to smoke. However, in *Drum Beat* (1954) Grant (Hayden Rorke) has an extended scene with Johnny MacKay (Alan Ladd). Rorke, a most believable Grant, mirrors the legendary general's remarkable face that was described by Dickens as "indicating courage, watchfulness, and certainly strength of purpose." Twain went on to pay tribute to "[h]is patience; his indestructible equability of temper; his exceeding gentleness, kindness, forbearance, lovingness, modesty, diffidence, self depreciation...."[6]

Grant and Lincoln (1911)

Grant: Unknown actor.

Grant plays the villain in this Lincoln clemency film. For details, see Chapter 16 on Abraham Lincoln.

Lieutenant Grey of the Confederacy (1911)

Grant: Alvin Wyckoff.

The only aspect of Grant's appearance that is known is that he was portrayed by Alvin Wyckoff. For details, see Chapter 16 on Abraham Lincoln.

The Battle of Shiloh (1913)

Grant: John Smiley. *Other Cast:* William Carr (Col. Bogard), Nell Craig (Martha Dunnell), James Daly (Col. Samson), Robert Drouet (Tom Winston), Clarence Elmer (Sgt.

Brown), Robert Graham Jr. (Pvt. Randall), Mildred Gregory (Ethel Whitcliff), John Ince (Frank Carey), Edgar Jones (Capt. Cook), Arthur Matthews (Lt. Cornell), Jennie Nelson (Jane Mathies), Peggy O'Neil (Ellen Winston), Blanche West (Ethel Carey), Ferdinand Tidmarsh (Gen. Joseph Johnston), Florence Williams (Clara Tolliver). *Director*: Joseph Smiley. *Writing Credits*: Emmett Campbell Hall. *Studio*: Lubin Manufacturing Co. *Length*: Four reels.

Sister against sister in the Civil War drives the plot of this silent film. Tom Winston's (Robert Drouet) sister Ellen (Peggy O'Neil) tries to talk him out of joining the Union Army while Frank Carey's (John Ince) sister Ethel (Blanche West) tries to talk him out of joining the Confederate Army. Winston learns that his sister has become a Southern spy when he seizes a message that she has given to Carey. He lets Carey escape but keeps the message.

During the battle of Shiloh (reportedly filmed at $21,000), Union soldiers find the message on Winston and, even though he is a hero, accuse him of being a traitor. He is sentenced to death but avoids the firing squad when Carey confesses. Prisons were lax, and Carey escapes to return home where he is recaptured by Union soldiers. Nobody seems to stay at the front, and when Winston visits his Southern spy sister Ellen he is captured by Southern troops. The sisters arrange for an exchange and reunite with their soldier sweethearts.

John Smiley appears as General Grant in the battle scene and performs well impersonating the general under great pressure during the first major battle of the war in the West. This film, one of the early successful "feature" films, commemorates the 50th anniversary of the Civil War. It was partially filmed in what today is Valley Forge National Park.

With Lee in Virginia (1913)

Grant: Unknown actor.

Grant is included among the uncredited historical personages depicted. For details, see Chapter 16 on Abraham Lincoln.

The Battle Cry of Peace (1915)

Grant: Paul Scardon.

Paul Scardon portrays Ulysses S. Grant in the film. For details, see Chapter 1 on George Washington.

The Birth of a Nation (1915)

Grant: Donald Crisp.

Donald Crisp plays Grant with great seriousness, as was his usual acting manner, in this epic film. Both actor and director since he came to the U.S. in 1906 after service in the Boer War, Crisp was Griffith's assistant on this film and *Broken Blossoms* (1919). In the latter he played the brutal father, showing his versatility as an actor. His most notable roles were the grand old man in *How Green Was My Valley* (1941) for which he won an Academy Award for Best Supporting Actor, and later in the *Lassie* series. For details, see Chapter 16 on Abraham Lincoln.

The Life of Abraham Lincoln (1915)

Grant: James Harris.

During one of the short episodes in the film, James Harris briefly appears as General

18—Ulysses Simpson Grant (1869–1877)

The Birth of a Nation (1915): D.W. Griffith's landmark film on the Civil War and its aftermath included many historical figures including President Lincoln and Gen. Grant. Donald Crisp (right) as Grant accepts the surrender of Lee at Appomattox Court House in Virginia. General Lee is played by Howard Gaye in the silent epic produced by Epoch Producing Corp. (Courtesy of George Eastman House.)

Grant in his role as the leader of Northern military forces during the Civil War. For details, see Chapter 16 on Abraham Lincoln.

Madam Who (1918)

Grant: Bert Hadley.
Bert Hadley as General Grant makes a cameo appearance. For details, see Chapter 16 on Abraham Lincoln.

My Own United States (1918)

Grant: Frank Murray.
Since Lt. Philip Nolan II served in the Civil War at some point he ran into General Grant (Frank Murray). For details, see Chapter 3 on Thomas Jefferson

In the Days of Buffalo Bill (1922)

Grant: Joel Day and J. Herbert Frank.
Grant appears as played by both Joel Day and J. Herbert Frank in this 18-episode serial. For details, see Chapter 16 on Abraham Lincoln.

Broadway Broke (1923)

Grant: Albert Phillips. Other Cast: Mary Carr (Nellie Wayne), Macklyn Arbuckle (P.T. Barnum), Edward Earle (Charles Farrin), Henrietta Crosman (Madge Foster), Leslie King (Mark Twain), Frederick Burton (Augustin Daly). Director: J. Searle Dawley. Writing Credits: Earl Derr Biggers, John Lynch. Studio: Selznick International. Length: 30 minutes.

Based on a Saturday Evening Post story by Earl Derr Biggers, this is a story of elderly vaudeville star Nellie Wayne (Mary Carr) who falls on hard times because of her villainous son-in-law. To cover up a forgery he sells his trained dog Lassie Bronte to a medical laboratory. Wayne is able to save the dog and the day by selling the film rights to a play that her late husband wrote. Moreover, she gets an offer to act in the film for $500 a week.

Albert Phillips portrays a vaudevillian who performs as General Grant in early scenes, setting the background for Wayne's fame on stage.

Dixie (1924)

Grant: Albert Phillips. Other Cast: Arthur Dewey (Maj. William Allan), Florence Johnstone (Mrs. Allan), J. Barney Sherry (Gen. Robert E. Lee), Brenda Bond (Ella Allan), May Blossom (Mary Allan), Lyons Wickland (James Allan), Antrim Short (Henry Allan), Allen Connor (Capt. Robertson). Director: Webster Campbell. Writing Credits: Martha Tucker Stephenson (adaptation). Studio: Chronicles of America Pictures, Yale University Press. Length: Approximately 30 minutes.

Adapted by Martha Tucker Stephenson from the book *The Days of the Confederacy*, the film purports to show the effect the Civil War has on plantation life. Unfortunately, the tale of the Allan family, beginning on their plantation in South Carolina in 1861, is so biased for the South that it loses any believability.

Maj. William Allan (Arthur Dewey) rides off to war with his eldest son James (Lyons Wickland). This leaves Mrs. Allan (Florence Johnstone) at home to manage the plantation and to supply goods to Robert E. Lee's troops. When her overseer leaves, Mrs. Allan's job is that much worse particularly since her loyal slaves are being enticed by black Northern spies wandering through the neighborhood telling them of Lincoln's freeing the slaves.

There are occasional shots of battles, including Petersburg. And we know that Maj. Allan has been wounded; son James killed; and younger son Henry (Antrim Short) has gone into the army. However, the most striking sequence of scenes in this silent is the surrender at Appomattox. A very distinguished Gen. Robert E. Lee (J. Barney Sherry), hand on sword, waits in a small parlor for the arrival of Gen. Grant (Albert Phillips). Grant arrives looking dusty and disheveled, then sits looking down with his hand in his vest. The two generals talk briefly. Then Grant writes out the surrender document that includes a phrase allowing Confederate officers to keep their side arms. Lee says this will please his men. They finish and sign the document. Grant comes out of the little house, stands on the front step, and raises his hat to Lee. This is one of the most accurate and realistic representations of the surrender ever to appear on film with even the Appomattox buildings looking authentic.

Phillips looks like Grant and handles the seriousness of the situation with great skill.

The Dramatic Life of Abraham Lincoln (1924)

Grant: Walter Rodgers.

The film rated as one of the top ten films of the year by the *New York Times*. For details, see Chapter 16 on Abraham Lincoln.

The Warrens of Virginia (1924)

Grant: Lt. Wilbur J. Fox. *Other Cast:* George Backus (Gen. Warren), Rosemary Hill (Betty Warren), Martha Mansfield (Agatha Warren), Robert Andrews (Arthur Warren), Wilfred Lytell (Lt. Burton), Harlan Knight (Pap), James Turfler (Danny), Helen Ray Kyle (The Little Reb), J. Barney Sherry (Gen. Robert E. Lee), Frank Andrews (Gen. Griffin). *Director:* Elmer Clifton. *Writing Credits:* William C. De Mille (also play). *Studio:* Fox Film Corp.

This silent film deals with a familiar story: love between a Union officer and a Confederate woman. But Betty Warren (Rosemary Hill) of the Warrens of Virginia saves Lt. Burton (Wilfred Lytell) as he is about to be executed and as Lee surrenders.

Of interest is a 1915 version of the same William C. De Mille stage play by his brother Cecil B. While Martha Mansfield was shooting a scene for this film adaptation, her period dress caught fire. Although the flames were extinguished and she was rushed to a hospital, she died of burns.

The Flaming Frontier (1926)

Grant: Walter Rodgers. *Other Cast:* Hoot Gibson (Bob Langdon), Anne Cornwall (Betty Stanwood), Dustin Farnum (Gen. George Armstrong Custer), Ward Crane (Sam Belden), Kathleen Key (Lucretia), Eddie Gribbon (Jonesy), Harry Todd (California Joe), Harold Goodwin (Lawrence Stanwood), George Fawcett (Senator Stanwood), Noble Johnson (Sitting Bull), Charles K. French (Senator Hargess), William Steele (Penfield), Ed Wilson (Grant's Secretary), Joe Bonomo (Rain in the Face). *Director:* Edward Sedgwick. *Writing Credits:* Charles Kenyon, Edward J. Montagne, Raymond L. Schrock, Edward Sedgwick. *Cinematography:* Virgil Miller. *Studio:* Universal Pictures. *Length:* 101 minutes.

Hoot Gibson, one of Hollywood's great early cowboys, could not save this pretentious (reported costing $400,000) silent western from being just another oater. Langdon is a Pony Express rider admitted to West Point through the influence of Sen. Stanwood (George Fawcett). Langdon falls in love with Stanwood's daughter Betty (Anne Cornwall) and saves Stanwood's son Lawrence (Harold Goodwin) from being shamefully dismissed from the Point by accepting the dismissal himself.

Returning to the West, Langdon is part of General Custer's command at Little Big Horn, escaping the massacre by riding for help. Lawrence is killed in the battle and is carrying evidence of Langdon's innocence at the Point. Langdon is ultimately reinstated.

One of the subplots is the corruption of the Indian Ring in Washington during Grant's administration. The Ring is out to get both Stanwood and President Grant (Walter Rodgers). Grant's appearance relates to the attempt to expose the Ring. Walter Rodgers is one of the original Grant imitators and we assume that he does his usual good job.

The Heart of Maryland (1927)

Grant: Walter Rodgers.
See the discussion of the 1915 and 1927 film versions in Chapter 16 on Abraham Lincoln.

The Little Shepherd of Kingdom Come (1928)
aka Kentucky Courage

Grant: Walter Rodgers. *Other Cast:* Molly O'Day (Melissa Turner), Nelson McDowell (Old Joel Turner), Martha Mattox (Maw Turner), Victor Potel (Tom Turner), Richard Barthelmess (Chad Buford), Gustav von Seyffertitz (Nathan Cherry), Claude Gillingwater (Maj. Buford). *Director-Producer:* Alfred Santell. *Writing Credits:* Dwinelle Benthall, John Fox Jr. *Cinematography:* Lee Garmes. *Film Editing:* Hugh Bennett. *Studio:* First National Pictures Inc. *Length:* 72 minutes.

A young orphan born in Kentucky, Chad Buford (Richard Barthelmess), is adopted by Maj. Buford (Claude Gillingwater) and sent to school in Lexington. When the Civil War breaks out, young Buford, in spite of the major's preference, joins the Union Army and becomes a captain. He is ordered back to his birthplace and falls in love again with childhood sweetheart Melissa Turner (Molly O'Day). After the war and upon the death of Maj. Buford, young Buford rejects the major's estate and remains with Turner.

Walter Rodgers is one of the better Grant impersonators and reportedly does an excellent job in his short appearance in this film. This is the second of four film versions of John Fox Jr.'s 1903 novel *The Little Shepherd of Kingdom Come*.

Two Americans (1929)

Grant: Unknown actor.
Supposedly the plot concerns the problems Lincoln (Walter Huston) encounters when naming Grant commander of the Northern forces. For details, see Chapter 16 on Abraham Lincoln.

Abraham Lincoln (1930)

Grant: Fred Warren.
Fred Warren plays Grant in two scenes, both with Lincoln. In the first he accepts command of the Union Army with the highest rank, lieutenant general, saying to the president, "Thy will be done." In the second scene, he tells the president, "The Union is saved" after the surrender at Appomattox. For details, see Chapter 16 on Abraham Lincoln.

Only the Brave (1930)

Grant: Guy Oliver. *Other Cast:* Gary Cooper (Capt. James Braydon), Mary Brian (Barbara Calhoun), Phillips Holmes (Capt. Robert Darrington), James Neill (Vance Calhoun), Morgan Farley (Tom Wendell), E.H. Calvert (The Colonel), Virginia Bruce (Elizabeth). *Director:* Frank Tuttle. *Writing Credits:* Richard H. Digges Jr., Agnes Brand

Leahy. *Cinematography:* Harry A. Fishbeck. *Editor:* Doris Drought. *Studio:* Paramount. *Length:* 66 minutes.

This film takes a new turn on the spy story. After Union Capt. James Braydon (Gary Cooper) finds his girlfriend with a civilian he despondently volunteers for spy duty on a mission behind enemy lines, and his chances of returning appear dire. However, he finds it difficult to get arrested with incriminating evidence because Barbara Calhoun (Mary Brian), the belle of the Southern plantation where he's ensconced, keeps defending him even after she learns he is a spy. To assure he is captured he resorts to leaping through a window. The Confederates believe his false orders, but when they discover he is a spy, they plan his execution. Just in time, a Union attack saves him, but he is wounded.

All is well for Braydon after the surrender at Appomattox in which Guy Oliver reportedly portrays Gen. Grant with commanding skill. The final scene is a military wedding for Braydon and Calhoun.

Secret Service (1931)

Grant: Fred Warren. *Other Cast:* Richard Dix (Capt. Lewis "Lew" Dumont, aka Capt. Thorne), William Post Jr. (Lt. Henry Dumont), Shirley Grey (Miss Edith Varney), Nance O'Neil (Mrs. Varney), Harold Kinney (Howard Varney), Gavin Gordon (Mr. Arlesford), Florence Lake (Miss Caroline Mitford), Frederick Burton (Gen. Randolph), Clarence Muse (Jonas Polk), Eugene Jackson (Israel Polk). *Director:* J. Walter Ruben. *Producers:* William LeBaron, Louis Sarecky. *Writing Credits:* William Gillette, Bernard Schubert, Gerrit J. Lloyd. *Music:* Max Steiner. *Cinematography:* Edward Cronjager. *Film Editing:* Jack Kitchin. *Costume Design:* Max Ree. *Studio:* RKO Pictures. Inc. *Length:* 68 minutes.

Based on a play of the same name by celebrated stage actor William Gillette, this film joined a number of full-length sound Civil War spy films that had been recently released. Lewis Dumont (Richard Dix) is a Yankee spy working in Richmond. He virtually moves in with a Southern family, including the love interest Edith Varney (Shirley Grey), when he brings her wounded brother home. She suspects him of being a Northern spy. She finally learns this to be true when the jealous intelligence officer, Mr. Arlesford (Gavin Gordon), captures Dumont as a spy, but she does not abandon him. Her affection keeps Dumont from sending a strategic message to Grant to show his love for her. As he goes to a Confederate prison he says, "Until we meet again." The illogical plot twists are difficult to follow.

Fred Warren, uncredited as Gen. Grant, conveys the single-mindedness of the Union commander who states in a short early scene "We've got to take Richmond now" after the heavy casualties at Cold Harbor and in the Wilderness. He enlists the Dumont brothers to gain him information, and shows his usual kindess by offering them a cigar in his tent as he gives them orders to intercept Confederate telegraphs. Later, in a shorter scene before he receives the spies' message, he urges, "We strike at 10 P.M. regardless." Although Warren appears too old for the role, he assumes Grant's posture and psychology of utter determination.

Silver Dollar (1932)

Grant: Walter Rodgers.

Grant (Walter Rodgers) visits Denver for the opening of the opera house donated by wealthy silver miner Yates Martin (Edward G. Robinson) to the new city. In this film Rodgers does not resemble Grant and does not speak a line. Actually he does not have a chance to speak because the blustery Martin character speaks non-stop throughout the extended scene. Grant is again shown in the opera box during a dream sequence in one of the final scenes in the film. For details, see Chapter 21 on Chester Arthur.

Operator 13 (1934)

Grant: Fred Warren. *Other Cast:* Marion Davies (Gail Loveless aka Operator 13, Lucille "Lucy," Anne Claiborne), Gary Cooper (Capt. Jack Gailliard), Jean Parker (Eleanor Shackleford), Katharine Alexander (Pauline Cushman, aka Mrs. Mary Vale, Operator 27), Henry Wadsworth (Lt. Gus Littledale), Douglass Dumbrille (Confederate Capt. John Pelham), Willard Robertson (Cornelius Channing), Fuzzy Knight (Pvt. Sweeney), Sidney Toler (Maj. Allen, aka Allen Pinkerton), The Four Mills Brothers (Medicine Show Singers), John Elliott (Gen. Robert E. Lee). *Director:* Richard Boleslavsky. *Producer:* Lucien Hubbard. *Writing Credits:* Robert W. Chambers (stories), Harvey F. Thew, Zelda Sears, Eve Greene (screenplay). *Music:* William Axt, Walter Donaldson. *Cinematography:* George J. Folsey. *Film Editing:* Frank Sullivan. *Art Direction:* Cedric Gibbons. *Costume Design:* Adrian. *Studio:* Cosmopolitan Pictures, MGM. *Length:* 85 minutes.

Once more a female becomes a Civil War spy on screen. Only this time it's Marion Davies, newspaper magnate and film producer William Randolph Hearst's blonde and blue-eyed favorite star-turned-blackface-into-Operator 13. Her charm, Gary Cooper's handsome and stalwart presence, and outstanding production values by Cosmopolitan Pictures under MGM elevate this pedestrian picture.

The cinematography by George Folsey shows how advanced the art became in 1934: frequent use of fast cuts from different points of view in battle scenes, soft focus in romantic and early morning scenes, shadows of key actors in tents for ominous effects, and backlighting of Davies to emphasize her blonde beauty.

An actress recruited by Allen Pinkerton aka Maj. Allen (Sidney Toler), Operator 13 blackens her face as an octoroon servant and heads behind Southern lines to learn Lee's "eyes of the army" Gen. J.E.B. Stuart's (Douglass Dumbrille) missions. The Civil War is going badly for the North and a quick shot of President Lincoln after the defeat at the Second Battle of Bull Run reveals the somber mood.

With her first success, Operator 13 assumes the identity of a Copperhead named Anne Claiborne to unveil the maneuvers of Capt. Jack Gailliard (Cooper), leader of this "Sons of Liberty" Copperhead movement. They fall in love aided by the Southern moonlight in a plantation garden (beautiful art direction by Cedric Gibbons) and her cascade of tulle (gowns by Adrian). "It is a night of stars," she says, Operator 13's password to reveal a battery installation. But she's found out and condemned by Gailliard, and she flees on horseback in Confederate disguise, claiming she despises war and destruction. Both are caught by Union troops, and with true love she urges him to go.

The war drags on until Appomattox, a poignantly directed scene by Richard Boleslavsky. Gen. Grant (Fred Warren) commands the canon firing as "foolishness" that must stop. "There's no North now and no South," he says, stepping down from the authentic-looking porch at Appomattox Courthouse to shake hands with Lee (John Elliott). As Grant, Fred Warren looks and acts the serious general's role. Shortly thereafter Operator 13 and Gailliard embrace, proclaiming "loyalty and love."

Frontier Scout (1938)

Grant: Jack Smith. *Other Cast:* George Houston (Wild Bill Hickok), Al St. John (Whiney Roberts), Beth Marion (Mary Ann Norris), Dave O'Brien (Steve Norris), Guy Chase (Mort Bennett), Jack Ingram (Folsom). *Director:* Sam Newfield. *Writing Credits:* Frances Guihan. *Producers:* Maurice Conn, Franklyn Warner. *Music:* Joseph Nussbaum. *Film Editing:* Richard G. Wray. *Art Department:* E.H. Reif. *Sound Department:* Hans Weeren. *Special Effects:* Howard A. Anderson. *Studio:* Fine Arts Film Co. *Length:* 61 minutes.

Wild Bill Hickok (George Houston) is sent on a dangerous mission behind Confederate lines by Gen. U.S. Grant (Jack Smith). Hickok is, of course, completely successful with the help of his sidekick Whiney Roberts (Al St. John), and the war comes to a quick end. This leaves sufficient time in the film for Hickok to accomplish normal western activities like catching cattle rustlers. He does this well and wins the heart of the ranch owner's sister, Mary Ann Norris (Beth Marion). Jack Smith as General Grant has a military bearing. Smith is no stranger to war as he was a World War I ambulance driver. He also was a graduate of the Juilliard School of Music.

Gold Is Where You Find It (1938)

Grant: Walter Rodgers. *Other Cast:* George Brent (Jared Whitney), Olivia de Havilland (Serena Ferris), Claude Rains (Col. Ferris), John Litel (Ralph Ferris), Marcia Ralston (Molly Featherstone), Barton MacLane (Slag Minton), Tim Holt (Lanceford Ferris). *Director:* Michael Curtiz. *Producers:* Hal B. Wallis, Jack L. Warner. *Writing Credits:* Clements Ripley, Warren Duff, Robert Buckner. *Music:* Max Steiner. *Cinematography:* Sol Polito. *Film Editing:* Clarence Kolster, Owen Marks. *Art Direction:* Ted Smith. *Costume Design:* Milo Anderson. *Studio:* Warner Bros. *Length:* 94 minutes.

Gold is not only where you find it but also how you define it. In this pretentious California gold-rush film, gold is the metal, gold is wheat, and ultimately, gold is the fruit from the orchards in the Sacramento Valley. This typical western pits the miners against the farmers rather than the ranchers versus the sheepherders. Gold miners using hydraulic mining methods are flooding the entire valley and ruining the farms. In this highly unlikely physical event, the chief technician for the miners is Jared Whitney (a bored looking George Brent) and the biggest farmer is Col. Chris Ferris (a very British Claude Rains). Naturally, Ferris has a young daughter, Serena (Olivia de Havilland in her first Technicolor role), an amateur fruit grower who falls for Whitney.

The federal courts step into the action and decide for the farmers. However, the miners don't immediately accept the ruling, and there is a major battle with Ferris's son Lance (Tim Holt) being killed. But in the end a changed Whitney dynamites a dam, drowning all of the evil miners ... and the farmers win. Under Michael Curtiz's deft direction and with scenic cinematography by Sol Polito, the action scenes provide great excitement.

Since the action takes place in 1879, the presidential appearance is actually ex-presidential when U.S. Grant (Walter Rodgers) appears at a lavish party given by Ferris's brother Ralph (John Litel), a farmer turned miner. Looking a bit like Grant, Rodgers only says "Hello" in the reception line. Max Steiner's original music, a variation on "America" ("My Country 'Tis of Thee"), signals his significance.

Geronimo (1939)

Grant: Joseph Crehan. *Other Cast:* Preston Foster (Capt. Starrett), Ellen Drew (Alice Hamilton), Andy Devine (Sneezer), Gene Lockhart (Gillespie), Ralph Morgan (Gen. John Steele), William Henry (Lt. Steele), Chief Thundercloud (Geronimo). *Director-Writer:* Paul Sloane. *Music:* Gerard Carbonara, John Leopold. *Cinematography:* Henry Sharp. *Film Editing:* John F. Link. *Art Direction:* Hans Dreier, Earl Hedrick. *Studio:* Paramount Pictures. *Length:* 89 minutes.

In the opening sequence of this purportedly A western, there is a montage of shots showing Indian raids on settlements in the West and newspapers describing vicious massacres of innocent people. The secondary title of the film is *The Story of a Great Enemy*. Obviously, political correctness is not a new development.

At a meeting in Washington, D.C., President Grant (Joseph Crehan) states that "our whole handling of the Indian problem has been wrong, unjust." After appointing Gen. John Steele (Ralph Morgan) to try to make peace with Geronimo (Native American Chief Thundercloud), Grant says, "Mr. Lincoln said that the frontiers of this country must be made safe; I can only repeat this sentiment."

From this point the film follows normal western formulas with Gen. Steele's son, John Jr. (William Henry), a shavetail lieutenant sent from West Point with a letter from Grant, ends up the hero and makes his duty-bound "Napoleonic" father show some humanity. He is aided by Captain Bill Starrett (Preston Foster) and his sidekick Sneezer (Andy Devine) in thwarting Gillespie, the Indian agent gun runner (a sniveling Gene Lockhart) and Geronimo. He's a modern Indian, using binoculars to observe his enemy. But that's not the only discrepancy in the film: Supposedly set in Arizona, the backgrounds are pure California, and the film uses much stock footage from existing films.

President Grant returns in the final scene to posthumously present the Congressional Medal of Honor to Capt. Starrett who has died in trying to save 16 soldiers from 3000 Indians! The medal then goes to his regiment, and Grant says, "So long as there are men such as you the frontiers of this country will always be safe." Crehan physically resembles Grant and handles the impersonation with ease.

Union Pacific (1939)

Grant: Joseph Crehan. *Other Cast:* Barbara Stanwyck (Mollie Monahan), Joel McCrea (Capt. Jeff Butler), Akim Tamiroff (Fiesta), Robert Preston (Dick Allen), Lynne Overman (Leach Overmile), Brian Donlevy (Sid Campeau), Robert Barrat (Duke Ring), Anthony Quinn (Jack Cordray), Stanley Ridges (Gen. Casement), Henry Kolker (Asa M. Barrows), Francis McDonald (Gen. Grenville M. Dodge), Willard Robertson (Oakes Ames), Harold Goodwin (E.E. Calvin), Evelyn Keyes (Mrs. Calvin), Richard Lane (Sam Reed), William Haade (Dusky Clayton), Regis Toomey (Paddy O'Rourke), J. M. Kerrigan (Monahan), Fuzzy Knight (Cookie), Harry Woods (Al Brett), Lon Chaney Jr. (Dollarhide), Julia Faye (Mame), Sheila Darcy (Rose). *Director:* Cecil B. DeMille. *Writing Credits:* Ernest Haycox, Jack Cunningham. *Studio:* Paramount Pictures. *Length:* 135 minutes.

This Cecil B. DeMille spectacular owes much to John Ford's *Iron Horse* (1924) on the same subject, the building of the first intercontinental railroad, the Union Pacific. President Lincoln authorized the railroad in one of the last bills he signed, but he does not appear in this film. In a brief appearance, Joseph Crehan as Gen. Grant coerces banker Asa M. Barrows (Henry Kolker) to lend money to the railroad. Barrows plans to recoup his loan through robbery of a payroll train by Sid Campeau (Brian Donlevy) and his sidekick Dick Allen (Robert Preston).

Fictional adventures interrupt the somewhat historical real-life spectacle as Jeff Butler (Joel McCrea), the Union Pacific troubleshooter, tries to stop the sabotage. Butler and Allen, old Army buddies, end up fighting over postmistress Mollie Monahan (Barbara Stanwyck). On the day in 1869 when the Golden Spike (the original on loan for filming) is driven in Ogden, Utah, Indians attack. Allen is killed by Campeau, and all obstacles are overcome for the union of the rails and the lovers.

President Franklin D. Roosevelt reportedly opened the premiere in Omaha, Nebraska, by pressing a button in Washington, D.C. The premiere was stated to be the biggest in motion picture history (at that time) with an antique train continuing on a 15-day coast-to-coast promotion tour.

Colorado (1940)

Grant: Joseph Crehan. *Other Cast:* Roy Rogers (Lt. Jerry Burke). George "Gabby" Hayes (Gabby), Pauline Moore (Lylah Sanford), Milburn Stone (Capt. Donald Mason), *Director-Producer:* Joseph Kane. *Writing Credits:* Harrison Jacobs, Louis Stevens. *Cinematography:* Jack A. Marta. *Film Editing:* Edward Mann. *Studio:* Republic Pictures. *Length:* 54 minutes.

In one of his early movies on his way to replacing Gene Autry as "King of the Cowboys," Roy Rogers portrays Lt. Jerry Burke as a military intelligence officer during the Civil War. He is sent to clean up a mess in Colorado—stop marauding Indians and bring needed Union troops back east. Carrying a letter from President Lincoln and with the support of Gen. Grant (Joseph Crehan) Burke does not need much more help than his sidekick Gabby (George "Gabby" Hayes, the Western character actor ironically born in Wellsville, New York) to immediately solve the problems in the territory.

The problems were made a bit more difficult in that Burke's black sheep older brother, Capt. Donald Mason (Milburn Stone), is the leader of the bad guys in addition to being the fiancé of the leading lady, Lylah Sanford (Pauline Moore). But all of these problems are quickly overcome (it is a 54-minute film) by the team of Burke and Gabby. Soon Burke and Lylah are boarding the stage to return to the East. More an action than a musical star like Autry, Rogers as Burke sings only one song, "Singing Alone in the Moonlight," by Peter Tinturin.

Crehan is one of the regulars at portraying Grant as either the general or the president. His physical appearance is similar to Grant's, and he invariably portrays the president as a strong, sincere leader. He displays anger at "the outlaws who engage marauding Indians" to control the territory and gives his "unequivocal authority" to Burke on this "man-sized assignment."

The Son of Davy Crockett (1941)

Grant: Harrison Greene. *Other Cast:* Bill Elliott (Dave Crockett), Iris Meredith (Doris Mathews), Dub Taylor (Cannonball), Kenneth MacDonald (King Canfield), Richard Fiske (Jesse Gordon), Eddy Waller (Grandpa Mathews), Donald Curtis (Jack Ringe), Paul

Scardon (Zeke), Edmund Cobb, Steve Clark (Henchmen), Lloyd Bridges (Sammy). *Director-Writer:* Lambert Hillyer. *Producer:* Leon Barsha. *Cinematography:* Benjamin H. Kline. *Film Editing:* Mel Thorsen. *Stunts:* Chuck Hamilton, Ted Mapes. *Studio:* Columbia Pictures Corp. *Length:* 55 minutes.

In a somewhat different opener for a western, Dave Crockett (Bill Elliott), son of Davy, sets up a gunfight and then guns down two men who poisoned a spring, forcing him to run from the law. He is quickly rescued from this odd situation by Union cavalrymen who take him to Washington, D.C.

President Grant (Harrison Greene) brings Crockett to the White House to ask his help in getting the "Upper Valley Strip" into the Union. The citizens of this small piece of land between two unnamed states want to be part of the U.S. but are cowed by King Canfield (Kenneth MacDonald), a local strongman. Grant wants Crockett to ensure that the local citizens get their opportunity to vote freely in a plebiscite. In true B western style, Crockett takes care of the problems. This, of course, includes a period when he appears to have sided with Canfield, but this is proven wrong at the crucial time. Greene does a reasonable job as Grant in his extended scene. With a Grant-style beard and cigar, it is hard not to look like the 18th president. However, it is unlikely that the victor at Vicksburg would have had a scene stolen by Grandpa Mathews (Eddy Waller) that was the case in this film when he took over the discussion of Crockett's task.

They Died with Their Boots On (1942)

Grant: Joseph Crehan. *Other Cast:* Errol Flynn (George Armstrong Custer), Olivia de Havilland (Elizabeth Bacon Custer), Arthur Kennedy (Ned Sharp), Regis Toomey (Fitzhugh Lee), Charles Grapewin (California Joe), Stanley Ridges (Maj. Romulus Taipe), Gene Lockhart (Samuel Bacon), Anthony Quinn (Crazy Horse), John Litel (Gen. Philip Sheridan), Sydney Greenstreet (Gen. Winfield Scott). *Director:* Raoul Walsh. *Producer:* Hal B. Wallis. *Writing Credits:* Wally Kline, Aeneas MacKenzie. *Music:* Max Steiner. *Cinematography:* Bert Glennon. *Film Editing:* William Holmes. *Art Direction:* John Hughes. *Costume Design:* Milo Anderson. *Stunts:* Yakima Canutt. *Studio:* Warner Bros. *Length:* 140 minutes.

This is a completely fictionalized biography of a real life soldier, George Armstrong Custer. Without any apparent attempt to make the simplest points of history, the film depicts Custer's life from his entrance into West Point until his death at Little Big Horn on June 25, 1876 (possibly the only accurate piece of history in the entire film). Critics call Little Big Horn the biggest and grandest battle scene of 1940s Hollywood films, enlarged by Max Steiner's music.

Despite the lack of historic accuracy or possibly because of it, the film is an exciting and, at times, funny recreation of events leading up to the tragic climax. The selection of Errol Flynn to play Custer was almost a given since Flynn was the swashbuckling hero of the cinematic day. As Custer's wife Libby, Olivia de Havilland performs her final role opposite Flynn in the sweet and supportive manner of her Oscar-nominated Melanie role in *Gone With the Wind* (1939). She then went on to more serious roles and two Oscars.

A director and actor since 1912, Raoul Walsh appeared as John Wilkes Booth in D.W. Griffith's *Birth of a Nation* (1915). As *They Died with Their Boots On* exemplifies, Walsh stressed unpretentious, smoothly paced films with the accent on entertainment and slick production values. Perhaps to keep his production costs low, he shot this film in California rather than on location in some place (without roads) that looks like the Dakota Territory. But the film cost $1.35 million.

The story is simple: Custer is a complete loss as a cadet at West Point and is fortunate to receive his lieutenant's bars when the Civil War starts. His academic record is "even worse than Ulysses S. Grant's" says one instructor (although Grant ranked 24th out of some 200). Completely by accident Custer becomes a brevet brigadier general but goes on to save the day in numerous battles, starting at Bull Run (Manassas) and extending through Gettysburg, thus becoming a national hero. He leaves the army at the end of the war but returns with his influential wife's intervention over his unhappy inactivity and becomes a commander of the 7th Cavalry in the Dakota Territory. There he and the Indians under Chief Crazy Horse (Anthony Quinn) get along, but the usual villains (ruthless land speculators) stir up trouble. In saving the lives of other soldiers in two other regiments against Crazy Horse's thousands, he sacrifices his own life and those of some 655 others in his command. All of the villains are defeated.

Grant (Joseph Crehan) appears in one scene in which he angrily accuses Custer of destroying his administration by publicly denouncing the land speculators. Grant then threatens Custer with a court martial. Custer convinces Grant to let him return to his command by reminding Grant that he, too, had experienced failure in his non-military life. In this well-staged and -played but completely fictitious scene, Grant is seen as tough and quite presidential.

The Adventures of Mark Twain (1944)

Grant: Joseph Crehan. *Other Cast:* Fredric March (Samuel Langhorn Clemens [Mark Twain]), Alexis Smith (Olivia Langdon Clemens), Donald Crisp (J.B. Pond), Alan Hale (Steve Gillis), C. Aubrey Smith (Oxford Chancellor), John Carradine (Bret Harte), William Henry (Charles Langdon), Robert Barrat (Horace E. Bixby), Walter Hampden (Jervin Langdon), Joyce Reynolds (Clara Clemens), Whitford Kane (Joe Goodwin), Percy Kilbride (Billings, Enterprise Typesetter), Nana Bryant (Mrs. Langdon), Jackie Brown (Samuel Clemens as a boy), Dickie Jones (Samuel Clemens at 13). *Director:* Irving Rapper. *Producer:* Jesse Lasky. *Writing Credits:* Harry Chandlee, Harry Sherman, Alan LeMay. *Cinematographer:* Sol Polito. *Musical Direction:* Leo F. Forbstein. *Editor:* Ralph Dawson. *Production Designer:* John Hughes. *Set Designer:* Fred MacLean. *Costume Designer:* Orry-Kelly. *Makeup:* Perc Westmore. *Studio:* Warner Brothers. *Length:* 130 minutes.

It is fortuitous that this film is called *The Adventures* rather than *The Life of Mark Twain* because, although it includes numerous events from his life, it in no way resembles his actual life. An enjoyable, well-acted film with Fredric March in the title role and Alexis Smith as his wife Olivia, it suffers by straying greatly from the truly adventurous life of Samuel Clemens.

Starting with his birth on the night that Halley's Comet crossed the sky and ending with his death 75 years later when the comet again appeared, the film ignores much of the actual chronology between these two events to present Mark Twain as alternately silly and serious. His stay in Nevada is presented as a series of misadventures with his partner Steve Gillis (Alan Hale), culminating in his jumping frog story that led to his literary fame but not soothing its readers during the Civil War as the film depicts. Director Irving Rapper takes the same excessively light approach in telling the story of Twain's romantic pursuit of

Olivia Langdon that took place in Elmira, New York. The lack of historicity or accuracy is exemplified by Olivia's father talking about Elmira being in New England.

The presidential segment of the film concerns the historically accurate fact of Twain/Clemens publishing *The Memoirs of Ulysses S. Grant*. The fact that Clemens published Grant is accurate, but the film's presentation of this event is completely wrong. In the film, Twain visits Grant (Joseph Crehan) and insists on publishing the mortally ill Grant's memoirs even though he knows that such a step will bankrupt him. In actuality, Grant's memoirs were very successful for Twain who did not go bankrupt until seven years later.

Crehan is a strong Grant look-alike and always plays the general/president with great skill. He was particularly good in portraying Grant toward the end of his life and at least attempts in his vocal delivery to show the effects of throat cancer that eventually killed Grant.

Centennial Summer (1946)

Grant: Reginald Sheffield. *Other Cast:* Jeanne Crain (Julia Rogers), Lois Austin (Mrs. Phelps), Cornel Wilde (Philippe Lascalles), Linda Darnell (Edith Rogers), Walter Brennan (Jesse Rogers), Constance Bennett (Zenia Lascalles), Dorothy Gish (Mrs. Rogers). *Director-Producer:* Otto Preminger. *Writing Credits:* Albert E. Idell, Michael Kanin. *Music:* Jerome Kern. *Cinematography:* Ernest Palmer. *Film Editing:* Harry Reynolds. *Art Direction:* Leland Fuller, Lyle R. Wheeler. *Set Decoration:* Thomas Little. *Studio:* 20th Century–Fox. *Length:* 102 minutes.

Twentieth Century–Fox tries to repeat the success of *Meet Me in St. Louis* (1944) in a similar story with the star (Jeanne Crain) of another film in the same tradition, *State Fair* (1945). Therefore, the plot is predictable: A family encounters new experiences at a fair. This time, it's the 1876 Centennial celebration in Philadelphia. Otto Preminger, the Viennese actor and director known for his serious work in this country since 1935, directs with his talent for narrative fluidity. His most lighthearted moment occurs at the costume ball opening the French pavilion when most of the men turn up dressed as Napoleon.

Preminger achieves this narrative fluidity by balancing the rivalry of two sisters, Crain as Julia (with dubbed singing) and Linda Darnell as Edith, over Philippe Lascalles (Cornel Wilde). He happens to come with his and the girls' aunt Zenia Lascalles (Constance Bennett) from Paris to take charge of the French pavilion. *Centennial Summer* features Jerome Kern's last musical score for the films. He wrote seven new songs for this musical: "Centennial," "Cinderella Sue," "Happy on the Railroad," "The Right Romance," "Up with the Lark," "To Be in Love in Vain," and "All Through The Day," which won him an Oscar for best song.

As the eccentric inventor of a synchronized clock for the railroad, Walter Brennan as Jesse Rogers displays the crustiness that makes him such an outstanding character actor. He won three Oscars within five years for his supporting roles. Brennan's barking comments about the softness of Grant's speech at the opening celebration prompts Brennan's wife (Dorothy Gish) to leave. Oblivious to this loss of audience, the president makes appropriate comments about the "specimens" of art, agriculture, etc., that this Centennial offers. Reginald Sheffield plays the part with the proper grandeur.

The Fabulous Texan (1947)

Grant: John Hamilton. *Other Cast:* Bill Elliott (Jim McWade), John Carroll (John Wesley Baker), Catherine McLeod (Alice Sharp), Albert Dekker (Gibson Hart), Andy Devine

(Elihu Mills), Patricia Knight (Josie Allen), Ruth Donnelly (Utopia Mills), Johnny Sands (Bud Clayton), Harry Davenport (Rev. Baker). *Director:* Edward Ludwig. *Producer:* Edmund Grainger. *Writing Credits:* Lawrence Hazard, Hal Long, Horace McCoy. *Cinematography:* Reggie Lanning. *Film Editing:* Richard Van Enger. *Art Direction:* James Sullivan. *Set Decoration:* John McCarthy Jr., George Milo. *Studio:* Republic Pictures Corp. *Length:* 95 minutes.

William "Wild Bill" Elliott takes on another task in this Republic big-budget film. Returning from the Civil War with his childhood buddy John Wesley Barker (John Carroll), Elliott as Jim McWade encounters corrupt, despotic carpetbaggers trying to take over the state. They assume the position of state troopers and even kill an outspoken, freedom-loving minister, the father of John Wesley, Reverend Barker (Harry Davenport).

Barker avenges his father's death by killing the leading trooper and wounding another. With a $1,000 reward on his head, he flees to the mountains with McWade and a band of sympathizers. There are more posses of horses riding at top speed than action by their riders, playing against painted backdrops that bear little resemblance to West Texas.

Eventually, McWade realizes he might accomplish more for his beloved state by becoming a federal marshal. He offers to bring in Barker if he will receive a fair trial. That doesn't happen and McWade ends up with the girl both men love, Alice Sharp (Catherine McLeod).

Grant (John Hamilton) takes his position on priorities during his one scene in this film. "My first obligation is to the nation," he responds in answer to a plea from McWade for protection for Texas from the lawless state police. In explaining his position, Grant, seated in his White House Office, goes on to say, "We're trying hard to be fair and just to the South."

Further questioning causes Grant to relent and say, "General [Philip] Sheridan is the commander and will have a look at the situation. If the people of Texas want action, they'll take action." Hamilton as Grant takes his part with commanding presence and bears a close resemblance to the president.

Silver River (1948)

Grant: Joseph Crehan. *Other Cast:* Errol Flynn (Capt. Mike McComb), Ann Sheridan (Georgia Moore), Thomas Mitchell (John Plato Beck), Bruce Bennett (Stanley Moore), Tom D'Andrea (Pistol Porter), Barton MacLane (Banjo Sweeney). *Director:* Raoul Walsh. *Producer:* Jack L. Warner. *Writing Credits:* Stephen Longstreet, Harriet Frank Jr. *Music:* Max Steiner. *Cinematography:* Sid Hickox. *Film Editing:* Alan Crosland Jr. *Art Direction:* Ted Smith. *Set Direction:* William Wallace. *Studio:* Warner Bros. *Length:* 110 minutes.

Outdoor action director Raoul Walsh and swashbuckler Errol Flynn get together for the seventh and last time in this western about the silver mining business shortly after the Civil War. It's an apparent retelling of the Bible story of King David, and not one of their more successful ventures, flawed by bad rear screen projections and California background for a Pennsylvania setting early in the film.

Flynn plays Mike McComb, a character basically identical to all of Flynn's roles: i.e., an essentially good person who makes some morally questionable decisions. In *Silver River* McComb falls in love with Georgia Moore (Ann Sheridan) who is already married to mining engineer Stanley Moore (Bruce Bennett). McComb sends Stanley off to a site where he knows renegade Indians are active and Stanley's chances of returning are slim. The Indians kill Stanley, and ultimately McComb marries Georgia, even though she claims he will "never change." Always in the background is McComb's nagging conscience, John Plato Beck (Thomas Mitchell). When Beck is killed by villain "Banjo" Sweeney (Barton MacLane), McComb recovers his moral direction and rides off with Georgia into the sunset.

In an attempt to convince the miners to increase silver production for the good of the country, Grant (Joseph Crehan) visits Silver City and is feted at a ball. Crehan, who looks like Grant, plays the president both seriously and with some humor. There is no attempt to indicate that the visit to Silver City has any historical basis.

Red Desert (1949)

Grant: Joseph Crehan. *Other Cast:* Don "Red" Barry (Pecos Kid), Tom Neal (John Williams), Jack Holt (Deacon Smith), Margia Dean (Hazel Carter), Byron Foulger (Sparky Johnson). *Directors:* Ford Beebe, Charles Marquis Warren. *Producer:* Ron Ormond. *Screenwriters:* Dan Ullman, Ron Ormond. *Cinematographer:* Ernest W. Miller. *Music:* Walter Greene. *Editor:* Hugh Wynn. *Studio:* Lippert Pictures Inc. *Length:* 60 minutes.

Lefty Jordan is considered by President Grant (Joseph Crehan) to be "the most dangerous man in the country." To track him down Grant reluctantly selects the Pecos Kid (Don "Red" Barry). Grant is reluctant because Lefty has already killed four U.S. marshals.

The nonsensical premise for the B western is compounded by the direction and pace of the film. A one-hour feature opening with a full five silent minutes (except for eerie organ music) of two men riding across desolate country, followed by a series of missed rifle shots by a marksman of the "Worst Shot in the West" quality, does not make for exciting action. The film ends with another desert trek by the same two men who have now lost their horses. This sequence lasts 15 minutes without a word being spoken. It appears that director Ford Beebe got his training for this 1949 film during the silent era by his use of sound and the old iris technique.

Much to the surprise of the Pecos Kid, a silly, weakling of a jeweler named Sparky Johnson (Byron Foulger) turns out to be Jordan, the dreaded gold thief with political ambitions. However, he is very tough in the last scene's fistfight with the hero.

Joseph Crehan had played Grant a number of times and does a better job in his measured portrayal in this film than would have been expected given its overall quality.

I Shot Billy the Kid (1950)

Grant: Archie Twitchell. *Other Cast:* Robert Lowery (Pat Garrett), Wally Vernon (Vicenti), Tom Neal (Bowdre), Wendy Lee (Francesca), Claude Stroud (Gen. Lew Wallace), Jack Perrin (Deputy), Richard Farmer (McSween), Felice Richmond (Mexican Girl), Jack Geddes (Sheriff), Tommy Monroe (Maxwell). *Director:* William Berke. *Producers:* Don "Red" Barry, William Berke, Robert L. Lippert. *Writing Credits:* Ford Beebe, Orville Hampton. *Music:* Albert Glasser. *Cinematography:* Ernest Miller. *Film Editing:* Carl Pierson. *Art Direction:* Fred Preble. *Makeup:* Ted Coodley. *Sound:* Harry Eckles, Harry Smith. *Studio:* Lippert Pictures. *Length:* 57 minutes.

The on-screen credits claim "This picture is based upon the true facts in the life of William H. Bonney, 'Billy the Kid,' outlaw and killer." It tells his story through flashback from the point of view of his killer Pat Garrett (Robert Lowery) whom Billy has saved from attacking Indians.

In a shootout Billy kills the sheriff and deputy, outraging the citizens of Lincoln County, scene of a cattle war in which Billy fought. Garrett is able to gain a pardon from territorial governor Gen. Lew Wallace (Claude Stroud). However, Billy rejects the pardon and begins a life of crime. Ultimately Pat Garrett is forced to kill Billy. Archie Twitchell, who is seen as Grant, played mostly in westerns, 67 films all told from 1937 to 1954.

San Antone (1953)

Grant: Unnamed actor.

Grant, uncredited, appears in a non-speaking cameo at the end of the Civil War. This scene finds him seated in a tent when Lee arrives for the surrender. With hardly any added expense, some degree of historical accuracy could have been possible for this scene. For details, see Chapter 16 on Abraham Lincoln.

Drum Beat (1954)

Grant: Hayden Rorke. *Other Cast:* Alan Ladd (Johnny MacKay), Audrey Dalton (Nancy Meek), Marisa Pavan (Toby), Robert Keith (Bill Satterwhite), Rodolfo Acosta (Scarface Charlie), Edgar Stehli (Jesse Grant), Peggy Converse (Julia Grant), Charles Bronson (Kintpuash, aka Captain Jack). *Director-Producer-Writer:* Delmer Daves. *Music:* Victor Young. *Cinematography:* J. Peverell Marley. *Film Editing:* Clarence Kolster. *Art Direction:* Leo K. Kuter. *Set Decoration:* William L. Kuehl. *Studio:* Jaguar/Warner Brothers. *Length:* 111 minutes.

Johnny MacKay (Alan Ladd) walks into the White House wearing an unconcealed six-gun. It is clear that the assassination of Lincoln has had little effect on security for the president. However, in this case it is all right since President Grant (Hayden Rorke) has asked to talk to veteran Indian fighter MacKay about ending the problems with the Modoc Indians in Oregon. Ladd also is a veteran of this peace-making role; he played it the year before in his memorable *Shane*.

Directed and produced by Delmer Daves, the film is "based on historical fact," and the extended scene with Grant instructing and questioning MacKay is one of the most believable film presentations of the great Civil War general in action as president. The meeting occurs in a sitting room with Grant's father Jesse (Edgar Stehli) and wife (Peggy Converse) in attendance. Grant tells MacKay that he wants "fair treatment for the Indians" and asks him to "bring peace to the Modoc country." Grant's kindliness and patience are much in evidence. He is most cordial to MacKay and to his father who interrupts the interview with his reminiscences.

On his return to Oregon, MacKay finds that renegade Modoc leader Captain Jack (a plum role for a young Charles Bronson) has no desire for peace with the white settlers. After many attempts to change Captain Jack's mind, MacKay finds his problems brought to a head when the Modocs kill all of the unarmed peace commissioners during a conference.

In a second scene, President Grant again makes his position clear that peaceful but just means must be used to settle the problems. This includes an upbraiding of General Sherman for his racist remarks suggesting that the Modocs be exterminated.

In line with the actual historical events, the renegade Modocs, including Captain Jack, are captured, tried in a federal court, and hung. The handling of these problems by Grant and his representatives apparently established a long-term peace between the Modocs and the settlers. The characterization of Grant by Rorke is excellent. Physically he looks like the general, and his actions in the film are serious, decisive and thoughtful.

Besides the effective presidential and battle scenes, there is some stunning exterior photography by J. Peverell Marley and a ballad-like musical score by Victor Young—not overlooking MacKay's love interest with Indian maiden Toby (Marisa Pavan) and brave new settler Nancy Meek (Audrey Dalton).

Sitting Bull (1954)

Grant: John Hamilton. *Other Cast:* Dale Robertson (Maj. Bob Parrish), Mary Murphy (Kathy), J. Carrol Naish (Chief Sitting Bull), Iron Eyes Cody (Chief Crazy Horse), John Litel (Gen. Howell). *Director:* Sidney Salkow. *Producer:* W.R. Frank. *Writing Credits:* Jack DeWitt, Sidney Salkow. *Music:* Raoul Kraushaar, Max Rich. *Cinematography:* Victor Herrera, Charles Van Enger. *Studio:* Tele-Voz, W.R. Frank Productions. *Length:* 105 minutes.

Director-writer Sidney Salkow threw together this retelling of Custer's Last Stand using a few reasonably good actors and as little actual history as possible. J. Carrol Naish in the title role brings a bit of decorum as a wise, pragmatic leader who pays great respect to President Grant. But given the script and cinematography reminiscent of the mid–1920s even Naish is a loss.

Sitting Bull (1954): John Hamilton as President Grant (right) sends Maj. Bob Parrish played by Dale Robertson off to face the title character Sitting Bull in this United Artists western. The Oval Office setting shows a Gilbert Stuart portrait of George Washington, a familiar prop in presidential films. Director/writer Sidney Salkow retells this fictional story of Custer's Last Stand against the Sioux with J. Carrol Naish in the title role. (Courtesy of George Eastman House.)

President Grant (John Hamilton) appears in two scenes. In Washington he gives the main protagonist Maj. Bob Parrish (Dale Robertson) the authority to begin talking to Sitting Bull about defusing a potential war with the Sioux in Dakota Territory. After failing in this effort and avoiding being with Custer in the fateful battle, Maj. Parrish is court-martialed and sentenced to death.

President Grant just happens to arrive at the fort and after hearing Sitting Bull, commutes Parrish's sentence. Parrish embraces the commander's daughter Kathy (Mary Murphy), and Grant shakes hands with the Indian leader and says, "To peace." The obvious California scenery, instead of Montana, provides a perfect cap to this disaster.

Run of the Arrow (1957) aka Hot Lead

Grant: Emile Avery. *Other Cast:* Rod Steiger (O'Meara), Sara Montiel (Yellow Moccasin), Brian Keith (Capt. Clark), Ralph Meeker (Lt. Driscoll), Jay C. Flippen (Walking Coyote), Charles Bronson (Blue Buffalo). *Director-Producer-Writer:* Samuel Fuller. *Cinematography:* Joseph Biroc. *Film Editing:* Gene Fowler Jr. *Art Direction:* Albert S. D'Agostino, Jack Okey. *Set Decoration:* Bert Granger. *Studio:* Globe Enterprises, RKO Radio Pictures, Inc. *Length:* 86 minutes.

In a film strikingly similar to *Dances With Wolves* (1990), a Southern sharpshooter, Private O'Meara (played with a strange Southern-Irish brogue accent by Rod Steiger), ends service in the Civil War with an intense hatred of Yankees and leaves for the West. After accidentally meeting Walking Coyote (a long-haired Jay C. Flippen), he learns the ways of the Sioux, thinking they have the Yankees as a common enemy. Through a bit of luck O'Meara survives a "run of the arrow" rite and is admitted into a Sioux village led by Blue Buffalo (Charles Bronson). Ultimately he marries Yellow Moccasin (Sara Montiel whose voice was dubbed by Angie Dickinson).

After talking to Northern Calvary Capt. Clark (Brian Keith), the head of an engineering group sent to build a fort in Sioux territory, O'Meara finds his hatred of Yankees lessening. He tries to save the villain of the film, Lt. Driscoll (Ralph Meeker), but Driscoll's troops are almost wiped out by the Indians. O'Meara realizes he will never completely be a Sioux and leaves.

From the quality of the cast, it is obvious that director-writer-producer Samuel Fuller had high aspirations. However the film ends up being little more than a B-western. Fuller concludes it ambiguously with a subtitle, "The end of this story can only be written by you."

Gen. Grant (Emile Avery) is shown briefly in the opening sequence with Robert E. Lee (Frank Baker) at the surrender at Appomattox Court House in Virginia. This short scene does not offer much to assess Grant's appearance.

From the Earth to the Moon (1958)

Grant: Morris Ankrum. *Other Cast:* Joseph Cotten (Victor Barbicane), George Sanders (Stuyvesant Nicholl), Debra Paget (Virginia Nicholl), Don Dubbins (Ben Sharpe), Patric Knowles (Josef Cartier), Carl Esmond (Jules Verne), Henry Daniell (Morgana). *Director:* Byron Haskin. *Producer:* Benedict Bogeaus. *Writing Credits:* Jules Verne, Robert Blees, James Leicester. *Music:* Louis Forbes. *Cinematography:* Edwin B. DuPar. *Production Design:* Hal Wilson Cox. *Costume Design:* Gwen Wakeling. *Studio:* RKO Radio Pictures. *Length:* 101 minutes.

Jules Verne is one of the original science fiction writers, and Hollywood has often turned to his stories for a script as it does here. The story of *From the Earth to the Moon* takes place in the late 1860s when Victor Barbicane (Joseph Cotten) discovers a new power source that looks suspiciously like nuclear energy. He feels that it could be used to send a rocket to the moon. In his endeavors, he is assisted by Ben Sharpe (Don Dubbins) but has to overcome interference from his righteous enemy, Stuyvesant Nicholl (George Sanders). There also is a love interest between Sharpe and Nicholl's daughter, Virginia, played by a blonde Debra Paget.

In order to develop financing for the moon shot, Barbicane demonstrates the extreme power of the new energy source, Power X. Because the demonstration is so successful, Barbicane is ordered to see President Grant (Morris Ankrum). In a very serious scene Grant asks him to drop his planned unmanned moon shot because "twenty-two nations are considering it an act of war by the United States." Barbicane reluctantly agrees to cancel the moon shot until he discovers that Nicholl has invented a ceramic material that would enable reentry into the Earth's atmosphere. Therefore a manned mission would be possible and President Grant's objections would be overcome.

The mission is a dramatic and cinematic disaster. About half of the running time of the film concerns Barbicane's attempt to solve the sabotage problems created by Nicholl on the completely mysterious equipment of the rockets (resembling 19th century factory equipment). The special effects in this portion of the film are completely inadequate even for a 1958 film and leave the viewer with many questions as to what exactly is happening.

But the money spent on the cast proves its worth. Cotten is an urbane, intense scientist and Sanders a religious, righteous one. Morris Ankrum as the president deports himself with the devotion to duty that characterized Grant. Even Henry Daniell in a supporting role shines with his suspicious nature about Barbicane's inventions. Paget and Dubbins provide window dressing for director Byron Haskin's weak attempt to make a Verne classic a political statement about the arms race.

The Horse Soldiers (1959)

Grant: Stan Jones. *Other Cast:* John Wayne (Col. John Marlowe), William Holden (Maj. Hank Kendall), Constance Towers (Hannah Hunter), William Forrest (Gen. Steve Hurlbut), Althea Gibson (Lukey). Hoot Gibson (Brown). *Director:* John Ford. *Producers:* John Lee Mahin, Martin Rackin. *Writing Credits:* Harold Sinclair, John Lee Mahin, Martin Rackin. *Music:* David Buttolph, Stan Jones. *Cinematography:* William H. Clothier. *Film Editing:* Jack Murray. *Art Direction:* Frank Hotaling. *Studio:* Mahin-Rackin, Mirisch Co. *Length:* 115 minutes.

Drama arises from the very first shot in the credits showing a long line of Union cavalry soldiers on their horses, riding single file and singing "I Left My Love" as they head 300 miles behind Southern lines to seize a Confederate railroad depot. Their objective, Newton Station, is to cut supply lines to Vicksburg. That's the plan of Gen. Grant (Stan Jones), who meets with Col. John Marlowe (John Wayne) and Gen. Steve Hurlbut (William Forrest) in the film's opening scene to discuss his strategy.

Grant, slumped in his office chair and smoking a cigar, admits that the war is "not going well, and if I take Vicksburg, the whole picture will change." Showing his command of the territory, he tells Marlowe to ignore the map. Marlowe then asks, "If you've thought about coming back?" Ever the sympathetic leader, Grant acknowledges he "asked for that" and expresses his worries about the hell hole that is Andersonville where federal troops are incarcerated and Marlowe's captured soldiers might end up.

In only a two-minute scene, Jones conveys Grant's openness, humanity, and brilliance as a general. Jones looks appropriately rumpled as Grant did (and still does on the newly designed $50 bill). This is one of director John Ford's last pictures and the only one to focus on the Civil War. It contains convincing action and spectacular cinematography, particularly of the pastoral scenes, by William Clothier.

Wayne, Ford's favorite star, gives a familiar performance as a tough guy who hates doctors as much as he hates to destroy the railroads he used to build. William Holden as Maj. Henry "Hank" Kendall, regimental surgeon, provides the humane foil for Wayne's toughness. Romance is provided by Constance Towers as Hannah Hunter of Greenbriar, a Southern lady who is taken prisoner after offering the Yankees hospitality and spying on them in her mansion. Towers, like many of the other supporting actors, overplays her role. Of note is tennis star Althea Gibson as Hunter's maid Lukey. Still, the film offers historical insight and gripping entertainment.

How the West Was Won (1962)

Grant: Harry Morgan.

Grant, as well played by Harry Morgan, makes one brief appearance in the section of this epic directed by John Ford. Filmed in Cinerama, featuring an all-star cast, and narrated by Spencer Tracy, this pretentious film even includes an intermission. Grant appears after that, following the first day of the bloody battle of Shiloh when he visits a hospital, bumps into a corporal and says a newspaper correspondent wrote he was "taken by surprise and was drunk. Win or lose, I will resign tomorrow." Gen. Sherman (John Wayne) insists he has no right to resign unless he is wrong. Although the scene is incorrect historically, Grant was not wrong, winning the battle the second day after more reinforcements arrived to replace his fallen numbers. Historian Gary W. Gallagher says in *The American Civil War, Part I*, that Grant's resolve and Buell's reinforcements eventually won the day for the Union.[7] For details, see Chapter 16 on Abraham Lincoln.

The Legend of the Lone Ranger (1981)

Grant: Jason Robards. *Other Cast:* Klinton Spilsbury (The Lone Ranger/John Reid), Michael Horse (Tonto), Christopher Lloyd (Maj. Bartholomew "Butch" Cavendish), Matt Clark (Sheriff Wiatt), Juanin Clay (Amy Striker), John Bennett Perry (Capt. Dan Reid), Richard Farnsworth (Wild Bill Hickok), Lincoln Tate (Gen. George A. Custer), Ted Flicker (Buffalo Bill Cody). *Director:* William A. Fraker. *Producer:* Martin Starger. *Writing Credits:* Ivan Goff, Michael Kane, William Roberts, George W. Trendle. *Music:* John Barry. *Cinematography:* Laszlo Kovacs. *Film Editing:* Thomas Stanford. *Production Design:* Albert Brenner. *Art Direction:* David M. Haber. *Set Decoration:* Phil Abramson. *Costume Design:* Noel Taylor. *Studio:* Incorporated Television Co., Wrather Corp. *Length:* 98 minutes.

Almost any boy growing up in the 1940s and 1950s was fully aware of the history and adventures of the Lone Ranger and his "faithful companion" Tonto. In many instances the Lone Ranger radio series also was the first introduction to classical music in the use of "The William Tell Overture."

The strongly criticized 1981 film uses all of the familiar ingredients: the exact introductory words of the radio program, "The William Tell Overture" at pertinent points in the story, and "Who was that masked man?" asked at the end. However, they were unable to make the film into an enjoyable reminiscence.

All members of a Texas Ranger posse are killed in an ambush led by "Butch" Cavendish (Christopher Lloyd) with the exception of John Reid (Klinton Spilsbury). Reid recovers from his wounds with the help of his boyhood Indian friend Tonto (Michael Horse), lives to avenge the ambush, and serves on the side of justice as the Lone Ranger.

Cavendish destroys the posse to advance his plan to kidnap President Grant (Jason Robards) and blackmail the government into letting him establish Texas as an independent country. In a wild ending that includes an unexpected "cavalry-to-the-rescue" charge, the Lone Ranger and Tonto save the president and bring Cavendish to justice.

The highlight of the film is Robards' portrayal of Grant. Robards seems to enjoy giving Grant a reasonable persona as a tough, hard-working and hard-playing individual. Grant is visiting Texas on a hunting trip with an historically unlikely group of notables: Wild Bill Hickok (Richard Farnsworth), Gen. George A. Custer (Lincoln Tate) and Buffalo Bill Cody (Ted Flicker). Spilsbury employs a style nothing like the legendary Lone Ranger portrayed by Clayton Moore, Horse is a cliché Indian, and Lloyd is an unbelievably sinister Cavendish. Robards as Grant has no difficulty in dominating each of the 11 scenes in which he appears, from trying out presidential speeches to battling with Cavendish.

It's a disappointing film for Lone Ranger fans but enjoyable for Jason Robards and cinematographer Laszlo Kovacs aficionados. Robards gets to say "Who is that masked man?" and Kovacs creates dazzling color effects, especially of sunsets.

Wild Wild West (1999)

Grant: Kevin Kline (also Artemus Gordon). *Other Cast:* Will Smith (Capt. James "Jim" West), Kenneth Branagh (Dr. Arliss Loveless), Salma Hayek (Rita Escobar), Ted Levine (Gen. McGrath). *Director:* Barry Sonnenfeld. *Producer:* Jon Peters. *Writing Credits:* Jim Thomas, John Thomas, S.S. Wilson, Brent Maddock, Jeffrey Rice, Peter S. Seaman. *Music:* Elmer Bernstein. *Cinematography:* Michael Ballhaus, Stefan Czapsky. *Film Editing:* Jim Miller. *Studio:* Warner Bros. *Length:* 107 minutes.

Like Grant's administration, this enterprise seems to have everything going for it: a star-studded cast, an experienced director, lavish special effects, a huge budget, and a legacy of a successful TV series. But nothing clicks. In a dual role as one of the two heroes and President Grant, the gifted Kevin Kline is much more believable as the authoritative, patriotic, and impatient Grant. Grant's character appears in an early scene authorizing Kline (as Artemus Gordon) and Will Smith (as James T. West) to save him from the mad scientist Dr. Loveless, much overplayed by the esteemed Shakespearean actor Kenneth Branagh.

Grant is next seen in Utah to drive the golden spike uniting two railroads. "Good Lord," he rightly says as an 80-foot mechanical tarantula arrives to capture him. Dr. Loveless masterminds this mechanical device in hopes of reconstructing the United States. Ever the soldier-president, Grant says, "Never will the U.S. surrender." Eventually, in the fourth of his five short scenes, Grant drives the golden spike, proclaiming, "May God continue the great unity of our country," and the tarantula hobbles off into the Western sunset. Most memorable is the theme song rendered by Smith and written by the estimable Elmer Bernstein.

19

Rutherford B. Hayes (1877–1881)

Taking office after a disputed election (as did John Quincy Adams), Rutherford Birchard Hayes did what he promised to do: conciliate the South; try to realize the party's reforms, especially civil service; and follow a conservative financial policy. Most of all, he restored presidential power and respect after the troubled terms of Johnson and Grant by breaking away from the old guard Republicans. Hayes did this in only one term, showing the moderation that governed his tenure by not running again.

He graduated first in his class from Kenyon College and from Harvard Law School and quickly ranked in the forefront of Cincinnati's young lawyers.[1] His wife Lucy, a college graduate and strong Methodist and reformer, urged him to be the same and encouraged his joining Ohio's 23rd volunteer company when the Civil War began. Rising to major general, he returned to Ohio politics and served as U.S. congressman and governor for three terms. The Republicans chose Hayes as a compromise candidate (over James G. Blaine) against Democrat Samuel J. Tilden who won the popular vote by 254,235. The disputed electoral votes of Florida, South Carolina, Louisiana, and Oregon were awarded to Hayes by a congressionally appointed commission.

Rutherford B. Hayes. (Courtesy of Library of Congress.)

Hayes shrewdly used his political power by his veto of numerous bills, especially a rider to a key House appropriations bill repealing federal enforcement over election. He called it "radical, dangerous, and unconstitutional"[2] as it could lead the Senate and the president to accept any rider. His civil service reform included the New York Custom House whereby he overrode a political tradition of senatorial courtesy on appointments (Chester Arthur's). In foreign affairs, Hayes strongest effort was his opposition to French entrepreneur Ferdinand-Marie de Lesseps's building a canal in Central America.

No president since Jefferson showed such a love of literature as Hayes who brought six thousand volumes of Americana to Washington. Although her teetotaler habit brought her the name of "Lemonade Lucy," Lucy's hospitality brought memories of Dolley Madison's White House soirees and the first usage of the title First Lady.

THE FILMS

The moderation for which Hayes is noted governs his role—a non-speaking one—in his biggest film, *Buffalo Bill*.

The Flag of Humanity (1940)

Hayes: Joseph King. *Other Cast:* Nana Bryant (Clara Barton), John Hamilton (General Garfield), Ted Osborne (Dr. Bellows), Robert Strange (Dr. Bradley), John Alexander (Robert Todd Lincoln). *Director:* Jean Negulesco. *Writing Credits:* Jean Negulesco, Charles L. Tedford. *Cinematography:* Charles Boyle. *Studio:* The Vitaphone Corp., Warner Brothers. *Length:* 2 reels.

From the little information available, this short would appear to concern Clara Barton's (Nana Bryant) efforts during the Civil War.

Buffalo Bill (1944): John Dilson as President Hayes, who makes just one appearance (seated, sixth from left), and a non-speaking one, in the second film on his presidency. Joel McCrea (in the title role) receives the Medal of Honor for the War Bonnet Gorge campaign at this banquet in Washington. In actuality the medal was for action against the Cheyenne in 1872. William Wellman directed this 20th Century–Fox production. (Photofest.)

Buffalo Bill (1944)

Hayes: John Dilson. *Other Cast:* Joel McCrea (William F. "Buffalo Bill" Cody), Maureen O'Hara (Louisa Frederici Cody), Linda Darnell (Dawn Starlight), Thomas Mitchell (Ned Buntline), Edgar Buchanan (Sgt. Chips), Anthony Quinn (Yellow Hand), Sidney Blackmer (Theodore Roosevelt). *Director:* William Wellman. *Producer:* Harry Sherman. *Writing Credits:* Cecile Kramer, Aeneas MacKenzie. *Music:* David Buttolph, Arthur Lange. *Cinematography:* Leon Shamroy. *Film Editing:* James B. Clark. *Art Direction:* James Basevi, Lewis Creber. *Set Decoration:* Thomas Little. *Costume Design:* Rene Hubert. *Studio:* 20th Century–Fox. *Length:* 90 minutes.

William Wellman is reported to have been embarrassed by the lack of historical accuracy in this life of "Buffalo Bill" Cody (Joel McCrea). As John Ford said of *The Man Who Shot Liberty Valance* (1962), "When the legend becomes fact, print the legend." With his concentration on a completely fictitious romance between Cody and his wife Louisa Frederici (Maureen O'Hara), Wellman, in his Technicolor western, ignores many of the more interesting aspects of the Buffalo Bill story.

Cody had a particularly exciting life; some biographers indicate that he was an experienced plainsman by the time he was 14. As a scout for the army, Cody was awarded a Congressional Medal of Honor for action against the Cheyenne in April 1872. (Because he had not been actually in the army, the award was withdrawn in 1916 but reinstated in 1989.) Wellman uses the Medal of Honor incident but for a completely different campaign in War Bonnet Gorge.

It is in the context of receiving the medal that Cody goes to Washington, D.C., and appears at a dinner with Hayes (John Dilson). Dilson, with a full beard, somewhat resembles pictures of Hayes. His role did not involve any speaking.

20

James A. Garfield (1881)

James A. Garfield. (Courtesy of Library of Congress.)

Just as he was preparing his education program to help African-Americans escape poverty as he had done, Garfield was assassinated by disgruntled office-seeker Charles J. Guiteau. Garfield was en route to his alma mater, Williams College, for an honorary degree. Only in office 120 days, this ambiguous man still is debated: Was he a Horatio Alger hero as purported in his biography, *From Canal Boy to President*, or merely an adept Ohio politician?

Garfield was a canal boy before he embraced the Disciples of Christ, viewing himself as an instrument of "God's destiny"[1] and later becoming an ordained minister. In between he taught high school and at Hiram College of which he later became president. He distinguished himself in the Civil War and in nine terms in the House of Representatives. Although elected senator by the Ohio legislature in 1880, he never took his Senate seat, as he became president.

Despite his legislative background, Garfield excelled more as conciliator— struggling over cabinet and other appointments to minimize the spoils system. His chief presidential initiative was a refunding of the national debt. In international policy, he supported Secretary of State James G. Blaine for a stronger presence in Western Hemisphere diplomacy and for opening more overseas markets. For a man whose oratory skills quieted a New York City mob the morning after Lincoln's assassination, his promise had he been a full-term president remains uncertain.

THE FILMS

For his short time in office, Garfield has proportionally more movies including him than many other presidents who served full terms. None, however, are biopics, but all use his assassination in the plot.

'Neath Western Skies (1929)

Garfield: Alfred Hewston. *Other Cast:* Tom Tyler (Tex McCloud), Hank Bell ("Wildcat" Riley), Harry Woods (Jim Canfield), J.P. McGowan (Dugan), Bobbie Dunn (Percival Givens), Lotus Thompson (Ann Givens), Barney Furey (Lem Johnson). *Director-Producer:* J.P. McGowan. *Writing Credits:* Sally Winters. *Cinematography:* Hap Depew. *Studio:* J.P. McGowan Productions. *Length:* 60 minutes.

Tom Tyler stars as rancher Tex McCloud who discovers oil on his property in this silent western. A gang of cutthroats led by Dugan (director-producer J.P. McGowan) attempts to spoil his development by stealing drills. Through some mix-up Lotus Thompson (Australian-born starlet Ann Givens) gets the drills and helps Tex succeed.

This film was not available for our viewing and we do not know if the Garfield character is actually the president. The same is true of *The Flag of Humanity* (1940) in which John Hamilton plays a character named Garfield. For details on that film, see Chapter 19 on Rutherford B. Hayes.

Angel of Mercy (1939)

Garfield: Emmett Vogan. *Other Cast:* Sara Haden (Clara Barton), John Nesbitt (Narrator), Ann Rutherford (Sister of Dead Soldier). *Director:* Edward Cahn. *Producer:* John Nesbitt. *Writing Credits:* Herman Boxer. *Music:* David Snell. *Cinematography:* Robert Pittack. *Film Editing:* Mildred Rich. *Studio:* MGM. *Length:* 10 minutes.

Narrator John Nesbitt takes a feminist point of view in this short from his "Passing Parade" series (he remade it in 1942 as *Flag of Mercy*). He stresses that men ran the world and shows how during the American Civil War women finally were permitted another occupation—that of nursing the wounded. Dramatizing his point in both oral and pictorial presentation, Nesbitt states how a boy is dead because for five days he lay unattended on the battlefield, denied medical care.

To the rescue of such boys comes Clara Barton (Sara Haden), born in 1821, a teacher and the first female clerk in the U.S. Patent Office (now the Patent and Trademark Office) before she turned to the field of health. For her work she was called "The Angel of the Battlefield." Struck by one of the diseases that ravaged many of the soldiers, one of her assistants, the sister of the dead boy, played by Ann Rutherford, also dies. It is like the death of a daughter to Barton.

Although the ten-minute film does not cover all her activities, Barton was appointed superintendent of nurses for the Army of the James. After the war, she formed a bureau that marked more than 23,000 graves in the Andersonville National Cemetery. Weakened by her war work, she went to Switzerland to recuperate.

The film shows that after receiving an appeal from the International Red Cross to promote its cause in the United States, Barton returns and visits President Garfield (Emmett Vogan). Receiving her with great dignity in his office, Garfield says he shares her anguish about war. Heartened that he will be behind her cause, Barton leaves only to soon learn of his assassination. The American branch of the Red Cross began in 1881, and she was its first president.

Barton continued her work of aiding victims of U.S. natural disasters such as the Johnstown flood with the help of the Canadian branch of the Red Cross. The film ends with

Nesbitt stating, "That a woman having given man life in the beginning fights to keep it to the end."

The Night Riders (1939) aka Lone Star Bullets

Garfield: Francis Sayles. *Other Cast:* John Wayne (Stony Brooke), Ray Corrigan (Tucson Smith), Max Terhune (Lullaby Joslin), Doreen McKay (Soledad), Ruth Rogers (Susan Randall), George Douglas (Talbot Pierce, aka Don Luis de Serrano), Tom Tyler (Henchman Jackson), Kermit Maynard (Sheriff Pratt), Sammy McKim (Tim Randall), Walter Wills (Hazleton), Ethan Laidlaw (Henchman Andrews), Edward Peil Sr. (Rancher Harper), Tom London (Rancher Wilson), Jack Ingram (Henchman Wilkins), William Nestell (Brawler). *Director:* George Sherman. *Producer:* William Berke. *Writing Credits:* William Colt MacDonald, Betty Burbridge, Stanley Roberts. *Music:* William Lava. *Cinematography:* Jack Marta. *Film Editing:* Lester Orlebeck. *Studio:* Republic Pictures Corp. *Length:* 56 minutes.

One of Republic Pictures' western series involving the adventures of "The Three Mesquiteers," *The Night Riders* has the three friends acting as Robin Hoods, dressed in white not green, against a major land swindler. Reportedly based on a historical event concerning James Addison Reavis and his attempt to steal Arizona from the United States, *The Night Riders* was remade by Republic as *Arizona Terrors* in 1942 also under the direction of the competent George Sherman. The Reavis character's story was again retold in Samuel Fuller's *The Baron of Arizona* (1950) starring Vincent Price. In *The Night Riders*, the con man Talbot Pierce (George Douglas) is able to convince the government that he has title to 13 million acres in an unnamed state.

Unfortunately for Pierce, the first settlers he attempts to evict are The Three Mesquiteers, Stony Brooke (John Wayne), Tucson Smith (Ray Corrigan), and Lullaby Joslin (Max Terhune). In an honest attempt to stop the land grab the three go to Washington and talk to President Garfield (Francis Sayles) who tells them there is nothing he can do officially, but he will overlook any "unofficial" action that they might take. The "unofficial" action takes the form of the Night Riders in a Robin Hood approach.

Ultimately the trio is arrested, tried, and given the death penalty. Just in the nick of time one of their friends uncovers evidence that the land grab is a fraud and presents the data to President Garfield. He is assassinated before taking any action. This results in the Three Mesquiteers dying before a firing squad. Not really, however; the bullets are blanks, and they live to see another day and ride.

Francis Sayles was a character actor who appeared in numerous films in the 1930s and reportedly did not improve his reputation by his impersonation of Garfield.

No More Excuses (1968)

Garfield: Lawrence Wolf. *Other Cast:* Robert Downey Sr. (Pvt. Stewart Thompson), Alan Abel (Himself), Prentice Wilhite (Charles Guiteau), Linda Diesem (Mrs. Garfield), Aimee Eccles (Chinese Girl), Don Calfa (Priest), Paula Morris (Priest's Woman/Prostitute). *Director-Writer:* Robert Downey Sr. *Film Editing:* Robert Soukis. *Studio:* Phantasma Film/Rogosin Films. *Length:* 62, 55, 52 minutes.

This New York underground film, released in three versions (62-, 55-, and 52-minute), involves elements of the surreal and absurd. Via time travel, wounded Confederate soldier

Pvt. Stewart Thompson (Robert Downey Sr.) flees to present-day New York City. He engages a prostitute, visits Yankee Stadium where he's thrown out as a lunatic, and returns to the Civil War and death.

In other flashbacks, Charles Guiteau (Prentice Wilhite) makes three unsuccessful attempts to assassinate President Garfield (Lawrence Wolf) and finally succeeds because the president takes a shortcut through the ladies room at the Washington D.C. Baltimore and Potomac Railroad Station. That historical deviation captures the tone of this film.

Il Prezzo del potere (1970) aka The Price of Power

Garfield: Van Johnson. *Other Cast:* Giuliano Gemma (Bill Willer), Fernando Rey (Pinkerton), Warren Vanders (Arthur McDonald), Benito Stefanelli (Sheriff Stefanel), Manuel Zarzo (Nick), Maria Cuadra (Lucrezia James), Ray Saunders (Jack Donavan), Jose Calvo (Dr. Strips). *Director:* Tonino Valerii. *Producer:* Bianco Manini. *Writing Credits:* Massimo Patrizi. *Cinematographer:* Stelvio Massi. *Music:* Luis Enriquez Bacalov. *Film Editing:* Franco Fraticelli. *Set Decoration:* Angel Arzuaga, Carlo Leva. *Studio:* Films Montana/Patry Film. *Length:* 108 and 90 minutes.

Occasionally the "spaghetti western" leaves the world of greed and gunfights and enters the political arena. By 1970 it was acceptable to use the Kennedy assassination as a basis for story telling, so director Tonino Valerii moves Garfield's assassination to Dallas to tell a parallel story.

By doing this Valerii immediately also tells his audience to forget any semblance of history. Van Johnson, in one of his few Italian appearances, plays Garfield with some vigor, but the dubbing does not do enough to convey this intelligent, well-educated president. Since the movie is set in Dallas in 1890, and Garfield was shot in 1881 at the Baltimore and Potomac Station in Washington, D.C., by an insane disgruntled office seeker, Charles Guiteau, an oversight like poor dubbing seems incidental to this fictitious story.

Despite all the historical inaccuracies and fabrications, the film is considered one of the better of the numerous spaghetti westerns shot in Spain in the 1960s and 70s because of the cinematography of Stelvio Massi.

21

Chester A. Arthur (1881–1885)

Chester A. Arthur (Courtesy of Library of Congress.)

Chester A. Arthur's self-justification for his conduct (presidential and personal) was that he never sought the presidency (as he succeeded the assassinated Garfield), he did not like it, and he did not intend to seek it again, actively at least. Yet this master of the spoils system astonished everyone by doing the unexpected—calling for civil service, post office, and tariff reform. He knew he was the Republican's compromise choice for the vice presidency on Garfield's ticket and while personally honest was considered only a party politician. Projecting presidential looks and confident independence, Arthur carried out a conservative program on currency and tariff reform and minimizing the role of government. He impressed the business community with his administrative skills as he had during the Civil War and in his New York law practice and in his payoff job as collector of New York Customs House. But he did not impress Congress enough to gain support of his calls for a repeal of revenue taxes, expansion of the army, and prevention of encroachment on lands marked for Indians. Although not the hardest working of presidents, he successfully used the veto against excluding Chinese immigration and citizenship. Toward African-Americans Arthur urged a general policy of conciliation under the Fourteenth Amendment. His foreign affairs were undermined by James G. Blaine, Garfield's Secretary of State, who retired to pursue a presidential nomination and attacked the European policies of Frederick Theodore Frelinghuysen. Arthur, recently widowed and lonely, did not like living in the White House, saying it was "depressing and fatiguing to live in the same house where you work."[1] So he refurbished and repaired it, extravagantly, and went to a cottage at the Soldiers Home when possible. He even suggested that Congress construct a separate presidential residence on Lafayette Square. For all his style, especially in dressing, "Beau Brummell" Arthur gained little respect—too many trousers were not befitting a democratic leader. Bright's disease restricted the last of his three-and-a-half years in office, and he died in 1886.

THE FILMS

The two films in which Arthur appears reflect two aspects of his character. In *Silver Dollar*, he shows his interest in style and society attending Yates Martin's lavish wedding. In *Cattle King* he displays his belief in minimizing the role of government wondering "where such a large operation of 265,000 head of cattle leaves the small farmer."

Silver Dollar (1932)

Arthur: Emmett Corrigan. *Other Cast:* Edward G. Robinson (Yates Martin), Bebe Daniels (Lily Owens Martin), Aline MacMahon (Sarah Martin), DeWitt Jennings (George, the Mine Foreman). *Director:* Alfred E. Green. *Writing Credits:* David Kaiser, Carl Erickson, Harvey F. Thew. *Music:* Cliff Hess, Milan Roder. *Cinematography:* James Van Trees. *Film Editing:* George Marks. *Art Direction:* Robert Haas. *Costume Design:* Orry-Kelly. *Studio:* First National Pictures Inc. *Length:* 83 minutes.

Based on the biography of H.A.W. Tabor by David Karsner, *Silver Dollar* details the rise and fall of Tabor's counterpart Yates Martin (Edward G. Robinson). An unsuccessful miner and a less-than-astute merchant, Martin builds a personal fortune by grub-staking silver miners.

Silver Dollar (1932): Emmett Corrigan as President Arthur (right) joins Edward G. Robinson as Yates Martin, the politically ambitious entrepreneur, in toasting his new bride Lily Owens Martin as played by Bebe Daniels. Alfred E. Green directed this First National Pictures biopic, based on the bio of H.A.W. Tabor. (Courtesy of George Eastman House.)

With his fortune assured he shifts to politics and becomes the first mayor of Denver and lieutenant governor of Colorado. By building Denver's opera house, Martin brings culture to the new city and aspires for higher political office. His plans are thwarted because of his unfaithfulness to his wife Sarah (Aline MacMahon) with "the other woman" Lily Owens (Bebe Daniels). In real life Lily was "Baby Doe" in the 1950s American opera "The Ballad of Baby Doe."

Martin is able to obtain an appointment as senator by the Colorado governor and moves to Washington where he marries Lily. President Arthur (Emmett Corrigan) attends the wedding, toasts and kisses the bride but refuses to have a private drink with Martin, possibly because of the scandal associated with the marriage or Martin's suspicious business practices. In his brief appearance Corrigan portrays Arthur as a cordial yet serious man but he does not have any resemblance to the twenty-first president.

The blustery, loud hubris of Martin throughout his life makes his fall a certainty. It happens with the silver panic in the Cleveland administration. Newspaper headlines show the passage of time until a mentally unbalanced Martin dies in the McKinley term. Supposedly McKinley appointed Martin Postmaster General just prior to his death. Director Alfred E. Green elicits the versatility of Robinson, the actor who embodied gangster roles as he did in *Little Caesar* (1931).

Cattle King (1963)

Arthur: Larry Gates. *Other Cast:* Robert Taylor (Sam Brassfield), Joan Caulfield (Sharleen Travers), William Windom (Harry Travers), Robert Loggia (Johnny Quatro), Robert Middleton (Clay Matthews), Virginia Christine (Ruth Winters). *Director:* Tay Garnett. *Producers:* Nat Holt, Thomas Thompson. *Writing Credits:* Thomas Thompson. *Music:* Paul Sawtell, Bert Shefter. *Cinematography:* William E. Snyder. *Film Editing:* George White. *Art Direction:* Walter Holscher. *Set Decoration.* Theodore Driscoll. *Studio:* MGM. *Length:* 88 minutes.

In his last appearance for MGM, Robert Taylor plays "Cattle King" Sam Brassfield in a somewhat different western. Different in that the heroine, Sharleen Travers (Joan Caufield), is gunned down by the villain, and her spineless brother, Harry (William Windom), survives to manage the ranch.

Arthur is played with great seriousness by Larry Gates, who although significantly lighter in weight than Arthur is equally presidential in his appearance. He arrives in Cheyenne, Wyoming, in 1883 to make a personal tour of Yellowstone Park. The park opened in 1872, and Arthur was the first president to visit it. He is feted by Clay Mathews (Robert Middleton), a Texas cattleman who wants the president's support for the National Cattle Trail Bill that would eliminate the fences that are impeding the movement of cattle from Texas to the Northwest. Brassfield arrives at the dinner uninvited and vehemently argues against the bill. Director Tay Garnett obviously filmed this Wyoming setting in California.

The action that follows is typical for westerns until Arthur arrives unexpectedly at Brassfield's ranch and requests a tour. During the tour and after dinner the president listens intently to Brassfield's position and departs, apparently having been convinced of grazing land control.

In the end, the film reverts to additional typical western fare with Brassfield beating Mathews to the draw and Brassfield's compadre Johnny Quatro (Robert Loggia) besting Texas gunman Vince Bodine (Richard Devon) in a showdown.

22 and 24

Grover Cleveland
(1885–1889 and 1893–1897)

Grover Cleveland. (Courtesy of Library of Congress.)

At last, an honest man running for the presidency—or was Grover Cleveland the father of Maria Halpin's son? The Republicans for James G. Blaine shouted: "Ma! ma!/ where's my pa?/ gone to the White House,/ ha! ha! ha!" and Cleveland Democrats retorted: "Blaine! Blaine!/ James G. Blaine!/ the con-ti-nental liar/ from the State of Maine."

Cleveland was exonerated by group of clergymen, led by Henry Ward Beecher.[1] But adultery ranked as a capital crime in an era of common bribery.[2] So Cleveland won by 219 to 182 electoral votes with the popular vote almost even. His electoral plurality was even higher in his second election, the largest since Grant's. Between his two terms, he ran and lost to Benjamin Harrison in 1888, although his popular vote was larger.

It was Joseph Pulitzer, the crusading owner of *The World*, who first raised the possibility of Cleveland's presidency. But Cleveland was particularly wary of newspapermen.[3] He tried to avoid them on his engagement and later marriage to Frances Folsom, his 21-year-old ward, but the "right to privacy" did not exist in the press's vocabulary. After the wedding, the former bachelor president, at 49, became more relaxed, but maintained his dutiful work schedule. From his early days as a lawyer in Buffalo, he always was an independent, honest administrator who hated corruption. The first term was occupied with two problems, patronage and the tariff.

Cleveland in the second term struggled with a country-wide depression by repealing the Silver Purchase Act of 1890. Abroad, he showed his respect of the law by insisting on a proper boundary between Venezuela and British Guiana by Great Britain on grounds it conflicted with the Monroe Doctrine.

THE FILMS

The characterization of Cleveland changes with the times in three main films including him: He has a regular presidential role in a western of the late 1930s and a satirical role in the western of the late 1970s. This is common with Hollywood presidential treatments in recent years, particularly with films about Richard Nixon.

The Oklahoma Kid (1939)

Cleveland: Stuart Holmes. *Other Cast:* James Cagney (Jim Kincaid), Humphrey Bogart (Whip McCord), Rosemary Lane (Jane Hardwick), Donald Crisp (Judge Hardwick), Harvey Stephens (Ned Kincaid), Hugh Sothern (John Kincaid). *Director:* Lloyd Bacon. *Producers:* Hal B. Wallis, Jack L. Warner. *Writing Credits:* Edward E. Paramore Jr., Wally Kline. *Music:* Max Steiner. *Cinematography:* James Wong Howe. *Art Direction:* Esdras Hartley. *Costume Design:* Orry-Kelly *Makeup:* Perc Westmore. *Studio:* Warner Bros. *Length:* 85 minutes.

Oklahoma, land of the Indians and the 1893 land rush, becomes the setting for normally urban gangster actors James Cagney and Humphrey Bogart in the last of three films that they did together in the 1930s. The others were *Angels With Dirty Faces* (1938) and *The Roaring Twenties* (1939). Cagney plays the Oklahoma Kid (aka Jim Kincaid), a prodigal son, and Bogart plays Whip McCord, the gang leader from whom Cagney steals money.

Even with the two stars it is a typical B-western that includes such scenery as Sierra-type mountains on the stagecoach route between Tulsa and Kansas City. The Oklahoma Kid is immediately known to be the top-rated star when in the opening sequence cinematographer James Wong Howe provide the audience with a stunning close-up.

The presidential scene is done with especially impressive makeup by Perc Westmore. President Cleveland (Stuart Holmes) presides at a meeting in his office with the press. "At your service," he says and announces that he has changed his policy about Western settlement. Previously, he believed the terms were unfavorable to the Indians. Now he issues a proclamation for adequate payment from the government to Indians in the Cherokee Strip for six million acres of the "finest farming country" because "I happen to believe in the will of the people, and Congress represents the will of the people."

Lillian Russell (1940)

Cleveland: William B. Davidson. *Other Cast:* Alice Faye (Lillian Russell), Don Ameche (Edward Solomon), Henry Fonda (Alexander Moore), Edward Arnold (Diamond Jim Brady), Warren William (Jesse Lewisohn), Leo Carrillo (Tony Pastor), Helen Westley (Grandma Leonard), Dorothy Peterson (Cynthia Leonard), Ernest Truex (Charles Leonard), Nigel Bruce (William S. Gilbert), Claud Allister (Arthur Sullivan), Lynn Bari (Edna McCauley), Joe Weber (Himself), Lew Fields (Himself), Eddie Foy Jr. (Eddie Foy Sr.), Joseph Cawthorn (Leopold Damrosch). *Director:* Irving Cummings. *Producer:* Darryl F. Zanuck. *Writing Credits:* William Anthony McGuire. *Music:* Mack Gordon, Charles Henderson, Bronislau Kaper, Alfred Newman, John Stromberg. *Cinematography:* Leon Shamroy. *Film Editing:* Walter Thompson. *Art Direction:* Richard Day, Joseph C. Wright. *Set Decoration:* Thomas Little. *Costume Design:* Travis Banton. *Sound:* Roger Heman, Arthur von Kirbach. *Studio:* 20th Century–Fox Film Corp. *Length:* 127 minutes.

Even with a cast of top Hollywood stars this biopic of Lillian Russell, one of the most notorious performers in the late 19th century, surprisingly turns out to be doggedly slow.

Born in Clinton, Iowa (where the film premiered in May 1940), as Helen Louise Leonard, the future Lillian Russell (Alice Faye) moves to New York City. She's taught by Leopold Damrosch (Joseph Cawthorn) and discovered by Tony Pastor (Leo Carrillo) and becomes one of the leading stage stars of her day. The film ignores her four marriages and numerous affairs, concentrating on her marriage to English composer Edward Solomon (Don Ameche) and her return to the love of her life Alexander Moore (Henry Fonda) in Pittsburgh after Solomon dies. Along the way she turns down a proposal from Diamond Jim Brady (Edward Arnold).

President Cleveland is played by William B. Davidson. The appearance of Weber & Fields as themselves in a classic routine was the highlight of the film, according to *Variety*.

Buffalo Bill and the Indians, or Sitting Bull's History Lesson (1976)

Cleveland: Pat McCormick. *Other Cast:* Paul Newman (William F. Cody), Joel Grey (Nate Salisbury), Kevin McCarthy (Maj. John Burke), Harvey Keitel (Ed Goodman), Allan Nicholls (Prentiss Ingraham), Geraldine Chaplin (Annie Oakley), John Considine (Frank Butler), Burt Lancaster (Ned Buntline), Shelley Duvall (Mrs. Cleveland), Frank Kaquitts (Sitting Bull), Evelyn Lear (Nina Cavalini). *Director-Producer-Screenwriter:* Robert Altman. *Writing Credits:* Arthur Kopit, Alan Rudolph. *Cinematography:* Paul Lohmann. *Composer:* Richard Baskin. *Editors:* Peter Appleton, Dennis M. Hill. *Production Designer:* Tony Masters. *Art Director:* Jack Maxsted. *Costume Designer:* Anthony Powell. *Studio:* United Artists. *Length:* 123 minutes.

Director Robert Altman's intention, as in previous films such as *McCabe and Mrs. Miller* (1971) and *Nashville* (1975), was to debunk western history and legend. He achieves his goal as megalomaniac "Buffalo Bill" Cody (Paul Newman) sustains the myths of white triumph over savage Indians in his Wild West show until Sitting Bull (Frank Kaquitts) joins the troupe and requests authenticity.

Cleveland (Pat McCormick) obviously enjoys the show with his bride (Shelley Duvall), an event of highly suspect historical possibility for the privacy-seeking president. Afterward, he affectionately slaps Sitting Bull on the arm and says, "You never miss." Cleveland also never misses a chance to collect lines he might use for political purposes. Later, at a party for him, Cleveland refuses to speak to Sitting Bull, an odd action. Still, McCormick looks the part except for his lesser girth.

Cleveland's bride, his former ward Frances Folsom, is played with simpering sweetness by Duvall whose only business is to introduce her friend, opera singer Nina Cavalini (Evelyn Lear). Director Altman's pageantry triumphs and however authentic his cinematic details, he reshapes history in his ironic indictment of western pop culture.

23

Benjamin Harrison (1889–1893)

Benjamin Harrison. (Courtesy of Library of Congress.)

Between Cleveland's terms of principled independence, Benjamin Harrison foreshadowed later American imperialism and cast more shadows with political patronage. He was said to have a fatal gift for doing the right thing in the wrong way.[1]

Campaigning for civil service reform, he disappointed reformers by cutting 55,000 patronage positions to 31,000 and offering them to so many newspapermen that there were not enough jobs to go around. Harrison's only criterion for his cabinet was Presbyterianism and a background similar to his except for being grandson of a former president, William Henry Harrison, great grandson of a signer of the Declaration of Independence and son of a congressman. Consequently, lawyers, Civil War generals, and Ohio natives dominated his administration. His obscure appointees disappointed many party leaders except James G. Blaine, whom he had defeated in the presidential party nomination and whom he reluctantly appointed Secretary of State.

In office, Blaine agreed with the president that the nation's industrial expansion required foreign markets and headed a Latin American conference that established the Pan-American Union. Blaine's ill health pushed his duties onto the president, enlarging his role in foreign affairs. Harrison won Congressional backing for the Navy that supported his belief in sea power as key to expansion. His expansion policies extended to Hawaii that he unsuccessfully tried to annex.

These initiatives gained Harrison subsequent esteem as did the Sherman Act that advocated competition and opposed monopolies. Lack of Congressional funds, however, prevented Harrison from enforcing the act against the trusts. He failed to stop Andrew Carnegie and his partner Henry Frick from their union-busting tactics in the Homestead steel strike. In other initiatives, Harrison supported bills that failed to protect black suffrage and enlist federal aid to combat illiteracy. He did enlist Frederick Douglass, the eminent black leader, to serve as minister to Haiti.

THE FILMS

If you are going to have only one major film about your presidency, nothing could be more stirring than *Stars and Stripes Forever*. The story of composer and conductor John Philip Sousa, it resounds with lively marches, ruffles and flourishes that served Harrison and many presidents since to underscore the ceremony of the office.

Stars and Stripes Forever (1952) aka *Marching Along*

Harrison: Roy Gordon: *Other Cast:* Clifton Webb (John Philip Sousa), Debra Paget (Lily Becker), Robert Wagner (Willie Little), Ruth Hussey (Jennie Sousa), Finlay Currie (Col. Randolph), Roy Roberts (Maj. Houston), Tom Browne Henry (David Blakely), Helen Van Tuyl (Mrs. President Harrison). *Director:* Henry Koster. *Producer:* Lamar Trotti. *Writing Credits:* John Philip Sousa, Ernest Vajda, Lamar Trotti. *Music:* Daniel Decatur Emmett. *Cinematography:* Charles G. Clarke. *Film Editing:* James B. Clark. *Art Direction:* Lyle Wheeler, Joseph C. Wright. *Set Direction:* Claude E. Carpenter, Thomas Little. *Costume Design:* Dorothy Jeakins. *Makeup:* Ben Nye. *Studio:* 20th Century–Fox. *Length:* 90 minutes.

As stirring as John Philip Sousa's marches, this film biography follows the composer from his early days in the Marine Corps Band through the Spanish-American War in 1898. It captures the drive of this bandmaster through the performance of Clifton Webb. Webb displays some of his well known acidulous and pedantic behavior that he epitomized as a babysitter, Mr. Belvedere, in *Sitting Pretty* (1948) and its sequels. Henry Koster, who began his directing career in Germany, is best known for his flair with light films and his craftsmanship that surface in this film.

Stars and Stripes Forever is historically accurate in following Sousa's career as written in Sousa's book *Marching Along* except for the addition of a subplot about a young musician who invents the Sousaphone and falls in love with a singer. Robert Wagner and Debra Paget handle these roles with charming enthusiasm. Ruth Hussey plays the other leading role, Sousa's wife Jennie, with grace and subtle wit.

Of course, it's the music that counts. Sousa's famous marches dominate the film that also includes one of the romantic ballads he loved to write. The final scene with Sousa leading his band in "Stars and Stripes Forever" between shots of Spanish-American and World War I soldiers marching as smartly as the band is filmmaking at its Technicolor red-white-and-blue best.

If Benjamin Harrison's gift was for doing the right thing in the wrong way, it certainly surfaced in *Stars and Stripes Forever* when he asked Sousa to play "livelier" at a White House reception so the pokey office-seekers might move along more quickly. Sousa's fast tempo works in this brief scene, beginning with the president's entrance with Mrs. Harrison to "Semper Fidelis" ("Always Faithful"). Harrison was the last of the presidents for whom Sousa's band played. From 1880 to 1892 the U.S. Marine Band under Sousa also performed for Hayes, Garfield, Arthur, and Cleveland. Roy Gordon and Helen Van Tuyl play the presidential couple with pomp perfection.

Independence (1976)

Harrison: Donald C. Moore.

This 30-minute short directed by John Huston for the U.S. Bicentennial celebration provides background on the development, writing, and signing of the Declaration of Independence. Benjamin Harrison (Donald C. Moore) appears with three other presidents and other founding fathers. For details, see Chapter 1 on George Washington.

25

William McKinley (1897–1901)

Reluctantly, William McKinley, an old-fashioned man, led the United States into the industrial age and foreign expansion. The last president who served in the Civil War—"one of the bravest and finest officers" said his commanding officer, Rutherford B. Hayes[1]—he was the third president to be assassinated. At the time, he was the most widely loved president in memory except for Washington and Lincoln, having always done what the people wanted.

Intelligent, quiet, hard-working, McKinley thought about becoming a minister before he turned to the law and eventually politics. He was governor of Ohio before he won the presidency over Williams Jennings Bryan who believed "You shall not crucify mankind upon a cross of gold." Besides the gold standard, McKinley supported protective tariffs and higher taxes. But the Spanish-American dispute was the key issue that McKinley hoped to achieve through negotiation; in his inaugural address he advocated "no wars of conquest; we must avoid the temptation of territorial aggression." Public, political, and press (Hearst and Pulitzer) pressures led to the Spanish-American War. Afterward, besides Cuban independence, McKinley's peace terms included transfer of Puerto Rico. Expansionism broadened to Hawaii and the Philippines "to uplift them and civilize and Christianize them," he said.[2] In the end, McKinley reversed American foreign policy from isolation and avoidance of entangling alliances to worldwide commitments. Of note also is McKinley's devoted commitment to his epileptic wife, Ida.

William McKinley. (Courtesy of Library of Congress.)

THE FILMS

McKinley appears in six films in minor roles mainly associated with the Spanish-American War or the effects of his assassination in the plot line. His appearances are short, the actors playing him often unconvincing, and the historical accuracy questionable for such a deserving president.

A Message to Garcia (1936)

McKinley: Dell Henderson. *Other Cast:* Wallace Beery (Sgt. Dory), Barbara Stanwyck (Raphaelita Maderos), John Boles (Lt. Andrew Rowan), Alan Hale (Dr. Krue), Herbert Mundin (Henry Piper). *Director:* George Marshall. *Producer:* Darryl F. Zanuck. *Writing Credits:* Gene Fowler, Sam Hellman, Elbert Hubbard, Gladys Lehman, W. Lipscomb, Lt. Andrew S. Rowan. *Music:* Louis Silvers. *Cinematography:* Rudolph Mate. *Film Editing:* Herbert Levy. *Art Direction:* William S. Darling, Rudolph Sternad. *Set Decoration:* Thomas Little. *Studio:* 20th Century–Fox. *Length:* 77 minutes.

With no thought of historical accuracy, appropriate casting, believable plotting or convincing dialogue, this film retells Elbert Hubbard's story of Lt. Andrew Rowan's (John Boles) delivery of McKinley's message to Garcia, the insurgent Cuban general in the Spanish-American War. In actual fact, the message was oral and delivered without incident; in the film it is written and winds up after much travail in Rowan's gun barrel.

A *Message to Garcia* (1936): Dell Henderson as President McKinley in this historically inaccurate retelling of the story of Lt. Andrew Rowan's (John Boles) delivery of McKinley's message of support to Garcia, the insurgent Cuban general in the Spanish-American War. George Marshall directed and Darryl F. Zanuck produced this 20th Century–Fox release. (Photofest.)

Many other historical changes occur in this melodrama: a rotten-to-the-core Marine deserter, Sgt. Dory (Wallace Beery), tries to help Rowan as does the sister of a Cuban fighter, Raphaelita Maderos (Barbara Stanwyck). Thrown in this odd mix for comic relief is an English tinware salesman, Henry Piper (Herbert Mundin). He's not even able to help Rowan and Dory fight the alligators in crossing a stream.

After even more trouble in the Cuban jungle and excruciating torture by hired gun Dr. Krue (Alan Hale), Rowan delivers the president's message. It had been written in the most authentic scene of the film. In his White House office, McKinley (Dell Henderson) learns from his military advisers that he needs to locate Garcia so that the American forces can unite with his insurgents. Soberly and succinctly the president asks his advisers if they have had any communication with Garcia and then if they have someone in mind to go to Garcia. In marches Rowan. McKinley stands, appraises Rowan, hands over the message, and advises him that he will have no support on this dangerous mission. After Rowan leaves, McKinley tells his advisers, "I think you picked the right man." Henderson seems the right actor for this role in his physical appearance. The *New York Times* review (April 10, 1936) found the film "as undocumented a piece of historical claptrap as Hollywood has produced."

This Is My Affair (1937)

McKinley: Frank Conroy. *Other Cast:* Robert Taylor (Lt. Richard L. Perry), Barbara Stanwyck (Lil Duryea), Victor McLaglen (Jock Ramsay), Brian Donlevy (Batiste Duryea), Sidney Blackmer (Theodore Roosevelt), John Carradine (Ed). *Director:* William A. Seiter. *Producer:* Darryl F. Zanuck. *Writing Credits:* Allen Rivkink, Lamar Trotti, Darryl F. Zanuck. *Music:* Mack Gordon, Harry Revel, Arthur Lange, Charles Maxwell. *Cinematography:* Robert H. Planck. *Film Editing:* Allen McNeil. *Art Direction:* Rudolph Sternad. *Set Direction:* Thomas Little. *Costume Design:* Royer. *Studio:* 20th Century–Fox. *Length:* 100 minutes.

Never go to a presidential ball if you want a quiet life. Navy Lt. Richard Perry (Robert Taylor) does and ends up working as an undercover agent for McKinley (Frank Conroy). Perry's job is to determine the identity of the so-called "Bank Bandits" who are supposedly about to ruin the entire U.S. economy because of their thievery.

This Is My Affair (1937): Frank Conroy (seated, center) plays President McKinley, who enlists an undercover agent, Navy Lt. Richard Perry (Robert Taylor), to identify the so-called "Bank Bandits" in this 20th Century–Fox film. McKinley, an old-fashioned man, sits stiffly surrounded by his Cabinet, and Vice President Theodore Roosevelt, played by Sidney Blackmer (left). Behind them are (from left) portraits of Grant, Washington, and William Henry Harrison. (Photofest.)

Of course, to accomplish his mission Perry can only be known to the president, thus following a plotline that is used for at least two other presidential movies, *Night Riders* (1939) and *Arizona Terrors* (1942). Perry, the undercover agent, is known only to the president, who dies in office but isn't trusting enough to bring any of his advisers into the scheme, thus leaving the agents out in the cold.

In this film, Perry easily determines the identity of the "Bank Bandits." It is difficult to believe by their petty activities that Batiste Duryea (Brian Donlevy) and Jock Ramsey (Victor McLaglen) are the caliber of thieves to threaten the U.S. economy. Perry informs McKinley of their "big" bank heist just before the president is assassinated in Buffalo. Naturally, Perry is captured, convicted, and almost hung before girlfriend Lil Duryea (Barbara Stanwyck), Batiste's sister, convinces Admiral Dewey (Robert McWade) and new President Theodore Roosevelt (Sidney Blackmer) of Perry's connection to McKinley.

Although the script denigrates the intelligence of McKinley, he is played with sincerity and seriousness by Conroy. McKinley is one of the lesser known presidents to the moviegoing public, and thus the use of Conroy, who looks nothing like the president, is not a problem. He appears in his White House Office, smoking a cigar, and attending to papers on his desk. Exuding efficiency, he says, "I give the parties and the vice president has all the fun. I bet Mr. Roosevelt hasn't missed a dance." On the other hand, Roosevelt's scene-stealing appearance and actions make his role more difficult. Of note: Stanwyck and Taylor wed in 1939, two years after this film's release.

Teddy the Rough Rider (1940)

McKinley: Douglas Wood.

At a cabinet meeting soon after President McKinley (Douglas Wood) appointed Roosevelt Assistant Secretary of the Navy, Roosevelt begs McKinley to act in Cuba. The president asks why the United States is endangered, and then he says he "fails to see any emergency." An aide brings news of the *Maine*'s explosion in Cuba. Upon this startling and empowering news, Roosevelt says, "From now on, remember the *Maine*." The capable Wood is convincing. For details, see Chapter 26 on Theodore Roosevelt.

Arizona Terrors (1942)

McKinley: Unnamed actor. *Other Cast:* Don "Red" Barry (Jim Bradley), Lynn Merrick (Lila Adams), Al St. John (Hardtack), Reed Hadley (Don Pedro aka Jack Halliday), John Maxwell (Larry Madden), Frank Brownlee (Henry Adams), Rex Lease (Henchman Briggs), Lee Shumway (Sheriff Wilcox), Tom London (Rancher Wade). *Director-Producer:* George Sherman. *Writing Credits:* Taylor Caven, Doris Schroeder. *Cinematography:* Ernest Miller. *Studio:* Republic Pictures Corp. *Length:* 56 minutes.

Republic Pictures decided that *The Night Riders* (1939) was so successful that a remake would make a great deal of sense (and dollars). To make it different but to tell the same story of illegal land grabs, the president is changed from Garfield to McKinley.

Don "Red" Barry plays Jim Bradley and Al St. John as Hardtack takes the places of "The Three Mesquiteers" in the original and do essentially the same Robin Hood job. After one of their night raids they are escaping from a posse and accidentally get on a train carrying President McKinley (actor unidentified) on a goodwill tour. They explain the problem they are facing to the president, and he gives his informal approval to their approach.

Ultimately they are captured and sentenced to death for killing one of the henchmen. Using evidence that the heroes have uncovered, ranch owner-romantic interest Lila Adams (Lynn Merrick) tries to get to President McKinley, but he is assassinated. As in *The Night Riders* the local sheriff fakes the execution of Bradley and Hardtack, and the heroes are able to capture the bad guys and save the state of Arizona from becoming an independent domain.

March On, America! (1942)

McKinley: Douglas Wood.
For details, see Chapter 5 on James Monroe.

The Adventures of Ociee Nash (2003)

McKinley: Daniel Burnley. *Other Cast:* Keith Carradine (Papa George Nash), Mare Winningham (Aunt Mamie Nash), Skyler Day (Ociee Nash), Ty Pennington (Wilbur Wright), Tom Key (Mr. Lynch), Janice Akers (Frances Murphy), Anthony P. Rodriguez (Gypsy John Leon), John Lawhorn (Conductor Mr. Charles), Jasmine Sky (Elizabeth Murphy), Charles Nuckols IV (Fred Nash), Jill Jane Clements (Miss June), Donna Wright (Nellie Bly), Charles McGary (Conductor Mr. Louis), Jamey Propst (Mr. Tift), Sean Daniels (Orville Wright). *Director:* Kristen McGary. *Producers:* Derek Kavanagh, Amy Gary. *Music:* Van Dyke Parks. *Film Editing:* Amy Carey. *Costume Design:* Shirley Mickey. *Makeup:* Judy Ponder-Patton. *Studio:* Cine Vita Productions.

Set in 1898, this family film relates the adventures of a bright nine-year-old tomboy, Ociee Nash (Skyler Day), who is sent by train from her rural Mississippi home to Asheville, North Carolina. Her father George Nash (Keith Carradine) feels that she needs the guidance and refinement of his prim and proper sister Mamie Nash (Mare Winingham) since Ociee's mother has died.

Despite an abundance of anachronisms and old-fashioned ideas, this film is good family fare, directed for sentimental appeal by Kristen McGary. Ociee meets the famous woman journalist/adventurer Nellie Bly (Donna Wright) while on the train and learns about early feminism. She also encounters the Wright Brothers (Ty Pennington and Sean Daniels) on the train, deep in conversation about their flying machine. Ociee's most memorable adventure during the train trip, however, is meeting President McKinley (Daniel Burnley). During a station stop McKinley makes a political speech, and the crowd accidentally knocks down Ociee. The president helps her to her feet, and they have a conversation about "haste." When she suggests it's best to "make haste slowly" McKinley tells her what a bright little girl she is.

Burnley in no way resembles McKinley, particularly since he appears to be in his late 30s or early 40s whereas McKinley was 55 in 1898. His acting, in line with that of the rest of the cast, is amateurish at best, and the role is so folksy that is difficult to consider him as a president. He later remembers Ociee with a commemoration on "Ociee Nash Day," a celebration of the little heroine who saved her more ladylike neighbor friend Elizabeth Murphy (Jasmine Sky) from her burning home.

26

Theodore Roosevelt (1901–1909)

The inauguration of Theodore Roosevelt initiated what is now popularly called "the imperial presidency," a phrase that came into use with the publication of Arthur Schlesinger Jr.'s book of the same name in 1973.[1] It meant supremacy of the president in foreign and domestic affairs that Roosevelt exhibited in his antitrust legislation and coal strike mediation at home, the construction of the Panama Canal abroad, and his single greatest gift to posterity, his conservation philosophy.[2] He redefined the presidency as an office that protects the public interest. All of this by a man who also arose at 6 A.M. for push-ups, boxed, hunted big game in Africa, explored rivers in South America, read a book in one of four languages daily, and wrote 38 books on his many other interests. He was second only to Niagara Falls among American natural phenomena.[3]

Theodore Roosevelt. (Courtesy of Library of Congress.)

Born to wealth but ill health, Roosevelt aimed to be a naturalist but turned to politics upon his father's death while a junior at Harvard. In 1882 at 23 Roosevelt won a seat in the New York assembly. He relinquished the seat in February 1884 upon the deaths of his mother and wife Alice on the same day, leaving him with an infant daughter and sorrow. As hyperkinetic as always, he sought comfort through "the strenuous life ... of labor and strife."[4] Lasting comfort came from his second wife Edith with whom he had five children.

He was appointed U.S. Civil Service commissioner, New York City police commissioner, and assistant secretary of the Navy before he became the Rough Rider hero of San Juan Hill during the Spanish-American War, "the greatest day" of his life. His popularity led Boss (New York Senator) Thomas Platt to support—with plans to control—him for vice president, but Roosevelt revolted and followed a West African proverb: "Speak softly and carry a big stick; you will go far." He did, replacing President William McKinley upon his assassination, at 42 the youngest president, politically, socially, and morally conservative—but a reformer and always for the public purpose.

Unabashedly using his presidential power, he shaped public opinion by controlling the press, except for Joseph Pulitzer's *World*. Yet the public ignored the most celebrated libel suit in presidential history: the *World*'s asking who got the $40,000 for the rights to build the Panama Canal. The public was more interested in what Roosevelt did, from prevailing on warring Japan and Russia to accepting international arbitration (for which he won the Nobel Prize), to dispatching the Navy Battle Fleet on a world cruise for a "pacific effect," to inspiring the "teddy bear."[5] Besides his paradoxical progressive politics and personal style in two terms (and hopes for a third), Roosevelt left a legacy of 150 million acres of timberland, 50 game preserves, 75 national parks, and 16 national monuments. In addition, he instituted a successful antitrust suit against J.P. Morgan's holding company, arbitration of mine employees' grievances, government control of railroad rates—in essence a legacy of domestic reform and enlightened internationalism.

THE FILMS

A life as complex, celebrated, and documented as Roosevelt's provides many opportunities for films and Hollywood recognized this. It is fitting that he appears, although briefly, in *Citizen Kane* (1941), the number one film of all time on many lists, and in a total of 33 films including at least one in every decade since 1911–20. Roosevelt has been the subject of four biopics with the first, *The Fighting Roosevelts*, produced in 1919 and the latest, *The Indomitable Teddy Roosevelt*, released in 1986. His distinctive appearance and enthusiastic vocal delivery made specialists of his portrayers like Sidney Blackmer with seven films. In recent years he has been impersonated by such known actors as Brian Keith and James Whitmore. Like cartoonists, movie makeup artists settled on TR's teeth and eyeglasses for characterization.

In most films his appearances are related to specific actions that defined his life style. Most recent scholarly treatment of Roosevelt stresses his strenuous life and his culture of masculinity. The most popular "embodying both an ideal type and the contemporary nation mood" is noted by Sarah Miles in *Rough Rider in the White House: Theodore Roosevelt and the Politics of Desire*. These aspects appear in the films about Roosevelt's Rough Rider exploits and *Brighty of the Grand Canyon* (1967) that concerns both his love of nature and practice of manliness. Yet, his preoccupation with manliness hid as much as it revealed about someone who wished to be seen as open, but was in fact more secretive, crafty, and politically cunning than many realized. That cunning appeared in some of his films. For example, when Vitagraph saw films of Roosevelt's charge up San Juan Hill that looked like a hike on a hot day, the battle was reenacted. Yet, what power loving Roosevelt declared the defining moment of his presidency—his election night statement not to run again—never appeared on film.

Why America Will Win (1918)

Roosevelt: W.E. Whittle. *Other Cast*: A. Alexander (Gen. John J. Pershing as a boy), Harris Gordon (Gen. John J. Pershing as a youth), Olaf Skavian (Gen. John J. Pershing), Ralph

C. Faulkner (President Wilson), Miss Irving (Mrs. Daniel Pershing), Frank McGlynn Sr. (John F. Pershing), Betty Gray (Ann Thompson Pershing), Ernest Maupain (The Kaiser/Field Marshal von Hindenburg), Harry Warwick (King George of England), Johnny Fox (Gen. Foch), Lt. Percy (Prince Frederick William of Germany), Johnny Hennessey (Premier Georges Clemenceau), George Humbert (Gen. Pancho Villa), A. Mintone (Emperor of Japan), William Canfield (Consul General von Keuk). *Director:* Richard Stanton. *Writing Credits:* Adrian Johnson. *Cinematographer:* Henry Cronjager. *Studio:* Fox Film Corp. *Length:* Six reels.

John J. Pershing's love for country is accentuated in this story of this famous military man. He graduates from West Point, fights the Apaches, and joins Col. Theodore Roosevelt (W.E. Whittle) at the Battle of San Juan Hill during the Spanish-American War. From there Pershing goes to the Philippines where he subdues the Moro tribe. President Roosevelt makes him a brigadier and places him in charge of the Presidio in San Francisco. After a fire consumes Pershing's entire family, he is sent to the Mexican-American border. With his proven skill as a military leader, Pershing becomes commander of the American Expeditionary Forces in France during World War I. There, according to *Variety* (Sept. 28, 1918), the film shows "how he has his own personal account to settle with the ruthless Hun."

This World War I propaganda film stresses one reason why America will win: General John J. Pershing. He is played as a boy by A. Alexander, as a youth by Harris Gordon, and as an adult by Olaf Skavian.

The Fighting Roosevelts (1919) aka *Our Teddy*

Roosevelt: Francis J. Noonan as a boy, Herbert Bradshaw as a young man, E.J. Ratcliffe as president. *Director:* William Nigh. *Writing Credits:* Charles Hanson Towne, Porter Emerson Browne (story). *Cinematography:* Charles J. Davis, R. Schellinger. *Studio:* McClure Publishing Co.

The emphasis of this film is on Roosevelt's life before he became president. The principal scenes are of the colonel as a child, a young man in the State Assembly, a cowboy, New York City police commissioner, assistant secretary of the Navy, lieutenant colonel of the Rough Riders, and president–all done in "frank Horatio Alger fashion" according to the *New York Times.*

The actors impersonating Roosevelt at different ages—Francis J. Noonan as a boy, Herbert Bradshaw as a young man, and E.J. Ratcliffe as president—suggest him strongly by their performances and makeup, according to the *Times.* Produced just before his death, this silent film was endorsed by Roosevelt. The plot follows the culture of masculinity theme of his life, suggesting that any American male could become president through hard work and strenuous exercise.

The Copperhead (1920)

Roosevelt: Archival footage and oratory by Jack Ridgeway.

In this spy film about the Civil War, Milt Shanks (Lionel Barrymore) suffers for his heroism. With son killed, wife dead, and all but his granddaughter Madeline (Anne Cornwall) despising him, Shanks, considered a Copperhead spy, passes the years withdrawn in silence. In 1904, his loyal granddaughter refuses marriage to Tom Hardy (William David), grandson of her grandfather's Union accuser Lt. Tom Hardy (William P. Carleton). It is "Reunion Day" and Theodore Roosevelt appears (in archival footage) and in oratory by Jack Ridgeway. His vocal ability is quite adequate. For details, see Chapter 16 on Abraham Lincoln.

Sundown (1924)

Roosevelt: E.J. Ratcliffe. *Other Cast:* Bessie Love (Ellen Crawley), Roy Stewart (Hugh Brent), Hobart Bosworth (John Brent), Arthur Hoyt (Henry Crawley), Charles Murray (Pat Meech), Jere Austin (John Burke), Charles Crockett (Joe Patton). *Directors:* Harry O. Hoyt, Laurence Trimble. *Writing Credits:* Kenneth B. Clarke, Earl Hudson (story), Frances Marion. *Cinematography:* David Thompson. *Film Editing:* Cyril Gardner. *Art Direction:* Milton Menasco. *Studio:* First National Pictures Inc. *Length:* 73 minutes.

"There was too much cattle stuff and not enough story to the picture," according to *Variety* (December 3, 1924). The story is about homesteaders in the West who are driving cattlemen from the land and into Mexico. A secondary story provides romance between Ellen Crowley (Bessie Love), one of the homesteaders, and Hugh Brent (Ray Stewart), a cattleman. The cattlemen's stampeding cattle have destroyed her home. But Brent must leave her and join his father John Brent (Hobart Bosworth) who leads the herds across the border, battling a stampede and a prairie fire along the way.

Lights of Old Broadway (1925)

Roosevelt: Buck Black. *Other Credits:* Marion Davies (Fely/Anne), Conrad Nagel (Dirk de Rhonde), Frank Currier (Lambert de Rhonde), George K. Arthur (Andy), Charles McHugh (Shamus O'Tandy), Eleanor Lawson (Mrs. O'Tandy), Julia Swayne Gordon (Mrs. de Rhonde), Mathew Betz ("Red" Hawkins), Wilbur Higby (Fowler), Bodil Rosing (Widow Gorman), George Bunny (Tony Pastor), George Harris (Joe Weber), Bernard Berger (Lew Fields), Frank Glendon (Thomas A. Edison), Karl Dane (Roosevelt's Father), William De Vaull (de Rhonde's Butler). *Director-Producer:* Monta Bell. *Writing Credits:* Laurence Eyre, Joseph Farnham, Carey Wilson. *Cinematography:* Ira H. Morgan. *Film Editing:* Blanche Sewell. *Art Direction:* Ben Carre, Cedric Gibbons. *Costume Design:* Ethel P. Chaffin. *Studio:* Cosmopolitan Pictures. *Length:* 77 minutes.

After the successful *Little Old New York* (1923) Marion Davies stars in another picturesque tale of New York. Based on the Laurence Eyre play *The Merry Wives of Gotham*, this silent film is set in 1870. In the midst of this black-and-white film, there is a five-minute Technicolor sequence during a riot scene.

Davies plays twins, a variation on her future spy role of many disguises in *Operator 13* (1934): Anne is adopted by the wealthy de Rhondes; Fely is a dancer in Tony Pastor's theater. Anne's stepbrother Dirk de Rhonde (Conrad Nagel) falls in love with Fely who rescues him in the Orangemen's riot. His parents, however, oppose his marriage to the impoverished Fely. While Fely's father becomes wealthy through his investment in Edison's incandescent light, Dirk's father is ruined. But Fely saves the de Rhondes and marries Dirk.

Roosevelt would have been 12 during the period of this film and could have accompanied his father to Thomas Edison's electric demonstrations.

The Rough Riders (1927) aka The Trumpet Calls

Roosevelt: Frank Hopper. *Other Cast:* Charles Farrell (Stewart Van Brunt), Charles Emmett Mack (Bert Henley), Mary Astor (Dolly), Noah Beery (Hell's Bells), George Bancroft (Happy Joe), Fred Kohler (Sgt. Stanton), Col. Fred Lindsay (Leonard Wood). *Director:* Victor Fleming. *Producer:* Lucien Hubbard. *Writing Credits:* John F. Goodrich (adaptation), Herman Hagedorn (story), Robert N. Lee, George Marion Jr. (titles), Keene Thompson. *Cinematography:* James Howe, E. Burton Steene. *Film Editing:* E. Lloyd Sheldon. *Studio:* Paramount Famous Lasky Corp. *Length:* 105 minutes.

Both history and romance figure in this silent film about Roosevelt's troops. The action takes place in the mobilization camp in Texas and in Cuba with the historical charge up San Juan Hill as the high point.

In between is the rivalry of two enlisted men, Stewart Van Brunt (Charles Farrell) and Bert Henley (Charles Emmett Mack who was killed in an automobile accident after filming) over Dolly (Mary Astor). Coupled with this competition are comedy scenes including a picnic when the Rough Riders mistake a gun firing in a band selection as a signal for shooting their own guns.

It is Roosevelt's glitter and pomp and command on horseback of the hand-to-hand fighting that sells the movie, according to *Variety* (March 30, 1927). Frank Hopper, who plays Roosevelt, was not a professional actor; he was a Los Angeles literary agent with an astonishing resemblance to the 26th president.

The Phantom President (1932)

Roosevelt: Unnamed actor.

Roosevelt appears in a portrait as do three other presidents—Washington, Jefferson, and Lincoln—in this satirical musical comedy singing a Rodgers and Hart song, "The Country Needs a Man." Similar in appearance and voice to their respective presidents, the actors do an animated rendition. For details, see Chapter 1 on George Washington.

I Loved a Woman (1933)

Roosevelt: E.J. Ratcliffe. *Other Cast:* Edward G. Robinson (John Hayden), Kay Francis (Laura McDonald), Genevieve Tobin (Martha Lane Hayden), J. Farrell MacDonald (Shuster), Henry Kolker (Sanborn). *Director:* Alfred E. Green. *Writing Credits:* David Krasner, Charles Kenyon, Sidney Sutherland. *Cinematography:* James Van Trees. *Film Editing:* Herbert Levy. *Art Direction:* Robert M. Haas. *Costume Design:* Earl Luick. *Studio:* Warner Bros. Pictures Inc. *Length:* 90 minutes.

It is 1892, the brink of American business expansion, and the son of a Chicago packing magnate is collecting antiquities in Athens. He, John Mansfield Hayden (Edward G. Robinson), receives two missives: the first, a letter from his father asking what he is going to do with life; the second, a cable, announcing his father's death. In the sweep of this biographical film, based on David Krasner's novel, that is operatic in its grand emotions, we see Hayden deal with his ambition, his desire to create something beautiful, and, finally, his fall to history and Roosevelt's reaction to bad meat-packing practices.

Back in the United States on his first day of work, Hayden helps a childhood friend,

Martha Lane (Genevieve Tobin), delivering food to the poor in Chicago's "packing town." They talk of a "reformer's campaign" and devoting themselves to it while "others mind the shop." But, as the title suggests, Hayden falls in love with a woman other than his wife, a woman who channels his desire to build something beautiful (her career) as well as building his business. While she, Laura McDonald (Kay Francis), becomes an opera star, Hayden becomes the meat-packing giant. He gets the largest share of the government's war contracts for the Spanish-American War and ends his firm's honorable method by selling contaminated meat.

When Roosevelt (E.J. Ratcliffe), all bully, finds as a colonel in the war that men are dying from "embalmed beef" he yells, "Someone's going to hang for this" and testifies before a governmental committee. Soon thereafter, Roosevelt confronts Hayden: "You packers murdered my boys in Cuba.... When I come into power I'm going to smash you and all those buccaneers." The buccaneers supported his candidacy for vice president upon Hayden's suggestion, thinking it will keep the feisty Roosevelt from crusading against their interests. When President McKinley's assassination catapults Vice President Roosevelt into the White House, Hayden is indicted for the Cuban bad meat episode but escapes conviction. Costumed appropriately for his soldier and statesman roles, Ratcliffe as Roosevelt conveys the crusading zeal of this reformer.

The end of World War I brings cancellation of Hayden's foreign contracts. Roosevelt appears no more, but the U.S. Attorney's Office investigates Hayden's intricate and fraudulent business practices in his mad drive to be the "man behind the food supply." Everyone deserts him: his bankers do him "a kindness" by refusing loans so he will go into receivership, and his humiliated wife of 20 years leaves him because of his adultery. Even the routine camera shots of director Alfred E. Green show Robinson behind the bars of a chair. There is nothing routine about his emotive performance, however, and he is shown, demented and dying in Athens, saying, "Who is this woman?" when McDonald calls on him.

The Silk Hat Kid (1935) aka *The Lord's Referee*

Roosevelt: Frank Genardi.
Frank Genardi portrays Roosevelt in this urban drama. For details, see Chapter 1 on Washington

End of the Trail (1936)

Roosevelt: Erle C. Kenton. *Other Cast:* Jack Holt (Dale Brittenham), Louise Henry (Belle Pearson), Douglass Dumbrille (Bill Mason), Guinn "Big Boy" Williams (Bob Hildreth), George McKay (Ben Parker), Gene Morgan (Cheyenne), John McGuire (Larry Pearson), Edward LeSaint (Jim Watrous), Frank Shannon (Sheriff Anderson). *Director:* Erle C. Kenton. *Producer:* Irving Briskin. *Writing Credits:* Zane Grey (novel *Outlaws of Palouse*), Harold Shumate. *Music:* Louis Silvers, William Grant Still. *Cinematography:* John Stumar, Benjamin H. Kline. *Film Editing:* Al Clark. *Art Direction:* Stephen Goosson. *Costume Design:* Lon Anthony. *Studio:* Columbia Pictures Corp. *Length:* 70 minutes.

"Remember the *Maine*" screams the banner over the Western town where ranchers are lamenting their stolen horses. While many townsmen including sheriff's deputy Bob Hildreth (Guinn "Big Boy" Williams) enlist for the Spanish-American War, Dale Brittenham

End of the Trail (1936): Erle C. Kenton as Col. Theodore Roosevelt (right) with two of his Rough Riders whom he leads in the Battle of San Juan Hill during the Spanish-American War in this Columbia Pictures Corp. film. It's a story of soldiers' continuing bravado after the war. (Courtesy of George Eastman House.)

(Jack Holt) one-handedly finds the eight stolen horses. He continues his bravado behavior but ends up on a train to Cuba and the Spanish-American War.

There, bristling Col. Theodore Roosevelt (played to toothy-smile bravado perfection by director Erle C. Kenton) rallies his Rough Riders for the "tough day" ahead: "We'll take San Juan Hill, then Santiago," he says. Using only his pistol he leads his troops in battle, but they soon are ordered to fall back. With Roosevelt's tacit permission—and horse—Brittenham saves Hildreth, his fallen buddy who has lost his eye during his gallantry. Prophetically, Brittenham tells his grave commander, "You'll be president some day."

The buddies return home, and in a completely different mood and pace under Kenton's direction, both romance Belle Pearson (Louise Henry). Hildreth becomes sheriff, and Brittenham returns to stealing horses. He amasses enough money to open the "Little Cuba" café and hire Pearson's ailing brother Larry (John McGuire) as manager. Brittenham follows his old rough ways and loses all, including Belle Pearson. Brittenham's wartime heroism and Roosevelt's stern portrait over his mantle do not save him from the comeuppance he is due for turning to a life of crime in this typical western ending.

The Lawless Nineties (1936)

Roosevelt: Earl Seaman. *Other Cast:* John Wayne (John Tipton), Ann Rutherford (Janet Carter), Harry Woods (Charles K. Plummer), George "Gabby" Hayes (Maj. Carter), Al

Bridges (Steele), Fred "Snowflake" Toomes (Moses), Etta McDaniel (Mandy Lou Schaefer), Tom Brower (Marshal Bowen), Lane Chandler (Bridges). *Director:* Joseph Kane. *Producer:* Trem Carr. *Writing Credits:* Scott Pembroke, Joseph F. Poland. *Cinematography:* William Nobles. *Stunts:* Yakima Canutt. *Studio:* Republic Pictures Corp. *Length:* 55 minutes.

Republic Pictures paired its up-and-coming cowboy star John Wayne with its ingénue Ann Rutherford for this western. Set in the Wyoming Territory on the eve of statehood, it takes John Tipton (John Wayne) and his partner Bridges (Lane Chandler) to Crockett City under the auspices of the Department of Justice. There they strive to destroy the political machine of Charles K. Plummer (Harry Woods) who also heads a vigilante army. Plummer manages to kill Bridges and Maj. Carter, the local newspaper owner. His daughter Janet (Ann Rutherford) takes over the paper.

Through clever bogus telegrams, Tipton foils the henchmen, and Wyoming becomes a state as Janet and John Tipton also unite.

This Is My Affair (1937)

Roosevelt: Sidney Blackmer.

As McKinley's vice president, Roosevelt is directed by William Seiter as a noisy, over-animated blowhard. He continually runs to and from White House meetings, talking about wrestling and going horseback riding. The script also gives him the opportunity to develop one of his famous lines, "Speak softly and carry a big stick."

However, after he becomes president in the final four of his six scenes, Blackmer as Roosevelt plays him in a much more subdued way as if his ascendancy after McKinley's assassination has sobered him. He acts with alacrity and displays Roosevelt's dynamic physicality. He also performs a key action, staying the execution of the hero Lt Richard Perry (Robert Taylor), saying, "This is one time when the president of the United States will have to apologize." Blackmer, in his first of many appearances as Roosevelt, handles both sides of the character with his usual adept acting skill. For details, see Chapter 25 on William McKinley.

The Monroe Doctrine (1939)

Roosevelt: Sidney Blackmer.

Roosevelt makes an appearance in this story of President Monroe's response to attempts by Spain to interfere in South America. In his presidency, Roosevelt impressed on the Kaiser that the violation of the Doctrine by territorial aggrandizement around the Caribbean meant war.

Teddy the Rough Rider (1940)

Roosevelt: Sidney Blackmer. *Other Cast:* Pierre Watkin (Senator), Theodore von Eltz (William), Arthur Loft (Rafferty), Paul Maxey (Second Slumlord), Edward Van Sloan (Secretary of State), Douglas Wood (President McKinley). *Director:* Ray Enright. *Producer:* Gordon Hollingshead. *Writing Credits:* Charles L. Tedford. *Cinematography:* Ray Rennahan. *Film Editing:* Everett Dodd. *Art Direction:* Charles Novi. *Studio:* The Vitaphone Corp., Warner Bros. *Length:* 20 minutes.

This sweeping view of Roosevelt's political career moves as quickly as this dynamo of a man. The accomplished actor Sidney Blackmer again plays the role of the 26th president with conviction, dramatic force, and a hoarse voice. Under Ray Enright's tight direction, the 20-minute Oscar–winning film covers all the positions and pronouncements of this charismatic figure.

It starts with Roosevelt as New York City police commissioner wiping out graft and corruption in defiance of the political bosses with his "big stick of reform." Although thinking himself "politically dead" as he is "considered too honest for politics," Roosevelt receives an appointment from President McKinley (Douglas Wood) to serve as Assistant Secretary of the Navy. Then man of action Roosevelt begs McKinley "to act" in Cuba; that he does when the *Maine* explodes.

After Roosevelt's success in the Spanish-American War, "the party needs him for governor" of New York State. When he becomes governor he refuses "to cooperate with the party." To control him, the party nominates him for vice president with McKinley who soon succumbs to an assassin's bullet in Buffalo.

Roosevelt's two-term presidential career flashes by in scenes of his intervention in a coal strike, support for the Panama Canal "lifeline," and legislation such as food laws backed by public opinion. He wins the Nobel Peace Prize. But he loses his third presidential election and more tragically his son Quentin in World War I, which he touchingly deals with in a press commentary. Then, in the final scene, Roosevelt turns to writing a stirring speech of patriotism.

Citizen Kane (1941)

Roosevelt: Thomas A. Curran. *Other Cast*: Orson Welles (Charles Foster Kane), Joseph Cotten (Jedediah Leland), Dorothy Comingore (Susan Alexander Kane), Agnes Moorehead (Mary Kane), Ruth Warrick (Emily Monroe Norton Kane), Ray Collins (James W. Gettys), Erskine Sanford (Herbert Carter), Everett Sloane (Mr. Bernstein), William Alland (Jerry Thompson), Paul Stewart (Raymond), George Coulouris (Walter Parks Thatcher), Fortunio Bonanova (Signor Matiste), Gus Schilling (The Headwaiter), Philip Van Zandt (Mr. Rawlstone), Georgia Backus (Bertha Anderson), Harry Shannon (Kane's father), Sonny Bupp (Charles Foster Kane III), Buddy Swan (Kane, age 8). *Director-Producer*: Orson Welles. *Writing Credits*: Orson Welles, Herman J. Mankiewicz. *Music*: Bernard Herrmann. *Cinematography*: Gregg Toland. *Film Editing*: Robert Wise. *Art Direction*: Van Nest Polglase. *Set Decoration*: Darrell Silvera. *Costume Design*: Edward Stevenson. *Makeup*: Mel Berns. *Production*: Pandro S. Berman. *Art Department*: Perry Ferguson. *Studio*: Mercury Productions/RKO. *Length*: 119 minutes.

Roosevelt (Thomas A. Curran) appears in one brief shot with Kane (Orson Welles) on the caboose of a train during the "News on the March" newsreel early in the celebrated film. Both wave wildly, Roosevelt smiling his toothy grin and appearing to show his political compatibility with the newspaper magnate and great "American." Curran, uncredited, resembles Roosevelt strongly in physique and facial features and appears as animated as the politically driven Roosevelt was.

The eight-minute newsreel, similar to the "March of Time" newsreels shown during the time of *Citizen Kane*, deals with the life of Charles Foster Kane and serves as an introduction to this complex, convoluted story of the failure of success. Kane runs for the New York State governorship—and loses—but he supports political figures in his many newspapers throughout his storied life. Before the train shot, there is another of troops, not identified as Rough Riders, but nevertheless soldiers going to the Spanish-American War that Kane (read William Randolph Hearst) championed.

As for *Kane*, it is no doubt the number one film of all time with its daring story of a great—perhaps even a real—man's life. The boy genius behind the film, Welles, says it was not Hearst, only partially of him, although Hearst used every means possible to stop the film. Of other note of this much discussed film are its technical innovations from deep focus shots to theatrical dissolves.

March On, America! (1942)

Roosevelt: Sidney Blackmer.

Blackmer plays Theodore Roosevelt in this patriotic story. For details, see Chapter 5 on James Monroe.

Yankee Doodle Dandy (1942)

Roosevelt: Wallis Clark.

The appearance of Roosevelt in *Yankee Doodle Dandy* is less than a one-minute cameo with Teddy being portrayed by an uncredited Wallis Clark. He is shown in the "You're a Grand Old Flag" production number of George M. Cohan's musical *George Washington, Jr.* For details, see *Yankee Doodle Dandy* in Chapter 32 on Franklin D. Roosevelt.

In Old Oklahoma (1943) aka War of the Wildcats

Roosevelt: Sidney Blackmer. *Other Cast:* John Wayne (Daniel F. "Dan" Somers), Martha Scott (Catherine Elizabeth Allen), Albert Dekker (Jim "Hunk" Gardner), George "Gabby" Hayes (Despirit Dean), Marjorie Rambeau (Bessie Baxter), Dale Evans (Cuddles Walker), Grant Withers (Richardson), Paul Fix (Cherokee Kid). *Director:* Albert S. Rogell. *Producer:* Robert North. *Writing Credits:* Thomson Burtis (story), Eleanore Griffith, Ethel Hill (screenplay). *Music:* Walter Scharf, Mort Glickman, Marlin Skiles. *Cinematography:* Jack Marta. *Film Editing:* Ernest Nims. *Art Direction:* Russell Kimball. *Set Decoration:* Otto Siegel. *Costume Design:* Walter Plunkett. *Stunts:* Yakima Canutt. *Studio:* Republic Pictures Corp. *Length:* 102 minutes.

According to this western, the oil industry in Oklahoma might never have started without the excitement of wagon chases and major fights between "Dan" Somers (John Wayne) and "Hunk" Gardner (Albert Dekker). Gardner is the president of Gardner Oil and the discoverer of major finds near Tulsa. In the opening scenes he and Somers, a Spanish-American War veteran, both fall in love with schoolteacher-author Catherine Allen (Martha Scott). This sets the stage for both love and oil conflict throughout the film. Dale Evans in her pre–Roy Rogers films co-stars as sexy dancehall singer Cuddles Walker.

Gardner wants an oil lease on Indian lands, but the tribe doesn't like him and offers it to Somers. This leads to a showdown in Washington where officials discover that Somers was "one of the toughest scrappers" for President Roosevelt (Sidney Blackmer) and was the first man to reach the top of San Juan Hill. Roosevelt gives the Indian lease to Somers with a four-month time limit. Quite naturally, he strikes oil and just barely meets the deadline despite dirty deeds by Gardner. The wagon race at the end of the film through desert country (probably Arizona and certainly not Oklahoma) to reach Tulsa on time provides the greatest excitement for this film and stock footage for other westerns.

Blackmer is the leading Theodore Roosevelt performer, and he does not disappoint with his close physical resemblance, gestures, and voice in this film.

Jack London (1943)

Roosevelt: Wallis Clark. *Other Cast*: Michael O'Shea (Jack London), Susan Hayward (Charmian Kittredge), Osa Massen (Freda Maloof), Harry Davenport (Prof. Hilliard), Frank Craven (Old Tom), Virginia Mayo (Mamie), Ralph Morgan (George Brett), Jonathan Hale (Kerwin Maxwell), Louise Beavers (Mammy Jenny), Leonard Strong (Captain Tanaka), Regis Toomey (Scratch Nelson), Albert Van Antwerp (French Frank), Paul Hurst ("Lucky Luke" Lannigan), Lumsden Hare (English Correspondent). *Director*: Alfred Santell. *Producer*: Samuel Bronston. *Writing Credits*: Isaac Don Levine, Charmian London, Ernest Pascal. *Music*: Freddie Rich. *Cinematography*: John W. Boyle. *Film Editing*: William Ziegler. *Art Direction*: Bernard Herzbrun. *Set Decoration*: Earl Wooden. *Costume Design*: Maria P. Donovan, Arnold McDonald. *Studio*: Samuel Bronston Productions/United Artists. *Length*: 82 minutes.

It would take a very long movie or a TV miniseries to cover, even briefly, the numerous adventures in Jack London's short but active life. This film, based on a book by Charmian London and directed by Alfred Santell, makes no attempt at completeness and touches only the highlights of London's life between 1890 and 1905.

Played in a less than dynamic manner by Michael O'Shea, London, at the age of 15 in 1891, becomes "Prince of the Oyster Pirates" in San Francisco Bay. He is able to purchase a small vessel for this purpose by borrowing money from Mammy Jenny (Louise Beavers), the woman who cared for him as a child. This profession, i.e., robbing oyster beds, becomes too dangerous even for London, and he signs on as an able-bodied seaman aboard a sealer bound for Northern Pacific waters. Returning from this adventure, he briefly attends a writing class at the University of California at Berkeley where he is criticized for writing with a "sledgehammer technique" but praised for his "courage." He abruptly leaves for the Yukon and its gold.

During all this period London writes and attempts to sell stories based on his experiences. After the Alaskan adventure, London returns to San Francisco and achieves some fame from his writing. Based on this celebrity he is offered a position as a journalist in the Boer War of 1892–1902. According to London's chronology this could not have actually happened. However, London did act as a correspondent during the Russo-Japanese War in 1904.

Much of the final half of the film amounts to an anti–Japanese diatribe since it was released in 1943 during World War II. This does provide the excuse for introducing President Roosevelt (Wallis Clark). Roosevelt uses his "big stick" approach to rescue London who has been jailed by the Japanese in Korea as a Russian spy, demanding "immediate release." Clark does an effective job of portraying Roosevelt as a strong, determined Rough Rider. No mention is made in the film of London's political ideals as the "Boy Socialist of Oakland" but it obviously had no effect on the literate Roosevelt's support for a well-known American writer.

The film ends with London returning to San Francisco and attempting to stir the

United States into an early awareness of the threats from Japan. He is accompanied in this effort by his admiring wife Charmian Kittredge (Susan Hayward) at fadeout.

Arsenic and Old Lace (1944)

Roosevelt/Brewster: John Alexander. *Other Cast*: Cary Grant (Mortimer Brewster), Josephine Hull (Aunt Abby Brewster), Jean Adair (Aunt Martha Brewster), Raymond Massey (Jonathan Brewster), Peter Lorre (Dr. Einstein), Priscilla Lane (Elaine Harper/Elaine Brewster), Jack Carson (Officer Patrick "Pat" O'Hara), Edward Everett Horton (Mr. Witherspoon). *Director*: Frank Capra. *Producers*: Jack L. Warner, Frank Capra. *Writing Credits*: Joseph Kesselring, Julius J. Epstein, Philip G. Epstein. *Music*: Max Steiner. *Cinematography*: Sol Polito. *Film Editing*: Daniel Mandell. *Art Direction*: Max Parker. *Costume Design*: Orry-Kelly. *Makeup*: Perc Westmore. *Studio*: Warner Bros. *Length*: 118 minutes.

Based on the highly popular play by Joseph Kesselring (and adapted by Julius J. and Philip G. Epstein), which opened on Broadway in 1941 and ran for 1444 performances, *Arsenic and Old Lace* became one of Frank Capra's most successful madcap comedies. With an all-star cast including Cary Grant, Priscilla Lane, Raymond Massey (not as Abe Lincoln), and Peter Lorre, it also included three of the Broadway performers: Josephine

Arsenic and Old Lace (1944): Although he plays the role of Theodore Brewster, John Alexander (right) knows that he is Theodore Roosevelt and is not disturbed by the gun in Raymond Massey's hand while Peter Lorre (center) and Josephine Hull observe the mayhem in this Frank Capra adaptation of the hit stage play, released by Warner Brothers Pictures. (Courtesy of George Eastman House.)

Hull, Jean Adair, and John Alexander who plays their brother Theodore "Teddy Roosevelt" Brewster.

The plotline of the movie is highly dependent on historical events in the life of Roosevelt and his well-known personal idiosyncrasies. Mortimer Brewster's (the great farceur Grant) dotty aunts Abby Brewster (Josephine Hull) and Martha Brewster (Jean Adair) give lonely old men "assistance" to achieve their final resting place. Mortimer's brother Teddy (John Alexander) thinks that he *is* Roosevelt and, since he is harmless (except for his loud bugle blowing), the family (and everyone else) plays along.

The basement of the lace-bedecked aunts' old-fashioned Victorian house in Brooklyn is the Panama Canal, the resting place of 12 of their "yellow fever" arsenic victims, as named by Teddy. Teddy is industrious in digging the locks for the canal and overseeing the burial of the yellow fever victims. In addition, every time he returns to his upstairs bedroom (his Oval Office) he recreates the charge up San Juan Hill.

Mortimer sees Teddy's nuttiness as a way to save his serial-killer aunts from prosecution, and when Teddy continues to blow his bugle to the neighbors' annoyance and complaints, Mortimer is able to arrange his admission to Happydale Rest Home. This move is broadly interpreted as Roosevelt's great African tour. The extent to which Theodore Roosevelt was still seen as a great, yet somewhat eccentric president in the early 1940s is illustrated when the director of Happydale (the funny and fusty Edward Everett Horton) asks if Teddy wouldn't like to be Napoleon because Happydale already has three Theodore Roosevelts in residence. (Mark Hanna, the Republican Party leader during Roosevelt's time, would agree about this institutionalization as he called Roosevelt a "mad man.") Another madman appears on this crazy scene in the person of Raymond Massey as the escaped convict killer brother Jonathan Brewster, returning to his childhood home to continue his "experiments" with the phony Dr. Einstein (Peter Lorre). Mortimer notes, "Insanity doesn't just run through my family, it gallops!" All of this mayhem prevents Mortimer from going on his honeymoon to Niagara Falls with lovely Elaine (Priscilla Lane).

John Alexander does an outstanding job of handling the serious yet highly comic role of Theodore "Teddy Roosevelt" Brewster. His part is central to making the play and film work with his "charges" up the stairs, his "dee-lighted" attitude about working on the Panama Canal, and his "bully" enthusiasm.

Buffalo Bill (1944)

Roosevelt: Sidney Blackmer.

Sidney Blackmer, in an uncredited appearance, plays his usual Roosevelt role during a cameo appearance in the audience at one of Buffalo Bill's Wild West shows. As usual, Blackmer does a good job of looking and acting like Teddy while saying his only line, "Bully." For complete details, see Chapter 19 on Rutherford B. Hayes.

Sun Valley Cyclone (1946)

Roosevelt: Edward Cassidy. *Other Cast:* Bill Elliott (Red Ryder), Robert Blake (Little Beaver), Alice Fleming (The Duchess), Roy Barcroft (Blackie Blake), Monte Hale (Jeff), Kenne Duncan (Dow), Eddy Waller (Maj. Harding), Edmund Cobb (Luce), Tom London (Sheriff), Rex Lease (Army Sergeant). *Director:* R.G. Springsteen. *Producer:* Sidney Picker.

Writing Credits: Fred Harman, Earle Snell. *Studio:* Republic Pictures Corp. *Length:* 56 minutes.

In another of Republic Pictures' B-westerns, Red Ryder (Bill Elliott) and his sidekick Little Beaver (Robert Blake) are asked by Col. Theodore Roosevelt (Edward Cassidy) to join his Rough Riders in order to catch a gang of horse thieves disrupting the shipment of horses to the army. All this action occurs in flashback in order to save Ryder's horse Thunder from destruction because of the horse's attack on a man who was going to shoot the sheriff.

This flashback is necessitated because Blackie Blake (Roy Bancroft) had escaped after beating Thunder, when Ryder broke up the rustling gang. As it turns out, the man attempting to shoot the sheriff is Blake in a disguise. That does not fool Thunder although it fools Ryder and Little Beaver. (You know it's a B-western when the horse is smarter than the heroes.)

I Wonder Who's Kissing Her Now (1947)

Roosevelt: John Merton. *Other Cast:* June Haver (Katie), Mark Stevens (Joe Howard), Martha Stewart (Lulu Madison), Reginald Gardner (Will Hough), Gene Nelson (Tommy Yale), Lenore Aubert (Fritzi Barrington), Truman Bradley (Martin Webb), George Cleveland (John McCullem). *Director:* Lloyd Bacon. *Producer:* George Jessel. *Writing Credits:* Lewis R. Foster, Marion Turk. *Music:* Frank Adams, Charles Henderson, Joe Howard, George Jessel, Alfred Newman, Will Hough. *Cinematography:* Ernest Palmer. *Film Editing:* Louis Loeffler. *Art Direction:* Richard Day, Boris Leven. *Set Decoration:* Thomas Little, Walter M. Scott. *Studio:* 20th Century–Fox. *Length:* 104 minutes.

Producer George Jessel made a career out of fictionalizing the lives of famous vaudevillians in a series of movies in the late 1940s and early 1950s. Besides *I Wonder Who's Kissing Her Now*, these include *The Dolly Sisters* (1945), *Oh You Beautiful Doll* (1949), and *The I Don't Care Girl* (1953).

This 1947 film covers what Jessel calls the life of Joe Howard (Mark Stevens), a turn-of-the-century songwriter whose work includes "What's the Use of Dreaming" and "Hello My Baby." But as producer Darryl F. Zanuck allegedly said to Jessel: Whenever we can use a similar locale without destroying our own story we have created, we should. The story deals with Joe's romances with Lulu Madison (Martha Stewart) and Fritzi Barrington (Lenore Aubert) before he settles down with his lifelong "kid sister," Katie (June Haver). None of this has anything to do with Howard's actual life that included several marriages during his 83 years, ending in 1961. In addition, there is some question as to whether he wrote the title song.

The presidential cameo is very brief as Roosevelt (John Merton) appears as a character saying "bully!" in one of the Howard and Hough (Reginald Gardiner) musicals that Lloyd Bacon directs with great authenticity by using lavish sets and period costumes.

My Girl Tisa (1948) aka Ever the Beginning

Roosevelt: Sidney Blackmer. *Other Cast:* Lilli Palmer (Tisa Kepes), Sam Wanamaker (Mark Denek), Akim Tamiroff (Mr. Grumbach), Alan Hale (Dugan), Hugo Haas (Tescu), Gale Robbins (Jenny Kepes), Stella Adler (Mrs. Faludi). *Director:* Elliott Nugent. *Producer:* Milton Sperling. *Writing Credits:* Lucille S. Prumbs, Sara B. Smith, Allen Boretz. *Music:* Max Steiner.

Cinematography: Ernest Haller. *Film Editing:* Christian Nyby. *Art Direction:* Robert M. Haas. *Set Decoration:* Fred M. MacLean. *Costume Design:* Leah Rhodes. *Makeup:* Perc Westmore. *Studio:* United States Pictures. *Length:* 95 minutes.

Once more, Teddy comes to the rescue. He saves the hero in the final scene, simultaneously honoring the virtues of the great democracy he loves and punctuating his actions with "Bully!" In this familiar turn-of-the-century story, written by Lucille S. Prumbs and Sara B. Smith after their play *Ever the Beginning*, a young Hungarian immigrant girl works to pay for her father's passage to the United States. She, Tisa Kepes, as poignantly played by Lilli Palmer, turns to the fast-talking Mark Denek (Sam Wanamaker) for aid—and eventually affection.

This was Wanamaker's screen debut. He moved to England because of his leftist political association although he was never called by the House Un-American Activities Committee (HUAC). Coincidentally, in *My Girl Tisa*, Wanamaker as Denek defends the politics of Roosevelt (played by Sidney Blackmer). In the final scene when his beloved Tisa is to be deported, he leaves the New York City Immigration Bureau to stumble upon a parade led by Roosevelt, meeting European royalty at a pier.

Roosevelt stands in a horse-drawn carriage waving to the crowd. The scene fades to immigration detention where Roosevelt enters, hearing the end of Tisa's plea to the Statue of Liberty about Liberty's "good son" Denek. She confides her desire to be a "good daughter," and Roosevelt agrees, "That's a pretty good lady." He acknowledges Denek as "the young man who broke up the parade" and admits that this is a "most peculiar situation." Then Roosevelt asks the advice of Denek, who in his fake bravura has told Tisa he would be a lawyer, a senator, and an advisor to the president. Ever believing in Denek, Tisa urges him on. Next they are seated with Roosevelt in his carriage approaching the pier where he will greet the dignitaries. "Mr. President," Denek says, "You certainly have a lot of influence." Roosevelt expounds, 'That's Bully!"

Akim Tamiroff appears as the anxious Mr. Grumbach, parsimonious necktie manufacturer and naturalized citizen, and Stella Adler shows her tremendous scope as the zesty Mrs. Faludi, boarding house owner. Max Steiner composed the effective original music.

Take Me Out to the Ball Game (1949)

Roosevelt: Ed Cassidy. *Other Cast:* Frank Sinatra (Dennis Ryan), Esther Williams (K.C. Higgins), Gene Kelly (Eddie O'Brien), Betty Garrett (Shirley Delwyn), Edward Arnold (Joe Lorgan), Jules Munshin (Nat Goldberg), Richard Lane (Michael Gilhuly), Tom Dugan (Slappy Burke). *Director:* Busby Berkeley. *Producer:* Arthur Freed. *Writing Credits:* Harry Tugend, George Wells, Gene Kelly, Stanley Donen, Harry Crane. *Music:* Roger Edens. *Lyrics:* Betty Comden, Adolph Green. *Cinematography:* George Folsey. *Film Editing:* Blanche Sewell. *Art Direction:* Daniel B. Cathcart, Cedric Gibbons. *Set Decoration:* Edwin B. Willis. *Costume Design:* Helen Rose, Valles. *Makeup:* Jack Dawn. *Art Department:* Henry W. Grace. *Sound:* Douglas Shearer. *Special Effects:* Warren Newcombe. *Gag Consultant:* Buster Keaton. *Studio:* MGM. *Length:* 93 minutes.

Forget about baseball but remember the song-and-dance routines in this flick and watch for the gags suggested by Buster Keaton. Dennis Ryan (Frank Sinatra) and Eddie O'Brien (Gene Kelly) are two sides of a double-play combination and a song-and-dance number "O'Brien to Ryan to Goldberg" with Jules Munshin playing Goldberg. As should be the case for this plot, Ryan and O'Brien are much more interested in show business than baseball even though they are members of the champion Wolves team.

Into this situation a new owner K.C. Higgins (Esther Williams) arrives, and the lives of our heroes are changed as both fall in love with her. Complications abound, but there is time for numerous song-and-dance routines as well as the obligatory swim by Williams. O'Brien gets Higgins in the end, but Ryan is compensated by capturing the hand of Shirley Delwyn (Betty Garrett) who is a much better singer and dancer than Williams.

Roosevelt (Ed Cassidy, previously seen in *Sun Valley Cyclone*) makes a brief appearance as a spectator at the big game and says one word when handed an oversized bat, "dee-lighted."

Fancy Pants (1950)

Roosevelt: John Alexander. *Other Cast:* Bob Hope (Humphrey aka Arthur Tyler), Lucille Ball (Agatha Floud), Bruce Cabot (Carl Belknap), Jack Kirkwood (Mike Floud), Lea Penman (Effie Floud), Hugh French (George Van Basingwell), Eric Blore (Sir Wimbley), Joseph Vitale (Wampum), Norma Varden (Lady Maude), Virginia Keiley (Rosalind), Colin Keith-Johnston (Twombley), Joe Wong (Wong). *Director:* George Marshall. *Producer:* Robert L. Welch. *Writing Credits:* Harry Leon Wilson, Edmund Hartmann, Robert O'Brien. *Music:* Ray Evans, Jay Livingston, Van Cleave. *Cinematography:* Charles B. Lang. *Film Editing:* Archie Marshek. *Art Direction:* Hans Dreier, Earl Hedrick. *Set Decoration:* Sam Comer, Emile Kuri. *Costume Design:* Mary K. Dodson, Gile Steele. *Makeup:* Wally Westmore. *Sound:* Don Johnson, Gene Merritt. *Special Effects:* Farciot Edouart, Gordon Jennings. *Studio:* Paramount Pictures. *Length:* 92 minutes.

In the 1950s Bob Hope made three movies with presidential characters, *Fancy Pants*, *My Favorite Spy* (1951) with Truman, and *Beau James* (1957) about Jimmy Walker with FDR, a biopic.

Using his patented campy approach, Hope plays Humphrey (aka Arthur Tyler), an English butler who in fact is a broke American actor stranded in London. Through a series of typically inept spills on his stage employer, Humphrey is fired but immediately rehired by Effie Floud (Lea Penman), a visiting American nouveau riche from Big Squaw, New Mexico. She is traveling in England with her daughter Agatha (Lucille Ball) in an attempt to land a titled Englishman for her.

Unsuccessful in finding a title, Mrs. Floud takes Humphrey home to New Mexico in order to civilize her husband Mike Floud (Jack Kirkwood). In a typical comedic case of mistaken identity Mr. Floud tells his Big Squaw neighbors that his wife is bringing an English earl home for their daughter Agatha. Hope is persuaded to play the earl for the neighbors and, except for his poor English accent (surprising for an English-born actor), does an acceptable job of convincing them, including Agatha's cowboy friend Carl Belknap (Bruce Cabot), who keeps trying to kill Humphrey.

The act is so convincing that President Roosevelt (John Alexander), who is traveling in the area, decides to detour to Big Squaw to meet the earl. Humphrey and Teddy get along famously—exchanging lots of "bully" and "dee-lighted" remarks—until arrangements are made for a fox hunt to be led by Humphrey—who cannot ride. This, of course, leads to a faked leg injury, followed by Humphrey's being chased by a motley collection of local dogs that have been pulled into service as fox hounds. After Belknap tells the president and the townspeople that Humphrey is an actor, the film ends with a disappointing final scene with Humphrey and Agatha escaping town on a hand-driven rail car.

This is the second, and final, appearance of Alexander as Roosevelt. As he did in his completely comic appearance in *Arsenic and Old Lace* (1944), Alexander both appears like and sounds like the president. He is not a gifted actor, but he makes this more serious appearance as Roosevelt believable by his forthright manner, stalwart carriage, and athletic prowess in the fox hunt—the manliness Roosevelt extolled.

The First Traveling Saleslady (1956)

Roosevelt: Ed Cassidy. *Other Cast:* Ginger Rogers (Rose Gillray), Barry Nelson (Charles Masters), Carol Channing (Molly Wade), David Brian (James Carter), James Arness (Joel Kingdom), Clint Eastwood (Lt. Jack Rice). *Director-Producer:* Arthur Lubin. *Writing Credits:* Devery Freeman, Stephen Longstreet. *Music:* Irving Gertz. *Cinematography:* William E. Snyder. *Film Editing:* Otto Ludwig. *Art Direction:* Albert S. D'Agostino. *Set Decoration:* Darrell Silvera. *Studio:* RKO Pictures, Inc. *Length:* 92 minutes.

Set in 1897, this romantic comedy purports to explain how the first traveling saleslady got that way. But there's little clear motivation for any of the characterization and action under Arthur Lubin's direction and production, even in the two-minute appearance by Roosevelt (Ed Cassidy) in his New York police commissioner days. Inexplicably, he appears as the dynamic politician urging steel magnate James Carter (David Brian) to continue manufacturing barbed wire. Eyeglasses flashing as much as his temper, Roosevelt counters, "You kind of like the idea of selling barbed wire and making a profit." Carter deplores the lack of protection and Roosevelt admits, "There just aren't enough federal marshals to do the job." He directed Agriculture Secretary James Wilson to conduct an investigation.

Rose Gillray (Ginger Rogers) happens by, upbeat as usual (and moreso than in her first presidential role as Dolley Madison) even though her corset business faces foreclosure by her latest venture, corset costumes for the musical *A Turkish Delight* that was closed by police order. Ever inventive, she asks Carter if she can be his saleslady in order to liquidate her debt to him. He is more interested in her as a lady as is Charley Masters (Barry Nelson), an auto enthusiast driving cross country, and Joel Kingdom (James Arness), a Texas rancher who wants to keep the government-ordained barbed wire from his ranch. Gillray outwits the men, sells the barbed wire to the cattlemen's wives, and drives off with Masters.

Not everyone is as strong a saleslady. Co-star Carol Channing in her first film role, Molly Wade, runs off with a Rough Rider, played by a youthful Clint Eastwood. In his third appearance as Roosevelt, Cassidy does a good, energetic job, glasses, mustache, and all.

Brighty of the Grand Canyon (1967)

Roosevelt: Karl Swenson. *Other Cast:* Joseph Cotten (Jim Owen), Pat Conway (Jake Irons), Dick Foran (Old Timer), Dandy Curran (Homer Hobbs). *Director-Writer:* Norman Foster. Based on a novel by Marguerite Henry. *Producer:* Stephen F. Booth. *Music:* Phyllis and Richard Lavsky. *Cinematography:* Ted and Vincent Saizis. *Film Editing:* Joseph Dervin. *Studio:* Stephen F. Booth Productions. *Length:* 89 minutes.

The central character in this family film is a burro, Brighty, who is part of a western adventure that takes place in the Grand Canyon. Based on a novel of the same name, the story involves an Old Timer (Dick Foran) who discovers gold in the Grand Canyon around the beginning of the 20th century. He is killed for the gold by Jake Irons (Pat Conway) who is then captured by Jim Owen (Joseph Cotten) with the help of Brighty.

Roosevelt (Karl Swenson) is brought into the story when he comes to the Canyon to hunt mountain lions with Owen. This gives conservationist Roosevelt an opportunity to orate on the grandeur of nature, particularly the Grand Canyon's. Swenson does a reasonable job of both appearing and sounding like the 26th president, saying the "Best way to live is close to earth and sky" and "The Canyon must be a park; man can only mar it." Among the interesting information in the Special Features on the DVD are the credits for Brighty. He belonged to writer Marguerite Henry and proved a natural for the role.

The Wind and the Lion (1975)

Roosevelt: Brian Keith. *Other Cast:* Sean Connery (Mulay Achmed Mohammed el Raisuli the Magnificent), Candice Bergen (Eden Pedecaris), John Huston (John Hay, Secretary of State), Shirley Rothman (Edith Roosevelt), Larry Cross (Sen. Henry Cabot Lodge), Alexander Weldon (Elihu Root, Secretary of War). Mark Zuber (Sultan of Morocco), Deborah Baxter (Alice Roosevelt). *Director-Writer:* John Milius. *Producer:* Herb Jaffe. *Music:* Jerry Goldsmith. *Cinematography:* Billy Williams. *Film Editing:* Robert L. Wolfe. *Production Design:* Gil Parrondo. *Art Direction:* Antonio Paton. *Costume Design:* Richard La Motte. *Makeup:* Jose Antonio Sanchez. *Studio:* MGM/United Artists. *Length:* 119 minutes.

Taking an obscure historical event, the kidnapping of an American man in Morocco by Berbers in the early 1900s, John Milius wrote and directed a political action film that he calls a Victorian Kiplingesque adventure. The Berber leader, Mulay Achmed Mohammed el Raisuli the Magnificent, is played (quite often with a Scottish burr) by Sean Connery and the American man, who has been replaced by a widowed American woman with two children, is played by Candice Bergen. The action is split between the spectacular desert scenery of Morocco (beautifully filmed in Spain) and the quiet beauty of Victorian Washington, D.C. (also filmed in Spain). It is the long distance adversary relationship between the "big stick" philosophy of President Roosevelt (Brian Keith) and the quiet desert wisdom of Raisuli (Connery) that gives the film its *raison d'etre*.

Raisuli is a Berber with a heart who kidnaps Eden Pedecaris (Bergen) in order to put pressure on his nephew, the Sultan of Morocco (Marc Zuber), to remove the Germans and French who are attempting to turn Morocco into a colony. In a daring use of artistic license, Milius has the U.S. Marines invading the country and taking over the government in order to rescue Mrs. Pedecaris and her children. All these maneuvers occur to maintain Roosevelt's renown as a military activist in his 1904 re-election year. This historical bravado continues right to the final scene when led by the spunky Mrs. Pedecaris the U.S. Marines join with the Berbers (in a scene reminiscent of the U.S. Cavalry coming to the rescue of Western settlers) to defeat the Germans who have captured Raisuli.

Despite the historical license, Keith does a credible job in presenting the dichotomies that were so evident in Roosevelt's life. He appears as a blustering warmonger in his political address concerning the kidnapping. Yet in a later scene he talks quietly and with obvious feeling to his daughter, Alice (Deborah Baxter), about his respect for Raisuli and Raisuli's goals. He is shown sitting next to a grizzly bear that he has just killed. Still he spends a great deal of time telling the omnipresent reporters why it was necessary to kill the magnificent animal that should be the symbol of the American people for its "strength, intelligence, and ferocity" rather than the bald eagle that is nothing more than a "big vulture." He obviously has a close personal and working relationship with John Hay, his Secretary of State (played with great skill by John Huston). On the other hand, Roosevelt sees no need to take Hay's advice to softpedal the reaction to the kidnapping. What Roosevelt wants, he says after boxing and while practicing archery and shooting bull's-eyes, is "respect for American life and property ... so the fleet sails."

Keith, who has a close physical resemblance to Roosevelt, does an excellent job in presenting the various sides of this highly popular but largely misunderstood president. In a role that could have been played too broadly, Keith is able to provide some understanding of Roosevelt's jingoistic thought processes.

The film resorts to much symbolism, from the first shot of the wind stirring the sea as Raisuli's Berbers ride through the waves. After his release Raisuli sends Roosevelt a message saying, "I am the lion and know my place and you are like the wind and will not know your place."

Bully (1978)

Roosevelt: James Whitmore. *Director*: Peter H. Hunt. *Producers*: Mel Marshall, Sam Maturo. *Screenwriter*: Jerome Alden. *Editor*: Terry Green. *Length*: 120 minutes.

In the manner of James Whitmore's one-man portrayal of Will Rogers and Harry Truman, this is a filmed performance of Whitmore at the Ahmanson Theater. The two-hour show enjoyed a long, very successful run on Broadway.

With only an artificially made resemblance to Roosevelt, Whitmore "still captures his blustering personality and coveys his love of nature and politics and devotion to duty and manliness," according to *Variety* (Oct. 4, 1978).

Ragtime (1981)

Roosevelt: Robert Boyd. *Other Cast*: James Cagney (Rheinlander Waldo), Thomas A. Carlin (Vice President Fairbanks), Brad Dourif (Younger Brother), Moses Gunn (Booker T. Washington), Elizabeth McGovern (Evelyn Nesbit Thaw), Kenneth McMillan (Willie Conklin), Pat O'Brien (Delmas), Donald O'Connor (Evelyn's Dance Instructor), James Olson (Father), Mandy Patinkin (Tateh), Howard E. Rollins (Coalhouse Walker Jr.), Mary Steenburgen (Mother), Debbie Allen (Sarah), Jeff DeMunn (Houdini), Robert Joy (Harry K. Thaw), Norman Mailer (Stanford White). *Director*: Milos Forman. *Producer*: Dino De Laurentiis. *Writing Credits*: E.L. Doctorow (novel), Michael Weller. *Music*: Randy Newman. *Cinematography*: Miroslav Ondricek. *Film Editing*: Anne V. Coates, Antony Gibbs, Stanley Warnow. *Production Design*: George DeTitta, John Graysmark, Peter Howitt, Anthony Reading, Patrizia von Brandenstein. *Set Decoration*: George DeTitta Jr. *Costume Design*: Anna Hill Johnstone. *Makeup*: Max Henriquez. *Studio*: Dino De Laurentiis Productions/Sunley Productions Ltd. *Length*: 155 minutes.

Using three of the storylines of E.L. Doctorow's sprawling period novel, director Milos Forman recreates the New York City area in the early 1900s by crisscrossing the lives of characters from three distinct socio-economic classes. The extremely wealthy are represented by lavish-living Harry K. Thaw (Robert Joy) and Stanford White (Norman Mailer), and Thaw's killing of White in his jealousy over his wife's, Evelyn Nesbit (Elizabeth McGovern), relationship with White. Immigrants are represented by Tateh (Mandy Patinkin) and his journey from the Jewish ghetto of New York City to successful film director. Finally, the plight of the Negro at the time is demonstrated by the story of Coalhouse Walker Jr. (Howard E. Rollins Jr.) and his attempt to obtain justice for a vicious racial attack on him and his car by Irish firemen led by Capt. Willie Conklin (Kenneth McMillan).

The stories intertwine and interrelate mainly through an upper-middle class family living in Westchester County. The mother (Mary Steenburgen) helps Sarah (Debbie Allen) who has just delivered Coalhouse's baby, and her brother (Brad Dourif) aids Coalhouse in his efforts for justice as well as being a lover of Evelyn Nesbit. The father (James Olson) aids the police in ending Coalhouse's standoff in the Morgan Library. In an inconclusive ending, Mother (no last name, making this family Every family) leaves on a family outing in a car with Tateh, whom the family had met while vacationing at the shore.

The presidential appearance is a brief period black-and-white newsreel-type film clip with the title "President hosts Booker T. Washington—a first at the White House." Roosevelt is portrayed by Robert Boyd (a non-speaking role). However, Roosevelt's Vice President Charles Fairbanks (Thomas A. Carlin) has two speaking appearances and is the central character in the scene when Sarah is mortally injured.

In the film's press coverage, the most attention was paid to the appearance of James Cagney as New York Police Commissioner Rheinlander Waldo—who does not appear in Doctorow's novel. This role was created with top billing specifically by director Forman for 81-year-old Cagney (his first acting in over 20 years). He is joined by his old Warner Bros. cohort Pat O'Brien as Delmas, a lawyer for Harry K. Thaw. In addition to other big names such as Norman Mailer, Donald O'Connor appears as Nesbit's dancing instructor. Besides Forman's superb cutting, the film benefits from good costumes and sets.

The Indomitable Teddy Roosevelt (1986)

Roosevelt: Bob Boyd and Harold Mark Kingsley as Young Roosevelt. *Other Cast*: Thomas Batty (Ted), Lisette Clemens (Alice), William Kapinski (Father), Sean Lavin (Kermit), Michael Roosevelt (Archie), Philippa B. Roosevelt (Edith), Pippi Roosevelt (Ethel), Theodore Roosevelt V (Quentin), George C. Scott (Narrator). *Director-Producer-Film Editing*: Harrison Engle. *Writing Credits*: Theodore Strauss. *Cinematography*: Tom Baer, Robert Ipcar, Jeri Suzanne. *Non-Original Music*: John Philip Sousa. *Sound*: Thelma Vickroy. *Studio*: Gannett/Anacapa/Signal Hill Entertainment. *Length*: 93 minutes.

Seamlessly produced with historical sounds and film footage, stills, narration (George C. Scott), and live dramatic action, this is an authentic and arresting biography of the 26th president. It opens with a Fourth of July parade in 1905 and shows Roosevelt celebrating it at Oyster Bay, Long Island, where he says, "I rose like a rocket." That characterizes his incredible energy described in the brief introduction to his personality by Scott: "He was not only president of the United States but the most entertaining ... and people love him."

Shots of Roosevelt's childhood capture his curiosity about any animal, and his college days at Harvard note the dandy and snob that he was there studying literature. The death of his father, "the best man I ever knew," he said, led to his life in politics, starting as New York State assemblyman at 23. Upon the death of his childhood love, wife Alice Lee, after childbirth and his mother on the same day, Roosevelt fled to North Dakota to find himself. Scenes from the film *Roosevelt and Friends* capture him with the wildlife he loved, but the lesson of that exile was "his mastery must be earned in the world of men."

Roosevelt soon married Edith Kermit Carow with whom he had five children. He lost the mayoralty but became New York City police commissioner and later governor of the state. His national celebrity sprang from his leading the Rough Riders during the Spanish-American War, captured in the film *The Rough Riders* (1927) included in this biopic. Some historical footage shows his campaigning for his vice presidency under McKinley and the funeral of the assassinated president that led to Roosevelt's ascendancy to the White House.

His presidency is covered in archival stills of him speaking, newsreels, cartoons, and dramatic footage of him—well played by look-alike Bob Boyd (also in *Ragtime*). Boyd also plays Roosevelt at home in Oyster Bay being the gentle, endlessly indulgent husband and father, notably leading his family on a very brisk point-to-point race through the woods, an enchanted scene. "It must be remembered," narrator Scott says about Roosevelt's childlike glee, "that the president is six [years old]."

The second administration of his presidency that he soundly won on his own deals with Roosevelt's foreign focus: the peace conference in New Hampshire, the Nobel Peace Prize, the Panama Canal, and the launch of a naval fleet around the world. "Did you ever see such a fleet or such a day?" he says. "Isn't it magnificent?"

Defeated in his Bull Moose campaign for another term, Roosevelt again found solace in travel, this time through the Brazilian wilderness, "my last chance to be a boy," he says. He lost his son Quentin in World War I, a terrible blow to a father who continues to rage against the world in his simple virtues. Death took Roosevelt in sleeping "or there would have been a fight," says Scott. This fine text by Theodore Strauss is accompanied by the music of John Philip Sousa, stirring marches for such a bombastic man.

Newsies (1992)

Roosevelt: David James Alexander. *Other Cast:* Christian Bale (Jack Kelly/Francis Sullivan), David Moscow (David Jacobs), Luke Edwards (Les Jacobs), Max Casella (Racetrack Higgins), Marty Belafsky (Crutchy), Arvie Lowe Jr. (Boots), Aaron Lohr (Mush), Trey Parker (Kid Blink), Gabriel Damon (Spot Conlon), Dee Caspary (Snitch), Joseph Conrad (Jake), Dominic Maldonado (Itey), Bill Pullman (Bryan Denton), Ann-Margret (Medda Larsen), Robert Duvall (Joseph Pulitzer). *Director-Choreographer:* Kenny Ortega. *Producer:* Michael Finnell. *Writing Credits:* Bob Tzudiker, Noni White. *Music:* Alan Menken. *Cinematography:* Andrew Laszlo. *Film Editing:* William Reynolds. *Production Design:* William Sandell. *Art Direction:* Nancy Patton. *Set Direction:* Robert Gould. *Costume Design:* May Routh. *Studio:* Touchwood Pacific Partners and Walt Disney Pictures. *Length:* 191 minutes.

In recent years it has been increasingly difficult to sell live-action (as opposed to animated) musicals to the filmgoing public. Using as a base an 1899 historical confrontation between press magnate Joseph Pulitzer (played by Robert Duvall) and his newsboy distributors, Kenny Ortega directed and choreographed a male version of *Annie* (1982) with references to the Dead End Kids films (1930s), and almost succeeded. Although the music composed by Alan Menken (*Beauty and the Beast*, *Little Shop of Horrors*) is catchy, it is not memorable nor original, and the storyline was so extremely close to *Annie's* that the film audience would not buy it. Like *Annie*, *Newsies* concerns orphans, bad-guy wardens, historical figures as saviors, and optimism, optimism, optimism for spunky American idealism.

Another of the similarities with *Annie* is to use a historical figure in solving the dramatic confrontation of the film. In *Newsies* the historical figure is Theodore Roosevelt (David James Alexander); his cousin Franklin Roosevelt was in *Annie*. Roosevelt appears in two short scenes. The few words he speaks in the first scene show his decisiveness as governor of New York in solving the problems that the leader of the newsboys, Jack Kelly, aka Francis Sullivan (Christian Bale), has with the police and Pulitzer. In the second scene Roosevelt waves to the crowd in front of Pulitzer's office as the newsboys win their strike against Pulitzer for raising the price one-tenth of one cent they pay as subcontractors. In neither scene was the actor able to show Roosevelt's strength of character, partially because he bore little physical resemblance to the vibrant soon-to-be president. The domestic gross of the film was $2,820,000 even with the talents of Ann-Margret as Medda Larsen, a dance-hall performer who unexplainably befriends the Newsies.

27
William Howard Taft (1909–1913)

In this immense man dwelt two Tafts—one who just wanted to practice law, particularly on the Supreme Court, and another whose wife and brother wanted him to be president.[1] That partially explains the changed behavior as serious president from his jolly self as friend and mentor while he was Theodore Roosevelt's Secretary of War. Or perhaps he could not compete with Roosevelt and did not want to; as he said, "There is no use trying to be William Howard Taft with Roosevelt's ways."[2]

Young lawyer Taft's political progress to the cabinet was rapid: assistant county prosecutor, district collector of internal revenue, judge of the Ohio State Superior Court, U.S. solicitor general, Federal Appeals Court judge in the Sixth Circuit, first U.S. civil governor of the Philippines.

Taft and Roosevelt split over their political views: Roosevelt's, the progressive Republican, and Taft's, the conservative,

William Howard Taft. (Courtesy of Library of Congress.)

particularly his advocacy of the Payne-Aldrich Tariff, another protectionist measure. Taft also opposed lowering the tariff for paper and pulp under the Dingley Tariff, creating animosity from the media he so scorned. He infuriated the press, especially the muckrakers, by calling for a substantial increase in postal rates, "a subsidy of fifty millions," he railed.[3]

This mounting irritability and indecision got Taft into more and more trouble with the progressive wing of the Republican Party. Although he carried on many of Roosevelt's policies, he lost to him, his closest friend turned progressive, and both Taft and Roosevelt lost to Woodrow Wilson in the 1913 election. Nevertheless, Taft became what he always wanted, Chief Justice of the Supreme Court when he was appointed to that position by Harding in 1921.

THE FILMS

For all his strong personal and political traits, Taft escaped celebration on celluloid. One film, *The Money Kings,* was not available for our viewing, and the other *The Greatest Game Ever Played* shows him in a cameo role.

The Money Kings (1912)

Taft: Frank A. Lyon. *Other Cast:* Rose Tapley (A Spy), Ralph Ince (The Aviator), Leo Delaney, William Humphrey, Lillian Walker, Dolores Costello, Clara Kimball Young, Maurice Costello. *Directors:* Van Dyke Brooke, William Humphrey. *Writing Credits:* Eugene Mullin. *Studio:* Vitagraph Company of America. *Length:* Three reels (2700 feet).

Not only is *The Money Kings* among the many missing films from the early years, but there is very little information about it. It was released on July 15, 1912, and portraying President Taft is Frank A. Lyon who appeared in a number of Edison films. The cast listing from IMDb is of interest for two reasons: It lists A Spy (Rose Tapley) and the Aviator (Ralph Ince, a very famous Lincoln portrayer), and it includes three actors with the last name of Costello. Among the Costellos is Maurice, the father, and his two daughters Dolores and Helene. Dolores was known as "Goddess of the Silent Screen." She lost this designation with the advent of talking pictures because of her very strong lisp. Director Van Dyke Brooke enjoyed an active career in films, directing seven from 1909 to 1917 and appearing in ten from 1910 to 1921.

The Greatest Game Ever Played (2005)

Taft: Walter Massey. *Other Cast:* Stephen Dillane (Harry Vardon), Stephen Marcus (Ted Ray), Francis Ouimet (Shia LaBeouf), Elias Koteas (Arthur), John Flitter (Eddie Lowery), Peyton List (Sarah Wallis). *Director:* Bill Paxton. *Writing Credits:* Mark Frost. *Producers:* David Blocker, Larry Brezner, Mark Frost, Jason Reed, David A. Steinberg. *Music:* Brian Tyler. *Cinematography:* Elliot Graham. *Production Design:* Francois Seguin. *Art Direction:* Pierre Perrault. *Set Decoration:* Anne Gallea. *Costume Design:* Renee April. *Studio:* Fairway Films Ltd., Touchstone Pictures, The Walt Disney Co. *Length:* 120 minutes.

Depending on one's interest in sports there can be great differences about the accuracy of the title of this film. However, a serious golfer would probably agree that the match here depicted between a young amateur, 20-year-old Francis Ouimet, and an experienced British professional in the 1913 U.S. Open has to rank near the top of spectator sport experiences.

Supposedly among the 10,000 spectators on that September 20, 1913 at the Country Club in Brookline, Massachusetts, was President Taft. Except by that time he was ex–President Taft, since Wilson was inaugurated March 3, 1913. Taft (Walter Massey) enjoyed his golf and would have undoubtedly been interested in the outcome of the match. Massey looks the part of the noted rotund ex-president in his cameo appearance.

28
Woodrow Wilson (1913–1921)

Woodrow Wilson. (Courtesy of Library of Congress.)

Rated among the top presidents by many scholars and many polls, the professor president began the transformation of the Democrat Party from the Jacksonian party of states' rights and limited government to the current-day party of federal initiative and government activism. He introduced more social legislation through Congress in his first term than Theodore Roosevelt and Taft in all their years in office. He ruined his health in trying to achieve his dream, the League of Nations, during his second term. Idealistic (he dreamed and fought for world peace), independent (he ignored the New Jersey bosses who helped elect him governor), intellectual (he wrote books, steered Princeton toward academics and away from social clubs), he appeared icy. Yet he needed the emotional support of a woman as demonstrated in his seemingly quick marriage to Edith Boling Galt after the death of his first wife Ellen Axson.

The social legislation he steered through Congress during his first term includes the Underwood Tariff Bill with a progressive income tax, antitrust initiatives by the Clayton Antitrust Act of 1914, and creation of the Federal Reserve Board and banks. Yet this Southerner's reform agenda lacked a program for African-Americans. He later supported women's suffrage.

Although he kept the country out of World War I in the early years, Germany's resumption of unrestricted submarine warfare and publication of plans (the Zimmerman telegram-note) that suggested that Mexico could recapture lost territory if the U.S. went to war forced him to declare war. Under war pressures, he suspended civil liberties and press freedom. His Fourteen Points peace proposal advocated open diplomacy, openly arrived at, freedom of the seas and trade, arms reduction, self-determination of peoples, an end to colonialism, territorial readjustments, and the establishment of a League of Nations. These progressive liberal values failed to gain Senate approval but became the basis for America's postwar vision. Wilson suffered a debilitating stroke and was incapacitated during his final months in office.

THE FILMS

Although there are 16 films that include a Wilson appearance, the majority of them are little more than propaganda films regarding World War I and World War II. The only meaningful one is the biographical film *Wilson*, one of the few about a president that presents him in a positive light, ignoring his arrogant dark side of "insufficient regard for those who had helped him and a greatly exaggerated view of what he had done for himself."[1]

The Sons of a Soldier (1913)

Wilson: Frederick C. Truesdell. *Other Cast*: Barbara Tennant, J.W. Johnston, Guy Hedlund, Alec B. Francis, Lamar Johnstone, Julia Stuart, Mildred Bright, Helen Marten, Will E. Sheerer, Clara Horton. *Director*: O.A.C. Lund. *Studio*: Éclair American.

Frederick C. Truesdell, who portrays Woodrow Wilson, was a very active character actor with 58 films in the period from 1912 through 1919. He played Wilson again in the 1919 film *The Great Victory, Wilson or the Kaiser?*

The Slacker's Heart (1917)

Wilson: T.H. Westfall.
For details, see Chapter 16 on Abraham Lincoln.

War and the Woman (1917)

Wilson: Ralph Faulkner. *Other Cast*: Florence La Badie (Ruth Norton), Ernest C. Warde (Lt. Fredericks), Tom Brooke (John Braun), Wayne Arey (John Barker), Grace Henderson (Barker's Mother), Arthur Bauer (Commander of Invading Army). *Director*: Ernest C. Warde. *Writing Credits*: Philip Lonergan. *Cinematography*: William M. Zollinger. *Studio*: Tannhouser Film Corp.

When World War I began, most movies tried to include a war theme. This one has a patriotic woman, Ruth Norton (Florence La Badie), who discovers that her stepfather, John Braun (Tom Brooke), is an enemy spy. Accused of being his accomplice, she escapes from him immediately and, in a stroke of good fortune, saves a wealthy, good-looking young aviator, John Barker (Wayne Arey), when his plane crashes in front of her.

As could be expected, this act of heroism ends in love, and after their marriage Norton is left at Barker's beautiful seaside estate while he goes off to save his country from an impending invasion. Unfortunately for Ruth and John Barker, the invasion takes place and his house becomes the headquarters for the lecherous leaders of the enemy forces. Things look bad for Ruth when she refuses to bend to the evil ways of the unnamed invaders, but she is adamant and is even able to hide dynamite in the cellar of the house. Barker is finally able to come to her rescue. As they leave in his flying machine the house is blown to bits along with its lecherous inhabitants.

Much to the chagrin of critics of the day one scene has President Wilson (Ralph Faulkner) purchasing a book in a shop. Faulkner was well-known for his impersonations of Wilson, particularly on the stage and in vaudeville. In its review, *Variety* notes that the character of President Wilson was introduced "for no particular reason excepting to pad out the picture to sufficient length." *Wid's Film and Film Folk* in its review (Sept. 13, 1917) states that, "In the first part of this they pulled an impersonation of President Wilson, which was not necessary from any angle and certainly seems to me to be very bad taste at this time." Times have changed when considering the usage of presidential images in modern films; they no longer serve as padding.

The Kaiser, the Beast of Berlin (1918)

Wilson: Orlo Eastman. *Other Cast:* Rupert Julian (The Kaiser), Elmo Lincoln (Marcas, the Blacksmith), Nigel De Brulier (Capt. von Neigle), Lon Chaney (Bethmann-Hollweg), Harry von Meter (Capt. von Hancke), Harry Carter (Gen. von Kluck), Joseph W. Girard (Ambassador Gerard), Harry Holden (Gen. Joffre), Ruth Clifford (Gabrielle), Gretchen Lederer (Bertha von Neigle), Betty Carpenter (Bride), Ruby Lafayette (Grandmother Marcas), Zoe Rae (Gretel), Mark Fenton (Adm. Von Tirpitz), Jay Smith (Marshal von Hindenburg), Alfred Allen (Gen. John Pershing). *Director-Producer:* Rupert Julian. *Writing Credits:* Elliott J. Clawson, Rupert Julian. *Cinematography:* Edward A. Kull. *Studio:* Jewel Productions, Inc. *Length:* Seven reels.

In what was obviously a propaganda piece aimed at stirring up the resentment of Americans toward Kaiser Wilhelm, director-producer-writer-actor Rupert Julian begins this silent with a look at the imperial palace and the joy of the people of Europe with the peace that they are experiencing. He then introduces the megalomaniac Kaiser and the impact of his mental attitude on the European continent and on individual events like the sinking of the *Lusitania*.

Julian portrays the Kaiser with great skill and uses a large cast to show both the German general staff and those opposing them throughout the world. President Wilson is portrayed in a short scene by Orlo Eastman who reportedly does a credible job. True to propaganda films, Julian is not averse to stretching a point to make the film more interesting than actual history. Toward the end of the film he has allied armies marching through Berlin, and the Kaiser put under the care of King Albert of Belgium.

On the Jump (1918)

Wilson: Ralph Faulkner. *Other Cast:* George Walsh (Jack Bartlett), Frances Burnham (Margaret Desmond), James Marcus (William Desmond), Henry Clive (Otto Crumley), Harold L. Lloyd (Bellhop). *Director:* Raoul Walsh. *Producer:* Hal Roach. *Writing Credits:* Ralph Spence (scenario), Raoul Walsh (story). *Cinematography:* Roy Overbaugh. *Studio:* Fox Film Corp.

Liberty Bond Sales for World War I provide the impetus for this silent propaganda film. Jack Bartlett (George Walsh, brother of director Raoul Walsh) shows his athletic ability when a bond campaign evolves into anti–German activity. He still is able to interview President Wilson about the Fourth Liberty Loan during the campaign. Veteran Wilson impersonator Ralph Faulkner again executes the role of the president.

The interview never appears in Bartlett's newspaper because new owner Otto Crumley (Henry Clive) is pro–German. Bartlett quits and continues his campaign for bonds and against Crumley's anti–American activities.

The Prussian Cur (1918) aka The Invisible Enemy

Wilson: Ralph C. Faulkner. *Other Cast:* Miriam Cooper (Rosie O'Grady), Sidney Mason (Dick Gregory), Capt. Horst von der Goltz (Otto Goltz), Leonora Stewart (Lillian O'Grady), James Marcus (Patrick O'Grady), Patrick O'Malley (Jimmie O'Grady), Walter McEwen (Count Johann von Bernstorff), William W. Black (Wolff von Eidel), Walter M. Lawrence (Emperor William II), Charles Reynolds (Emperor William I), William Harrison (Crown Prince Frederick), James Hathaway (Field Marshal von Hindenburg), P.C. Hartigan (Adm. von Tirpitz), John E. Franklin (James W. Gerard), John W. Harbon (U.S. Congressman). *Director-Writer:* Raoul Walsh. *Cinematography:* Roy Overbaugh. *Studio:* Fox Film Corp.

"Upsetting all Records!

"In Springfield, Mass., people stood three abreast a block long, from 11 A.M. to 9:30 P.M. in spite of temperature of 103 degrees!" read an ad in *Motion Picture World* (Sept. 14, 1918) for this film. Capt. Horst von der Goltz (as Otto Goltz), an actual German spy operating in North and South America before World War I, is the "Prussian cur" whose spy network causes labor strikes, factory explosions, and transportation disasters. His dastardly treatment of his wife Lillian O'Grady (Leonora Stewart) is avenged by young American soldier Dick Gregory (Sidney Mason) who is in love with her sister Rosie (Miriam Cooper).

The villain's ally Wolff von Eidel (William Black) is arrested and shot by a patriotic group when German sympathizers try to rescue him. The silent film ends as U.S. forces storm France, and Kaiser Wilhelm grows desperate.

Why American Will Win (1918)

Wilson: Ralph Faulkner.
For details, see Chapter 26 on President Theodore Roosevelt.

The Great Victory, Wilson or the Kaiser?
The Fall of the Hohenzollerns (1919)

Wilson: Frederick C. Truesdell. *Other Cast:* Creighton Hale (Conrad Le Brett), Florence Billings (Vilma Le Brett), E.J. Connelly (Paul Le Brett), Helen Ferguson (Amy Gordon), Frank Currier (William Gordon), Henry Kolker (Kaiser Wilhelm II), Joseph Kilgour (Gen. Von Bissing), Margaret McWade (Nurse Edith Cavell), Earl Schenck (Lt. Ober/Crown Prince), H. Carvill (Count von Bismarck), Florence Short (Elaine), Charles Edwards (Rev. Joseph Wilson), May Allen (Mrs. Joseph Wilson). *Director:* Charles Miller. *Producer-Writing Credits:* Maxwell Karger. *Cinematography:* George K. Hollister. *Studio:* Screen Classics. *Length:* Seven reels.

In a silent propaganda film that was a little late for effect, released in January 1919 after the Armistice in November 1918, the Germans again take a great berating. Opening with a quick comparison between the birth of the Kaiser in a Hohenzollern palace and Wilson in a minister's manse in Virginia, the action moves to Alsace-Lorraine where Paul Le Brett (Edward Connelly) is forced to join the German army.

Le Brett is wounded but brought back to health by the famous Edith Cavell (Margaret McWade) and American nurse Amy Gordon (Helen Ferguson). Cavell is shot and Le Brett ends up in the U.S. where he convinces President Wilson (Frederick C. Truesdell) to allow Alsatians to enlist. Returning to Europe, Le Brett avenges the rape and death of his sister Vilma (Florence Billings). After the Armistice, Le Brett comes back to America and Amy.

The Road Is Open Again (1933)

Wilson: Samuel S. Hinds.

Wilson appears in this short about the National Recovery Act with fellow Presidents Washington and Lincoln, reading a newspaper about how the NRA has created one million jobs. All the presidents address star Dick Powell, a songwriter, in historically telling terms.

Wilson (Samuel S. Hinds) explains what the NRA will do: end unemployment. He also says the act will work "if every man, woman, and child can do his part." Hinds looks and sounds much like Wilson. For details, see Chapter 1 on Washington.

Turn Back the Clock (1933)

Wilson: Unnamed actor. *Other Cast*: Lee Tracy (Joseph "Joe" Gimlet), Mae Clarke (Mary Gimlet/Mary Wright), Otto Kruger (Ted Wright), George Barbier (Pete Evans), Peggy Shannon (Elvina Evans Wright/Elvina Gimlet), C. Henry Gordon (Dave Holmes), Clara Blandick (Mrs. Gimlet). *Director*: Edgar Selwyn. *Producer*: Harry Rapf. *Writing Credits*: Edgar Selwyn, Ben Hecht. *Music*: Herbert Stothart. *Cinematography*: Harold Rosson. *Film Editing*: Frank Sullivan. *Art Direction*: Stanwood Rogers. *Costume Design*: Adrian. *Art Department*: Edwin B. Willis. *Sound*: Douglas Shearer. *Studio*: MGM. *Length*: 79 minutes.

The story of this film appears time and time again: It's the return to the past to live life over. In Ben Hecht and Edgar Selwyn's screenplay, hero Joseph "Joe" Gimlet (Lee Tracy) dines with his boyhood friend Ted Wright (Otto Kruger) and their wives. The wealthy bank president Wright offers Gimlet a chance to invest $4,000 in an aluminum-underwriting venture. Before he can accept, Gimlet is injured in an automobile accident and finds himself transported back in time. He becomes a millionaire and pledges one million dollars to aid returning World War I veterans. For this generosity, President Wilson offers him a job as head of the War Industry Board.

You Can't Buy Everything (1934)

Wilson: Fred Lee. *Other Cast*: May Robson (Hannah Bell), Jean Parker (Elizabeth Burton Bell), Lewis Stone (John Burton), Mary Forbes (Kate Farley), Reginald Mason (Dr. Lorimer), William Bakewell (Donny Bell as a Man), Tad Alexander (Donny Bell as a Boy), Walter Walker (Josiah Flagg), Reginald Barlow (Tom Sparks), Claude Gillingwater (Banker Asa Cabot), Bruce Bennett (Bank Clerk), Walter Brennan (Train Vendor). *Director*: Charles Reisner. *Producer*: Lucien Hubbard. *Writing Credits*: Eve Greene, Dudley Nichols, Zelda Sears, Lamar Trotti. *Music*: William Axt. *Cinematography*: Leonard Smith. *Film Editing*: Ben Lewis. *Art Direction*: David Townsend. *Set Decoration*: Edwin B. Willis. *Costume Design*: Dolly Tree. *Studio*: Cosmopolitan Pictures, MGM. *Length*: 80 minutes.

While Wilson is president of Princeton, upright Donny Bell claims in his valedictory that you "must break down the walls of materialism." Although he does not resemble the president, Fred Lee takes on the Wilson role credibly as he sits erect at the center of the podium and applauds Bell's speech.

The money that Bell (William Bakewell) disdains obsesses his widowed mother Hannah Bell (May Robson) who is so frugal she waits a week after he injures his leg before she takes him to a hospital, and a charity ward at that. She inquires whether he will get the same care as the rich patients. "Money has nothing to do with care," Dr. Lorimer (Reginald Mason) assures her.

Everything she saves and does is for her Donny who's more interested in writing than banking. At a house party attempting to reunite his mother and her former lover John Burton (Lewis Stone), Donny meets Burton's daughter Elizabeth (Jean Parker). They end up singing a love duet.

The well-written story by the respected screenwriters Dudley Nichols and Lamar Trotti takes unexpected turns: Donny proposes to Elizabeth, and his mother immediately accuses her father of "sneaking behind my back to get my money." Most kindly, Burton tells her she was "as nice a girl a man could want," but she inherited her father's avarice.

"Pickled on her own sour juice" (as her girlhood friend says), Hannah observes the wedding behind the church gate and soon learns she can avenge Burton, her former lover, in a stock deal after the crash. Her son learns of her shameful act, and in her bank's vault (a well-chosen setting) accuses her of never loving him, only money, and shows her the incredible nuptial agreement her father wanted Burton to sign.

Stunned and distraught, Hannah leaves the bank, throws her money to a scrambling crowd (another well-directed and -photographed scene), and ends up on a park bench, contracting pneumonia. While all parties reconcile and Hannah returns Burton's stock, she utters the last selfish word to her solicitous doctor about her condition, "Whose pneumonia is this—yours or mine?"

Espionage Agent (1939)

Wilson: Lloyd Ingraham. *Other Cast:* Joel McCrea (Barry Corvall), Brenda Marshall (Brenda Ballard), Jeffrey Lynn (Lowell Warrington), George Bancroft (Dudley Garrett), Stanley Ridges (Hamilton Peyton), James Stephenson (Dr. Rader), Howard C. Hickman (Walter Forbes), Martin Kosleck (Karl Mullen), Nana Bryant (Mrs. Corvall), Rudolph Anders (Paul Strawn), Hans Heinrich von Twardowski (Dr. Helm), Lucien Prival (Decker), Addison Richards (Bruce Corvail), Edwin Stanley (Secretary of State), Granville Bates (Phineas T. O'Grady), Grace Hayle (Mrs. O'Grady), Egon Brecher (Larsch), Emmett Vogan (Instructor). *Director:* Lloyd Bacon. *Producer:* Hal B. Wallis. *Writing Credits:* Frank Donaghue, Warren Duff, Michael Fessier. *Music:* Adolph Deutsch. *Cinematography:* Charles Rosher. *Film Editing:* Ralph Dawson. *Art Direction:* Carl Jules Weyl. *Costume Design:* Milo Anderson. *Makeup:* Perc Westmore. *Studio:* Warner Brothers. *Length:* 83 minutes.

This spy film diverts from the usual plot in clearly identifying the villains, Germans. The conventions of newspaper headlines and ticker tape herald the forthcoming event—World War II—for which the United States is unprepared. Barry Corvall (Joel McCrea) serves as a Spanish legation officer dealing with unhappy Americans. He befriends Brenda Ballard (Brenda Marshall), an opera star without a passport by taking her aboard the *Fredo-*

nia (overtones of freedom and the Marx Brothers). In record movie time he asks her to marry him, but she won't tell him why she can't.

In Washington, Corvall, son of a distinguished diplomat, attends the Foreign Service Training School with his buddy, Lowell Warrington (Jeffrey Lynn). For his diligence, Corvall pulls a top post, Paris, and gets a "special" assignment: obtain complete information on the Germans' industrial mobilization plan. He marries Ballard who confesses she's a German spy. Her activities are known and revealed to Corvall who resigns. Distraught, his new wife bewails her situation to Corvall's mother (Nana Bryant). He finds a new career as a spy and with his wife's help unearths the Germans' plan, all suspenseful action.

Published castlists credit Lloyd Ingraham with playing Wilson but he does not appear.

Wilson (1944)

Wilson: Alexander Knox. *Other Cast*: Charles Coburn (Prof. Henry Holmes), Geraldine Fitzgerald (Edith Bolling Galt Wilson), Thomas Mitchell (Joseph Tumulty), Ruth Nelson (Ellen Wilson), Sir Cedric Hardwicke (Sen. Henry Cabot Lodge), Vincent Price (William Gibb McAdoo), William Eythe (Lt. George Felton), Mary Anderson (Eleanor Wilson), Ruth Ford (Margaret Wilson), Sidney Blackmer (Josephus Daniels), Madeleine Forbes (Jessie Wilson), Stanley Ridges (Dr. Cary Grayson), Eddie Foy Jr. (Eddie Foy), Charles Halton (Colonel House. *Director*: Henry King. *Producer*: Darryl F. Zanuck. *Writing Credits*: Lamar Trotti. *Music*: Alfred Newman. *Cinematography*: Leon Shamroy. *Film Editing*: Barbara McLean. *Art Direction*: James Basevi, Wiard Ihnen. *Set Decoration*: Thomas Little. *Costume Design*: Rene Hubert. *Makeup*: Guy Pearce. *Sound Department*: Edmund H. Hansen, Roger Heman, E. Clayton Ward. *Studio*: 20th Century–Fox/Darryl F. Zanuck Productions. *Length*: 154 minutes.

Winner of five Academy Awards but little box office success, this celebratory study of the 28th president's rise to power and two terms in office faithfully portrays the political idealism and intellectualism of this complex man. Producer Darryl F. Zanuck's serious historical intent surfaces in the intertitle opening the film about Wilson's shaping the "destiny of our country" and showing how "sometimes the life of a man mirrors the life of a nation." But while *Wilson* is a one-man film it is more about a peace treaty than a president's administration.

Prophetic of the film's positive rendering of Wilson is his remark in the opening scene to the quarterback who lost the Princeton football game to Yale (by six points), "Anyone can fumble." Wilson's rigidity and his admitted inability to change shaped his idealism, particularly about war and his treaty (The Fourteen Points) to end wars, but it also limited his ability to deal with a recalcitrant Senate about passing the treaty and to work with a persistent press.

As Wilson, Alexander Knox creates a credible likeness in his stiff carriage and speech. Knox appears in almost every scene of the film. Although not as tall as Wilson, Knox remains convincingly imposing, especially in his delivery of several of Wilson's speeches—to the German ambassador about Germany's resumption of submarine warfare, to Congress announcing war, to Clemenceau about France's (and England's) greed in reclaiming German territory after the war, and to the American public in urging their support of his peace plan in 40 speeches during his 22-day tour of 17 states. Equally adept is Knox at conveying Wilson's didactic, professorial nature, evident in his lecture about the meaning of World War I to

Wilson (1944): Alexander Knox is as serious as President Wilson while he performs his duties in the Oval Office as head of state in Darryl F. Zanuck's production of this biopic for 20th Century–Fox. (Courtesy of George Eastman House.)

American doughboys embarking at a train station where Wilson himself (to the soldiers' awe) is serving coffee. While Wilson and his family (of three daughters) resented press reportage about their family life, their close relationship surfaces in several scenes of their singing popular songs around the piano. Wilson's love of his first—and second—wife also gets revealing treatment, especially when his dying (of Bright's disease) first wife tells her daughters how he "needs a woman's love."

But the film focuses on the election of Wilson to public office, first to the governorship of New Jersey, then to two terms as president of the United States, and his lasting efforts to effect world peace through a League of Nations. With Zanuck's noted concern for historical detail, the film's scenes of the 1912 Democratic convention and the signing of the Treaty of Versailles in that magnificent palace burst with authenticity (in color). Adding to the historical treatment of Wilson are clips from newsreels of the period about inductees leaving the training camps, celebrities participating in Liberty Bond drives, and the President and Mrs. Wilson arriving in Paris for the peace conference.

To underline the positive portrayal of this anti-war president during a period of war (it was released in 1944 during World War II) is Alfred Newman's original music, frequently variations on American patriotic songs such as "Yankee Doodle Dandy" and "The Battle Hymn of the Republic." *Wilson*'s Academy Awards are for Best Original Screenplay, Best Cinematography, Best Editing, Best Art Direction, and Best Sound Recording.

Wilson failed historically ...

• By not emphasizing Wilson's legislative accomplishments in his first term. The film quickly only shows a series of shots of his signing bills establishing the Federal Reserve Board and banks, the Federal Trades Commission, reduced tariffs, and shorter working hours;

• By ignoring the early medical problems that led to his final debilitating stroke, especially bouts of psychological depression, and the White House cover-up of his illness;

• By minimizing his close relationship with his alter ego, Colonel Edward M. House, until their break over the Versailles Peace Treaty negotiations;

• By limiting the scandal caused by his courtship of Edith Bolling Galt seven months after his first wife's death. It prompted his secretary Joseph Tumulty to suggest he not marry Edith until after the second election. Edith's dislike of the effective and faithful Tumulty because he was uncouth and a Catholic led Wilson to fire him. This is only one example of Edith's influence that is not treated;

• By simplifying the speeches, the social issues, and political processes of Wilson's administration.

The film was made at a cost of $5 million, a large amount in 1944, with a cast of 13,000. Accused of being "propaganda" for Franklin D. Roosevelt's 1944 presidential campaign, it drew millions of moviegoers in its first five weeks and recovered $3 million in box office sales in two years. Zanuck, however, denied he was a Democrat. He said he was a Republican and voted for FDR's opponent Wendell Wilkie and said the film was his "personal crusade for world peace."[2] Nevertheless, the film was not shown before the 1944 election to armed forces as it was considered "too partisan." *The New York Times* judged *Wilson* one of the ten best films of the year and considered its handling of the political process "authentic," especially the 1912 Democratic convention.

Nezabyvayemyj god (1919) aka *The Unforgettable Year* (1952)

Wilson: L. Korsakov. *Other Cast*: Boris Andreyeve Mikheil Gelovani (Stalin), Viktor Koltsov (Lloyd George), M.I. Molchanov (V.I. Lenin), Viktor Stanitsyn (Sir Winston Churchill), Gnat Yura (Clemenceau). *Director*: Mikheil Chiaureli. *Writing Credits*: Mikheil Chiaureli, A. Filimonov, Vsevolod Vishnevsky. *Music*: Dmitri Shostakovich. *Cinematography*: Leonid Kosmatov, Vitali Nikolayev. *Production Design*: Vladimir Kaplunovsky. *Studio*: Mosfilm.

Very little information was available to us on Mikheil Chiaureli's story of the beginnings of the Soviet Union in the immediate post–World War I era. After performing in silent films as an actor in the 1920s, Chiaureli became one of Stalin's favorite directors with films stretching from 1928 until 1973. In 1949 Chiaureli released two films *Padeniye Berlina I* and *II* (*The Fall of Berlin*) in which he pictures Stalin as almost godlike. This is the same Stalin who is reported to have eliminated 20 million of his countrymen during his reign. It is assumed that Chiaureli's treatment of the events of 1919 is along the same lines as these two earlier films. He is known for his technical skill, attention to detail, and strong dramatic narratives.

In both of those 1949 films Roosevelt and Churchill are presented as pawns in the hands of the revered Soviet leader. Again the assumption is that Wilson (L. Korsakov) is presented in much the same manner in the 1952 film.

Of interest: Chiaureli won the Czech Karlovy Vary Film Festival crystal bowl award for his directorial work on *The Unforgettable Year,* and Dmitri Shastokovich composed original music for the film. If it approaches the score he composed for the *Padeniye Berlina* films, it is moving indeed.

The Story of Will Rogers (1952)

Wilson: Earl Lee. *Other Cast:* Will Rogers Jr. (Will Rogers), Jane Wyman (Betty Rogers), Carl Benton Reid (Clem Rogers), Slim Pickens (Dusty Donovan), Steve Brodie (Dave Marshall), Eddie Cantor, Fanny Brice, Al Jolson (Themselves). *Director:* Michael Curtiz. *Producer:* Robert Arthur. *Writing Credits:* Frank Davis, Jack Moffitt, Stanley Roberts, Betty Blake Rogers. *Music:* Victor Young. *Cinematography:* Wilfred M. Cline. *Film Editing:* Folmar Blangsted. *Art Direction:* Edward Carrere. *Set Decoration:* George James Hopkins. *Makeup:* Gordon Bau. *Sound:* Charles Lang. *Studio:* Warner Bros. *Length:* 109 minutes.

Will Rogers Jr. as his father Will Rogers creates authenticity in this biopic. Based on a magazine story by Rogers's wife, it moves fluidly through Rogers's life as cowboy, rodeo entertainer, and vaudeville comedian, basing his jokes on newspaper material. Rogers then gained fame as a star comedian in Ziegfeld's *Follies* and grew into an aviation enthusiast and an American goodwill ambassador. His fame brought him a favorite son nomination for president in 1932 at the Democratic National Convention.

Oh! What a Lovely War (1969)

Wilson: Frank Forsyth. *Other Cast:* Paul Daneman (Czar Nicholas II), Ian Holm (President Poincare), Joe Melia (The Photographer), Guy Middleton (Gen. Sir William Robertson), Dirk Bogarde (Stephen), Phyllis Calvert (Lady Haig), John Gielgud (Count Leopold Von Berchtold), Jack Hawkins (Emperor Franz Josef), Kenneth More (Kaiser Wilhelm II), Laurence Olivier (Field Marshal Sir John French), Michael Redgrave (Gen Sir. Henry Wilson), Vanessa Redgrave (Sylvia Pankhurst), Ralph Richardson (Sir Edward Grey), Maggie Smith (Music Hall Star), Susannah York (Eleanor), John Mills (Field Marshal Sir Douglas Haig). *Director:* Richard Attenborough. *Producers:* Richard Attenborough, Brian Duffy, Len Deighton. *Writing Credits:* Charles Chilton, Len Deighton, Joan Littlewood. *Music:* Alfred Ralston. *Cinematography:* Gerry Turpin. *Production Design:* Donald M. Ashton. *Art Direction:* Harry White. *Set Decoration:* Peter James. *Costume Design:* Anthony Mendleson. *Makeup:* Stuart Freeborn. *Studio:* Accord Productions. *Length:* 144 minutes.

Frank Forsyth as Wilson joins a cast of historical figures in this expansive musical satire of World War I. Forsyth's brief appearance parallels Wilson's limited expectations for a League of Nations following the World War I treaty signing. Wilson's look-alike appears in only one brief scene toward the end of the film, silently signing documents with other heads of state to end this "war to end all wars," in an all-white Victorian solarium symbolically covered in red tape. His brief appearance is typical of those by many stars as historical figures and stars in the film: Laurence Olivier, Ralph Richardson, John Gielgud (before they all became titled), Michael Redgrave, Vanessa Redgrave, Jack Hawkins, John Mills, Ian Holm, Kenneth More, Susannah York, Maggie Smith, Dirk Bogard, and Phyllis Calvert. Despite this brevity, their roles are sharply shaped, as are their few lines.

What carries the anti-war saga are the songs, all World War I songs or familiar songs with pacifist lyrics, such as "Onward Christian Soldiers" with the final line changed to "We are all commanders, safely in the rear." The jubilant patriotism, really jingoism, of the British citizenry comes through in an early large production number with everyone singing.

Throughout all the stylistic interpretation of "The Great War," the camera focuses on a middle-class family named Smith, whose five sons die in battle. They first appear at Brighton Amusement Pier for the new attraction, "World War One," in bright lights over the entrance to shooting galleries and a merry-go-round with toy figures that turn into live soldiers that turn into live soldiers in combat.

Segues abound from Brighton to battlefield following the course of the war. Red poppies also abound, the motif for the dying and later the English symbol for its war dead. The film ends with Mrs. Smith, her daughter, and two granddaughters having a proper picnic in a field of poppies. The youngest asks. "Grandma, what did Daddy do in the war?" The camera pulls back to acres and acres of white crosses as a group of soldiers sing "We'll never tell them ... there was a front but damned if we knew where."

Richard Attenborough's directorial debut met with much acclaim, for example *Variety*'s "It may be a long time before a better, more moving and significant film emanates from a British (or, indeed, any studio)." Some critics, such as the *New York Times*'s, found it too "inflated" from the stage play. *Oh! What a Lovely War* is based on Charles Chilton's play of the same name that Joan Littlewood staged before they teamed with Len Deighton for this film.

Polonia Restitua (1981)

Wilson: Jerzy Kaliszewski. *Other Cast:* Krzysztof Chamiec (Paderewski), Edmund Fetting (David Lloyd George), Jozef Fryzlewicz (Dmowski), Kirill Lavrov (Lenin), Ignacy Gogolewski (Stefan Zeromski), Emil Karewicz (Edward House), Zdzislaw Mrozewski (Arthur Balfour), Zygmunt Malanowicz (Franek Pawlak). *Director:* Bohddan Poreba. *Music:* Czeslaw Niemen. *Cinematography:* Waclaw Dybowski. *Set Designer:* Andrzej Plocki. *Studio:* Film Polski/Profil. *Length:* 230 minutes.

This long Polish film covers the developments in the creation of the modern Polish state in the period from 1914 to 1919. The All Movie Guide notes that with 45 minutes per year there is a great deal of historical detail including "large crowd scenes, and hundreds of period costumes." As one of the major players in this time period, Wilson (Jerzy Kaliszewski) is occasionally shown, particularly regarding his relationship with important Polish individuals of the time such as Paderewski (Krzysztof Chamiec).

29

Warren Gamaliel Harding (1921–1923)

Harding gained office because the public wanted a president who would leave them alone,[1] normalcy after Wilson's idealism. If Harding had paid more attention to his cabinet and other appointees who felt free to engage in corruption, he might have escaped being called "the most scandalous president" for decades. Still, other presidents before him did less for the country, and other presidents since him have also had problems with scandals.

In the 1920 campaign Harding used his favored alliteration to tell the country what to expect: "not heroics, but healing; not nostrums, but normalcy; not revolution, but restoration; not agitation, but adjustment; not surgery, but serenity; not the dramatic, but the dispassionate; not experiment, but equipoise; not submergence in internationality but sustainment in triumphant nationality."[2] And he did by disarming the navy, supporting the highest tariff act in history, and retreating into isolation. His affability offset his "bungalow mind" as Wilson described him. But personal charm could not overcome the natural inertia of a man who said he found "being president is rather an unattractive business unless one relishes the exercise of power. That is a thing which has never greatly appealed to me."[3]

Warren Gamaliel Harding. (Courtesy of Library of Congress.)

Clouding his administration is Teapot Dome, the shape and name of an oil lease for which Secretary of the Treasury Albert B. Fall accepted $400,000. The political corruption was widespread—in the Veteran's Bureau, Attorney General Harry M. Daugherty's department and among minor appointed cronies. Harding's personal life also was tainted with more than the alcohol and tobacco he consumed: a ten-year love affair with his best friend's wife, another love affair (often in a White House closet)—and allegedly a child—with Nan Britton. Even his misdiagnosed death during a transcontinental "voyage of understanding" led to suspicion that his wife Florence, "The Duchess," poisoned him.

THE FILMS

There are no films about or with Harding. There's a theory called the "Warren Harding Error: Why We Fall for Tall, Dark, and Handsome Men" espoused by Malcolm Gladwell in *Blink*.[4] It was applied to Harding, called "Roman" in descriptions of him, in choosing him to run for president. It might be applied to movie stars, too. But as Gladwell and most historians agree, Harding, "a model of normal mediocrity,"[5] was one of the worst presidents in American history. And in spite of the drama involved in his administration, Hollywood never chose to use it in any films although Broadway presented *The Gang's All Here*, a semi-fictionalized account of the Teapot Dome scandal, in 1959.

30

Calvin Coolidge (1923–1929)

After the Harding scandals, Calvin Coolidge, like the silent man he was, presided over a quiet interval in the presidency. A New England lawyer with a natural reserve and a laconic wit that made him seem more silent than he really was, he believed the chief business of America was business.[1] To achieve prosperity in business he believed in good community behavior.

The public liked his one-liners and elected him on his own after he fulfilled the term of the deceased Harding. Coolidge had become Harding's running mate after a career in Republican Massachusetts politics as mayor of Northampton, state senator, lieutenant governor, and governor when he made a name for using the state militia to end a police strike. With the same coolness he handled the Harding scandals so that the corruption charges clung to individuals, not to the Republican Party.

While journalists such as the wordsmith H.L. Mencken observed that Coolidge's ideal day was "one on which nothing whatever happens,"[2] Coolidge opposed the Immigration Act of 1924 that banned Japanese whom he aided after the Yokohama earthquake and typhoon. He also strove to improve South American relations by sympathetic emissaries and supported the Dawes Plan that loaned Germany $2.5 billion for its reparations debt to the Allies.

Calvin Coolidge. (Courtesy of Library of Congress.)

THE FILMS

There is only one film involving Calvin Coolidge. Appropriately, it depicts him as taciturn, to-the-point, and stringent in upholding the honor of the country. Coolidge took particular interest in movies that had become the nation's fourth-largest business enterprise with a capital investment of more than $1.5 billion during his administration. However, he was more a 19th century man than 20th.

The Court-Martial of Billy Mitchell (1955)

Coolidge: Ian Wolfe. *Other Cast:* Gary Cooper (Col. Billy Mitchell), Charles Bickford (Gen. Guthrie), Ralph Bellamy (Congressman Frank Reid), Fred Clark (Col. Moreland), Rod Steiger (Maj. Allan Gullion), Jack Lord (Cmdr. Zach Lansdowne), Elizabeth Montgomery (Margaret Lansdowne), Dayton Lummis (Gen. Douglas MacArthur), Tom McKee (Capt. Eddie Rickenbacker), Steve Roberts (Maj. Carl Spaatz), Herbert Heyes (Gen. John J. Pershing), Robert Brubaker (Maj. H.H. Arnold), Phil Arnold (Fiorello LaGuardia), Will Wright (Adm. William S. Sims). *Director:* Otto Preminger. *Producer:* Milton Sperling. *Writing Credits:* Ben Hecht, Emmett Lavery, Milton Sperling, Dalton Trumbo, Michael Wilson. *Music:* Dimitri Tiomkin. *Cinematography:* Sam Leavitt. *Film Editing:* Folmar Blangsted. *Art Direction:* Malcolm Bert. *Set Decoration:* William Kuehl. *Costume Design:* Howard Shoup. *Makeup:* Gordon Bau. *Studio:* Warner Bros. *Length:* 100 minutes.

Director Otto Preminger's courtroom drama *The Court-Martial of Billy Mitchell* is gripping and far-reaching in its importance. Followers of this sub-genre of films will find many characteristics of the courtroom drama: the wily bullying prosecutor; the struggling defense lawyer; the battle of will and words between lawyers presided over by an unbending tribunal; and the evidence that might save the case.

The case is Hollywood's story of Brigadier General Billy Mitchell (Gary Cooper) who wants to strengthen and modernize the Army Air Force. Producer Milton Sperling demurred from changing his Zanuck-inspired story when told by the head of research for Warner Brothers that the actual events of Mitchell's life "were *so* dramatic, that it would be difficult indeed to improve on the drama through fictionalization."[3]

After the needless death of a young friend who followed orders to fly a decrepit dirigible, Mitchell calls a press conference. In a few words he calls this accident a "direct result of the almost treasonable attitude of the military." As he knows will be the case, he is court-martialed by a military establishment rooted in the past and mindless of the future possibilities of flight.

Mitchell calls on his friend Congressman Frank Reid (Ralph Bellamy) to defend him. That he ably and nobly does, bringing the widow (Elizabeth Montgomery in her screen debut) to testify about the negligence that caused her husband's death. To prove the justification of Mitchell's charges against the military, Reid brings distinguished witness after distinguished witness, from Capt. Eddie Rickenbacker (Tom McKee) to Fiorello La Guardia (Phil Arnold).

Finally Mitchell takes the stand against the expert prosecuting attorney, Maj. Allan Gullion (Rod Steiger). Gullion's menacing accusations include calling Mitchell a madman, making Mitchell's stoic and simple defense seem even more heroic. Mitchell knows that his proof of military incompetence and negligence cannot outweigh his insubordination. Gen. John J. Pershing (Herbert Heyes) defines Mitchell's position well: "There is no progress without discipline." So Mitchell is found guilty except by Gen. Douglas MacArthur (Dayton Lummis), suspended from his rank, command, duty, and salary. Of course, he was right as he had forecast: The Japanese did bomb Pearl Harbor. He was the good soldier fighting for a higher cause.

As commander-in-chief of the Armed Forces, President Calvin Coolidge (Ian Wolfe) was subpoenaed to testify at the court-martial of Billy Mitchell. But the president declined. Later, when press and public opinion rises in support of Mitchell, the chief prosecuting officer of the court-martial, Col. Moreland (Fred Clark), goes to the president to assert that the army "will not be on the defensive." Sitting straight in his office chair behind his imposing desk, Coolidge states that "the prestige of the armed forces is affected all over the world" by this case. He closes his brief statement by announcing that he wants "this over as soon as possible." The part is well played by Wolfe, upholding Coolidge's public reserve and caution.

31

Herbert Hoover (1929-1933)

Herbert Hoover. (Courtesy of Library of Congress.)

The case for or against the presidency of Herbert Hoover now rests mainly on his inflexible character and personality in a difficult time. While acclaimed as a brilliant engineer, master organizer, and supreme economist in his admittedly overblown campaign material, these virtues that made him a multi-millionaire as an engineer and an acclaimed organizer of food relief after World War I ironically did not serve him during the Depression he inherited seven months into his administration. Yet, he was no "fat Coolidge" as H.L. Mencken described him.[1]

After his international efforts in food relief, Stanford engineer graduate Hoover served Harding and Coolidge as Secretary of Commerce, reviving the moribund department. To combat the Depression in his presidential role he cut already low taxes (to no avail), conferred with business leaders to uphold wages and production levels, and advocated a one-year moratorium on international World War I debt payments (too late to save Germany's economy). His recent biographer Craig Lloyd says Hoover failed because he was "unsuited for the times—his distaste for public exposure, his inability to dramatize his leadership, his dogmatic individualism and antistatism, his sensitivity to criticism...."[2]

Rejecting public works for fear of budget deficits and federal relief as undermining self-government and rugged individualism, Hoover emphasized volunteerism as a means for economic recovery, as did his engineer wife Lou. Then involved with the Girl Scouts, she had been his helpmate since their 1912 translation of Georgius Agricola's 1556 *De re metallica*, the standard European text on salt making.[3] Change and experiments were ignored for creation of the Reconstruction Finance Corporation for business—an act, along with Hoover's use of the military against the Bonus March of veterans for immediate payment that contributed to his reelection defeat. His innate courage, integrity, and humanitarian service were rewarded by President Truman who restored him to respectability by asking him to repeat his World War I success in feeding the hungry after World War II.[4]

THE FILMS

In this one film Hoover shows his humanity.

Angel of Pennsylvania Avenue (1996)

Hoover: Thomas Peacocke. *Other Cast:* Robert Urich (Angus Feagan), Diana Scarwid (Mrs. Annie Feagan), Tegan Moss (Bernice), Margaret (Camille Mitchell), Jack (Alexander Pollock). *Director:* Robert Ellis Miller. *Producers:* Craig Anderson, Rider McDowell, Tom Rowe, Lisa Towers. *Writing Credits:* Rider McDowell, Michael De Guzman. *Music:* Simon Kendall, Al Rodger. *Cinematography:* David Geddes. *Film Editing:* Robert K. Lambert. *Production Design:* David Fischer. *Art Direction:* Nancy Ford. *Set Decoration:* Cynthia T. Lewis. *Costume Design:* Susan De Laval. *Length:* 93 minutes.

In a Depression-era story that appears to be made for TV, unemployed electrician Angus Feagan (Robert Urich) leaves his family in Detroit just before Christmas to try to find a job in Kansas City. Since this is a family film his three children are adorable and his wife is strong and determined. Feagan runs into trouble in Kansas City and is jailed for a crime he didn't commit.

There is considerable discussion in the Detroit area about the problems that President Hoover is having coping with the Depression. In a radio address the president repeats two of his most quoted lines: "a chicken in every pot" and "prosperity is just around the corner." Although Feagan's eldest daughter Bernice (Tegan Moss) hears many complaints about Hoover, her mother Annie (Diana Scarwid) tells her that he is "the most powerful man in the world." Since nothing seems to help her father, Bernice decides to go to Washington, D.C., to ask for Hoover's help. Without telling her mother and letting the other two children, Margaret (Camille Mitchell) and Jack (Alexander Pollock), go with her, she sets out for the capital. In a parallel plot, Annie goes to find them.

Most of the film covers the adventures the children have on their trip including meeting a puppeteer who happens to have a Hoover puppet. Naturally, they finally get to meet with Hoover (Thomas Peacocke) who, in a variation on the Lincoln clemency theme, promises to help their father. Dad returns to his family—in church—just in time for Christmas.

Peacocke does not look like Hoover but plays the role with sincerity and seriousness. When first seen in the White House (the interior of which bears a striking resemblance to a hotel), Hoover is shooting billiards and smoking a cigar. His advisers are telling him "to loosen up with the public" and "to pay attention to appearances." Because of this previous discussion, it is ambiguous as to whether Hoover acts out of compassion for the family or to meet the suggestions of his advisors, but he certainly appears to be sincere as portrayed by Peacocke. In the final shot he looks out a White House window at the snow that reminds him of his childhood.

32

Franklin D. Roosevelt (1933–1945)

Franklin D. Roosevelt. (Courtesy of Library of Congress.)

To millions of Americans alive today, Franklin Delano Roosevelt was *the* president, the man who led the U.S. out of the Great Depression and steered it through World War II in four unprecedented terms during 12 of the most fateful years in the country's history. Wealthy and socially privileged, "he was brought up," said an aunt, "in a beautiful frame."[1] Paradoxically, he appealed to the common man as he did to the cynical press through his jauntiness, cockiness, and self-confidence.[2] He was superbly confident that he was the best political strategist in American history.[3]

Accompanying him throughout was his wife Eleanor with whom he had one daughter and four sons. Eleanor was as much an innovator in her role as he, especially for civil and social rights, despite her knowledge since 1918 of his liaison with Lucy Mercer, the household social secretary. It was Eleanor—not his possessive mother Sara—who urged him to continue in politics after he contracted infantile paralysis in 1921. FDR had been elected twice to the New York State Senate, then served as Assistant Secretary of the Navy to Woodrow Wilson, and in 1928 was elected to his first of two terms as governor of New York State. As governor, FDR initiated at the state level what he later became famous for at the national level: New Deal programs and fireside chats.

As president, FDR introduced a New Deal system of governmental programs to fight the Great Depression. He revitalized the Democratic Party, realigned the electorate, and transformed the role of the federal government and the presidency itself. During his first "Hundred Days," Congress passed 15 major bills addressing the banking crisis, repealing prohibition, creating substantial relief and public works programs, establishing recovery programs for agriculture and industry, and promoting the people's faith in government. A second series of New Deal legislation following the midterm election included work and entitlement programs and support for labor. His most enduring program was the Social Security Act.

FDR did falter with his "court-packing" campaign to increase the number of Supreme Court justices to counter the conservative majority. Through retirements FDR ironically got his majority, but the "court packing" campaign ended his dominance of Congress. World War II eventually returned national and party support, and FDR again dominated in shaping U.S. war strategy as well as postwar world order, notably in the establishment of the United Nations, an act that shows him as the heir to Wilson. He died in office, leaving his Vice President Harry S Truman to deal with ending the war—and dropping the atomic bomb.

THE FILMS

Among other initiatives, FDR was the first president to give the film industry precise instructions to develop a cinema that would glorify law and American values.[4] He made a direct appeal to Frank Capra to bring life to the production of patriotic films in the "Why We Fight" series and others he supervised.[5] He also appeared in newsreel after newsreel and in many short features. Shortly after his first election Edwin C. Hill narrated *The Fighting President*, a 65-minute film compiled from newsreels covering the major incidents in FDR's life. One *Pete Smith Special*, "Fala at Hyde Park," shows the president's pet on a daily round at the Hudson River estate of the Roosevelts. With a voice-over by Smith, the film includes two shots of FDR greeting his dog as he arrives by car at Hyde Park.

In most of the 22 films in which Roosevelt was portrayed, he has minor roles. The most comprehensive film depicts his fight with polio early in his political life, *Sunrise at Campobello*.

The Man Who Dared (1933)

Roosevelt: Unnamed actor. *Other Cast:* Preston Foster (Jan Novak), Zita Johann (Teena Pavelic), Joan Marsh (Joan), Iren Biller (Tereza Novak), Phillip Trent (Dick), June Lang (Barbara), Leon Ames (Yosef Novak), Douglas Cosgrove (Dan Foley), Douglass Dumbrille (Judge Collier), Frank Sheridan (Sen. "Honest John" McGuiness), Leonid Snegoff (Posilipo), Matt McHugh (Karel), Jay Ward (Jan as a Boy). *Director:* Hamilton MacFadden. *Producer:* Sol M. Wurtzel. *Writing Credits:* Dudley Nichols, Lamar Trotti. *Cinematography:* Arthur C. Miller. *Film Editing:* Alfred DeGaetano. *Costume Design:* Royer. *Studio:* Fox Film Corp. *Length:* 72 minutes.

This drama is based on the life of Anton Cermak, son of East European immigrants. Cermak rose to become mayor of Chicago; an anarchist killed him accidentally while trying to kill president-elect Roosevelt. Other evidence indicates that anarchist Giuseppe Zangara deliberately killed Mafioso member Cermak but faked the FDR attempt to avoid reprisal against the Mob by the government. Well-known writers Dudley Nichols and Lamar Trotti do not deal with this. Instead Cermak is Jan Novak (Preston Foster), whose career is followed and ends with his traveling to Miami to invite Roosevelt to the Chicago World's Fair. As he is dying, Novak tells Roosevelt that he is glad it was he, not the leader of his country, who was shot.

Cash and Carry (1937)

Roosevelt: Al Richardson. *Other Cast:* Curly Howard (Curly), Larry Fine (Larry), Moe Howard (Moe), Sonny Bupp (Jimmie), Nick Copeland, Lew Davis (Con Men), Harlene Wood (Jimmie's Sister). *Director:* Del Lord. *Producer:* Jules White. *Writing Credits:* Clyde

Bruckman, Elwood Ullman. *Cinematography:* Lucien Ballard. *Film Editing:* Charles Nelson. *Studio:* Columbia Pictures. *Length:* 18 minutes.

A Three Stooges short with a presidential appearance is impossible to ignore. Larry (Larry Fine), Moe (Moe Howard), and Curly (Curly Howard) attempt to help a crippled orphan, Jimmie (Sonny Bupp), and his sister (Harlene Wood). Jimmie needs $500 for an operation on his disabled leg.

After their typical trail of silly misfortunes including being taken in by con men, the comics accidentally break into a U.S. Treasury vault and are arrested. Their story reaches President Roosevelt (Al Richardson) who not only gives Moe, Larry, and Curly clemency but says that Jimmie will have his operation, paid by the president himself.

Richardson has his back to the camera and appears considerably smaller than FDR. However, he gives a reasonably good representation of Roosevelt's voice and gestures.

The Reluctant Dragon (1941)

Roosevelt: Art Gilmore, voice. *Other Cast:* Robert Benchley (Himself), Frances Gifford (Doris), Buddy Pepper (Buddy), Nana Bryant (Mrs. Benchley), Claud Allister (Sir Giles), Barnett Parker (The Dragon), Alan Ladd (Animator). *Directors:* Ford Beebe, Jasper Blystone. *Writing Credits:* Robert Benchley, Erdman Penner, T. Hee, Joe Grant, Dick Huemur, John P. Miller. *Music:* Frank Churchill, Larry Morey, Charles Wolcott. *Cinematography:* Bert Glennon, Winton C. Hoch. *Film Editing:* Earl Rettig, Paul Weatherwax. *Art Direction:* Ken Anderson, Hugh Hennesy, Charles Philippi, Gordon Wiles. *Set Decoration:* Earl Wooden. *Sound:* Frank Maher. *Studio:* Walt Disney Pictures. *Length:* 72 minutes.

Robert Benchley leads the audience on an extended tour of the Walt Disney Studios that includes screening of two cartoons, *The Reluctant Dragon* and *Baby Weems*. This last segment has an appearance of a FDR character whose voice is supplied by Art Gilmore.

March On, America! (1942)

Roosevelt: Unnamed actor.
Roosevelt's voice is heard in this film about the story of America. For details, see Chapter 6 on John Quincy Adams.

Yankee Doodle Dandy (1942)

Roosevelt: Jack Young and Art Gilmore (voice). *Other Cast:* James Cagney (George M. Cohan), Joan Leslie (Mary), Walter Huston (Jerry Cohan), Richard Whorf (Sam Harris), Irene Manning (Fay Templeton), George Tobias (Dietz), Rosemary DeCamp (Nellie Cohan), Jeanne Cagney (Josie Cohan), Frances Langford (Singer), George Barbier (Erlanger), S.Z. Sakall (Schwab), Walter Catlett (Manager), Douglas Croft (George M. Cohan at 13), Eddie Foy Jr. (Eddie Foy), Minor Watson (Albee), Chester Clute (Guff), Odette Myrtil (Madame Bartholdi), Patsy Lee Parsons (Josie Cohan at 12). *Director:* Michael Curtiz. *Producers:* Hal B. Wallis and Jack L. Warner. *Writing Credits:* Robert Buckner, Edmund Joseph. *Music:* George M. Cohan, Ray Heindorf, Heinz Roemheld. *Cinematography:* James Wong Howe. *Film Editing:* George Amy. *Art Direction:* Carl Jules Weyl. *Costume Design:* Milo Anderson. *Makeup:* Perc Westmore. *Studio:* Warner Bros. *Length:* 126 minutes.

Probably the greatest biopic in an era of numerous biopics is *Yankee Doodle Dandy*. The portrayal of George M. Cohan, the early 20th century song-and-dance man, by James Cagney is outstanding and resulted in Cagney's receiving a Best Actor Oscar for his performance. The biographical vignettes are presented in flashbacks that are bookended at the beginning and ending of the film in an upstairs office at the White House with excerpts from the actual two-hour visit between Cohan and President Roosevelt.

The purported reason for Cohan's visit to Washington is an invitation from FDR that Cohan receives after portraying the president in the Broadway musical *I'd Rather Be Right*. Since the musical (with segments shown on screen) both parodies and extols FDR, Cohan was concerned that he was being invited to the White House to receive a dressing-down from the president. As it turns out, Cohan has been invited in order to receive from the president a Congressional Medal of Honor (the first for an entertainer) for his lifelong patriotism and the writing of the stirring songs, "Over There" and "You're a Grand Old Flag."

The portrayal of FDR was obviously a problem because he was continually visible to the public in the news in the early days of World War II, the days of the filming of *Yankee Doodle Dandy*. Captain Jack Young was chosen but is only seen in profile in a darkened Oval Office. Although Young looked like Roosevelt, at least in profile, he did not sound like him and the president's voice is provided by Art Gilmore. FDR has the usual FDR charm, telling Cohan, "You Irish-Americans carry your flag" and "Your songs were a symbol of the American spirit."

Although accurate in period detail, the film is not noted for its biographical accuracy. Cohan's life is sugar-coated, including the fact that he never happily married anyone named Mary (who combines the positive attributes of his two wives) as he does on screen. Joan Leslie, a trooper at 17, embodies this role. Nor does the film depict his stinginess and disdain for fellow actors. His acceptance of the Congressional Medal of Honor in a tear-inducing private ceremony with FDR is also a bit misleading. Congress voted for the award in 1936 to honor Cohan for his work in World War I. He thought so little of it that he waited until 1940 to pick it up. At least part of the reason for the delay was Cohan's well-known contempt for FDR (although Cohan was a life-long Democrat) mainly because of the serious differences of opinion concerning unionism that FDR supported. Cohan strongly opposed Actor's Equity.

The overall portrayal of President Roosevelt is completely in character—the great man behaving as the great host to his fellow American. However, Cagney's sprightly dancing as FDR in *I'd Rather Be Right* seems ironical since the crippled president remained confined to a wheelchair. The dancing, choreographed by Jack Boyle, is in Cohan's stiff-legged style, rather than Cagney's usual loose-limbed technique. But there's nothing stiff about this flag-waving musical that grossed $5 million and won Oscars for Ray Heindorf and Heinz Roemheld, who wrote the music not by Cohan himself.

Mission to Moscow (1943)

Roosevelt: Jack Young. *Other Cast:* Walter Huston (Ambassador Joseph E. Davies), Ann Harding (Marjorie Davies), Oskar Hook (Maxim Litvinov), George Tobias (Freddie), Gene Lockhart (Vyacheslav Molotov), Eleanor Parker (Emlen Davies), Richard Travis (Paul Grosjean), Helmut Dantine (Maj. Kamenev), Victor Francen (Vyshinsky), Henry Daniell (Minister Joachim von Ribbentrop), Barbara Everest (Mrs. Ivy Litvinov), Dudley Field Malone

(Prime Minister Winston Churchill), Roman Bohnen (Krestinsky), Maria Palmer (Tanya Litvinov), Moroni Olsen (Col. Faymonville), Minor Watson (Loy Henderson), Vladimir Sokoloff (Michail Kalinin), Maurice Schwartz (Dr. Botkin). *Director*: Michael Curtiz. *Producer*: Robert Buckner. *Writing Credits*: Joseph E. Davies, Howard Koch. *Music*: Max Steiner. *Cinematography*: Bert Glennon. *Film Editing*: Owen Marks. *Production Design*: Carl Jules Weyl. *Studio*: Warner Brothers. *Length*: 123 minutes.

Prior to the development of the Cold War and toward the end of World War II there was already considerable animosity toward the Soviet Union within the United States. In an attempt to reduce this animosity, President Roosevelt convinced Jack Warner of Warner Brothers to produce a decidedly propagandistic film concerning the Communist state. The book *Mission to Moscow* was written by Ambassador Joseph E. Davies and became the basis for this propaganda film introduced by Davies and directed by Michael Curtiz, whose importance as a studio director signals the importance of the film.

The story concerns Davies's (Walter Huston) assignment as ambassador to Moscow in the late 1930s. As enacted, Davies displays appalling naiveté as a new ambassador, even in a propaganda film. For example, he refuses to worry that the embassy might have been "bugged" by the Soviets (which it was). He says his "purpose is to see everything with an open mind" and everything he sees is beautiful, wonderful, and taken as true without question. Supported by a strong international cast including Ann Harding as Mrs. Davies, Eleanor Parker as daughter Emlen Davies, Gene Lockhart as Molotov, and Oscar Homolka as Litvinov, Davies reports on the intrigues leading up to World War II. One suspects that an intelligent audience watching the film when it was released in 1943 would immediately see it for what it was and would worry about the quality of FDR's choice of ambassadors. If not, the final scene with people walking to a backlit city on a hill to Davies's exhortation about "making an end to wars forever" certainly challenges some credibility.

Jack Young portrays Roosevelt in a short scene at the beginning of the film giving Davies his "blessing" as ambassador and saying he was going to ask Congress to extend lend lease aid to Russia. As was the case of his role in *Yankee Doodle Dandy*, he is filmed only from the rear probably because he does not really resemble the president. However, his voice is very good in this film and the general demeanor is that of FDR.

This Is the Army (1943)

Roosevelt: Jack Young. *Other Cast*: George Murphy (Jerry Jones), Joan Leslie (Eileen Dibble), George Tobias (Maxie Twardofsky), Alan Hale (Sgt. McGee), Charles Butterworth (Eddie Dibble), Dolores Costello (Mrs. Davidson), Una Merkel (Rose Dibble), Stanley Ridges (Maj. Davidson), Rosemary DeCamp (Ethel), Ruth Donnelly (Mrs. O'Brien), Dorothy Peterson (Mrs. Nelson), Frances Langford (Herself), Gertrude Niesen (Singer), Kate Smith (Herself), Ronald Reagan (Johnny Jones), Joe Louis (Himself), Ezra Stone (Sgt. Stone), Tom D'Andrea (Tommy), Irving Berlin (Himself). *Director*: Michael Curtiz. *Producers*: Hal B. Wallis, Jack L. Warner. *Writing Credits*: Irving Berlin, Casey Robinson, Claude Binyon. *Music*: Irving Berlin. *Cinematography*: Bert Glennon, Sol Polito. *Film Editing*: George Amy. *Art Direction*: John Hughes, John Koenig. *Set Decoration*: George James Hopkins. *Costume Design*: Orry-Kelly. *Makeup*: Perc Westmore. *Studio*: Warner Bros. *Length*: 121 minutes.

This is an unusual film in that it consists mainly of a Broadway musical, *This Is the Army*, and it features a one-shot appearance of FDR, the 32nd president, and a featured role for Ronald Reagan, the 40th president. The musical is Irving Berlin's World War II hit, a reworking of his World War I "barracks musical," *Yip Yip Yaphank*. The jingoistic film is directed by Michael Curtiz, the year after he directed *Yankee Doodle Dandy* and *Casablanca* for which he won an Academy Award. A Warner Brothers studio director with credits for more than a hundred films, Curtiz so employs his creativity it outdoes his technical skill. For *This Is the Army* Curtiz frames the musical with a sentimental love story.

The story centers on Jerry Jones's (George Murphy) directing and dancing in the World War I musical and enlisting many servicemen from that show to appear in the World War II extravaganza. Because Jones has been wounded he can't perform, but he directs with his son's help. The son, Johnny Jones (Ronald Reagan), political colleague and nine years Murphy's junior, shows his dedication to military duty by postponing marrying Eileen Dibble (Joan Leslie). Reagan's celebrated geniality dominates his romantic role.

Besides Reagan, the cast includes Kate Smith, Joe Louis, and Irving Berlin as well as the many servicemen performers from the only integrated Army company. Nevertheless, there are no integrated numbers in the review format of the musical, and there is one blackface and three drag numbers. All proceeds from the film went to the Army Emergency Relief Fund

Jack Young plays the part of President Roosevelt who attends the final performance of the cross-country tour of *This Is the Army*. Although his presence generates great excitement among the cast and a stirring rendition of "Hail to the Chief," Roosevelt only appears as he enters his box seat. Young makes a believable FDR.

Up in Arms (1944)

Roosevelt: Jack Young, voice. *Other Cast:* Danny Kaye (Danny Weems), Dinah Shore (Nurse Lt. Virginia Merrill), Dana Andrews (Joe Nelson), Constance Dowling (Mary Morgan), Louis Calhern (Col. Ashley), The Goldwyn Girls. *Director:* Elliott Nugent. *Writing Credits:* Owen Davis, Don Hartman. *Producer:* Samuel Goldwyn. *Music:* Sylvia Fine, Max Liebman, Howard Jackson, Max Steiner. *Non-Original Music:* Harold Arlen. *Cinematography:* Ray Rennahan. *Film Editing:* Daniel Mandell, James Newcom. *Art Direction:* Stewart Chaney, Perry Ferguson. *Set Decoration:* Howard Bristol. *Costume Design:* Miles White. *Makeup:* Nina Roberts, Robert Stephanoff. *Special Effects:* R.O. Binger. *Studio:* Samuel Goldwyn Co. *Length:* 106 minutes.

Hypochondriac Danny Weems (Danny Kaye) gets drafted into the army and survives a number of unlikely comic incidents before capturing a Japanese regiment and becoming a hero on a South Sea island. Jack Young as the convincing voice of President Roosevelt congratulates the hero.

Weems is on the island with his girl friend, Mary Morgan (Constance Dowling), who has stowed away on his transport ship; Virginia Merrill (Dinah Shore) who's in love with Weems; and Nelson (Dana Andrews) who's in love with Morgan.

This action provides the reason for Kaye to sing a number of songs including the rapid patter "Theater Lobby Number" and "Melody in 4-F" written by his wife Sylvia Fine (and Max Liebman). The Goldwyn Girls, including Virginia Mayo, Kaye's future co-star, also appear. This is a remake of Eddie Cantor's *Whoopee*.

The Beginning or the End (1947)

Roosevelt: Godfrey Tearle. *Other Cast:* Brian Donlevy (Maj. Gen. Leslie R. Groves), Robert Walker (Col. Jeff Nixon), Tom Drake (Matt Cochran), Beverly Tyler (Anne Cochran),

Audrey Totter (Jean O'Leary), Hume Cronyn (Dr. J. Robert Oppenheimer), Hurd Hatfield (Dr. John Wyatt), Joseph Calleia (Dr. Enrico Fermi), Victor Francen (Dr. Marre), Richard Haydn (Dr. Chisholm), Jonathan Hale (Dr. Vannevar Bush), John Litel (K.T. Keller), Henry O'Neill (Gen. Thomas F. Farrell), Warner Anderson (Capt. William S. Parsons), Barry Nelson (Col. Paul Tibbetts Jr.), Art Baker (President Harry S Truman), Ludwig Stossel (Dr. Albert Einstein), John Hamilton (Dr. Harold C. Urey), Frank Ferguson (Dr. James B. Conant), Tom Stevenson (Dr. E. P. Winger), John Gallaudet (Dr. Leo Szilard). *Director*: Norman Taurog. *Producer*: Samuel Marx. *Writing Credits*: Robert Considine, Frank Wead. *Music*: Daniele Amfitheatrof. *Cinematography*: Ray June. *Film Editing*: George Boemler. *Art Direction*: Cedric Gibbons, Hans Peters. *Set Decoration*: Keogh Gleason, Edwin B. Willis. *Costume Design*: Irene. *Makeup*: Jack Dawn. *Sound*: Douglas Shearer. *Special Effects*: A. Arnold Gillespie, Donald Jahrus, Warren Newcombe. *Studio*: MGM. *Length*: 112 minutes.

Although there is a meaningless romance added for interest, this film directed by Norman Taurog, relates in a more or less factual manner the development of the atomic bomb. The romance enables writer Robert Considine to raise the moral questions related to the creation of such a destructive weapon.

Starting with pre–World War II research into the energy potential of the atom by mainly university scientists, Albert Einstein (Ludwig Stossel) is convinced to approach President Roosevelt (Godfrey Tearle) concerning the potential of atom-splitting as a military weapon. Roosevelt agrees to finance such a research effort and the principals in the development of the atomic bomb are put to work: Enrico Fermi (Joseph Calleia), General Groves (Brian Donlevy), Harold Urey (John Hamilton), James B. Conant (Frank Ferguson), etc. Using all of these scientists and military men who were actually involved in the Manhattan Project at both Oak Ridge, Tennessee, and Los Alamos, New Mexico, the film takes on realism necessary for believability, particularly since the film was made shortly after the actual events.

After the death of Roosevelt, President Truman (Art Baker) continues support for the project and authorizes the use of the bomb at Hiroshima and Nagasaki in a successful attempt to shorten the war in the Pacific. To satisfy the storyline implied in the title of the film, one of the characters involved in the fictional romance, Matt Cochran (Tom Drake), is exposed to radioactivity and dies. Thus we have the "beginning" of the Atomic Age with its impact in ending the Pacific War and the "end" with its impact on human life.

Padeniye Berlina (1-r seria) (1949) aka *The Battle of Berlin*

Roosevelt: Oleg Frelikh. *Other Cast*: Mikheil Gelovani (Marshal Iosef Stalin), Boris Andreyev (Alexei Vane), M. Kovalyova (Natasha Vasilnyeva), V. Savelyev (Adolf Hitler), G. Timoshenko (Kostya Zavchenko), A. Urrasalyev (Yusupov), Nikolai Bogolyubov (Factory Superintendent Kumchinsky), Y. Verikh (Hermann Goering), S. Giatsintova (Mother Vane), K. Roden (Charles Bedston), Viktor Stanitsyn (Prime Minister Winston Churchill), M. Novakova (Eva Braun). *Director-Screenwriter*: Mikheil Chiaureli. *Writing Credits*: Pyotr Pavlenko. *Music*: Dmitri Shostakovich. *Cinematography*: Leonid Kosmatov. *Film Editing*: T. Likhachyova. *Production Design*: Vladimir Kaplunovsky, Aleksei Parkhomenko. *Sound*: Boris Volsky. *Studio*: Mosfilm. *Length*: 124 minutes.

Although the Library of Congress copy runs only 40 of this film's 124 minutes, it contains the propaganda the Soviets wanted to convey about their urgency to take embattled

Berlin during World War II. Filmed on a grand scale with stirring original music by Dmitri Shostakovich, the film, under director-screenwriter Mikheil Chiaureli, always pictures Stalin (Mikheil Gelovani) as a methodical martinet with a will of iron.

In a flashback scene of the Yalta Conference, Stalin asserts his position on Berlin and confronts those of his allies. FDR (Oleg Frelikh) says, "Eisenhower considers activation impossible." Churchill (Viktor Stanitsyn) says he doesn't like "haste or force. If we all enter together, it would be splendid propaganda for the United Nations." Both of the Russian actors in this all-Russian cast bear strong resemblances to their real-life counterparts.

Stalingradskaya bitva I, II (1949) / The Battle of Stalingrad, Part I and II (1950)

Roosevelt: Nikolai Cherkasov. *Other Cast:* Mikhail Astangov (Adolf Hitler), Aleksei Dikij (Josef Stalin), Vladimir Gajdarov (Gen. Von Paulus), M. Garkavij (Hermann Goering), N. Kolenikov (Col. Gen. Yeremenko), Nikolai Komissarov (Field Marshal Wilhelm Keitel), Boris Livanov (Lt. Gen Rokossovsky), Vasili Merkuryev (Col. Gen. Voronov), K. Mikhajlove (Ambassador W. Averill Harriman), Yuri Shumsky (Col. Gen. Vasilyevsy), Nikolai Simonov (Lt. Gen. Churkov), Viktor Stanitsyn (Winston Churchill). *Director:* Vladimir Petrov. *Writing Credits:* Nikolai Virta. *Music:* Aram Khachaturyan. *Cinematography:* Yuri Yekelchik. *Art Direction:* Leonide Mamaladze. *Costume Design:* Vasili Kovrigin. *Makeup:* Anton Andhra. *Sound:* Valeri Popov. *Studio:* Gosudarstvenii Komitet po Kinematografii. *Length:* 81 minutes.

Vladimir Petrov's two-part presentation of *The Battle of Stalingrad* is generally seen as a continuation of the Soviet propaganda effort and the extolling of Stalin. With these two goals in mind the other historical characters including Roosevelt (Nikolai Cherkasov, one of the preeminent Russian actors in the first half of the 20th century) were written to fit the party line. The subtitles so inform: "The First Front," "The Victors," and "The Vanquished." Stalin is the hero so the actual military leader of the battle, Marshal Zhukov, is not even mentioned in this film as his fame had increased to Stalin's displeasure. But the First Front Generals Vasiliyevsy, Voronov, Rokossovsky, Yeremenko, and Churkov appear.

To the credit of Petrov he was able to obtain the services of Aram Khatchaturyan to create a moving score for the films.

Beau James (1957)

Roosevelt: Dick Nelson. *Other Cast:* Bob Hope (Mayor James J. "Jimmy" Walker), Vera Miles (Betty Compton with Imogene Lynn as singing voice), Paul Douglas (Chris Nolan), Alexis Smith (Allie Walker), Darren McGavin (Charley Hand), Joe Mantell (Bernie Williams), Horace McMahon (Prosecutor), Richard Shannon (Dick Jackson), Willis Bouchey (Arthur Julian), Sid Melton (Sid Nash), George Jessel (Himself), Walter Catlett (Gov. Alfred E. "Al" Smith), Jack Benny, Jimmy Durante, and Walter Winchell (Themselves). *Director:* Melville Shavelson, *Producer:* Jack Rose. *Writing Credits:* Gene Fowler, Jack Rose, Melville Shavelson. *Cinematography:* John F. Warren. *Film Editing:* Floyd Knudtson. *Art Direction:* John B. Goodman, Hal Pereira. *Set Decoration:* Sam Comer, Frank R. McKelvy. *Costume Design:* Edith Head. *Makeup:* Wally Westmore. *Sound:* Charles Grenzbach, Hugo Grenzbach. *Special Effects:* John P. Fulton. *Studio:* Hope Enterprises/Paramount Pictures. *Length:* 105 minutes.

Faithful to Gene Fowler's biography, this biopic of James J. "Jimmy" Walker, the colorful and corrupt Mayor of New York City from 1926–32, captures the tone of the era. Bob Hope plays it straight as the Tin Pan Alley songwriter-turned-politician who campaigns by singing his own composition; "Will You Love Me in December as You Do in May?" in Yiddish, Polish, and Italian. True to his and Walker's nature, he makes many humorous asides from asking the cat as he pours himself a drink, "What do you want, milk on the rocks?" to his reaction to the initial crowd's booing him at Yankee Stadium, "Maybe they think I'm going to umpire." Still, he wins and wins, but is summoned by the investigatory Seabury Committee and Gov. Roosevelt about his acceptance of stocks and bonds from political associates. Although he proclaims himself guilty of stupidity, he is denounced for causing a split in the Democrat Party vote that may damage Roosevelt's chances in the presidential election. When Walker realizes he lost his constituents' support, he resigns at a Yankee baseball game.

Alexis Smith appears as his faithful wife and Vera Miles as his most faithful love interest. Several celebrities appear as themselves. FDR is first seen in brief archival footage of his acceptance speech for the New York gubernatorial nomination. Later, Dick Nelson, back to camera with an approximation of Roosevelt's patrician accent, authoritatively presides over Walker's investigation during which Walker pleads his case.

Sunrise at Campobello (1960)

Roosevelt: Ralph Bellamy. *Other Cast:* Greer Garson (Eleanor Roosevelt), Hume Cronyn (Louis McHenry Howe), Jean Hagen (Missy Le Hand), Ann Shoemaker (Sara Delano Roosevelt), Alan Bunce (Gov. Alfred E. Smith), Tim Considine (James Roosevelt), Zina Bethune (Anna Roosevelt/Sis), Frank Ferguson (Dr. Bennett), Pat Close (Elliott Roosevelt), Robin Warga (Franklin Roosevelt Jr.), Tom Carty (Johnny Roosevelt), Lyle Talbot (Mr. Brimmer), Walter Sande (Capt. Skinner), Janine Grandel (Marie the Housekeeper), Otis Greene (Edward the House Butler), Ivan Browning (Charles the Butler), Al McGranary (Sen. Walsh), Herbert Anderson (Daly), Jerry Crews (Speaker). *Director:* Vincent J. Donehue. *Producer-Writing Credits:* Dore Schary. *Music:* Franz Waxman. *Cinematography:* Russell Harlan. *Film Editing:* George Boemler. *Production Design:* Edward Carrere. *Set Decoration:* George James Hopkins. *Costume Design:* Marjorie Best. *Studio:* Warner Bros. *Length:* 144 minutes.

Franklin D. Roosevelt contracted infantile paralysis (polio) in the summer of 1921 while he was vacationing with his family at the Roosevelt summer home on Campobello Island, New Brunswick, Canada. At the age of 40 he was already an important figure in Democrat Party politics having been the Navy's assistant secretary under Wilson and a candidate for vice president of the United States in 1920. This film, based on a Tony Award–winning play by Dore Schary, who wrote the script, depicts FDR's struggle to recover from this crippling disease and return to his prior personal and political life. As his alter ego Louis McHenry Howe (Hume Cronyn) said to him, "You can be a country squire and write books or be the president of the United States."

The opening scenes show a healthy, relaxed FDR enjoying Campobello with his large family (four sons and a daughter) and his cousin-wife Eleanor (Greer Garson) whom he affectionately calls Babs. Having established their characters, director Vincent J. Donehue turns to the onset of the disease. In a short time, FDR becomes paralyzed. Although the local doctor is uncertain at first, it is soon established that FDR has infantile paralysis, which at that time and until the 1960s was dreaded for its highly contagious nature, mortality rate, and the lifetime paralysis which normally accompanied it.

32—*Franklin D. Roosevelt (1933–1945)* 267

Sunrise at Campobello (1960): Ralph Bellamy as Franklin D. Roosevelt shows his determination to conquer all handicaps while Ann Shoemaker as Sara Delano Roosevelt (left) and Greer Garson as Eleanor Roosevelt (right) show their concern about his safety in his new wheelchair. Vincent J. Donehue directs this biopic concerning Roosevelt's struggle with polio, produced and written by Dore Schary for Warner Bros. Pictures. (Courtesy of George Eastman House.)

Eleanor is shown working continuously to make her husband comfortable, assisted by Howe, FDR's friend and political advisor, when he arrives on the island. Their efforts are stymied somewhat with the arrival of Sara Roosevelt (Ann Shoemaker), FDR's "Mama"— accent on the last syllable in the French manner for this aristocratic family. Since she has raised her only child herself for years, Mama displays her propensity to want to take charge of everything and particularly to baby her Franklin. But even in the early stages of the disease, when he is sickest and in constant pain, FDR will have neither the babying nor the thought that he wouldn't return to a normal life.

After the family moves back to New York and ultimately to the Roosevelt estate at Hyde Park, much of the film centers on FDR's struggles—both physical and psychological—to accept and live within the limitations of his wheelchair-bound existence. The primary scene during this portion of the film is a major confrontation between FDR and his mother. She has tried to convince him to give up his aspirations and retire "for his own good" at Hyde Park. In addition, she is highly critical of Howe for his efforts to push Franklin. "That dirty little man," she calls Howe, although she never says "Jew." FDR not only defends Howe but makes it clear to his mother that he has no intentions of rusticating in Hyde Park or giving up his lifelong ambitions supported by his recounting to her his inspiring meeting with President Cleveland when he was a child. He says he does not want to quarrel and intends to work as hard as necessary to lead as normal a life as possible. One long scene, completely silent (no background music), shows his determination as he (in the usual long shots of this film) struggles to walk alone on his crutches. After one painful attempt ending in a fall, he succeeds.

The final sequence of scenes show the extent to which FDR has been able to meet his goals. They culminate with his active return to politics in 1924 when Al Smith (Alan Bunce) is attempting to obtain the Democrat Party presidential nomination. Smith asks FDR to give his nominating speech at the convention. Even though the speech would require that he stand for 45 minutes, FDR is encouraged by both Eleanor and Howe to accept the challenge. In the final scene of the film, at a stirring party convention, FDR walks on crutches the ten feet leading to the rostrum at the convention and, upon reaching it, raises a hand and gives the conventiongoers the famous Roosevelt grin. They burst into "Happy Days Are Here Again," Smith's signature campaign song.

Ralph Bellamy gives a performance in which he looks, speaks, and acts like FDR, not the frequent mama's boy and bumbling guy-who-loses the girl as in *His Girl Friday* (1940). This excellent performance, particularly in the scenes depicting FDR with paralyzed legs, leads one to question why Bellamy was not recognized more by the critics when the film was released.

Greer Garson, in her last major screen role, is exceptional as Eleanor and more than deserved her Oscar nomination as Best Actress (beaten by Elizabeth Taylor for *BUtterfield 8*). The makeup department under Gordon Bau reportedly had a difficult time in turning Miss Garson's beauty into the plainness of Eleanor Roosevelt, and the addition of protuberant front teeth couldn't quite do the job. On the other hand, Garson's acting skill enabled her to approach Eleanor's speech cadence.

FDR's friendship with Louis Howe is central to the film's story. Cronyn captures the essence of this relationship—honest advice and cutting humor—with his extraordinary skill. A 2005 TV drama, *Warm Springs*, recounts this event with Kenneth Branagh and Cynthia Nixon as the Roosevelts.

The Pigeon That Took Rome (1962)

Roosevelt: Dick Nelson. *Other Cast*: Charlton Heston (Capt. Paul MacDougall/Benny the Snatch/Narrator), Elsa Martinelli (Antonella Massimo), Harry Guardino (Sgt. Joseph Contini), Gabriella Pallotta (Rosalba Massimo), Brian Donlevy (Col. Sherman Harrington), Arthur Shields (Monsignor O'Toole), Salvatore Baccaloni (Ciccio Massimo), Marietto (Livio Massimo), Rudolph Anders (Col. Wilhelm Krafft), Vadim Wolkowsky (Conte Danesi). *Director-Producer-Writer*: Melville Shavelson. *Music*: Alessandro Cicognini. *Cinematography*: Daniel L. Fapp. *Film Editing*: Frank Bracht. *Art Direction*: Roland Anderson, Hal Pereira. *Set Direction*: Sam Comer, Frank R. McKelvy. *Makeup*: Wally Westmore, Giancarlo De Leonardis. *Studio*: Paramount Pictures. *Length*: 103 minutes.

Charlton Heston shifts from ancient Rome *Ben-Hur* (1959) and plays Capt. Paul MacDougall, aka Benny the Snatch, in this 1962 black-and-white comedy set in modern Rome during World War II. Assisted by Sgt. Joseph Contini (Harry Guardino), MacDougall spies on the Germans prior to the Allied attack on the city. The Americans' radio creates problems so communication with headquarters is by carrier pigeon. The Italian Resistance—that aids and houses the Americans-consists of an Irish priest, Monsignor O'Toole (Arthur Shields), and an Italian family, including Ciccio Massimo (Metropolitan Opera basso Salvatore Baccaloni) and his children: Antonella (Elsa Martinelli), Rosalba (Gabriella Pallotta), and Livio (Marietto). Difficulties occur when all of the carrier pigeons except one are eaten at a family Easter celebration to announce Rosalba's engagement to Contini. Director Melville Shavelson, who also wrote the script based on Donald Downes' novel, delightfully captures the hunger of the war-starved family consuming the birds. The missing pigeons are replaced by carrier pigeons stolen from German intelligence, thus delivering messages from MacDougall directly to the enemy.

Fortunately, the final message is put on the right pigeon; the Americans capture Rome with minimal casualties; Contini marries Rosalba; and MacDougall eyes Antonella very seriously. According to the credits, there was an appearance by FDR (Dick Nelson), but the scene obviously was deleted. The only logical place for an FDR scene in this farce would be for him to be presenting a medal to the pigeon (Geronimo II) who saved Rome. The movie received an Academy Award nomination for art direction by Roland Anderson and Hal Pereira.

First to Fight (1967)

Roosevelt: Stephen Roberts. *Other Cast:* Chad Everett (Jack Connell), Marilyn Devin (Peggy Sanford), Dean Jagger (Lt. Col. Baseman), Bobby Troup (Lt. Overman), Claude Akins (Capt. Mason), Gene Hackman (Sgt. Tweed), James Best (Sgt. Carnavan), Norman Alden (Sgt. Schmidtmer), Bob Watson (Sgt. Maypole), Ken Swofford (O'Brien), Ray Reese (Hawkins), Gary Goodgion (Karl), Robert Austin (Adams), Clint Ritchie (Sgt. Slater). *Director:* Christian Nyby. *Producer:* William Conrad. *Writing Credits:* Gene L. Coon. *Music:* Fred Steiner. *Cinematography:* Harold E. Wellman. *Film Editing:* George R. Rohrs. *Art Direction:* Art Loel. *Set Decoration:* Hal Overell. *Makeup:* Gordon Bau. *Studio:* Warner Bros. *Length:* 92 minutes.

With a theme involving cowardice during battle and action scenes staged at Camp Pendleton Marine Base in Oceanside, California, Bell Ranch in the San Fernando Valley, and Africa plus clips from *Casablanca,* this drama deals realistically with World War II.

The story concerns Marine Sgt. Jack Connell (Chad Everett) who's called back to Washington, D.C., to receive the Congressional Medal of Honor for his distinguished combat in Guadalcanal. He falls in love and marries public relations woman Peggy Sanford (Marilyn Devin) with the promise not to engage in combat because she had lost a fiancé in battle. When Connell suffers guilt as a "slacker," his wife releases him from his promise. He returns to the Pacific and freezes on his first mission. Slowly he overcomes this fear and leads his men to a Japanese island stronghold.

The plot suggests that Roosevelt (Stephen Roberts) awarded Connell the medal.

Vybor tseli (1974) aka Choice of Purpose

Roosevelt: Innokenti Smoktunovsky. *Other Cast:* Sergei Bondarchuk (Kurchatov). Sergei Yursky (Oppenheimer). *Director:* Igor Talankin. *Writing Credits:* Daniil Granin, Igor Talankin. *Music:* Alfred Shnitke. *Cinematography* Naum Ardashnikov. *Production Design:* Tatyana Lapshina, Aleksandr Myagkov. *Studio:* Mosfiilm. *Length:* 158 minutes.

The cast listing for this Russian film from the middle of the Cold War includes both Roosevelt and Oppenheimer; one would surmise that it concerns work on the atomic bomb.

MacArthur (1977)

Roosevelt: Dan O'Herlihy.

Although President Roosevelt (Dan O'Herlihy) does not appear as often as President Truman in this drama of Gen. Douglas MacArthur's military life, he does have revealing encounters with the flamboyant, strong-minded military man. Short as these encounters are, they show the similarities of the two stubborn men; Roosevelt generally agrees with MacArthur's military plans. Yet these two egotists rarely condescend to another person, no matter how important. While FDR seems to agree with MacArthur, he did not in reality but left the communication of the disagreement to subordinates. O'Herlihy gives a convincing, but not altogether psychologically revealing portrait of the World War II president. For details, see Chapter 33 on Harry S Truman.

MacArthur (1977): Gregory Peck in the title role as General Douglas MacArthur and Dan O'Herlihy as President Franklin D. Roosevelt. Joseph Sargent directed this Universal production of the military life of the fabled general. (Courtesy of George Eastman House.)

The Private Files of J. Edgar Hoover (1977)

Roosevelt: Howard Da Silva. *Other Cast:* Broderick Crawford (J. Edgar Hoover), Jose Ferrer (Lionel McCoy), Michael Parks (Robert F. Kennedy), Ronee Blakley (Carrie DeWitt), Rip Torn (Dwight Webb), Celeste Holm (Florence Hollister), Michael Sacks (Melvin Purvis), Dan Dailey (Clyde Tolson), Raymond St. Jacques (Martin Luther King Jr.) Andrew Duggan (Lyndon B. Johnson), June Havoc (Hoover's Mother), James Wainwright (Young Hoover), Lloyd Nolan (Attorney General Stone), Ellen Barber (FBI Secretary), Lloyd Gough (Walter Winchell), George Plimpton (Quentin Reynolds), Jack Cassidy (Damon Runyon). *Director-Writer-Producer:* Larry Cohen. *Music:* Miklos Rozsa. *Cinematography:* Paul Glickman. *Film Editing:* Chris Lebenzon. *Production Design:* Cathy Davis. *Set Decoration:* Carol Loewenstein. *Studio:* American International Pictures. *Length:* 112 minutes.

As the director of the Federal Bureau of Investigation for 48 years, J, Edgar Hoover did enough, both good and bad, to generate both powerful friends and enemies. Writing, producing, and directing this historically limited biopic, Larry Cohen attempts to maintain a somewhat balanced view of this enigmatic figure.

Cohen presents Hoover as a young man (James Wainwright) who is a dedicated, sincere new lawyer in the Immigration Department worried about the civil rights of aliens about to be deported because of Communist activities.

Attorney General Harlan Stone (Lloyd Nolan) appoints Hoover to head the organization that was the forerunner of the FBI. This occurs in the Harding administration and highlights and lowlights of Hoover's career until his death in 1972 are shown, including his relationship with four presidents: Franklin Roosevelt, John Kennedy, Lyndon Johnson, and Richard Nixon.

FDR is portrayed by Howard Da Silva, who neither looks like Roosevelt nor, despite some effort, sounds like him. By the time Roosevelt asks Hoover (now played by Broderick Crawford) to use wiretaps on Nazi sympathizers, Hoover has turned the FBI into a highly professional organization. The use of wiretaps and bugs becomes a lifelong obsession with Hoover, and he apparently takes advantage of information obtained in this manner to put pressure on politicians as well as criminals.

Da Silva as FDR appears briefly in two scenes concerning wiretapping and incarcerating Japanese living in the U.S. Of the later, FDR says, "Edgar realizes right must yield to the necessities of war." He seems to take Hoover somewhat lightly, telling him, "Be a good soldier and stand silent." As the remainder of the film indicates, this was a mistake.

Annie (1982)

Roosevelt: Edward Hermann. *Other Cast:* Albert Finney (Daddy Warbucks), Carol Burnett (Miss Hannigan), Ann Reinking (Grace Farrell), Tim Curry (Rooster), Bernadette Peters (Lily), Aileen Quinn (Annie), Geoffrey Holder (Punjab), Roger Minami (Asp), Toni Ann Gisondi (Molly), Rosanne Sorrentino (Pepper), Lara Berk (Tessie), April Lerman (Kate), Robin Ignico (Duffy), Lucie Stewart (July), Lois De Banzie (Eleanor Roosevelt). *Director:* John Huston. *Producer:* Ray Stark. *Writing Credits:* Thomas Meehan, Carol Sobieski, Harold Gray. *Music:* Charles Strouse. *Cinematography:* Richard Moore. *Film Editing:* Michael A. Stevenson. *Production Design:* Dale Hennesy. *Set Decoration:* Marvin March. *Studio:* Columbia Pictures. *Length:* 126 minutes.

John Huston, the versatile director, screenwriter, and actor, played the part of Lincoln in a WPA production three years after his celebrated father did the role in the D.W. Griffith film *Abraham Lincoln* (1930). In directing *Annie*, the younger Huston upholds his reputation as an impulsive and unpredictable individual. *Annie* drew bad notices, for Huston's "Bigger is better approach" to playwright Thomas Meehan and screenwriter Carol Sobieski's Depression story of innocence and warmth. Nevertheless, Huston achieves convincing performances from Aileen Quinn in the title role, based on the Harold Gray cartoon strip, *Little Orphan Annie*, and Albert Finney as the cold-money-hearted Oliver "Daddy" Warbucks. The story concerns the young orphan's adventures in finding her family. Tough with tousled red hair, she befriends her fellow orphans in evading Miss Hannigan, the orphanage headmistress, played brilliantly as a drunken floozy by Carol Burnett.

Along their song-and-dance–strewn way, there are many Charles Strouse songs from the original musical except "We'd Like to Thank You Herbert Hoover" and "N.Y.C." Substituting for them are "Dumb Dog" (named for Sandy, Annie's adopted pet) and "Let's Go to the Movies," which sets up a lavish dance number, led by the talented Ann Reinking. Best known as a dancer, Reinking plays Warbucks's secretary Grace Farrell with elegant efficiency. In fact, much is elegant about this musical.

FDR behaves as the antithesis of Warbucks, the conservative billionaire businessman, in promoting his ideas of social welfare. He's mentioned twice by Warbucks before he appears. First, that FDR called Warbucks three times, saying it was urgent; then, that he'd get a lot more done if FDR "would leave me alone." When he does appear in a five-minute scene, FDR receives Annie on the White House lawn, cigarette and holder jutting out on screen left, granting the orphan her greatest wish. FDR remarks to Eleanor about the private helicopter, "Aren't Republicans ostentatious." As played by Edward Hermann, FDR is very patrician (except for the unbelievable red hair) in appearance yet populist in manner. "My pleasure, Annie," FDR says when he meets her. He then relates to the child, saying, "My uncle [Theodore Roosevelt] used to teach his children to walk on stilts, I can teach you to roll in a chair with wheels, my own private rollercoaster."

They repair to the White House where FDR tells Warbucks that he "intends to take people off the dole and put them to work ... and he was hoping you, Oliver [Warbucks], could organize it with Annie." Precocious Annie says she cheers up her poor orphan friends by singing "Tomorrow," which she then does with FDR, Eleanor, and Warbucks joining in, eventually in harmony at FDR's request. The Stuart portrait of George Washington observes the songfest. Later, in the final celebration of Annie's return to Daddy Warbucks, FDR and Eleanor join the multitudes at the extravagant lawn party, replete with circus performers and fireworks. Smiling at Warbucks and Annie's rendition of "Together at Last," FDR says she's "The Fourth of July kid."

For All: O Trampolim da Vitoria (1997) aka *For All: Springboard to Victory*

Roosevelt: Guaracy Picado. *Other Cast:* Betty Faria (Lindalva), Jose Walker (Giancarlo), Paulo Gorgulho (Joao Marreco), Caio Junqueira (Miguel), Erik Svane (Sgt. Frank Donovan). *Directors:* Buzza Ferraz, Luiz Carlos Lacerda. *Writing Credits:* Joaquim Assis, Buzza Ferraz. *Producers:* Luiz Carlos Lacerda, Bruno Stroppiana. *Cinematography:* Guy Goncalves. *Film Editing:* Ana Mariz Diniz. *Art Direction:* Alexander A. Mayer. *Costume Design:* Marilia Carneiro. *Studio:* Columbia TriStar Filmes do Brasil. *Length:* 95 minutes.

This Portuguese-language film from Brazil is based on a true event, the story of the relationships between GIs and locals when the United States set up a military base in Natal, Brazil, during World War II. It would appear to be a comedy of the "make love, not war" variety. The reason for the appearance of Franklin Roosevelt played by Brazilian actor Guaracy Picado is not known.

Pearl Harbor (2001)

Roosevelt: Jon Voight. *Other Cast:* Ben Affleck (Capt. Rafe McCawley), Josh Hartnett (Capt. Danny Walker), Kate Beckinsale (Nurse Lt. Evelyn Johnson), Cuba Gooding Jr. (Petty Officer Doris "Dorie" Miller), Alec Baldwin (Lt. Col. James "Jimmy" Doolitte), Tom Sizemore (Sgt. Earl Sistern), William Lee Scott (Lt. Billy Thompson), Greg Zola (Lt. Anthony Fusco), Ewen Bremner (Lt. Red Winkle), Jaime King (Nurse Betty Bayer), Catherin Kellner (Nurse Barbara), Jennifer Garner (Nurse Sandra), Sara Rue (Nurse Martha), Michael Shannon (Lt. Gooz Wood). *Director:* Michael Bay. *Producer:* Jerry Bruckheimer. *Writing Credits:* Randall Wallace. *Studio:* Touchstone Pictures. *Length:* 183 minutes.

Given a great deal of pre-release hype, *Pearl Harbor* was expected to be the blockbuster of 2001, Jerry Bruckheimer's big budget and special effects showpiece. Michael Bay, the director, was known for his ability to direct great action scenes and the work he did in the attack on Pearl Harbor in this film proved that he had not lost his touch. However, Randall Wallace, who wrote *Braveheart* (1995) and *The Man in the Iron Mask* (1998), was unable to provide Bay with a script that gives meaning to the action scenes. Critics almost unanimously panned what was basically a romantic soap opera that tied together two of the most dramatic events in early World War II: the attack on Pearl Harbor and the Doolittle (Alec Baldwin) Raid.

Rafe McCawley (Ben Affleck) and Danny Walker (Josh Hartnett) are lifelong friends and are serving as Army Air Corps pilots prior to the beginning of World War II. McCawley falls in love with Evelyn Johnson (Kate Beckinsale) and then goes off to defend Britain from the Nazis. Everybody thinks he died when his plane crashed in the English Channel. Now stationed in Hawaii, Walker and Johnson commiserate for a while, and then they fall in love (prompted by a clichéd scene about a dropped handkerchief). McCawley "returns from the dead," and he and Walker fight over Johnson. The Japanese attack on Pearl Harbor interrupts this string of clichés, and it takes the Japanese's killing of Walker in China after the Doolittle raid to solve the eternal triangle.

President Roosevelt (Jon Voight) is used throughout the film to illustrate Washington's involvement both before the war started and in the executive planning leading up to the Doolittle raid. The six scenes in which the president appears are brief but meaningful in the development of the story, especially his "Day of Infamy" speech to Congress. They also seem to be historically accurate. However, it is highly unlikely that FDR had to resort to the emotional stunt of standing up from his wheelchair to convince his military chiefs of staff that a major moral booster (i.e., the Doolittle Raid) was necessary for the American people's war morale. He says, "We have to do more.... We are building refrigerators while our enemies are building bombs." It is also unlikely that a general would tell the president the enemy would "be in Chicago" before we could stop them if they invaded the U.S. in early 1942.

From his appearance Voight obviously spent a great deal of time with the makeup people to prepare for his scenes as the president, but neither his physical appearance nor his voice is particularly reminiscent of Roosevelt's. Overcoming these shortcomings his interpretation of the role is still quite convincing.

Pearl Harbor II Pearlmageddon (2001)

Roosevelt: Bryan Clark. *Other Cast:* Chip Chinery (Advisory), Seth Goldstein (Adm. Oldgard), Butch Hammett (Marine), Hallieaune Jacobson (Gwen), Hugh Lewis (Adm. Connery), Byrne Offutt (Aide), Greg Wendell Reid (MP), Jim Rothman (Matt Ripley), Nicholas Shaffer (Scientist), Nicholas Shinners (Ben). *Director–Film Editing:* Robert Moniot. *Producer:* Taz Goldstein. *Writing Credits:* Taz Goldstein, Robert Moniot. *Music:* Mark Snow. *Cinematography:* Mark Doering-Powell. *Studio:* Built-d Media.

Director-writer-film editor Robert Moniot put together this very short spoof of *Pearl Harbor* (2001) and *Armageddon* (1998). It basically substitutes the arrival of a meteor for the Japanese December 7, 1941, attack on Pearl Harbor. Those who have seen the film are divided over it as a very funny take-off on modern action films or a tasteless satire of the American losses at Pearl Harbor.

33

Harry S Truman (1945–1953)

This most plain-speaking man of Missouri really was not so plain.

A common but complex man, denied higher education because of his father's financial difficulties and admission to West Point because of his poor eyesight, Truman worked in clerical jobs and on his father's farm before World War I. In France as an artillery officer he demonstrated leadership abilities under fire and was discharged as a captain in May 1919. Connections through an Army buddy led to his election as district judge in Missouri. Better connections with Tom Pendergast, the Kansas City political boss, led to Truman's election as senator.[1]

But, from the first, Truman voted for the New Deal measures that Pendergast opposed, showing his independence. As Roosevelt's successor, Truman upheld the New Deal and contended after only three months in office "with a greater surge of history, with larger, more difficult, more far-reaching decisions than any President before him. Neither Lincoln after first taking office nor FDR in his tumultuous first hundred days, had to contend with issues of such magnitude and coming all at once."[2] One of Truman's first initiatives was a 21-point domestic program that included increases in unemployment compensation, minimum wage, housing, and fair employment practices, among other measures.

Harry S Truman (Courtesy of Library of Congress.)

Truman was ridiculed for his mid–American mannerisms, his Missouri pals, and his devotion to his mother. For the first time since before the Depression, the Republicans swept the election with a 246 to 188 margin in the House and a 51 to 45 margin in the Senate. The questions persisted: Was Harry Truman an ordinary provincial American sadly miscast in the presidency? Or was he a man of above-average, even exceptional qualities and character, who had the makings of greatness?[3] The answer, historians now say, is that he was a great president, citing such actions as the Truman Doctrine and the Marshall Plan. One of Truman's brilliant appointments, Clark Clifford, would say that what happened

275

during 1947 and '48 "was that Harry Truman and the United States saved the free world."[4] As legal counsel, Clifford served on Truman's small staff of 13, only two more than on Roosevelt's, and Truman acted as his own chief of staff. To his staff Truman inspired devotion and love by his hard work and soft-spoken and even-tempered professional manner. That temper did erupt occasionally as when his daughter Margaret was panned about her singing by *Washington Post* critic Paul Hume. But Truman was reluctant to fire anyone—even MacArthur—and saved his outbursts for what he called "longhand spasms" entries in his private diary.

He undertook his famous Whistle-stop Campaign, traveling 33 days by railroad over 21,928 miles in search of votes for the 1948 presidency. "I'm going to give 'em hell," Truman said to Alban Barkley, his running mate, voicing the theme of his campaign. Truman's pithy comments, such as how the Republican Congress had "stuck a pitchfork in the farmer's back,"[5] marked his style and strategy of attack. He pulled off the biggest upset in American political history and won by just over 2,100,000 popular and 303 electoral votes from 28 states.

The photograph after the election of a beaming Truman holding the Chicago *Tribune* with a front page headline DEWEY DEFEATS TRUMAN illustrated the spirit of this president. His inaugural address—his first inauguration on his own terms—concerned foreign policy and unveiled his Point Four Program. These four years were marked by the establishment of the North Atlantic Treaty Organization (NATO), China's fall to the forces of Mao tse-tung, Russia's development of the Atomic Bomb, McCarthy, "a ballyhoo artist who had to cover up his shortcomings by wild charges,"[6] as Truman said—and the Korea "police action." While Palestine was the most difficult, the Korean action was the most important decision of his presidency, he believed.[7] His seizure of the steel mills proved equally controversial.

In a presidency with no preparation from his predecessor, Truman restored the nation's military power, reduced the national debt—until the onset of Korea ("the supreme test," he said), changed the structure of power in Washington, and furthered the cause for civil rights.

THE FILMS

Except for *MacArthur* and *Give 'Em Hell Harry*, the films including Harry S Truman show him in brief sequences performing official business. Among these films are three in which only his voice is used, *Call Me Madam*, *My Favorite Spy*, and *Bye Bye Blues*. Yet these actual voice excerpts are integral to these films' storylines. He also appears in a post-modern, satirical film, *Brenda Starr*.

The Beginning or the End (1947)

Truman: Art Baker.
For details, see Chapter 32 on Franklin D. Roosevelt.

Go for Broke! (1951)

Truman: Voice. *Other Cast*: Van Johnson (Lt. Michael Grayson), Lane Nakano (Sam), George Miki (Chick), Akira Fukunaga (Frank), Ken K. Okamoto (Kaz), Henry Oyasato

(Ohara), Harry Hamada (Masami), Henry Nakamura (Tommy), Warner Anderson (Col. Charles W. Pence), Don Haggerty (Sgt. Wilson I. Culley), Gianna Canale (Rosina), Dan Riss (Capt. Solari). *Director-Writer:* Robert Pirosh. *Producer:* Dore Schary. *Music:* Alberto Colombo. *Cinematography:* Paul Vogel. *Art Direction:* Cedric Gibbons, Eddie Imazu. *Set Decoration:* Edwin B. Willis. *Makeup:* William Tuttle. *Studio:* MGM. *Length:* 92 minutes.

During World War II the 442nd Regimental Combat Team was formed and made up entirely, except for officers, of Japanese-Americans—an astounding development, considering the treatment, especially incarceration, of Japanese-Americans, at that time. *Go for Broke!*, recounts the experiences of the 442nd with particular emphasis on their training in Mississippi and their combat in Italy and Southern France. A number of the GIs who were actually assigned to the 442nd during the war play roles in the film.

War films of the 50s usually have the same basic story: Tough officers and GIs learn to love each other by living together in combat. One of the platoons in the 442nd is commanded by a hard-nosed, bigoted Texan, Lt. Michael Grayson (Van Johnson), who wants to have nothing to do with a bunch of "Japs." All of the good-guy senior officers in the unit tell him to forget his bias, and over time he learns to love his men and, of course, they learn to love him.

As a result of the 442nd men's bravery in action, at the end of the film there is an archival scene of President Truman presenting a Presidential Unit Citation for outstanding action to them. This postscript includes an uncredited (obviously not Truman's) voiceover of the president's words on the citation.

My Favorite Spy (1951)

Truman. Other Cast: Bob Hope (Peanuts White/Eric Augustine), Hedy Lamarr (Lily Dalbray), Francis L. Sullivan (Karl Brubaker), Arnold Moss (Tasso), John Archer (Henderson), Luis Van Rooten (Rudolf Hoenig), Stephen Chase (Donald Bailey), Morris Ankrum (Gen. Frazer), Angela Clarke (Gypsy Fortune Teller), Iris Adrian (Lola), Frank Faylen (Newton), Mike Mazurki (Monkara), Marc Lawrence (Ben Ali), Tonio Selwart (Harry Crock), Ralph Smiley (El Sarif), Joseph Vitale (Fireman), Nestor Paiva (Fire Chief). *Director:* Norman Z. McLeod. *Producer:* Paul Jones. *Writing Credits:* Edmund Beloin, Lou Breslow, Edmund Hartmann, Jack Sher, Hal Kanter. *Studio:* Paramount Pictures Corp. *Length:* 93 minutes.

Bob Hope plays a double role—international playboy spy Eric Augustine and burlesque comedian Peanuts "Boffo" White—in this spy comedy. En route to Tangier, White is picked up as spy Augustine and then released. The captors, Donald Bailey (Stephen Chase) and Gen. Frazer (Morris Ankrum), press White to retrieve some top secret microfilm that another spy, Rudolph Hoenig (Luis Van Rooten), agrees to turn over to Augustine for one million dollars. White declines, then decides it his patriotic duty after President Truman telephones him and commands him to cooperate. Much fast-moving fun and intrigue follows involving Lily Dalbray (Hedy Lamarr) and White dressed in a camel suit and the two of them in a barrel, contentedly kissing.

Truman's only appearance in the film is in the telephone conversation although he is a major element in the story, initiating the action.

Call Me Madam (1953)

Truman: Unidentified. *Other Cast:* Ethel Merman (Sally Adams), Donald O'Connor (Kenneth), Vera-Ellen (Princess Maria), George Sanders (Cosmo Constantine), Billy De Wolfe (Pemberton Maxwell), Helmut Dantine (Prince Hugo), Walter Slezak (August Tantinnin), Steven Geray (Sebastian), Ludwig Stossel (Grand Duke), Lila Skala (Grand Duchess), Charles Dingle (Sen. Brockway), Emory Parnell (Sen. Charlie Gallagher), Percy Helton (Sen. Wilkins). *Director:* Walter Lang. *Producer:* Sol Siegel. *Writing Credits:* Russel Crouse, Howard Lindsay, Arthur Sheekman. *Music:* Irving Berlin, Alfred Newman. *Cinematography:* Leon Shamroy. *Film Editing:* Robert L. Simpson. *Art Direction:* John de Cuir, Lyle R. Wheeler. *Studio:* 20th Century–Fox. *Length:* 117 minutes.

Truman appears via telephone in this dynamic adaptation of Irving Berlin's Broadway hit musical. Oops, his hands also appear playing "The Missouri Waltz" on the piano of Sally Adams (Ethel Merman) at her farewell party for herself. The president has appointed this wealthy "hostess with the mostest" ambassador (in real life Perle Mesta) to Lichtenburg (in real life Liechtenstein) for her (Democrat) party support. She has no idea even where Lichtenburg is and makes three *faux pas* including calling the inhabitants of the duchy "Dutch." But she has a big Oklahoman heart, hires Kenneth (Donald O'Connor) on the spot, takes him with her, and helps his romance with Princess Maria (Vera-Ellen). That proves her undoing when the persnickety *charge d'affaires* Pemberton Maxwell (Billy De Wolfe) complains to Truman that she interfered with Maria's engagement to another man, Prince Hugo (Helmut Dantine), and she's ordered home.

In between, Truman telephones Adams several times to report on his daughter Margaret's critical reception in the press (a running gag), and Adams falls in love with Gen. Cosmo Constantine (George Sanders), the principled foreign minister. She does her ambassadorial duties in perfect pitch with her clarion clear voice, perfect (albeit Queens-accented) diction, and sassy delivery of Berlin's songs: "I'm the Hostess with the Mostest," "Can You Use Any Money Today?," "The International Rag," and the show- and-film-stopping "You're Just in Love."

The central issue is, as always, money for poor Lichtenburg. Constantine insists his country should solve its problems without foreign aid; Adams misunderstands his protest, and calls Truman for a $100 million loan. When three U.S. senators come to investigate the feasibility of a loan, they are so impressed with Constantine's statesmanship they offer $200 million. He gets transferred as ambassador to the U.S, and all ends in song.

Give 'Em Hell, Harry! (1975)

Truman: James Whitmore. *Director:* Steve Binder. *Adaptation:* Samuel Gallu based on the stage play by Gallu and Thomas J. McErlane. *Director:* Peter H. Hunt. *Producers:* Al Ham, Joseph E. Bluth. *Cinematography:* Ken Palius. *Studio:* Avco Embassy Pictures. *Length:* 104 minutes.

Give 'Em Hell, Harry! is a filmed version of James Whitmore's acclaimed one-man stage play. In 104 minutes, this so-called "political cabaret" dramatizes the one-man show that Truman was in the White House. It is marked by the personal vitality, equally strong language, and moral courage that characterized this president. And it is generally historically accurate, using language found in the major Truman biographies.

With an appearance and a voice similar to Truman's, Whitmore covers the entire Truman Administration in direct and telephone conversation to unseen persons, letters, speeches, and comments. The dynamism, the outspoken directness, and the devotion to the people—as well as his family—emerge in this entertaining historical portrait. It's a fine picture, never varnished, always true to the subject. Unlike the other major film including Truman, *MacArthur* that deals with only one aspect of Truman's administration, this biographical picture gives as close a look at the man in office as any presidential film.

As Truman, Whitmore looks, talks, and acts the part as if he, too, came from Missouri. *Give 'Em Hell, Harry!* begins with Truman seated upright at his desk writing to his daughter Margaret about what it takes to be a good president. With typical modesty he says he *won't* be a good president but he's having a lot of fun, then affixes his own stamp. Next he telephones the heads of the railroad unions to ask if they've worked out the proposed settlement. "I'm going to teach them some lessons in social responsibility," says the fast-talking, finger-pointing Whitmore, "and that goes for management. I may have inherited this job, but I'm in charge."

While contending with the ghost of Franklin D. Roosevelt to whom he later explains how he had no options but to use the atom bomb on Japan, Truman confers with Herbert Hoover about tackling human hunger. Other presidents are invoked in Truman's fond history of the White House including Thomas Jefferson and the physical pain of migraine headaches he suffered because of his conflicts over the Constitution and slavery. Quoting Shakespeare, Truman says "the elements were so mixed in him ... this was a man." To Truman one of his biggest headaches was that "too much money is in the hands of too few," reciting his 1937 Senate speech.

Although the office set remains foremost on the stage, lighting changes signal passage of time and place—to his front lawn in Independence, Missouri, for example, where he complains about the "isolation" of the White House and his need "to get home." Other changes include Truman's World War I uniform that he dons to give his views on military discipline. Another change reveals a white shirt, natty, of course, like the haberdasher he was, and further revelations about his early career as a judge. "Roads," he says, "were the biggest job," and Tom Pendergast, "my secret partner, never bothered me."

Truman next stands before a black curtain stating his belief in the "brotherhood of man" and scolds the Ku Klux Klan for "calling yourselves the invisible empire." The scolding never stops with this tough, honest, and outspoken man as he teases his secretary, Rose, asking if he should delete "bastard" from the letter he is dictating to John L. Lewis (on this occasion she says keep it). Truman then jokes about how it took his wife Bess forty years to get him to say "manure." But *Give 'Em Hell, Harry!* does delete the last line of Truman's letter to music critic Hume, calling him "a gutter snipe" rather than "a reflection on [his] ancestry" for his damning review of Margaret's singing.

Even though Five-Star General Douglas MacArthur defied Truman's orders and the government's decisions by attacking beyond the prescribed boundary in Korea, this president never spoke or wrote to him in terms of derision—to his face. Rather, he compared his problems with the general to Lincoln's reverse problems with General George B. McClellan for *not* attacking and cited Lincoln's story of the man who when his horse kicked up and stuck a foot through the stirrup, said to the horse, "If you are going to get on, I will get off." In one of the few historical lapses in the film, the dropping of the historical reference of this joke glosses over Truman's love of history and his sense of place in it.

But for other military such as Gen. George C. Marshall, Truman calls him "the most dedicated and greatest American I've ever known" and Gen. Omar Bradley "brilliant." As for Gen. Dwight D. Eisenhower, Truman rails against his "dirty politics" during the 1952 campaign versus Democratic candidate Adlai Stevenson, and says when Ike got into politics he "lost his guts."

To dramatize Truman's remarks against Joe McCarthy's calling Marshall (among others) "soft on Communism," the format changes with superimposed images of Truman appearing on a rear screen while he "takes on" McCarthy in a public address in Boston. He stresses the threat of Communism "must not make us lose common sense," and calls McCarthy's accusations of Communism "the big lie ... so monstrous that it stuns...."

Always driven by common sense and faith, Truman's "happiest time" during his Whistle-stop Campaign is recounted by Whitmore, on the back of a train talking to crowds, like the 9,600 farmers in Dexter, Iowa. ("There must have been a run on buttermilk" after that, he quips.) "No mister," he continues, "I don't give 'em hell, just tell the truth, and it makes them feel that they are in hell." His subsequent election victory flashes before the audience when he holds up the Chicago *Tribune* newspaper with the DEWEY DEFEATS TRUMAN headline. Then Whitmore as Truman plays a satire of a Dewey campaign song.

With a hat on, he assumes the pose of Truman's walking and talking to the press whom he (erroneously, another historical lapse) says he likes. Ever showing the breadth of his self-education he quotes the poem he always carries, Tennyson's *Locksley Hall*, on the future, and signals his leaving of office as "My promotion ... to be one of you."

The Front (1976)

Truman: Himself in archive footage. *Other Cast*: Woody Allen (Howard Prince), Zero Mostel (Hecky Brown), Herschel Bernardi (Phil Sussman), Michael Murphy (Alfred Miller), Andrea Marcovicci (Florence Barrett), Remak Ramsay (Hennessey), Marvin Lichterman (Myer Prince), Lloyd Gough (Delaney), David Margulies (Phelps), Joshua Shelley (Sam), Norman Rose (Prince's Attorney). *Director*: Martin Ritt. *Producer*: Jack Rollins. *Writing Credits*: Walter Bernstein. *Music*: Dave Grusin. *Cinematography*: Michael Chapman. *Film Editing*: Sidney Levin. *Art Direction*: Charles Bailey. *Set Decoration*: Robert Drumheller. *Costume Design*: Ruth Morley. *Studio*: Columbia Pictures Corp. *Length*: 95 minutes.

In a rare occurrence, Woody Allen only acts rather than writes, directs, and produces this film. But this film is rare: It deals with this historically serious subject with some comic touches, mainly supplied by Allen. He plays Howard Prince, deli cashier–bookie, always the neurotic nebbish and always down on his luck until he fronts for a friend who is blacklisted by a TV network as a suspected Communist. Prince's TV scripts get raves and he soon fronts for others.

That he never reads the scripts is implausible. So is script editor Florence Barrett's (Andrea Marcovicci) romantic interest in him, really for his "talent." But this is a film, written by Walter Bernstein, directed by Martin Ritt, and produced by Ritt, and others who were blacklisted as well as actors Herschel Bernardi, Lloyd Gough, Joshua Shelley, and Zero Mostel.

While the romance detracts from the political message of Sen. Joseph McCarthy's Red-baiting witch hunts, Mostel's role as a down-and-out comedian forced to spy on Prince and ultimately driven to suicide illustrates the tragedy of McCarthy's political machinations.

Finally, Prince appears before the House Un-American Committee and exposes the hypocrisy of the government's attempt to control the entertainment industry while condemning Communism with its state control. Because of this film's importance (it was named one of the year's ten best by the National Board of Review), the non-dramatic appearance of Cold War presidents Truman and Eisenhower deserve mention. Both appear in archival footage in a black-and-white newsreel montage during the credits: Truman in a quick clip, Ike with Lily Pons. The background music is Frank Sinatra singing "Young at Heart."

MacArthur (1977)

Truman: Ed Flanders. *Other Cast:* Gregory Peck (MacArthur), Dan O'Herlihy (Franklin D. Roosevelt), Ivan Bonar (Gen. Richard K. Sutherland), Ward Costello (Gen. George C. Marshall), Nicolas Coster (Maj. Sidney Huff), Marj Dusay (Mrs. Jean MacArthur), Sandy Kenyon (Maj. Gen./Lt Gen. Jonathan M. Wainwright), Robert Mandan (Rep. Martin), Allan Miller (Col. Legrande A. Diller), Dick O'Neill (Col. Courtney Whitney), Addison Powell (Fleet Adm. Chester W. Nimitz), Tom Rosqui (Gen. Sampson). *Director:* Joseph Sargent. *Producer:* Frank McCarthy. *Writers:* Hal Barwood, Matthew Robbins. *Music:* Jerry Goldsmith. *Cinematography:* Mario Tosi. *Film Editing:* George Jay Nicholson. *Production Design:* John Lloyd. *Set Direction:* Hal Gausman. *Costume Design:* Larry Harnell. *Studio:* Universal. *Length:* 130 minutes.

MacArthur uses a speech the American five-star general gave at West Point as the vehicle for his reflections on his military life, a life that was bound by the Academy's credo of duty, honor, and country. While the film is about MacArthur, President Franklin D. Roosevelt figures briefly (see Chapter 32 on Franklin Roosevelt), and President Harry S Truman figures highly in their encounters with this ambitious, arrogant, brilliant military leader.

The film follows MacArthur's military career from his last days on Corregidor in the Philippines in 1942 through his recall by Truman to the United States during the Korean conflict in 1951. In subtitles before the credits, the question is raised whether MacArthur was "one of the greatest men who ever lived" or a "demagogue." The film never answers that question, focusing instead on his military strategies and accomplishments.

President Truman receives respectful treatment. His portrayal by Ed Flanders follows historical fact and personal behavior—Truman offers MacArthur a plum cake "for the missus" when he arrives to confer with him on Wake Island about the course of the Korean conflict. His appearances all deal with the Korean conflict, 19 in all. While brief, sometimes lasting only thirty seconds, the appearances convey Truman's constant battles with this stubborn general, battles as complex as any that occurred in the Pacific.

As stated above, MacArthur receives almost reverential treatment. Star Gregory Peck employs the same determination he displayed in *Twelve O'Clock High* (1949) and dignified manner he used in his Academy Award performance as lawyer Atticus Finch in *To Kill a Mockingbird* (1962). Although Peck assumes the carriage and mannerisms (including the corncob pipe-smoking) of MacArthur, his voice is much richer and deeper than the general's, making his farewell speech especially moving.

Ed Flanders as Harry S Truman approaches FDR's successor very closely in physical appearance and behavior with almost staccato speech, straight posture, and piercing gaze through steel-rimmed eyeglasses. Even his expressions smack of the man from Missouri's: "Ever had a load of hay fall on you?" he says in his first scene when he learns of his ascendancy to the White House upon FDR's death.

MacArthur (1977): Ed Flanders as Harry S Truman and Gregory Peck as General Douglas MacArthur meet on Wake Island in the Pacific to discuss the Korean War in this biopic of MacArthur's military career. (Courtesy of George Eastman House.)

In his second scene, Truman sits in the Oval Office, a sign saying "The Buck Stops Here" on his desk, authorizing the atomic bomb attack, and says FDR "never told me," an understatement about the lack of Roosevelt's communication with his vice president. Throughout the following scenes dealing with MacArthur, alternating with shots of the general, the president demonstrates his growing frustration with MacArthur's behavior, beginning by saying it's "damn embarrassing" when MacArthur says he's too busy to come home to discuss post–World War II strategy.

The remaining scenes deal with Truman's stance on Korea—first his stating publicly, "We are not at war ... we are engaged in a police action." Then Truman angrily deals with MacArthur's plans to involve Chiang Kai-Chek and MacArthur's ("his majesty" he says bitingly) audacious plan to attack Inchon. Truman finally gives him "cringing approval."

Next Truman appears with Vice President Alban Barkley discussing the U.S. victory in Inchon and MacArthur's wanting to expand the war into China. Truman's effort to stop MacArthur by dealing with him face to face gets treated with three short scenes of Truman's plane trip to Wake Island. He fumes when it first appears that MacArthur is making him wait to be greeted on the tarmac: "He can do that to Harry Truman but not to his commander in chief," Truman barks. The ever smartly dressed former haberdasher then comments to his aides how MacArthur always dresses in "costume" with his rumpled cap and then openly criticizes him by making a dig at MacArthur's political ambitions as they ride off in a car by saying, "I've read a little of military history ... and congratulate you. But I've heard it's a bad idea to dabble in politics."

But civility and cordiality rule. The two men meet in an enormous hangar to discuss their enormous problems; Truman bluntly states "I've got the whole United Nations on my back, and I'm scared stiff of war. The Soviets also promise the A-Bomb to China."

In three more short scenes—again almost one-liners from Truman—his reaction to MacArthur's persistent appeals to bomb China and expand the war surface. Finally, Truman explodes in anger over MacArthur's message about negotiating with the Chinese. The president wants a political solution, not a military one.

Truman's dismissal of the insubordinate MacArthur gets treated indirectly (as Truman liked to do in such matters) with MacArthur's wife Jean interrupting him with a presidential message in the middle of an Army-Navy baseball game story at a dinner party. Newsreels clips—with shots of Peck as MacArthur inserted—convey the hero's welcome that the U.S. gave the returning MacArthur. Truman's reaction is typically indignant: "When people think they're god," he says. The final scenes of Truman show him listening to MacArthur's speech to Congress, his "Old Soldiers Never Die" sentimental plea about how he didn't scuttle the Pacific. When MacArthur says goodbye, a reaction shot shows Truman stating "Goodbye, hell; he's running for president," his final word on this man who would be king.

Inchon (1981)

Truman: Ed Flanders (voice). *Other Cast:* Laurence Olivier (Gen. Douglas MacArthur), Jacqueline Bisset (Barbara Hallsworth), Ben Gazzara (Maj. Frank Hallsworth), Toshiro Mifune (Saito-San), Richard Roundtree (Sgt. Augustus Henderson), David Janssen (David Feld, scenes deleted), Rex Reed (Longfellow, scenes deleted), Kung-won Nam (Park), Dorothy James (Jean MacArthur), Kwang Nam Young (President Synghman Rhee). *Director:* Terence Young. *Producers:* Sidney Beckerman, Mitsuhari Ishii. *Writing Credits:* Laird Koenig, Robin Moore, Paul Savage. *Music:* Jerry Goldsmith. *Cinematography:* William A. Fraker, Bruce Surtees. *Film Editing:* John W. Holmes, Dallas Puett, Michael J. Sheridan, Peter Taylor. *Art Direction:* Juichi Ikuno. *Set Decoration:* Francesco Chianese, Ho-Kil Kim. *Costume Design:* Donfeld. *Studio:* MGM/One Way Productions/Unification Church. *Length:* 140 minutes.

One of the riskiest tactical moves in military history was the landing at Inchon on the Korean Peninsula planned by General Douglas MacArthur. One of Hollywood's greatest flops was this approximately $50 million film produced by One Way Productions and the Reverend Moon's Unification Church. It reportedly grossed less than $2 million. The film exists in at least three versions: a 90-minute British video called *Operation Inchon*, a 105-minute version, and a full 140-minute version released theatrically in 1981.

With an all-star cast headed by Laurence Olivier as General MacArthur, it is difficult to imagine how director Terence Young managed to turn out such an artistic and financial disaster. However, a bad script and poor, almost uninterested acting can go a long way to create a dud out of an exciting historical event. The best that can be said about the film is already said in the Plot Synopsis in the *All Movie Guide*: "[T]he film presents one of your only opportunities to see Olivier, the greatest actor of his generation, talk like W.C. Fields while smoking a corn-cob pipe." Although Truman does not appear, there is a voice characterization of him done by Ed Flanders.

Brenda Starr (1989)

Truman: Ed Nelson. *Other Cast:* Brooke Shields (Brenda Starr), Timothy Dalton (Basil St. John), Tony Peck (Mike Randall), Diana Scarwid (Libby "Lips" Lipscomb), Nestor Serrano (Jose), Jeffrey Tambor (Vladimir), June Gable (Luba), Charles Durning (Editor Francis I. Livright), Kathleen Wilhoite (Reporter Hank O'Hare), John Short (Cub Reporter Pesky Miller), Eddie Albert (Police Chief Maloney), Mark von Holstein (Donovan O'Shea, Public Enemy #3), Henry Gibson (Prof. Gerhardt Von Kreutzer). *Director:* Robert Ellis Miller. *Producers:* John D. Backe, Alana H. Lambros. *Writing Credits:* Noreen Stone, James D. Buchanan, Jenny Wolkind. *Music:* Johnny Mandel. *Cinematograhy:* Freddie Francis. *Film Editing:* Mark Melnick. *Production Design:* John J. Lloyd. *Costume Design:* Peggy Farrell, Bob Mackie. *Studio:* AM-PM/New World/Tribune Entertainment. *Length:* 93 minutes.

Journalists suffered from lack of public esteem at the time of this film's making, 1986. When it was released three years later, the film suffered even more, getting scathing reviews. The consensus was that Brooke Shields, who stars as the girl reporter, was a completely untalented actress, and that "Brenda Starr," the 1940s Dale Messick cartoon on which the film is based, was antiquated.

But why not suspend all disbelief and watch Starr save herself from German mercenaries and Russian spies by water-skiing on the backs of two crocodiles in the deepest South American jungle? She's on a quest to save her newspaper, *The Flash,* by finding a German scientist who has invented a rocket fuel. Joining her is her cartoonist, Mike Randall (Tony Peck), whom she has berated for making her pocketbooks too small for her notebooks, among other serious slips of the pen. He draws himself into the strip as the film shifts from cartoon to 1948 reality. Adding to the action is Basil St. John (Timothy Dalton before 007), the mystery man who must use the serum from black orchids to prevent madness. To which Starr replies in innocent understatement, "Nobody's perfect."

That kind of dialogue comes from the rewrite of Noreen Stone and James D. Buchanan's original script by the talented Delia Ephron under the name of Jenny Wolkind. She also supplies Starr with such epithets as irreverent as "golly" and "gosh" to add to her unbelievable character. When she's not uttering such lines that would nicely fit in a cartoon frame, Starr's changing clothes. Her costumes are designed by Bob Mackie and seem more fit for the stage than the jungle. Among the other characters are Diana Scarwid as Libby "Lips" Lipscomb, Starr's rival; Charles Durning as the tough newspaper editor; a bunch of "dumbell" Russian spies, and wild circus performers, including Brazilian combat dancers.

Brenda Starr's never-ending talents appear as she plays the piano with President Truman (Ed Nelson) in a short scene in the White House. He's sitting there, looking very much like Truman, giving a rendition of "Carolina Moon" and asks her to play bass which, being Brenda Starr, she does very well. She's there because in her quest to find the missing German scientist, she leaves no source untapped. In Truman's usual Missouri style, he replies he's "halfway between the breakup of the OSS and the start of this new CIA but I'd be a suck egg mule if I wasn't upset about rocket fuel." Demonstrating Truman's down-home sense, he shows her something he learned in Boy Scouts: how sunlight through glass ignites paper. He fears if the "Ruskies" get the fuel, they might go into space and harness the sun's rays; then the free world will be "up the creek." Superman, Batman, Spider-Man, or Dick Tracy she is not, but *Brenda Starr* shows how some things, including that comic strip, endure.

Bye Bye Blues (1989)

Truman: Himself (voice). *Other Cast:* Michael Ontkean (Teddy Cooper), Rebecca Jenkins (Daisy Cooper), Chad Krowchuk (Richard Cooper at 5), Vincent Gale (Will Wright), Leslie Yeo (Arthur Wright), Kate Reid (Mary Wright), Robyn Stevan (Frances Cooper), Luke Reilly (Max Gramley), Stuart Margolin (Slim Godfrey). *Director-Writer:* Anne Wheeler. *Producers:* Tony Allard, Arvi Liimatainen, Anne Wheeler. *Music:* George Blondheim. *Cinematography:* Vic Sarin. *Film Editing:* Christopher Tate. *Production Design:* John Blackie. *Art Direction:* Scott Dobbie. *Costume Design:* Maureen Hiscox. *Studio:* Alberta Motion Picture Development Corp. *Length:* 117 minutes.

This Canadian film is mentioned only because the voice of Truman is heard over the radio. *Bye Bye Blues* (1989) has a story loosely based on the life of writer-director Anne Wheeler's mother. It is about how World War II affects a young Canadian doctor's wife. She joins a local dance band as pianist and singer to support herself and her two children; hence the title from a song. Rebecca Jenkins won a Genie award, the Canadian Oscar, for portraying Daisy Cooper. Late in the war, playing cards with her family in Western Canada, Cooper hears the radio announcement of the first atomic bomb explosion. The voice of President Truman soon comes on the air as he explains the use of the bomb: "We shall continue to use it ... until we completely destroy Japan's power to make war." Truman's voice is his only presence as in two other films, *My Favorite Spy* and *Call Me Madam*.

34

Dwight D. Eisenhower (1953–1961)

Dwight D. Eisenhower. (Courtesy of Library of Congress.)

"I like Ike," the 1952 campaign slogan of Dwight D. Eisenhower, describes the American public's attitude toward the 34th president and the tone of his two-term administration—an affable administrator bringing what he promised, peace and prosperity.

His early reputation as an inarticulate leader relying on his subordinates changed to what now is considered a "hidden hand" president whose desire for precision governed his executive decisions and public pronouncements. Although his career was with the military, he will be remembered for the warning in his farewell address "against the acquisition of unwarranted influence, whether sought or unsought, by the military-industrial complex."

Eisenhower's military career began at West Point and reached its highest point in his planning and managing the D-Day invasion of Europe on June 6, 1944. After World War II he served as chief of staff for the demobilization of American forces and then for two years as president of Columbia University. His final Army assignment in 1950 was to head the creation of military forces for the North Atlantic Treaty Organization (NATO).

The platform of his first presidential campaign—Korea, Communism, and Corruption—was partially realized when the Korean War ended by armistice during Eisenhower's first term. He had taken the step of threatening the use of atomic bombs if the stalemate over prisoners of war continued between the United States and Chinese Communists. In fighting Communism, Eisenhower supported a policy of containment based on the domino theory (if one domino in a row falls, they all fall). He helped establish the Southeast Asia Treaty Organization (SEATO) to thwart Communist expansion, he sent arms and advisors to Vietnam, and he supported coups to overthrow Communism in Iran and Guatemala. But with the Communist un–American activity investigation of Senator Eugene McCarthy,

Eisenhower took a different approach and tried to ignore him, thinking he would destroy himself.

On another civil rights issue of the time—integration of public schools—when Governor Orval Faubus of Arkansas called out the National Guard to block African-American students from entering the Central High School in Little Rock, Eisenhower sent in troops, upholding the position of the Supreme Court.

While Eisenhower's foreign policy during his first term was mainly influenced by the Cold War, he did work toward reducing tensions, proposing universal disarmament. But he decided not to risk an encounter with the Soviets when they overran Hungary in its move for independence. Nor did he counter Soviet interference during the Suez Crisis when he urged British, French, and Israeli withdrawal.

In internal affairs during both terms, Eisenhower maintained his position against a welfare state, yet he expanded Social Security, created student loans through the National Defense Education Act of 1958, and established the Department of Health, Education and Welfare. During his second term Eisenhower faced further Soviet challenges especially the launching of *Sputnik I* that led to the establishment of the National Aeronautics and Space Administration (NASA). The Eisenhower Administration appeared to follow a policy of reaction to Russian initiative and response to American pressure groups.

In one of his most memorable acts, he decreed what became the Eisenhower Doctrine that offered American financial and military aid to any Middle Eastern country threatened by any other country controlled by international Communism. American military support of Lebanon in 1958 demonstrated this doctrine in action. Similarly Eisenhower backed the Chinese government of Taiwan in the Quemoy and Matsu affair.

Ironically, Eisenhower, the beloved general who made his career in the military, left public office with that ringing Farewell Address warning against the implications of the influence of the military-industrial complex. He also left the legacy of the institutional presidency.[1]

THE FILMS

There are only eight feature-length films with Eisenhower appearing always as a minor character. They treat his military career and his administration with respect but not with the veneration of our first president/general—Washington.

Beyond Glory (1948)

Eisenhower: Unidentified. *Other Cast:* Alan Ladd (Capt. Rockwell "Rocky" Gilman), Donna Reed (Ann Daniels), George Macready (Maj. Gen. Bond), George Coulouris (Lew Proctor), Harold Vermilyea (Raymond Denmore Sr.), Henry Travers (Pop Dewing), Luis Van Rooten (Dr. White), Tom Neal (Capt. Henry Daniels), Conrad Janis (Raymond Denmore Jr.), Margaret Field (Cora), Paul Lees (Miller), Dick Hogan (Cadet Sgt. Eddie Loughlin), Audie Murphy (Thomas). *Director:* John Farrow. *Producer:* Robert Fellows. *Writing Credits:* William Wister Haines, Jonathan Latimer, Charles Marquis Warren. *Music:* Victor Young. *Cinematography:* John Seitz. *Film Editing:* Eda Warren. *Art Direction:* Franz Bachelin, Hans Dreier. *Set Decoration:* Sam Comer, Ray Moyer. *Costume Design:* Edith Head. *Makeup:* Wally

Westmore. *Sound:* Hugo Grenzbach, Walter Oberst. *Special Effects:* Farciot Edouart. *Studio:* Paramount Pictures. *Length:* 82 minutes.

West Point upperclassman Rockwell "Rocky" Gilman (Alan Ladd) is accused of being unfit and perhaps criminally liable by Plebe Cadet Raymond Denmore Jr. (Conrad Janis). All of these troubles started when "Rocky" was an officer battling General Rommel's Panzer division in Tunisia. He felt personally responsible for the death of his friend, Captain Henry Daniels (Tom Neal), during the fighting.

Even though he was completely exonerated and a recipient of the Distinguished Service Medal, it takes the love of a woman, Daniels's widow Ann (Donna Reed), and a medical determination to convince him of his innocence. This persuades "Rocky" to remain in West Point, and when he graduates General Eisenhower is present.

The Stars Are Singing (1953)

Eisenhower: Unidentified. *Other Cast:* Rosemary Clooney (Terry Brennan), Anna Maria Alberghetti (Katri Walenska), Lauritz Melchior (Jan Poldi), Bob Williams (Homer Tirdell), Tom Morton (Buddy Fraser), Fred Clark (McDougall), John Archer (Dave), Mikhail Rasumny (Ladowski), Lloyd Corrigan (Miller), Don Wilson (Himself), Otto Waldis (Ship's Captain Goslak), Henry Guttman (Ship's Mate), Paul E. Burns (Henryk, the Ship's Messboy), Freeman Lusk (Conway), Red Dust (Homer's Dog). *Director:* Norman Taurog. *Producer:* Irving Asher. *Writing Credits:* Paul Hervey Fox, Liam O'Brien. *Music:* Ray Evans, Jay Livingston, Victor Young. *Cinematography:* Lionel Lindon. *Film Editing:* Arthur P. Schmidt. *Art Direction:* Henry Bumstead, Hal Pereira. *Set Decoration:* Sam Comer, Ray Moyer. *Costume Design:* Edith Head. *Makeup:* Wally Westmore. *Sound:* John Cope, Harold Lewis. *Special Effects:* Gordon Jennings. *Studio:* Paramount Pictures. *Length:* 99 minutes.

This musical teamed Metropolitan Opera star Lauritz Melchior as Jan Poldi and Rosemary Clooney as Terry Brennan in her first film (after her song hit, "Come-On-A-My-House"). The story centers on Anna Maria Alberghetti as 15-year-old Katri Walenska who jumps a Polish ship and swims to freedom in New York City. She does not find freedom readily as her old family friend Jan Poldi (Melchior) is alcoholic, although he can sing "Vesti la giubba" from *I Pagliacci*. His neighbors, led by Brennan (Rosemary Clooney), try to keep her in the country legally by making recordings. Walenska's a big hit on a TV talent show, and a telephone call from President Eisenhower, responding to the public support, assures her staying in America.

The Long Gray Line (1955)

Eisenhower: Harry Carey Jr. and Elbert Steele. *Other Cast:* Tyrone Power (Martin "Marty" Maher), Maureen O'Hara (Mary O'Donnell), Robert Francis (James "Red" Sundstrom Jr.), Donald Crisp (Old Martin), Ward Bond (Capt. Herman J. Kohler), Betsy Palmer (Kitty Carter), Philip Carey (Charles "Chuck" Dotson), William Leslie (Red Sundstrom), Patrick Wayne (Abner "Cherub" Overton), Sean McClory (Dinnny Maher), Peter Graves (Cpl. Rudolph Heinz), Milburn Stone (Capt. John Pershing), Erin O'Brien-Moore (Mrs. Kohler), Walter D. Ehlers (Mike Shannon). *Director:* John Ford. *Producer:* Robert Arthur. *Writing Credits:* Nardi Reeder Campion from his book with Martin Maher and Edward Hope. *Music:* W. Franke Harling, Herbert S. Shipman. *Cinematography:* Charles Lawton Jr., Charles Lang.

Film Editing: William A. Lyon. *Art Direction:* Robert Peterson. *Set Decoration:* Frank Tuttle. *Costume Design:* Jean Louis. *Makeup:* Clay Campbell, Helen Hunt. *Sound:* George Cooper, John P. Livadary. *Studio:* Columbia Pictures Corp., Rota Productions. *Length:* 138 minutes.

This is a sentimental story of 10,000 cadets, as the voiceover on the trailer states, and a man who knows them all, based on his book, *Bringing Up the Brass*. The man, Martin Maher, is a fabled athletic trainer. He is played with bumbling Irish charm by Tyrone Power. The film promises to show that his story is the story of West Point from the time of Maher's arrival until the middle of the 20th century. Under John Ford's direction it is, in that it shows the hard work, discipline, and caring that goes to making a plebe into a West Point officer.

The film follows Maher from his arrival at the Point to work as a busboy, shortly after his landing in the U.S. from Ireland. Proving to be an inept busboy, he joins the army and is quickly noticed by the Master of the Sword during a fistfight with Maher's nemesis, Cpl. Rudolph Heinz (Peter Graves). Ward Bond, one of Ford's familiar actors, plays Capt. Herman J. Kohler, the modern version of the Master of the Sword upholding old West Point traditions through athletics.

Maher's spunk also wins him the hand of Mary O'Donnell (Maureen O'Hara), a beautiful Irish redhead hired by Kohler as a household cook. After an incredibly brief courtship masterminded by the Master of the Sword, they marry. From this point the movie focuses more on them than the cadets, touching on O'Hara's bringing Maher's brother to start life in the new world and his father to live with them, the death of their only child, a newborn infant, and their relationships with numerous cadets.

Ford's direction presents grand spectacles—many scenes of cadets marching in formation—from the credits until the final scene with the band playing both Irish and Scottish tunes ("Auld Lang Syne") in a tribute to Maher. Again Ford frames his characters in their chosen settings that symbolize their destiny—Power through the imposing arches of West Point.

Eisenhower actually appears in two roles in *The Long Gray Line*. In the opening and closing scenes only the back of his head is seen as he sits at a dining table in the White House listening to Marty Maher's pleas to not be retired from the Military Academy. Maher may be 70 as he says but he feels as fit as the day he arrived. Ike—as played by the uncredited Elbert Steele—listens attentively and says such warm things as, "Go ahead and smoke your pipe, Marty. I'd hardly know you without it." That visit to Eisenhower provides the excuse for Maher to tell his story.

Included, naturally, is Maher's relationship with Eisenhower as a cadet. Following the humorous vein of the film, he—as played by Harry Carey Jr.—is presented as an eager young man, mostly worried about the pace at which he is losing his hair. When young Ike beckons Maher in the locker room to note how well his hair is doing by his use of a special tonic, exuberant Maher says, "Keep it up."

After the story of Maher at West Point, the scene shifts back to the White House, where we again see Eisenhower in rear view. He orders one of his military aides to find out what Maher's "snafu" is all about—a familiar working pattern of Eisenhower who is known for his great ability at designating authority. Maher thanks Eisenhower profusely, and the president replies, "I hope I'll always have time for old friends."

The character of Eisenhower as a cadet in the Class of 1915 that "the stars fell upon" is somewhat lightly handled, i.e., the hair loss problem, but in line with a cadet with a cadet-type problem. (Neither the problems nor the early successes of other 1915 star cadets Omar

Bradley and James Van Fleet are mentioned.) On the other hand, as president, Eisenhower is depicted as having the time and desire to listen to and solve an old friend's problem. The portrait of Eisenhower seems to be in line with his actual personality.

When Hell Broke Loose (1958)

Eisenhower: Archival footage. *Other Cast:* Charles Bronson (Steve Boland), Violet Rensing (Ilsa), Richard Jaeckel (Karl), Arvid Nelson (Ludwig), Robert Easton (Jonesie), Dennis McCarthy (Capt. Melton), Robert Stevenson (Capt. Grayson), Eddie Foy III (Brooklyn), John Morley (Chaplain). *Director:* Kenneth G. Crane. *Producers:* Oscar Brodney, Sol Dolgin. *Writing Credits:* Oscar Brodney, Ib Melchior. *Cinematography:* Hal McAlpin. *Music:* Albert Glasser. *Film Editing:* Asa Boyd Clark, Kenneth G. Crane. *Production Design:* G.W. Berntsen. *Studio:* Paramount Pictures. *Length:* 78 minutes.

While–then-General Eisenhower figures highly in the plot of this World War II story, he only appears once—and in archival footage in a one-shot leaving his headquarters and getting into his car. He is the target of the "Werewolves," Nazi assassins dedicated to kill the Allied Commander and to terrorize Allied troops. Eisenhower's fate crosses that of self-described "sharp operator" Steve Boland (Charles Bronson), a bookie sent to the Army where a chaplain prays he'll find "his reason for being." Boland continues his nefarious ways, betting on anything possible including the time the Allies will enter Paris, using his gains to amass goods desired by the Germans, and proclaiming he "ain't gonna bust my back for nothin.'"

Boland's fellow soldiers see him as privileged, and the military police accuse him of being "yellow" by spending so much time in the guard house for his illegal gambling. As the war progresses, indicated by the familiar device of newspaper headlines, Boland advances to a small town near the Rhine where he befriends a hungry German girl who stole meat. Infatuated, Boland showers Ilsa (Violet Rensing) with food and affection. She rebukes him, and he leaves her in anger.

Boland cannot forget Ilsa and returns to learn that her brother Karl (Richard Jaeckel) and his fellow Nazi Ludwig (Arvid Nelson) are "Werewolves." To shorten the war and to save her brother's life, Ilsa reports their assassination plan to Allied Intelligence. She and Boland join the search for them in the neighboring forest. The "Werewolves" ambush them but Boland saves the approaching Ike's life in a tense action scene, as the narrator says, "Sometimes history is changed by a handful of men." The film ends with the chaplain's invocation about Boland finding his reason for being.

The Longest Day (1962)

Eisenhower: Henry Grace. *Other Cast:* John Wayne (Lt. Col. Benjamin Vandervoort), Robert Mitchum (Brig. Gen. Norma Cota), Henry Fonda (Brig. Gen. Theodore Roosevelt), Robert Ryan (Brig. Gen. James M. Gavin), Rod Steiger (Destroyer Commander), Richard Todd (Maj. John Howard), Richard Burton (R.A.F. Pilot David Campbell), Robert Wagner (U.S. Ranger), Mel Ferrer (Maj. Gen. Robert Haines), Jeffrey Hunter (Sgt. Fuller), Paul Anka (U.S. Ranger), Sal Mineo (Pvt. Martini), Roddy McDowall (Pvt. Morris), Stuart Whitman (Lt. Sheen), Eddie Albert (Col. Tom Newton), Edmond O'Brien (Gen. Raymond O. Barton), Fabian (U.S. Ranger), Red Buttons (Pvt. John Steele), Tom Tryon (Lt. Wilson),

34—Dwight D. Eisenhower (1953–1961)

The Longest Day (1962): Dwight David Eisenhower was the Supreme Allied Commander at the time of the Normandy invasion. Played by little known actor Henry Grace (left) because of his close resemblance, Eisenhower obviously controls the meeting of the general staff. This Darryl F. Zanuck Production for 20th Century–Fox had four other directors—Ken Annakin, Andrew Marton, and Bernhard Wicki—and an all-star cast. (Photofest.)

Alexander Knox (Maj. Gen. Walter Bedell Smith), Tommy Sands (U.S. Ranger), Arletty (Madame Barrault), Jean-Louis Barrault (Father Louis Roulland), Bourvil (Mayor of Colleville), Sean Connery (Pvt. Flanagan), Curt Jurgens (Maj. Gen. Gunther Blumentritt), Peter Lawford (Lord Lovat), Richard Todd (Maj. John Howard), Gert Frobe (Sgt. Kaffekanne). *Directors:* Ken Annakin, Andrew Marton, Bernhard Wicki. *Producer:* Darryl F. Zanuck. *Music:* Paul Anka, Maurice Jarre. *Cinematography:* Jean Bourgoin, Pierre Levent, Henri Persin, Walter Wottitz. *Film Editing:* Samuel E. Beetley. *Art Direction:* Leon Barsacq, Ted Haworth, Vincent Korda. *Studio:* 20th Century–Fox. *Length:* 179 minutes.

This film reprises the events of June 5 and 6, 1944, and the preparations for the Allied invasion of Europe during World War II—the greatest amphibious landing in history. The directors use a documentary style to underline authenticity with subtitles for the actors and times of the operations. An international cast of 42 stars and an estimated 23,000 U.S., English, and French troops provide further authenticity of the vastness of this military operation, the effect it produces on the Allies as well as the Germans and French civilians, and the role of military leaders, particularly Eisenhower.

The title comes from a German officer's prescient comment that this will be "the longest day," a phrase that is repeated and rephrased in many reflections on this historical military event. Adding to the epic nature of the title and the production is the music, beginning with the opening passages of Beethoven's Symphony No. 5 and resounding with Paul Anka's theme music that was later (1968–95) used as the Regimental March of the Canadian Airborne Regiment.

Even the first shot—a lone American helmet on a Normandy beach—interprets the intention of the film: both epic sweep and personal statement. The film concludes with that image. The plot follows preparations for the June 6, 1944 Allied invasion of Europe and the actual day. Poor weather was delaying the invasion and it continues throughout the day of June 5. On the Allied side the story is told through the events as they affected five different attacking groups. They are: the 82nd Airborne paratroopers led by Lt. Col. Benjamin Vandervoort played by John Wayne, the 505th Infantry Battle Group led by Brig. Gen. Norman Cota played by Robert Mitchum, the RAF with Richard Burton taking the lead role of David Campbell, a British glider and parachute group commanded by Richard Todd as Maj. John Howard, and a British special forces group led by Lord Lovat played by Peter Lawford. On the German side the anxiety and uncertainty is well portrayed by a strong group of German actors including Curt Jurgens as Maj. Gen. Gunther Blumentritt, Werner Hinz as Field Marshal Erwin Rommel, and Gert Frobe as Sgt. Kaffekanne.

Throughout the day the scenes switch back and forth among all of these groups showing their impatience and dread. Also shown is the work proceeding at headquarters in preparation for a 9:30 P.M. decisive meeting with the top brass. Several German officers worry and ask that a Panzer division be rushed to the English Channel shore area. No decision on this request can be made until Hitler (who has taken a sleeping pill) awakens.

Across the English Channel at Allied headquarters the weather clears somewhat and Eisenhower, played by Henry Grace, gravely and reluctantly makes the decision to go forward with the invasion. Most important is the advice of meteorologists on the tides, the moon, and the winds. Waiting for good weather as the Allies had for invasions of Africa and Italy would delay the European invasion until July. "I don't like it," says Ike, "but I don't see how we can possibly do anything else." His general staff supports him.

The remainder of this long film of the longest day follows the action of the invasion and how it affects the five aforementioned groups. The invasion scenes are strong and realistic but do not approach those achieved by Steven Speilberg's *Saving Private Ryan* (1998) in the 20-minute opening sequence of the landing. Still, the Allies in *The Longest Day* face one mishap after another and relentless German firepower. However, the desire of the filmmakers was to cover in the broadest way the whole of the event and not just the landings at Omaha and Utah beaches.

So convincing are the actors in their roles that even John Wayne's swaggering seems appropriate as the tough "old man" who, as his men note, changes as do they all during this battle. Richard Todd, leader of the glider assault on the Orne River Bridge, actually served during that assault. Joseph Lowe was a Ranger at Ponte du Hoc.

German officers get equal, balanced treatment and convincing interpretation. They are shown doubting such an "illogical" landing site as Normandy (they predicted Calais) and illogical bad-weather invasion time taken by the Allies (they predicted the fair weather previously favored by the Allies). Much is made by the use of Verlaine's poetry in coded messages intercepted over French Resistance radio broadcasts.

Both sides employ similar doubts: "Whose side is God on?"

But it is the soldiers in the trenches who make war and movies as they have since *All*

Quiet on the Western Front (1930), winner of one of the first Academy Awards and one of the best pictures about war. Interspersed between battle scenes are such vignettes as the humor and frustration shown by Red Buttons as Pvt. John Steele who lands on the church tower of St. Mere-Eglise and watches the action of his comrades.

Among these comrades are well-known international actors such as Arletty, Jean-Louis Barrault (in French roles), and Sean Connery, Mel Ferrer, Sal Mineo, George Segal, and Rod Steiger (as Allied troops in credits order).

Dwight David Eisenhower was the Supreme Allied Commander at the time of the invasion. As such he chaired the June 5 meeting at which the decision was made to go ahead with the invasion. In his only appearance in this film, played by little-known actor Henry Grace for his close resemblance, Eisenhower obviously controls the meeting of the general staff. Eisenhower offered to play the role but makeup experts felt it too difficult to make him appear younger. Grace, however, shows the careful probity and consideration of this soon-to-be five-star general.

This landmark day in the history of World War II and in the history of many associated with the war and its effects remains etched in memory. With such expectations for historicity, producer Darryl F. Zanuck shows his usual attention to authenticity (as he did in *The Long Gray Line*), going over his $8 million budget and employing shooting locales in Cyprus, Corsica, and France. He hired the book's authors, Cornelius Ryan and Romain Gary, with two other writers, David Pursall and Jack Seddon. Zanuck also employed Sir Frederick Morgan and Vice Admiral Friedrich Ruge as Allied and German military consultants, respectively. The film won Oscars for Best Cinematography in Black and White, Best Effects, Special Effects, and Best Art Direction-Set Decoration Black and White.

The Front (1976)

Eisenhower: Archival Footage.

Because of this film's importance (it was named one of the year's ten best by the National Board of Review), the appearance of Cold War presidents Truman and Eisenhower deserves mention. Both are seen in archival footage in a black-and-white newsreel montage during the credits of the Technicolor film, Ike with Lily Pons, the opera singer. The background music during this sequence is Frank Sinatra singing "Young at Heart." For complete details on the film, see Chapter 33 on Harry S Truman.

The Right Stuff (1983)

Eisenhower: Robert Beer. *Other Cast:* Sam Shepard (Capt./Col. Chuck Yeager), Scott Glenn (Capt. Alan Bartlett Shepard Jr.), Ed Harris (Maj. John Herschel Glenn Jr.), Dennis Quaid (Capt. Leroy Gordon Cooper Jr.), Fred Ward (Capt. Virgil Ivan "Gus" Grissom), Barbara Hershey (Glennis Yeager), Kim Stanley (Pancho Barnes), Veronica Cartwright (Betty Grissom), Pamela Reed (Trudy Cooper), Scott Paulin (Capt. Donald Kent "Deke" Slayton), Charles Frank (Lt. Cmdr. Malcolm Scott Carpenter), Lance Henriksen (Lt. Cmdr. Walter Martin Shirra Jr.), Donald Moffat (Lyndon B. Johnson), Levon Helm (Capt. Jack Ridley), Mary Jo Deschanel (Annie Glenn). *Director:* Philip Kaufman. *Producers:* Robert Chartoff, Erwin Winkler. *Screenplay:* Philip Kaufman, Tom Wolfe, William Goldman. *Cinematography:*

Caleb Deschanel. *Music:* Bill Conti. *Art Director:* W. Stewart Campbell, Richard J. Lawrence. *Special Effects:* Jordan Belson, Gary Gutierrez. *Studio:* Ladd Co./Warner Bros. *Length:* 193 minutes.

The Right Stuff is the fictionalized yet reasonably accurate story of the first days of the American space program. Based on the Tom Wolfe novel of the same name, the film begins with a look at the poorly financed but personally rewarding life of the test pilots who, in the years immediately following World War II, worked to see how far and how fast the new jet engines would take them. This early portion of the film centers on the best and brightest test pilot, Chuck Yeager, played by Sam Shepard. Brilliant a pilot as he is, he lacks the college degree needed for the space program.

Even though Wolfe receives screenwriting credit with director Philip Kaufman, the film fails to capture the dark and dangerous side of flying that Wolfe describes. Missing is his signature stylistic phrase-making—"the right stuff" that the astronauts have—and repetitive phrases such as the allusion to *Ten Little Indians* used at the funerals of the pilots. What remains includes a minister who first appears in an early scene at the door of a houseful of crying women and resurfaces in other somber scenes.

Under Kaufman's direction the acting does capture the camaraderie (and the competition) among the pilots, their seat-of-the-pants, gum-chewing (Beemans is the chosen gum) approach to their craft, and the loathing their wives have for such exploits. Shepard stands out in his easy, earnest fearlessness—he chases the sound barrier in a plane as effortlessly as he chases women on a horse.

Russian space advances and the accelerated Cold War demands for an American response interrupt the dangerous but relatively isolated life of test pilots. The careful selection and rigorous training of the first seven astronauts takes up the rest of the first half of the film. Emphasis is on four of the seven: John Glenn, played by Ed Harris; Alan Shepard, played by Scott Glenn; Gordon Cooper, played by Dennis Quaid; and Gus Grissom, played by Fred Ward. Cooper and Grissom come from the old group of Air Force test pilots and represent a different lifestyle from the other astronauts. This difference causes early tension within the group of seven.

The second half of the movie relates the difficulties of the early space program, particularly the development of a reliable rocket. Included are shot after shot of the early flights of the four main protagonists: Shepard and Grissom with their sub-orbital flights (even Grissom's misadventure and loss of his capsule) and Glenn and Cooper with their multi-orbital flights (especially the dramatic need to cut short Glenn's flight to three orbits due to an instrument indication of a malfunctioning heat shield). Interspersed throughout the film are numerous strains the astronauts experienced with their families, the everpresent press, politicians, and rocket scientists.

America didn't get a man up there first; the Russians beat them. This led to much American scientific testing of even monkeys for missions—that the astronauts deplored. So does President Eisenhower in the one short scene in which he's featured. Played by Robert Beer, he nods his head and clenches his teeth.

Among the other authentic aspects of this film are archival footage of presidents John F. Kennedy and Lyndon B. Johnson, plus LBJ as portrayed by an actor. Added are spectacular shots of test planes and missiles in flight and the first realistic shots of spacecraft entry. The film won Academy Awards for Best Effects, Sound Effects Editing, Best Film Editing, and Best Music, Original Score.

My Science Project (1985)

Eisenhower: Robert Beer. *Other Cast:* John Stockwell (Michael Harlan), Danielle von Zerneck (Ellie Sawyer), Fisher Stevens (Vince Latello), Raphael Sbarge (Sherman), Dennis Hopper (Bob Roberts), Richard Masur (Detective Jack Nulty), Barry Corbin (Lew Harlan). *Director-Writer:* Jonathan R. Betuel. *Producer:* Jonathan T. Taplin. *Music:* Peter Bernstein, Bill Heller. *Cinematography:* David M. Walsh. *Film Editing:* Carroll Timothy O'Meara. *Production Design:* David L. Snyder. *Set Decoration:* Jerry Wunderlich. *Studio:* Silver Screen Partners/Touchstone Pictures. *Length:* 94 minutes.

This kid-flick begins as a reasonable teenage sci-fi film but loses its way about halfway through and has a disappointing ending. The story revolves around car fanatic Michael Harlan (John Stockwell) who has not completed his high school science project for his fading flower-child teacher, Bob Roberts (Dennis Hopper). Harlan plans to use a piece of equipment he finds in an Air Force disposal facility to meet the project requirement. It turns out that the equipment is from an alien spaceship and, in addition to causing time warps, it seeks out all the energy it can consume, from batteries, electric power grids, etc. After meeting all of the warriors and monsters, both historical and future, that any teenage sci-fi film should have, Harlan is finally able to turn off the machine, but not before it virtually destroys the high school.

President Eisenhower (Robert Beer) is used in the first sequence, which is set in 1957, 28 years before the main action, to establish the premise of the film. It is a portentous beginning. As the credits roll over approaching darkness, a motorcade winds through the Western mountainous desert country. Soon two motorcycles, followed by two limousines enter Dawson Air Force Base. In a shot reminiscent of Alfred Hitchcock's introduction of the two leading characters in *Strangers on a Train* (1951), the camera tilts to Ike's golf shoes as he steps from his limo. He tells the general (John Carter) he doesn't mind being called on the hot line as his "golf game isn't what it used to be." The general shows Ike an alien spacecraft. After ensuring that the press had not been informed, Ike tells the general to "get rid of it" and leaves. The logic of this statement is a bit hard to understand, and the military obviously didn't succeed or there would not have been a film because Harlan finds a piece of the spacecraft that he calls in his simplistic fashion, a "gizmo."

Robert Beer, also seen as Ike in *The Right Stuff*, has a slight physical resemblance to Eisenhower and carries off the brief appearance, key statement included, reasonably well. The rest of director-writer Jonathan R. Betuel's film lacks any semblance of reasonable development.

35

John Fitzgerald Kennedy (1961–1963)

John Fitzgerald Kennedy. (Courtesy of Library of Congress.)

Despite the tarnished image that became known after his assassination, the glow of Camelot illuminates John F. Kennedy because of his handling of the Cuban Missile Crisis, considered the most dangerous event of the Cold War[1]; his development of the Civil Rights Act of 1964, and his inspiriting inaugural call to "ask what you can do for your country." This second son of wealthy Joseph P. Kennedy openly acknowledged how the family fortune aided his ascent in politics: from congressman and senator to president of the "New Frontier."

Political commentators wrote of a Hundred Days that would duplicate or even surpass those of Franklin Roosevelt.[2] JFK established the Peace Corps by executive order; ordered a review of the Food for Peace program; established presidential commissions on the status of women, on space and on employment discrimination; and expanded food assistance to the war-torn Congo.[3]

Determined to take the initiative in the Cold War, JFK ordered an invasion of Cuba by exile forces that ended in disaster (the Bay of Pigs) but continued by confronting Nikita Khrushchev, the then–Soviet leader; containing the Cuban missile crisis with the Communists; negotiating the first arms control treaty; expanding American presence in Vietnam, and launching the space program to the moon.

JFK's wife Jacqueline brought culture and style to the White House and abroad. Such was her impact that JFK remarked he was the man who accompanied Jackie to Paris. His intellectual speed and vivacity, remarkable mastery of the data of government, terse, self-mocking wit, and exhilarating personal command drew the admiration of the press corps that kept his private life, notably his extramarital sexual activities, private until after his untimely death.[4] He leaves an unfulfilled legacy to many Americans.

35—*John Fitzgerald Kennedy (1961–1963)* 297

THE FILMS

Although there have been a number of serious films with Kennedy as a character including two biopics, *PT-109* and *JFK*, the vast majority of JFK films particularly in recent years have JFK in a minor role in satire or teenage films. Thus the powerful drama of *Thirteen Days* is more than offset by the silliness of *Company Man* or *Bubba Ho-tep*.

PT 109 (1963)

Kennedy: Cliff Robertson. *Other Cast:* Ty Hardin (Ensign Leonard J. Thom), James Gregory (Cmdr. Ritchie), Robert Culp (Ensign George "Barney" Ross), Grant Williams (Lt. Alvin Cluster), Lew Gallo (Yeoman Rogers). *Director:* Leslie H. Martinson. *Producer:* Bryan Foy. *Writing Credits:* Richard L. Breen, Robert J. Donovan, Vincent Flaherty, Howard Sheehan. *Music:* David Buttolph, Howard Jackson, William Lava. *Cinematography:* Robert Surtees. *Film Editing:* Folmar Blangsted. *Art Direction:* Leo K. Kuter. *Set Decoration:* John P. Austin. *Makeup:* Gordon Bau. *Studio:* Warner Bros. *Length:* 140 minutes.

Kennedy dominates this film as he did the American public's imagination during his truncated administration. In this re-enactment of the young ensign's heroic action during World War II, Cliff Robertson exudes the athleticism, charm, courage, and grace (under pressure, one of JFK's favorite lines) although he lacks the Boston accent of the 35th president.

PT 109 (1963): Cliff Robertson as John Fitzgerald Kennedy appears ready to take on anybody in this biopic concerning Kennedy's World War II experience in the Pacific Theater. Under the supervision of Jack L. Warner, this was a Warner Bros. Pictures release. (Courtesy of George Eastman House.)

The action occurs in the Solomon Islands where the Japanese Imperial Fleet is bombarding the ill-prepared American Navy. JFK (Robertson) shows his patriotism from the beginning of the film when he questions the spirit of a seaman who wants to be transferred to Hawaii for safer duty. On the contrary, JFK wants to command a boat and goes to tough Commander Ritchie (James Gregory) for permission. Because of JFK's low rank, Ritchie says he "does not want to know about him ... just run a boat."

Using the only men available, JFK develops a crew of 13 for the Patrol Torpedo (PT) Boat 109. On a mission to rescue some stranded Americans on a small Pacific island, they face Japanese gunfire that hits PT 109. JFK springs to action, jumping into the water to pull an injured man to shore, then returns for another through the burning debris of his boat. Encamped on a remote island, some of the men argue about surrendering, but JFK says, "Knock it off." He jokes that he "can't send for room service" even when radio reports announce that their boat has no survivors.

In desperation, JFK swims the legendary miles to Ferguson Passage for help. He leaves a message in a coconut and returns, exhausted but stalwart about not giving up. Eventually an Australian boat arrives and takes them to a rescue ship. On board JFK refuses to take leave and tells his men, "I just hope I have more men like you." He then is given charge of a new boat with three of his PT 109 crew. The always tough Comdr. Ritchie jokes, "Just a bunch of jockeys."

Eat Your Makeup (1968)

Kennedy: Howard Gruber. *Other Cast:* Lizzy Temple Black (The Child Star), Divine (Jacqueline Kennedy), David Lochary (Governess's Boy Friend), Mary Vivian Pearce (Kidnapped Model), John Waters. *Director-Writer-Producer-Cinematographer-Film Editor:* John Waters. *Studio:* Dreamland. *Length:* 45 minutes.

This film has never been shown commercially but word-of-mouth about a two-day run in a Baltimore church basement makes it most sought after by John Waters diehards. It is his first 16mm film and he directs, writes, producers, films, edits, and stars in it. The basic story has a deranged nanny kidnapping models and forcing them to eat their makeup before being "modeled to death." John F. (Howard Gruber) and Jacqueline Kennedy (Divine) appear.

Gas-s-s-s ... or It May Become Necessary to Destroy the World to Save It! (1971)

Kennedy: Unnamed actor. *Other Cast:* Bob Corff (Coel), Elaine Giftos (Cilla), Bud Cort (Hooper), Talia Shire (Coralee), Ben Vereen (Carlos), Cindy Williams (Marissa), Alex Wilson (Jason), Lou Procopio (Marshal McLuhan), Phil Borneo (Quant), Alan Braunstein (Dr. Drake). *Director-Producer:* Roger Corman. *Writing Credits:* George Armitage. *Music:* Country Joe McDonald, Barry Melton. *Cinematography:* Ron Dexter. *Film Editing:* George Van Noy. *Art Direction:* David Nichols. *Set Decoration:* Stephan Graham. *Makeup:* Dean Cundey. *Art:* Peter Fain. *Sound:* James M. Tannenbaum. *Special Effects:* Conrad Rothmann. *Studio:* San Jacinto Productions. *Length:* 79 minutes.

Roger Corman, prolific producer and director of mainly low-budget films in many genres, ended his association with American International Pictures after its elimination of

"God" and the original ending of this comedy-drama. The "Jewish comic" type voice of God was considered sacrilegious and the ending panorama shot with Cilla (Elaine Giftos) and Coel (Bob Corff) walking into the sunset with marching bands and the complete cast was considered a cliché. Corman then formed New World Pictures.

This counter-culture story follows Cilla and Coel to a safe haven hippie commune in New Mexico after experimental nerve gas accidentally released from an Alaskan defense plant speeds up the aging processes of everyone over 25 to early death. Facing expulsion, the couple is saved by lightning that suddenly strikes. The earth opens up from which emerges a procession of legendary heroes, including Kennedy.

Executive Action (1973)

Kennedy: Archival footage. *Other cast:* Burt Lancaster (Farrington), Robert Ryan (Foster), Will Geer (Ferguson), Gilbert Green (Paulitz), John Anderson (Halliday), Paul Carr (Gunman Christ), Deanna Darrin (Stripper), James MacCall (Oswald Imposter). *Director:* David Miller. *Producer:* Edward Lewis. *Writing Credits:* Donald Freed, Mark Lane, Dalton Trumbo. *Cinematography:* Robert Steadman. *Music:* Randy Edelman. *Film Editing:* George Grenville. *Art Direction:* Kirk Axtell. *Studio:* Executive Action Enterprises, Wakefield-Orloff Productions. *Length:* 91 minutes.

Although not falling within the strict definition of the films covered in this work, because Kennedy is not portrayed by an actor, *Executive Action* is included because Kennedy is the main character and the film is the precursor to Oliver Stone's *JFK* (1991).

The cast of sinister conservatives is outstanding with Burt Lancaster, Robert Ryan, and Will Geer trying to make some sense of Dalton Trumbo's dialogue. This was one of Trumbo's last screenplays. It is based on Mark Lane's *Rush to Judgment*, considered the JFK conspiracy theorist's bible. The story is that a right-wing cartel of military and industrial interests was behind the JFK assassination.

All Movie Guide's Hal Erickson classified the dialogue as "silly and sophomoric" and added, "The microphone boom makes so many unexpected appearances that it should have been given Special Guest Star billing." He also noted that conspiracy theorists should have had a field day noting the similarities between *Executive Action* and *JFK*.

President Kennedy appears throughout the film in archival footage.

The Private Files of J. Edgar Hoover (1977)

Kennedy: Unnamed actor.

One of the central subplots in the film concerns the relationship between Hoover (Broderick Crawford) and Attorney General Robert Kennedy (Michael Parks). By 1961 Hoover has been in his job as head of the FBI for 35 years and obviously does not appreciate being ordered around by a young Kennedy. To alleviate this unpleasantness he subtly, yet thoroughly, informs RFK that he has files on his brother Jack's sexual activity and his relationship with the Mafia.

JFK convinces Robert that he can handle Hoover. This actor has some physical resemblance to Kennedy, but his Boston accent is very poor. He does, however, exude JFK's charm and confidence in his actions. For details, see Chapter 32 on Franklin D. Roosevelt.

Impure Thoughts (1985)

Kennedy: Bob Flor (voice). *Other Cast:* John Putch (Danny Stubbs), Terry Beaver (William Miller), Brad Dourif (Kevin Harrington), Lane Davies (Steve Barrett), Judith Anderson (The Sister of Purgatory voice). *Director-Producer:* Michael A. Simpson. *Producer:* Michael J. Malloy. *Writing Credits:* Michael J. Malloy, Michael A. Simpson. *Composer:* David Kurtz, James Oliverio. *Editor:* Wade Watkins. *Production Designer:* Guy Tuttle. *Studio:* ASA Communications. *Length:* 87 minutes.

Four men who attended a Catholic school together as children all die from various causes and find themselves seated around a table in a nondescript room. They are Danny Stubbs (John Putch), William Miller (Terry Beaver), Kevin Harrington (Brad Dourif), and Steve Barrett (Lane Davies). The location is clear when narrator Dame Judith Anderson asks the question, "What is Purgatory?"

From this point the film becomes a series of flashbacks, some comic, some serious, illustrating the relationship of the men while they attended school. Most of the situations relate to events that would be common to any child who attended a Catholic school in the 1950s and 1960s.

The only factor that seems to tie their lives together is the election, presidency, and assassination of Kennedy, the first (and only) Roman Catholic president of the United States. As the men talk about their lives together, the only time that they can remember when they acted in concert was the day that Kennedy was assassinated. It was then when they all drank sacramental wine in the sacristy of the church. This must have been the problem event because three of the four disappear after remembering the incident.

In Catholic theology, purgatory is an interim place between death and Heaven that serves as punishment for those who die with venial (not serious) sins on their souls and must await atonement for these small sins before being allowed into Heaven. For the three men, it appears that remembering the incident with the sacramental wine was sufficient to achieve atonement.

Although President Kennedy is central to the plot, he mainly appears in archival footage. However, there is a credited voice for Kennedy by Bob Flor. Unfortunately, Flor was not good enough with Kennedy's Boston accent to fool anybody who ever heard the real president.

JFK (1991)

Kennedy: Archival footage, Steven Reed. *Other Cast:* Kevin Costner (Jim Garrison), Sissy Spacek (Liz Garrison), Tommy Lee Jones (Clay Shaw), Gary Oldman (Lee Harvey Oswald), Michael Rooker (Bill Broussard), Jay O. Sanders (Lou Ivon), Laurie Metcalf (Suzie Cox), Beata Pozniak (Marina Oswald), Brian Doyle-Murray (Jack Ruby), Jim Garrison (Chief Justice Earl Warren), Gary Grubbs (Al Oser). *Director:* Oliver Stone. *Producer:* A. Kitman Ho. *Writing Credits:* Jim Marrs, Jim Garrison, Zachary Sklar. *Cinematography:* Robert Richardson. *Music:* John Williams. *Film Editor:* Frank Corwin, Joe Hutshing, Pietro Scalia. *Art Direction:* Derek R. Hill, Alan Tomkins. *Set Designer:* Crispian Sallis. *Costume Design:* Marlene Stewart. *Sound:* Todd A. Maitland. *Makeup:* Craig Berkeley. *Studio:* Alcro Films/Canal Plus/Ixtlan Corp./Regency Enterprises/Warner Bros. *Length:* 189 minutes.

Oliver Stone directs this dramatic political thriller based on Jim Garrison's conspiracy theory about the investigation and subsequent Warren Commission report on the assassination of President Kennedy. It is less of a character study of the president than Stone's politically moralistic view of JFK's untimely death. Stone, in his DVD commentary, notes the many other theories about JFK's death and accepts the critical and historical criticism of his film. Most balanced is Desson Howe's in *The Washington Post*: "[Stone] exercised his full prerogative to use poetic license. He should feel more than mere craftsman's satisfaction in the result." Shot in only 72 days, the film combines Stone's dramatic license (composite characters, combination of text and original script, compression of events) and modern film techniques (mixture of black-and-white and color film, both archival and fictional; real-life photos; TV footage; and lifelike models) as well as thematic music by John Williams. Nominated for eight Academy Awards, *JFK* received one for Best Photography and another for Editing.

Stone's story begins with New Orleans District Attorney Jim Garrison's (Kevin Costner) investigation of the New Orleans connections to the Dallas assassination, particularly of Clay Shaw (Tommy Lee Jones), a New Orleans international businessman and *bon vivant*. The investigation leads to Shaw's trial in the final (50-minute) courtroom scene. Garrison's investigation stops for three years until he runs into Sen. Russell Long (Walter Matthau, one of the many familiar stars in the film) on a flight to Washington, D.C. The senator asserts that Lee Harvey Oswald, the murdered assassin of JFK, was "a patsy." Garrison, aided by his small team of dedicated assistant district attorneys (with one defection), begins his obsessive quest, his role as the surrogate for national doubts about the Oswald theory (73 percent of the U.S. public in a Gallup poll were against the Oswald theory). "We're through-the-looking-glass people," Garrison says to his team, "white is black and black is white." Depicted as driven by the search for truth and love for country with a wonderful memory, wry humor, and decency (he will not tolerate infighting and profanity), Costner as Garrison gives an arresting and convincing performance, his best since *Dances with Wolves* (1990). Garrison ironically appears as Chief Justice Earl Warren. Eventually Garrison documented his theory in *On the Trail of Assassins*, the basis for the screenplay by Stone and Zachary Sklar along with Jim Marrs's *Crossfire: The Plot That Killed Kennedy*.

JFK appears mostly in archival footage with a few reenacted scenes in which Steven Reed stands in as his double. The theme of this film is that there was a conspiracy to kill JFK by those who opposed his policies in Cuba (not to invade) and in Vietnam (to withdraw)—what Garrison movingly calls in his trial summation "a *coup d'etat*, a secret murder at the heart of the American dream." *JFK* was termed a "masterpiece of film assembly" by Roger Ebert of the *Chicago Sun Times* (12/20/91) who asserted, "The important point is that Stone does not subscribe to all of Garrison's theories and rewrites history to make Garrison the symbolic center of his film because Garrison is the only man who attempted to bring anyone into court about this political murder."

Of the many critical comments about the film, Robert A. Rosenstone's best summarizes the controversy: "[T]he reaction it has evoked makes it seem like a very successful piece of historical work. Not a work that tells us the truth about the past, but one that questions the official truths about the past so provocatively that we are forced once again to look to history and consider what those events mean to us today."[5]

Love Field (1992)

Kennedy: Bob Gill, archival footage. *Other Cast*: Michelle Pfeiffer (Lurene Hallett), Dennis Haysbert (Paul Cater), Stephanie McFadden (Jonell), Brian Kerwin (Ray Hallett), Louise

Latham (Mrs. Enright), Peggy Rea (Mrs. Heisenbuttal), Beth Grant (Hazel), Johnny Ray McGhee (Mechanic), Cooper Huckabee (Deputy Swinson), Troy Evans (Lt. Galvan), Mark Miller (Trooper Exley), Pearl Jones (Mrs. Baker), Rhoda Griffis (Jacqueline Kennedy). *Director:* Jonathan Kaplan. *Producers:* George Goodman, Kate Guinzburg. *Writing Credits:* Don Roos. *Music:* Jerry Goldsmith. *Cinematography:* Ralf D. Bode. *Film Editing:* Jane Kurson. *Production Design:* Mark S. Freeborn. *Art Direction:* Lance King, David Willson. *Set Decoration:* Jim Erickson. *Costume Design:* Colleen Atwood, Peter Mitchell. *Studio:* Orion/Sanford-Pillsbury Productions. *Length:* 102 minutes.

In an Academy Award–nominated role, Michelle Pfeiffer plays a sweet, naïve Texas hairdresser named Lurene Hallett obsessed by Jacqueline Kennedy. Hallett shows her special bond with the First Lady in her hairdo, clothes, and devotion to President Kennedy whom she goes to see at Love Field, the airport in Dallas where the Kennedys arrived that fateful day. Bob Gill as a look-alike JFK and Rhoda Griffis as a similarly convincing Jackie appear briefly, getting off the plane and mingling with the crowd. Even with neighbor Mrs. Heisenbuttal (Peggy Rea) in a wheelchair, Hallet does not get to shake hands with Jackie.

Driving through Dallas, a well-constructed simulation of the city, Hallett senses something wrong and learns of the assassination. Despite the objection of her redneck husband Ray (Brian Kerwin), she goes "to my president's funeral." "You go too far," says her husband. And she does: On a bus to D.C. she befriends a black man, Paul Cater (Dennis Haysbert), and his daughter Jonell (Stephanie McFadden) and volunteers him to give an eyewitness account of an accident.

The simple hero-worship plot becomes more complicated than many critics feel necessary. Now it's a road movie with romantic undertones as Hallet, Cater, and Jonell flee the FBI and other law enforcement officers in a stolen car. Hallet seems as unaware of the problems created by her white presence with a black man in the 1963 South with such behavior as her heartfelt but naïve utterance, "Kennedy did a lot for your people." However, the film reveals race relations of this period and also presents a fine period recreation as well as apt archive footage of JFK's assassination.

Malcolm X (1992)

Kennedy: Steve Reed. *Other Cast:* Denzel Washington (Malcolm X), Spike Lee (Shorty), Angela Bassett (Betty Shabazz), Al Freeman Jr. (Elijah Muhammad), Delroy Lindo (West Indian Archie), Albert Hall (Baines). Christopher Plummer (Chaplain Gill), William Kunstler (Judge), Ossie Davis (Eulogy Performer). *Director:* Spike Lee. *Producers:* Spike Lee, Marvin Worth. *Writing Credits:* Alex Haley, Malcolm X, Arnold Perl, Spike Lee. *Music:* Terence Blanchard, John Coltrane, Ella Fitzgerald, Chick Webb, Lionel Hampton. *Cinematography:* Ernest R. Dickerson. *Film Editing:* Barry Alexander Brown. *Production Design:* Tom Warren. *Set Direction:* Ted Glass. *Costume Design:* Ruth Carter. *Studio:* 40 Acres and a Mule Filmworks/Largo International/Warner Bros. *Length:* 205 minutes.

This is an epic story of an important American historical figure (Malcolm X) by one of America's finest filmmakers (Spike Lee) starring one of its best actors (Denzel Washington). In telling this life story, Lee stresses man's ability to change—from a Nebraska preacher's son to a criminal and cocaine user to a charismatic leader of the Nation of Islam who finds his true faith by journeying to Mecca.

Using Alex Haley and Malcolm X's *The Autobiography of Malcolm X,* Lee wrote his screenplay with Arnold Perl in three "acts." The first deals with the murder of Malcolm X's father, the institutionalizing of his mother for insanity, and the "parceling out" of their five children with Malcolm treated as "invisible" and encouraged to "work with his hands" rather than be the lawyer he wishes. So Malcolm gets a job as a Pullman porter but soon involves himself with a Harlem gangster and finds himself in prison. The second act shows Malcolm in prison, defiant as ever, eventually turning to the teachings of the Nation of Islam as explained by fellow inmate Baines (Albert Hall). The third act, the most dramatic, involves Malcolm's break with the Nation of Islam, his journey to Mecca, and, tragically, his death.

Lee, as director, creates a man of many parts that Washington handles with equal skill. Lee never allows his sympathy to surface and, with cinematographer Ernest Dickerson, creates a somber mood of darkness and shadows. Intercuts of black-and-white archival footage reveal how Malcolm's public image was being shaped.

But a sequence on JFK's assassination is not archival; it is restaged in black and white with actors closely resembling the president (Steve Reed) and the First Lady (Jodie Farber). Short as it is, this sequence is so placed that its impact is enhanced. It recreates the political excitement of the president's visit to Dallas, the reaction of the populace, and the shocking effect of the shooting itself. The actors move as if they were there, a true reproduction of archival footage.

Ruby (1992)

Kennedy: Gerard David (in Las Vegas), Kevin Wiggins (in Dallas). *Other Cast:* Danny Aiello (Jack Ruby), Sherilyn Fenn (Candy Cane), Arliss Howard (Maxwell), Tobin Bell (David Ferrie), Willie Garson (Lee Harvey Oswald), Joe Viterelli (Joseph Valachi), Sean McGraw (Governor Connally), Terri Zee (Mrs. Connally). *Director:* John Mackenzie. *Producer:* Michael Kuhn. *Writing Credits:* Stephen Davis. *Music:* John Scott. *Cinematography:* Phil Meheux. *Film Editing:* Richard Trevor. *Production Design:* David Brisbin. *Art Direction:* Ken Hardy. *Set Decoration:* Lauri Gaffin. *Costume Design:* Susie DeSanto. *Studio:* Kuzui Enterprises/Polygram/PropagandaFilms/The Rank Organisation Film Productions Ltd. *Length:* 111 minutes.

Released a year after Oliver Stone's *JFK*, *Ruby* is essentially the same conspiracy theory film. But the story is told from Jack Ruby's point of view. Ruby (Danny Aiello) is portrayed as a longtime criminal (and a Mafia hit man) with a heart of gold who wanders in and out of high level Mafia meetings. Ultimately, he is selected to be one of the "patsies" in the Kennedy assassination.

A completely fictional character, a stripper at Jack Ruby's nightclub, Candy Cane (Sherilyn Fenn), appears in an attempt to tie this confusing theory together. Cane becomes a friend of one of the Mafia bosses and is used by him as Mafia bait for President Kennedy (the reason for this is never explained).

The film proceeds through the assassination of Kennedy and Ruby's killing of Lee Harvey Oswald. Although in the context of the film it is never made clear what Ruby hopes to accomplish, it is surmised that he kills Oswald to get away from the conspirators and into the hands of the police so that he could tell the full story of the conspiracy. Unfortunately, this is not the only unclear aspect of the film as it points a finger, rather a whole hand, at the Mafia, the anti–Castro Cubans, the CIA, and the FBI without actually showing (and explaining) the interrelationships of the accused. In the end, Ruby's attempt at clarification fails because of conspirators in the justice and penal systems.

In addition to archival footage of the president leading up to and including the assassination, JFK appears in two different fictional scenes played by two different actors. Gerard David portrays Kennedy in a Las Vegas nightclub scene in which he is introduced to Candy Cane, who then joins him at his table with implications for a later liaison. Kevin Wiggins plays Kennedy in a Dallas scene that also has implications that he deals with the Mafia. Why director Mackenzie and writer Davis made this casting decision is unclear.

Although the film is confusing and poorly produced, Aiello gives an estimable portrayal of Ruby, even if one believes that lowlife Ruby did not deserve any sympathy.

Forrest Gump (1994)

Kennedy: Archival footage and Jed Gillin (voice). *Other Cast*: Tom Hanks (Forrest Gump), Robin Wright Penn (Jenny Curran), Gary Sinise (Lt. Dan Taylor), Mykelti Williamson (Pvt. Benjamin Buford "Bubba" Blue), Sally Field (Mrs. Gump), Rebecca Williams (Nurse at Park Bench), Michael Conner Humphreys (Young Forrest Gump). *Director*: Robert Zemeckis. *Producers*: Wendy Finerman, Steve Starkey, Steve Tisch. *Writing Credits*: Kinston Groom, Eric Roth, Charlie Peters, Ernest Thompson. *Music*: Joel Sill, Alan Silvestri. *Cinematography*: Don Burgess, David M. Dunlap. *Film Editing*: Arthur Schmidt. *Production Design*: Rick Carter. *Art Direction*: Leslie McDonald, William James Teegarden. *Set Decoration*: Nancy Haigh. *Costume Design*: Joanna Johnston. *Studio*: Paramount. *Length*: 142 minutes.

Although he's sub-normal IQ, Forrest Gump (Tom Hanks) follows his mother's (Sally Field) philosophy of "Stupid is as stupid does" and lives an innocent life becoming a football star, Vietnam hero, table-tennis champion, shrimp boat millionaire, and cross-country runner with a following. While doing this he is present, thanks to archival footage, but not quite cognizant at many historical events and meets three American presidents and finally weds his childhood sweetheart Jenny (Robin Wright Penn). Hanks won an Oscar as he had the year before for *Philadelphia*. *Forrest Gump* received many Oscar nominations and won other awards for best picture, director Robert Zemeckis, screenplay based on material previously produced (Winston Groom's novel), film editing, and visual effects (digitally computerized imaging that allows Gump to meet the presidents). It was a technique pioneered in Woody Allen's *Zelig* (1983).

One of the most commercially successful films of all time, *Forrest Gump* grossed more than $300 million in its first year. It also caused a merchandising phenomenon including a line of "Bubba Gump" (Gump's trade name) seafood.

When Gump meets JFK in a one-shot scene, the president (in superimposed documentary footage with a voice by Jed Gillin) asks, "How does it feel to be an All American?" (football player). Gump, who has been awed by the food and drink available to the All-American football players, has drunk 15 Dr. Peppers. By the time he shakes hands with the president, he can only answer, "I gotta pee." This scene embodies a postmodern reading of the film as part allegory of Gump as Everyman and as a satire of America, particularly the importance of electronic media and the ideology of conformity vs. the culture of individualism and the American dream.[6]

The Misery Brothers (1995)

Kennedy: Jed Gillin. *Other Cast*: Leo Rossi (Michael Misery), Lorenzo Doumani (Angelo Misery), Gary Ross (Redwood Stump), Pollo Loco (Riddler), Andres Leithe (Blonde Bus

Babe), Kristi Ducati (Brunette Bus Babe), Robert Costanzo (Grandpa Miserio), Linda Lutz (Hilda Hindenberg), Michael Tylo (Minister), Paula Barbieri (Mary Kay Misery), Lou Ferrigno (Quazzie), Mother Love (Herself), Abe Vigoda (Don Frito Layleone). *Director-Writer:* Lorenzo Doumani. *Script Supervisor:* Liz Graham. *Songwriter-Composer:* Sidney James. *Sound:* Andrew DeCristofaro. *Stunts:* Leslie Hoffman. *Cinematography:* Ken Blakely. *Length:* 87 minutes.

This is basically a collection of teenage bathroom humor, sexual innuendo, and double entendres. It is also one of the top contenders for the title of "Worst Films with a President as a Character."

Taking advantage of Kennedy's reputation as a womanizer, the long opening scene has the president (Jed Gillin, previously heard in *Forrest Gump*) in his bedroom with an uncredited Marilyn Monroe look-alike playing with JFK's phallic symbol, a toy rocket. Forecasting one of his administration's accomplishments, he says, "One of these days we'll launch a rocket to the moon." Although Gillin does not look like Kennedy he does an excellent job with the JFK voice and action. MM leaves when they are interrupted by the arrival of Mary Kay Misery (Paula Barbieri), the daughter of a Mafia boss. JFK's reaction is, "Thank God, you're not Jackie." Misery asks Kennedy's help in getting her twin sons, Michael (Leo Rossi) and Angelo (director Doumani), out of Cuba. After ensuring that the boys are not his children, Kennedy agrees to help.

Beyond this point, the plot and the musical accompaniment (Sidney James is the songwriter-composer) become completely nonsensical. The surprising aspect of the film and possibly an indication of the changing media world are the cameo and extended appearances by older TV stars Dr. Joyce Brothers, Abe Vigoda, Norm Crosby, Pat Morita, Nell Carter, and Erik Estrada.

The End of a Dynasty (1998)

Kennedy: Greg S. Campbell. *Other Cast:* Joe Adkins (Jack Ruby), Cortnie Campbell (Jacqueline Kennedy), Brian Klapstein (Lee Harvey Oswald), Mike A. Martinez (Third Gunman on Grassy Knoll), George N. Thompson (Sirhan Sirhan), David Wood (David Kennedy). *Director-Writer-Producer-Cinematography-Film Editing:* Mike A. Martinez. *Music:* Walter Rizzati. *Studio:* Scythe Productions.

The ability to create a comedy out of two of the least comedic events in American history requires a great deal of skill that writer-producer-director Mike A. Martinez does not demonstrate. This recreation of a series of terrible events that befell the family, "The Kennedy Curse," is reported to be amateurish and to have been developed with a low budget.

The low budget is illustrated by the utilization of one actor, Greg S. Campbell, to portray Robert, Michael, and John F. Kennedy. Martinez also is the cinematographer and film editor and an actor, playing third Gunman on Grassy Knoll.

Norma Jean, Jack and Me (1998) aka *The Island*

Kennedy: Michael Murphy. *Other Cast:* David de Vos (Helicopter Pilot), Kai Lennox (Rob), Sally Kirkland (Norma Jean). *Director-Screenwriter-Producer:* Cyrus Nowrasteh. *Producers:* David de Vos, Paul Seydor. *Editor:* Paul Seydor. *Cinematograpy:* Nils Erickson. *Costume Designer:* Kristen Anacker. *Studio:* New Path Pictures. *Length:* 95 minutes.

Rob (Kai Lennox) washes up on a deserted Caribbean island (actually it wasn't far from Santa Barbara, California) with a bag full of drugs and money and discovers that it isn't deserted. Living on the island is an aging couple who could well be Norma Jean aka Marilyn Monroe (Sally Kirkland) and Jack Kennedy (Michael Murphy).

Rob has inadvertently stumbled onto one of the nation's top secrets. Now Jack and Norma Jean have to determine what to do to Rob in order to maintain their secret.

Director Cyrus Nowrasteh teamed with short story writer James Trivers to develop this unlikely comedic scenario.

Da Di Qin Qing (1999) aka *Love in the Big Country*

Kennedy: Mikel Short. *Other Cast:* Buxx Banner (Jack Ruby), Mic Nuggette (Lee Harvey Oswald), Carmella N. Hall (Marina Oswald—1963), Suzi Noroki (Marina Oswald—1977), Tonto Clarkton (Dave Ferry), Tom Yu (Frenchy), Tony Okabi (Agent X), Don Fung (Roc White), Pei Taki (Larry Howard), Bok Taki (CIA Agent), Tu Li (CIA Agent). *Directors:* Ng Loo, Mic Nuggette. *Producers:* Buxx Banner, Ng Loo. *Writing Credits:* Buxx Banner, Ng Loo, Mic Nuggett. *Music:* Buxx Banner, Tonto Clarkton, Mic Nuggette. *Cinematography:* Lee Loo, George "Vilmos" Todd. *Film Editing:* Harry John Stites. *Studio:* Dragon Banner Productions. *Length:* 112 minutes.

One of the viewers commenting on this film at IMDb says, "It was the worst of the JFK movies." Another viewer notes that the film is "told in a flashback and double and triple flashbacks" making it "like the *Slaughterhouse Five* of JFK flicks." These flashbacks involve Lee Harvey Oswald (Mic Nuggette) and Jack Ruby (Buxx Banner) who are hiding in Asia from a Senate investigation of the JFK assassination. Between flashbacks, they break into song.

Evil Hill (1999)

Kennedy: Jed Gillin. *Other Cast:* Timothy Dowling (Mr. Evil), Kim Little (Marilyn Monroe), Ezra Buzzington (Jeremy the Customer), Blair Hickey (Number 2). *Director:* Ryan Schifrin. *Writing Credits:* Timothy Dowling. *Music:* Deborah Lurie. *Cinematography:* Brian Baugh. *Length:* Approximately 30 minutes.

Dedicated to "the genius of Mike Myers," this comedy employs one of Myers's characters and some of his plot characteristics to make its shallow point. It runs approximately 30 minutes although various sources list it at 9 and 12 minutes.

The Myers character is Mr. Evil before he became Dr. Evil, the repulsive tyrant in *The Spy Who Shagged Me* (1999). This Mr. Evil, enacted by the film's writer Timothy Dowling, is a kindly young man whose dress (the gray Nehru-like suit worn by Dr. Evil) and appearance (bald head, intense facial expressions, and robot-like step walk) cause the town children to call him "freak."

Into his bookstore, Evil Books for Children, somewhere near Bavaria, Marilyn Monroe (Kim Little) wanders. In true Myers fashion he woos her with his naiveté and innocence, and he gives her a copy of "one of his favorites," *The Ugly Duckling*. Subsequently they bump into each other on the street and dine.

During this strangely filmed dining sequence of different costume changes by Monroe (to show time passing), Evil reveals his bizarre childhood. It seems his mother was a "hunter-gatherer" and his father a "slasher-burner," and their activities often twisted these roles. Nevertheless, she kisses him. The next day Evil goes to Monroe's hotel room, flowers in hand, for brunch. Monroe explains her boyfriend is there as JFK (Jed Gillin, doing Kennedy for the third time) comes into view, wine bottle in hand. He asks who's there, and thinking Evil a waiter says he'll "have a cup of chowder; no, lobster thermidor." Gillin, although fuller faced, resembles JFK in actions, appearance and voice enough to make his short appearance credible.

Company Man (2000)

Kennedy: Tuck Milligan. *Other Cast:* Paul Guilfoyle (Officer Hickle), Jeffrey Jones (Sen. Biggs), Reathel Bean (Sen. Farwood), Harriet Koppel (Stenographer), Douglas McGrath (Alan Quimp), Sigourney Weaver (Daisy Quimp), Terry Beaver (Ms. Judge), Kathleeen Chalfant (Mother Quimp), John Turturro (Crocker Johnson), Woody Allen (Lowther). *Directors-Writers:* Peter Askin, Douglas McGrath. *Producers:* Guy East, Rick Leed, John Penotti, James W. Skotchdopole. *Music:* David Nessim Lawrence. *Cinematography:* Russell Boyd. *Film Editing:* Camilla Toniolo. *Production Design:* Jane Musky. *Art Direction:* Patricia Woodbridge. *Costume Design:* Ruth Myers. *Makeup:* Randy Mercer. *Studio:* Foundry Film Partners/Intermedia Films/Union Generale Cinematographique. *Length:* 86 minutes.

This spoof of the Bay of Pigs and Castro assassination attempts is almost as embarrassing a comedy as the events were to President Kennedy. The fault may rest in the lack of comic timing by Douglas McGrath, who plays the lead (and co-directed and co-wrote the vehicle). McGrath is better known for *Bullets Over Broadway* (1994). As Alan Quimp, he lies (not lays as he will tell anyone interested in English grammar) to his avaricious wife Daisy (Sigourney Weaver) telling her he teachers English and Driver's Ed as a cover for his CIA job.

He does land with the CIA in backwater Cuba where he's involved in several wacky schemes to get Castro (LSD-laced drinks, defoliation, loaded cigars) with rabid anti–Castroite Crocker Johnson (John Turturro) and ennui station head Lowther (Woody Allen). Several critics suggested Allen did this as a payback for *Bullets*.

Yet Quimp wins commendation and a promotion from President Kennedy (sound-alike Tuck Milligan). During their White House meeting, the president also stumbles into a closet of three young beauties, his "3:30s," and apologies for another mishap, the arrest of Quimp's wife. That's JFK's only scene. The film was reportedly shot several years earlier, and the filmmakers' lawsuit with the production company over final editing as well as forced reshoots led to the long delay.

Thirteen Days (2000)

Kennedy: Bruce Greenwood. *Other Cast:* Kevin Costner (Kenneth P. O'Donnell), Steve Culp (Atty. Gen. Robert F. Kennedy), Walter Adrian (Vice President Lyndon B. Johnson), Dylan Baker (Secretary of Defense Robert McNamara), Michael Fairman (U.S. Ambassador to the U.N. Adlai Stevenson), Henry Strozier (Secretary of State Dean Rusk), Frank Wood (National Security Adviser McGeorge Bundy), Kevin Conway (Air Force Chief of Staff Gen. Curtis LeMay), Bill Smitrovich (Chairman of the Joint Chiefs of Staff Gen. Maxwell Taylor), Len Cariou (Dean Acheson), Stephanie Romanov (Jacqueline Kennedy). *Director:* Roger Donaldson. *Producers:* Peter O. Almond, Kevin Costner, Armyan Bernstein. *Writing Credits:* Ernest

R. May, Philip D. Zewlikow, Davis Self. *Music*: Trevor Jones. *Cinematography*: Andrzej Bartkowiak, Roger Deakins, Christopher Duddy. *Film Editing*: Conrad Buff IV. *Art Direction*: Ann Harris, Thomas T. Taylor. *Set Decoration*: Denise Pizzini. *Costume Design*: Isis Mussenden. *Special Effects Supervisor*: Grant McCune. *Studio*: Beacon Pictures. *Length*: 145 minutes.

Following the 13 days in 1962 when President Kennedy faced the Cuban missile crisis in which the U.S. and the Soviet Union approached nuclear war because of the Soviets' supplying offensive nuclear arms to its satellite, this film documents, with considerable drama, how the president, aided by his brother Robert and his special assistant, handle the literally explosive situation. It is a political thriller with insight on how the president acts and thinks as well as on how he must deal with conflicting forces in his administration, namely the military command and the State Department.

Director Roger Donaldson creates a sense of impending doom from an opening shot of nuclear explosions. He accomplishes the difficult job of showing one White House meeting after another without picturing "talking heads." And he highlights Kennedy, the center of this crisis, without diminishing the narrative role of Kevin Costner, the film's producer, as Kenny O'Donnell, Special Assistant to the president and longtime friend. Donaldson's switch from color to black-and-white confuses the viewer because the b&w drama sequences don't seem to follow any pattern and can't be discerned from newsreel footage.

The story is told through O'Donnell's involvement from his first breakfast with his wife and five children until he's called by Attorney General Bobby Kennedy (Steven Culp) to join him and the president on the portico, showing O'Donnell's influential position with the Kennedys. An earlier TV drama, "The Missiles of October," that tells the same story gets higher ratings than this film by *Salon* critic Michael Sragon (Dec. 25, 2000). Other critics give the film similar reviews. The *Boston Review*'s Alan A. Stone gave the film one of its few lesser reviews. He noted that the events precipitating Fidel Castro's asking the Soviets for offensive weapons were not stressed. He's right, there's only brief mention of the U.S. failed Cuban invasion of the Bay of Pigs.

Playing Kennedy with reserve and elegance *and* a consistent Boston accent unlike Costner's, Bruce Greenwood uses understatement: "We've no choice" on an early plan for invasion; a slight wince when he sits down reacting to his painful back; or when he questions former Secretary of State Dean Acheson's (Len Cariou). Greenwood never appears weak, just serious, worried, and not as witty as Kennedy usually was.

But who could be witty during those 13 days? Only Adlai Stevenson, who suggests a U.S. military withdrawal from Turkey in return for a Soviet one from Cuba and later, at a party, admits to O'Donnell he's "cut his political throat." This film is a man's world: Jackie (Stephanie Romanov) only appears once, pushing her party plans; O'Donnell's wife Helen (Lucinda Jenney) pops up occasionally in a domestic role. Rather than showing the confrontation between Khrushchev and Kennedy, the film deals with the best and brightest new frontier brinksmanship vs. the old men in the State and War Departments. It's based on *The Kennedy Tapes—Inside the White House During the Cuban Missile Crisis*, a documented view of those 13 days by Ernest R. May.

Bubba Ho-tep (2002)

Kennedy: Ossie Davis. *Other Cast*: Bruce Campbell (Elvis Presley/Sebastian Haff), Reggie Bannister (Rest Home Administrator), Ella Joyce (Nurse), Heidi Marnhout (Callie), Bob

Ivy (Bubba Ho-tep). *Director-Producer*: Don Coscarelli. *Writing Credits*: Joe R. Lansdale, Don Coscarelli. *Music*: Brian Tyler. *Cinematography*: Adam Janeiro. *Film Editing*: Scott J. Gill, Donald Milne. *Production Design*: Daniel Vecchione. *Art Direction*: Justin Zaharczuk. *Costume Design*: Shelley Kay. *Makeup*: Robert Kurtzman. *Studio*: Silver Sphere Corp. *Length*: 92 minutes.

Possibly the strangest role for a president in film goes to the work by Ossie Davis as John F. Kennedy in this horror comedy, based on a short story by cult author Joe R. Lansdale. Producer-director Don Coscarelli specializes in this type of film (*Phantasm* [1979]) and has surprisingly reaped broad critical acclaim for this satirical effort.

Working with "Jack," the president, is Elvis Presley, played by B-film great Bruce Campbell. Although "Jack" explains having a black body as evidence of the cleverness of his abductors, Elvis claims that he changed places with an Elvis impersonator and was never able to reverse the ruse before the impersonator died.

These two elderly gentlemen are living out their lives in a nondescript, dreary convalescent home in Mud Creek, Texas. A number of the rest home guests have died suddenly and our heroes discover that the departeds' lives and souls have been "sucked" from them by an Egyptian mummy, Ho-tep (Bob Ivy), who somehow was lost in East Texas. Ho-tep has obviously taken to East Texas since he wears snakeskin cowboy boots and a twenty-gallon Stetson. In the end and for the good of the remaining souls in Mud Creek, the mummy is sent to a more final resting place at the cost of the lives of Elvis and Jack. Ossie Davis as the black JFK plays the role with as much dignity and sincerity as possible under these cinematic circumstances.

Timequest (2002)

Kennedy: Victor Slezak. *Other Cast*: Caprice Benedetti (Jacqueline Kennedy), Vince Grant (Robert F. Kennedy), Bruce Campbell (William Roberts), Barry Corbin (Lyndon Johnson), Larry Drake (J. Edgar Hoover), Ralph Waite (The Time Traveler), Joseph Murphy (Raymond Mead), Rick Gianasi (James Robert Kennedy), Jeffrey Steiger (Lee Harvey Oswald), Marty Bufalini (Walter Cronkite), Dan Miller (Dan Rather). *Director-Writer*: Roger Dyke. *Producer*: Mary Petryshyn. *Music*: Dan Kolton. *Cinematography*: Lon Stratton. *Film Editing*: Joseph Kleinman. *Production Design*: Larry Fox. *Set Decoration*: Eric Seppi. *Costume Design*: Scarlett Jade, Chrissy Pavlick. *Makeup*: Carol Branston. *Studio*: Destination Earth LLC. *Length*: 92 minutes.

Alternative history is an often-used technique in fiction to explore the possibilities that might have ensued if an event in history had turned out differently. *Timequest* is an attempt to look at our world if the Kennedy assassination had not occurred on November 22, 1963. Although the concept provides a potentially interesting sci-fi story, such is not the case in this inexpensive and sloppily made film.

Jacqueline Kennedy (Caprice Benedetti) is in her hotel room preparing to join the motorcade in Dallas when she is visited by a Time Traveler (Ralph Waite from *The Waltons*). In a short time she and the Time Traveler are joined by her husband John Kennedy (Victor Slezak) and ultimately by Robert Kennedy (Vince Grant). After initial disbelief the Kennedy brothers are convinced of the reality of the tale told by the Time Traveler. And the Kennedy assassination is avoided. Thus begins the alternative history.

In convincing the Kennedys of his prescience, the Time Traveler also shows the brothers the effects of JFK's association with the Mafia and his unfaithfulness to Jackie. These revelations obviously make the president a changed man, and also help Robert Kennedy prevent J. Edgar Hoover (Larry Drake) from pressuring the Kennedys by exposing JFK's affair with Marilyn Monroe. Hoover doesn't because Robert Kennedy possesses photographs of Hoover in drag. All these historical possibilities are presented in a confusing, disjointed manner using three time periods: past, present, and future. Most of the future scenes occur around the time of the death of Jacqueline Kennedy who is instrumental in finding and protecting the Time Traveler. Yet, he no longer exists because of his interference with history by traveling to the past. Although everything appears the same in this future sequence, it seems that the major developments for mankind are a city on the moon, the Beatles are unknown (how the 1963 event affected the music of the 1950s is not explained), and William Jefferson Clinton is an author, not a president. One might have a different feeling as to how good the film is depending on how one feels about Clinton and the Beatles. The acting is as far from reality as the plot, and the direction only confuses the viewer. The film was given limited distribution.

Cover-Up '62 (2004)

Kennedy: Allan Cooke. *Other Cast:* David Beren (Sergeant Clemmons), Tim Furlong (Robert Kennedy), Stefan Gierasch (Dr. Greenson), John Gilbert (Chief Abernathy), Brodie Nelson (Peter Lawford), Carla Orlandi (Marilyn Monroe). *Director-Producer-Writer:* Carla Orlandi. *Music:* Jonathan Barrick, Joey Melotti. *Cinematography:* Markus Davids. *Film Editing:* Kate Christensen. *Studio:* Golden Girl Productions.

In this conspiracy story, Marilyn Monroe's death was not suicide but murder—a fatal injection of Nembutal administered by Robert Kennedy (Tim Furlong) and a Dr. Greenson (Stephan Gierasch). They did this to quiet her after an argument. With the help of Peter Lawford (Brodie Nelson) and the Secret Service, her death is called a suicide. A budget of $8,000 was enough to produce the film, released in October 2004 at the Smmash (sic) Film Festival.

36

Lyndon Baines Johnson (1963–1969)

As outsized as his native Texas, Lyndon Baines Johnson was so delusional and obsessive about the Vietnam War that he never achieved the greatness he deserved for his changes in race relations and his Great Society program Medicare and Head Start.[1] A master manipulator,[2] LBJ rose from a poor rural childhood to become a successful six-term congressman, senator, and the youngest Senate majority leader in history, moving from Texas to New Deal liberalism. He also was the youngest National Youth Administration director in the nation under his hero Franklin D. Roosevelt and the first congressman to enlist in World War II.

He achieved a remarkable legacy for a Senate leader whose party did not control the presidency. When he became president himself upon the assassination of JFK,[3] LBJ began the greatest legislative initiative in the history of the country. His legislative triumph was the landmark omnibus Civil Rights Act of 1964. It created a Fair Employment Practices Committee, barred discrimination in public accommodation, and included provision to speed desegregation of schools and promote fair voting practices. Upon winning a landslide term on his own, he continued his war on poverty, his enactment of the 1965 Voting Rights Act, and his legislation for the environment, consumerism, and the arts and humanities.

Lyndon Baines Johnson. (Courtesy of Library of Congress.)

But the Vietnam War undermined the war on poverty. The gap between expectations and reality in both these areas led to countrywide riots and protests. Inheriting the Vietnam policies of Eisenhower and Kennedy, Johnson chose to escalate the American military presence, particularly with the Gulf of Tonkin Resolution giving LBJ the greatest ever presidential war power. His lifelong closed nature led to a "credibility gap" between the administration's constant prediction of enemy defeat and the reality of the enemy's ability. As criticism of the war rose, LBJ announced he would not seek reelection. Throughout it all, his wife, Claudia Taylor ("Lady Bird"), considered the almost perfect first lady by Margaret Truman, always stood by him.

THE FILMS

For a legendary political figure such as Johnson, his cinematic legacy is slight. Although he is chronicled in book after book, especially by the Boswellian Robert Caro, there is no biopic about Johnson. Nor are there films about his efforts in building a Great Society by the greatest legislative initiative in the history of the country. He survives mainly in short scenes in films centering on other presidents.

The Private Films of J. Edgar Hoover (1977)

Johnson: Andrew Duggan.

In one brief scene in this historically limited biopic of FBI head Hoover (Broderick Crawford), he provides the new President Johnson (Andrew Duggan) with pictorial proof of JFK's extracurricular activities. Johnson is interested but changes the subject to suggest that Hoover consider retiring. Hoover, again using some of his wiretap and bugging files, convinces LBJ that he should stay in the job. Duggan does a reasonable job of portraying Johnson, but he is at a loss to project LBJ's Texas accent. For details, see Chapter 32 on FDR.

The Right Stuff (1983)

Johnson: Archival footage and Donald Moffat.

Vice President Johnson joins Presidents Eisenhower and Kennedy in this film about the original seven U.S. Mercury astronauts and their space program, based on the Tom Wolfe book of the same name. Johnson appears in archival footage as well as in two scenes impersonated by Donald Moffat. (Kennedy only appears in archival film, and Eisenhower also is impersonated.) In an unusual directorial choice for such a serious film, the imperial Johnson, then vice president, is played as an errand boy, paying sympathy calls on the widows of the astronauts. Not only is Johnson portrayed as a fool, Moffat gives him no stature in his performance. For details, see Chapter 34 on Dwight D. Eisenhower.

JFK (1991)

Johnson: Archival footage, Tim Howard, John Galt, voice.

Then–Vice President Johnson appears in archival footage and some reconstructed scenes in Oliver Stone's film about the investigation of President John F. Kennedy's assassination. LBJ's appearance is important in that, according to Jim Garrison's conspiracy theory, Johnson is one of Garrison's suspects. Johnson is seen consorting with his own military and espionage sources about the need to continue the war in Vietnam to maintain the American industrial-military complex. He does not follow JFK's policies.

The key archival scene is his being sworn in as the 36th president aboard Air Force One. The other scenes show him at the above-mentioned meetings. John Galt is credited

36—Lyndon Baines Johnson (1963–1969) 313

The Right Stuff (1983): Lyndon Baines Johnson joins Presidents Eisenhower and Kennedy in this fictionalized story of the original U.S. Mercury Astronauts in the early days of the space program. Donald Moffat portrays then–Vice President Johnson, who handles the difficult task of informing astronauts' wives of their husbands' deaths. It's a Ladd Company release through Warner Brothers. (Photofest.)

as the voice of LBJ and Tim Howard (although not credited) routinely plays LBJ. For full details on *JFK*, see Chapter 35 on John F. Kennedy.

Forrest Gump (1994)

Johnson: Archival footage, John Galt, voice.

In technically assisted footage, President Johnson plays himself pinning a Medal of Honor on Forrest Gump for his service in Vietnam. John Galt provides the voice of Johnson with some skill and proper accent. For details, see Chapter 35 on John F. Kennedy.

The Collegians Are Go!! (1999)

Johnson: Vince Flueck. *Other Cast:* Dean Collegian (Dean Collegian PhD), Tad Collegian (Tad Collegian), Johnny Hardwick (Sleepy Student), Aaron LTG (Muy Sucio), Chris LTG (El Hombre Sin Nombre), Peter LTG (El Hispanico Santanico), Vance LTG (El Que Bolear), Ben III Rogers (Conspiracy Guy), Patty S. (Patty S.). *Directors:* Scott Calonico, Chuck Collegian, Dean Collegian, Robert Timbrook. *Producers:* Eileen and Fred Calonico, Kathy Hull, Jeff Radice, Ben Rogers. *Writing Credits:* Scott Calonico, Robert Timbrook. *Music:* Peter Nurzynski. *Cinematography:* Kevin Sharon. *Film Editing:* Nathan McGinty. *Studio:* AD&D Productions/Slowkid Productions. *Length:* 30 minutes.

Part of the current wave of insipid, silly movies, this short film follows the adventures of Los Tigres Guapos, an evil musical group, who want to raise former President Kennedy from the dead and turn him into a zombie. They have already turned current President Johnson into a mummy. They are blocked by the Collegians—Dean, Chuck, and Tad—who take a road trip to Dallas to defeat Los Tigres on their own ground.

Thirteen Days (2000)

Johnson: Walter Adrian.

Then–Vice President Johnson as played by Walter Adrian appears in two brief shots in this film about how President Kennedy handled the Cuban missile crisis in 1962. In the first shot he sits at the conference table with other key administrators during one of the many conferences concerning the crisis. He does not speak. The second shot is near the end of the film when Kennedy learns that the Soviets have withdrawn their offensive missiles from Cuba. His advisors applaud him in the Oval Office, and LBJ enthusiastically says, "There's no stopping us now." That statement could be prophetic because LBJ continued the Cold War policies of JFK, mainly in Vietnam, when he became president.

Adrian closely resembles the tall Texan, especially his hewn facial features. He also sounds like LBJ. For details, see Chapter 35 on John F. Kennedy.

Timequest (2002)

Vice President Johnson (Barry Corbin) plays an insignificant role in *Timequest*, Robert Dyke's inexpensive sci-fi film. Since in the film John F. Kennedy was not assassinated, Lyndon Johnson never became president. For details, see Chapter 35 on John F. Kennedy.

37

Richard Milhous Nixon (1969–1974)

Watergate, the burglary that stands as the symbol of Nixon's fall, also was a critical episode in his plan to exalt the presidency. Press reportage, a Congressional investigative committee, and impeachment proceedings stopped Nixon's grand plan and led to his resignation.

Nixon's morality divides historical appraisal of the man and his administration. One of the most complex presidents, he is described as "socially awkward yet fiercely other-directed, humble but grandiose, combative yet clueless, suspicious, secretive and endlessly self-revealing."[1] Nixon himself lamented that he was "an introvert in an extrovert's profession."[2] Yet, after service in the Navy during World War II, he won election to Congress. There he gained national attention as a member of the House Un-American Activities Committee, developing charges against Alger Hiss, former FDR–appointed State Department official. For his subsequent role of vice president to Eisenhower, Nixon gained the Republican nomination in 1960 against Kennedy but didn't win the presidency until 1968, against Hubert Humphrey. Nixon's domestic policy, "new Federalism" or state power, still involved a federal role in welfare and the environment. Of more interest to him, his foreign policy embraced gradual withdrawal of American troops from Vietnam and normalization of relations with China, which he visited. He also achieved warmer relations with the Soviet Union.

Richard Milhous Nixon. (Courtesy of Library of Congress.)

Despite Watergate and Nixon's obstruction of justice over the Pentagon Papers, he was elected to a second term, during which time he mainly involved himself with manipulations to suppress his tapes that criminally involved him in the Watergate scandal. Nixon's paranoia can be considered as "see[ing] the fate of conspiracy in apocalyptic terms ... always manning the barricades of civilization," as *New York Times* columnist David Brooks quotes Richard Hofstadter.[3] Nixon remains the only American president to resign.

THE FILMS

The major films about Nixon relate to his resignation. *Nixon* and *Secret Honor* deal with the president's psychological makeup—secretive, scheming, devious, and insecure—particularly during this event.[4] *Born Again* treats Nixon seriously as does *The Private Files of J. Edgar Hoover*, although contemptuously. But the majority of the 25 films with Nixon are inept parodies.

This most complex of presidents is the reason for such enduring fascination and in a book about his movie-watching, *Nixon at the Movies*, its author, Mark Feeney, analyzes Nixon through the films he screened in the White House. By Feeney's count, Nixon watched more than 500 movies during the 67 months of his presidency, making him our Number One presidential film buff. His favorite was *Around the World in 80 Days* (1956), but Nixon was not without taste, Feeney says.[5]

Made in U.S.A. (1966)

Nixon: Jean-Pierre Biesse. *Other Cast:* Anna Karina (Paula Nelson), Jean-Pierre Leaud (Donald Siegel), Richard Widmark (Lazlo Szabo), Marianne Faithfull (Herself), Ernest Menzer (Edgar Typhus), Kyoko Kosaka (Doris Mizoguchi), Yves Afonso (David Goodis), Marc Dudicourt (Barman), Remo Forlani (Workman in Bar), Jean-Luc Godard (Richard Politzer, voice), Sylvain Godet (Robert MacNamara), Claude Bouillon (Inspector Aldrich), Claude Bakka (Man with Faithfull), Philippe Labro (Himself). *Director:* Jean-Luc Godard. *Producer:* Georges de Beauregard. *Writing Credits:* Jean-Luc Godard, Donald E. Westlake (novel). *Cinematography:* Raoul Coutard. *Film Editing:* Francoise Collin, Agnes Guillemot. *Studio:* Anouchka Films, Rome Paris Films, S.E.P.I.C. *Length:* 90 minutes.

Jean-Luc Godard made 15 feature films in the period between 1960 and 1967 and this one is probably the least understandable. Godard indicated that it was a political film based on Donald E. Westlake's novel *The Jugger*, but it's basically Walt Disney plus blood.

Using a film noir theme close to *The Big Sleep* (1946), this is the story of female detective Paula Nelson (Anna Karina) who is investigating the death of her lover Richard Politzer (Jean-Luc Godard's voice). To satisfy Godard's need to justify the political speeches within the film, the killers are named: Richard Nixon (Jean-Pierre Biesse) and Robert MacNamara (Sylvain Godet).

Is There Sex After Death? (1971)

Nixon: Jim Dixon. *Other Cast:* Alan Abel (Dr. Rogers), Harry Bangel (Round Table Discussion/Man on Table), Janet Banzet (Clinic patient), Iris Brooks (Breast Development Student), Marshall Efron (Vince Domino), Buck Henry (Dr. Manos), Mary Elaine Monti (Stag Film Scene/Sue), Jim Moran (Dr. Elevenike), Mink Stole (Dominatrix), K.C. Townsend (Round Table Discussion/Woman on Table), Jennifer Welles (Magic Act/Merkin's Assistant). *Directors:* Alan Abel, Jeanne Abel. *Producers:* Alan Abel, Jeanne Abel, Michael Rothchild. *Writing Credits:* Alan Abel, Jeanne Abel, Buck Henry. *Cinematography:* Arthur Albert, Gerald Cotts. *Studio:* Abel-Child Productions. *Length:* 97 minutes.

The answer to the title's question, *Is There Sex After Death?*, is "yes." That is not the silliest answer to the many silly questions in this film posed by Dr. Harrison Rogers of the Bureau of Sexological Investigation. In his Sexmobile, Alan Abel, writer, director, producer, and star, travels from Grant's Tomb, site of his bureau, to seek answers to all sorts of sex questions. They range from the "What is the average calorie content of male ejaculation?" to "Are wet dreams dangerous if you sleep under an electric blanket?"

Dr. Rogers visits an erotic art gallery, a magician, a nudist colony, a topless string quartet, and the International Sex Bowl where American, French, German, Italian, and Russian teams compete. His most famous encounter is with President Nixon (Jim Dixon) in front of the White House. Using clips from Nixon's comments to other questions, Dr. Rogers asks the president his views on sex—from his attitude about his relations with women ("immoral"), birth control ("no reason for encouraging withdrawal"), sex education ("no comment"), and what next after his presidency? Looking much like Nixon with his signature nose, rigid posture, stiff hand gestures, and formal dress, Dixon as Nixon then breaks into a tap dance outside the White House gates.

The Million Dollar Duck (1971)

Nixon: Unnamed actor. *Other Cast:* Dean Jones (Professor Albert Dooley), Sandy Duncan (Katie Dooley), Joe Flynn (Finley Hooper), Tony Roberts (Fred Hines), James Gregory (Rutledge), Lee Harcourt Montgomery (Jimmy Dooley), Jack Kristen (Dr. Gottlieb), Virginia Vincent (Eunice Hooper), Jack Bender (Arvin Wadlow), Billy Bowles (Orlo Wadlow), Sammy Jackson (Frisby), Arthur Hunnicutt (Mr. Purdham), Frank Wilcox (Bank Manager), Bryan O'Byrne (Bank Teller), Ted Jordan (Mr. Forbes), Bing Russell (Mr. Smth), Pete Renoudet (Mr. Beckert), Frank Cady (Assayer), George O'Hanlon (Parking Attendant), Jonathan Daly (Purchasing Agent), Hal Smith (Courthouse Guard), Edward Andrews (Morgan). *Director:* Vincent McEveety. *Producer:* Bill Anderson. *Writing Credits:* Ted Key, Roswell Rogers. *Music:* Buddy Baker. *Cinematography:* William Snyder. *Film Editing:* Lloyd L. Richardson. *Art Direction:* John Mansbridge, Al Roelofs. *Set Decoration:* Hal Gausman, Emile Kuri. *Costume Design:* Chuck Keehne, Emily Sundby. *Sound:* Robert O. Cook, Dean Thomas. *Makeup:* Robert J. Schiffer. *Special Effects:* Eustace Lycett, Hans Metz. *Stunts:* Denny Arnold. *Studio:* Walt Disney Pictures. *Length:* 89 minutes.

This typical Disney film of the period features a typical Disney star of the period, Dean Jones, as Professor Albert Dooley, owner of an irradiated duck that lays golden eggs. The movie employs the familiar film device of calling on the president to save the situation. There are two conflicts in this vehicle: First, the U.S. government doesn't want an unlimited supply of gold to upset the currency value, and second, the question arises as to whether the greed for the duck's gold is overshadowing the love that Dooley and his wife Katie (Sandy Duncan) have for their son Jimmy (Lee Harcourt Montgomery). As with all Disney films of this period, the problems are solved with a minimum of logic and a maximum of hysterics.

President Nixon appears in one scene to support the level of importance the gold-producing duck ($40,000) has to the U.S. economy. The scene is played relatively straight for this genre of film, and the actor sounds like Nixon although his face is never shown. He sits at his desk in the Oval Office talking on the telephone to Treasury Department officials to "Get the duck. Do you understand? Get the duck."

Tricia's Wedding (1971)

Nixon: Kreemah Ritz. *Other Cast:* Goldie Glitters (Tricia Nixon), Steven Arnold (Joan Kennedy), Frank Bouquin (Mrs. Cox Sr.), Bobby Cameron (Patricia Nixon), Pristine

Condition (Rose Kennedy), Dusty Dawn (Julie Nixon Eisenhower), Anton Dunnigan (Eartha Kitt), John Flowers (Phyllis Diller), Marta Gomez (Indira Gandhi), Chris Kilo (Rev. Billy Graham), Richard Koldewyn (Pope Paul VI), Michael Lyons (Prince Charles), Link Martin (Madame Nu), Johnny McGowan (Jackie Onassis & bridesmaid), Milton Miron (Announcer, BB Rebozo), Marshall Olds (Edward Cox, the groom), John Rothermel (Mamie Eisenhower), Lendon Sadler (Mahalia Jackson & bridesmaid), Michael Shane (Lady Bird Johnson), Sylvester (Coretta King & Delegate from Uma Guma), Pamela Tent-Carpenter (Golda Meir & bridesmaid), Steven Walden (Queen Elizabeth II & bridesmaid), Daniel Ware (Martha Mitchell), Roger Webster (David Eisenhower), Martin Worman (Sen. George Murphy). *Director:* Milton Miron. *Producer:* Mark L. Lester. *Writing Credits:* Milton Miron, Robert Patteson, Kreemah Ritz. *Cinematography:* Paul Aratow. *Length:* 30 minutes.

An over-the-top spoof starring the members of a San Francisco drag group, *Tricia's Wedding* does little to add thoughtful comments about the Nixon administration. As if the whole concept was not bad enough, things start to get even worse after the drag queen playing Eartha Kitt (Anton Dunnigan) adds LSD to the punch. President Nixon is portrayed by Krenmah Ritz, and his performance is hardly presidential in this ridiculous exercise.

Another Nice Mess (1972)

Nixon: Rich Little. *Other Cast:* Herb Voland (Spiro Agnew). *Director-Writer:* Bob Einstein. *Producers:* Tom Smothers, Jonathan Haze. *Music:* Bob Emenegger. *Studio:* Smo-Bro International Productions. *Length:* 66 minutes.

The title is a clue to the contents of this film released and directed by Bob Einstein and co-produced by Tom Smothers, both of TV comedy fame. Yes, this feature film has impersonator Rich Little playing Nixon as Stan Laurel and Herb Voland playing Spiro Agnew as Oliver Hardy.

It appears that shortly after its 1972 release, the film quickly disappeared from sight. Co-producer Jonathan Haze is quoted as saying that there are 100 prints in existence in Smothers' basement. Rich Little's other impersonations of Nixon were always good but never gentle.

Hail (1972) aka Hail to the Chief

Nixon: Dan Resin. *Other Cast:* Richard B. Shull (Secretary of Health), Dick O'Neill (Attorney General), Joseph Sirola (Rev. Jimmy Williams), Pat Ripley (First Lady), Gary Sandy (Tom), Willard Waterman (Vice President), K. Callan (Burd), Constance Forslund (Sara), Phil Foster (Michael). *Director:* Fred Levinson. *Producers:* Paul Leaf, Roy Townshend. *Writing Credits:* Phil Dusenberry, Larry Spiegel. *Music:* Trade Martin. *Cinematography:* William Storz. *Film Editing:* Robert DeRise. *Studio:* Cine Globe, Hail. *Length:* 85 minutes.

Although completed in 1972, i.e., before Watergate, this film was not released until 1973 when it became more reasonable to viciously lampoon a sitting president. The story basically entails the establishment of concentration camps in the U.S. to hold political protesters and the problems such an action causes for the president (Dan Resin).

President Nixon is not specifically identified in the film, but there is no doubt as to whom writers Phil Dusenberry and Larry Spiegel were referring. Although Dan Resin does not resemble Nixon, his voice echoes Nixon's in its tone, inflection, and modulation. Most importantly, Resin exhibits the paranoia ("There's a cancer eating away at the heart of the American principles"), vindictiveness ("The justice was cut down by some son of a bitch"), ego ("Read me the part about how I 'electrified the crowd'"), love of sports and Chinese food (He watches a televised football game while eating Chinese spareribs, "bridge to our yellow friends"), and inferiority complex ("They've never liked me").

The "hero" is Burd (K. Callan), the president's old war buddy and Secretary of Health, Education, and Welfare. Because Burd will not go along with the concentration camp scheme, Nixon and the remainder of his cabinet and his military leaders plot to set up Burd. Realizing that he is to be the fall guy, and that this insane behavior about civil unrest, especially among the young (read "hippies"), and dictatorial plans to do away with election, Congress, etc. will continue, Burd has the last laugh. In a cynical Walter Matthau style (his look-alike), he fools the plotters and ends up killing the entire group including the president.

Richard (1972)

Nixon: Richard M. Dixon, Dan Resin. *Other Cast:* Vivian Blaine (Herself), Imogene Bliss (Mother), Marvin Braverman (Hardhat), John Carradine (Plastic Surgeon), Paul Ford (Washington Doctor), Paul Forrest (Advisor), Hank Garrett (Advisor), Hazen Gifford (Advisor), Lynn Lipton (Young Pat), Kevin McCarthy (Washington Doctor), Mickey Rooney (Guardian Angel). *Directors:* Harry Hurwitz, Lorees Yerby. *Producer:* Bertrand Castelli, Lorees Yerby. *Music:* Bertrand Castelli, Galt MacDermot. *Cinematography:* Victor Petrashevic. *Film Editing:* Emil Haviv. *Set Decoration:* Raymond Maynard. *Studio:* Aurora City Group. *Length:* 83 minutes.

Even before Watergate became a major political problem for Nixon, he was a major target of the Hollywood world. This film uses an episodic approach to covering the entire career of then President Nixon.

Employing archival film clips of Nixon as well as dramatic appearances of young Nixon (Dan Resin) and mature Nixon (Richard M. Dixon), the satire follows the major steps in Nixon's political career. Nixon is assisted along the way by three ethnic advisors and a guardian angel (Mickey Rooney). However, to ultimately make him acceptable to the American public, a bit of plastic surgery is done by four Washington M.D.s (Vivian Blaine, Kevin McCarthy, John Carradine, and Paul Ford).

Although released in an election year and with reasonable critical reviews, *Richard* did not do well at the box office. Richard M. Dixon made a career out of comedic portrayals of Richard M. Nixon.

Top of the Heap (1972)

Nixon: Richard M. Dixon. *Other Cast:* Christopher St. John (George Lattimer), Paula Kelly (Black Chick, Singer), Florence St. Peter (Viola Lattimer), Leonard Kuras (Bobby Gelman), Patrick McVey (Tim Cassidy), John Alderson (Capt. Walsh), Ingeborg Serensen (Nurse Swenson), Allen Garfield (Taxi Driver), Ron Douglas (Hip Passenger), Almeria Quinn (Valerie Lattimer), Beatrice Webster (George's Mother), Essie McSwine (African Dancer), Jerry Jones (Club Owner), Willie Harris (Bouncer). *Director-Producer-Writer:* Christopher St. John. *Music:* J.J. Johnson. *Cinematography:* Richard Kelley. *Film Editing:* Mike Pozen. *Art Direc-*

tion: Normand Houle. *Set Decoration:* Robert Signorelli. *Costume Design:* Eddie Marks. *Makeup:* Maurice Stein. *Studio:* St. John Unlimited, Unicorn. *Length:* 83 minutes.

While Christopher St. John—the director, producer, writer, and star—displays a "powerful presence" (*New York Times*), he overdoes it. His excesses as a D.C. cop who thinks he "can do anything he wants" lead to audience incredulity at his close-mindedness. This derivative film is one of the few black-themed pictures of its period that isn't completely sympathetic to its central character.

When St. John, as George Lattimer, isn't raging relentlessly about everything in his circumscribed world, he engages in fantasy as a NASA astronaut, a black Walter Mitty. In these fantasies he basks in private sexual satisfaction and public glory. That's where President Nixon appears in two shots at the end of the film giving his victory sign and a raised arm in salute to Lattimer, the astronaut parading in a white convertible through his hometown in Alabama. Richard M. Dixon, the most frequent movie Nixon, earnestly conveys the president's feelings.

Good to See You Again, Alice Cooper (1974)

Nixon: Richard M. Dixon. *Other Cast:* Alice Cooper (Himself), Dennis Dunaway (Himself), Michael Bruce, Neal Smith, Glen Buxton, Mick Mashbir, Bob Dolin (Themselves), James Randi (Dentist/Executioner), Cindy Smith (Dancing Tooth). *Director:* Joe Gannon. *Producers:* Joe Gannon, Shep Gordon, Herb Margolis. *Writing Credits:* Joe Gannon, Shep Gordon, Fred Smoot. *Studio:* Penthouse Productions Ltd. *Length:* 81 minutes.

Good to See You Again, Alice Cooper is not good if you want to see Richard M. Dixon as President Nixon. He doesn't appear until the final minutes in the Library of Congress's version of this documentary color footage of the Alice Cooper Band in concert. The real Nixon does appear more often in two filmclips from his well-known commentary after losing the California gubernatorial elections: "That's the way the game is played," he says, along with "You [the press] won't have Nixon to kick around any more." These and other clips employ lines that are generally used in suggestive or scatological sequences to complement Cooper's songs.

Richard M. Dixon, the frequent Nixon impersonator because of his close physical resemblance and ability to act like the 37th president, comes on stage with both arms and fingers raised in Nixon's signature victory salute. Cooper and company pummel him and take him off stage horizontally yet still holding his victory pose.

White House Madness (1975)

Nixon: Steve Friedman. *Other Cast:* Patti Jerome (Martha Mitchell), Dennis Fimple (Bob Haldeman), Perry Cook (John Mitchell), Rusty Blitz (John Erlichman), George Skaff (King Feisal), Lesley Woods (Pat Nixon). *Director:* Mark L. Lester. *Producers:* Phil Gramm, Mark L. Lester. *Film Editing:* Marvin Walowitz. *Studio:* Program Power Entertainment. *Length:* 121 minutes.

If there is any redeeming feature in this political satire, it is President Nixon's current dog Timaho (sic?) that cavorts and condescends to wearing outlandish clothing without a bark. Otherwise, this work of Mark L. Lester, the director and producer, is tasteless, trite, and dull—poor in every aspect.

Its plot concerns finding the famous Nixon tapes of his misdemeanors that have been hidden in his dead dog Checkers, now stuffed and enshrined in a secret room in the White House. When Senators Goldwater and Irvine lead a senatorial inspection of the White House, Checkers is whisked away to safety by Nixon's friend Bebe Rebozo and press secretary Ron Ziegler. In a series of parallel plots that would make D.W. Griffith writhe, the capture of Checkers and the party that Nixon stages for his supporters ensue.

Steve Friedman, alas, remains on screen for most of the film, exhibiting his approximations of Nixon's movements and voice, albeit garbled. Lester previously spoofed the nuptials of Nixon's daughter in *Tricia's Wedding* (1972) and should have stopped then.

The Faking of the President (1976)

Nixon: Richard M. Dixon. *Other Cast:* William J. Daprato (Lincoln), Marshall Efron (Donald Segretti), Alan Barinholtz (Ronald Ziegler), Robert Staats (G. Gordon Liddy). *Director-Writing Credits:* Alan Abel, Jeanne Abel. *Producer:* Alan Abel, Jeanne Abel, Alan Barinholtz. *Cinematography:* Arthur Albert. *Studio:* Spencer Productions. *Length:* 90 minutes.

"Crazy, clumsy" satire of President Nixon, according to *Variety* (May 19, 1976), describes this $100,000 pseudo-documentary in which Nixon admits to all clandestine acts, including Watergate.

The film uses Nixon's voice from 250 hours of taped speeches and press conferences, re-edited word by word, resulting in the 37th president making the most outrageous accusations, confessions, *faux pas* and *non-sequiturs*. Visuals come from newsreel stock footage and comic vignettes created for actor Richard M. Dixon. This frequent Nixon impersonator bears an uncanny resemblance to Nixon and capitalizes upon it. In these vignettes the fake Nixon siphons gas from a senator, and steals flowers from the grave of Fala, FDR's Scottish terrier, to place on that of his own dog Checkers. Other Nixon associates—Segretti, Liddy, and Ziegler—engage in similar comic escapades. This comedy style dominates the Abels' earlier film, *Is There Sex After Death?* (1971).

The Cayman Triangle (1977)

Nixon: Anderson Humphreys. *Other Cast:* Reid Dennis (Dirty Reid), John Morgan (Gen. Smithe), Ed Beheler (Jimmy Carter), Jules Kreitzer (Henry Kissinger), Dale Reeves (Herbo), Dick Barker (Crachit), Mary Gillooly (Virgin), Arek Joseph (Arab), Ryhal Gallagher (Blackbeard), Ron Sinclair (Adm. Gumfault), Bob Ankrom (Gen. Eastlesslin), Brian Uzzell (Hunchback), Steve Foster (Nazrat), Tian Giri (Scarlett O'Tara), Noel Spencer-Barnes (Maj. Limey), Michael Blackie (Capt. Smedley), Emily Hector (Hot Lips Hector). *Director-Writing Credits:* Ralph Clemente, Anderson Humphreys. *Producer:* Anderson Humphreys. *Cinematography:* Ed Paveitti, Tom Rosseter, Egon Stephan. *Film Editing:* Ralph Clemente. *Studio:* Hefalump Pictures. *Length:* 92 minutes.

This is an "oddball feature," *Variety* says, that would appeal only to the high school and college satire trade. The quality of the humor appears in the punning names (Nazrat, Major Limey, Scarlett O'Tara) for mostly amateur actors from the British Island's Cayman Drama Society. The action, nevertheless, involves the Bermuda, not the Cayman Triangle.

The plot is an investigation of missing vessels in the "Cayman Triangle" that involves flashbacks to pirates. Authenticity is assured by footage of unpopulated Georgetown streets due to the cooperation of Bermuda authorities.

Dale Reeves, a Miami radio personality, provides the voices of Carter, Nixon, and Kissinger. Anderson Humphreys plays Nixon and also directed, wrote, and produced the film.

The Private Files of J. Edgar Hoover (1977)

Nixon: Unnamed actor.

In this biopic about the FBI head, a Nixon characterization appears in two scenes, both concerning the use of wiretapping. In the second, Hoover refuses to allow the FBI's bugging of political enemies, thus leading to Nixon's bugging of Watergate and the ultimate downfall of Nixon after Hoover's death. The portrayal is difficult to judge because he is generally shown in shadow in these scenes and has very little to say. For details see Chapter 32 on FDR.

Born Again (1978)

Nixon: Harry Spillman. *Other Cast:* Dean Jones (Charles Colson), Anne Francis (Patty Colson), Jay Robinson (David Shapiro), Dana Andrews (Tom Phillips), Raymond St. Jacques (Jimmy Newsom), George Brent (Judge Gerhard Gesell), Harold Hughes (himself), Scott Walker (Scanlon), Robert Gray (Kramer), Arthur Roberts (Al Quie), Ned Wilson (Douglas Coe), Dean Brooks (Dick Howard), Peter Jurasik (Henry Kissinger), Christopher Conrad (Chris Colson), Stuart Lee (Wendell Colson), Alicia Fleer (Emily Colson), Richard Caine (H.R. Haldeman), Brigid O'Brien (Holly Holm), Robert Broyles (John Erlichman), Byron Morrow (Archibald Cox), Bill Zuckert (E. Howard Hunt), William "Billy" Benedict (Leon Jaworski). *Director:* Irving Rapper. *Producers:* Frank Capra Jr., Robert Munger, Paul Temple. *Writing Credits:* Walter Bloch. *Music:* Les Baxter. *Cinematography:* Harry Stradling Jr. *Film Editing:* Axel Hubert Sr. *Production Design:* Bill Kenney. *Studio:* AVCO Embassy Pictures. *Length:* 110 minutes.

Charles Colson's rise and fall from his work as counsel to the president in the Nixon administration unfolds in this minor biopic based on Colson's book. Best known for his Disney films, Dean Jones gives a convincing performance of this cynical lawyer's religious conversion ("born again") after he left the White House and before he was imprisoned for his involvement in maligning Daniel Ellsberg for his revelation of the Pentagon Papers.

During Colson's White House tenure, President Nixon appears in five scenes. He's played by Harry Spillman whose voice and physical movements closely resemble Nixon's. He first welcomes Colson "aboard" in the Oval Office stating, "We have historical opportunity to turn this country around" and lauding Colson as being "tough" and "smart." The embattled president keeps turning to Colson, first to "bring in line" Arthur Burns, head of the Federal Reserve; then to "expose that son of a bitch" Ellsberg; and finally in a discussion about "taking our loses over Watergate."

After Nixon's re-election he allows Colson to resign, which he happily does, feeling "dead inside." While on a "getaway" with his wife, Colson visits esteemed old friend Tom Phillips (Dana Andrews) who "accepted Jesus Christ" and changed his life. So does Colson, later joining former political enemy Sen. Harold Hughes (played by himself) in prayer meetings. Despite being urged to plea bargain by his law partner David Shapiro (Jay Robinson), Colson serves time in prison, winning friends and influencing convicts to also accept Jesus Christ.

Where the Buffalo Roam (1980)

Nixon: Richard M. Dixon as Candidate; Brian Cummings as Nixon voice. *Other Cast:* Peter Boyle (Carl Lazlo, Esq.), Bill Murray (Dr. Hunter S. Thompson), Bruno Kirby (Marty Lewis), Rene Auberjonois (Harris from the *Post*), R.G. Armstrong (Judge Simpson), Danny Goldman (Porter), Rafael Campos (Rojas), Leonard Frey (Desk Clerk), Leonard Gaines (Blackie), DeWayne Jessie (Superfan), Mark Metcalf (Dooley), Jon Shear (Billy Kramer), Joe Ragno (Willins), Quin K. Redeker (Pilot), Lisa Taylor (Ruthie), Danny Tucker (Narcotics Agent), Jon Acevedo (Hippie). *Director-Producer:* Art Linson. *Writing Credits:* Hunter S. Thompson (book and stories), John Kaye (screenplay). *Cinematographer:* Tak Fujimoto. *Composer:* Neil Young. *Editor:* Christopher Greenbury. *Production Designer:* Richard Sawyer. *Set Designer:* Barbara Krieger. *Costume Designer:* Eddie Marks. *Studio:* Universal Pictures. *Length:* 96 minutes.

Considered a cinematic tribute to Hunter S. Thompson, the dean of gonzo guerrilla journalism, this anarchic comedy appears as aimless in theme and direction as its hero's mission. Bill Murray as Thompson goes on this drunken, drug-saturated foray with his attorney (Peter Boyle), a Mexican-American who wants to form a new hippie nation. During their frantic adventures, Thompson "writes" his version of the 1972 Super Bowl in Los Angeles between Dallas and Miami from his hotel room (he's traded his tickets and press passes to some passersby), addresses college students who ask why he's not seeing The Candidate (Nixon) to which he replies, "We are on different schedules," and covers the 1972 presidential campaign.

Enter Nixon in the similar person of Richard M. Dixon to a men's washroom. There he meets Thompson who's stolen the suit and credentials of Harris of the *Post* (Rene Auberjonois) and asks him, "How's the family?" Thompson breaks into a tirade about what the country's doing for the doomed—"the young, the honest, the weak, the Italians—who are lost and helpless like pigs in the wilderness." Nixon pounds his hands on the washroom mirror as Thompson expands on how the country is divided between screwheads and the doomed ("who really hate you, sir," he says to Nixon as he dries his shoes on the hand blowers). Nixon responds with one of his familiar expletives, "[Bleep] the doomed." Richard M. Dixon's similar appearance and Brian Cummings's similar voice make this a realistic, if not weird, Nixon portrayal.

Secret Honor (1984)

Nixon: Philip Baker Hall. *Director:* Robert Altman. *Producers:* Robert Altman with Scott Bushnell. *Writing Credits:* Donald Freed, Arnold M. Stone. *Music:* George Burt. *Cinematography:* Pierre Mignot. *Film Editing:* Juliet Weber. *Production Design:* Stephen Altman. *Costume Designer:* Philip Baker Hall. *Sound Designer:* Bernard Hajdenberg: *Studio:* Los Angeles Actors' Theatre/Sandcastle 5 Productions/University of Michigan Department of Communications. *Length:* 90 minutes.

Richard Nixon's resignation provided grist for numerous films and other media events. Perhaps none of these are as explicit as that written as a one-man show by Donald Freed and Arnold M. Stone. Robert Altman, while working at the University of Michigan, used the same actor, Philip Baker Hall, to turn this stage piece into a 90-minute film. Briefly, Nixon is in his personal office, some time after his resignation, recollecting both true and untrue events in his career that led up to his final decision to resign the presidency.

In a rambling and often almost incoherent tirade, the ex-president explains his life to a microphone, which is connected to a tape recorder. Quite often the objects of conversation are pictures on the wall, including Eisenhower, Lincoln, Kissinger, Woodrow Wilson, and his (Nixon's) mother. In an essentially paranoiac rant he blames the media for saying he talks to pictures on the wall; he blames corporate greed and machinations for both his defeats and his elections; he blames the Kennedys for being the Kennedys; he blames J. Edgar Hoover for everything else, except he blames his mother for making him feel like a dog. Since Nixon has been drinking throughout the film, it would be possible that the ranting is the result of this, but Hall's performance convinces the audience that Nixon truly believes what he is saying.

Hall does not physically resemble Nixon; nor does he sound like him. However, by the end of the film, he *is* Nixon and the audience knows it. His use of laughter and sobbing, frustration and gleeful conniving enables Hall to persuade the anti–Nixon audience that they are right about this man while the pro–Nixon audience probably understands why they have sympathy for the ex-president.

Horror House on Highway Five (1985)

Nixon: Ronald Reagan. *Other Cast:* Phil Therrien (Dr. Marbuse), Max Manthey (Gary), Irene F. (Sally Smith), Michael Castagnolia (The Pothead), Susan Leslie (Louise), Kathleen Battersby (Housewife). *Director-Writer:* Richard Casey.

Don't be misled by a Ronald Reagan playing Nixon. It's a different one from the president and he's in a rubber mask doing murderous deeds. Parodying *The Texas Chainsaw Massacre* films, psycho serial killers go on a rampage. According to IMDb, the plot includes college students in a van, Nazis, rape, mysterious rooms, and chase scenes involving Nixon.

Bebe's Kids (1992)

Nixon: Rich Little.

This is the first mainstream animated feature film developed for African-American audiences. Based on a comedy routine by the late Robin Harris (Faizon Love), it is a romantic comedy gone crazy. To woo Jamika (Vanessa Bell Colloway), Harris takes her son as well as her friend Bebe's three kids on their date. They careen from one childhood amusement to another, satirizing hip-hop music, urban riots, and white bread theme parks. Understandably, they are charged with aggression. President Lincoln (Pete Renaday) defends them as the kids present their Rap defense with a chorus about freedom. President Nixon (Rich Little) waves his arms in familiar gestures in his prosecution of the case.

Hot Shots! Part Deux (1993)

Nixon: Buck McDancer. *Other Cast:* Charlie Sheen (Topper Harley), Lloyd Bridges (President Thomas Benson), Valeria Golino (Ramada Ronham Hayman), Richard Crenna (Col. Denton Walters), Brenda Bakke (Michelle Rodham Huddleston), Miguel Ferrer (Cmdr. Arvid Harbinger), Rowan Atkinson (Dexter Hayman), Jerry Haleva (Saddam Hussein), David

Wohl (Gerou), Larry Lindsey (Gerald Ford), Ed Beheller (Jimmy Carter), Daniel T. Healy (George Bush), Jay Koch (Ronald Reagan). *Director:* Jim Abrahams. *Producer:* Bill Badalato. *Writing Credits:* Jim Abrahams, Pat Proft. *Music:* Basil Poledouris. *Cinematography:* John R. Leonetti. *Film Editing:* Malcolm Campbell. *Production Design:* William A. Elliott. *Art Direction:* Greg Papaila. *Set Decoration:* Jerie Kelter. *Costume Design:* Mary Malin. *Makeup:* David LeRoy Anderson, John Blake. *Studio:* 20th Century–Fox, Sidley Wright and Associates. *Length:* 86 minutes.

Operation Desert Storm left some unanswered questions in the Middle East, and one of them was what to do about Saddam Hussein. Jim Abrahams and Pat Proft came up with the answer and used "Rambo" wannabe Topper Harley (Charlie Sheen) as their instrument of destruction. In a continuation of Abrahams's hit spoofs including *Airplane!* (1980) and the *Naked Gun* series, *Part Deux* solves all of the Middle East problems while using bits and pieces of almost every movie series produced in the 1980s and early 1990s.

As is his practice Abraham involves actual individuals in his films to double the fun. In this case he introduces five U.S. presidents in a scene showing the beginning of construction on the presidential library for fictional President Thomas "Tug" Benson (Lloyd Bridges). Benson is presented throughout the film as being both stupid and inept, a typical post-modern portrayal of the president, sort of deconstructed to nothingness. In this outdoor presidential library groundbreaking scene, while using a shovel to break the ground, Benson accidentally hits all of the attending ex-presidents including Nixon (Buck McDancer). The only assessment of McDancer's performance is that he looks like he has been hit by a shovel.

Nixon (1995)

Nixon: Anthony Hopkins, David Barry Gray (Nixon at 19), Corey Carrier (Nixon at 12). *Other Cast:* Joan Allen (Pat Nixon), Powers Boothe (Alexander Haig), Ed Harris (E. Howard Hunt), Bob Hoskins (J. Edgar Hoover), E.G. Marshall (John Mitchell), David Paymer (Ron Ziegler), David Hyde Pierce (John Dean), Paul Sorvino (Henry Kissinger), Mary Steenburgen (Hannah Nixon), J.T. Walsh (John Ehrlichman), James Woods (H.R. Haldeman), Brian Bedford (Clyde Tolson), Kevin Dunn (Charles Colson), Ed Hermann (Nelson Rockefeller), Madeline Kahn (Martha Mitchell), George Plimpton (President's lawyer). *Director:* Oliver Stone. *Producer:* Oliver Stone, Clayton Townsend, Andrew G. Vajna. *Writing Credits:* Stephen J. Rivele, Christopher Wilkinson, Oliver Stone. *Music:* John Williams. *Cinematography:* Robert Richardson. *Film Editing:* Brian Berdan, Hank Corwin. *Production Design:* Victor Kempster. *Art Direction:* Richard F. Mays, Donald B. Woodruff, Margery Zweizig. *Set Decoration:* Merideth Boswell. *Costume Design:* Richard Hornung. *Makeup:* John Blake. *Studio:* Buena Vista. *Length:* 192 minutes.

Oliver Stone, the controversial political filmmaker of the 1980s and 1990s, again uses his virtuoso film techniques to create a personal biography. His view of John F. Kennedy's assassination appears in the film on Jim Garrison's legal pursuit of conspirators in *JFK* (1991). While the earlier film dealt with one event in the life of an American president, *Nixon* covers many different periods and events in the life of Nixon, starting on June 17, 1972, the night of the second break-in at the Watergate, and ending Aug. 8, 1974, with Nixon's departure from D.C. after his resignation, interspersed with flashbacks of his early life.

Following the character-as-destiny theme of a man destroyed by himself and using beast imagery and a death motif, key events of Nixon's life surface in this film as Stone's reasons

Nixon (1995): Academy Award winner Anthony Hopkins as President Nixon dances with his wife Pat (Joan Allen) in a biography of many different periods and events in the life of the 37th president, starting on June 17, 1972, the night of the second Watergate break-in and ending August 8, 1974, with Nixon's departure from D.C. after his resignation, interspersed with flashbacks. A Buena Vista release. (Photofest.)

for Nixon's political policies and personal qualities. Nixon's politics get more favorable treatment than his personality, portrayed by Anthony Hopkins as resentful and paranoiac. An impressive actor in wide-ranging roles from *Hamlet* (1969) to *The Silence of the Lambs* (1991), Hopkins gives his Nixon interpretation a range of emotions and postures, including Nixon's noted slouch, head hunched into shoulders, and use of profanity to great advantage to portray Nixon's paranoia. Hopkins also gives pathos to the role, evoking sympathy from the film audience over this fatally flawed antihero who truly does himself in because of his paranoia about his "enemies" and the "imperial" presidency itself.

In main supportive roles are Joan Allen as a strong, even more politically aware helpmate than the real-life Pat Nixon; Powers Boothe, an ambitious, self-assured Alexander Haig; Ed Harris, a conniving E. Howard Hunt; and Bob Hoskins, a burlesqued J. Edgar Hoover.

Stone's voiceover in the credits opens the film saying that scenes are fabricated, speculated, or hypothesized. Indeed they are, from Nixon's Checkers speech to his praying on his knees with Henry Kissinger (Paul Sorvino). Stone's postmodernist style of shifting film stocks (newsreels to dramatic portrayals) and crazy camera cuts and angles create a thick cinematic web that fails as a balanced view of Nixon.

Roger Ebert of the *Chicago Sun-Times* observed that *Nixon* was flavored by the greatest biography in American film history, *Citizen Kane* (1941). He cites: along with an opening upward pan from outside the White House fence, gothic music on a cloudy night, the "March of Time"–style newsreel, and an eating scene with President and Mrs. Nixon separated by a long table. Ebert also says Stone employs Orson Welles's "Rosebud" missing

Nixon (1995): Anthony Hopkins as Richard Nixon accepts the Republican nomination for president at the party's 1968 convention. This marked one of the most startling comebacks in presidential history. He's backed by his family including Pat as portrayed by Joan Allen (third from left). (Photofest.)

piece of information that might explain the man's mystery (Nixon's early stern Quaker childhood and death of two brothers). But, as Christopher Sharrett asserts in the *Cineaste* (v22, n1 [Wntr, 1966]:4) "Stone never gives his protagonist the nuance that Welles allowed his."

Other critics see even more similarities to *Kane*: the character as destiny. Tony Barta notes how Pat's words in the eating scene recall Jedediah Leland's to Kane after a lost election, "You don't care about anything except you. You just want to persuade people that you love them so much they ought to love you back."[6] Thomas Monsell in his *Nixon on Stage and Screen* gives a scene-by-scene summary as well as extensive excerpts from a range of film critics.

Stone's conspiracy theory, that of the "beast," applies to Nixon, too. It is the secret government apparatus, especially against Cuba, that turned on its own leader. Nixon's obsessive jealousy of JFK permeates the film and concludes it when Nixon stalks the White House halls as Watergate encloses him. He stops before a portrait of Kennedy and says, "When they look at you they see what they want to be; when they look at me they see what they are."

Long as the film is, it avoids the "deep politics of Nixon's career that seem ready-made for Stone's scenario," says Sharrett. He concludes his insightful critique with, "Nixon, more than any modern politician, is a symbol of the deligitimization of the standing political order."

Dick (1999)

Nixon: Dan Hedaya. *Other Cast:* Kirsten Dunst (Betsy Jobs), Michelle Williams (Arlene Lorenzo), Will Ferrell (Bob Woodward), Bruce McCulloch (Carl Bernstein), Teri Garr (Helen

Lorenzo), Dave Foley (Bob Haldeman), Jim Breuer (John Dean), Ana Gasteyer (Rose Mary Woods), Harry Shearer (G. Gordon Liddy), Devon Gummersall (Larry Jobs), Ted McGiley (Roderick), Ryan Reynolds (Chip), Saul Rubinek (Henry Kissinger), G.D. Spradlin (Ben Bradlee), Len Doncheff (Leonid Brezhnev). *Director-Screenwriter:* Andrew Fleming. *Producer:* Gale Anne Hurd. *Cinematography:* Alexander Gruszynski. *Music:* John Debney. *Film Editing:* Mia Goldman. *Production Designer:* Barbara Dunphy. *Art Director:* Lucinda Zak. *Set Decoration:* Donald Elmblad. *Costume Design:* Deborah Everton. *Studio:* Canal & Da/Pacific Western/Phoenix Pictures. *Length:* 94 minutes.

Part political satire and much teen farce with characterization as in *Bill & Ted's Excellent Adventure* (1989), this film solves the mystery of the missing 18½ minutes on one of Nixon's White House tapes. Two bumbling teenage girls (like Bill & Ted), Betsy Jobs (Kirsten Dunst) and Arlene Lorenzo (Michelle Williams), get lost in the White House on a high school field trip. They bump into Checkers, Nixon's dog, and then meet the owner, the president (Dan Hedaya). Lorenzo, obsessed with singer Bobby Sherman, turns her obsession to Nixon whom she sees as caring (at least for his dog).

The girls become official White House dog watchers and eventually learn that the president has a short temper and a foul mouth that he uses to abuse *Washington Post* reporters Bob Woodward (Will Ferrell) and Carl Bernstein (Bruce McCulloch) who, even though they are portrayed as dull, are trying to uncover the president's dirty tricks. The girls prove trickier. They help the reporters, explaining that while singing love songs to "Dick," the president, on his tape recorder they heard the president in playback as his profane and paranoiac worst.

Hedaya gives a winning portrayal of Nixon, even down to the peace sign. On screen throughout, he slumps, he bullies, he schemes—asking the girls to be Secret Youth Advisers. He even eats the girls' "Holly Dolly" marijuana cookies with Brezhnev (Len Doncheff) and breaks into song. While this scene and others involving the cookies are broadly satirical, director Andrew Fleming's underlying theme of the young girls' honesty betrayed triumphs in a star-spangled ending, all crisply filmed by Alexander Gruszynski.

Ultrachrist (2003)

Nixon: Jurgen Fauth. *Other Cast:* Jonathan C. Green (Jesus/Ultrachrist), Celia A. Montgomery (Molly), Samuel Bruce Campbell (A.C. Meany), Dara Shindler (Jadda Jennsen), Jordan Hoffman (Archangel Ira), Danielle Langlois (Jane), Samantha Dark (Paula), Nathaniel Graves (Tommy), Michael R. Thomas (Vlad the Impaler). *Director–Film Editing:* Kerry Douglas Dye. *Producer:* Jordan Hoffman. *Writing Credits:* Kerry Douglas Dye, Jordan Hoffman. *Music:* Howard Leshaw. *Cinematography:* Peter Olsen. *Art Direction:* Ann Farrell. *Costume Design:* Catherine Barinas. *Makeup:* Michael R. Thomas. *Sound:* Byrant Musgrove. *Studio:* LeisureSuit Media. *Length:* 92 minutes.

Nixon was the only president to be forced to resign and leave the White House in shame. Even he does not deserve the treatment given him in this amateurish satire on the second coming of Christ.

It involves the simplest of stories with Jesus (Jonathan C. Green) returning to Earth and finding that the only way he can communicate with people in the 21st century is to become, or appear as, a superhero. In a film that is obviously made on a misspent shoestring, Christ wanders about New York City less looking to save the world than to find the

30 cheap locations for filming. Using an idea that could be both funny and interesting, writer-director Kerry Douglas Dye and his cohort writer-actor Jordan Hoffman (Archangel Ira) miss the mark completely and produce a film that can't even be called sacrilegious because it is theologically misinformed, slowly paced, and relying on obvious sex jokes, i.e.: Ultrachrist says his palms bleed when he's sexually aroused.

President Nixon (Jurgen Fauth) is brought into the film, along with two other evildoers, Adolf Hitler (Steve Montague) and Vlad the Impaler (Michael R. Thomas), by Antichrist A.C. Meany (Samuel Bruce Campbell) to distrupt Christ's efforts to save the world. Hitler impersonator Montague does not bear the slightest resemblance to the dictator and the same is probably true of Fauth although he plays the ex-president in a Nixon Halloween mask. Needless to say, this performance does not further cinematic understanding of the presidents.

The Assassination of Richard Nixon (2004)

Nixon: Archival TV footage. *Other Cast:* Sean Penn (Samuel Bicke), Naomi Watts (Maire Bicke), Don Cheadle (Bonny Simmons), Jack Thompson (Jack Jones), Brad Henke (Martin Jones). *Director:* Niels Mueller. *Producers:* Doug Bernheim, John Limotte. *Music:* Steven M. Stern. *Cinematography:* Emmanuel Lubezki. *Film Editing:* Jay Lash Cassidy. *Production Design:* Lester Cohen. *Set Decoration:* Barbara Munch. *Costume Design:* Aggie Guerard Rogers. *Special Effects:* Frank Ceglia. *Visual Effects:* Erik Dehkhoda. *Studio:* Anhelo Productions, Appian Way. *Length:* 95 minutes.

The power of the media drives this film through the televised presence of President Nixon as the telephone voice of President Truman does in *Call Me Madam* and Truman's radio voice does in *Bye, Bye Blues*. Seamlessly intertwined with the disintegration of Samuel Bicke, the TV pronouncements and presence of Nixon impel the possessed Bicke to "destroy the seat of government ... to make a change." Starting with closeups of Nixon's hands pointing and his voice stating, 'Tell them that. Tell them my reasons," the short TV shots that Bicke sees as he hopelessly tries to save his marriage and his office furniture salesman job underline his sense of powerlessness in American society. Nixon's TV commentary falls in ironic counterpoint to Bicke's situation as the president says, "Justice will be preserved."

The archival Nixon footage tracing the president's career as "the greatest salesman who sold us twice on how he'd end the war in Vietnam," as Bicke's boss says, to Nixon dancing happily at his daughter's wedding as Bicke struggles to get his estranged wife to even have dinner with him, makes Bicke more and more determined to try to control his destiny. His is a warped version of the American dream that he wants Leonard Bernstein to understand. "A man is only remembered for his work," says Bicke as he tries to hijack an airplane. Penn is pathetically magnificent in this role, similar to many of his dark underdog characterizations. He slumps and stutters throughout the film, symbolically revealing his ineptitude. After three Oscar nominations, for *Dead Man Walking* (1995), *Sweet and Low Down* (1999), and *I Am Sam* (2001), he won for *Mystic River* (2003). His performance receives outstanding reviews in this 2004 venture, although Roger Ebert of the *Chicago Sun-Times* suggests the title should be changed to *The Assassination of Samuel Bicke* because of the self-destructive nature of Penn's character.

She Hate Me (2004)

Nixon: Keith Jochim. *Other Cast:* Anthony Mackie (John Henry "Jack" Armstrong), Kerry Washington (Fatima Goodrich), David Bennent (Dr. Herman Schiller), Ellen Barkin (Margo Chadwick), Monica Bellucci (Simona Bonasera), Jim Brown (Geronimo Armstrong), Ossie Davis (Judge Buchanan), Jamel Debbouze (Doak), Brian Dennehy (Chairman Billy Church), Woody Harrelson (Leland Powell), John Turturro (Don Angelo Bonasera), Peter Michael Marino (John Dean), Don Harvey (G. Gordon Liddy), Gary Evans (H.R. Haldeman), Murphy Guyer (John Erlichman), Brian Simons (Jeb Stuart Magruder), Jeff Hughes (Oliver North). *Director:* Spike Lee. *Producers:* Jean Cazes, Djamel Debbouze. *Writing Credits:* Michael Genet, Spike Lee. *Music:* Terence Blanchard. *Score Musician:* Bradford Marsalis. *Cinematography:* Matthew Libatique. *Film Editing:* Barry Alexander Brown. *Production Design:* Brigitte Broch. *Costume Design:* Donna Berwick. *Special Effects:* Drew Jiritano. *Studio:* 40 Acres and a Mule Network. *Length:* 138 minutes.

What reads like a grammatical disaster for a title reveals what many critics call a disaster of a film that addresses current feminine issues with strong pornographic undertones. Directed by Spike Lee, it's about a successful young African-American executive, John Henry "Jack" Armstrong (Anthony Mackie), who is fired from his top job in biotechnology after informing the SEC of insider trading. His company developed an AIDS vaccine that has been rejected by the FDA, leading to the suicide of the company's principal scientist Dr. Herman Schiller (David Bennent). Because Armstrong finds his bank accounts frozen, he accepts the monetary offer of his former fiancée Fatima (Kerry Washington) if he successfully impregnates her and her new girlfriend Alex (Dania Ramirez). Armstrong soon is deluged by other lesbians who want babies and will pay $10,000. No questions arise about single-sex marriage or other cultural and moral issues.

Nixon appears in a flashback about Watergate whose guard appears as a scapegoat like Armstrong. Wearing the familiar Nixon mask, Keith Jochim appeals to his staff, "Damn it, I told them I didn't erase the tape ... kill him." In frenzied reaction, the staff includes John Dean (Peter Michael Marino), G. Gordon Liddy (Don Harvey), H.R. Haldeman (Gary Evans), John Erlichman (Murphy Guyer), Jeb Stuart Magruder (Brian Simons), and Oliver North (Jeff Hughes). McGruder pulls the gun.

Later in the film, after Armstrong's defiant appearance at the SEC, Nixon appears in another shot, newsreel footage of him with Vice President Spiro Agnew, looking triumphant.

38

Gerald Ford (1974–1977)

Gerald Ford literally and figuratively stumbled into the White House. He was named, not elected, vice president when Spiro Agnew resigned and Ford's first move—pardoning Richard Nixon—reversed the good feeling in Washington that his "nice guy" presence brought.[1] He earned that from his long career in government, culminating as speaker of the house. Furthermore, his lack of physical balance gave him a public image as a stumbling bumbling president.[2] However, Ford's decency and simple virtues currently receive praise for restoring Americans' faith in political leaders.[3]

With these virtues, Ford struggled with administration infighting between Alexander Haig and other Nixon stalwarts despite liberal Republican Nelson A. Rockefeller as appointed vice president. Ford also struggled with the American economy, urging economic restraint. In foreign affairs he oversaw the fall of Saigon, making Vietnam the first military defeat in American history. He participated with Soviet and Western European leaders in signing the Helsinki accords and ratifying World War II boundaries.[4]

Gerald Ford. (Courtesy of Library of Congress.)

Ford's wife, Betty, aired her progressive views on cultural and political matters, including support of the Equal Rights Amendment. They had met after his first political victory for the House of Representatives in which he served 13 terms. In retirement, Ford raised money for his presidential library and museum in his native Michigan where he had graduated (and starred as a football center) from the University of Michigan.

THE FILMS

Two of the three films containing a Ford portrayal rely on his reputation as an inept bumbler and the third, although serious, has never been released to the public. He is hardly one of Hollywood's heroes. This honest, long-serving political leader suffers from the film industry's turn to satire and ridicule in portraying presidents.

The Pink Panther Strikes Again (1976)

Ford: Dick Crockett. *Other Cast:* Peter Sellers (Inspector Jacques Clouseau), Herbert Lom (Chief Insp. Charles Dreyfus), Burt Kwouk (Cato), Colin Blakely (Alec Drummond), Leonard Rossiter (Inspector Quinlan), Lesley-Anne Down (Olga). *Director:* Blake Edwards. *Producers:* Blake Edwards, Tony Adams. *Writing Credits:* Blake Edwards, Frank Waldman. *Music:* Henry Mancini. *Cinematography:* Harry Waxman. *Film Editing:* Alan Jones. *Production Design:* Peter Mullins. *Art Direction:* John Siddall. *Set Decoration:* Fred Carter. *Costume Design:* Tiny Nicholls, Bridget Sellers. *Studio:* Amjo Productions. *Length:* 103 minutes.

Inspector Jacques Clouseau's boss, Charles Dreyfus (Herbert Lom) escapes from a mental asylum, commandeers a death ray, and tries to kill the clumsy Parisian detective (Peter Sellers). Clouseau adopts one obvious but funny disguise after another as he is hunted by paid assassins. He is rescued by Soviet spy Olga (Leslie-Anne Down).

Dick Crockett, identified only in the credits as The President but obviously Gerald Ford, appears in two brief scenes as a stumbling fool. In the first he is watching a Michigan football game with his staff, including Secretary of State Henry Kissinger (Byron Kane), and the game is interrupted by a newsflash from Dreyfus. In the second scene, Ford is awakened by a telephone call in his bedroom, lit by a lamp with a football-helmet-shade and decorated with a University of Michigan blanket.

The farcical nature of this "comeback" Pink Panther film, the third in the series, with its many sight gags and pain-and-destruction jokes, adds little to a serious understanding of Ford.

Hot Shots! Part Deux (1993)

Ford: Larry Lindsey.

Appearing in a scene in which fictional President Benson (Lloyd Bridges) accidentally hits all the living five ex-presidents with a shovel at a groundbreaking ceremony for his presidential library is Larry Lindsey as Ford. Lindsey's acting as Ford is not readily discernable in this scene, filmed in long shot. For details, see Chapter 37 on Richard Nixon.

The Commission (2003)

Ford: Corbin Bernsen. *Other Cast:* Martin Landau (Sen. Richard Russell), Sam Waterson (J. Lee Rankin), Alan Charof (Chief Justice Earl Warren), Martin Sheen (Deputy Attorney General Nicholas Katzenbach), Edward Asner (Capt. J.W. "Will" Fritz), Joe Don Baker (Rep. Hale Boggs), Lloyd Bochner (John J. McCloy), Stephen Collins (Joseph A. Ball), Paul Morgan Fredrix (Commission Counsel Leon Hubert), Henry Gibson (Police Chief Jesse Curry), Don Moss (Sen. John Sherman Cooper), D.C. Douglas (Staff Lawyer), Glenn Morshower (Commander James J. Humes), Jim Beaver (Howard L. Brennan). *Director-Writer-Cinematographer-Film Editor:* Mark Sobel.

Although this film has not been as yet released for general viewing in commercial theaters, it has been shown at film conferences and festivals. As of August 2004 it was reported to be in the final stages of post-production. Regardless of the lack of general release it has already created a great number of both pro and con comments on IMDb.

The basic premise is to take the actual documentation of the Warren Commission investigation of the assassination of President Kennedy and to present it in a docu-drama form. The Commission members are portrayed by major Hollywood actors. Corbin Bernsen portrays then–Representative Gerald Ford. As would be expected from this controversial topic, the comments received depend on either the bias of the viewer or the actual amount of knowledge the viewer has concerning the work of the Warren Commission.

Since the film was started in 1998 and missed the 40th anniversary of Kennedy's death, the final release to the theaters may be delayed until the 50th anniversary.

39

Jimmy Carter (1977–1981)

Jimmy Carter's presidency could take the title of his 18th book, *The Hornet's Nest*,[1] so roiled was it by his excessive morality and religious self-righteousness. These characteristics contributed to what James Wooten of the *New York* Times analyzed as his clinging to power.[2] Another Timesman, the esteemed James Reston, summed up Carter by writing, "There has always been this puzzle about Jimmy Carter—whether the smile on his face or the chip on his shoulder would prevail."[3] Still, Carter achieved success, at least temporary success, in the Camp David Agreements, the Panama Canal Treaties, the human rights campaign, and the fight for an energy plan.

But Carter suffered from too many Georgians in his administration, especially budget director Bert Lance, whose questionable banking practices forced his resignation—and, of course, Jimmy's brother Billy, who took advantage of his elevated position from Plains, Georgia, gas station owner. Most damaging was Carter's inability to free the 63 Americans taken hostage by followers of the Ayatollah Khomeini in retaliation for Carter's humanitarian admission of the Shah of Iran to the U. S. for a cancer operation.

Jimmy Carter. (Courtesy of Library of Congress.)

His wife since 1946, Rosalynn earned the sobriquet of "the steel magnolia" and much admiration for her political partnership in championing for the mentally ill, conducting lobbying efforts, and campaigning.

THE FILMS

There's a tendency toward the ridiculous interpretation of Jimmy Carter in films about him. *Sextette* and *The Lonely Guy*, in particular, paint a picture of the 39th president as a simple, smiling fool. His appearance in all seven films is brief and never serious.

The Cayman Triangle (1977)

Carter: Ed Beheler.

Ed Beheler plays the role of Carter in this satire although Carter's voice is by Dale Reeves, a Miami radio personality. Beheler, a close look-alike, works for the Veterans Administration in Waco, Texas, and reportedly was working on an act. For details, see Chapter 37 on Richard Nixon.

Sextette (1978)

Carter: Ed Beheler. *Other Cast:* Mae West (Marlo Manners), Timothy Dalton (Sir Michael Barrington), Dom DeLuise (Dan Turner), Tony Curtis (Alexei Karansky), Ringo Starr (Laslo Karolny), George Hamilton (Vance Norton), Alice Cooper (Waiter), Walter Pidgeon (The Chairman), Rona Barrett, Regis Philbin, George Raft, Gil Stratton (Themselves). *Director:* Ken Hughes. *Producers:* Daniel Briggs, Robert Sullivan, Warner G. Toub. *Writing Credits:* Mae West (play), Herbert Baker (screenplay). *Music:* Artie Butler, Gene S. Cantamessa, Van McCoy. *Cinematography:* James Crabe. *Film Editing:* Art J. Nelson. *Art Direction:* James F. Clayton. *Set Decoration:* Reg Allen. *Costume Design:* Edith Head. *Studio:* Crown International Pictures. *Length:* 91 minutes.

Jimmy Carter with Mae West? Yes! Almost as ridiculous as Jimmy Carter as a lonely guy. That's the premise of this film, *Sextette,* adapted from the play *Sex* by Mae West. At 85, West makes her final film appearance in her usual sex goddess role as movie star Marlo Manners, on her honeymoon with husband number six, Sir Michael Barrington, played by 32-year-old Timothy Dalton with more bravado than his 007 persona. The other husbands and West's manager, the irrepressible Dom DeLuise, interrupt their wedding night with preparations for another film. Flatteringly filmed in long shot and soft focus by James Crabe, West is indiscernible in some shots. She slowly sashays across the screen, constantly poses seductively, lip-synchs more than sings, and delivers her old lascivious one-liners ("It's not the men in my life but the life in my men") as if she's parodying herself. *Sextette* is an embarrassment of a script by Herbert Baker and performance by West, the vaudevillian-turned outrageous film star. As directed by Ken Hughes, the film is neither a humorous, farcical, campy, or racy musical comedy. It's barely saved by West's gorgeous costumes designed by the award-winning Edith Head and the brief turns by stars such as Tony Curtis as a Russian, Ringo Starr as an East European filmmaker, George Hamilton as a former husband, Alice Cooper as a waiter, and Rona Barrett, Regis Philbin, and George Raft as themselves. Paramount, which filmed it, refused to release it, and it was finally distributed by Crown International Pictures, an independent. Reviews were so bad one critic gave it a "O" out of "5."

Carter appears briefly in three shots during the final scene of the international summit conference with Walker Pidgeon as the Chairman. To conclude their successful negotiations, the delegates exchange national dishes such as octopus and unmentionable but appetizingly presented foodstuffs that make even diplomatic Pidgeon vomit. Carter smilingly says, "Billy was right. These people are nuts" as he eats his peanuts. He refuses an international dish and cracks another peanut; "I'm doing fine." When West appears to retrieve her audio cassette containing her memoirs and pronounces, "Get together or they'll be more war," Carter rises and kisses her hand. He also appears in a group shot of the delegates at the table. Ed Beheler handles his role well, looking and acting like the Man from Plains.

Used Cars (1980)

Carter: Carter in archival footage. *Other Cast:* Kurt Russell (Rudolph "Rudy" Russo), Jack Warden (Roy/Luke Fuchs), Gerrit Graham (Jeff), Frank McRae (Jim, the Mechanic), Deborah Harmon (Barbara Jane Fuchs). *Director:* Robert Zemeckis. *Producer:* Bob Gale *Screenwriters:* Bob Gale, Robert Zemeckis. *Cinematography:* Donald M. Morgan. *Music:* Patrick Williams. *Studio:* Columbia Pictures. *Length:* 111 minutes.

Brotherly love is not the theme of this early Robert Zemeckis film in which two competing brothers, Roy and Luke Fuchs (both played by a frenetic Jack Warden), struggle to sell useless used cars. They are aided in their outrageous sales schemes by a sleazy group of salesmen led by Rudy Russo (Kurt Russell) and Jeff (Gerrit Graham). The plot of the film is typical teenage farce, concentrating on sales techniques that include strippers, guns, and breaking into live TV broadcasts to steal air time for advertising.

It is the TV broadcasts that introduce President Carter (and in archive footage) into the activities. Russo decides to take advantage of the president's live economic address to the nation to sell more cars. The only interesting aspect of this sequence is the obvious effort to tie the president's actual words into the words being spoken by the actors at both the break-in point and the ending of the break. Such presidential phrases as "What is the solution?," "... cannot cope with inflation," and "... we run an honest ..." get ridiculous endings.

Only in America would the gratuitous use of actual footage of a sitting president be used to advance the commercial interests of a ridiculous film.

Good-bye Cruel World (1983)

Carter: Walt Hanna. *Other Cast:* Dick Shawn (Rodney Pointsetter/Ainsley Poinsetter), Cynthia Sikes (Joyce), Pierre Jalbert (Pierre), Pamela Brull (Alice), LaWanda Page (Wilma), Marius Mazmanian (Rabbi Bandini), Pricilla Pointer (Myra), Chuck Mitchell (Larry Locatelli). *Director:* David Irving. *Producer:* Stephen L. Newman. *Writing Credits:* Nicholas Niciphor, Dick Shawn. *Music:* Tom Jenkins. *Cinematography:* Jerry Hartleben. *Film Editing:* Marshall Harvey, Rob Smith. *Art Direction:* Paul Zacha. *Studio:* NSN Productions/Newman/Sardonis. *Length:* 100 minutes.

Writers Nicholas Niciphor and Dick Shawn attempt to cover all possible aspects of a dysfunctional family in this story of a TV anchorperson, Rodney Pointsetter (Dick Shawn), who delays committing suicide so that he can film his wild family. What the viewer sees is a series of raunchy skits that have little reason to exist. The appearance of Jimmy Carter (Walt Hannah) allows Shawn and company to do a little political satirizing with such characters as Joy Crotch (sic) Jeans Woman, Norman Bates in "Psycho Soap," Waitress on Skates, Pervert in Theatre, and Dancing Nun.

An IMDb review notes the film's non–PC humor, raunchy jokes, and dysfunctional family, hardly material for a better understanding of President Carter.

The Lonely Guy (1984)

Carter: Ed Beheler. *Other Cast:* Steve Martin (Larry Hubbard), Charles Grodin (Warren Evans), Judith Ivey (Iris), Steve Lawrence (Jack Fenwick), Robyn Douglass (Danielle),

Merv Griffin (Himself), Dr. Joyce Brothers (Herself). *Director:* Arthur Hiller. *Producers:* Arthur Hiller, William E. McEuen, Dorothy Wilde, C.O. Erickson, Judy Gordon. *Writing Credits:* Bruce Jay Friedman (book), Neil Simon (adaptation), Stan Daniels and Ed Weinberger (screenplay). *Music:* Jerry Goldsmith. *Cinematography:* Victor J. Kemper. *Film Editing:* Raja Gosnell, William Reynolds. *Production Design:* James Dowell Vance. *Set Decoration:* Linda DeScenna. *Costume Design:* Betsy Cox. *Studio:* Aspen Film Society, Universal Pictures. *Length:* 90 minutes.

Jimmy Carter as a lonely guy? Yes! There are a lot of lonely guys out there, Larry Hubbard (Steve Martin) discovers after his initial happiness in New York City with Robyn Douglass as Danielle, a ballerina who turns out to have other guys in *their* bed. Hubbard, a writer for a greeting card company, finds another lonely guy, Warren Evans, drolly played by Charles Grodin, and the two search for happiness ... and a girl.

Directed with sophistication and without sympathy, sentiment, or platitudes by Arthur Hiller, the film, with adaptation by Neil Simon, is based on the book by Bruce Jay Friedman. That book is called *The Lonely Guy's Way of Life*, a title similar to *A Guide for the Lonely Guy*, the book that turns Hubbard into a best-selling sensation via the cover of *Time*, TV's *The Merv Griffin Show*, etc. Still, he can't connect: He tries plants, card tricks, celebrity cutouts, dogs, giving blood, jogging with canned sweat, psychiatry.

Then he meets six-time wedded Iris, played with charming kookiness by Judith Ivey. She can't commit because she "loves him too much" and is afraid of losing him. Hubbard also meets but doesn't recognize Jimmy Carter in the long line at Doubleday's for an autographed copy of Hubbard's book.

Grinning broadly in a blue suit, shirt and tie to match his eyes, Carter says, "Hi. Could you just put 'To Jimmy'?" That's all he wants and gets in this one-shot appearance by Ed Beheler, a real look- and-talk alike, as seen in *Sextette*. Even with the wacky talents of Martin, *Lonely Guy* received mixed reviews and grossed only $4,800,000 in the U.S.

Hot Shots! Part Deux (1993)

Carter: Ed Beheler.

Appearing in a scene in which fictional President Benson (Lloyd Bridges) accidentally hits all five ex-presidents with a shovel at a groundbreaking ceremony for his presidential library is Ed Beheler. For details, see Chapter 37 on Richard Nixon.

40

Ronald Reagan (1981–1989)

Ronald Reagan. (Courtesy of Library of Congress.)

As the "Great Communicator" Ronald Reagan used his movie acting skills to suspend disbelief and to make illusion seem like reality in creating a happier America than his immediate predecessors. The former radio announcer, movie actor, and president of the Screen Actors Guild moved to the conservative side as the corporate spokesman for General Electric in a TV series that he hosted. This led to an active political career starting with two terms as governor of California before finally being elected to the presidency at 69.

Reagan's presidency was guided by his personal belief in a few, simple, conservative principles and his ability to achieve them through both negotiation and compromise. In his first term, Reagan addressed the failing economy, utilizing tax cuts to implement "supply side" economics and in effect start the "Reagan Revolution." During his second term, he struggled with the Iran-Contra scandal, but the "Teflon President" was able to overcome this problem through the ending of the Cold War and continuing improvement in the national economy.

Throughout both terms Reagan maintained high personal marks from the American public despite criticism that his was a scripted presidency, controlled by media experts to overcome Reagan's misinformation, twisted history, poor syntax, and plain misstatements. Reagan had the communicator's ability to both make and define news in a simple manner that ultimately dazzled the public. The "Great War Against Granada" and the firing of all 13,000 air traffic controllers are examples of situations in which his approval ratings went up in questionable circumstances. However, in each of these instances he was able to communicate a simple, patriotic message that resonated for Americans wishing to believe in their national virtue and uniqueness.

In retirement as in office, his devoted wife Nancy upheld him, particularly in his struggle with Alzheimer's until his death in 2004.

THE FILMS

Reagan noted he first worried that because he was "only an actor" he was not prepared for politics. Later, he came to wonder, "How you could be president and not be an actor."[1] With the exception of *Panther*, all of the films including a Reagan character are of the silly or satiric type. The deeper respect for Reagan that has evolved in the past ten years has not been reflected in these mainly teenage films.

Sailor's Holiday (1944)

Reagan: Paul Bradley. *Other Cast:* Arthur Lake (Marblehead Tomkins), Jane Lawrence (Clementine Brown), Bob Stanton (Bill Hayes), Shelley Winters (Gloria Flynn), Lewis

This Is the Army (1943): In a reversal of his presidential role, Ronald Reagan plays Private Johnny Jones in the World War II revue on Irving Berlin's Broadway musical of the same name, which in turn was a reworking of his World War I "barracks musical" *Yip Yip Yaphank*. Most of the cast members were servicemen. Reagan figures in the romantic subplot with Joan Leslie as Eileen Dibble and there is a cameo appearance by FDR played by Jack Young. (Courtesy of George Eastman House.)

Wilson (Iron Man Collins), Edmund MacDonald (Fred Graham), Pat O'Malley (Studio guide), Herbert Rawlinson (Director), George Tyne (Assistant Director), Vi Athens (Maid), George Ford (Ronald Blair). *Director:* William Berke. *Producer:* Wallace MacDonald. *Writing Credits:* Manny Seff. *Cinematography:* Burnett Guffey. *Film Editing:* Paul Borofsky. *Art Direction:* Lionel Banks, Victor Greene. *Set Decoration:* Lew Deeds. *Makeup:* Robert Cowan, Ida Forgette. *Art Department:* Harold Pann. *Sound:* Lee Colby. *Studio:* Columbia Pictures. *Length:* 60 minutes.

It's the middle of World War II and two merchant marines, Marblehead Tomkins (Arthur Lake) and Iron Man Collins (Lewis Wilson), are on leave in Hollywood. Tomkins's only ambition (similar to the singular sleeping ambition of his Dagwood characterization) is to kiss Rita Hayworth while Collins wants to marry his longtime girlfriend Clementine Brown (Jane Lawrence). After meeting a sailor on leave, Bill Hayes (Bob Stanton), Tomkins arranges a date for him with Gloria Flynn (a new arrival from Broadway, Shelley Winters). Although there are numerous misadventures, the basic story is the switching of girlfriends with Hayes ending up with Brown and Collins with Flynn.

The double wedding is attended by a long list of star impersonators including Jimmy Cagney, Errol Flynn, Peter Lorre, Boris Karloff, Veronica Lake, Loretta Young, and ZaSu Pitts. In addition, to complete the story, the double for Rita Hayworth kisses Tomkins who, as the comic lead, faints.

The most meaningful star double for this book's purposes is Paul Bradley portraying Ronald Reagan.

Airplane II: The Sequel (1982) aka Flying High II

Reagan: Rip Torn. *Other Cast:* Robert Hays (Ted Striker), Julie Hagerty (Elaine Dickinson), Lloyd Bridges (Steven McCroskey), Chad Everett (Simon Kurtz), Peter Graves (Capt. Clarence Oveur), Chuck Connors (The Sarge), William Shatner (Cdr. Buck Murdock), Raymond Burr (Judge D.C. Simonton), John Vernon (Dr. Stone), Stephen Stucker (Controller Jacobs/Courtroom Clerk), Kent McCord (Navigator Dave Unger), James A. Watson Jr. (First Officer Dunn), John Dehner (The Commissioner), Sonny Bono (Joe Seluchi). *Director-Writer:* Ken Finkleman. *Producer:* Howard W. Koch. *Cinematography:* Joseph Biroc. *Music:* Elmer Bernstein. *Visual Effects:* Phillip C Kellison, Joseph Rayner. *Production Design:* William Sandell. *Studio:* Paramount Pictures. *Length:* 85 minutes.

New writer and director Ken Finkleman can't make the old *Airplane* (1980) gags soar again. Much missed are Jerry Zucker, Jim Abrahams, and David Zucker of the first flight into lunacy that inspired many other film parodies. The sequel's sight gags, puns, and *double entendres* go on and on in this spoof, such as the exchange among the airplane's officers Unger and Dunn about who served under Dunn, much in the manner of Abbott and Costello's famous exchange "Who's on First?" That is to say, most of the characters are comic stereotypes of ineptitude. Critics, such as Roger Ebert, consider the first ten minutes funny—about passengers being checked aboard and a paging system announcing "E.T., please phone home" which he does with a three-fingered hand and is told to "Please insert six billion dollars for three minutes."

Once in orbit, things go awry for hero Ted Striker (Robert Hays) and his former lover Elaine Dickinson (Julie Hagerty). They play their roles straight, therefore becoming the cause of much comedy. Striker is trying to recover his reputation as a space pilot and his love relationship by leaping from his mental home bed to take over *Mayflower I*, the doomed space shuttle—with paying passengers. The ROK 9000 (a spoof on the H.A.L. 9000) computer explodes, jamming the shuttle on a course to the sun and—most disturbing to the passengers—the kitchen runs out of coffee.

Everyone blames someone else for the disaster, thus making an opening for a cameo appearance of President Reagan, played by Rip Torn who also plays Bud Kruger, a space shuttle bigwig. Torn doesn't even resemble Reagan, nor do his words and actions.

Pandemonium (1982)

Reagan: David Becker. *Other Cast:* Tom Smothers (Sgt. Reginald Cooper), Carol Kane (Candy Jefferson), Miles Chapin (Andy Jackson), Debralee Scott (Sandy), Marc McClure (Randy), Judge Reinhold (Glenn Dandy), Teri Landrum (Mandy North), Candy Azzara (Bambi), Eve Arden (Warden June), Kaye Ballard (Mrs. Dandy), Tab Hunter (Blue Grange), Donald O'Connor (Glenn's Dad). *Director:* Alfred Sole. *Producer:* Doug Chapin. *Writing Credits:* Jaime Barton Klein, Richard Whitley. *Music:* Dana Kaproff. *Cinematography:* Michael Hugo. *Film Editing:* Eric Jenkins. *Production Design:* Jack De Shields. *Art Direction:* Jamie Claytor. *Set Decoration:* Charles Graffeo. *Costume Design:* Roberta Weiner. *Makeup:* Bob Mills. *Studio:* TMC Venture. *Length:* 82 minutes.

Even with a cast of strong comedians—Tom Smothers, Candy Azzara, Debralee Scott, Marc McClurg, Paul Reubens, and Eve Arden—it is difficult to make much of this film. It is basically a spoof of slasher films that telegraphs too long in advance what is coming next. A mad slasher has been killing cheerleaders for 20 years, and this is the story of how he handles the next six individuals (victims) who go to a new cheerleader school.

The presidential scene occurs when one of the new cheerleaders hitchhikes to the school but asks for three references from anybody who offers her a ride. She arrives at the school in a presidential motorcade and gets out of the limousine. President Reagan (David Becker) says, "You forgot your candy." She replies, "No thanks, even if Nancy does it for jellybeans, I don't." Becker does not look like Reagan.

Didi—Der Doppelganger (1984)

Reagan: David Becker. *Other Cast:* Dieter Hallervorden (Bruno Koob/Hans Immer), Ruth Maria Kubitschek (Heidi Immer), Tilo Pruckner (Bazille), Gotz Kaufmann (Heinrich), Hans Joachim Grubel (Otto), Gert Burkard (Poldi von Posel). *Director:* Reinhard Schwabenitzky. *Producer:* Wolf Bauer. *Writing Credits:* Dieter Hallervorden, Walter Kempley. *Music:* Harold Faltermeyer, Arthur Lauber. *Cinematography:* Charly Steinberger. *Film Editing:* Clarissa Ambach. *Production Design:* Klaus Michael Kuhn. *Art Direction:* Albrecht Konrad. *Costume Design:* Rotraud Braun. *Special Effects:* Michel Norman. *Studio:* Universum Film A.G./Zweites Deutsches Fernsehen. *Length:* 96 minutes.

This slapstick German comedy concerning role-switching by two individuals is the story of lookalike identical twins, Bruno Koob (a poor bartender) and Hans Immer (a wealthy businessman). They both are played by one of the top German comedians, Dieter Hallervorden. The comic situation develops when Koob does better and better as a businessman and Immer does poorer and poorer as a bartender.

A review of the English version states that the translation is very poor, and that none of the humor that makes it one of the better German comedies seems to have survived in English.

Obviously one of the jokes concerns Reagan since the president appears in both archival footage and in a portrayal by David Becker.

Je hais les acteurs (1986) aka I Hate Actors

Reagan: Andre Aventin, Jacques Deschamps (voice). *Other Cast:* Jean Poiret (Orlando Higgins), Michel Blanc (Monsieur Albert), Bernard Blier (Jerome B. Cobb), Patrick Floershein (Korman), Michael Galabru (Bison), Pauline Lafont (Elvina), Dominique Lavanant (Miss Davis), Sophie Duez (Bertha), Guy Marchand (Egelhofer), Wojtek Pszoniak (Hercule Potnik), Jean-Francois Stevenin (Chester Devlin), Patrick Braoude (Fineman), Jezabel Carpi (Caroma), Claude Chabrol (Lieberman), Jean-Paul Comart (Bizzel), Alex Descas (Allan), Allan Wenger (Humphrey Bogart), Gerard Depardieu. *Director:* Gerard Krawczyk. *Producers:* Jean Nainchrik, Alain Poire. *Writing Credits:* Ben Hecht (novel), Gerard Krawczyk. *Music:* Roland Vincent. *Cinematography:* Michel Cenet. *Film Editing:* Marie-Josephe Yoyotte. *Production Design:* Jacques Dugied. *Costume Design:* Rosine Lan. *Studio:* Films A2, Gaumont International, Septembre Productions. *Length:* 90 minutes.

This is a satire of Ben Hecht's *I Hate Actors* using the mystery genre to depict a top talent agent who becomes the prime suspect in the murder of several male stars during the filming of a Hollywood spectacular. *Variety* says, "It's a meek French stand-in" because of director Krawczyk's misconception of Hecht's barbs that he replaces with a "caricature style."

Kinnikuman: New York kiki ippatsu! (1986)

Reagan: Yonehiko Kitagawa. *Other Cast:* Akira Kamiya (Kinnikuman), Minori Matsushima (Alexandria Meat), Hideyuki Tanaka (Terryman), Daisuke Gori (Robin Mask). *Writing Credits:* Kenji Terada. *Studio:* Toei Doga. *Length:* 45 minutes.

Kinnikuman is an animated Japanese TV superhero who has been serving the needs of justice in Japan since the early 1980s. Over the years feature-length films have been created using the TV series characters. In this film one of the characters is Reagan (voice by Yonehiko Kitagawa).

Back to the Future Part II (1989)

Reagan: Jay Koch. *Other Cast:* Michael J. Fox (Marty McFly/Marty McFly Jr./Marlene McFly/Middle-Aged Marty McFly), Christopher Lloyd (Dr. Emmett Brown), Lea Thompson (Lorraine Baines/McFly/Tannen), Thomas F. Wilson (Biff Tannen/Griff), Elisabeth Shue (Jennifer Parker/McFly), James Tolkan (Mr. Strickland), Jeffrey Weissman (George McFly). *Director:* Robert Zemeckis. *Producers:* Neil Canton, Bob Gale. *Writing Credits:* Robert Zemeckis, Bob Gale. *Music:* Sammy Hagar, Alan Silvestri. *Cinematography:* Dean Cundey. *Film Editing:* Harry Keramidas, Arthur Schmidt. *Production Design:* Rick Carter. *Art Direction:* Margie Stone McShirley. *Set Decoration:* Linda De Scenna. *Costume Design:* Joanna Johnston. *Studio:* Amblin Entertainment/Universal. *Length:* 108 minutes.

Although filmed at the same time as the original *Back to the Future*, in *Part II* director-writer Robert Zemeckis was unable to sustain the logic for a triple time-travel film and the wacky but simple enjoyment that made the original such a success.

McFly (Michael J. Fox) and Dr. Brown's (Christopher Lloyd) time travels take them from 1985 to 2015 and back to 1955 in an attempt to prevent 1955 bully Biff Tannen (Thomas F. Wilson) from becoming unimaginably wealthy by using a 2015 sports almanac for betting. Our heroes are able to keep the time continuum straight through a series of wild and confusing adventures. While frenetic, they are not funny. Ultimately, the film sets the stage for a return to 1885 and *Back to the Future Part III* (1990), the final film of the series.

The presidential appearance comes during a short scene in the 2015 period when McFly is waited on in a soda fountain by a "Ronald Reagan Video Waiter," a TV set showing Reagan as a waiter urging McFly to note that it's "morning in America." Jay Koch's close physical resemblance gives credulity to his brief appearance.

Bumbledown: The Lives and Times of Ronald Reagan (1989)

Director: Geoffrey Perkins. *Producer:* John Lloyd. *Cast:* Cliff Taylor (as a puppet doll), Geoffrey Perkins (puppeteer). *Studio:* Spitting Image Productions. *Length:* 76 minutes.

The DVD jacket says it's "The life and times of Ronald Reagan, a B-Movie Actor and a B-Awful President." That blurb does not say it all, but this British film captures the tone of this short satirical, cynical, farcical, humorous insight into Ronald Reagan—and Margaret Thatcher.

Bumbledown follows the life of Reagan as performed by puppet dolls from its "humble beginnings." Lincoln asks him if he cut down the cherry tree, and Reagan responds, "I can not tell the truth." Turning to Reagan's athletic success, it mentions his 77 rescues as a lifeguard showing him in strange life-saving situations. As an actor, his most famous role was president of the United States, and he dealt with auditions for all movies—*Gone With the Wind, Casablanca, The Wizard of Oz,* and silents—with the same line, "Frankly, my dear, I don't give a damn," twisting its delivery in every take.

There is Reagan's World War II action on the set and "a bit more" on his position during the HUAC hearings: "I plead the ninth; my arithmetic was never my strength." Some scenes may be offensive, particularly those about Margaret Thatcher's excessive groupie behavior: "Whenever the president did anything at all, she was behind him—literally—before, after, and during Irangate."

Still, emanating from the acclaimed British Spitting Image team, the film won the Bronze Lion Award at Cannes, the Cleo in New York City, and the Gold Comedy Award at the Houston International Film Festival.

Pizza Man (1991)

Reagan: Bryan Clark. *Other Cast:* Bill Maher (Elmo Bunn), Annabelle Gurwitch (The Dame), David McKnight (Vince), Bob Delegall (Mayor Tom Bradley), Andy Romano (The Hood), Simon Richards (Donald Trump), John Moody (Bob Woodward), Sam Pancake (Kid), Cathy Shambley (Geraldine Ferraro), Arlene Banas (Marilyn Quayle), Clyde Kusatsu (Former Prime Minister Nakasone), Ron Darian (Michael Dukakis), Jim Jackman (Mike Milken). *Director-Writer:* J.F. Lawton, *Producer:* Gary W. Goldstein. *Cinematography:* Fred Samia. *Production Design:* Ted Smudde. *Costume Design:* Debra Goold. *Studio:* Megalomania. *Length:* 90 minutes.

In an after-midnight Los Angeles, the super pizza delivery man, Elmo Bunn (Bill Maher), delivers a sausage and anchovy extra large pizza and inadvertently becomes involved in an international conspiracy. The future host of TV's *Politically Incorrect* is only trying to be paid $15.23 for the delivery. This leads him into numerous conflicts with political celebrities of the day. Unfortunately, Maher is the only bright light in this dimly lit film noir version of a political satire.

Bunn's meeting with Reagan (Bryan Clark) takes place in a bedroom with Reagan in bed with Geraldine Ferraro (Cathy Shambley). In an aside, Reagan calls her a "tax-and-spend slut." Rather than pay the $15.23, Reagan and Ferraro attempt to kill Bunn.

Clark has problems in being an impersonator of Reagan. He has only a passing facial resemblance; he is at least six inches shorter; and he looks like he weighs more. With a voice that only vaguely resembles Reagan's, he is at best a pudgy facsimile without any of Reagan's acting ability. J.F. Lawton, the *Pretty Woman* screenwriter, wrote this under the name J.D. Athens and directed under his own name.

Hot Shots! Part Deux (1993)

Reagan: Jay Koch.

Appearing in a scene in which fictional President Benson (Lloyd Bridges) accidentally hits all five ex-presidents with a shovel at a groundbreaking ceremony for his presidential library is Jay Koch as Reagan. For details, see Chapter 37 on Richard Nixon.

Panther (1995)

Reagan: Jay Koch. *Other Cast:* Kadeem Hardison (Judge), Bokeem Woodbine (Tyrone), Joe Don Baker (Brimmer), Courtney B. Vance (Bobby Seale), Tyrin Turner (Cy), Marcus Chong (Huey Newton), Anthony Griffith (Eldridge Cleaver), Bobby Brown (Rose), Angela Bassett (Betty Shabazz), Nefertiti (Alma), James Russo (Rodgers), Richard A. Dyssart (J. Edgar Hoover), Melvin Van Peebles (Old Jailbird). *Director:* Mario Van Peebles. *Producers:* Tim Bevan, Mario Van Peebles, Melvin Van Peebles, Robert De Niro. *Writing Credits:* Melvin Van Peebles from his novel. *Music:* Stanley Clarke, Usher Raymond. *Cinematography:* Edward J. Pei. *Film Editing:* Earl Watson. *Production Design:* Richard Hoover. *Art Direction:* Bruce Robert Hill, Carol Lavoie. *Set Decoration:* Bob Kensinger. *Costume Design:* Paul Simmons. *Studio:* Grammercy Pictures. *Length:* 123 minutes.

Mario Van Peebles directs this simplistic and less than complete history of the founding of the Black Panther Party of Self Defense. He also appears (as Stokely Carmichael), as does his father, Melvin Peebles, in the role of Old Jailbird in the script written by the senior Peebles, based on his novel of the same name.

This dramatized account starts in the late 1960s when a small group of blacks in Oakland, California, founded an organization called "The Black Panther Party for Self-Defense." It was led by Bobby Seale (Courtney B. Vance) and Huey Newton (Marcus Chong) and, along with militant confrontations with local authorities, it provided help within the black community: free lunch to children, education in African-American awareness, removal of drug dealers from the streets.

The true story of the Black Panthers is much more complex and problematic than is shown in this film. On both sides of the racial conflict there were bad guys and good guys, never clearly drawn in Van Peebles's film. One of the villains in a short appearance in the film is then-governor Ronald Reagan (Jay Koch). Reagan is shown talking to an all-white crowd in front of the California State House as a group of the Black Panthers storm into a legislature meeting to ask for an inquest about police brutality toward the blacks. Reagan is avuncular, casually and intimately chatting with the youngsters gathered around him. In counterpoint, the 29 Panthers raise their arms and demand retribution. The shortness of the scene and the fact that all of the shots are from the rear make it impossible to assess Koch's ability to impersonate the late president.

In addition to the characterization of Reagan by Koch, the film uses archival footage that shows Presidents Kennedy, Nixon, and Reagan.

Knutschen, kuschen, jubiliener (1998)

Reagan and Nancy Reagan: Lonny Warnowski. *Other Cast:* Peter Jansen (Charlotte), Johann Jaquemont (Hennes), Udo Jermann (Mutter Colonia), Wolfgang Rendat (Biene), Jurgen Wolf (Mutter Wolf). *Director-Writer:* Peter Kern. *Producer:* Till Ulenbrock. *Cinematography:* Sven Kierst. *Film Editing:* Jean Christopher Buurger. *Studio:* Alma Film. *Length:* 87 minutes.

This is a film released in Germany and reportedly seen in Vienna, Austria, at the "Identities: Queen Film Festival." The story concerns how five elderly homosexuals get together regularly in a small bar. Then one of them wins a trip to Venice. This pseudo documentary follows the group's enjoyable trip; one of the participants goes by the name of both Ronald and Nancy Reagan.

41

George Herbert Walker Bush (1989–1993)

George Herbert Walker Bush. (Courtesy of Library of Congress.)

Reared in an established family headed by his Senator-father, Preston Bush, and educated at Phillips Academy and Yale University, George H.W. Bush served his country in World War II and, with the exception of one term as congressman and the vice presidency under Reagan, in appointive positions—delegate to the United Nations, Republican National Committee chairman, liaison to China, and director of the CIA—before he defeated Michael S. Dukakis for the presidency. Bush pledged "read my lips, no new taxes"[1] in his campaign for a "kinder, gentler nation" through volunteerism and charitable acts that created "a thousand points of light."[2]

More interested in foreign than domestic policy, Bush triumphed in his leading an international defense of Kuwait from an Iraqi invasion in the five-day Operation Desert Storm in 1991. It involved General Colin L. Powell, chairman of the Joint Chiefs of Staff, the first African-American in the post. Powell also planned the capture of General Manuel Noriega, the Panamanian leader and drug trafficker.

That same year Bush signed the Strategic Arms Reduction Treaty (START) with Soviet president Mikhail S. Gorbachev, ending the Cold War weapons race. But the Soviet Union and Gorbachev disappeared and Boris Yeltsin emerged as leader. Bush oversaw the end of the Cold War and a new internationalism—with student uprisings for democracy in China's Tiananmen Square and ethnic and religious upheavals in Yugoslavia. But the economy plagued Bush and he reversed his pledge on taxes. He also faced the controversial nomination of Clarence Thomas to the Supreme Court.

His wife, Barbara, played an influential role during Bush's presidency; her favorite cause was literacy. The Bushes have four sons (President George W. Bush, Florida Governor Jeb Bush, Neil, and Marvin) and a daughter (Dorothy). Another daughter, Robin, died at three from leukemia. "Forty-one" and "forty-three," as the Bushes call themselves, are the first father-and-son elected president since John Adams and his son John Quincy. Forty-one contended with terrorism but never initiated policies to control it,[3] giving forty-three a beleaguered legacy.

THE FILMS

Typical of his time—the active 1990s—the films involving Bush are action and satirical films, geared to the teenage moviegoing audience with the exception of *Hero* in which he reacts to a news event.

Naked Gun 2½: The Smell of Fear (1991)

Bush: John Roarke. *Other Cast:* Leslie Nielsen (Lt. Frank Drebin), Priscilla Presley (Jane Spencer), George Kennedy (Capt. Ed Hocken), O.J. Simpson (Nordberg), Robert Goulet (Quentin Hapsburg), Richard Griffiths (Dr. Albert S. Mainheimer/Earl Hacker), Jacqueline Brookes (Commissioner Annabell Brumford), Anthony James (Hector Savage), Lloyd Bochner (Baggett), Tim O'Connor (Fenzwick), Ed Williams (Ted Olsen), Margery Ross (Barbara Bush), Peter van Norden (John Sununu), Gail Neely (Winnie Mandela), Mel Torme, Zsa Zsa Gabor (Themselves). *Director:* David Zucker. *Producers:* Jim Abrahams, Gil Netter, Jerry Zucker, Robert K. Weiss. *Writing Credits:* Jim Abrahams, Jerry Zucker, David Zucker, Pat Proft. *Music:* Ira Newborn. *Cinematography:* Robert M. Stevens. *Film Editing:* Christopher Greenbury, James R. Symons. *Production Design:* John J. Lloyd. *Set Decoration:* Michael S. Michaels. *Costume Design:* Taryn De Chellis. *Studio:* Paramount Pictures. *Length:* 85 minutes.

President George H.W. Bush (John Roarke) has appointed a new energy czar, Dr. Albert S. Mainheimer (Richard Griffiths), who becomes the target of old-line oil, coal, and electric industries. Stepping in to save Mainheimer is Lt. Frank Drebin (Leslie Nielson). He joins in the conspiracy to substitute a fake Meinheimer who will keep the existing energy system, not alternative energy policy.

This is the second of the *Naked Gun* trilogy, based on a failed 1982 TV series called *Police Squad!* Taking off from the satirical TV series, the film uses broad farce to send-up detective dramas through sight gags, wordplay, overacting, profanity, bodily functions, and celebrity cameos. George Kennedy, Priscilla Presley, O.J. Simpson, and Robert Goulet return to the series to lampoon their public images. This style of lowbrow humor characterizes the work of director David Zucker, his brother Jerry Zucker and their partner Jim Abrahams of *Airplane!* (1980) fame. *Gun 2½* grossed $44.2 million at the box office, ranking among the top films of 1991.

President and Mrs. Bush (Margery Ross) become the fall guys for the inept and dangerous Drebin throughout the film. In the first scene at a White House dinner, Mrs. Bush is the victim of numerous Drebin mishaps. While being made up for a speech on energy, Bush humorously briefs himself on his famous phrases, such as "a thousand points of light." At the podium Bush again deals in doubletalk, saying cutting is the only way to go forward in the strained oil situation. In the Bushes' final scene, Drebin kisses Mrs. Bush and accidentally pushes her off the balcony. As Bush, John Roarke physically resembles the president and comports himself much in the manner of the relaxed and aristocratic leader.

Hero (1992) aka Accidental Hero

Bush: Daniel T. Healy. *Other Cast:* Dustin Hoffman (Bernard "Bernie" Laplante), Geena Davis (Gale Gayley), Andy Garcia (John Bubber), Joan Cusack (Evelyn Laplante), Kevin J. O'Connor (Chucky), Maury Chaykin (Winston), Stephen Tobolowsky (James Wallace), Christian Clemenson (James Conklin, Channel 4 News Reporter), Tom Arnold (Chick the Bartender), James Madio (Joey Laplante), Chevy Chase. *Director:* Stephen Frears. *Producers:* Joseph M. Caracciolo, Laura Ziskin. *Writing Credits:* Laura Ziskin, Alvin Sargent, David Webb Peoples. *Music:* George Fenton. *Cinematography:* Oliver Stapleton. *Film Editing:* Mick Audsley. *Production Designer:* Dennis Gassner. *Art Director:* Leslie McDonald. *Set Designers:* Gina B. Cranham, Nancy Haigh, Lawrence Hubbs. *Costume Designer:* Richard Hornung. *Sound Designer:* Steve Maslow. *Makeup:* Christina Smith. *Special Effects:* Keith Shartle. *Studio:* Columbia Pictures Corp. *Length:* 117 minutes.

This is a Cinderella story of the modern world of media. Contrary to some reviews, as directed by Stephen Frears, it is no Frank Capra fantasy or Preston Sturges satire. While Frears directed *Dangerous Liaisons* (1988) and *The Grifters* (1990) with clarity, he approaches *Hero* as he did *Mary Reilly* (1996), with uncertainty of form. Does it laud or lampoon TV news?

Hero is the sad story of Bernie Laplante, as played by Dustin Hoffman in his best "little man" manner. He's awaiting sentencing as a petty thief when his car breaks down at the scene of an airplane crash. Reluctantly, Laplante breaks open the plane's door, then saves some passengers, including ace reporter Gale Gayley (Geena Davis). He flees with the passengers' wallets and only one of his beloved expensive shoes. Homeless John Bubber (Andy Garcia) befriends the careless Laplante and is mistaken as the one who has saved the passengers.

In quick succession through the wiles of ace and ambitious reporter Gayley, Bubber becomes a national hero, receiving a million dollars from her ratings-conscious TV station, the best hotel room in town (the setting for a rags-to-riches TV story), a new wardrobe and haircut, and dinner with Gayley. Laplante learns on TV of the million-dollar award as he's seized by undercover agents at his favorite bar. Handsome, humble Bubber becomes the perfect hero, admitting on TV that he "was trying to save my [own] life more than anything else...."

President George H.W. Bush and Barbara Bush, appropriately played in this slick story by lookalikes Daniel T. Healy and Margery Ross (the latter previously seen in *Naked Gun 2½*), join the thousands of Americans who watch the overplayed TV story of the Angel of Flight 104. They are seen in only one shot, at long range, with Bush sitting at his desk and his wife standing, as usual, beside him, watching Bubber explain why he saved 54 people. The presidential couple's shot is one in a montage; they join a slovenly landlord, homeless people, men in jail, the real hero's son, and Gayley and the Channel 4 News staff. The film slowly winds to an anticlimax as Laplante once more makes a deal, this time with the guilty, suicidal Bubber, on his hotel balcony. Laplante is reunited with his son who believes him the hero.

Hot Shots! Part Deux (1993)

Bush: Daniel T. Healy.

Appearing in a scene in which fictional President Benson (Lloyd Bridges) accidentally hits all five ex-presidents with a shovel at a groundbreaking ceremony for his new presidential library is Daniel T. Healy as George H.W. Bush. For details, see Chapter 37 on Richard Nixon.

Silence of the Hams (1994) aka Il Silenzio dei prociutti

Bush: John Roarke. *Other Cast:* Pat Rick (President Bill Clinton), Dom DeLuise (Dr. Animal Cannibal Pizza), Ezio Greggio (Antonio Motel), Billy Zane (FBI Agent Jo Dee Fostar), Joanna Pacula (Lily Wine), Charlene Tilton (Jane Wine), Martin Balsam (Detective Balsam), Mel Brooks (Guest Checking Out), Stuart Pankin (Inspector Pete Putrid), John Astin (The Ranger), Phyllis Diller (Old Secretary), Bubba Smith (Olaf), Larry Storch (The Sergeant), Rip Taylor (Mr. Laurel), Shelley Winters (Mrs. Motel, the mother). *Director-Writer:* Ezio Greggio. *Producers:* Ezio Greggio, Julie Corman, Luca Oddo. *Music:* Parmer Fuller. *Cinematography:* Jacques Haitkin. *Film Editing:* Robert Barrere, Andy Horvitch. *Production Design:* James William Newport. *Art Direction:* Russell J. Smith. *Set Decoration:* Natalie Pope. *Costume Design:* Leesa Evans. *Studio:* Silvio Berlusconi Communication, Thirtieth Century Wolf. *Length:* 81 minutes.

The Italian title may be the funniest element of this foreign-made spoof of *The Silence of the Lambs* (1991) and Hitchcock's *Psycho* (1960). Director-writer-producer Ezio Greggio steals from *Airplane!* (1980) and the *Naked Gun* series, borrows old prop jokes and sight gags, and begs for laughs. Greggio as Antonio Motel is stabbed *a la Psycho*, and FBI Agent Jo Dee Fostar (yes, the spelling is correct), as overearnestly conceived by Billy Zane, searches for the serial killer.

While training, Fostar runs into fellow joggers, former President George H.W. Bush (John Roarke) and President Bill Clinton (Pat Rick). The two leaders of our country quickly get into a fistfight over Clinton's "inhaling." While Roarke closely resembles Bush, Rick appears much too thin and small to be Clinton. Nevertheless, neither wins. For details on Clinton, see Chapter 42 on Bill Clinton.

More mayhem ensues, the zaniest character being Dom DeLuise as Dr. Animal Cannibal Pizza, incarcerated in the Hollywood Nuthouse's Unbelievably Bad Maniacs Wing. He's lost his psychic powers but finally gives Zane three clues. While Fostar's girlfriend Jane (Charlene Tilton) absconds with $400,000, a slew of stars appear: John Astin, Mel Brooks, Phyllis Diller, Joanna Pacula, Stuart Pankin, Larry Storch, and, most effectively, Martin Balsam and Shelley Winters.

American Virgin (2000)

Bush: John Roarke. *Other Cast:* John Roarke (Jerry Springer/Maury Povitch/Tom Snyder), Bob Hoskins (Joey Quinn), Robert Loggia (Ronny Bartolotti), Mena Suvari (Katrina), Sally Kellerman (Quaint McPerson), Lamont Johnson (Nick), Gabriel Mann (Brian), Alexandra Wentworth (Mitzi), Bobbie Phillips (Raquel). *Director:* Jean-Pierre Marois. *Producers:* Jean-Pierre Marois, Aissa Djabri, Farid Lahouassa, Manuel Munz. *Writing Credits:* Jean-Pierre Marois, Ira Israel. *Cinematography:* Egil Orn Egilsson. *Film Editing:* George Klotz. *Production Design:* Christian Wagener. *Art and Set Direction:* Lisa Deutsch. *Costume Design:* Deborah Everton. *Studio:* M6 Films/TPS Cinema/Vertigo Films. *Length:* 105 minutes.

Of the many fine films with *American* in their title, this should not be listed. It is not the esteemed *American Beauty* (1991) in which Mena Suvari also plays an important role. Nor is it the equally raunchy but funny *American Pie* (1999) that follows a similar theme of youth losing virginity.

American Virgin is the story of Katrina (Suvari) who is disgusted with her father's (Robert Loggia) double standards. He, Ronny Bartalotti, is a porn baron rivaling Joey Quinn (Bob Hoskins). To avenge her father, Katrina agrees to appear on rival Quinn's national TV show, losing her virginity. The ensuing efforts of her father and her former boyfriend, Brian (Gabriel Mann), to save her involve more yelling and screaming and disjointed actions than ever occurred on even the poorest playing field. Jean-Pierre Marois, director and writer with Ira Israel, attempt satire but create vulgarity.

President George Bush, Jerry Springer, Maury Povitch, and Tom Snyder are all played by the same actor, John Roarke. But they are not seen in the DVD release.

42

Bill Clinton (1993–2001)

Bill Clinton was the second U.S. president to be impeached despite the public's general disapproval of his trial. He was acquitted and left a record of domestic prosperity and foreign policy initiatives of questionable long-term value, especially the Israel-Jordan peace agreement, the restoration of Haiti's president, Jean-Bertrand Aristide, his support of Russian president, Boris Yeltsin, and a peace accord on Bosnia.

He came to the presidency after a campaign of charges against his character, principally infidelity, the same charge that led to his impeachment. His wife Hillary, whom he met in Yale Law School, remained loyal. He also graduated from Georgetown University and was a Rhodes Scholar. His supporters considered him one of the most intelligent, articulate, and politically agile presidents of the 20th century; his detractors labeled him "Slick Willy."[1]

Bill Clinton. (Courtesy of Library of Congress.)

In his first term, a health care reform package formulated by Hillary failed to get sufficient Congressional support. Yet, Clinton did get support for the North American Free Trade Agreement (NAFTA) and the Global Agreement on Tariffs and Trade (GATT) that led to the formation of the World Trade Organization (WTO) as well as a deficit reduction bill, rules allowing abortion counseling, the Brady Bill for controlling handgun purchases, and a national service program. In midterm, Representative Newt Gingrich (R-GA) offered a conservative "Contract with America" that made Clinton seem a left liberal. He reacted by making Republican issues his own and captured the middle ground of American politics.

In his second term, the first for a Democratic president since FDR, continued economic prosperity allowed Clinton to reach an agreement that forecast a balanced federal budget over the next three decades. But character issues (investigated by Kenneth Starr) continued with the Whitewater land deal, the death of Vince Foster, and more allegations of sexual misconduct, namely with 22-year-old White House intern Monica Lewinsky. Although the impeachment trial dominated his activities, Clinton contended with Saddam Hussein who refused weapons inspection that led to a 78-day bombing campaign. His purported lack of strategic vision failed him personally and politically.[2] During his last years in office he took several major trips overseas and supported Al Gore and Hillary in their political campaigns.

THE FILMS

This president who loved flamboyant risk-taking in the secret "parallel life" he lived, provides ample experience for the many outrageous films about him, including a video game, not included here, "Spy Fox: Dry Cereal" (1997). The most thorough in treatment about his talents as a politician, *Primary Colors*, uses a fictional name, but it is evident in every political act, action and accent that Jack Stanton, as played by John Travolta, is Clinton. With the sole exception of *Primary Colors*, all of the 12 films with a Clinton character are basically for the teenage audience. To paraphrase an old line, the rest (of these films) is *not* history.

Naked Gun 33⅓: The Final Insult (1994)

Clinton: Timothy Watters. *Other Cast:* Leslie Nielsen (Lt. Frank Drebin), Priscilla Presley (Jane Spencer Drebin), George Kennedy (Capt. Ed Hocken), O.J. Simpson (Nordberg), Fred Ward (Rocco Dillon), Kathleen Freeman (Muriel Dillon), Anna Nicole Smith (Tanya Peters), Mary Lou Retton, Vanna White, Florence Henderson, James Earl Jones, Mariel Hemingway, Olympia Dukakis, Morgan Fairchild, Elliot Gould, Raquel Welch (Themselves). *Director:* Peter Segal. *Producers:* Jim Abrahams, Gil Netter, Jerry Zucker. *Writing Credits:* Jim Abrahams, David Zucker, Jerry Zucker, Pat Proft, Robert LoCash. *Music:* Erroll Garner, Ira Newborn. *Cinematography:* Robert M. Steven. *Film Editing:* James R. Symons. *Production Design:* Lawrence G. Paull. *Art Direction:* Bruce Crone. *Set Direction:* Kathe Klopp. *Costume Design:* Mary E. Vogt. *Studio:* Paramount Pictures. *Length:* 83 minutes.

Los Angeles police Lieutenant Frank Drebin in the deadpan and dead perfect persona of Leslie Nielsen returns in this extension of the *Police Squad!* TV series. Although Jim Abrahams, David Zucker, and Jerry Zucker produce again, David Zucker does not direct as he did the previous two. Peter Segal is the new director, playing for fast gags from satirical lampoons of cop movies to broad slapstick and word play.

The plot involves Drebin leaving his happy house-husband retirement to stop an evil terrorist organization that threatens Los Angeles and the Academy Award ceremonies. The final scene of the Awards involves several celebrities including President Clinton (Timothy Watters). Watters gives a credible performance, joining in the fun.

Silence of the Hams (1994) aka Il Silenzio dei prociutti

Clinton: Pat Rick.

Clinton (Pat Rick) joins former President George H.W. Bush (John Roarke) and a host of celebrities playing themselves in this Italian-made spoof of *The Silence of the Lambs* (1991) and *Psycho* (1960). The two former presidents run into a fellow jogger, FBI Agent Jo De Fostar (Billy Zane), who's in training for a search for a serial killer. The leaders of our country almost kill each other when Bush makes a remark about Clinton's "inhaling," and Clinton retaliates with a profane one about saving him from Saddam Hussein. Rick appears much too thin and small to be Clinton. Nevertheless, neither wins.

For more details, see Chapter 41 on George H.W. Bush.

Gordy (1995)

Clinton: Jim Meskimen (voice). *Other Cast*: Hamilton Camp (Gordy's Father), Doug Stone (Luke MacAllister), Kristy Young (Jinnie Sue MacAllister), James Donadio (Gilbert Sipes), Deborah Hobart (Jessica Royce), Tom Lester (Cousin Jake), Louis Rukeyser (Himself), Michael Roescher (Hanky Royce), Tom Key (Brinks), Ted Manson (Henry Royce). *Director*: Mark Lewis. *Producer*: Sybil Robson. *Writing Credits*: Jay Sommers, Dick Chevillat, Leslie Stevens. *Music*: Tom Bahler, Charles Fox. *Cinematography*: Richard Michalak. *Film Editing*: Lindsay Frazer, Duane Hartzell. *Production Design*: Philip Messina. *Set Decoration*: Kristen Toscano Messina. *Costume Design*: Barcie Waite. *Studio*: RAS Robson. *Length*: 90 minutes.

Gordy is not to be confused with *Babe* (1995), the charming U.S.–Australian film (about a pig taken in by an eccentric farmer) that won an Academy Award for special effects. In a dozen reviews, *Gordy* evoked such obvious and descriptive puns as "porker" and "sausage meat." It's the story of another little pig whose father, mother, and five siblings have been shipped "up north," the politically correct term for sausage factory. In seeking to find his folks, Gordy meets a country singer (Doug Stone) and his daughter (Kristy Young) and a rich little boy named Hanky (Michael Roescher) whom he saves from drowning.

That rescue brings Gordy the position of CEO of the Royce food industries owned by the little boy's grandfather (Ted Manson). It also brings Gordy fame on the cover of *Time*, on TV with Louis Ruykeser, and a phone call from President Clinton. Jim Meskimen provides the voice. He says he understands "piggy talk" and unveils Gordy's "very own postage stamp," a 29-center. But there's no connection between Gordy, who is from a farm in Arkansas, and Clinton's nearby home town of Hope; Gordy only passes through it.

In fact, there are many disconnected elements in this film: Kristy Young's singing, the maternal intentions of the rich little boy's mother (Deborah Hobart), and the romance between her and Doug Stone as the country and western singing father of the young girl. But it adds up to triumph for the value of the family and triumph over a backstabbing PR man (Gilbert Sipes) who hopes to take over Royce industries.

The film is directed by Australian Mark Lewis with badly synched voices by Paul Mejias and cinematography by Richard Michalak that looks like a child's coloring book about farm animals. Screenwriter Leslie Stevens based *Gordy* on the *Green Acres* TV series in which Tom Lester plays Ed, a similar role to his dumb Uncle Jake film role.

Beavis and Butt-head Do America (1996)

Clinton: Dale Reeves, voice. *Other Cast*: Mike Judge (Beavis, Butt-head, Tom Anderson, Mr. Van Driessen, Principal McVicker voices), Cloris Leachman (Old Woman on Plane and Bus voices), Robert Stack (ATF Agent Flemming voice), Jacqueline Barba (FBI Agent Hurly voice), Bruce Willis (Muddy Grimes voice), Demi Moore (Dallas Grimes voice), Greg Kinnear (FBI Agent Bork voice), Pamela Blair (Flight Attendant, White House Tour Guide voices), Eric Bogosian (Ranger at Old Faithful, White House Press Secretary, Lieutenant at Strategic Air Comand voices), David Letterman (Motley Crue Roaddie #1 voice). *Director*:

Mike Judge, Vyette Kaplan (animation). *Producers:* David Gale, Van Toffler, Mike Judge, Abby Terkkuhle. *Writing Credits:* Mike Judge, Joe Stillman. *Music:* Tim Armstrong, Lars Fredriksen, John Frizzell, Isaac Hayes, Mike Judge, Anthony Kiedis, LL Cool J, Ozzy Osbourne, Ronald Belford Scott, Gwen Stefani, Angus Young, Malcolm Young, Rob Zombie. *Film Editing:* Gunter Glinka, Terry Kelley, Neil Lawrence. *Art Direction:* Jeff Buckland. *Special Effects:* Dave Hughes, Norman Rompre. *Studio:* Geffen Pictures, MTV Productions, Paramount Pictures. *Length:* 81 minutes.

This is an animated buddy film, a road flick, a fantastic and foul-mouthed (but no violence, thank you) movie about the two TV characters. Directed, written, and produced by Mike Judge, who did the TV series, the story concerns the anti-heroes' attempt to find their stolen TV set and "do" a mobster's wife. In typical fashion, high hormone level Beavis and Butt-head's understanding of "do" is different from the mobsters.' In so "doing," they cross the country, evade professional killers and lawmen, and in their warped minds, define a busload of nuns as "chicks."

True to the low level of this film, a cartoon President Clinton (Dale Reeves, voice) in what Stephen Holden of the *New York Times* calls "dripping platitudes," gives "deepest thanks" to these "great Americans" Beavis and Butt-head and makes them honorary gents in the Bureau of Alcohol, Tobacco, and Firearms (ATF). This scene of satiric ceremony precedes the end of the film in which the dumb duo find their TV set but still wonder about "scoring." The president's voice is employed as are many others of well known but not always credited stars: Cloris Leachman, Robert Stack, Eric Bogosian, Richard Linkletter, Bruce Willis, Demi Moore, and Greg Kinnear. Those who like this toilet humor of Generation X might find Robert Stack as the voice of ATF Agent Flemming amusing. Obviously, there is a following for Beavis and Butt-head as their TV ratings reveal. On the bigger screen, their redeeming feature is their embodiment of teenage angst about sexuality.

The Godson (1998)

Clinton: Craig Barnett. *Other Cast:* Rodney Dangerfield (The Rodfather), Kevin McDonald (Guppy Calzone), Dom DeLuise (The Oddfather), Fabiana Udenio (Don Na), Lou Ferrigno (Bugsy/Alice), Paul Greenberg (Frito Calzone), Carol DeLuise (Mama Calzone), Barbara Crampton (Goldy), Bob Hoge (Sunny Calzone), Irwin Keyes (Tracy Dick), Eileen Keeney (Agent Hoover), Bobbie Brown (Sunny's Babe), Carlos Alazraqui (Tony "Flock You" Montana), Perry Stephens (Father O'Connell), Jerry Lambert (Professor), Jerry Douglas (Freddie Gilen), Dom Irrerar and Joey Buttafuoco as themselves. *Director-Writer:* Bob Hoge. *Producers:* Don Dunn, Kevin Flint, George Marinos, Lynn Mooney, Jeff Ritchie, Morris Ruskin, Mary Skinner. *Music:* Robert Backus, Boris Elkis, Max Raxley, Roy Rede, Brent Walker. *Cinematography:* Tom Lappin. *Film Editing:* Tracy Curtis. *Production Design:* Deren Abram. *Art Direction:* Flip Filippelli. *Set Decoration:* Jon Joseph Glover. *Costume Design:* Mandi Line, Leesa-Rae Sandoval. *Studio:* Shoreline Entertainment, Three Spear Productions. *Length:* 100 minutes.

A satire on Mafia films, namely the *Godfather* series, this film uses every trick in the comic bag to evoke humor. The result is an empty sack of a story about the Calzone mob family's trying to build a future after the death of son Sunny (Bob Hoge). Hoge also wrote and directed. The future rests on the success of the dumb son Guppy (Kevin McDonald) who goes to Mafia school to "be a contender," as his father The Oddfather (Dom DeLuise) quotes Marlon Brandon from *On the Waterfront* (1954) in his Brando-like voice, one of too many such references in this film.

Everything Guppy tries fails—a nightclub, a phone sex service, a romance with the daughter of rival mobster Rodfather (Rodney Dangerfield)—to make his father disown him, *Romeo and Juliet* style. But Guppy does outwit his jealous brother Frito (Paul Greenberg) and win the affection of Don Na (Fabiana Udenio).

The humor descends to the lowest level in the party scene with Craig Barnett as President Clinton. With the build and voice of Clinton, he indulges in the spread, getting red sauce all over his face. He also indulges in the female guests, offering to show one his "Washington monument" (she then hits him) and asking another's name. It's Sue, and he says, "You can sue me any time." There is no end to these jokes and seemingly no end to the film as it continues even after the final credits.

Jesus 2000 (1998)

Clinton: Kelley Johnson. *Other Cast:* Jim Abbott (Rev. Jesse Jackmon Jr.), Cristina Alvarez Cox (Salma Yakyak), Elaine Andrews (Airport Official), Derek Annunciation (Jess Jabberjaw), Andrea Anthony (Mary Hark), Nikki Arlyn (Nikki Nak), Robert Backus (Letterboy), Clorina Bassolino (Jane D'Ho), Nelson Bennett (Oren), Carole Bergeron (Natalie Nytnite), Alex Boling (Reggie Cartwright), Laura Bossis (Ruth Norman), N.D. Brown (Bertha Baditude), Joseph Calvino (Brett Cummings), John Silbert (Walter Crumbkite), Frank Hotchkiss (Ted Poppel). *Director-Producer-Writer:* Eric Cooper. *Cinematography:* Garrick Wilkie. *Film Editing:* Eric Cooper, Adrian Lawson. *Production Design:* Linda Shockley. *Makeup:* Laura Irwin. *Art Department:* Dean McReary. *Sound:* Robert Backus. *Studio:* OK, Maybe a Little (but don't make a) Production. *Length:* 30 minutes.

In a spoof of current television news casting director-producer-writer Eric Cooper covers the last week of the life of Jesus as if he were alive today. In his own plot summary for IMDb Cooper notes that "rumors, facts, and half truths fly around interchangeably on nightly news, talk shows, and even commercials. Questions about Jesus' nationality, race, sexual orientation, and birth are posed by the media."

Although all of the many characters are given readily decoded fictional names like Walter Crumbkite and Ted Poppel, the name of Bill Clinton (Kelley Johnson), comes through loud and clear. Because the film is not available for viewing, it is impossible to assess the appearance of Clinton.

Michael Kael Contre La World News Company (1998)
aka Michael Kael vs. The World News Company

Clinton: Pat Rick. *Other Cast:* Benoit Delepine (Michael Kael), Marine Delterme (Paola Maertens), Victoria Principal (Leila Parker), William Atherton (James Denit), Mickey Rooney (Griffith), Elliott Gould (Coogan), Feodor Atine (Maj. Sylvain), Yves Jacques (Charles Robert), Alix De Konopka (Miss Picottte), Michael Morris (Robert Kipp), Luc Bernard (Steve Walsh), Paul Van Mulder (Jean Crevier). *Director:* Christophe Smith. *Producers:* Dominique Brunner, Charles Gassot. *Writing Credits:* Benoit Delelpine. *Cinematography:* Pascal Gennesseaux. *Film Editing:* Veronique Parnet. *Art Direction:* Jean-Marc Kerdelhue. *Costume Design:* Jacqueline Bouchard. *Studio:* Canal Plus/France 2 Cinema/France 3 Cinema/Telema Productions. *Length:* 86 minutes.

It is hard to believe historically, but this French film directed by Christophe Smith shows a major TV news network working with Washington to enable President Clinton to be elected for a third term. To do this the head of the network, Griffith (Mickey Rooney) sends incredibly naïve French reporter Michael Kael (script writer Benoit Delepine) to Africa where he is to report on a fake story in which a crazy Japanese scientist is going to destroy the world. Kael figures the whole scheme out, and things do not go as Griffith expected.

In a cameo appearance Pat Rick plays President Clinton. Rick made a career of portraying Clinton, mainly in TV productions. Because this film is not available for viewing it is impossible to assess the appearance of Rick as Clinton.

Primary Colors (1998)

Gov. Jack Stanton/Clinton: John Travolta. *Other Cast:* Emma Thompson (Susan Stanton), Billy Bob Thornton (Richard Jemmons), Kathy Bates (Libby Holden), Adrian Lester (Henry Burton), Maura Tierney (Daisy), Larry Hagman (Gov. Fred Picker), Diane Ladd (Mamma Stanton), Paul Guilfoyle (Howard Ferguson), Caroline Aaron (Lucille Kaufman), Tommy Hollis (Fat Willie), Rob Reiner (Izzy Rosenblatt), Ben Jones (Arlen Sporken), J.C. Quinn (Uncle Charlie), Allison Janney (Miss Walsh), Robert Klein (Norman Asher). *Director:* Mike Nichols. *Producers:* Michael Haley, Michele Imperato, Jonathan D. Krane, Neil Machlis. *Writing Credits:* Joe Klein (novel), Elaine May (screenplay). *Cinematography:* Michael Ballhaus. *Film Editing:* Arthur Schmidt. *Casting:* Juel Bestrop, Ellen Lewis, Juliet Taylor. *Production Design:* Bo Welch. *Art Direction:* Tom Duffield. *Set Decoration:* Cheryl Carasik. *Studio:* Mutual Film Company. *Length:* 143 minutes.

Primary Colors (1998): John Travolta assumes the role of Jack Stanton, a Clinton act-alike. He's an ambitious progressive governor of a small Southern state, running for the presidency. Mike Nichols directs this adaptation of the book of the same name by "Anonymous," later identified as political columnist Joe Klein who shares writing credits with Elaine May. (Photofest.)

Although this is a fiction film about the presidency, actually, the presidential campaign, it certainly doesn't deserve the title "Anonymous" that the author of the book on which it was based is named. It's a study of Bill Clinton's 1992 run for the presidency, a textbook example of campaigning. Elaine May wrote the screenplay based on

Top: Primary Colors (1998): John Travolta as Jack Stanton with his wife and political partner Susan played by Emma Thompson. *Bottom: Primary Colors* (1998): Adrian Lester (left) as Henry Burton, a young idealist, joins the presidential campaign of Jack Stanton, played by John Travolta in the Bill Clinton–inspired story. (Both photographs Photofest.)

the bestseller by Joe ("Anonymous") Klein, then political reporter of *New York* magazine. In turn, director Mike Nichols gets superb performances and much comedy from the script.

John Travolta, in one of his best roles, stars as Jack Stanton, a Southern governor who has a way with the people and the ladies. Emma Thompson plays his wife Susan with all the smarts and political savvy of Hillary Clinton. Stanton's confidant Libby Holden (Kathy Bates) acts as "dust buster" and truly gives her life for him. And Billy Bob Thornton as Richard Jemmons, one of Stanton's advisors, allows his morality to triumph. Yes, the campaign is contrived: "sex, drugs, venality," in Libby Holden's characterization.

It's full of drama, suspense, and wonderful turns of Travolta speaking to crowds, dealing with contenders, inspiring his workers, and eating doughnuts alone late at night with only the franchise's cook to chat with. It's a superb characterization. The evolution of idealistic campaign worker Henry Burton (Adrian Lester) provides yet another insight into the political process.

Austin Powers: The Spy Who Shagged Me (1999)

Clinton: Tim Watters. *Other Cast:* Mike Myers (Austin Powers/Dr. Evil/Fat Bastard), Heather Graham (Felicity Shagwell), Michael York (Basil Exposition), Robert Wagner (Number Two), Rob Lowe (Young Number Two), Seth Green (Scott Evil), Mindy Sterling (Frau Farbissina), Verne Troyer (Mini-Me), Elizabeth Hurley (Vanessa Kensington), Kristen Johnston (Ivana Humpalot), Gia Carides (Robin Swallows), Burt Bacharach, Elvis Costello, Will Ferrell, Woody Harrelson, Charles Napier, Willie Nelson, Jerry Springer (Themselves). *Director:* Jay Roach. *Producers:* Michael De Luca, Donna Langley, Erwin Stoff. *Writing Credits:* Mike Myers, Michael McCullers. *Music:* George S. Clinton, John Flansburgh, Susanna Hoffs, Lenny Kravitz, John Linnell, Madonna, Mike Myers, Debbi Peterson, Victoria Peterson, Michael Steele, Neil Diamond, Mike Dirnt, Marvin Gaye, Marvin Hamlisch, Quincy Jones, Pete Townshend. *Cinematographer:* Ueli Steiger. *Film Editing:* Debra Neil-Fisher, Jon Poll. *Production Design:* Rusty Smith. *Art Direction:* Alec Hammond. *Set Decoration:* Sara Andrews. *Costume Design:* Deena Appel. *Studio:* Eric's Boy, Moving Pictures, Team Todd. *Length:* 95 minutes.

Austin Powers is back, that fashion photographer, party man of Swingin' London, and international espionage agent. Between squeals of "baby" to his ever-present harem of beautiful girls, he discovers he has lost his "mojo," the secret to his sex appeal for "shagging." Stranded in 1999, he goes back to 1969 to find the thief. He's the fey Dr. Evil, his nemesis (also played by Myers), who wants to take over the world. Helping him is his dwarf clone Mini-Me (Verne Troyer) and the Scottish Fat Bastard (Myers's third role).

Powers enjoys the benefits and beauty of Felicity Shagwell (Heather Graham), a "shagadelic" secret agent. They zip to the moon and back, leaving a trail of gross and goofy gags, some familiar to fans of *Austin Powers: International Man of Mystery* (1997). Several brief star cameos from a Bill Clinton lookalike (Tim Watters), Jerry Springer, Burt Bacharach, and Elvis Costello provide some change of pace from the sexual silliness.

The president of the United States—an unnamed and different character from Clinton—undergoes blackmail via a TV visit from Dr. Evil who will destroy Washington and one city every hour unless he receives $100 billion. The president and his staff laugh. So Dr. Evil feigns a laser attack and says, "I think we have an understanding." On TV, the president later tells Dr. Evil, "We have your money" and exclaims, "I can't believe we're doing this." Tim Robbins handles this role with his youthful good looks and energy.

42—Bill Clinton (1993–2001)

The Extreme Adventures of Super Dave (2000)

Clinton: Pat Rick. *Other Cast:* Bob Einstein (Super Dave Osborne), Dan Hedaya (Gil Ruston), Gia Carides (Sandy), Don Lake (Donald), Art Irizawa (Fuji), Mike Walden (Michael), Carl Michael Lindner (Little Timmy), Teresa Barnwell (Hillary Clinton). *Director:* Peter MacDonald. *Producers:* Larry Brezner, Lorne Cameron, David Hoselton, Mike Marcus, Richard H. Prince, David Sternberg. *Writing Credits:* Bob Einstein, Allan Blye, Don Lake, Lorne Cameron, David Hoselton. *Music:* Flaviano Giorgini, Andrew Gross. *Cinematography:* Bernd Heinl. *Film Editing:* Mike Murphy. *Production Design:* Scott Chambliss. *Studio:* Metro-Goldwyn-Mayer. *Length:* 91 minutes.

The stunt crew deserves the credit, and 18 are credited in the Internet Movie Database material on this film. They perform all the accidents that happen to daredevil ace Super Dave Osborne (Bob Einstein). These accidents serve as the action of this film about Super Dave's challenge by his former pupil. It requires Supe, as Super Dave is known to his friends, to go over a host of vehicles, measuring a half mile. He only does it to raise money for a heart operation on Little Timmy (Carl Michael Lindner), son of Supe's love interest, Sandy (Gia Carides).

But before that great leap, Supe performs his "most death-defying stunt," a shot from a cannon to trampolines mounted on the ceiling and floor of a gigantic stadium. Predictably, it goes wrong. The audience watching this includes President Clinton (Pat Rick), Hillary Clinton (Teresa Barnwell), Queen Elizabeth, and The Pope. Clinton, wearing a tuxedo, appears in four different shots, chatting with his seat mates and expressing great emotion at Super Dave's misfiring. Rick looks and moves very much like Clinton and adds an historical touch to this tasteless film.

Einstein assisted in the writing of this feature-length extension of the TV series. It never made the theaters and was released on video instead—perhaps because it includes one of the longest and vilest of bathroom jokes.

Life or Something Like It (2002)

Clinton: Tim Watters. *Other Cast:* Angelina Jolie (Lanie Kerrigan), Edward Burns (Pete Scanlon), Tony Shalhoub (Prophet Jack), Christian Kane (Cal Cooper), Stockard Channing (Deborah Connors), Melissa Errico (Andrea), James Gammon (Lanie's Father), Lisa Thornhill (Gwen), Greg Itzin (Dennis), Max Baker (Vin). *Director:* Stephen Herek. *Producers:* Kenneth Atachity, Rick Kidney, Teddy Zee. *Writing Credits:* John Scott Shepherd, Dana Stevens. *Cinematography:* Stephen H. Burum. *Music:* David Newman. *Editor:* Trudy Ship. *Production Designer:* Bill Groom. *Art Director:* Helen Veronica Jarvis, Gary Myers. *Studio:* Davis Entertainment/Epsilon Motion Pictures/Monarchy Enterprises/New Regency Pictures/Regency Enterprises. *Length:* 103 minutes.

The best way to describe this stale romantic comedy is A.O. Scott's in the *New York Times* (April 26, 2004). He asks how Angelina Jolie, the star, is like an Altoids mint. He replies with the line of Edward Burns, the co-star love interest, "Curiously strong." And Scott concludes that the mint comparison is the most thoughtful aspect of this film.

The film does not get "curioser and curioser" as Alice in Wonderland would say. It gets more mundane in its treatment of the female career vs. romance dilemma. Most reviewers agree, even the *Seattle-Post Intelligencer's* William Arnold. He expected something like the director Stephen Herek's life-affirming *Mr. Holland's Opus* (1995) but got even wrong references to Seattle streets and institutions in this film. *Life* was partly filmed there by cinematographer Stephen H. Burum. Lanie Kerrigan (Jolie) lives and works there as a TV personality in line for a network job. She's engaged to baseball pitcher Cal Cooper (Christian Kane) but falls for her TV cameraman Pete Scanlon (Ed Burns) and debates what to do with her life when a street prophet (Tony Shalhoub) tells her she will die in a week.

Stockard Channing as Deborah Connors, the star of the network that wants to hire Kerrigan, displays the only realistic character traits of the film in her Barbara Walters–like role. She's assertive, steely, and touchingly human, all in a course of the few minutes she appears on screen. She also shows how TV stars frequently treat presidents in her two interviews of Presidents Bill Clinton (Tim Watters) and George W. Bush (Brent Mendenhall). To Clinton, Connors asks probing questions, verging on invasion of privacy. Watters, a real Clinton lookalike, handles himself smoothly, like Clinton. For details on President Bush, see Chapter 43.

43

George W. Bush (2001–2009)

Bush Two, forty-three, or Shrub, as he's been called, depending on one's political persuasion, nevertheless is the first president to gain office by a U.S. Supreme Court decision. He also was the first president since 1877 to gain admission to the White House by an Electoral College majority that overcame the loss he suffered in the popular vote (to Al Gore). More significant, he was the only president since 1825 to be elected to the office his father had held. He is "best understood as the political son of Ronald Reagan."[1]

Upon inauguration, in a stolen election according to most liberal Americans, Bush was faced with an economy moving into recession and a world facing a growth in terrorism. His tax cut policy and Congressional legislation began to turn the economy around. However, the terrorist attack on New York City and Washington on September 11, 2001, demonstrated the need for increased efforts in domestic defense and international cooperation against terrorism, in particular Al Qaeda.

George W. Bush. (Photofest.)

Although the bipartisan support after 9/11 faded over time, particularly with the invasion of Iraq and the deposing of long-time despot Saddam Hussein, Bush tended to retain the support of the American voting public. His reelection to a second term in 2004 was not sullied by the question of being stolen as in 2000. As a lame duck president Bush, in addition to a continuing defense of his unpopular actions in Iraq and Afghanistan, has taken on other controversial issues such as the politically sensitive Social Security reform. At this writing, serious political commentators are mostly concerned by what appears to be a widening ideological split between the Democrats and Republicans that is leading to gridlock in the Congress.

THE FILMS

The film media manipulates Bush almost as much as he is accused of manipulating the news media. He appears as a character in only six films. They all fall into the silly, satirical mode, made for a teenage audience.

361

The Crocodile Hunter: Collision Course (2002)

Bush: Timothy Bottoms. *Other Cast:* Steve Irwin (Himself), Terri Irwin (Herself), Magda Szubanski (Brozzie Drewitt), David Wenham (Sam Flynn), Lachy Hulme (Robert Wheeler), Aden Young (Ron Buckwhiler), Kenneth Ransom (Vaughn Archer), Kate Beahan (Jo Buckley). *Director:* John Stainton. *Producers:* Judy Bailey, Arnold Rifkin, John Stainton, Bruce Willis. *Writing Credits:* John Stainton (story), Holly Goldberg Sloan (screenplay). *Music:* Mark McDuff. *Cinematography:* David Burr. *Film Editing:* Suresh Ayyar, Bob Blasdall. *Production Design:* Jon Dowding. *Art Direction:* Jon Dowding. *Set Direction:* Chrissy Feld. *Costume Design:* Jean Turnbull. *Studio:* Best Picture Show Co./Cheyenne Enterprises/MGM. *Length:* 90 minutes.

Steve and Terri Irwin play themselves in this fictional elongation of their *The Crocodile Hunter* TV series. The story, written by John Stainton, who also directs the film, is of little importance other than providing the Irwins with a reason to demonstrate their handling of dangerous Australian animals. These number crocodiles, poisonous snakes, and large, ugly spiders. However, given the Irwins' enthusiasm, the whole effort is an authentic and exciting naturalist foray.

President George W. Bush, played by lookalike Timothy Bottoms, is introduced late in the film to illustrate the importance of a communications device that is lost when a satellite breaks up over Australia, and, when it lands on earth, is swallowed by a large crocodile. Bush appears very serious while sitting at his desk, talking on the phone about the device to the head of the CIA recovery team. So intent is Bush on recovering the capsule that he says, "I don't care if you have to send in the Marines." The interplay between the Irwins, the crocodile, and the inept U.S. government agents sent to recover the device is the excuse for this lighthearted and well-photographed look by David Burr at Australian animal life.

Life or Something Like It (2002)

Bush: Brent Mendenhall.

Stockard Channing as Deborah Connors, the star of a TV network, interviews presidents Bill Clinton and George W. Bush in this romantic comedy. Her technique reveals how TV stars frequently treat presidents in their baiting questions. For example, she asks President Bush (Brent Mendenhall), "Have you ever doubted yourself?" His answer is cut by a special report on an earthquake. For details, see Chapter 42 on Bill Clinton.

The Master of Disguise (2002)

Bush: Dana Carvey.

President Bush shows his command by pushing villain Devlin Bowman (Brent Spiner) into a swimming pool in Costa Rica where he's fled to avoid the master of disguise. The master, Dana Carvey, plays Bush with great swagger, saying, "Folks around here call me W., but you can call me King George." Carvey seizes the stolen Constitution from the villain, gets the girl, and concludes this madcap parody. For details, see Chapter 1 on George Washington.

Mobilising the Troupes (2004)

Bush: Jamie Bower. *Other Cast:* Ron Hulton (Michael Panton), Michael Jeffries (Vadim Flanders), Eliot Hill (Sam), Daniel Higley (Tom), George Nicolas (Saddam Hussein), Nick

Smithers (Theatre Manager). *Director:* Chris Lightwing. *Writing Credits:* Stephen Follows, Toby Oliver. *Producers:* Stephen Follows, Yang Xu. *Music:* Matthew Board. *Cinematography:* Samuel O. Norman. *Film Editing:* Chris Lightwing. *Studio:* Catsnake Studios. *Length:* 20 minutes.

There are any number of films that unfold as a play within a play. *Mobilising the Troupes* (sic) is a mock documentary involving the production of a musical, *The War Against Terror: The Musical,* for the London stage by an Anglo-American team. It is a political satire by a London group headed by a classically trained and celebrated Shakespearean actor. He has troubles with the nuances of his character, President Bush. Song numbers include *The Republi-can-can* and *This Has Absolutely Nothing Whatsoever to Do with Oil.* The satirizing of both President Bush and Prime Minister Blair strive for broad British appeal but apparently did not catch on after opening in London in July 2004.

Nyocker! (2004) aka *The District!*

Bush: Istvan Orosz, voice. *Other Cast:* Lajos Csuha (Tony Blair, voice), Zoltan Katona (The Prime Minister, voice), Imre Szalai (The Cardinal, voice), Robert Kajtar (The Pope, voice). *Director:* Aron Gauder. *Writing Credits:* Mariusz Bari, Viktor Nagy. *Producer:* Erik Novak. *Music:* Zsolt Hammer, Alex Hunyadi, Adam Javorka, Viktor Laszlo, Spacecafe. *Film Editing:* Kincso Palotas. *Studio:* Lichthof Productions Ltd. *Length:* 87 minutes.

Yes, this is an animated Hungarian film that has won international critical acclaim since its release in the Czech Republic in 2004. An English version is being prepared and will be released in the UK in 2006.

The film has been described as an updated remake of *Romeo and Juliet* or *West Side Story* in *South Park* style. It's about two gangs in Budapest fighting over their oil supplies. However, it includes time travel, sex and drugs, political satire, and animation. According to critics, the cameos of President Bush, Prime Minister Blair, and Osama bin Laden in the finale are explosive and explosively funny.

Switch (2005)

Bush: Jeremy Saville. *Other Cast:* Brian Lynch (Wilbur Wallace), Javarus Brown (Jamal McComb), Bridget Oberlin (Inge/Klaus), Michele Persley (Ashley), Leah Warren (Tanya), Nobel Lee Lester (George Robertson). *Director:* Jeremy Saville. *Writing Credits:* Brian Lynch, Jeremy Saville. *Cinematography:* Adam Teichman. *Film Editing:* Jeremy Saville. *Length:* 93 minutes.

The only information available on this comedy short states that it concerns "a man [who] becomes the object of a global tug of war between telecoms."

Chapter Notes

Introduction

1. In a 1999 study of "The Literary Presidency," Warren G. Rochelle, following Marshall McLuhan's influential theories on the media, contends that the messages delivered by fiction, educational textbooks, and televised images govern public perception. He concludes by suggesting that further study of cinematic presidencies is warranted as "this impossible mythos continues to shape and define our expectations of the president as a 'superstar,' as the American national hero." Warren G. Rochelle, "The Literary Presidency," *Presidential Studies Quarterly*, vol. 29, issue 2 (June 1999), 407.
2. Robert Sklar, *Movie-Made America: A Social History of American Movies* (New York: Random House, Inc., 1975), 12.
3. Merrill D. Peterson, *The Jefferson Image in the American Mind* (New York: Oxford University Press, 1960), 42.
4. Joseph J. Ellis, *American Sphinx: The Character of Thomas Jefferson* (New York: Alfred A. Knopf, 1997).
5. Thomas Schatz, *Hollywood Genres: Formulas, Filmmaking, and the Studio System* (New York: Random House, 1981).
6. David Bordwell, *On the History of Film Style*. Cambridge: Harvard University Press, 1997, 259.
7. Myron Levine, "The Transformed Presidency: The *Real* Presidency and Hollywood's *Reel* Presidency," in *Hollywood's White House: The American Presidency in Film and History*, eds. Peter C. Rollins and John E. O'Connor (Lexington: The University Press of Kentucky, 2003), 352.
8. George Bluestone, *Novels into Film* (Berkeley: University of California Press, 1961).
9. Ibid.; Henry Adams, *History of the United States*, vol. I (CITY OF PUBLICATION: PUBLISHER, 1889), 227.
10. Natalie Zemon Davis, *Slaves on Screen: Film and Historical Vision* (Cambridge: Harvard University Press, 2000), vi.
11. Ibid., 136–37.
12. Ron Chernow, *Alexander Hamilton* (New York: The Penguin Press, 2004), 4.
13. Robert K. Murray and Tim H. Blessing, *Greatness in the White House: Rating the Presidents*, second updated edition (University Park: The Pennsylvania State University Press, 1994), 7.
14. James Coombs, *American Political Movies: An Annotated Filmography of Feature Films* (New York: Garland Publishing, Inc., 1990), v.

Chapter 1

1. David McCullough, *1776* (New York: Simon & Schuster, 2005), 247.
2. Michael Beschloss, (*The Presidents* New York: ibooks, 2000), 25.
3. Edmund S. Morgan, "A Tract for the Times," review of Gore Vidal's *Inventing a Nation: Washington, Adams, Jefferson* (New Haven: Yale University Press, 2003), in *The New York Review of Books*, 18 Dec. 2003: 28.
4. Richard Brookhiser, *Founding Father: Rediscovering George Washington* (New York Free Press Paperbacks, 1996), 5.
5. McCullough, 213–14.
6. John Tebbel and Sarah Miles Watts, *The Press and the Presidency From George Washington to Ronald Reagan* (New York: Oxford University Press, 1985), 16.

Chapter 2

1. David McCullough, *John Adams* (New York: Simon & Schuster, 2001), 67.
2. Tebbel and Watts, 27.
3. McCullough, *Adams*, 192.
4. Ibid., 285.
5. Ibid., 429.
6. Ibid., 476.
7. Peter Stone and Sherman Edwards *1776: A Musical Play* (New York: Viking, 1970), 162.
8. McCullough, *Adams*, 344.
9. Ibid., 127.
10. Ibid., 120.
11. Ibid, 163.

Chapter 3

1. Gary Wills, "The Negro President," *The New York Review of Books*, 6 Nov. 2003: 45.
2. Joseph J. Ellis, *American Sphinx: The Character of Thomas Jefferson* (New York: Alfred A. Knopf, 1997), 227.
3. Ibid.
4. Ibid., 228.
5. Tebbel and Watts, 30.
6. Dumas Malone, *Jefferson and His Time—Volume 1, Jefferson the Virginian* (Boston; Little, Brown and Company, 1948).

Chapter 4

1. Tebbel and Watts, 44.
2. Ralph Ketcham, *James Madison: A Biography* (Charlottesville and London: University Press of Virginia, 1990), 473.
3. Ibid., 481.

Chapter 5

1. Tebbel and Watts, 54.
2. Ibid.
3. *Webster's Guide to American History* (Springfield, MA: G. & C. Merriam Co., Publishers, 1971), 129.

Chapter 6

1. Tebbel and Watts, 64.
2. Lynn Hudson Parsons, *John Quincy Adams* (Lanham, MD: Rowman & Littlefield, 2001), xvii.
3. Ibid.
4. Ibid., xvi.
5. Ibid., 165.
6. A.O. Scott, "The Studio-Indie, Pop-Prestige, Art-Commerce King: Why Steven Spielberg really is the greatest living American director," *The New York Times Magazine*, 9 Nov. 2003: 62.
7. Natalie Zemon Davis, *Slaves on Screen: Film and Historical Vision* (Cambridge: Harvard University Press, 2000), 79–80.
8. John Quincy Adams, *Argument of John Quincy Adams before the Supreme Court of the United States, in the Case of the United States, Appellants, vs. Cinque, and Others, Africans, Captured in the Schooner Amistad* (New York: Negro Universities Press, 1969).

Chapter 7

1. Tebbel and Watts, 76.
2. Arthur Schlesinger, Jr. . "The Democratic Autocrat," *The New York Review of Books*, 15 May 2003: 18.
3. Robert V. Remini, *The Legacy of Andrew Jackson* (Baton Rouge: Louisiana State University Press, 1988), 9.

Chapter 8

1. Tebbel and Watts, 89.
2. Beschloss, 123.
3. John L. Silber, *Martin Van Buren and the Emergence of American Popular Politics* (Lanham, MD: Bowman & Littlefield, 2002).
4. Ted Widmer, *Martin Van Buren* (New York: Henry Holt, 2005).
5. Ibid., xiii.
6. Davis, 126.

Chapter 9

1. Beschloss, 131.
2. Tebbel and Watts, 101.
3. Ibid., 103.
4. Beschloss, 131.

Chapter 10

1. Tebbel and Watts, 104.

Chapter 11

1. Tebbel and Watts, 112, and Paul H. Bergeron, *The Presidency of James K. Polk* (Lawrence: University of Kansas Press, 1987), xi.
2. Frank P. King, *America's Nine Greatest Presidents* (Jefferson, NC: McFarland, 1997), and Allan Lichtman, *Great Presidents Part II* (Chantilly, VA: The Teaching Company, 2000).
3. Beschloss, 141.
4. Ibid., 146.

Chapter 12

1. Tebbel and Watts, 136.
2. Beschloss, 159.

Chapter 13

1. Tebbel and Watts, 148.

Chapter 14

1. Tebbel and Watts, 149.
2. Beschloss, 172.

Chapter 15

1. Tebbel and Watts, 180.
2. Beschloss, 181.

Chapter 16

1. Beschloss, 190.
2. Jacques Barzun, *On Writing, Editing, and Publishing* (Chicago: The University of Chicago Press, 1986), 81.
3. Tebbel and Watts, 179,
4. Barzun, 80.
5. From Lincoln's Second Inaugural Address.
6. Richard Hofstadter, *The American Political Tradition: And the Men Who Made It* (New York: Alfred A. Knopf, 1967), 93.
7. Doris Kearns Goodwin, *Team of Rivals: The Political Genius of Abraham Lincoln* (New York: Simon & Schuster, 2005), 507.
8. Mark S. Reinhart, *Abraham Lincoln on Screen* (Jefferson, NC: McFarland, 1999), 1.
9. Thomas Keneally, *Abraham Lincoln* (New York: Viking Penguin, 2003), 27, 150.

10. Carl Sandburg, *The Prairie Years and the War Years*, One-Volume Edition. (San Diego: A Harvest Book, Harcourt, 1954), 401–402.
11. George F. Custen, *BIO/PICS: How Hollywood Constructed Public History* (New Brunswick, NJ: Rutgers University Press, 1992), 135–136.
12. Gerald Mast and Bruce F. Kawin, *A Short History of the Movies* (New York: Longman, 2003) 115.
13. Russell Baker, "The Entertainer," *The New York Review of Books*, 3 November 2005: 10.

Chapter 17

1. Tebbel and Watts, 214–215.
2. Beschloss, 209.

Chapter 18

1. Tebbel and Watts, 227.
2. James Marshall-Cornwall, *Grant as Military Commander* (New York: Barnes & Noble Books, 1995) 221.
3. Beschloss, 232.
4. Graham Fuller, "Sending Out a Search Party for the Western," *The New York Times*, 3 March 3, 2000: 13, 16.
5. Grayson Cooke, "Willing to Explode: The American Western as Apocalypse-Machine," in *Bang Bang, Shoot Shoot! Essays on guns and popular culture*, second edition, eds. Murray Pomerance and John Sakeris (Needham Heights, MA: Pearson Education, 2000), 1–10.
6. *Mark Twain's Letters, Vol. II* (New York: Harper & Brothers, 1988), 460, and James Marshall-Cornwall, *Grant as Military Commander* (New York: Barnes & Noble Books, 1995), 224.
7. Gary W. Gallagher, *The American Civil War, Part 1* (Chantilly, VA: The Teaching Company, 2000).

Chapter 19

1. Beschloss, 235.
2. Ibid., 241.

Chapter 20

1. Beschloss, 247.

Chapter 21

1. Tebbel and Watts, 251.

Chapter 22 and 24

1. Tebbel and Watts, 262.
2. Ibid., 264.
3. Ibid., 270.

Chapter 23

1. Tebbel and Watts, 279.

Chapter 25

1. Beschloss, 289.
2. Tebbel and Watts, 308.

Chapter 26

1. Tebbel and Watts, 318.
2. Edmund Morris, *Theodore Rex* (New York: Random House, 2003).
3. Richard Hofstadter, *The American Political Tradition* (New York: Alfred A. Knopf, 1967), 225.
4. Bechloss, 300.
5. Stephen Graubbard, *Command of Office* (New York: Basic Books, 2004), 81.

Chapter 27

1. Tebbel and Watts, 349.
2. Graubard, 110.
3. Tebbel and Watts, 358.

Chapter 28

1. Gaubard, 131.
2. Terry Christensen, *Reel Politics: American Political Movies from Birth of a Nation to Platoon* (New York: Oxford University Press, 1987), 69–70.

Chapter 29

1. Russell Baker, "Back to Normalcy," review of John W. Dean's *Warren G. Harding* (New York: Times Books, 2004) in *The New York Review of Books*, 12 Feb. 2004: 12.
2. Ibid., 14.
3. Tebbel and Watts, 399.
4. Malcolm Gladwell, *Blink* (New York: Little, Brown and Company, 2005), 72–75.
5. Hofstadter, 278.

Chapter 30

1. Tebbel and Watts, 403.
2. Ibid, 410.
3. Custen, 116–17.

Chapter 31

1. Tebbel and Watts, 418.
2. Ibid., 432.
3. Mark Kurlansky, *Salt: A World History* (New York: Penguin Books, 2002), 327–328.
4. Tebbel and Watts, 433.

Chapter 32

1. Beschloss, 361.
2. Tebbel and Watts, 438.
3. Ibid., 452.
4. Marc Fero, *Cinema and History* (Detroit: Wayne State University Press, 1988), 113.
5. Ibid., 150.

Chapter 33

1. Beschloss, 375.
2. David McCullough, *Truman* (New York: Simon & Schuster, 1992), 463.
3. Ibid., 525.
4. Ibid., 554.
5. Ibid., 659.
6. Ibid., 768.
7. Ibid., 860.

Chapter 34

1. R. Gordon Hoxie, "About This Issue," *Presidential Studies Quarterly*, Eisenhower Centennial Issue, vol. XX, number 2 (Spring 1990): 247–251.

Chapter 35

1. Allan Lichtman, *Great Presidents, Part IV* (Chantilly, VA: The Teaching Company, 2000), 14; and Tebbel and Watts, 480.
2. Beschloss, 407.
3. Lichtman, 10.
4. Tebbel and Watts, 482.
5. Robert A. Rosenstone, *Visions of the Past: The Challenge of Film to Our Idea of History* (Cambridge, MA: Harvard University Press, 1995), 130.
6. Steven D. Scott, "'Like a Box of Chocolates': *Forrest Gump* and Postmodernism," *Literature/Film Quarterly*, vol. 29, no. 1 (2001): 23–31.

Chapter 36

1. Tebbel and Watts, 500.
2. Lichtman, 17.
3. Ibid., 21.

Chapter 37

1. J. Hoberman, *London Review of Books*, 17 Feb. 2005: 25.

2. Beschloss, 427.
3. David Brooks, "The Prosecutor's Diagnosis: No Cancer Found," *The New York Times*, 30 Oct. 2005: IV, 13.
4. Graubard, 379.
5. Gwen Barry, "All the President's Movies," review of Mark Feeny's *Nixon at the Movies* (Chicago: The University of Chicago Press, 2004), *New York Times*, 12 Dec. 2004.
6. Tony Barta, *Screening the Past: Film and the Representation of History* (Westport, CT: Praeger, 1998).

Chapter 38

1. Tebbel and Watts, 517.
2. Ibid., 519.
3. Beschloss, 447.
4. Ibid., 445.

Chapter 39

1. Jimmy Carter, *The Hornet's Nest: A Novel of the Revolutionary War* (New York: Simon & Schuster, 2003).
2. Tebbel and Watts, 525.
3. Ibid., 523.

Chapter 40

1. Custen, 205.

Chapter 41

1. Beschloss, 477.
2. Ibid., 478.
3. Graubard, 494.

Chapter 42

1. Beschloss, 495.
2. Graubard, 529.

Chapter 43

1. Graubard, 534.

Bibliography

Adams, John. *The Life and Works of John Adams.* Edited by Charles Francis Adams. Boston: Little, Brown, 1856.
Adams, John Quincy. *Argument of John Quincy Adams before the Supreme Court of the United States, in the Case of the United States, Appellants, vs. Cinque, and Others, Africans, Captured in the Schooner Amistad.* New York: Negro Universities Press, 1969.
____. *The Diary of John Quincy Adams.* Edited by Allan Nevins. New York: Longmans, Green, 1928.
____. *Memoirs of John Quincy Adams.* Edited by Charles Francis Adams. 1874–77. Reprint: Freeport, N.Y.: Books for Libraries Press, 1969.
____. *Writings of John Quincy Adams.* Edited by W.C. Ford, 1913–17. Reprint: New York: Greenwood Press, 1968.
Alkana, Linda. "The Absent President." In *Hollywood's White House: The American Presidency in Film and History,* edited by Peter C. Rollins and John E. O'Connor. Lexington: The University Press of Kentucky, 2003.
The American Film Institute Desk Reference. London: DK, 2002.
Ammon, Harry. *James Monroe: The Quest for National Identity.* New York: McGraw-Hill Book Company, 1971.
Anderson, Donald F. *William Howard Taft: A Conservative's Perception of the Presidency.* Ithaca: Cornell University Press, 1973.
Anderson, Paul Y. "Hoover and the Press." *Nation,* October 14, 1931.
Andrews, J. Cutler. *The North Reports the Civil War.* Pittsburgh: University of Pittsburgh Press, 1955.
Armstrong, William M. *E.L. Godkin and American Foreign Policy, 1865–1900.* New York: Bookman Associates, 1957.
Baer, Harr. *The New York Tribune Since the Civil War.* New York: Octagon Books, 1972.
Baker, Ray Stannard. *Woodrow Wilson: Youth.* Garden City: Doubleday, 1927.
____. *Woodrow Wilson and World Settlement,* 1922.
Baker, Russell. "Back to Normalcy." Review of *Warren G. Harding,* by John W. Dean. *The New York Review of Books,* 12 Feb. 2004.
Barnes, Thurlow Weed. *Memoir of Thurlow Weed.* Boston: Houghton Mifflin, 1884.
Barrett, James Wyman. *Joseph Pulitzer and His World.* New York: Vanguard Press, 1941.
Barry, David S. *Forty Years in Washington.* Boston: Little, Brown, 1924.
____. "News-Gathering at the Capital." *Chautauquan* (December 1897): 282–86.
Barry, Gwen. "All the President's Movies." Review of *Nixon at the Movies,* by Mark Feeny. *New York Times,* 12 Dec. 2004.
Barta, Tony. *Screening the Past: Film and the Representation of History.* Westport, CT: Praeger, 1998
Barzun, Jacques. *On Writing, Editing, and Publishing.* Second edition. Chicago: University of Chicago Press, 1986.
Bassett, John Spencer. *The Life of Andrew Jackson.* New York: Macmillan, 1925.
Bauer, K. Jack. *The Mexican War, 1846–1848.* New York: Macmillan, 1974.
Beirne, Francis. *The War of 1812.* New York: E.P. Dutton, 1949.
Bemis, Samuel Flagg. *John Quincy Adams and the Foundations of American Foreign Policy.* New York: Alfred A. Knopf, 1949.
____. *John Quincy Adams and the Union.* New York: Alfred A. Knopf, 1956.
Bergeron, Paul H. *The Presidency of James K. Polk.* Lawrence: University of Kansas Press, 1987.
Beschloss, Michael. *The Presidents.* New York: ibooks, 2000.
Bishop, Joseph Bucklin. "Newspaper Espionage." *Forum,* vol.1, 528–37.
Bluestone, George. *Novels into Film.* Berkeley: University of California Press, 1961.

Borck, Jr., Oscar Theodore, and Manfred Blake Nelson. *Since 1900: A History of the United States in Our Times.* New York: Macmillan, 1947.
Bordwell, David. *On the History of Film Style.* Cambridge: Harvard University Press, 1997.
Bowers, Claude G. *Jefferson and Hamilton.* Boston: Houghton Mifflin, 1925.
____. *Jefferson in Power.* Boston: Houghton Mifflin, 1936.
____. *The Tragic Era.* Cambridge: Riverside Press, 1929
____. *The Party Battles of the Jackson Period.* New York: Octagon Books, 1965.
Brookhiser, Richard. *Founding Father: Rediscovering George Washington.* New York: Free Press Paperbacks, 1996.
Brooks, David. "The Prosecutor's Diagnosis: No Cancer Found." *The New York Times,* 30 Oct. 2005, IV, 13.
Brooks, Noah. *Washington in Lincoln's Time.* Edited by Herbert Mitgang. Chicago: Quadrangle Books, 1971.
Buell, Richard, Jr. "Freedom of the Press in Revolutionary America." In *The Press and the American Revolution,* edited by Bernard Bailyn and John Henry. Worchester, MA: American Antiquarian Society, 1980.
Burns, David. *Herbert Hoover: A Public Life.* New York: Alfred A. Knopf, 1979.
Butt, Archibald W., ed. *Taft and Roosevelt: The Intimate Letters of Archie Butt, Military Aide.* Garden City: Doubleday, Doran, 1930.
Caldwell, Robert Granville. *James A. Garfield, Party Chieftain.* 1931. Reprint: Hamden, CT: Archon Books, 1965.
Cameron, Kenneth M. *America on Film: Hollywood and American History.* New York: The Continuum Publishing Company, 1997.
Carlson, Oliver. *The Man Who Made News.* New York: Duell, Sloan & Pearce, 1941.
Carnes, Mark C. *Past Imperfect History According to the Movies.* New York: Henry Holt and Company, Inc., 1996.
Caroli, Betty Boyd. *First Ladies.* New York and London: Oxford University Press, 1987.
Carter, Jimmy. *The Hornet's Nest: A Novel of the Revolutionary War.* New York: Simon & Schuster, 2003.
Cartmell, Deborah, I.Q. Hunter, and Imelda Whelehan. *Retrovisions: Reinventing the Past in Film and Fiction.* London: Pluto Press, 2001.
Castel, Albert. *The Presidency of Andrew Johnson.* Lawrence: University Press of Kansas, 1979.
Chace, James. *1912: Wilson, Roosevelt, Taft and Debs—The Election That Changed the Country.* New York: Simon & Schuster, 2004.
Chadwick, Bruce. *The Reel Civil War: Mythmaking in American Film.* New York: Alfred A. Knopf, 2001.
Chernow, Ron. *Alexander Hamilton.* New York: The Penguin Press, 2004.
Chitwood, Oliver Perry. *John Tyler.* New York: Russell and Russell, 1939.
Christensen, Terry. *Reel Politics: American Political Movies from Birth of a Nation to Platoon.* New York: Oxford University Press, 1987.
Cleveland, Grover. *Letters of Grover Cleveland.* Edited by Allan Nevins. Boston: Houghton Mifflin, 1933.
Clinton, Bill. *My Life.* New York: Knopf, 2004.
Coletta, Paoela E. *The Presidency of William Howard Taft.* Lawrence: University Press of Kansas, 1973.
Cooke, Grayson. "Willing to Explode: The American Western as Apocalypse-Machine." In *Bang, Bang, Shoot Shoot! Essays on guns and popular culture,* second edition, edited by Murray Pomerance and John Sakeris. Needham Heights, MA: Pearson Education, 2000.
Coolidge, Calvin. *Autobiography of Calvin Coolidge.* New York: Cosmopolitan Book Corporation, 1929.
Coombs, James E. *American Political Movies: An Annotated Filmography of Feature Films.* New York: Garland Publishing, Inc., 1990.
Cornwell, Jr., Elmer E. *Presidential Leadership of Public Opinion.* Bloomington: Indiana University Press, 1965.
Cresson, W.P. *James Monroe.* Chapel Hill: University of North Carolina Press, 1946.
Crozier, Emmet. *Yankee Reporters, 1861–65.* New York and London: Oxford University Press, 1856.
Cuneo, Sherman. *From Printer to President.* Philadelphia: Dorrance, 1922.
Curtis, George Ticknor. *Life of James Buchanan.* New York: Harper & Bros., 1883.
Custen, George F. *BIO/PICS: How Hollywood Constructed Public History.* New Brunswick, NJ: Rutgers University Press, 1992.
Dangerfield, George. *The Era of Good Feelings.* New York: Harcourt Brace, 1952.
Davis, Natalie Zemon. *Slaves on Screen: Film and Historical Vision.* Cambridge: Harvard University Press, 2000.
Davison, Kenneth C. *The Presidency of Rutherford B. Hayes.* Westport, CT: Greenwood Press, 1972.
Deakin, James. *Johnson's Credibility Gap.* Washington, D.C.: Public Affairs Press, 1968.
____. *Straight Stuff: The Reporters, the White House, and the Truth.* New York: William Morrow, 1984.
Decatur, Stephen, Jr. *The Private Affairs of George Washington. Documents Relating to the Colonial History of the State of New York.* Vol. 3. Albany: n.p., 1953.

Doenecke, Justin D. *The Presidencies of James A. Garfield and Chester A. Arthur.* Lawrence: Regents Press of Kansas, 1981.
Donavan, Robert J. *Eisenhower: The Inside Story.* New York: Harper & Bros, 1956.
Dunn, Arthur Wallace. *From Harrison to Harding: A Personal Narrative of a Third of a Century, 1888–1921.* New York: G.P. Putnam's Sons, 1922. Reprint: Port Washington: Kennikat Press, 1971.
Dyer, Brainerd. *Zachary Taylor.* New York: Barnes & Noble, 1946.
Eisenhower, Dwight D. *The White House Years: Mandate for Change, 1953–1956.* New York: Doubleday, 1966.
Ellis, Joseph J. *American Sphinx: The Character of Thomas Jefferson.* New York: Alfred A. Knopf, 1997.
____. *His Excellency: George Washington.* New York: Alfred A. Knopf, 2004.
Evans, Rowland, and Robert Nowak. *Lyndon B. Johnson: The Exercise of Power.* New York: New American Library, 1966.
Feeney, Mark. *Nixon at the Movies.* Chicago: The University of Chicago Press, 2005.
Fero, Marc. *Cinema and History.* Detroit: Wayne State University Press, 1988.
Filler, Louis. *The Muckrakers: Crusaders for American Liberalism.* 1939. Paperback ed. Chicago: Henry Regnery, 1958.
Fillmore, Millard. *Millard Fillmore Papers.* Edited by Frank H. Severance. Buffalo: Buffalo Historical Society, 1907.
Ford, Gerald R. *A Time to Heal.* New York: Harper & Row and Reader's Digest Association, 1979.
Fraser, Hugh Russell. *Democracy in the Making: The Jackson-Tyler Era.* New York: Bobbs-Merrill, 1938.
Freeman, Douglas Southall. *George Washington.* Vol. 6, *Patriot and President.* New York: Charles Scribner's Sons, 1954.
Fuess, Claude M. *Calvin Coolidge: The Man from Vermont.* 1940. Reprint: Hamden, CT: Archon Books, 1965.
Fuller, Graham. "Sending Out a Search Party for the Western." *The New York Times,* 3 March 2000.
Gallagher, Gary W. *The American Civil War, Part I.* Chantilly, VA: The Teaching Company, 2000.
Garfield, James A. *The Diary of James A. Garfield.* Edited by Harry James Brown and Frederick D. Williams. East Lansing: Michigan State University Press, 1967.
____. *Works of James Abram Garfield.* Edited by Burke Aaron Hinsdale. Boston: J.R. Osgood, 1882.
Gianos, Phillip. L. *Politics and Politicians in American Film.* Westport, CT: Praeger, 1999.
Glad, Paul W. *McKinley, Byran, and the People.* Philadelphia: J.B. Lippincott, 1964.
Gladwell, Malcolm. *Blink.* New York: Little, Brown and Company, 2005.
Goldman, Eric. *The Tragedy of Lyndon Johnson.* New York: Alfred A. Knopf, 1969.
Goodwin, Doris Kearns. *Team of Rivals: The Political Genius of Abraham Lincoln.* New York: Simon & Schuster, 2005.
Graubard, Stephen. *Command of Office.* New York: Basic Books, 2005.
Greeley, Horace. *Recollections of a Busy Life.* New York: J.B. Ford, 1868.
Green, Horace. "Grant's Last Stand." *Harper's Weekly,* 6 January 1887, 315.
Grossman, Michael Baruch, and Martha Joynt Kumar. *Portraying the President: The White House and the News Media.* Baltimore: Johns Hopkins University Press, 1981.
Gwen, Barry. "All the President's Movies." Review of *Nixon at the Movies,* by Mark Feeny. *New York Times,* 12 Dec. 2004.
Hale, William Harlan. *Horace Greeley: Voice of the People.* New York: Harper & Bros., 1950.
Harper, Robert S. *Lincoln and the Press.* New York: McGraw-Hill, 1951.
Hawthorne, Nathaniel. *Life of Franklin Pierce.* Papers of the People, no. 2. New York: 1852.
Hayes, Rutherford B. *Diary and Letters of Rutherford B. Hayes.* Edited by C.R. Williams. N.p.: Ohio Archaeological and Historical Society, 1922–26.
____. *Hayes: The Diary of a President.* Edited by T. Harry Williams. New York: David McKay, 1963.
Heller, Francis H. *The Truman White House: The Administration of the Presidency, 1945–1953.* Lawrence: Regents Press of Kansas, 1980.
Herndon, William H., and Jesse William Wilk. *Herndon's Lincoln: The True Story of a Great Life.* Chicago: Belford, Clark, 1889.
Higashi, Sumiko. *Cecil B. DeMille and American Culture: The Silent Era.* Berkeley: University of California Press, 1994.
Hilderbrand, Robert C. *Power and the People: Executive Management of Public Opinion in Foreign Affairs, 1897–1921.* Chapel Hill: University of North Carolina Press, 1981.
Hoberman, J. *London Review of Books.* 17 Feb. 2005, 25.
Hofstadter, Richard. *The American Political Tradition.* New York: Alfred A. Knopf, 1967.
____. *Anti-Intellectualism in American Life.* New York: Alfred A. Knopf, 1963.
Holmes, Alexander. *The American Talleyrand.* New York: Harper & Bros., 1935.
Hoover, Herbert. *Memoirs.* New York: Macmillan, 1951–52.

Hoover, Ike. *Forty Years in the White House*. Boston: Houghton Mifflin, 1934.
Horner, Harlan Hoyt. *Lincoln and Greeley*. Urbana: University of Illinois Press, 1953.
Howe, George Frederik. *Chester A. Arthur: A Quarter Century of Machine Politics*. New York: Frederick Ungar, 1935.
Howells, William Dean. *Sketch of the Life and Character of Rutherford B. Hayes*. New York: Hurd and Houghton, 1876.
Hoxie, R. Gordon. "About This Issue." *Presidential Studies Quarterly*. Eisenhower Centennial Issue, Vol. XX, Number 2 (Spring 1990).
Hudson, Frederic. *Journalism in the United States from 1690 to 1872*. New York: Harper & Bros., 1873. Reprint: New York: Harper & Row, 1969.
Hughes, Emmet John. *The Ordeal of Power: A Political Memoir of the Eisenhower Years*. New York: Atheneum Press, 1963.
Ickes, Harold. *The Secret Diary of Harold L. Ickes*. Vol. 1, *The First Thousand Days, 1933–36*. New York: Simon & Schuster, 1953.
Ireland, John R. *History of the Life, Administration and Times of Zachary Taylor*. Chicago: Fairbanks and Palmer, 1888.
Jefferson, Thomas. *Letters and Addresses of Thomas Jefferson*. Edited by William B. Parker and Jonas Vilas. New York: West, 1905.
_____. *The Portable Thomas Jefferson*. Edited by Merrill D. Peterson. New York: Viking Press, 1975.
_____. *Writings of Thomas Jefferson*. Edited by Paul Leicester Ford. New York: G.P. Putnam's Sons, 1892–99.
Johnson, Paul. *Modern Times: The World from the Twenties to the Eighties*. New York: Harper & Row, 1983.
Jones, Alfred Haworth. *Roosevelt's Image Brokers: Poets, Playwrights, and the Use of the Lincoln Symbol*. Reprint: Port Washington, N.Y.: National University Publications, Kennikat Press, 1974.
Juergens, George. *News from the White House: The Presidential-Press Relationship in the Progressive Era*. Chicago: University of Chicago Press, 1981.
Katz, Ephraim. *The Film Encyclopedia*. Fourth edition. New York: HarperResource, 2001.
Kearns, Doris. *Lyndon Johnson and the American Dream*. New York: Harper & Row, 1975.
Keneally, Thomas. *Abraham Lincoln*. New York: Viking Penguin, 2003.
Keogh, James. *President Nixon and the Press*. New York: Funk & Wagnalls, 1972.
Kern, Montague, Patricia W. Levering, and Ralph B. Levering. *The Kennedy Crisis: The Press, the Presidency, and Foreign Policy*. Chapel Hill: University of North Carolina Press, 1983.
Ketcham, Ralph. *James Madison: A Biography*. Charlottesville and London: University Press of Virginia, 1990.
King, Frank P. *America's Nine Greatest Presidents*. Jefferson, N.C.: McFarland, 1997.
Klein, Philip Shriver. *President James Buchanan: A Biography*. University Park: Pennsylvania State University Press, 1926.
Kurlansky, Mark. *Salt: A World History*. New York: Penguin Books, 2002.
Kutter, Stanley I., and Stanley N. Katz, eds. "The Promise of American History: Progress and Prospect." *Reviews in American History* 10, no. 4 (December 1982).
Larson, Arthur. *Eisenhower: The President Nobody Knows*. New York: Charles Scribner's Sons, 1968.
Lee, A.M. "Dunlap and Claypoole: Printers and News-Merchants of the Revolution." *Journalism Quarterly*, vol. 11, no. 2, 160–78.
Leech, Margaret. *In the Time of McKinley*. New York: Harper & Row Bros., 1959.
Levine, Myron. *The Transformed Presidency: The Real Presidency and Hollywood's Reel Presidency*. " In *Hollywood's White House The American Presidency in Film and History*, edited by Peter C. Rollins and John. H. O'Connor. Lexington: The University Press of Kentucky, 2003.
Lichtman, Allan. *Great Presidents*. Parts I, II and IV. Chantilly, VA: The Teaching Company, 2000.
Link, Arthur S. *Wilson: The New Freedom*. Princeton: Princeton University Press, 1956.
Lipsky, George A. *John Quincy Adams: His Theory and Ideas*. New York: Thomas Y. Crowell, 1950.
Lloyd, Craig. *Agressive Introvert: A Study of Herbert Hoover and Public Relations Management, 1912–1932*. Columbus: Ohio State University Press, 1972.
Lodge, H.C. *George Washington*. Boston: Houghton Mifflin, 1889.
Lorant, Stefan. *The Presidency*. New York: Macmillan, 1951.
Loucheim, Katie, ed. *The Making of the New Deal: The Insiders Speak*. Cambridge: Harvard University Press, 1983.
Lowry, Edward. *Washington Close-ups: Intimate Views of Some Public Figures*. Boston: Houghton Mifflin, 1921.
Lynch, Denis Tilder. *Grover Cleveland: A Man Four-Square*. New York: Horace Liveright, 1932.

Bibliography

Madison, James. *The Writings of James Madison.* Edited by Gaillard Hunt. New York: G.P. Putnam's Sons, 1900.
Magill, Frank. *Magill's Survey of Cinema.* Volumes 1 and 2. Englewood Cliffs, N.J.: Salem Press, 1980.
Maglish, Bruce, and Edwin Diamond. *Jimmy Carter: A Character Portrait.* New York: Simon & Schuster, 1979.
Malone, Dumas. *Jefferson the President: First Term.* Boston: Little, Brown, 1970.
____. *Jefferson and His Time. Volume One Jefferson the Virginian.* Boston: Little, Brown and Company, 1948.
____. *Jefferson and The Rights of Man.* Boston: Little, Brown, 1951.
Marshall-Cornwall, James. *Grant as Military Commander.* New York: Barnes & Noble Books, 1995.
Martin, Fenton S. and Robert U. Goehlert. *American Presidents: A Bibliographpy.* Washington, D.C.: Congressional Quarterly Inc., 1987.
Mast, Gerald, and Bruce F. Kawin. *A Short History of the Movies.* Eighth edition. New York: Longman, 2003.
May, Ernest R. *The Making of the Monroe Doctrine.* Cambridge: Harvard University Press, 1975.
McAdoo, Eleanor Wilson. *The Woodrow Wilsons.* New York: Macmillan, 1937.
McAuliffe, Mary S. "Eisenhower the President." *Journal of American History,* December 1981.
McCoombs, William F. *Making Woodrow Wilson President.* New York: Fairview, 1921.
McCormac, Eugene Irving. *James K. Polk.* New York: Russell and Russell, 1965.
McCoy, Donald R. *Calvin Coolidge: The Quiet President.* New York: Macmillan, 1967.
McCullough, David. *John Adams.* New York: Simon & Schuster, 2001.
____. *Mornings on Horseback.* New York: Simon & Schuster, 1981.
____. *1776.* New York: Simon & Schuster, 2005.
____. *Truman.* New York: Simon & Schuster, 1992.
McFeeley, William S. *Grant.* New York: W.W. Norton, 1981.
Merrill, Horace Samuel. *Bourbon Leader: Grover Cleveland and the Democratic Party.* Boston: Little, Brown, 1957.
Meyer, Peter. *James Earl Carter: The Man and the Myth.* Kansas City: Sheed, Andrews and McMeell, 1978.
Miller, John C. *Alexander Hamilton: Portrait in Paradox.* New York: Harper & Bros., 1959.
Miller, Merle. *Lyndon: An Oral Biography.* New York; G.P. Putnam's Sons, 1980.
Milton, George F. *The Age of Hate.* New York: Coward McCann, 1930.
Mitgang, Herbert. *Abraham Lincoln: A Press Portrait.* Chicago: Quadrangle Books, 1971.
Monroe, James. *The Writings of James Monroe.* Edited by Stanislaus Murray Hamilton. New York: 1969.
Monsell, Thomas. *Nixon on Stage and Screen.* Jefferson, N.C.: McFarland, 1998.
Morgan, Edmund S. "A Tract for the Times." Review of *Inventing a Nation: Washington, Adams, Jefferson,* by Gore Vidal. *The New York Review of Books,* 18 Dec. 2003: 28.
Morgan, H. Wayne. *William McKinley and His America.* Syracuse: Syracuse University Press, 1963.
Morris, Edmund. *The Rise of Theodore Roosevelt.* New York: Coward, McCann & Geoghegan, 1979.
____. *Theodore Rex.* New York: Random House, 2003.
Morse, John T. *John Quincy Adams.* New York: Chelsea House, 1980.
Mott, Frank Luther. *American Journalism.* Third edition. New York: Macmillan, 1962.
____. *Jefferson and the Press.* Baton Rouge: Louisiana State University Press, 1943.
____, ed. *Oldtime Comments on Journalism.* Vol. L, no.5. Columbia, MO: Press of the Crippled Turtle, 1955.
Murray, Robert K., and Tim H. Blessing. *Greatness in the White House Rating the Presidents.* Second updated edition. University Park: The Pennsylvania State University Press, 1994.
____. "The Presidential Performance Study: A Progress Report." *Journal of American History,* vol. 70, no. 3.
Nevins, Allan, ed. *American Press Opinion. Washington to Coolidge.* Boston: D.C. Heath, 1928.
____. *The Emergence of Lincoln.* New York: Charles Scribner's Sons, 1950.
____. *Grover Cleveland: A Study in Courage.* New York: Dodd, Mead, 1933.
Nichols, Peter M., Vincent Canby, Janet Maslin, and the film critics of *The New York Times. The New York Times Guide to the Best 1,000 Movies Ever Made.* New York: Random House, 1999.
Nichols, Roy F. *Franklin Pierce: Young Hickory of the Granite Hills.* Philadelphia: University of Pennsylvania Press, 1958.
Nixon, Richard M. *Memoirs of Richard Nixon.* New York: Grosset & Dunlap, 1978.
Nowell-Smith, Geoffrey, ed. *The Oxford History of World Cinema.* New York: Oxford University Press, 1997.
Olcott, Charles A. *William McKinley.* Boston: Houghton Mifflin, 1916.
Osborn, John. *White House Watch: The Ford Years.* Washington, D.C.: New Republic Books, 1977.
Parsons, Lynn Hudson. *John Quincy Adams.* Lanham, MD: Rowman & Littlefield Publishers, Inc., 2001.
Parton, James. *Life of Andrew Jackson.* Boston: Houghton Mifflin, 1888.

Perkins, Bradford. *Castlereagh and Adams: England and the United States.* Berkeley: University of California Press, 1964.
Perkins, Dexter. *The Monroe Doctrine.* Cambridge: Harvard University Press, 1932.
Peskin, Allan. *Garfield.* Kent: Kent State University Press, 1978.
Peterson, Merrill. D. *The Jefferson Image in the American Mind.* New York: Oxford University Press, 1960.
Platt, David. *Celluloid Power: Social Criticism from The Birth of a Nation to Judgment at Nuremberg.* Metuchen, NJ: The Scarecrow Press, Inc., 1992.
Polk, James K. *Polk: The Diary of a President, 1845–1849.* Edited by Allan Nevins. New York: Longmans, Green, 1952.
Pollard, James E. *The Presidents and the Press.* New York: Macmillan, 1947. Supplement: New York: Macmillan, 1972.
Poore, Benjam Perley. *Perley's Reminiscences of Sixty Years in the National Metropolis.* Philadelphia: Hubbard Bros, 1886.
Pringle, Henry F. *Theodore Roosevelt.* New York: Harcourt Brace & World, 1931.
Rayback, Robert J. *Millard Fillmore.* Buffalo: Henry Stewart, 1959.
Reeves, Richard. *A Ford, Not a Lincoln.* New York: Harcourt Brace Jovanovich, 1975.
_____. "The Prime-Time President." *New York Times Magazine.* 15 May 1977: 18.
Reeves, Thomas C. *Gentleman Boss: The Life of Chester Alan Arthur.* New York: Alfred A. Knopf, 1975.
Reinhart, Mark S. *Abraham Lincoln on Screen.* Jefferson, NC: McFarland, 1999.
Remini, Robert V. *Andrew Jackson and the Course of American Freedom, 1822–1832.* New York: Harper & Row, 1983.
_____. *The Legacy of Andrew Jackson.* Baton Rouge: Louisiana State University Press, 1988.
_____. *Martin Van Buren and the Making of the Democratic Party.* New York: Columbia University Press, 1951.
_____. *The Revolutionary Age of Andrew Jackson.* New York: Harper & Row, 1976.
Reynolds, Donald E. *Editors Make War: Southern Newspapers in the Secession Crisis.* Nashville: Vanderbilt University Press, 1966.
Richardson, Elmo. *The Presidency of Dwight D. Eisenhower.* Lawrence: Regents Press of Kansas, 1979.
Ritchi, Thomas. *Unpublished Letters of Thomas Ritchie.* Edited by Charles H. Ambler. John P. Branch Historical Papers 3 (June 1911).
Rochelle, Warren. "The Literary Presidency." *Presidential Studies Quarterly*, vol. 29, issue 2 (June 1999): 407.
Rollins, Peter C., ed. *Hollywood As Historian: American Film in a Cultural Context.* Lexington: The University Press of Kentucky, 1983.
_____, and John E. O'Connor. *Hollywood's White House: The American Presidency in Film and History.* Lexington: The University Press of Kentucky, 2003.
Romasco, Albert U. *The Poverty of Abundance: Hoover, the Nation, and the Depression.* New York: Oxford University Press, 1965.
Rosenstone, Robert A. *Visions of the Past: The Challenge of Films to Our Idea of History.* Cambridge: Harvard University Press, 1995.
Rovere, Richard. *Final Reports.* New York: Doubleday, 1984.
Russell, Francis. *The Shadow of Blooming Grove.* New York: McGraw-Hill, 1968.
Sandburg, Carl. *Abraham Lincoln: The Prairie Years.* New York: Harcourt Brace, 1926.
_____. *Abraham Lincoln: The Prairie Years and the War Years.* One-Volume Edition. San Diego: Harcourt, Inc., 1954.
_____. *Abraham Lincoln: The War Years.* New York: Harcourt Brace, 1939.
Schatz, Thomas. *The Genius of the System: Hollywood Filmmaking in the Studio Era.* New York: Pantheon Books, 1988.
_____. *Hollywood Genres: Formulas, Filmmaking, and the Studio System.* New York: Random House, 1981.
Schell, Jonathan. *The Time of Illusion.* New York: Alfred A. Knopf, 1976.
Schiller, Dan. *Objectivity in the News: The Public and the Rise of Commercial Journalism.* Philadelphia: University of Pennsylvania Press, 1981.
Schirmer, Daniel B. *Republic or Empire: American Resistance to the Phillippine War.* Cambridge: Schenkman, 1972.
Schlesinger, Arthur M., Jr. *The Age of Jackson.* Boston: Little, Brown, 1946.
_____. "The Democratic Autocrat." Review of *The Passion of Andrew Jackson*, by Andrew Burstein. *The New York Review of Books*, 15 May 2003.
_____. *The Imperial Presidency.* Boston: Houghton Mifflin, 1973.
_____. *A Thousand Days: John F. Kennedy in the White House.* Boston: Houghton Mifflin, 1965.
Schroeder, John J. *Mr. Polk's War: American Opposition and Dissent.* Madison: University of Wisconsin Press, 1973.

Scott, A.O. "The Studio-Indie, Pop-Prestige, Art-Commerce King: Why Steven Spielberg really is the greatest living American director." *The New York Times Magazine*, 9 November 2003.

Scott, Steven D. "'Like a Box of Chocolates': *Forrest Gump* and Postmodernism." *Literature/Film Quarterly*, vol. 29, no. 1 (2001): 23–31.

Seager, II, Robert. *And Tyler Too*. New York: McGraw-Hill, 1963.

Seitz, Don C. *The James Gordon Bennetts*. Indianapolis: Bobbs-Merrill, 1928.

Sellers, Jr., Charles Grier. *James K. Polk*. Princeton: Princeton University Press, 1957.

Shoup, Laurence H. *The Carter Presidency and Beyond*. Palto Alto: Ramparts Press, 1980.

Sidey, Hugh. *John F. Kennedy, President*. New York: Atheneum Press, 1963.

———. *Lyndon Johnson*. New York: Atheneum Press, 1968.

Sievers, Harry J. *Benjamin Harrison*. Indianapolis: Bobbs-Merrill, 1968.

Silber, John. L. *Martin Van Buren and the Emergence of American Popular Politics*. Lanham, MD: Rowman & Littlefield Publishers, Inc., 2002.

Sklar, Robert. *Movie-Made America A Social History of American Movies*. New York: Random House, 1975.

Skowronek, Stephen. *The Politics Presidents Make: Leadership from John Adams to Bill Clinton*. Cambridge: The Belknap Press of Harvard University Press, 2001.

Smith, Culver Haygood. "The Washington Press in the Jacksonian Period." Ph.D. dissertation, New York University.

Smith, Elbert B. *The Presidency of James Buchanan*. Lawrence: University Press of Kansas, 1975.

Smith, James Morton. *Freedom's Fetters*. Ithaca: Cornell University Press, 1956. Reprint: Ithaca: Cornell University Paperback, 1966.

———, and Paul L. Murphy, eds. *Liberty and Justice: American Constitutional Development to 1869*. New York, 1965.

Smith, Page. *John Adams*. Garden City: Doubleday, 1962.

Smith, Theodore Clarke. *The Life and Letters of James Abram Garfield*. 1925. Reprint: Hamden, CT: Archon Books, 1968.

Smith, William E. *The Francis Preston Blair Family in Politics*. New York: Da Capo Press, 1969.

Sorenson, Theodore G. *Kennedy*. New York: Harper & Row, 1965.

Sorlin, Pierre. *The Film in History: Restaging the Past*. Totowa, NJ: Barnes & Noble Books, 1980.

Spragens, William C., and Carole Ann Terwoord. *From Spokesman to Press Secretary: White House Media Operations*. Washington, D.C.: University Press of America, 1980.

Steinberg, Alfred. *The Man from Missouri: The Life and Times of Harry Truman*. New York: G.P. Putnam's Sons, 1962.

Stevens, Michael G. *Reel Portrayals*. Jefferson, NC: McFarland, 2003.

Stoddart, Scott. F. "The Adams Chronicles: Domesticating the American Presidency." In *Hollywood's White House: The American Presidency in Film and History*, edited by Peter C. Rollins and John E. O'Connor. Lexington: The University Press of Kentucky, 2003.

Stone, Peter, and Sherman Edwards. *1776: A Musical Play*. New York: Viking, 1970.

Stryker, Lloyd Paul. *Andrew Johnson*. New York: Macmillan, 1929.

Sullivan, Mark. *Our Times*. Vol. 3, *Pre-War America*. New York: Charles Scribner's Sons, 1930.

Tarbell, Ida M. "President McKinley in War Times." *McClure's Magazine* (July 1898): 2080–86.

Tebbel, John. *A Compact History of the American Newspaper*. New York: Hawthorn Books, 1963.

———. *The Media in America*. New York: Thomas Y. Crowell, 1974.

———, and Sarah Miles Watts. *The Press and the Presidency from George Washington to Ronald Reagan*. New York: Oxford University Press, 1985.

Thomas, Lately. *The First President Johnson*. New York: William Morrow, 1968.

Thompson, David. *The Whole Equation: A History of Hollywood*. New York: Alfred A. Knopf, 2005.

Toplin, Robert Brent. *History by Hollywood: The Use and Abuse of the American Past*. Urbana: University of Illinois Press, 1996.

Townsend, George Alfred. *Washington Outside and Inside*. Hartford: James Betts, 1873.

Truman, Harry S. *The Autobiography of Harry S Truman*. Edited by Robert H. Ferrell. Boulder: Associated University Press, 1980.

Truman, Margaret. *First Ladies*. New York: Fawcett Columbine, 1995.

Tugwell, Rexford G. *Grover Cleveland*. New York: Macmillan, 1968.

Tumulty, Joseph P. *Woodrow Wilson as I Knew Him*. Garden City: Doubleday, 1924.

Tyler, John. *The Letters and Times of the Tylers*. Edited by L.G. Tyler. New York: Da Capo Press, 1970.

Van Buren, Martin. *Autobiography of Martin Van Buren*. Washington, D.C.: Government Printing Office, 1920.

Van Deusen, Glyndon G. *The Jacksonian Era*. New York: Harper & Row, 1959.

Vidal, Gore. *Screening History*. Cambridge: Harvard University Press, 1992.
Washington, George. *Writings of George Washington*. Boston: Russell, Odiorne and Metcalf, 1838.
Watts, Sarah. *Rough Rider in the White House: Theodore Roosevelt and the Politics of Desire*. Chicago: University of Chicago Press, 2005.
Webster, Daniel. *Letters of Daniel Webster*. Edited by C.H. Van Tyne. 1902.
Webster's Guide to American History. Springfield, Mass.: G & C Merriman Co., 1971.
Weinstein, Edwin A. *Woodrow Wilson: A Medical and Psychological Biography*. Princeton: Princeton University Press, 1981.
Weisberger, Bernard A. *Reporters for the Union*. Boston: Little, Brown, 1953.
White, Theodore H. *The Making of the President, 1964*. New York: Signet Books, 1966.
White, William Allen. *Calvin Coolidge*. New York: Macmillan, 1925.
____. *Masks in a Pageant*. New York: Macmillan, 1928.
Widmer, Ted. *Martin Van Buren*. New York: Henry Holt & Company, 2005.
Wills, Gary. "The Negro President." *The New York Review of Books*, 6 Nov. 2003: 45.
Wilmerding, Jr., Lucius. *James Monroe, Public Claimant*. New Brunswick, NJ: Rutgers University Press, 1960.
Wilson, Woodrow. *The New Freedom*. 1913. Reprint: Englewood Cliffs, N.J.: Prentice-Hall, 1961.
____. *The Public Papers of Woodrow Wilson*. Edited by Ray Stannard Baker and William C. Dodd. New York: Harper & Bros., 1926.

Index

Names in **bold** indicate main entries. Numbers in ***bold italics*** indicate pages with photographs.

Abe Lincoln in Illinois (1940) 4, 106, 148, **149**
Abel, Alan 316, 321
Abel, Jeanne 316, 321
Abraham Lincoln (1930) 4, 106, 127, 131, ***132***, 178, 272
Abraham Lincoln's Clemency (1910) 108
Abrahams, Jim 325
Ace of Spades (1925) 47, 62
Acord, Art 126
Acosta, Rodolfo 155
Adams, Henry 6, 45
Adams, John 5, 38–44, 50, 66
Adams, John Quincy 8, 61, 65, 66–69, 86, 88, 103, 195
Adams, Kathryn 29
Adams, Lionel 20, 22, 47
Adler, Stella 230
Adolfi, John G. 24
Adrian 180
Adrian, Walter, as Lyndon Johnson 314
The Adventures of Mark Twain (1944) 185
The Adventures of Ociee Nash (2003) 215
Affieck, Ben 273
Aiello, Danny 303
Airplane II: The Sequel (1982; aka *Flying High II*) 340
Alberghetti, Anna Maria 288
Albright, Hardie 52
Alderson, Erville: as Andrew Jackson 74; as Thomas Jefferson 50, 54
Aldon, Mari 96
Alexander, A., as Theodore Roosevelt 216
Alexander, David James, as Theodore Roosevelt 236
Alexander, Edward 14
Alexander, John, as Theodore Roosevelt 227, 231
Alexander Hamilton (1924) 18
Alexander Hamilton (1931) 24, 47, 62, ***63***

Allen, Debbie 235
Allen, Irwin 157
Allen, Joan 325
Allen, Woody 5, 293, 304, 307
Altman, Robert 207, 323
Altur, Alan 165
Ameche, Don 207
America (1924) 4, 12, 19, 47
American Film Institute (AFI) 6
American Virgin (2000) 349
Ames, Leon 145
Amistad (1997) 8, 67, **68**, 85
Anderson, John 159, 160
Anderson, Dame Judith 300
Anderson, Sherwood 147, 149
Andre, Major 12, 13
Andrews, Dana 263, 322
Andrews, Stanley 150
Angel of Mercy (1939) 199
Angel of Pennsylvania Avenue (1996) 257
Ankrum, Morris, as Ulysses Grant 169, 192, 277
Ann-Margret 237
Annakin, Ken 6
Annie (1982) 271
Another Nice Mess (1972) 318
Apache Ambush (1955) 155
Appomattox 179, 180, 191
Arbuckle, Macklyn 20
Arden, Eve 341
Are We Civilized? (1934) 26, 106, 134
Arizona Terrors (1942) 200, 214
Arletty 293
Arliss, George 24
Arness, James 232
Arnold, Benedict 13
Arnold, Edward 207
Arnold, Phil 254
Arsenic and Old Lace (1944) **227**, 228
Arthur, Chester 195, 202–204, 209
Arthur, Jean 141
Ashley, Arthur 17
Askin, Peter 307

The Assassination of Richard Nixon (2004) 329
Astor, Mary 220
Attenborough, Richard 249, 250
Aubert, Lenore 229
Auer, Mischa 28
Austin, Frank, as Abraham Lincoln 130, 131
Austin Powers: The Spy Who Shagged Me (1999) 358
Aventin, Andre, as Ronald Reagan 342
Avery, Emile, as Ulysses Grant 191
Ayres, Lew 27, 137, 154
Ayres, Robert 40
Azzara, Candy 341

Bacharach, Burt 358
Back to the Future Part II (1989) 342
Bacon, Kevin 161
Bacon, Lloyd 206, 229, 245
Badger, Clarence 129
Bainter, Fay 80
Baker, Art, as Harry Truman 264, 276
Baker, Bob 139
Baker, Frank 191
Baker, Herbert 335
Bakewell, William 245
Baldwin, Alec 273
Bale, Christian 237
Ball, Lucille 231
Ballew, Smith 143
Balsam, Martin 349
Bancroft, Roy 229
Banderas, Antonio 167
Banner, Buxx 306
Barbara Frietchie (1924) 126
Barbary Pirate (1949) 53
Barbieri, Paula 305
Baring, Mathlide 14
Barker, Bob 164
Barker, Lex 97, 158
Barker, Reginald 123
Barnes, George 150
Barnett, Craig, as Bill Clinton 354, 355

377

Barnwell, Teresa 359
Barr, Clarence 123
Barrat, Robert 75; as Abraham Lincoln 96, 138, 139
Barrault, Jean-Louis 293
Barrett, Rona 335
Barrick, Jonathan 310
Barriscale, Bessie 123
Barron, Robert V., as Abraham Lincoln 162
Barry, Don "Red" 188, 214
Barrymore, Lionel 124, 171, 218; as Andrew Jackson 19, 72, 78, 171, 218
Barta, Tony 327
Barthelmess, Richard 178
Barton, Clara 199
Bates, Kathy 358
Battistini, Pat 166
The Battle Cry of Peace (1915) 15, 115, 174
Battle Hymn of the Republic (1911) 109
The Battle of Bull Run (1913) 111
The Battle of China (1944) 152
Battle of Gettysburg (1913) 111
The Battle of Shiloh (1913) 173
Baxter, Deborah 233
Baxter, Warner 138
Bay, Frances 164
Bay, Michael 273
Beals, Dick 32
Beau James (1957) 231, 265
The Beautiful Mrs. Reynolds (1918; aka *The Adventurer*) 4, 17, 39, 46, 62
Beavers, Louise 226
Beavis and Butt-head Do America (1996) 353
Bebe's Kids (1992) 163, 324
Becker, David, as Ronald Reagan 341
Beckinsale, Kate 273
Beebe, Ford I. 188, 260
Beecher, Henry Ward 205
Beer, Robert, as Dwight Eisenhower 294, 295
Beery, Noah, Jr., as George Washington 12, 17
Beery, Wallace 212
The Beginning or the End (1947) 5, 263, 276
Beheler, Ed, as Jimmy Carter 335, 336, 337
Belasco, David 117, 130
Bell, Monta 219
Bellamy, Ralph 254; as Franklin Roosevelt 266
Belmore, Lionel 23
Ben and Me (1953) 54
Benchley, Robert 260
Benedetti, Caprice 310

Benedict Arnold and Major Andre (1909) 12
Benét, Stephen Vincent 132
Benham, Harry 110
Bennent, David 330
Bennett, Bruce 150, 187
Bennett, Constance 186
Bennett, Enid 23
Bennett, Joe 127
Bennett, Spencer G. 88
Beren, David 310
Berenger, Tom 98
Bergen, Candice 233
Berke, William 188, 340
Berkeley, Busby 230
Berlin, Irving 263, 278
Bernardi, Herschel 280
Bernsen, Corbin, as Gerald Ford 332
Bernstein, Elmer 194
Bernstein, Walter 280
Berry, Ken 160
Betsy Ross (1917) 16
Betuel, Jonathan R. 295
Bey of Tripoli 53
Beyond Glory (1948) 287
Bickford, Charles 141
Biesse, Jean-Pierre, as Richard Nixon 316
The Big Picture (1989) 161
Bill & Ted's Excellent Adventure (1989) 106, 162, **163**
The Bill of Rights 58
Billings, Florence 244
Billings, George A., as Abraham Lincoln 126, 127, 129, 130
Binder, Steve 278
The Birth of a Nation (1915) 4, 6, 115, 174, **175**, 184
The Birth of a Race (1918) 122
Bixby, Lydia Mrs. 111
Black, Buck, as Theodore Roosevelt 219
Black, William 243
Black Hawk War 104, 106, 110, 146, 150
Black Hills 3
Blackmer, Sydney, as Theodore Roosevelt 64, 214, 217, 223, 225, 226, 228, 229
Blackton, J. Stuart 13, 15, 109, 111
Blackwell, Carlyle 17
Blaine, James G. 195, 198, 202, 205, 208
Blaine, Vivian 324
Blake, Peter Andelin 37
Blake, Richard, as Abraham Lincoln 162
Blake, Robert 229
Blanc, Mel 32, 152
Blandick, Clara 48

The Blue and the Gray (1908; aka *The Days of '61*) 107
Bluestone, George 6
Blystone, Jasper 260
Boccaloni, Salvatore 269
Boetticher, Budd 96
Bogard, Dirk 249
Bogart, Humphrey 141, 151, 206
Boggs, Francis 110
Boland, Mary 28
Boles, John 105, 135, 212
Boleslavsky, Richard 180
Bolton, Buddy, as Abraham Lincoln 165
Bonaparte, Jerome 48
Bonaparte, Napoleon 47, 48, 156
Bond, Ward 289
Bondi, Beulah 72, 74, 78, 144
Bonney, William H. 188
Boone, Daniel 62, 120
Booth, Adrian 153
Booth, John Wilkes 133, 138, 156, 160, 184
Boothe, Powers 326
Born Again (1978) 322
Borzage, Frank 48, 59
Borzage, Raymond, as Abraham Lincoln 27
Boston Tea Party 51
Bosworth, Hobart 133, 219
Bottoms, Timothy, as George W. Bush 362
Boulton, Matthew 53
Bowen, Julie 164
Bower, Jamie, as George W. Bush 362
Bowers, John 16
Boyd, Robert, as Theodore Roosevelt 234, 235
Boyd, William 95
Boyer, Charles 82
Boyhood Daze (1957) 32
Boyle, Jack 261
Boyle, Peter 323
Brabin, Charles, as Abraham Lincoln 109
Bradbury, Robert N. 137
Braddock, Gen. Edward 22
Bradley, Paul, as Ronald Reagan 339, 340
Bradshaw, Herbert, as Theodore Roosevelt 218
Brady, Alice 16
Brady, William A. 16, 17
Brame, Charles, as Abraham Lincoln 164, 165, 166
Branaugh, Kenneth 194, 268
Brandon, David, Sr. 128
Brandt, Charles, as James Monroe 17, 62
Brave Warrior (1952) 88
Brenda Starr (1989) 284

Index

Brennan, Walter 74, 136, 186
Brenon, Herbert 116
Brent, George 181
Brenton, Herbert 124
Bretherton, Howard 143
Brian, David 232
Brian, Mary 179
Brice, Pierre 98
Bridges, Lloyd 53, 325, 332
Brighty of the Grand Canyon (1967) 217, 232
Brinley, Charles 18
Broadway Broke (1923) 176
Bronson, Charles 189, 191, 290
Brooke, Tom 241
Brooke, Van Dyke 108, 239
Brooks, David 315
Brooks, Mel 349
Brothers, Dr. Joyce 305, 337
Brown, Clarence 72, 144
Bryan, William J. 211
Bryant, Nana 76, 196, 200, 246
Brynner, Yul 82
Bubba Ho-tep (2002) 308
The Buccaneer (1938) 74, **75**
The Buccaneer (1958) 82
Buchanan, James 7, 103
Buckley, Kay 153
Buffalo Bill (1944) 197, 228
Buffalo Bill and the Indians, or Sitting Bull's History Lesson (1976) **196**, 207
Bull, Charles Edward, as Abraham Lincoln 128, 130
Bully (1978) 8, 234
Bumbledown: The Lives and Times of Ronald Reagan (1989) 343
Bunce, Alan 268
Burke, John P. 4
Burnett, Carol 272
Burnley, Daniel, as William McKinley 215
Burns, Bob 143
Burns, Edward 359
Burr, Aaron 39, 46, 53, 59, 62, 72, 129, 140
Burr, David 362
Burton, Richard 156, 292
Burum, Stephen H. 360
Bush, George H. W. 5, 346–350, 352
Bush, George W. 5, 346, 360, 361–364
Bushman, Francis X., as George Washington 12, 22, 23
Buster, Budd 137
Butler, David 134
Butler, Daws, as George Washington 32, 33
Buttons, Red 293
Bye Bye Blues (1989) 285
Byington, Spring 74

Cabot, Bruce 153, 231
Cabrerra, John 166
Cagney, James 206, 235, 261, 340
Cahn, Edward 30, 199
Calhoun, Alice 23
California (1947) 92
Call Me Madam (1953) 278, 285
Callan, K. 319
Calleia, Joseph 264
Callow, Simon 56
Calonico, Scott 313
Calvert, Phyllis 249
Cameron, Rod 153, 155
Camilleri, Terry 163
Campbell, Bruce 309
Campbell, Colin 121
Campbell, Greg S., as John F. Kennedy 305
Campbell, Martin 166
Campbell, Samuel Bruce 329
Campbell, Webster 19, 22
Cansino, Rita (aka Rita Hayworth) 50, 95
Can't Help Singing (1944) 92, 152
Caplan, Jonathan 302
Capra, Frank 152, 227, 259
Carewe, Edwin 26
Carey, Harry, Jr. 288
Carides, Gia 359
Cariou, Len 308
Carleton, William P. 125, 219
Carlin, George 162
Carlin, Thomas A. 235
Carlson, Richard 50, 51, 96
Carlyle, Thomas 12
Carnegie, Andrew 208
Caro, Robert 312
Carr, Mary 176
Carradine, John 138, 319; as Abraham Lincoln 143
Carradine, Keith 215
Carrier, Corey, as Richard Nixon 325
Carrillo, Leo 207
Carroll, Anna Ellis 145
Carroll, John 187
Carter, Jimmy 5, 9, 334–337
Carter, Mrs. Leslie 117
Carter, Nell 305
Carvey, Dana 37, 165, 362
Casewell, Lincoln, as Abraham Lincoln 130
Casey, Richard 324
Cash and Carry (1937) 259
Cassidy, Edward, as Theodore Roosevelt 228, 229, 230, 232
Castle, Mary 32
Cattle King (1963) 204
Caufield, Joan 31, 204
Cavalry (1936) 137
Cavan, Allan, as Zachary Taylor 49, 50, 95

The Cayman Triangle (1977) 321, 335
Centennial Summer (1946) 186
Chalmers, Lionel 22
Chamiec, Krzysztof 250
Chandler, Lane 223
Channing, Carol 232
Channing, Stockard 360
Chapin, Benjamin, as Abraham Lincoln 117, 118, 119, 120, 121
Chase, Stephen 277
Chatterton, Tom 50
Chautard, Emile 46
Chave, Kotti 140
Cherkasov, Nikolai, as Franklin Roosevelt 265
Chester, Howard, as Abraham Lincoln 165
Chiaureli, Mikheil 248, 265
Chief John Big Tree 23
Chief Thundercloud 182
Chong, Marcus 344
Christensen, Kate 310
Citizen Genet 11
Citizen Kane (1941) 6, 217, 224, 326
Clare, Madelyn 118
Clark, Bryan: as Franklin Roosevelt 274; as Ronald Reagan 343
Clark, Fred 255
Clark, Wallis, as Theodore Roosevelt 225, 226
Clarke, Mae 27, 137
Clay, Henry 58, 61, 66, 87, 90, 94
Clemens, Samuel *see* Twain, Mark
Clemente, Ralph 321
Cleveland, George 155
Cleveland, Grover 65, 204, 205–207, 208, 209, 268
Clifford, Clark 275, 276
Clifford, William, as Abraham Lincoln 109, 113
Clifton, Elmer 177
Cline, Edward F. 29
Clinton, Bill 1, 5, 9, 310, 349, 351–360, 362
Clive, Henry 243
Clooney, Rosemary 288
Clothier, William 193
Coburn, Charles 33, 144
Cody, William "Buffalo Bill" 126, 140, 194
Cohan, George M. 25, 225, 261
Cohen, Larry 271
Cohn, Art 154
Colbert, Claudette 25
Collegian, Chuck 313
Collegian, Dean 313
The Collegians Are Go!! (1999) 313
Collins, Ray 92

Colloway, Vanessa Bell 163, 324
Collum, John 41
Collyer, June 24
Colman, Ronald 33, 157
Colorado (1940) 183
Colson, Charles 322
The Commission (2005) 332
Company Man (2000) 307
Compson, Betty 131
Congressional Medal of Honor 197
Connelly, Edward 242
Connery, Sean 233, 292
Connor, Allen 18
Conried, Hans: as Thomas Jefferson 54; as Abraham Lincoln 153, 154
Conroy, Frank 52; as William McKinley 213
Considine, Robert 264
Converse, Peggy 189
Conway, James L. 160
Conway, Kevin 508
Conway, Pat 233
Cook, Lillian 16
Cooke, Allan, as John F. Kennedy 310
Coolidge, Calvin 7, 253–255, 256
Cooper, Alice 320, 335
Cooper, Eric 355
Cooper, Gary 31, 96, 141, 179, 180, 254
Cooper, Miriam 115, 243
The Copperhead (1920) 124, 218
Corbin, Abel Rathbone 172
Corbin, Barry, as Lyndon Johnson 314
Corey, Jeff, as Abraham Lincoln 152, 153, 158
Corff, Bob 299
Corman, Roger 298
Cornwall, Anne 124, 177, 218
Corrigan, Emmett, as Chester Arthur 203
Corrigan, Ray 200
Cortez, Ricardo 71
Coscarelli, Don 309
Costello, Dolores 130, 239
Costello, Elvis 358
Costello, Helene 239
Costello, Maurice 109, 239
Costner, Kevin 301, 308
Cosway, Maria 56
Cotton, Joseph 191, 192, 232, 233
Coulouris, George 92
The Country Needs a Man 4
Courage of the West (1937) 139
Court-Martial (1928) 130
The Court-Martial of Billy Mitchell (1955) 254
Courtney, Erik 167

Courtney, William B. 19
Cover-Up '62 (2004) 310
Cowl, George 16
Cox, Betsy 337
Crabe, James 335
Craft, William James 18
Crain, Jeanne 186
Crawford, Broderick 78, 271, 299, 312
Crawford, Jack, as George Washington 33
Crawford, Joan 23, 72, 85
Craycroft, Richard, as Abraham Lincoln 161
Credit Mobilier Affair 172
Cregar, Laird 88
Crehan, Joseph, as Ulysses Grant 173, 182, 183, 185, 186, 187, 188
The Crisis (1916) 121
Crisp, Donald, as Ulysses Grant 174
Crockett, Davy 81
Crockett, Dick, as Gerald Ford 332
The Crocodile Hunter: Collision Course (2002) 362
Cromwell, John 148, 150
Cronyn, Hume 266, 267
Crosby, Norm 305
Crosland, Ivan 36, 44
Crowther, Bosley 34
Culp, Steven 308
Cummings, Brian 323
Cummings, Irving 206
Cunard Grace 15, 112, 116
Curran, Thomas A., as Theodore Roosevelt 224
Currier, Frank 23
Curry, Tim 272
Curtis, Tony 335
Curtiz, Michael 28, 151, 181, 182, 249, 260, 262, 263
Custer, George Armstrong 141, 173, 177, 184, 191, 194
Czarodziej z Harlemu (1988) 160

Da di qin qing (1999; aka *Love in the Big Country*) 306
Dalton, Timothy 335
Daly, Arnold 47
Dangerfield, Rodney 355
Daniell, Henry 192
Daniels, Bebe 204
Daniels, Sean 215
Daniels, Stan 337
Daniels, William 40, 41
Danner, Blythe 43
Dantine, Helmut 278
Daprato, William J., as Abraham Lincoln 159
D'Arcy, Roy 23
Darnell, Linda 52, 187

Darwell, Jane 52
Da Silva, Howard, as Franklin Roosevelt 5, 31, 41, 271
Davenport, Harry 187
Daves, Delmer 189
David, Gerard, as John F. Kennedy 303, 304
David, William 125, 218
Davids, Markus 310
Davidson, John 31
Davidson, William B., as Grover Cleveland 206
Davies, Joseph 5, 262
Davies, Lane 300
Davies, Marion 20, 48, 180, 219
Davis, Bette 34
Davis, Geena 348
Davis, Natalie Zemon 7
Davis, Ossie, as John F. Kennedy 308, 309
Davy Crockett, King of the Wild Frontier (1954) 81
Dawley, J. Searle 176
The Dawn of Freedom (1916) 15
Day, Gerald, as Abraham Lincoln 46, 124
Day, Joel: as Abraham Lincoln 125; as Ulysses Grant 176
Day, Skyler 215
Dayton, James, as Abraham Lincoln 109
De Alsif, Ferdinand-Marie 195
Dean, Sydney 19
Declaration of Independence 7, 51
The Declaration of Independence (1938) 39, 50
De Corsia, Ted 154
Dee, Francis 143
Dee, Ruby 154
De Havilland, Olivia 181, 184
Dehner, John 160
Deighton, Len 249
Dekker, Albert 225
Delaney, Charles 127
Delephine, Benoit 356
DeLuise, Dom 335, 349, 354
Demarest, William 102
DeMille, Cecil B. 5, 74, 95, 140, 141, 177, 182
DeMille, William C. 177
Demunn, Jeffrey, as Abraham Lincoln 167
Derek, John 156
DeScenna, Linda 337
Deschamps, Jacques, as Ronald Reagan 342
Desmond, William 47
DeVaul, William 47
Devin, Marilyn 269
Devine, Andy 145, 182
DeVinna, Clyde 24, 144

Devon, Richard 204
Dewey, Arthur 19, 176
Dewolfe, Billy 278
Dick (1999) 1, 327, 328
Dickens, Charles 90, 168, 173
Dickinson, Angie 191
Dickinson, John 43
Didi—Der Doppelganger (1984) 341
Dieterle, William 169
Diller, Phyllis 349
Dillman, Bradford 160
Dilson, John, as Rutherford Hayes 197
Dinehart, Alan, as George Washington 25, 26
Disney, Walt 81
Distant Drums (1951) 96
Dix, Richard 75, 179
Dixie (1924) 176
Dixon, James, as Richard Nixon 317
Dixon, Richard M., as Richard Nixon 159, 319, 320, 321, 323
Doctorow, E.L. 234
Donaldson, Roger 308
Doncheff, Len 328
Donehue, Vincent J. 266
Donlevy, Brian, as Andrew Jackson 30, 53, 77, 183, 264
Don't You Believe It (1943) 30
Doucette, Jeff 161
Douglas, George 200
Douglas, Melvyn 72
Douglas, Stephen 112, 122, 149
Douglass, Frederick 208
Doumani, Lorenzo 305
Dourif, Brad 235, 300
Dowling, Constance 263
Dowling, Joseph J. 124
Dowling, Timothy 306
Down, Leslie-Anne 332
Downey, Robert, Sr. 200
Drake, Larry 309–310
Drake, Tom 264
The Dramatic Life of Abraham Lincoln (1924) 106, 127, 177
Drane, Sam D., as Abraham Lincoln 121
Dreville, Jean 34
Drew, Ellen 77
Driscoll, Tex 126
Drouet, Robert 174
Drum Beat (1954) 173, 189
Drumier, Jack 17, 39
Dubbins, Don 192
Dudley, Charles, as Abraham Lincoln 128
Dugan, Dennis 164
Duggan, Andrew, as Lyndon Johnson 312
Dumbrille, Douglas 180; as George Washington 31; as William Henry Harrison 88
Duncan, Sandy 317
Dunn, James 134
Dunne, Philip 156
Dunst, Kirsten 328
Durante, Jimmy 25
Durbin, Deanna 92
Durlam, George Arthur 133
Durning, Charles 284
Duvall, Robert 236
Duvall, Shelley 207
Dye, Kerry Douglas 328
Dyke, Roger 309, 314

The Eagle of the Sea (1926) 71
Earle, Edward, as James Polk 92
Earle, F.C., as Andrew Jackson 46, 71
Eason, B. Reeves 27, 52
Eastman, Orlo, as Woodrow Wilson 428
Eastwood, Clint 232
Eat Your Makeup (1968) 298
Ebert, Roger 301
Ebsen, Buddy 81
Edgren, Gustaf 140
Edwards, Aaron, as George Washington 26
Edwards, Blake 332
Edwards, George C. II 4
Edwards, Sherman 40, 43
Einstein, Bob 318, 359
Eisenhower, Dwight D. 1, 5, 265, 280, 286–295, 311, 312, 315, 323
Elliot, Gordon 139
Elliott, John 180
Elliott, William "Wild Bill" 187, 229
Ellis, Edward, as Andrew Jackson 76
Ellis, Joseph 3, 12
Elvidge, June 17
Emery, Gilbert, as Thomas Jefferson 52, 53
Emmerich, Roland 37
The End of a Dynasty (1998) 305
End of the Trail (1936) 221, **222**
Engle, Harrison 235
English, John 150
Enright, Ray 223, 224
Erickson, C. O. 337
Ericsson, Amelia 140
Ericsson, John, as Abraham Lincoln 140
Ernest, George 245, 316
Esdale, Charles 22
Espionage Agent (1939) 245
Estrada, Erik 305
Evans, Gary 330
Everett, Chad 269

Evil Hill (1999) 306
Executive Action (1973) 299
The Extreme Adventures of Super Dave (2000) 359
Eyton, Bessie 121

The Fabulous Texan (1947) 186
A Failure at Fifty (1940) 150
Fair, Elinor 95
The Faking of the President (1976) 321, 159
The Fall of Black Hawk (1912) 110
Fancy Pants (1950) 231
Fapp, Daniel L. 55
The Far Horizons (1955; aka *Blue Horizons, Untamed West*) 54, 93
Farber, Jodie 303
Farley, James 126
Farnsworth, Richard 194
Farnum, William 26, 134
Farrow, John 33, 92
Faulkner, Ralph, as Woodrow Wilson 218, 241, 242, 243
Fauth, Jurgen 328
Fawcett, Charles 98
Fawcett, George, as Zachary Taylor 121, 177
Faye, Alice 207
Feeney, Mark 316
Fenn, Sherilyn 303
Ferguson, Frank 264
Ferguson, Helen 244
Ferguson, William J., as Abraham Lincoln 115
Ferraz, Buzza 272
Ferrell, Will 328, 165
Ferrer, Mel 292
Field, Betty 102
Field, Sally 304
Fields, W. C. 22
Fifteenth Amendment 172
The Fighting Roosevelts (1919; aka *Our Teddy*) 218
Fillmore, Millard 65, 99
Fine, Larry 259, 260
Finkleman, Ken 340
Finney, Albert 272
The First Texan (1956) 81
First to Fight (1967) 269
The First Traveling Saleslady (1956) 232
Fish, Hamilton 172
Fisher, Louis 4
Fisk, Jim 172
Fiske, Robert 50
Fitch, Clyde 127
Fitzgerald, Barry 92
Fitzgerald, F. Scott 3
The Flag: A Story Inspired by the Tradition of Betsy Ross (1927; aka *The Flag*) 22

The Flag of Freedom (1913) 14
The Flag of Humanity (1940) 196
The Flaming Frontier (1926) 177
Flanders, Ed, as Harry Truman 281, 282
Fleming, Andrew 328
Fleming, Victor 220
Flicker, Ted 194
Flippen, C. Jay 191
Flor, Bob, as John F. Kennedy 300
Fluek, Vince, as Lyndon Johnson 313
Flynn, Errol 151, 184, 187, 340
Folsey, George 134, 180
Folsom, Frances 205, 207
Fonda, Henry, as Abraham Lincoln 147, 157, 207
Fontaine, Joan 76
For All: O Trampolim da Vitoria (1977) aka *For All: Springboard to Victory* (1997) 272
Foran, Dick 139, 233
Ford, Francis 130; as Abraham Lincoln 15, 111, 112, 113, 116
Ford, Gerald 1, 331–333, 570
Ford, Harrison 20
Ford, Hugh, as Abraham Lincoln 114
Ford, John 4, 128, 138, 147, 148, 157, 158, 192, 193, 197
Ford, Paul 319
Forman, Milos 234, 235
Forrest Gump (1994) 304, 313
Forrest, William 192
Forsyth, Frank, as Woodrow Wilson 249
The Fortune Cookie (1966) 106, 158
The Fortunes of War (1911) 109
Foster, Norman 232, 281
Foster, Preston 172, 259
Foulger, Byron 188
Fowle, John Mrs. 113
Fowler, Gene, Jr. 93, 265
Fox, Michael J. 343
Fox, Lt. Wilbur J., as Ulysses Grant 177
Fraker, William A. 193
Francis, Kay 220
Francis, Mark, as Abraham Lincoln 164
Frank, J. Herbert, as Ulysses Grant 126, 175
Franklin, Benjamin 5, 41, 50, 52, 53, 54, 77
Frears, Stephen 348
Freeman, Morgan 68
Fregonese, Hugo 97
Frelang, Friz 32
Frelikh, Oleg, as Franklin Roosevelt 264–265
Frelinghuysen, Frederick 202

Frick, Henry 208
Friedman, Bruce Jay 337
Friedman, Steve, as Richard Nixon 320, 321
Frobe, Bert 292
From Rail Splitter to President (1913) 112
From the Earth to the Moon (1958) 119
From Surveyor to President (2003) 166
The Front (1976) 5, 280, 293
Frontier Scout (1933) 181
The Frontiersman (1927) 71
Fuller, Samuel 191, 200
Furlong, Tim 310

Gaall, Franciska 75
Gable, Clark 78
Gaines, Richard, as George Washington 31
Gallagher, Gary 193
Gallatin, Alfred 58
Galt, John, as Lyndon Johnson 312, 313
Gammon, James, as Zachary Taylor 98
Gannon, Joe 320
Garcia, Andy 348
Gardiner, Reginald 229
Gardner, Ava 78
Garfield, James 198–201, 202, 209
Garnett, Tay 141, 204
Garrett, Betty 231
Garrison, Jim 301, 325
Garson, Greer 266, 267
Gas-s-s-s or It May Become Necessary To Destroy the World To Save It! (1971) 298
Gates, Larry, as Chester Arthur 204
Gateway to the West (1924) 19
Gaye, Howard 16
Gazzara, Ben 283
Geer, Will 299
Gelovani, Mikheil 265
Genardi, Frank, as Theodore Roosevelt 27, 221
Geronimo (1939) 182
Gettysburg Address 112, 127, 130, 136, 145, 151, 155, 161, 162
Gibbons, Cedric 144, 180
Giblyn, Charles 112
Gibson, Althea 193
Gibson, Hoot 177
Gibson, Mel 37
Gierasch, Stefan 310
Gierasch, John 310
Giftos, Elaine 299
Giggers, Earl Derr 176
Gilbert, John 249

Gill, Bob, as John F. Kennedy 301
Gillette, William 179
Gilliam, Seth 56
Gillin, Jed, as John F. Kennedy 304, 305, 306, 307
Gillingswater, Claude 178
Gilmore, Art, as Franklin Roosevelt 260
Gilmore, Virginia 52
Girard, William 114
Gish, Dorothy 186
Gish, Lillian 115
Give 'Em Hell, Harry! (1975) 8, 278
Give Me Liberty (1936) 27
Givens, Ann 199
Gleason, Adda 16
Glenn, Scot 194
Glover, Edmund 150
Go for Broke (1951) 276
Godard, Jean-Luc 316
Goddard, Paulette 31
Godet, Sylvain 316
The Godson (1998) 354
Gold Is Where You Find It (1938) 181
Goldsmith, Jerry 337
Goldstein, Robert 17
Goltz, Otto 243
Good to See You Again, Alice Cooper (1974) 320
Good-bye Cruel World (1983) 336
Goodwin, Harold 177
Gordon, Gavin 179
Gordon, Judy 337
Gordon, Julia Swayne 109, 111
Gordon, Roy, as Benjamin Harrison 209
Gordon, Ruth 149
Gordy (1995) 353
The Gorgeous Hussy (1936) 72, **73, 84**, 85
Gorky, Maxim 9
Gosnell, Raja 337
Gough, Lloyd 80
Gould, Jay 172
Goulet, Robert 347
Grace, Henry, as Dwight Eisenhower 290
Graham, Charles 46
Graham, Gerrit 336
Graham, Heather 358
Grahame, Margot 75
Grandin, Ethel 113
Grant, Cary 56, 57, 227
Grant, Ulysses S. 7, 15, 117, 131, 141, 158, 172–194, 195, 205
Grant, Vince 310
Grant and Lincoln (1911) 109, 173
Graves, Peter 289
Gray, David Barry, as Richard Nixon 325
Gray, Harold 272

Index

Gray, Shirley 179
Great Crash 4
The Great Moment (1944) **101**
The Great Victory, Wilson or the Kaiser? The Fall of the Hohenzollerns (1919) 243
The Greatest Game Ever Played (2005) 239
Greeley, Evelyn 17
Green, Alfred E. 25, 203, 220
Green, Austin, as Abraham Lincoln 156, 157
Green, Jonathan C. 328
Greenberg, Paul 355
Greene, Harrison 184
Greenwood, Bruce, as John F. Kennedy 307, 308
Greggio, Ezio 349
Gregory, James 298
Griffin, Merv 337
Griffis, Rhoda 302
Griffith, D.W. 4, 6, 10, 115, 121, 174, 184, 272
Griffith, James 82; as Abraham Lincoln 153, 155
Griffith, Raymond 129
Griffiths, Richard 347
Grodin, Charles 337
Groom, Winston 304
Gruber, Howard, as John F. Kennedy 298
Gruszynaki, Alexander 328
Guardian of the Wilderness (1977; aka *Mountain Man*) 159
Guardino, Harry 268
Guest, Christopher 161
Guiteau, Charles J. 198, 201
Gunn, Moses 235
Guyer, Murphy 330

Haden, Sara 199
Hadley, Bert, as Ulysses Grant 175
Hagerty, Julie 340
Hagney, Frank 72
Hail (1972; aka *Hail to the Chief*) 318
Hale, Alan 151, 185, 212
Hale, Barbara 55, 97
Hale, Edward Everett 46, 74, 129, 140
Hale, Nathan 46
Hale, Richard, as Abraham Lincoln 154, 155
Hall, Albert 203
Hall, Ella 14
Hall, Jon 32, 89
Hall, Philip Baker, as Richard Nixon 323, 324
Hall, Porter, as Pierce 102
Hall, Stanley, as Abraham Lincoln 156

Hallerworden, Dieter 341
Hamilton, Alexander 7, 39, 62
Hamilton, George 335
Hamilton, John: as James Garfield 264; as Ulysses Grant 186, 187, 190
Hammond, Kay 133
Hancock, John 38, 43
Hands Up! (1926) 129
Hanks, Tom 304
Hannah, Walter, as Jimmy Carter 336
Happy Gilmore (1996) 161, 164
Harding, Ann 262
Harding, Warren G. 7, 251–252, 253, 256, 271
Hardwick, Cedric 157
Harmon, Pat 126
Harolde, Ralf 27
Harrigan, Nedda 27
Harrigan, William 27
Harris, Ed 294, 326
Harris, James, as Ulysses Grant 174
Harrison, Benjamin 205, 208–210
Harrison, William Henry 87–89, 90, 94, 208
Hart, Albert 17, 46
Hart, Gordon 50
Hart, William S. 126
Hartnett, Josh 273
Harvey, Don 330
Haskin, Byron 81, 191
Hathaway, Henry 88
Haver, June 30, 229
Hawkins, Jack 34, 249
Hawthorne, Nigel, as Martin Van Buren 85, 86
Hay, John 105, 118, 234
Hayes, George "Gabby" 75, 183
Hayes, Rutherford B. 195–197, 211
Hays, Robert 340
Haysbert, Dennis 302
Hayward, Susan 80
Hayworth, Rita 50
Haze, Jonathan 318
Head, Edith 335
Healy, Daniel T., as George H. W. Bush 348
Hearn, Edward 129, as George Washington 23
Hearst, William Randolph 20, 211, 225
The Heart of a Hero (1916) 46
The Heart of Lincoln (1915) 116
The Heart of Maryland (1915) 116
The Heart of Maryland (1927) 130, 178
Hearts Divided (1936) 48, **49**
Hearts in Bondage (1936) 127

Hecht, Ben 244, 342
Hedaya, Dan, as Richard Nixon 327, 328
Heflin, Van, as Andrew Johnson 169, 171
Heindorf, Ray 261
Heisler, Stuart 77
Hemings, Sally 45, 56
Henabery, Joseph, as Abraham Lincoln 115
Henderson, Dell, as William McKinley 212
Henley, Bert 220
Henry, Charlotte 137
Henry, Louise 222
Henry, Marguerite 232
Henry, Patrick 27
Henry, William 136
Herbert, Holmes 72, 95; as Thomas Jefferson 53
Herbert, Hugh "Woo Woo" 28, 29
Herdman, John, as Thomas Jefferson 47
Herek, Stephen 162
Hermann, Edward, as Franklin Roosevelt 271, 272
Hernden, William 108, 133, 149
Hero (1992; aka *Accidental Hero*) 348
Herrmann, Bernard 156
Heston, Charlton 55, 71; as Andrew Jackson 79, 82
Hewston, Alfred, as James Garfield 199
Heyes, Herbert 54, 55, 254
Hickey, John 20, 207,
Hickman, Howard 124
The Higher Mercy (1912) 110
The Highest Law (1921) 106, 125
Hill, Edwin C. 259, 259
Hill, Ramsay, as James Madison 59
Hill, Rosemary 177
Hiller, Arthur 337
Hillyer, Lambert 126, 184
Hinds, Samuel S., as Woodrow Wilson 25, 244
Hingle, Pat 35, 44
Hinz, Werner 292
His First Commission (1911) 109
Hiss, Alger 315
Hi-Yo Silver (1940) 150
Hoffman, Dustin 248
Hoffman, Jordan 329
Hoge, Bob 354
Holden, Gloria 74, 140
Holden, Harry, as Zachary Taylor 95
Holden, William 30, 53, 77, 193
Holgate, Ron 42
Holiday Highlights (1940) 29

Holm, Ian 249
Holmes, Stuart, as Grover Cleveland 64, 206
Holt, Jack 131, 135, 221
Holt, Tim 181
Homalka, Oscar 262
Hool, Lance 98
Hoover, Herbert 256–257, 272
Hope, Bob 31, 231, 265, 277
Hopkins, Anthony: as John Quincy Adams 8, 67, 68, 86; as Richard Nixon 8, 325
Hopkins, Miriam 151
Hopper, E. Mason 20
Hopper, Frank, as Theodore Roosevelt 220
Horror House on Highway 5 (1985) 324
Horse, Michael 194
The Horse Soldiers (1979) 192
Horton, Edward Everett 48, 88, 228
Hoskins, Bob 326
Hot Shots! Part Deux (1993) 324, 332, 337, 344, 348
House, Edward M. 248
Houston, George 181; as George Washington 29
Houston, Sam 75, 81
How the West Was Won (1962) 157, 193
Howard, Arlis 86
Howard, Curly 260
Howard, Ken, as Thomas Jefferson 35, 41, 55, 56
Howard, Leslie 141
Howard, Lewis 29
Howard, Mary 53, 149
Howard, Moe 260
Howard, Tim, as Lyndon Johnson 312
The Howards of Virginia (1940) 5, 29, 50, **51**
Howe, James Wong 150, 206
Howe, Julia Ward 109
Howe, Louis 267
Hoyt, Harry O. 219
Hudson, Hugh 35
Hudson, Rock 96
Hughes, Jeff 330
Hughes, Ken 335
Hull, Josephine 228
Humberstone, H. Bruce 27
Humphrey, William 239
Humphreys, Anderson, as Richard Nixon 321
Hunnicutt, Arthur 96
Hunt, Madge 130
Hunt, Peter H. 40, 234
Hurwitz, Harry 319
Hussey, Ruth 169, 209

Huston, John 35, 44, 55, 210, 234, 271
Huston, Walter 144, 262; as Abraham Lincoln 131, 132, 133, 152, 178

I Loved, as Woman (1933) 220
I Shot Billy the Kid (1950) 188
I Wonder Who's Kissing Her Now (1947) 229
Impure Thoughts (1985) 300
In the Days of Buffalo Bill (1922) 4, 125, 169, 175
In the Days of Daniel Boone (1923) 18, 62
In Old Oklahoma (1943; aka *War of the Wildcats*) 225
Ince, John. 174
Ince, Ralph, as Abraham Lincoln 106, 109, 110, 111, 112, 113, 114, 125, 239)
Ince, Thomas 109, 111
Inchon (1981) 283
Independence (1976) 35, 44, 55, 210
The Indomitable Teddy Roosevelt (1986) 235
Ingraham, Lloyd, as Woodrow Wilson 245
Ireland, Frederick 122
The Iron Horse (1924) 128
Irving, David 336
Irving, George, as Andrew Jackson 48, 71
Irwin, Steve 362
Irwin, Terri 362
Is There Sex After Death? (1971) 316, 321
Israel, Ira 350
Ivey, Judith 337
Ivory, James 56
Ivy, Bob 309

Jack London (1943) 226
Jackson, Andrew 4, 7, 65, 66, 70–83, 84, 140, 146
Jackson, Charles, as Thomas Jefferson 46
Jaeckel, Richard 290
James, Sidney 305
Janice Meredith (1924; aka *The Beautiful Rebel*) 12, 20, **21**, 47,
Janis, Conrad 288
Jason, Will 150
Jay, John 11
Je hais les acteurs (1986; aka *I Hate Actors*) 342
Jefferson, Thomas 3, 4, 6, 7, 11, 22, 38, 39, 45–57, 58, 61, 62, 70, 84, 87, 133, 195, 220, 279
Jefferson in Paris (1995) 56
Jenkins, Allen 28

Jenkins, Rebecca 285
Jenks, Frank 145
Jenney, Lucinda 308
Jessel, George 229
Jesus 2000 (1998) 355
JFK (1991) 5, 6, 300, 312
Jhabvala, Ruth Prawer 56
Jochim, Keith, as Richard Nixon 330
John Ericsson—Victor at Hampton Roads (1937) 139
John Paul Jones (1959) 33, 40
Johnson, Andrew 136, 152, 168–171, 195
Johnson, Kelley, as Bill Clinton 355
Johnson, Lyndon B. 5, 271, 294, 311–314
Johnson, Nunnally 138
Johnson, Peter N. 36
Johnson, Tefft 111
Johnson, Van 277; as James Garfield 201
Johnstone, Florence 176
Jolie, Angelina 359
Jones, Chuck 32
Jones, Dean 317, 322
Jones, James Earl 57
Jones, Okon, as Abraham Lincoln 160
Jones, Stan, as Ulysses Grant 192, 193
Jones, Tommy Lee 301
Jovovich, Milla 165
Joy, Robert 234
Joyce, Alice 14
Judge, Mike 353, 354
Julian, Rupert 95, 242
Jurado, Katy 155
Jurgens, Kurt 292

Kaaren, Suzanne 50
The Kaiser, the Beast of Berlin (1918) 5, 242
Kaliszewski, Jerzy, as Woodrow Wilson 250
Kane, Byron 332
Kane, Christian 360
Kane, Gail 46
Kane, Joseph 153, 155, 183, 223
Kane, Michael 193
Kaplan, Jonathan 302
Kaplan, Vyette 608
Kaquitts, Frank 207
Karina, Anna 316
Karpinski, Pawel 161
Katsis, Tom, as Abraham Lincoln 164, 166
Katzman, Sam 53
Kaufman, Philip 293
Kaye, Danny 263
Keene, Tom 50, 95

Keith, Brian 191; as Theodore Roosevelt 217, 233
Keith, Ian 74, 133
Kelly, Gene 230
Kelly, Paul 27
Kemper, Victor J. 337
Kennedy, George 347
Kennedy, John F. 5, 7, 9, 160, 201, 271, 296–310, 311, 312, 314, 315, 324, 325, 333, 345
Kent, Dorothea 145
Kenton, Erle C., as Theodore Roosevelt 221
Kern, Jerome 92, 136
Kerwin, Brian 302
Kesselring, Joseph 227
Kilgour, Joseph, as George Washington 12, 13, 15, 16, 20
Kilian, Victor, as Abraham Lincoln 151
Kimmell, Leslie, as Abraham Lincoln 154
King, Emmett, as James Monroe 129
King, Henry 114, 246
King, Joseph, as Rutherford Hayes 196
Kingsford, Walter, as George Washington 30
Kingsley, Harold Mark, as Theodore Roosevelt 235
Kinnear, Greg 354
Kinnikuman: New York kiki ippatsu! (1986) 342
Kinski, Natassja 36
Kirkland, Sally 306
Kirkwood, Jack 231
Kitagawa, Yonehiko, as Ronald Reagan 342
Klein, Joe 358
Kline, Kevin 194
Knox, Alexander 246, 247
Knutschen, kuschen, jubiliener (1998 German) 345
Koch, Jay, as Ronald Reagan 342, 343, 344, 345
Kohler, Fred 128
Kolker, Henry 183
Korsakov, L., as Woodrow Wilson 248
Koster, Henry 209
Kostner, Kevin 301, 308
Kovacs, Laszlo 194
Krawczyk, Gerard 342
Kruger, Otto 244

La Badie, Florence 241
Lacerda, Luiz Carlos 273
Lachman, Harry 52
Ladd, Alan 173, 189, 283
Laemmle, Carl 126
Laemmle, Edward 126

La Fayette (1962) 12, 34
LaGallienne, Eva 156
Lake, Arthur 340
Lamarr, Hedy 157, 277
Lancaster, Burt 299
The Land of Opportunity (1920) 125
Landers, Lew 32, 53
Landon, Hal, Jr. 162
Lane, Mark 299
Lane, Priscilla 228
Lang, Walter 278
Lansing, Secretary of State Robert 15
Lasky, Jesse, Jr. 33
Launsdale, H.G., as Abraham Lincoln 110
Lawford, Peter 292, 309
The Lawless Nineties (1936) 222
Lawrence, Jane 340
Lawson, Robert 54
Lawton, Charles, Jr. 153
Lawton, J.F. 343
Layman, Terry 37
Leachman, Cloris 354
League of Nations 240
Lee, Duke R., as George Washington 18
Lee, Earl, as Woodrow Wilson 249
Lee, Fred, as Woodrow Wilson 244
Lee, Richard Henry 11, 42, 50
Lee, Robert E. 129, 130, 133, 176, 180, 189, 191
Lee, Rowland V. 129
Lee, Spike 302
Lee, William 110
The Legend of the Lone Ranger (1981) 193
The Legend of Zorro (2005) 166
Leiber, Fritz 137
Lemmon, Jack 159
Lennox, Kai 306
Leon, Peter 15
Le Royer, Michel 34
Leslie, Joan 30, 261, 263
Leslie, Rolf, as Abraham Lincoln 124
Lester, Adrian 358
Lester, Mark L. 320
Lester, Tom 353
Levin, Henry 79
Levine, Myron A 6
Levinson, Fred 318
Lewis, Jack, as James Monroe 18, 62
Lewis, Joseph H. 139
Lewis, Mark 353
Lewis and Clark Expedition 55, 93
Lieutenant Grey of the Confederacy (1911) 110, 173

The Life of Abraham Lincoln (1908) 208
The Life of Abraham Lincoln (1915) 174
The Life of George Washington (1909) 13
The Life of Lincoln (1915) 106, 117
Life or Something Like It (2002) 359, 362
Lights of Old Broadway (1925) 219
Lightwing, Chris 363
Lillian Russell (1940) 206
Lincoln, Abraham 3, 4, 7, 8, 9, 11, 12, 15, 45, 70, 104–167, 178, 220, 244, 257, 275, 279, 323
Lincoln, Mary Todd 104, 127, 130, 133, 138, 141, 149, 165
The Lincoln Conspiracy (1977) 160
The Lincoln Cycle (1915–1917) aka *The Cycle of Photodramas Based on the Adventures of Abraham Lincoln* and aka *Son of Democracy* 117
Lincoln for the Defense (1913) 112
Lincoln in the White House (1939) 106, 145
Lincoln the Lover (1914) 106, 114
Lincoln Vs Bush (2004) 166
Lincoln's Clemency (1910) 108
Lincoln's Eyes (2005) 167
Lincoln's Gettysburg Address (1912) 111
Lincoln's Gettysburg Address (1927) 130
Lindner, Carl Michael 359
Lindsey, Larry, as Gerald Ford 332
Linkletter, Richard 354
Linson, Art 323
Litak, Anatol 152
Litel, John 27, 40, 52, 74, 140, 181
Little, Kim 306
Little, Rich, as Richard Nixon 164, 318, 324
Little Big Horn 177, 184
The Little Shepherd of Kingdom Come (1928; aka *Kentucky Courage*) 178
The Littlest Rebel (1935) 134, **135**
Littlewood, Joan 249
Livingston, Robert 39, 48, 50
Lloyd, Christopher 194, 343
Lloyd, Craig 256
Lloyd, Frank, as Andrew Jackson 50, 71, 142
Lockhart, Gene 182, 262
Loggia, Robert 204
Lom, Herbert 332
Lone Star (1952) 78, **79**

The Lonely Guy (1984) 336
The Long Gray Line (1955) 288
The Longest Day (1962) 290, **291**
Longstreth, Emily 162
Loo, Ng 306
Lord, Del 259
Lorraine, Louise 72
Lorre, Peter 228, 340
Louis, Joe 263
Louisiana Purchase 45, 47
Love, Bessie 219
Love, Faizon 163, 324
Love, Montagu 74; as George Washington 28, 30; as Thomas Jefferson 24, 47, 48
Love Field (1992) 301
The Loves of Edgar Allan Poe (1942) 52
Lowe, Edmund 127
Lowe, Joseph 292
Lowery, Robert 188
Lubin, Arthur 232
Ludwig, Edward 187
Lummis, Dayton 254
Lund, O.A.C. 241
Luske, Hamilton 54
Lutic, Bernard 36
Lynch, Brian 363
Lynn, Jeffrey 246
Lyon, Frank A., as William Taft 239
Lytell, Wilfred 177

MacArthur (1977) **270**, 279, 281, **282**
MacArthur, Dougas 5, 254, 270, 279, 281, 283
MacDonald, J. Farrell 117, 139
MacDonald, Kenneth 184
MacDonald, Peter 359
MacFadden, Hamilton 259
Mack, Charles Emmett 19
Mack, Willard 111
MacKenzie, John 303
Mackie, Anthony 330
MacLane, Barton 188
MacMahon, Aline 204
MacMurray, Fred 30, 55, 93
MacQuarrie, George, as George Washington 16, 17
MacRae, Henry 47
The Mad Empress (1939) 146
Madam Who (1918) 123, 175
Madden, Donald 41
Made in U.S.A. (1966) 316
Madison, Dolley 53, 196
Madison, Guy 97, 98
Madison, James 49, 58–60
The Magistrate's Story (1915) 121
Magnificent Doll (1948) 53, 59, 60
Maher, Bill 344

Maigne, Charles 124
Mailer, Norman 234
Malcolm X (1992) 302
Malden, Karl 158
Maltese, Michael 32
Man of Conquest (1939) 75
The Man Who Dared (1933) 259
The Man Who Invented the Moon (2003) 166
The Man Who Knew Lincoln (1914) 114
Man Without a Country (1925) 129
The Man Without a Country (1937) 62, 72, 74, 140
Mann, Anthony 154
Mann, Gabriel 350
Manners, David 137
Mansfield, Martha 177
Manson, Ted 353
Mara, Adele 153
March, Fredric 74, 185
March On, America! (1942) 64, 65, 67, 77, 106, 152, 215, 225, 260
Marcovicci, Andrea 280
Marietto, Livio 269
Marino, Peter Michaell 330
Marion, Beth 181
Markopoulos, Robert 36
Marley, J. Peverell 190
Marois, Jean-Pierre 349
Marry the Girl (1937) 27
Marshall, Brenda 245
Marshall, E.G. 82
Marshall, George 31, 212, 231
Marshall, Trudy 53
Marston, Theodore 15
Martin, Bev 164
Martin, Steve 337
Martinelli, Elsa 269
Martinez, Mike A. 305
Martinson, Leslie H. 297
Marx Brothers 157
Mason, LeRoy 26, 143
Mason, Reginald 245
Mason, Sidney 243
Massey, Raymond 227, 228; as Abraham Lincoln 106, 148, 149, 157, 158
Massey, Walter, as William Taft 239
Massi, Stelvio 201
The Master of Disguise (2002) 37, 165, 362
Mate, Rudolph 54
Matthau, Walter 158, 159, 301
Maude, Arthur 22
Maurice, Mary 111
Maxwell, Marilyn 154
May, Elaine 356
May, Karl 97, 158

Mayer, Gerald 53
Maynard, Ken 20
Mayo, Frank 16
Mayo, Virginia 157, 263
McCarthy, Kevin 319
McClure, A.K. 109
McClurg, Marc 341
McCormick, Pat 207
McCoy, Gertrude 121
McCoy, Tim 23, 72
McCrea, Joel 81, 101, 106, 142, 143, 183, 197, 245
McCullers, Michael 358
McCulloch, Bruce 328
McCullough, David 39, 43
McDancer, Buck, as Richard Nixon 324, 325
McDonald, Chris 164
McDonald, Kevin 354
McEuen, William E. 337
McEveety, Vincent 317
McFadden, Stephanie 302
McGann, William 27, 145
McGary, Kristen 215
McGlynn, Frank, Sr. 26; as Abraham Lincoln 65, 106, 117, 134, 135, 136, 137, 138, 140, 141, 142, 143, 145, 146, 150, 151, 152
McGovern, Elizabeth 235
McGowan, J.P. 199
McGuire, John 222
McGuire, Michael, as George Washington 36
McGrath, Douglas 307
McGrath, J.B. 161
McKee, Tom 254
McKenzie, Robert, as Zachary Taylor 95
McKinley, William 65, 204, 211–215, 216, 224, 236
McLaglen, Victor 214
McLeod, Catherine 187
McLeod, Norman Z. 277
McMillan, Kenneth 235
McNally, Stephen 59
McNamara, Maggie 156
McQuarrie, George, as George Washington 16, 17
McWade, Margaret 244
McWade, Robert 214
Meehan, John 131
Meeker, Ralph 191
Meet the Chump (1941) 29
Melchior, Lauritz 288
Melotti, Joey 310
Memoirs of Ulysses S. Grant 186
Mencken, H.L. 253, 256
Mendelsohn, Jack 35
Mendenhall, Brent, as George W. Bush 360, 362
Menjou, Adolphe 154

Menken, Alan 236
Mercer, Lucy 258
Merchant, Ismail 56
Meredith, Burgess, as James Madison 59, 60
Merkel, Una 133
Merman, Ethel 278
Merrick, Lynn 215
Merton, John, as Theodore Roosevelt 229
Meskimen, Jim, as Bill Clinton 353
A Message to Garcia (1936) **212**
Michael Kael contre la World News Company (1998; aka *Michael Kael vs. The World News Company*) 355
Michalak, Richard 353
Middleton, Charles B., as Abraham Lincoln 25, 133, 140, 141, 144
Middleton, Robert 160, 204
Miles, Sarah 217
Miles, Vera 266
Milius, John 233
Miljan, John 95
Milland, Ray 92
Miller, Charles 29, 243
Miller, David 299
Miller, Robert Ellis 251, 284
Miller, Sidney: as Abraham Lincoln 137; as George Washington 26
Miller, William 300
Milligan, Tuck, as John F. Kennedy 307
The Million Dollar Duck (1971) 317
Mills, Joe, as Abraham Lincoln 113
Mills, John 249
Mineo, Sal 293
Mira, Pedro, as Abraham Lincoln 166
Miron, Milton 318
The Misery Brothers (1995) 304
Mission to Moscow (1943) 5, 261
Mr. Whitney Has a Notion (1949) 53
Mitchell, Camille 257
Mitchell, Grant, as John Quincy Adams 65
Mitchell, Thomas 188
Mitchum, Robert 292
Mobilising the Troupes (2004) 362
Moffat, Donald, as Lyndon Johnson 312
The Money Kings (1912) 239
Mong, William V. 136
Moniot, Robert 274
Monroe, James 11, 47, 48, 50, 61–65, 68, 140

The Monroe Doctrine (1939) 63, **64**, 67, 92, 99, 223
Monsell, Thomas 327
Monsieur Beaucaire (1946) 31
Montague, Steve 329
Montiel, Sara 191
Montgomery, Elizabeth 254
Montgomery, Frank 16
Montgomery, George 88, 150
Montgomery, Lee 317
Moore, Clayton 194
Moore, Demi 354
Moore, Dickie 146
Moore, Donald C., as Benjamin Harrison 210
Moore, Pauline 183
Moorehead, Agnes 157
Mooreland, Sherry 32
More, Kenneth 249
A More Perfect Union: America Becomes a Nation (1989) 36, 44, 56, 60
Morgan, Harry 193
Morgan, J.P. 217
Morgan, Ralph 75, 182
Morita, Pat 305
Morley, Jay 126
Morley, Karen 135
Morris, John W. 126
Morris, Robert 43
Morris, Wayne 153
Morrison, James 111
Moss, Tegan 257
Mostel, Zero 280, 281
Mount Rushmore 3
Mowbray, Alan, as George Washington 12, 24, 25, 30, 31, 142
Mudd, Dr. "Sam" Samuel Alexander 138
Mueller, Niels 329
Mundin, Herbert 212
Munshin, Jules 230
Murphy, George 263
Murphy, Mary 191
Murphy, Michael, as John F. Kennedy 305
Murphy, Ralph 153
Murray, Bill 323
Murray, Frank, as Ulysses Grant 46, 175
Murray-Blessings Ratings 7, 8
My Favorite Spy (1951) 231, 277, 285
My Girl Tisa (1948; aka *Ever the Beginning*) 229
My Own United States (1918) 46, 71, 124, 175
My Science Project (1985) 295
Myers, Harry, as Andrew Johnson 126, 169
Myers, Mike 306, 358

Nagle, Conrad 146, 219
Naish, J. Carroll 190
Naked Gun 2½: The Smell of Fear (1991) 347
Naked Gun 33⅓: The Final Insult (1994) 352
Nash, George, as George Washington 18, 22
Neagle, Anna 142
Neal, Tom 287
'Neath Western Skies (1929) 199
Neesen, Liam 167
Negulesco, Jean 196
Neilan, Marshall 121, 124
Nelson, Arvid 290
Nelson, Barry 232
Nelson, Bobby 133
Nelson, Brodie 310
Nelson, Dick, as Franklin Roosevelt 265, 266, 268, 269
Nelson, Ed, as Harry Truman 284
Nesbitt, John 54, 199
New Mexico (1951) 154
Newfield, Sam 181
Newman, Paul 207
Newsies (1992) 236
Newton, Thandie 56
Nezabyvayemyj god ([1919]; aka *The Unforgettable Year* [1952]) 248
Nichols, Dudley 245, 259
Nichols, George, Jr. 75
Nichols, Mike 356
Niciphor, Nicholas 337
Nicolay, John G. 107
Nielsen, Leslie 164, 347
Nigh, William 218
The Night Riders (1939; aka *Lone Star Bullets*) 200, 214
Niven, David 59
Nixon (1995) 5, 6, 8, 325, **326**, **327**
Nixon, Cynthia 268
Nixon, Richard M. 1, 5, 6, 7, 8, 9, 164, 271, 315–330, 331, 345
No More Excuses (1968) 200
Noble, John W. 46, 122
Nolan, Lloyd 271
Nolan, Philip 46, 124, 129, 140, 175
Nolte, Nick, as Thomas Jefferson 56
Noonan, Francis J., as Theodore Roosevelt 218
Norma Jean, Jack and Me (1998; aka *The Island*) 305
North, Wilford 15
Norton, Ed, as Harry Truman 284
Nowrasteh, Cyrus 305, 306
Nugent, Elliott 229, 263
Nuggette, Mic 306

Nyby, Christian 269
Nyocker! (2004; aka *The District!*) 363

O'Brien, George 128
O'Brien, Pat 235
O'Connor, Donald 235, 278
O'Day, Molly 178
Of Human Hearts (1938) 105, 143
Oh! What a Lovely War (1969) 249
O'Hara, Maureen 88, 197, 289
O'Herlihy, Dan, as Franklin Roosevelt 270
The Oklahoma Kid (1939) 206
Old Hickory (1939) 76, 89, 146
Old Louisiana (1937; aka *Louisiana Gal*) 49, 59
Old Shatterhand (1964) 97
Oliver, Guy, as Ulysses Grant 178
Olivier, Laurence 249, 283
Olkewicz, Walter 162
Olmstead, Lyndall 22
Olson, James 235
Olson, Moroni 78
O'Malley, David 160
On the Jump (1918) 242
One Man's Hero (1990) 98
O'Neal, Patrick 35
O'Neil, Peggy 174
O'Neill, Ed 152, 169
Only the Brave (1930) 178
Operator 13 (1934) 134, 180
The Oregon Trail (1959) 93
Orlandi, Carla 310
Ormond, William 39
Orrosz, Istvan, as George W. Bush 363
Ortega, Kenny 236
Osborne, Ted 39, 50
O'Shea, Michael 226
Osmond, Cliff 159
O'Toole, Ollie 93
Ott, Charles, as Abraham Lincoln 164
Owen, Sid 36

Pacino, Al 36
Pacula, Joanna 349
Padden, Sarah 156
Padeniye Berlina (1949; aka *The Battle of Berlin*) 264
Paget, Debra 192, 209
Paine, Tom 11, 39
Pallotta, Gabriella 269
Palmer, Lilli 229, 230
Palmieri, Vince, as George Washington 36
Paltrow, Gwyneth 56
Pandemonium (1982) 34
Pankin, Stuart 349
Panther (1995) 344

Parker, Eleanor 262
Parker, Fess 81
Parker, Jean 245
Parks, Michael 299
Parsons Percy, as Abraham Lincoln 142
The Passing Parade (1912) 14
Patinkin, Mandy 235
The Patriot (2000) 12
Paul, Logan 14
Pavan, Marissa 190
Paxton, Bill 239
Payne, Louis 95
Peace Corps 296
Peacocke, Thomas, as Hoover 257
Pearl Harbor (2001) 273
Pearl Harbor II: Pearlmageddon (2001) 274
Peck, Gregory 157, 158, 281
Peck, Tony 284
Penman, Lea 231
Penn, Robin Wright 304
Penn, Sean 329
Pennington, Ty 215
The Perfect Tribute (1935) 136
Perkins, Geoffrey 343
Pershing, John J. 218, 254
The Persistence of Dreams (2005) 167
Peters, Bernadette 272
Peterson, Merrill D. 3
Petrov, Vladimir 265
Pfeiffer, Michelle 302
The Phantom President (1932) 4, 25, 48, 133, 220
Phelbin, Regis 335
Phillips, Albert, as Ulysses Grant 176
Picado, Guaracy, as Franklin Roosevelt 272, 273
Pierce, Franklin 100–102
Pigeon, Walter 335
The Pigeon That Took Rome (1962) 268
Pike, J.W. 14
The Pink Panther Strikes Again 1, 332
Pirosh, Robert 277
Pizza Man (1991) 343
The Plainsman (1937) 140
Platt, Thomas 216
Poe, Edgar Allan 52
Polito, Sol 181
Polk, James K. 63, 91–93
Pollock, Alexander 257
Polonia Restitua (1981) 250
Pons, Lily 281
Pontiac's Rebellion 5
Poreba, Bohddan 250
Porter, Edwin S. 107
Powell, Dick 25, 48, 106, 133, 154, 244

Power, Tyrone 289
Preminger, Otto 186, 254
The President's Lady (1953) 5, 79, **80**
Presley, Priscilla 347
Preston, Robert 183
Il Prezzo del potere (1970; *The Price of Power*) 201
Price, Vincent 157, 200
Primary Colors (1998) 1, **356**, **357**
Prince of Players (1955) 156
Prisoner of Shark Island (1936) 138
The Private Files of J. Edgar Hoover (1977) 5, 271, 299, 312, 322
Proft, Pat 164, 165, 325
The Prussian Cur (1918; aka *The Invisible Enemy*) 5, 243
PT 109 (1963) 5, **297**
Pulitzer, Joseph 205, 211, 217, 236
Putch, John 300
Pyle, Denver 160

Quaid, Dennis 294
Quinn, Aileen 272
Quinn, Anthony 74, 75, 82, 83, 96, 141, 185

Raft, George 335
Ragtime (1981) 234
Rainey, Ford, as Abraham Lincoln 160
Rains, Claude 28, 49, 181
Ramirez, Dania 330
Randall, Henry S. 45
Ranous, William V. 110
Rapper, Irving 322, 185
Ratcliff, E.J., as Theodore Roosevelt 218, 219, 220
Ratoff, Gregory 30
Rawlinson, Herbert 14
Raymond, Paula 154
Rea, Peggy 302
Reagan, Ronald 5, 6, 263, 338–345, 346, 361
Reagan, Ronald, as Richard Nixon 324
Reavis, James Addison 200
Rebellion (1936; aka *Lady from Frisco*) 95
Red Desert (1949) 188
Redgrave, Michael 249
Redgrave, Vanessa 249
Reed, Donna 55, 288
Reed, Steve, as John F. Kennedy 302, 303
Reeves, Dale, as Bill Clinton 353, 354; as Jimmy Carter and Richard Nixon 322, 335
Reeves, Keanu 162
Reid, Carl Benton 81, 82

Index

Reid, Hal 111
Reinhart, Mark S. 105, 108, 110, 117, 130, 132, 145, 171
Reis, Irving 154
Reisner, Charles 244
The Reluctant Dragon (1941) 260
The Remarkable Andrew (1942) 30, 53, 77
Renaday, Pete, as Abraham Lincoln 163, 324
Renaldo, Duncan 95
Renavent, George 76
Rensing, Violet 290
The Reprieve: An Episode in the Life of Abraham Lincoln (1908) 108
Resin, Dan, as Richard Nixon 318, 319
Reubens, Paul 341
Revolution (1985) 35
Reynolds, Debbie 157
Reynolds, Mrs. Moira 17, 18, 24, 62
Reynolds, William 337
Rhodes, Grandon 53
Rich, Ron 158
Richard (1972) 319
Richards, Addison: as James Monroe 50, 63; as James Polk 93
Richardson, Al, as Franklin Roosevelt 259, 260
Richardson, Ralph 249
Richman, Charles 16
Rick, Pat, as Bill Clinton 349, 352, 355, 356, 359
Ridgeway, Jack, as Theodore Roosevelt 218
The Right Stuff (1983) 5, 293, 312, **313**
Ritt, Martin 280
Ritz, Kreemah, as Richard Nixon 317, 318
Roach, Hal 128
Roach, Jay 358
The Road Is Open Again (1933) 25, 133, 244
Roarke, John, as George H. W. Bush 347, 349, 350, 352
Robards, Jason, as Ulysses Grant 193, 194
Robards, Jason, Sr. 130, 133, 146
Roberts, Stephen, as Franklin Roosevelt 269
Robertson, Cliff, as John F. Kennedy 297, 298
Robertson, Dale 191
Robinson, Bill "Bojangles" 135
Robinson, Edward G. 179, 203, 204, 220
Robinson, Jay 322
Robson, May 245

Rock Island Trail (1950) 153
Rodgers, Walter, as Ulysses Grant 130, 173, 177, 178, 179, 181
Rodgers and Hart 133, 220
Rodney, Caesar 39, 40, 50
Roemheld, Heinz 261
Roescher, Michael 353
Rogell, Albert S. 225
Rogers, Ginger 59, 232
Rogers, Roy 183
Rogers, Will 234, 249
Rogers, Will, Jr. 249
Rollins, Howard E. Jr. 235
The Romance of Louisiana (1938) 50, 62
A Romance of the 60's (1911) 110
Romanov, Stephanie 308
Rooney, Mickey 319, 356
Roope, Fay 96, 97
Roosevelt, Eleanor 258
Roosevelt, Franklin D. 4, 7, 8, 11, 15, 70, 183, 237, 248, 258–274, 275, 279, 281, 296, 311, 315
Roosevelt, Theodore 3, 4, 7, 8, 15, 70, 125, 133, 214, 216–237, 238, 240
Rorke, Hayden, as Ulysses Grant 173, 189, 190
Rosen, Phil 127
Ross, Betsy 14, 22
Ross, Margery 347, 348
Rossi, Leo 305
The Rough Riders (1927; aka *The Trumpet Calls*) 220
Royle, William 95
Ruben, J. Walter 179
Ruby (1992) 303
Ruggles, Charles 48, 54
Run of the Arrow (1957) 191
Russell, Albert, as Abraham Lincoln 139
Russell, Kurt 336
Russell, Lillian 206
Rutherford, Ann 199, 223
Rutledge, Ann 106, 127, 132, 133, 148, 149
Rutledge, Edward 41
Ruysdael, Basil, as Andrew Jackson 81
Ryan, Frank 92
Ryan, Robert 299

Sailor's Holiday (1944) 339
St. John, Al 181, 214
St. John, Christopher 320
St. John, Howard, as George Washington 12, 34, 35
Sale, Charles "Chic," as Abraham Lincoln 136
Salkow, Sidney 190

San Antone (1953) 154, 189
Sandburg, Carl 105, 110, 132, 141
Sanders, George 192
Santell, Alfred 178, 226
Santschi, Tom 121
Sargent, Joseph 281
Saville, Jeremy, as George W. Bush 363
Sayles, Francis, as James Garfield 200
Scaddhi, Greta 56
Scammon, P.R. 46, 47
Scardon, Paul, as Ulysses Grant 16, 177
Scarwid, Diana 257, 284
Schallert, William, as Abraham Lincoln 167
Schary, Dore 266
Schatz, Thomas 6
Schifrin, Ryan 306
Schlesinger, Arthur, Jr. 104, 216
Schnabel, Stefan 53
Schroell, Nicholas, as Abraham Lincoln 124
Schuum, Harry 15
Schwabenitzky, Reinhard 341
Scott, A.O. 68, 359
Scott, Debralee 341
Scott, George C. 235
Scott, Martha 51, 225
Scott, Randolph 151
Scott, William 108, 113, 128
Scrap Happy Daffy (1943) 152
Seaman, Earl, as Theodore Roosevelt 222
Sears, Fred S. 155
Seay, James: as George Washington 32; as William Henry Harrison 88
Second Continental Congress 5
Secret Honor (1984) 323
Secret Service (1931) 179
Sedgwick, Edward 177
Segal, George 293
Segal, Peter 352
Seiter, William A. 213, 223
Seitz, George B. 130, 131
Sellers, Peter 332
Selwyn, Edgar 244
Seminole (1951) 96, **97**
1776 (1972) 5, 6, 7, 40, **42**, 55
The Seventh Son (1912) 111
Seward, William Henry 105, 111, 146, 168
Sextette (1978) 335
Shalhoub, Tony 360
Shambley, Kathy 344
Shanks, John 47
Sharrett, Christopher 327
Shavelson, Melville 265, 268
Shawn, Dick 337
Shay, William E. 117

She Hate Me (2004) 330
Sheen, Charlie 325
Sheffield, Reginald, as Ulysses Grant 186
Sheldon, Gene 30
Shelley, Joshua 280
Shelton, Marla 142
Shepard, Sam 294
Shepherd, John Scott 359
Sheridan, Ann 187
Sheridan, Gen. Philip 133, 187
Sherman, George 200, 214
Sherman, Vincent 78
Sherry, J. Barney 176
Shields, Arthur 269
Shields, Brooke 284
Shoemaker, Ann 267
Shore, Dinah 263
Shores, Lynn 95
Short, Antrim 176
Short, Martin 162
Short, Mikel, as John F. Kennedy 306
Shostakovich, Dimitri 249, 265
Silence of the Hams (1994; aka *Il Silenzio dei prociutti*) 349, 352
The Silk Hat Kid (1935; aka *The Lord's Referee*) 26, 137, 221
Silver Dollar (1932) 179, **203**
Silver River (1938) 187
Silverheels, Jay 89
Simon, Neil 337
Simons, Brian 330
Simpson, Michael A. 300
Simpson, O.J. 347
Simpson, Russell, as Andrew Jackson 71, 72
Sinatra, Frank 230, 231
Siodmak, Robert 158
Sipes, Gilbert 353
Sitting Bull (1954) **190**
Skavian, Olaf, as Theodore Roosevelt 218
Sklar, Robert 3
Skowronek, Stephen 4
Sky, Jasmine 215
The Slacker's Heart (1917) 122, 241
The Sleeping Sentinel (1910) 103
Slezak, Victor, as John F. Kennedy 309
Sloan, Paul 82
Sloman, Edward 136
Smiley, John, as Ulysses Grant 174
Smiley, Joseph 174
Smith, Al 268
Smith, Alexis 186, 266
Smith, Bruce W. 163
Smith, Christophe 356
Smith, Clifford 126
Smith, Jack, as Ulysses Grant 181
Smith, Kate 263

Smith, Maggie 249
Smith, Noel 138
Smith, Paul J. 33
Smith, Pete 259
Smith, Will 194
Smitrovich, Bill
Smoktunovsky, Innokenti, as Franklin Roosevelt 269
Smoot, Reed 167
Smothers, Tom 318, 341
Snyder, Matt 121, 122
Sobel, Mark 332
Sole, Alfred 341
Some Kinda Joke (2001) 165
Sometimes Santa's Gotta Get Whacked (1998) 36, 164
The Son of Davy Crockett (1941) 183
Song Bird of the North (1913) 112
Sonnenfeld, Barry 194
The Sons of a Soldier (1913) 241
Sons of Liberty (1939) 28
Sorvino, Paul 326
Sothern, Hugh, as Andrew Jackson 65, 74, 75, 76, 77
Sousa, John Phillip 209, 236
Sperling, Milton 254
Spiegel, Larry 318
Spielberg, Steven 254, 292
Spillman, Harry, as Richard Nixon 322
Spiner, Brent 362
The Spirit of '76 (1917) 16
Springer, Jerry 350
Springsteen, R.G. 228
Sprotte, Bert, as James Monroe 47, 62
The Spy (1914) 14
Stack, Robert 33, 34, 354
Stage to Tucson (1950) 153
Stainton, John 362
Stalingradskaya bitva I (1949) The Battle of Stalingrad, Part I 265
Stand-In (1937) 141
Stanitsyn, Viktor 265
Stanley, Edwin 76; as James Polk 64, 92
Stanton, Bob 349
Stanton, Edwin M. 119, 125, 160, 168
Stanton, Richard 218
Stanwyck, Barbara 92, 183, 213, 214
Starke, Pauline 129
Starr, Ringo 335
Stars and Stripes Forever (1952; aka *Marching Along*) 209
The Stars Are Singing (1953) 288
Steele, Bob 137
Steele, Elbert 288, 289
Steenburgen, Mary 235
Stehli, Edgar 189
Steiger, Rod 191, 254, 293

Steiner, Max 181, 191, 229, 230
Stephenson, Henry 48
Stevens, Dana 359
Stevens, Inger 82
Stevens, Leslie 353
Stevens, Mark 229
Stewart, Anita 109, 113, 114
Stewart, James 72, 105, 144, 148, 157
Stewart, Leonora 243
Stewart, Martha 229
Stewart, Ray 219
Stille, George 108
Stiller, Ben 165
Stiller, Jerry 165
Stockwell, John 295
Stone, Doug 353
Stone, Lewis 245
Stone, Milburn 183
Stone, Oliver 5, 300, 301, 312, 325, 327
Stone, Paula 139
Stone, Peter 40, 43
Storch, Larry 349
Storey, Edith 109
The Story of George Washington (1965) 35
The Story of Mankind (1957) 33, 156
The Story of Will Rogers (1952) 249
Stossel, Ludwig 264
Stowe, Leslie 14
Strange Faces (1938) 144
Strange Glory (1938) 145
Stroud, Claude 189
Strouse, Charles 272
Strudwick, Shepperd 52
Stuart, Gloria 138
Sturges, Preston 101, 102
Sun Valley Cyclone (1946) 228
Sundholm, William, as Abraham Lincoln 152
Sundown (1924) 219
Sunrise at Campobello (1960) 5, 266, **267**
Suvari, Mena 350
Swenson, Karl, as Theodore Roosevelt 232, 233
Switch (2005) 363

Tabor, H.A.W. 203
Taft, William Howard 238-239, 240
Taggert, Earl 144
Take Me Out to the Ball Game (1949) 230
Talankin, Igor 269
Taliaferro, Mabel 18
The Tall Target (1951) 5, 106, 154
Talleyrand 47, 50
Tamiroff, Akim 75, 230
The Tanks Are Coming (1941) 52

Tapley, Rose 110, 239
Tarbell, Ida M. 114
Tashlin, Frank 152
Tate, Lincoln 194
Taurog, Norman 25, 264, 288
Taylor, Christine 165
Taylor, Deems 20
Taylor, Ferris, as John Adams 39, 40
Taylor, Robert 72, 204, 213, 223
Taylor, Zachary 91, 94–98, 99
Teal, Ray 155
Tearle, Godfrey, as Franklin Roosevelt 264
Tebbel, John 1
Teddy the Rough Rider (1940) 213, 223
Temple, Shirley 105, 134, 135, 136
Ten Gentlemen from West Point (1942) 88, **89**
Tennessee Johnson (1942) 152, 169, **170**
Terhune, Max 200
They Died with Their Boots On (1942) 184
Thirteen Days (2000) 307, 314
This Is My Affair (1937) **213**, 223
This Is the Army (1943) 262, **339**
Thomas, Edward 109
Thomas, Michael R. 329
Thompson, Emma 358
Thompson, Hunter S. 323
Thompson, Marshall 154
Thornton, Billy Bob 358
Tilden, Samuel J. 195
Tilton, Charlene 349
Timbrook, Robert 313
Timequest (2002) 309, 314
Tissier, Alain 98
Tobin, Genevieve 221
Todd, Richard 292
Toler, Sidney 180
The Toll of War (1913) 113
Tombes, Andrew 29
Tone, Franchot 72
Top of the Heap (1972) 319
Torn, Rip, as Ronald Reagan 341
Torres, Miguel Contreras 146
Tourneur, Jacques 145
Towers, Constance 193
Towne, Rosella 39
Tozzi, Fausto 158
Tracy, Lee 244
Tracy, Spencer 157, 193
Trailin' West (1936; aka *On Secret Service*) 138
Travolta, John 356, 358
Treacher, Arthur 48
Treasure of the Aztecs (1965) aja *Der Schatz der Azteken* 158
Treaty of London 172
Treen, Mary 145

Tricia's Wedding (1971) 317
Trimble, Laurence 109, 219
Trotti, Lamar 147, 209, 245, 259
Trowbridge, Charles, as Martin Van Buren 72, 85
Troyer, Verne 358
Truesdell, Frederick C., as Woodrow Wilson 241, 243
Truman, Harry S. 7, 8, 257, 259, 264, 275–285, 293, 329
Trumbo, Dalton 78, 299
Trumbull, John 44
Tucker, Forrest 153
Tucker, Richard 121, 129
Turn Back the Clock (1933) 4, 244
Turner, Otis 14
Turturro, John 307
Tuttle, Frank 178, 179
Twain, Mark 118, 173, 186
Twitchell, Archie, as Ulysses Grant 188
Two Americans (1929) 131, 178
Two-Fisted Justice (1931) 133
Two Idiots in Hollywood (1988) 161
Tyler, John 7, 90
Tyler, Tom 133, 199

Udenio, Fabiana 355
Ultrachrist (2003) 328
The Unbearable Salesman (1957) 33
Uncle Tom's Cabin (1903) or *Slavery Days* 107
Unconquered (1947) 5, 31
Under One Flag (1911; aka *One Flag at Last*) 106, 110
Union Pacific (1939) 182
Untitled Steven Spielberg/Abraham Lincoln Project (2007) 167
Up in Arms (1944) 263
Urich, Robert 257
Used Cars (1980) 336

Vale, Travers 16
Valerii, Tonino 201
Valley Forge National Park 174
Van Brunt, Stewart 220
Van Buren, Martin 4, 78, 84–86
Vance, Courtney B. 344
Vance, James Dowell 337
Van Dyke, W.S. 23
Van Loon, Henrik 157
Van Peebles, Mario 344
Van Rooten, Luis 277
Varhol, Michael 161
Vera-Ellen 278
Verne, Jules 192
Vicksburg 192
Victoria the Great (1937) 142
Victory and Peace (1918) 124
Vidal, Gore 11
Vidor, Florence 71, 127

Vigoda, Abe 305
Vincent, Millard, as Millard Fillmore 99
Vinton, Arthur, as George Washington 19, 20
Virginia City (1940) 151
Vogan, Emmett 76; as James Garfield 199
Voight, Jon, as Franklin Roosevelt 273
Voland, Herb 318
Vybor tseli (1974; aka *Choice of Purpose*) 269

Wagner, Robert 209
Wainright, James 271
Waite, Ralph 310
Waldron, Charles, as James Monroe 63, 64, 65
Walker, Mrs. Allen 46, 47
Walker, James J. "Jimmy" 265, 266
Walker, Johnny 23
Walker, Walter 40, 50, 52
Wallace, Morgan, as James Monroe 24, 42, 47, 62
Wallace, Randall 273
Waller, Eddy 184
Walling, William 23, 133
Walsh, Frank 19, 47
Walsh, George 242
Walsh, J.T. 161
Walsh, Raoul 96, 116, 184, 187, 242, 243
Wanamaker, Sam 230
War and the Woman (1917) 241
Warde, Ernest C. 241
Warden, Jack 336
Warner, Jack 262
Warnowski, Lonny, as Ronald Reagan 345
Warren, Charles Marquis 188
Warren, Fred, as Abraham Lincoln 133, 178, 179, 180
The Warrens of Virginia (1924) 177
Warwick, Robert 146, as George Washington 27, 46
Washington, Denzel 302, 303
Washington, George 3, 7, 8, 11–37, 45, 53, 61, 133, 157, 220, 244, 272, 287
Washington, Kerry 330
Washington, Martha 22
Washington at Valley Forge (1908) 12
Washington at Valley Forge (1914) 15
Washington Under the American Flag (1909) 12, 13
Washington Under the British Flag (1909) 13

Wasson, Craig, as James Madison 36, 60
Watergate 315, 321
Waters, John 298
Watters, Timothy, as Bill Clinton 352, 358, 359, 360
Wayne, Fredd 36
Wayne, John 157, 192, 193, 200, 223, 225, 292
Weathers, Carl 164
Weaver, Signourney 307
Webb, Clifton 209
Webb, Kenneth S. 18
Webster, Daniel 76, 87, 90
Weinberger, Ed 337
Welch, Jim 130
Welles, Orson 6, 34, 224
Wellman, William 197
Wells Fargo (1937) 106, 142
West, Blanche 174
West, Judi 159
West, Langdon 117
West, Mae 335
West, Tony 122
Western Gold (1937; aka *The Mysterious Stranger*) 143
Westfall, T. H., as Woodrow Wilson 241
Westmore, Perc 206
Wharton, Theodore 108
Whelen, Arleen 155
When Hell Broke Loose (1958) 290
When Lincoln Paid (1913) 113
When Lincoln Was President (1913) 113
When the Redskins Rode (1951) 32
Where Do We Go from Here? (1945) 30
Where the Buffalo Roam (1980) 5, 323
Whiskey Rebellion 11
White House Madness (1975) 320
Whitman, Walt 104, 115
Whitmore, James: as Harry Truman 8, 278, 279, 280; as Theodore Roosevelt 8, 217, 234
Whitney, Eli 53, 54
Whittier, John Greenleaf 126
Whittle, W.E., as Theodore Roosevelt 217, 218

Why America Will Win (1918) 217, 243
Why We Fight series 152, 259
Wide Open Spaces (1924) 128
Wiggins, Kevin 303, 304
Wilbur, Crane 28, 50, 63, 64, 74, 76
Wilcox, Frank, as Abraham Lincoln 146
Wilcox, Herbert 142
Wilcox, S.D. 130
Wild Bill Hickok (1923) 126
Wild Wild West (1999) 194
Wilde, Cornell 186
Wilde, Dorothy 337
Wilder, Billy 159
Wilhite, Prentice 201
Wilkinson, Scott, as Thomas Jefferson 36, 56
Willat, Irvin 49
William, Michelle 328
Williams, Bill 155
Williams, Dean 166
Williams, Earle 110
Williams, Esther 231
Williams, George A 126
Williams, Guinn "Big Boy" 151, 221
Willis, Bruce 354
Wills, Chill 153
Wilson (1944) 5, 6, 246, **247**
Wilson, Lewis 340
Wilson, Owen 165
Wilson, Thomas F. 343
Wilson, Woodrow 4, 5, 7, 15, 17, 70, 115, 118, 120, 122, 133, 238, 240–250, 251, 266, 324
The Wind and the Lion (1975) 233
Windom, William 204
Windsor, Claire 72
Windsor, Frank, as George Washington 35, 36
Winingham, Mare 215
Winners of the Wilderness (1927) 23
Winter, Alex 162
Winters, Shelley 340, 349
With Lee in Virginia (1913) 114, 174
Withers, Grant 153

Wolf, Lawrence, as James Garfield 200, 201
Wolfe, Ian: as James Polk 92, as Calvin Coolidge 254, 255
Wolfe, Tom 294
Wood, Douglas, as William McKinley 65, 214, 215, 224
Wood, Peggy 59
Woodard, Jode, as Abraham Lincoln 166
Woods, Donald 53
Woods, Dorothy 126
Woods, Harry 223
Worthington, William, as George Washington 14, 28
Wright, Donna 215
Wright-Penn, Robin 304
Wrongfully Accused (1998) 164
Wyckoff, Alvin, as Ulysses Grant 174

The Yankee Clipper (1927) 95
Yankee Doodle Bugs (1954) 32
Yankee Doodle Dandy (1942) 225, 260
Yates, George Worthington 154
Yeager, Chuck 294
Yerby, Lorees 319
York, Susannah 249
Yorktown (1924) 22
You Can't Buy Everything (1934) 244
Young, Jack, as Franklin Roosevelt 260, 261, 262, 263
Young, James 111
Young, Kristy 353
Young, Terence 283
Young, Victor 190
Young Mr. Lincoln (1939) 4, 106, 146, **147**

Zane, Billy 349, 352
Zanuck, Darryl F. 138, 147, 229, 246, 254, 291, 293
Zemeckis Robert 304, 336, 342
Zeta-Jones, Catherine Jones 167
Zoolander (2001) 165
Zuber, Marc 233
Zucker, David 340, 347, 352
Zucker, Jerry 340, 347, 352